# A History of the Modern British Isles, 1914–1999

## Circumstances, Events and Outcomes

Arthur Marwick

BLACKWELL PUBLISHING
350 Main Street, Malden, MA 02148-5020, USA
9600 Garsington Road, Oxford OX4 2DQ, UK
550 Swanston Street, Carlton, Victoria 3053, Australia





First published 2000

2 2006

*Library of Congress Cataloging-in-Publication Data*

Marwick, Arthur, 1936–
A history of the modern British Isles, 1914–1999 : circumstances, events and outcomes / by Arthur Marwick.
p. cm. — (History of the Modern British Isles)
Includes bibliographical references and index.
ISBN 0-631-19521-1 (hardbound : alk. paper). — ISBN 0-631-19522-X (pbk. : alk. paper)
1. Great Britain—History—20th century. 2. Ireland—History—20th century.
I. Title. II. Series.
DA566.M345 2000
941.082—dc21
99-43623
CIP

ISBN-13: 978-0-631-19521-4 (hardbound : alk. paper). — ISBN-13: 978-0-631-19522-1 (pbk. : alk. paper)

A catalogue record for this title is available from the British Library.

Set in 10 on 12 pt Plantin
by Ace Filmsetting Ltd, Frome, Somerset

The publisher's policy is to use permanent paper from mills that operate a sustainable forestry policy, and which has been manufactured from pulp processed using acid-free and elementary chlorine-free practices. Furthermore, the publisher ensures that the text paper and cover board used have met acceptable environmental accreditation standards.

For further information on
Blackwell Publishing, visit our website:
www.blackwellpublishing.com

# A History of the Modern British Isles, 1914–1999

# A History of the Modern British Isles

Founding Editor: Sir Geoffrey Elton
General Editor: John Stevenson

This series will cover the history of the British Isles from 1529 to the present. The books will combine the results of the latest scholarship and research with clear, accessible writing.

**Published**

A History of the Modern British Isles, 1529–1603:
The Island of Britain
*Mark Nicholls*

A History of the Modern British Isles, 1603–1707:
The Double Crown
*David L. Smith*

A History of the Modern British Isles, 1914–1999:
Circumstances, Events and Outcomes
*Arthur Marwick*

**In Preparation**

A History of the Modern British Isles, 1707–1815:
The Age of Wars
*John Stevenson*

A History of the Modern British Isles, 1815–1914:
Liberal Britain
*James Webster*

The British Empire, 1500–1997
*T. N. Harper*

In association with the series:

Ireland 1798–1998:
Politics and War
*Alvin Jackson*

# Contents

# List of Plates

*The authors and publishers gratefully acknowledge the following for permission to reproduce copyright material:*

*The publishers apologize for any errors or omissions in the above list and would be grateful to be notified of any corrections that should be incorporated in the next edition or reprint of this book.*

# List of Maps

# List of Tables

# Preface

There are many types of history, each one legitimate if carried out in accordance with the long-established, though constantly developing, canons of the historical profession. I have written this book because I was invited to do so by the late Sir Geoffrey Elton, for whom I had an enormous admiration, though his approaches to history were very different from mine. His idea was that the new Blackwell Series should essentially consist of political narratives (excluding foreign policy). My own interest has long been in opening up new areas in social and cultural history and I am happiest when working with the non-conventional primary sources which are the raw material of that kind of history. However, I have come more and more strongly to feel that, traditionally, social historians have been too preoccupied with 'general forces' and 'long-term trends', ignoring the significance of events themselves. I don't think historians should write too many books which are based on other people's researches, yet I do think it is important from time to time to bear testimony to the fact that history is a cumulative activity, that we trust the work of our colleagues, and that we are, observing the proper conventions, happy to make use of it. For the period covered in this book there are the magnificent monographs by Peter Clarke, David French, John Turner, Ben Pimlott, Kenneth Morgan, Paul Addison, Peter Hennessy, Anthony Seldon, Hugo Young, and many, many more.

As it happened, when John Stevenson took over the series, he injected into it the notion of a 'history of the British Isles'. Since I had been the person responsible for insisting that the Penguin Social History of England, planned in the late seventies, was in fact titled The Penguin Social History of Britain, I was delighted with this expansion of aims. John was also keen that there should be more social history, which did not bother me at all since I had already, in my synopsis, spelled out the need to discuss the relationship between political actions and other 'forces', 'circumstances' and 'consequences' (the words are imperfect, but then we have to live with the imperfections of language, controlling it – if we have the brains – rather than permitting it, in any sense, to control us).

I am aware that the market I am plunging into is already a very crowded one, with many excellent books selling well in the shops. Acknowledging the guidance from both Sir Geoffrey Elton and John Stevenson, I have tried:

1. To write a clear, comprehensible account, featuring those things that I feel students and general readers should want to know;
2. To give a sense of the unrelenting succession of events, the greatest cause (as Harold Macmillan remarked) of prime ministerial angst, and to bring out that events can have considerable effects on social and cultural developments;
3. To give due weight to the different experiences of the different component parts of the British Isles;
4. To show how far the British experience was unique and how far it was a shared one by providing some comparative information from France, Germany, the United States and other countries;
5. Above all, to provide a clear sense of historical explanation* by examining the structural, ideological, and institutional circumstances which determine both the possibilities for change, and the limits upon change. (There can, of course, be no mechanistic cause-and-effect model – circumstances are constantly being acted upon, outcomes quickly become circumstances, contingency and 'accident' are often critical.)

There is nothing particularly original, nor, I hope, eccentric in my account of circumstances, events and outcomes. For most statements, quotations, statistics one could find a dozen or more secondary authorities. I have tried to keep my chapter notes short and simple, citing only one or two accessible books.

My subtitle will seem austere. Originally, Sir Geoffrey envisaged each book in the series being called 'The Age of . . . ' ('Wars', 'Illusions', etc.). In the past I have written of 'The Age (or Century) of Total War', but, then, fortunately, it has turned out to have been only a 'Half-Century of Total War'.

I am still convinced of the significance of war as cataclysmic event, but have sought not to sing that tune too tiresomely. It is true that, forced to put a title to my synopsis, I did come up with 'The Age of Missed Opportunities'. That, however, is a title for a polemical essay, not a balanced book. Furthermore, though historians should know more than the politicians they write about, they should not affect superior wisdom in discussing the problems these politicians had to grapple with.

The austerity of my subtitle is intended to signify my belief that history should have more in common with the sciences than with literature: it should depend on evidence, system and the precise use of language, not on metaphysics, rhetoric, ambivalence and invention. That belief has also resulted in a large number of statistical tables being woven into my text, not dumped in appendices. They are not repositories of truth, but are there to be analysed and thought about.

My overall plan is, in each sub-period, to take the circumstances (structural, ideological and institutional) making for, or limiting, change, before moving on to a narrative of (more-or-less) willed political actions, then concluding with 'outcomes', mainly social and cultural. But the 'circumstances' I privilege in chapters 1 and 3 are those of the two wars. And I start, as I very nearly finish,

* I have never been fully persuaded by the model of explanation offered by Sir Geoffrey – G. R. Elton, *Political History: Principles and Practice* (1970), pp. 138–42.

with the United Kingdom's relationship with Ireland. What I actually finish with, of course, is the United Kingdom's relationship with the rest of Europe.

This book is almost entirely based on secondary sources, sharpened by occasional bouts of primary research carried out at various times over the past forty years. I'd like to express a special word of thanks for their efficiency and courtesy to the staff of the new British Library; also to James Walsh of Conservative Central Office and Jill Davidson of the Conservative Party Archives in the Bodleian Library, Oxford. Deploying her great managerial and secretarial skills, Margaret Marchant has been indispensable in seeing this book through the many processes from first beginnings to final handover. As series editor John Stevenson has been the soul of helpfulness and consideration, my publishers consistently supportive. Colleagues Tony Lentin, Bill Purdue and Henry Cowper have generously taken time to read through my text and provide helpful suggestions and constructive criticisms. Otiose to say the final responsibilities are mine: could it ever be otherwise?

# 1 War, 1914–1918

## Irish Nationalists, Ulstermen and the War Against the German Empire

### *Ireland and Germany*

In 1914, the whole island of Ireland was part of the United Kingdom of Great Britain and Ireland, being represented in the House of Commons in London by 84 Irish Nationalist MPs, 17 Unionists, one Liberal and one Independent. So strong was the Irish Catholic element in Liverpool that the Scotland constituency there returned one Irish Nationalist (till 1927). The Liberal government of Henry Asquith, which was dependent for its majority on the support of the Irish Nationalists, was in the process of enacting the Irish Home Rule Bill, introduced in 1912. This would have created a bicameral legislative body in Dublin, confined to internal Irish matters, including considerable powers of taxation; Ireland would continue to send 42 MPs (reduced from 103) to the Imperial Parliament. Amendments had been proposed, though so far not accepted by the government, to exclude, in the one case, the six counties of Ulster with clear Protestant majorities, and, in the other, the entire nine counties of historic Ulster (see map 1). The Conservative party (usually at this time calling themselves Unionists), who had an overwhelming majority in the House of Lords, were deeply opposed to Home Rule, as were most of the big Protestant landowners in the southern parts of Ireland, together with the Protestant majority in the north. Early in 1913, a landowner in County Clare instructed his solicitor to withdraw his investments in major British stocks, in view 'of the possibility of my death in the Ulster War, and of the national break-up which I regard as inevitable in the near future . . . '.[1] Already, a well-organized Ulster Volunteer Force (UVF), dedicated to resisting Home Rule, was in existence, and by April 1914 it had 90,000 men. That month, in the spectacular Larne gun-running, it brought in substantial quantities of up-to-date weaponry. The rival Irish Volunteers responded with their own gun-running at Howth on 26 July (which, in fact, yielded only a small amount of obsolete weaponry). British troops (there were 1,000 of them stationed in Ireland) became involved, and shot dead three unarmed civilians at Batchelor's Walk in Dublin. However, it should be kept in mind that there had always been a strong non-sectarian

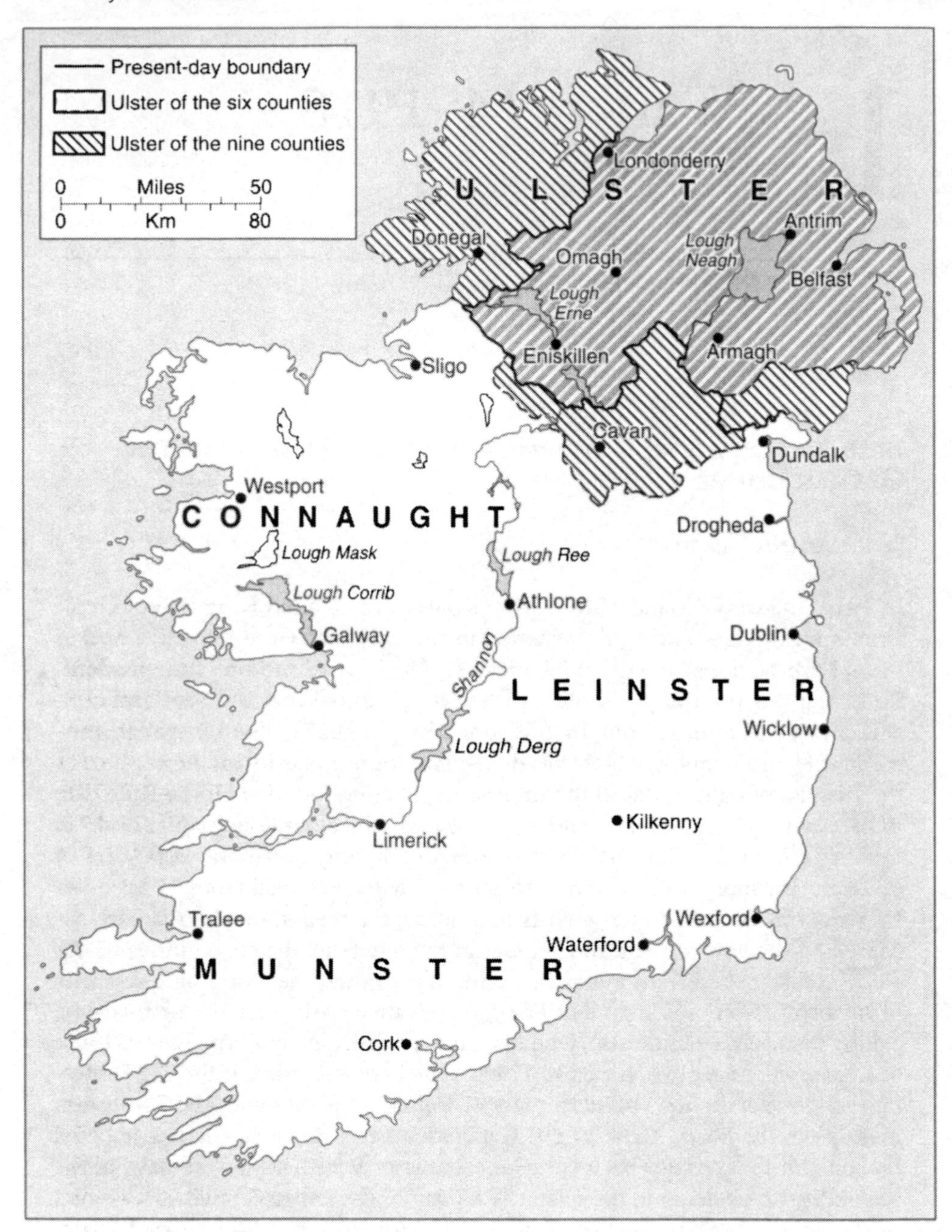


**Map 1** Partitioned Ireland (based on map in A. J. P. Taylor, *English History 1914–1945*, Oxford: Oxford University Press, 1965).

element in modern Irish nationalism: two leading figures of the eighteenth century, and nineteenth century, respectively, Wolfe Tone and Charles Parnell, had both been Protestants. The Nationalist leader in Parliament, John Redmond, actually had the rather wild hope that the Ulster Volunteers could be brought behind the Home Rule movement. On the Nationalist side, the body which was most extreme in its advocacy of complete separation from Britain was the tiny, conspiratorial, Irish Republican Brotherhood.

The idea of Germany as a potential international enemy had surfaced from time to time in previous years, not least in popular novels. The assassination of the heir to the throne of the Austro-Hungarian Empire at Sarajevo by a Serbian nationalist on 28 June, and the events which followed, did suggest to the well-informed the imminence of a European war; but it was the prospect of civil war in Ireland which continued to command the headlines. Austria-Hungary, having first secured German backing, invaded and overran Serbia. Russia, protector of fellow Slavs and Orthodox co-religionists, began to prepare for mobilization. On Saturday, 1 August Germany declared war on Russia. Meeting on the evening of Sunday, 2 August, the British Cabinet learned that Germany had invaded Luxembourg, clear evidence of the intention to march through Belgium. It was on this evening that the Prime Minister gave written authority for the mobilization of the British army. On the morning of Bank Holiday Monday, 3 August, news reached the Cabinet that Germany had issued an ultimatum to Belgium demanding unresisted passage for the German troops. That afternoon, the House of Commons, in emergency session, received its first account of the international crisis. As Germany declared war on France, the British government served an ultimatum on Germany to halt their invasion by 11.00 p.m. (midnight in Germany) the following day. On the morning of 4 August, Field-Marshal Lord Kitchener, Consul-General in Egypt, who had been briefly in London to collect an earldom, was on his way to Dover, prior to embarking for Egypt. Kitchener was intercepted at Dover and invited to take office as Secretary of State for War. Meantime the Cabinet received definite news of the German invasion of Belgium, while not receiving any reply at all to the ultimatum. The date 4 August 1914 is one everybody knows; actually, the state of war between Britain and Germany only began in the very last hour of that day. An act of 1871 had provided that in the event of war the railways would be put at the disposal of the government. Thus on 4 August, even before war had been declared, the railways passed into the control of the government, to be run as a unified system by the Railway Executive Committee, of which the official Chairman was the President of the Board of Trade. Receipts were pooled, and the individual railway companies were guaranteed the same level of profits as they had enjoyed in 1913. The first British Council of War was held on the afternoon of 5 August, with Kitchener taking his place as Secretary of State for War. On 8 August the Channel Fleet was fully mobilized and standing guard over the Channel crossing. Between 12 and 22 August the first British Expeditionary Force (BEF) was transported to France, with a small number travelling by aeroplane.[2]

The crowds which had been gathering in Trafalgar Square on the evening of 4 August greeted the declaration of war with cheering, flag waving and a great show of patriotic enthusiasm. People in crowds do not necessarily behave as they would at home; thus there is no need to believe that the involvement of Britain in war was greeted with universal jubilation and delirium. Yet the evidence is overwhelming that throughout the United Kingdom the feeling was this was a war that had to be fought. Individuals could, of course, be enthusiastic for the war and not actually want to fight themselves, or have sons or husbands taken from them. Men might quite decidedly feel it a duty to fight, yet, quite understandably, be overwhelmingly fearful of military discipline, of injury, of death. The 'recruiting boom' of August–September 1914 (the phrase is used by Peter Simkins, in his excellent *Kitchener's Army*[3]) is in some ways most impressive, and in others rather less so. When, on the morning of 4 August, with war still fifteen hours away, the recruiting officer arrived at the main London office in Great Scotland Yard, it took him twenty minutes to get in, so large was the crowd of eager volunteers outside. Across the country, between 4 and 8 August, an average of 1,640 men enlisted each day; on Sunday, 9 August the figure was 2,433.

After 7 August, many more recruiting offices were opened in London and throughout the country. Recruiting actually slackened somewhat. However, towards the end of the month, news of the engagement of the BEF in the Battle of Mons, and their subsequent retreat, produced another spurt of volunteers. Britain had never subscribed to the French Revolutionary tradition of the nation in arms, always relying on the professional army: many young men evidently continued to believe that, however just the war, it was for others to fight. Those who would in no circumstances be called upon waxed indignant. A self-styled 'British Matron' referred in the *Brighton Herald* (5 September 1914) to 'hundreds of cowardly young male curs (I cannot call them men) perambulating the streets daily, apparently ignoring their obligations to their country'; she recommended that English women should learn to use revolvers, 'so that' – the reference is to the threat of rape, though the language is that of Victorian delicacy – 'when England is invaded by a horde of German barbarians they could at least account for one the less and save their own honour'. A male playwright, writing from his gentlemen's club, called in *The Times* (1 September 1914) for English girls to shun young men not taking up arms without good reason, while a crusty admiral reminded them of the white feather as a traditional symbol of cowardice (*Daily Mail*, 31 August 1914).

Right up until 5 August there had been demonstrations and appeals against British involvement in the war; the Labour party was formally committed to the notion that if all workers refused to fight there would be no wars; but, several thousand courageous pacifists apart, opposition to the war very quickly evaporated. There were volunteers from both communities in Ireland, though it was the Ulster Volunteers who found their numbers most rapidly depleted. Home Rule was enacted in September, but was not to come into effect until the end of the war.

Events are important. The Great War (alias the First World War) was a very big event, and ultimately was to transform developments in Ireland; for the time being, it completely eclipsed them. The actual decision to go to war was made by two or three Liberal Cabinet ministers; they already knew they could count on the support of practically all Conservative politicians; and, very quickly, they got the approval of practically all politicians across the parties. Their belief was that Britain could not tolerate a German domination of the European continent. For many ordinary people the cry of 'King, God, and Country', of rallying to the flag, was enough; then there was the threat of German (and Austrian) barbarism, whether felt vicariously on behalf of Belgians and Serbs, or perceived as entailing invasion of Britain itself, the sense of taking up 'The Sword of Justice' (see plate 1). It has been argued that since German dominance of Europe was inevitable anyway, Britain's politicians would have been wiser to bow to the inevitable and stay out of the war.[4] Given the pressures on them (channelled in particular through the press), given their conviction that Britain could never acknowledge being second to any other power, and given the sense of obligation to support France, this was scarcely an option that any but the most exceptional, or most deeply pacifist, politician of the time could have entertained. Thus, as they saw it, the politicians, with their generals, had one overriding task: to wage war as effectively as they could. They had the advantage of an almost totally unified country – the (almost) uncomplaining efforts and sacrifices of the British people throughout the war explode any thesis about Britain being a deeply divided society, or being on the verge of revolution. A political truce was declared; any parliamentary seats falling vacant would be filled by the incumbent party.

Was the challenge of this war greatly in excess of anything which had gone before? One certainly does not need to belittle the challenges faced by British politicians during the Revolutionary and Napoleonic wars, which lasted for over twenty years, as compared with four years, three months, and one week for the Great War; nor to ignore the American Civil War. But, despite

**Plate 1** Taking the Oath: Recruiting Office at White City, London, June 1915. Courtesy of Hulton Getty

fashionable quibbles,[5] the notion of the Great War as 'the first total war' is entirely justified, for at least three overlapping reasons:

1 This was a war between industrialized nations, covering the whole of Europe, and parts of the world outside (the American Civil War had been waged between the industrialized and the non-industrialized parts of the same country).
2 Science and technology were thoroughly integrated into the waging of war.
3 Everyone, in every country, became in some way affected by, or implicated in, the war – it became necessary for governments to control and to mobilize their domestic fronts.

Britain was not invaded. Though disastrous interruptions of her supply lines came close, she was never blockaded into continuous near-starvation, as were the countries of Central and eastern Europe. She did not have to fight other major powers on two different European fronts. On the other hand, at the beginning of the war, Britain, unlike friend and foe alike, had no mass conscript army – just a mighty navy, and a small professional army basically designed for policing the Empire. Just precisely what effects the Great War had on British politics, the economy, society and British culture continues to be a matter for legitimate debate. But it can scarcely be denied that without an understanding of the dimensions and nature of the Great War, there can be no complete understanding of Britain in the twentieth century.[6]

## *War*

The Admiralty knew what to do on the outbreak of war, and did it: the Grand Fleet was quickly at its battle stations in the North Sea ready for any encounter with the German navy. The only plans for the army were those which Sir Henry Wilson, Director of Military Operations, had developed in discussions with French staff officers. These were basically to send the BEF (Commander-in-Chief, Sir John French, ambitious and affable, self-serving but considerate towards his men), established in 1910 out of all the troops that could be spared from Imperial duties, to join the French left flank. By Lord Kitchener's orders of 14 August Sir John was to cooperate fully with the French army: on 21 and 22 August the French Fifth Army and the BEF marched together across the frontier into Belgium. The German plan (the famous 'Schlieffen Plan') was to defeat the French as quickly as possible (Teutonic logic thus dictating passage through Belgium), so that the German armies could then face up to Russia in the east. The French plan was, with great *élan*, to strike rapidly into Germany through Lorraine, which the Germans had captured in 1870 (the upshot being that the French threw away vital industrial territory of their own). At the time of Mons the BEF encountered the massive German First Army, and though acquitting itself well, was forced into a retreat which, in wearisome heat, continued until early September; meantime the French Fifth Army suffered crushing defeat at the Battle of Charleroi. The French Commander-in-Chief, General J. J. C. Joffre, saw that plans for dramatic attack must be scrapped for inspirational defence (including the use of Paris taxis to carry troop reinforcements), successfully implemented at the Battle of the Marne, generally accepted by those historians who care about such things as the crucial turning point which prevented the rapid German conquest of France, and led to the war turning into a prolonged and bloody stalemate. The BEF played only a marginal role in this battle, but its retreat had come to an end. There then followed what is always, slightly misleadingly, termed 'the race to the sea' as the Germans sought to get round the left flank of the Allied line. Now the BEF had a major part to play in what came to be known as the First Battle of Ypres (18 October–18 November), where it brought the German outflanking movement to a halt despite losses which were so heavy that they amounted to the destruction of the old professional army.[7] The war of movement in the west had come to an end six weeks before the year did (see map 2).

Although frustrated in the west, the Germans had by the end of 1914 inflicted some devastating defeats on the Russians. Thus, in a reversal of strat-

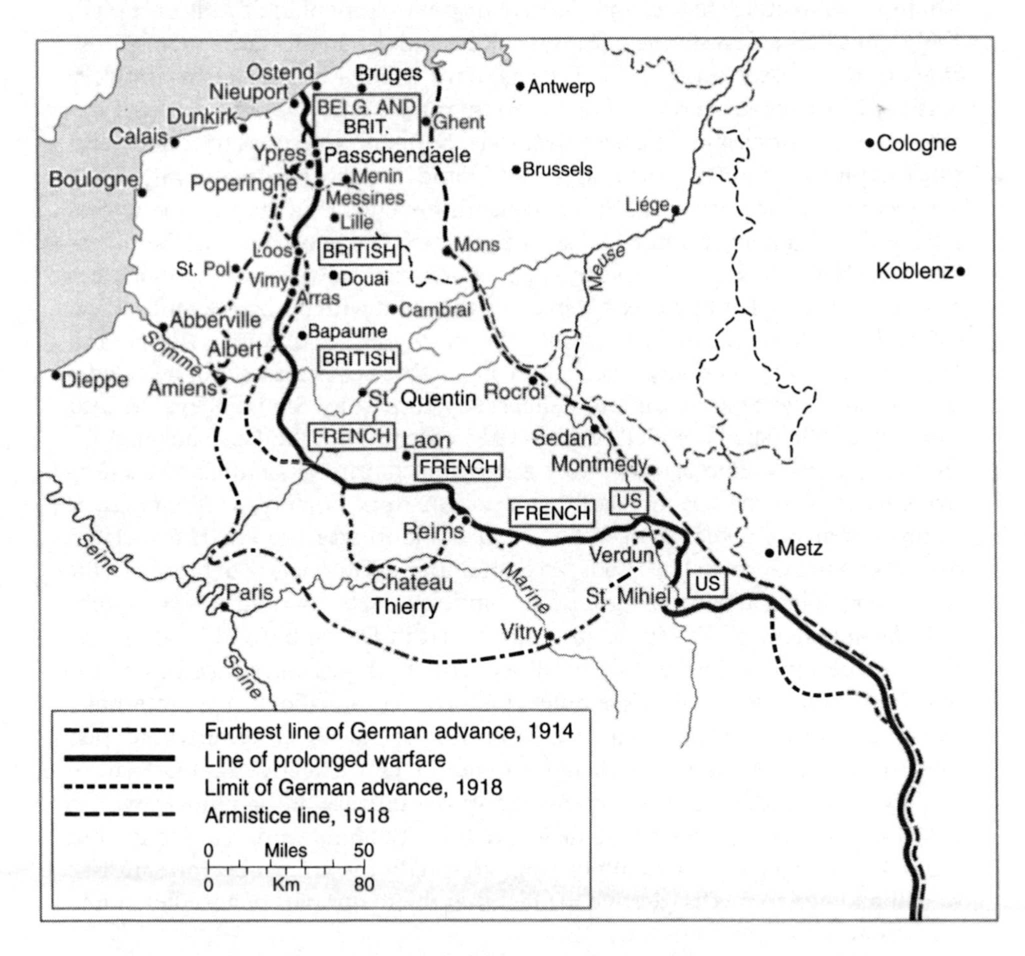


**Map 2** First World War: The Western Front (based on map in Trevor Lloyd, *Empire, Welfare State, Europe*, Oxford: Oxford University Press, 1993).

egy, they planned for further advances in the east, while defending in strength in the west. Already French casualties were enormous: two-fifths of what they were to be after nearly four more years. The BEF had performed honourably, but in the entire perspective of the war its part so far had been very small. What the British authorities had to do was to raise a mass army; at the same time they had to decide what, if anything, could be done to break the commanding position held by the Germans. The BEF had exploited the potential of the formidable Lee-Enfield rifle to the full, but had been shown to be woefully short of heavy guns and high explosives. Not only would the British government have to massively expand the British army, it would have to ensure that it was fully equipped to meet German firepower on equal terms.

In addition to occupying the whole of Belgium, save for the small area round La Panne, where about half of the line was manned by Belgian troops, the Germans occupied one-tenth of the national territory of France. Despite the fact that barbed-wire emplacements and machine-gun nests gave the advantage to the defence, attack for the French was a moral imperative. So the British, too, had to attack to keep the German troops in front of them fully occupied. Field guns had a devastating effect on soldiers advancing towards them across the 'no-man's land' between the two sets of front-line trenches. Heavy artillery was used, particularly prior to attempted infantry advances, to weaken the enemy's fortifications and defensive positions. Sappers were used to tunnel, and place explosives, under enemy lines. Aeroplanes quickly became so important for reconnaissance work that life-and-death air engagements became a vital part of the war: being burned to death in your aeroplane became another alternative to being blown to pieces by high explosives, mown down by machine-gun fire, or being left to die slowly in no-man's land with perhaps a limb blown off. British offensives at Neuve Chapelle in March, and Aubers Ridge and Festubert, in May, not only incurred the inevitable heavy losses, but revealed a serious shortage of ammunition, deliberately turned by Sir John French into the very public 'shell scandal' of May 1915. Meantime, the Germans had introduced a new technological horror, employing chlorine gas in their own short-lived advance at the Second Battle of Ypres in April, mainly, as it happened, against French colonial troops. The same weapon was used in Haig's 1915 assaults on the German line (Loos, 25 September–8 October). For those caught unawares, chlorine could do gruesome, and for those who did not succumb, long-lasting damage. Phosgene gas, introduced in December 1915, was many times more toxic. Most deadly of all was mustard gas, introduced in 1917, which not only did not disperse quickly, but raised horrific blisters, internally as well as externally. The first advice for protection against chlorine was to 'piss on your handkerchiefs and tie them over your faces'.[8] Effective gas masks were rapidly developed, so that, while gassing for the unwary or the unlucky was as atrocious as popular memory of the war tells us, the final verdict has to be that the risk of being gassed was minor compared with the almost everpresent risk of being blown to pieces (despite the fact that the major part of a soldier's time was spent out of the front line).

Should 'the Great War' ever have been christened 'the First *World* War' – as it was as early as 1920?[9] When Turkey entered the war on the German side on

5 November 1914 this was immediately perceived as a threat to the British position in Egypt, and, indeed, in India. But Winston Churchill, First Lord of the Admiralty, also saw it as an opportunity to open up another front against the Central Powers, particularly as the western stalemate became apparent: furthermore, the Russians, in January, specifically requested British and French action against Turkey. A combined British and French force (including the poet Rupert Brooke, and strong contingents of Australians and New Zealanders) sailed forth for Gallipoli, landing on 23 April. But, woefully inadequate to the stated task of knocking Turkey out of the war, the Imperial and French forces became bogged down in an impasse just as horrific as that on the Western Front, and finally had to be withdrawn on 8 January 1916. British forces also landed in Mesopotamia, suffering early reverses, before eventually being materially assisted by the Arab Revolt against Turkish rule (in which Lawrence of Arabia played his celebrated role).

It was in 1916, according to many of today's military historians, that true total warfare began. The phrase was actually coined by General Ludendorff, who, nominally as Adjutant to Field-Marshal Hindenberg, ran the German war effort from August 1916. If we are interested in the principles of *waging* war, in the conscious decisions of generals and politicians, in the absence of the likelihood of a decisive blow, to bleed the enemy to death, to subordinate flesh and blood completely to machines, to be quite explicit in incorporating the home front in the war effort, then 1916 is the year. If, on the other hand, we are interested in the overall effects of the war on society, then individual years are of less significance: the entire war, from August 1914 to November 1918, can be rated a 'total war', even if (a phrase permitted to historians if not to philosophers) it became 'more total' from 1916 onwards.

Probably General von Falkenhayn was not a complete total warrior in the sense just expounded, but he saw that what he must do was break the French army. If he mounted a massive attack on the great French defensive system around Verdun, the French sense of national honour would compel them to defend it at all costs, and thus Falkenhayn would 'bleed France white'. An intense artillery bombardment signalled the commencement of the German attack on 21 February. By May the French had lost nearly 200,000 men. The Italians, having just entered the war on the side of the Western Allies, had already suffered a heavy defeat at the hands of the Austrians. Planning a major offensive in Galicia, the Russians wanted the Germans to be fully stretched in the west. Earlier in the year, a massive joint offensive had been planned for the Somme, the main point of junction between the British and French armies, with the clearly stated purpose of achieving a decisive victory. Verdun changed all that, and when, on 1 July 1916, the British launched into a battle unprecedented in its magnitude, the basic objective was to relieve the pressure on the French at Verdun, while inflicting as much damage as possible on the Germans; it would, Haig fully recognized, be a 'wearing out fight'.[10] Before what, to optimistic British troops, was to be the 'Great Push', there took place the only major naval engagement of the war, when the German High Seas Fleet came out of port for the first and only time. At the Battle of Jutland (31 May–1 June) the British Grand Fleet suffered far heavier losses than the Germans,

112,000 tons to 61,000, and 6,000 men to 2,500. But, the crucial upshot was that the German fleet retreated to port, where it remained for the rest of the war. Four days later the ship in which Lord Kitchener was travelling on a mission to Russia hit a mine off the Orkneys; the War Secretary's body was never recovered.

Whatever his other failings, Kitchener had from the start seen the need to create a mass army, and he had certainly proved to be 'a magnificent poster'. The brunt of the Battle of the Somme was borne by 'Kitchener's Army' or 'The New Army', the idealistic, or simply duty-conscious, men, young and not so young, who had volunteered to fight for King and Country. The first day, 1 July 1916, was horrendous. A week-long barrage, marred by an insufficiency of heavy guns and far too many faulty shells, had failed to clear the way for the infantry advance: almost 20,000 men were cut down by relentless machine-gun fire, with 60,000 casualties in all. Thereafter there was more tactical flexibility, and some local gains were achieved, though always with heavy losses, three British for every two German. As early as 11 July, the Germans did break off the offensive against Verdun. One technological response to the stalemate of trench warfare was the 'tank', an armoured vehicle on tracks which could move forward against machine-gun fire across barbed wire and pock-marked terrain. Britain was the first to develop the new concept, but, in fact, of the 150 Haig had been promised for the opening of the Somme, only 60 had arrived by late August. Tanks, mechanically unreliable and with a maximum speed of half a mile per hour, were deployed for the first time on 15 September, having just about enough of an effect on the Germans (mainly surprise) to indicate their potential for the future, if intelligently used. At best, the Somme gained a maximum of 10 miles, at a cost of 400,000 casualties for the British. Appalling all round, the blood-letting was even more serious for the Germans. The Somme offensive was kept going until, with winter victorious, it was closed down on 18 November.

With respect to total war, in the military sense, another arm was the unrestricted use of submarines. In February 1915 Germany had declared the waters around the British Isles a war zone, where submarine attacks could be carried out without prior warning; in part, at least, this was a response to the British naval blockade, which prevented vital materials of all types from getting through to Germany. On 7 May the British liner *Lusitania*, carrying 2,000 passengers, but also some munitions, was torpedoed: 1,198 passengers were drowned, of whom 128 were American citizens, 291 were women and 94 children. In September, following American protests, Germany drew back from unrestricted submarine warfare, and thereafter policy oscillated. On 1 February 1917, the new Hindenberg–Ludendorff regime made itself felt with the introduction of completely unrestricted submarine warfare, rendered devastating by the arrival of a new generation of submarines which could operate submerged for long periods as far afield as the Atlantic seaboard of the United States.

The slaughter on the Somme created one kind of rumbling crisis for the British government: how could this go on? Was there any alternative? Could generals who lost so many lives for so little perceptible gain be trusted? But the catastrophic shipping losses by April 1917 created a crisis of an altogether more desperate sort: quite literally, within weeks vital supplies would run out, and Britain would have lost the war. This is a crucial fact which must always be placed at the centre of any discussion of the political direction of the war. The war could have been lost; it wasn't. Massive reorganization to conserve resources was essential (discussed later). More important, the submarine threat itself had to be directly countered. The only solution which offered itself was that of organizing shipping into convoys, a solution fraught with problems: speeds would be reduced to those of the slowest ship; congestion would be created; merchant ships would have the greatest difficulty in keeping close formation. The Admiralty reasoning, though undoubtedly defeatist (itself a measure of the crisis), was not absurd. However, thanks to the support of two eminent seamen, Captain Richmond and Admiral Hamilton, Lloyd George, now Prime Minister, secured acceptance of the convoy system on 27 April. Convoy, deploying battleships as escorts, was an offensive, as well as defensive (its principal purpose), measure. In July and August, only five merchant ships were lost out of the eight hundred convoyed; meantime German submarine losses mounted, so that by September they were in excess of new launchings. Britain's desperate situation was also eased by the entry into the war of the United States, on 6 April, following the breaking of diplomatic relations with Germany on 3 February.

French politicians shared Lloyd George's revulsion at the fruitless bloodletting. The new French Commander-in-Chief, General Robert Nivelle, promised a new approach. As a gunner, he put his faith in creating crushing artillery bombardments, followed by breakthrough and rapid pursuit of the Germans. If the breakthrough failed to materialize, then the engagement would immediately be stopped. Lloyd George was impressed, and at the Calais Conference of 26/27 February 1917, he committed the British forces to full cooperation under Nivelle's command. Aided by greatly improved ammunition, the British had a modest success at the Battle of Arras. Nivelle's offensive on the Aisne, beginning on 16 April, was a failure. There were three principal reasons: already the Germans had made a strategic withdrawal to the heavily fortified 'Siegfried Line'; they had managed to capture the detailed plans of the French Fifth Army; and Nivelle's opening bombardment was nowhere as effective as he had promised. French soldiers endured the usual heavy losses, accompanied by the usual absence of any recognizable gain. The conscript 'peasants' (i.e. mainly small landowners who farmed their own land) had had enough. Across 68 out of 112 army divisions, soldiers refused to obey orders, sang the song of international working-class solidarity, the *Internationale*, and even threatened to march on Paris. These were the famous 'mutinies', which reached their peak in June and July. The Germans never got to hear of them; despite the fears of generals and politicians, they were not revolutionary in intention; they were expressions of extreme war weariness and desire for an end to futile slaughter. Nivelle was dismissed in May (as A. J. P. Taylor pointed out, he was one of the few generals so chastened as not to burden posterity with his memoirs).[11] The cautious Pétain took over. The main consequence of the mutinies was that the British were forced to extend the area of their own offensive, producing a steep rise in casualties, and delaying the offensive which Haig had long planned in Flanders.

Haig's ultimate objective in the Flanders campaign was the capture of Bruges, 30 miles away, which would certainly have undermined the entire German position in Belgium. If one accepts that this was a war which the British had to fight, and that, on the Western Front, it could only be fought in a particular way, then the opening battle, the Battle of Messines, was the very model of a successful battle. At Messines, the Royal Flying Corps had air supremacy, and thus provided accurate information about the German rear areas. General Sir Herbert Plumer, known to his troops as 'Daddy', lacked the handsome, martial features of a Kitchener, French or Haig. He had amassed the greatest concentration of heavy artillery in the war so far, and this was used with great deliberation, exploiting to the full the knowledge of German dispositions in the rear areas. The bombardment lasted for eight days, then at 3.10 a.m. on 7 June almost a million pounds of explosive in tunnels under the German front line were set off, causing havoc. Preceded by a devastating creeping barrage, and accompanied by 72 efficient Mark IV tanks, the infantry of Plumer's Second Army advanced steadily to take all of their objectives. Plumer had taken great care to master the typography of the terrain, and had had his troops practise assaults against facsimile objectives. As J. M. Bourne sums up, the 'Battle of Messines was a vindication of careful planning, overwhelming concentration of artillery, limited objectives and methodical advance'.[12]

The campaign ended in the Third Battle of Ypres of 31 July to 10 November, always known as Passchendaele, one of the most emotive names in the geography of the Western Front. August was very wet; October and November were even worse. Well-directed artillery barrages could have a devastating effect on the enemy; but they also shattered the drainage system in this territory where water was always close to the surface. The battlefield became a swamp of liquid mud, often waste-high. Tanks were useless. Guns sank; sometimes men too. When, on 6 November, the Canadians captured the devastated village of Passchendaele, the Allied line had moved forward by four miles. Given the atrocious conditions, should the campaign have been persisted with? One possible explanation certainly is not available: treating the French mutinies with restraint (only a few activists were executed), Pétain was very successful in restoring French morale by the autumn, so it was no longer vital, as defenders of the Flanders campaign have argued, that the British keep the Germans under persistent attack. The Germans, of course, suffered immensely too, many soldiers deserting into neutral Holland.

In the summer of 1916 the Russians had enjoyed some successes on the Eastern Front, though with very high casualties. The simple fact was that the inflexible and autocratic Tsarist regime ultimately could not stand the demands and stresses of war. Riots broke out in Petrograd in March 1917, leading to the formation of a Provisional Government, under Kerensky, supported by the middle-class 'voluntary organizations' who had contributed much to the national effort, and who wanted to see the war prosecuted with greater efficiency; the Tsar abdicated on 15 March. But the new Russian offensive in July was a disaster, leaving Ludendorff free to transfer his strategic reserve of seven divisions to support the Austrians on the Italian front, materially contributing to the rout of the Italian army at Caporetto. Hastily despatched British and French troops prevented an invasion of Italy. In November, the Bolsheviks, dedicated believers in revolution on the Marxist model, overthrew the Kerensky regime. Within a month, Russia was out of the war. French generals and politicians feared that 'the Bolshevik infection' would revive mutinous tendencies: in fact soldiers' letters show their detestation of the Bolsheviks for making it possible for the Germans to transfer their full weight to the Western Front.

In his Flanders Campaign ('Passchendaele') Haig had singly-and-narrow-mindedly sought decisive victory in Belgium. In a rather similar kind of way, Ludendorff convinced himself that Germany must, in the first months of 1918, deliver a decisive blow in the west, before the American armies arrived in strength (in fact, the Americans produced a mass army quicker than anyone expected). He had other good reasons. Austria-Hungary was near to collapse and, with the defeat of Russia, was looking for a way of ending the war, while Turkey looked almost certain to succumb to renewed British action in Palestine. Even with troops transferred from the Eastern Front, Germany could hope for no more than numerical parity with the British and French forces. Germany had so few tanks that Ludendorff did not feel it worthwhile to deploy them. He did have an effective railway system, and he intended to make the most of motor transport. A mighty artillery force of 5,500 guns and 3,500 mortars was assembled. The point carefully chosen for attack was that of the junction between the main British and the main French armies. To retain as much of the surprise element as possible, Ludendorff eschewed what had become the almost standard lengthy period of bombardment. His heavy guns went into action at 4.40 a.m. on 21 March 1918; just five hours later the German infantry were on the move. The British Fifth Army, under General Gough, collapsed into disorderly retreat; the French Third Army failed to provide the expected reinforcements. By 27 March the German army had advanced 40 miles to within 12 miles of the strategic rail centre at Amiens. Paris would fall; the British would have to get their forces out while they still held the Channel ports; the war would be lost. This time, as had not happened with the case of the disastrous shipping losses, the sense of desperate crisis reached the newspapers, which published special editions on Good Friday (29 March). Lloyd George himself took over the War Office and rushed men on leave back across the Channel at a rate of 30,000 a day instead of the standard 8,000. Doing a salutary U-turn, Haig recommended that Foch be given powers to 'coordinate' Allied action – that is, become Allied supreme commander. This was effected on 26 March; on 28 March General Gough was sacked. Reluctantly, but decisively, Haig moved 46 of his 58 divisions to Amiens. The German attempt to capture the vital communications centre was beaten off (4/5 April). Ludendorff immediately turned against the weakened line in Flanders; he could still win the war by capturing the Channel ports.

When Haig issued his famous Order of the Day of 11 April, he really meant it: 'With our backs to the wall and believing in the justice of our cause each one of us must fight to the end.' The German advance continued until 27 April. On 29 April the British 21st, 49th and 25th Divisions inflicted heavy losses and brought the German advance towards the Channel ports to an end. But German offensive power had not yet been neutralized. After almost a month, and to the complete surprise of the French, Ludendorff launched a new advance towards Paris (27 May). On 31 May, the Germans were once more on the Marne, less than 40 miles from Paris. But by now the Americans were arriving in considerable numbers. Combined French and American counter-attacks blocked the advance. But again (15 July) the Germans attempted that crucial breakthrough. They were met by the French Fourth Army, deploying 'elastic defence', which meant a lightly held forward zone where land-mines and mustard gas were used to devastating effect. Foch's counter-attack, employing hundreds of small 'whippet' tanks, followed. By 20 July, the four-month-long 'Ludendorff offensive' was over. Ludendorff's achievements were considerable, but he was consistently beset by the problem of his army outrunning its supplies; motor lorries were not yet able to deliver what he hoped of them. But pushing the German armies back towards Germany was still going to be an extremely difficult task. Still, lessons had been learned by the generals: the British and French points of attack were constantly varied, no offensive being persisted with if it was not immediately successful. Then individual divisions were ordered to get as far forward as possible, without worrying about the rest of the line. There was a halt as the Germans withdrew behind the formidable Hindenburg Line. But British victories on 27 September prepared the way for the breaching of the line by 9 October – a cataclysmic defeat for the Germans.

Everywhere Germany's allies were collapsing. On 23/24 October the Italians crushed the Austrians at Vittoria Veneto. Having already concluded that the Germans must seek an armistice, Ludendorff resigned on 27 October. On 8 November a civilian delegation joined Marshal Foch in a railway carriage in the Forest of Compiègne to sue for peace. Hostilities, it was agreed, were to end on the Western Front at the eleventh hour of the eleventh day of the eleventh month.

### *Ireland*

Irish Home Rule had been enacted in 1914, but implementation was to remain in abeyance for the duration of the war. Now that the war was over, the politics of Ireland, unfortunately, had changed, utterly. The war, Professor R. F. Foster has told us unambiguously, 'should be seen as one of the most decisive events in modern Irish history'.[13] Unionists and many moderate Nationalists enlisted; fundamentalist Nationalists did not. For them, it was a truism that 'England's danger is Ireland's opportunity'. It was a fundamentalist who spoke of (postponed) Home Rule as 'a cheque continually post-dated', but as more and more Unionists joined Britain's Coalition Governments, that thought became real to moderates as well. Generally, Ireland's peasant small-holders and land workers grew in self-confidence as they benefited from high agricultural prices, while simultaneously feeling resentment at the British government's insistence that they dig up their pasture, and the imposition of production quotas. None of that created what might be called a revolutionary situation. What was true was that, as in every sphere, the horrors and excitements of the battles in France created a quickening of the pulse, felt strongly by those in the Irish Republican Brotherhood (IRB) who envisaged insurrection against the British; more, there was now a very real prospect of serious German support, in men as well as arms, for such an insurrection.

In late 1914–15, Sir Roger Casement, former British Consular official, born in County Dublin, and internationally renowned for his exposure of slave-labour conditions in Africa and South America, was in Berlin seeking German support for an Irish rising against the British, and endeavouring to raise an Irish Brigade among early volunteers from Ireland who were already prisoners of war. The decision for an insurrection at Easter 1916 was taken by a minority within the IRB. Socialist ideas and trade-union organization had been spreading rapidly in Ireland in the years before the war, and the element of socialist revolution was brought in by trade-union organizer and author of the song 'The Red Flag', James Connolly (who, revealingly, said he had always found it easier to explain socialism to the Irish than the Irish to socialists). But the strongest flavouring in this tiny little coterie was that of a mystic Catholic Gaelic nationalism, most obviously represented by law graduate and playwright Patrick Pearse. Casement believed that without a force of 50,000 German troops, a rising would be pointless; in fact, 20,000 rifles and ten machine-guns were to be delivered off County Kerry, but no troops. The overwhelming majority of Nationalists believed that the Irish Volunteers should be kept in reserve to be used as a bargaining counter with the British, or possibly in a future guerrilla war; they were certainly opposed to an insurrection based on Gaelic romanticism. The arms never reached their destination, and the steamer carrying them was scuttled. Insurrections planned for country areas were nearly all called off, so that the famous Easter Rising was almost exclusively a Dublin affair. Even that was postponed from Easter Sunday to Easter Monday. A force of up to 1,600 took over the General Post Office in O'Connell Street and other main buildings. Government forces, put on the alert earlier, had assumed that the whole thing had been called off: troops were belatedly rushed in, including new conscripts who, it was said, thought they were arriving in France. Many were shot down at the Battle of Mount Street Bridge. Dublin became a tiny corner of the Western Front, heavy shells destroying much of the city centre. But, of course, this was a minuscule engagement. The fighting ended the following Monday with 116 soldiers and 16 policemen dead, and Irish casualties of 450 dead, and 2,614 wounded, many having been uninvolved citizens.

Without the war, this event would not have taken place; without this event, and without the ill-advised reactions of the British authorities (themselves partly conditioned by the sense of war emergency), the politics of Ireland would not have been transformed to the extent that they were. Courts martial sentenced 90 leading insurrectionaries to death; 15 executions by firing squad were actually carried out, early in May. In addition, Casement, who had come to Ireland in a German submarine to advise against the rising, and had been captured, was hanged as a traitor. Worse still, martial law was imposed on all Ireland and implemented in such a brutal way that middle-class, pro-British Catholics were totally alienated. Large-scale deportations led to the deportees, often in fact without strong political views, being indoctrinated into extreme nationalism by fellow prisoners in the Frongoch distillery in Wales where they were interned; at which point they were often released back to Ireland by the hard-pressed British authorities.

So, throughout 1917 and on into 1918 a new broadly based, integrated, well-organized movement came into being, taking its name from the pre-war extreme nationalist, but non-violent party founded by Arthur Griffith, Sinn Féin. Those who once would have condemned anything like the Easter Rising as irrational and counter-productive now began to see it as a mighty moral blow on behalf of Irish national identity.

And national identity was something strongly espoused by the newest ally of the western powers, America under President Wilson. Here was another war-related stimulus to a more fundamentalist Irish nationalism. But there was a still more important one. Conscription had been introduced in Britain in two stages in 1916, but, by general consent among the politicians, Ireland had been excluded (Protestants, and many Catholics, had volunteered enthusiastically; conscription would needlessly antagonize the others, whom it might not be wise anyway to equip with arms). But, as we saw, the British need for re-inforcements became more and more acute during 1917. As it began to contemplate extending conscription to Ireland, the government also perceived that with the substantial change in sentiment throughout Ireland it might be a good idea to get Home Rule put into practice as quickly as possible. There were two problems: the new sentiment in Ireland now went far beyond Home Rule to the idea of complete separation; but any discussion of even Home Rule made immediately pressing the issue of excluding the six Ulster counties which had clear Protestant majorities – that is to say, the issue of 'partition'. This resulted in the conviction that if conscription in Ireland was to be successful, then Home Rule very certainly must be implemented at the same time; even Unionists began to accept this, taking it for granted, of course, that Ulster would be excluded.

The Military Service Bill drawn up by Lloyd George in April 1918 was intended to open the way for conscription in Ireland, linked with the implementation of Home Rule. The constitutional Irish Nationalist party in parliament, under John Redmond, felt they were promised Home Rule already. Most of the new Sinn Féin movement wanted far more than Home Rule. Everybody could unite in passionate opposition to conscription. The government at Westminster had succeeded in intensifying the alienation of every nationalist interest; then the authorities in Dublin carried out a series of arrests of Sinn Féiners, on the basis of an alleged 'German Plot'. Home Rule might just have been a practical proposition before the war broke out, though it would probably have provoked the Ulster Volunteers into armed resistance. In a thoughtful article, Alvin Jackson has suggested that even if Irish Home Rule had been enacted in 1912, outcomes in the embattled isle would have been broadly the same.[14] For those with eyes to see, Home Rule was a highly unlikely proposition now that the war had ended.

## THE LIMITS ON, AND THE POSSIBILITIES OF, CHANGE

### *FUNDAMENTAL CIRCUMSTANCES GOVERNING CHANGE*

Of the period of around 84 years covered by this book, the crises of total war occupied well over 10 per cent (and throw in a few more per cent for the Korean, Argentine, Gulf and Yugoslav wars), while the lesser, but more persistent, crises of Irish politics were major preoccupations for a good deal more than a third. But we must now turn from great events to the longer-term circumstances, which both create the possibilities for change and impose the limits upon it, which set the context for both change and stagnation. For analytical purposes, these 'circumstances' can be divided into three: structural, ideological, and institutional. Human development, manifestly, is governed by geography, demography, economics and technology; these are basic structural circumstances. But ideas, beliefs and values are very important as well. Religious faith, pride in the nation, political principles, can be powerful motivators. More, ideas cannot be fully acted upon till they have been fully formulated. There can be no democracy, until someone has thought up the idea of democracy; nor equality for women till the belief that women are inherently inferior to men has been destroyed. Without a concept of change itself, there would be very little change. The importance of changing ideological circumstances was wittily brought out in a *Punch* cartoon of 26 August 1926, by Pat Keely (see plate 2). A 'bright young thing' is lolling in a hammock being lectured by her mother:

**Plate 2** *Punch* cartoon, 25 August 1926, by Pat Keely. Courtesy of Punch, University of Kent

But the nature and extent of change, or the lack of it, is often determined by institutions: parliament, the electoral system, political parties, the Bank of England, the Church of England. Thus it is important, thirdly, to establish the institutional framework. Few would disagree that British parliamentary institutions, with all their faults, were more conducive to change than the Russian autocracy, for example.

That the United Kingdom of Great Britain and Ireland was two islands was certainly helpful in insulating Britain from foreign invasion; though the fact that Ireland was a second island did make the prospect of German landings there rather more realistic than the prospect, say, of such landings in Wales. As is well known, appropriate coal and mineral deposits, natural harbours and a terrain upon which communications networks could relatively easily be constructed, assisted Britain in becoming the world's first industrialized nation. The exact role of population change in that has been much debated, but there can be no debating the overarching significance of 'vital statistics' – civil service prose for the bare demographic facts: birth rates, death rates, the rise and decline, and the structure, of population. Matters of this sort are best set out in tables (e.g. table 1.1); and then (believe me!) it is quite fun working out what major implications for the development and wellbeing of the country one can draw out from them.

I suggest that you, the reader, now ponder the implications of these figures. But before that, two words of caution. First, it is dangerous to interpret statistics without being in command of all the relevant contextual information. Second, broad statistical trends can be the sum of several mini-trends, not all of them necessarily going in the same direction. As well as births and deaths, crude population figures reflect the balance of emigration against immigration. Before 1914 emigration caused a net loss of up to around 200,000 a year – mainly, though not exclusively, young men. In the twenties this figure halved, and in the thirties there was a small inward balance. Then we have the loss of life caused by war, almost exclusively among young men. And to that add the effects of the influenza epidemic at the end of the war, which was pretty indiscriminate as to age and sex. All that said, I hope that you spotted the following crucial trends:

1 Although total population continues to grow slowly, the annual rate of increase by 1921 is less than half what it had been before 1911, and this low rate of increase continues throughout the inter-war years.
2 The proportion of old people is continually going up, while the proportion of young people (not, of course, the total number) is dropping.
3 While women are always in a majority (because, at all ages, women have better survival rates than men), the balance is much more sharply distorted in 1921 (because of the war losses) – many young women were not going to be able to find husbands – even though the loss due to emigration was diminishing. The phenomenon of the 'lost generation' has perhaps been exaggerated – the top politicians *after* 1945, Attlee and Macmillan, for instance, came from this generation – but it can be said that there was a gap in what should have been the rising cohort of political and business leaders in the thirties, and, more generally, that a population loss of this sort tended to generate pessimism.

**Table 1.1** United Kingdom population statistics, 1901–1931

| *Year* | *Total population (in millions) in Great Britain (including Northern Ireland after 1922)* | *Total population (in millions) in Ireland (up to 1921)* | *Annual percentage growth rates over previous ten years (excluding Ireland)* |
|---|---|---|---|
| 1901 | 37.00 | 4.6 | |
| 1911 | 40.83 | 4.4 | 1.04 |
| 1921 | 42.77 | 1.3, North (3.0, South) | 0.47 |
| 1931 | 46.04 (44.80 Great Britain only) | | 0.47 |

| *Year* | *Males females* | *Married females* | *Unmarried females* | *Total (years of age percentage)* | *Under 15 (years of age percentage)* | *Over 65* |
|---|---|---|---|---|---|---|
| 1901 | 17.9 | 6.41 | 12.69 | 19.1 | 32.5 | 4.7 |
| 1911 | 19.75 | 7.39 | 13.68 | 21.07 | 30.8 | 5.2 |
| 1921 | 20.42 | 8.44 | 13.91 | 22.77 | 27.9 | 6.0 |
| 1931 | 21.46 | 9.49 | 13.85 | 23.24 | 24.2 | 7.4 |

| | *Birth rates per thousand of population* | | |
|---|---|---|---|
| *Year* | *England and Wales* | *Scotland* | *Ireland* |
| 1901 | 28.5 | 29.5 | 22.7 |
| 1911 | 24.3 | 25.6 | 23.2 |
| 1921 | 22.4 | 25.2 | 20.8 |
| 1931 | 15.8 | 19.9 | 20.5 (Northern Ireland only) |

*Source:* B. R. Mitchell, with Phyllis Deane, *Abstract of British Historical Statistics* (Cambridge: Cambridge University Press, 1962).

A moment ago I mentioned that Britain was the world's first industrialized nation. How was she faring at the outbreak of war in 1914? For that we need to start with the basic economic facts.

The comparative statistics were the ones which worried politicians. Prior to 1913 Germany, most notably, and also the United States, were beginning to eat into Britain's share of world exports of manufactured goods. However, on the figures given in tables 1.2, 1.3 and 1.4 (other authorities give slightly more pessimistic ones) Britain still seems to be doing pretty well. The trend continues, but we can see how Germany obviously suffers from being defeated in the war. Growth in British productivity is clearly sharply in decline after the turn of the century, and the challenge from other countries is obvious, though again

**Table 1.2** World exports of manufactured goods (percentage shares), 1899–1937

| | *UK* | *US* | *Germany* | *Italy* | *France* | *Japan* |
|---|---|---|---|---|---|---|
| 1899 | 34.5 | 12.1 | 16.6 | 3.8 | 14.9 | 1.6 |
| 1913 | 31.8 | 13.7 | 19.9 | 3.5 | 12.8 | 2.5 |
| 1929 | 23.8 | 21.7 | 15.5 | 3.9 | 11.6 | 4.1 |
| 1937 | 22.3 | 20.5 | 16.5 | 3.7 | 6.2 | 7.4 |

*Source:* R. C. O. Matthews, C. H. Feinstein and J. C. Odling-Smee, *British Economic Growth, 1856–1973* (Oxford: Clarendon Press, 1982), p. 435.

**Table 1.3** Growth of Gross Domestic Product per man-year (annual percentage growth rates), 1873–1937

| | *UK* | *US* | *Sweden* | *France* | *Germany* | *Italy* | *Japan* |
|---|---|---|---|---|---|---|---|
| 1873–99 | 1.2 | 1.9 | 1.5 | 1.3 | 1.5 | 0.3 | 1.1 |
| 1899–1913 | 0.5 | 1.3 | 2.1 | 1.6 | 1.5 | 2.5 | 1.8 |
| 1913–24 | 0.3 | 1.7 | 0.3 | 0.8 | –0.9 | –0.1 | 3.2 |
| 1927–37 | 1.0 | 1.4 | 1.7 | 1.4 | 3.0 | 1.8 | 2.7 |

*Source:* R. C. O. Matthews, C. H. Feinstein and J. C. Odling-Smee, *British Economic Growth, 1856–1973* (Oxford: Clarendon Press, 1982), p. 31.

**Table 1.4** British balance of payments, 1901–1938 (annual average in £million)

| | *Visible* | *Invisible* | *Investments* | *Balance* |
|---|---|---|---|---|
| 1901–5 | –174.5 | 110.6 | 112.9 | 49.0 |
| 1906–10 | –142.1 | 136.5 | 151.4 | 145.8 |
| 1911–13 | –134.4 | 152.6 | 187.9 | 206.1 |
| 1920–9 | –205.0 | 100.0 | 219.0 | 114.0 |
| 1930–8 | –255.0 | 33.0 | 183.0 | –40.0 |

*Source:* B. R. Mitchell and Phyllis Deane, *Abstract of British Historical Statistics* (Cambridge: Cambridge University Press), p. 334; Sean Glynn and John Oxborrow, *Interwar Britain: A Social and Economic History* (Allen and Unwin, 1976), p. 71.

Germany is set back by the war, with only the United States doing well then. The balance of payments figures, certainly up to the war at least, are those of a rich country. With respect to actual goods ('visible' imports and exports) Britain can afford to import more than she exports. The differences were far more than compensated for by 'invisible' exports (banking and insurance services etc.), which were, of course, concentrated in the City of London, and by returns from overseas investments. Some historians have recently suggested that we should concentrate on British successes in finance and trade and ignore failings in manufacture;[15] this book takes a contrary view. The balance of payments is very healthy in 1913, and continues to be so for the first half of the inter-war years; thereafter we can see recession and the big crisis of 1931 reacting with the longer-term trends.

We have already had evidence of the awesome importance of technology in our study of the war. As between the industrial powers, levels of technological innovation and exploitation tend to even out. In pure science (not the same thing as technology) the British record in 1914 was certainly not behind that of the French and the Germans (there were, for example, Lord Kelvin and Clerk Maxwell, pioneers of the theory of electromagnetic waves in electrical theory; J. J. Thomson, who in 1897 proved the existence of the electron; and Ernest Rutherford who constructed a model of the atom just before the war). Undoubtedly Britain was behind France and Germany in the development and exploitation of the internal combustion engine, as her chemicals industry lagged behind the German one (two prime examples of technology). Probably there would have been a catching-up process anyway; the war provided an immediate and desperate stimulus.

Such as it was, the domestic motor-car industry came to a standstill with the outbreak of war. But the War Office intervened directly, first of all subsidizing the production of vehicles, then requisitioning the whole output of all factories able to produce suitable machines, of which a great variety were developed, ranging from lorries and ambulances to – eventually – tanks. Still, a government report in 1914 had commented on the astonishing rise of 'the mechanically-propelled vehicle for passenger purposes' (generally known as the bus) which already accounted for 'fully 94 percent of the passenger vehicles met with on the roads round London'.[16] The horse continued to be very important to commercial transport until well after the Second World War, steam trains went on connecting up villages and suburbs, as well as major cities, the electrified London Underground system and the Southern Railway were crucial to the inter-war development of London's commuter suburbs, but still the motor bus, across the same period, was to play a vital part in increasing mobility for ordinary people, in the countryside and in the towns.

Before the war Britain was so heavily dependent on other countries for aero-engines that in the Aerial Derby of 1911 only one of the 11 machines had a British engine. By the end of the war, as the British Association for the Advancement of Science reported in 1919, 'British aero-engines had gained the foremost place in design and manufacture, and were well up to requirements as regards supply' – a touch of patriotic bombast no doubt, but indeed the British in their island had been best-placed to respond to necessity. The aeroplanes sent out with the BEF in 1914 had a maximum speed of 80 m.p.h., a rate of climb from ground level of 300 or 400 feet per minute, and were equipped with engines of 60 to 100 horsepower. In 1918 the fastest machines could reach 140 m.p.h. and had a rate of climb from ground level of 2,000 feet per minute. The Handley–Page V/1500, which had its first test flight in May 1918, was capable of developing over 1,300 horsepower. The maximum flying height had been raised from 5,000 to 25,000 feet. Three days before the armistice, two Handley–Page bombers stood fully equipped awaiting the order to start for Berlin. By this time there was considerable interest in the possible civilian uses of aircraft. In April 1918 the government formed a Civil Aerial Transport Committee under Lord Northcliffe. Anxious to exploit their new productive capacity, Handley–Page, together with another leading manufacturer, Holt Thomas, announced their plans for the development of civil aviation.[17]

Wireless likewise proclaimed its potential during the war, with British valve transmitters being developed for the first time, mainly for contact between the ground and planes on reconnaissance. As supplies from the main pioneer companies in the field, Marconi, Edison, Swann, and A. C. Cosser, were insufficient, contracts for radio valves were given to the main manufacturers of electric light bulbs: the General Electric Company Limited, the British Thompson Houston Company Limited, and the British Westinghouse Electrical and Manufacturing Company Limited. The commitment of these three companies to the nascent radio industry was, by the end of the war, so great that it was they who exerted some of the strongest pressure on the government to permit broadcasting in the post-war years. The first actual broadcasters were in many cases men who had gained experience of wireless during the war. Telephonic and telegraphic communication already existed from before the war, as indeed did the technological innovations which had made possible the most important means of communication of all – the cheap, mass-circulation press. The *Daily Mirror*, conceived of as a picture paper aimed at the relatively prosperous middle classes, overtook the *Daily Mail*, aimed at a lower middle-class, and upper working-class readership, and in 1912 became the first daily to achieve a circulation of one million.

At the outset of the war, a Chemical Products Supply Committee was set up 'to consider and advise as to the best means of obtaining for the use of British industries sufficient supplies of chemical products, colours and dye stuffs of kinds hitherto largely imported from countries with which we are at present at war'. The result was the setting-up of the not very successful National Dye Company. In May 1915 a deputation of professional scientists called for the establishment of a National Chemical Advisory Committee; a government White Paper of July went beyond that in outlining a form of 'permanent organization for the promotion of industrial and scientific research'. In 1916 this proposed organization was merged with the National Physical Laboratory and emerged as the Department of Scientific and Industrial Research. The National Insurance Act of 1911 (coming into effect in 1913) made provision for the establishment of a Medical Research Committee. Its annual reports referred to the war as 'a great stimulus', providing 'unequalled opportunities for study and research': work of the utmost value was indeed sponsored on dysentery, typhoid, cerebral-spinal fever, and new antiseptics. Seventeen months after the end of the war, the new status and new permanency was recognized in the new title Medical Research Council.[18]

In two rather different spheres, technological advances directly affected the amenities of ordinary life. Condoms, an invention of the nineteenth century, though greatly improved in the twentieth by advances in rubber technology, were distributed to British troops – not to encourage promiscuity, or family planning (as in fact was the consequence after the war), but to prevent the catching of disabling disease. In 1919 a reasonably efficient diaphragm for women was developed in the Netherlands – the Dutch cap; its reliability was enhanced after 1932 when a suitable spermicidal jelly was invented in Oxford.[19] More mundanely, existing electrical power resources were inadequate to the new demands of war. Thus, between 1914 and 1919, the capacity of electrical generating stations, both municipal and private, had to be doubled.[20] In the inter-war years, America streaked far ahead of Britain in the development of modern conveniences for the home: still, there could have been no conveniences for British housewives without adequate electricity supplies.

## *Ideologies*

In elaborating the circumstances defining the limits for political action, social improvement, and cultural development, it will be essential for me to say something about class structure. For reasons to be explained, class arises from structural and ideological imperatives, but it will be convenient to discuss it later as part of the institutional context. The point to make here is that when we are talking about ideologies, values and beliefs, we have to be clear whether we see these as being espoused by all sections of society, or only by certain classes or groups. That said, there can be no question but that the responses to the war emergency, across the classes, demonstrated that the British people were united behind certain simple, almost simplistic, values: Country, King and God (this is almost certainly the right order from the point of view of the vast majority) – 'Country', more than anything else, meant one's own way of life in one's own little community. Everyone, inevitably, had several identities: and it was not difficult to be a Cockney and British; a Geordie and British; a Scot and British. For most, hostility towards 'the Hun', or indeed the 'Froggies', was easily aroused. Whether among ordinary people there really was an imperialism which can be separated from nationalism and a sense, born of ignorance, of superiority towards all non-Europeans is open to some doubt.

Sectarian hostility was strong in parts of Scotland (where there was considerable immigration from Catholic Ireland and Catholic areas of the Highlands of Scotland), in Lancashire, and obviously, in Ulster. Ulstermen were the most vehement in the expression of their Britishness; yet, before the transforming blasts of war, most Irish Catholics seemed able to accommodate to the idea of Home Rule within a British framework. Anglicanism was a tolerant religion, and that tolerance had began to permeate Presbyterianism, the established religion in Scotland: there was placid coexistence for nonconformists, Baptists, Methodists, and so on. Actually, from the time of the growth of the great industrial towns, formal religion had ceased to be at the very core of the lives of everybody. Even at the beginning of the century, membership figures for the various religious denominations were not overwhelmingly impressive. Yet, older traditions continued to influence British attitudes and beliefs, obviously so at times of birth, marriage, death, and war (even in 1947, 84 per cent of people polled said they believed in God, and the figure is still almost 70 per cent today). Anglicanism spilled over into ordinary life in what I have termed 'secular Anglicanism', entailing an easy-going spirit of tolerance, contained within a broad sense of hierarchy, often marked by formal shows of deference.[21] Nonconformity, and Presbyterianism in Scotland, had left a legacy of respect for individual rights and democratic ideals, though all contained within the bounds of moderation.

Statistics for church membership are not easy to come by, but the table I have compiled is basically correct in the proportions and relative changes it indicates.[22]

**Table 1.5** Membership of main religious denominations, 1900–1939, in millions with percentages of total populations in brackets – for the Church of England the population is England, for the Church of Scotland, Scotland, for the other denominations, the whole of Great Britain

| | *Church of England* | *Church of Scotland* | *Methodists* | *Congregationalists* | *Baptists* | *Catholics* |
|---|---|---|---|---|---|---|
| 1900 | 2.90 (8.9) | 1.15 (25.7) | 0.77 (2.1) | 0.29 (0.9) | 0.25 (0.8) | 1.8 (3.9) |
| 1924 | 3.54 (9.3) | 1.30 (26.6) | 0.83 (1.9) | (0.9) | (0.8) | 2.0 (4.1) |
| 1939 | 3.39 (6.7) | 1.29 (26.2) | 0.80 (1.7) | (0.9) | (0.8) | 3.0 (6.0) |

The potency of religious ideology, particularly that derived from the Old Testament, in governing the decisions of politicians and the lives of ordinary people, is seen most markedly in attitudes towards sexual behaviour, the family, gender roles, children and crime. Obviously the realities of life, and of human nature, were often at odds with publicly asserted moral principles. The rich and powerful could indulge in extra-marital liaisons, working-class young women in times of trade depression could be forced into prostitution. The material penalties for sexual transgression, particularly for women, of course, were so severe as to ratify the sense of their inherent sinfulness: venereal diseases, unwanted pregnancies, social ostracism and total destitution. Most feminists in the Edwardian period believed in what they called 'purity'; their aim was to get all men to observe the ideal standard that respectable women themselves had to observe.[23] 'Christian marriage' was seen as the fundamental unit of society: a woman should see her duty and her fulfilment as being a wife and mother. Many women did hard, unpleasant work outside the home, but the duty for the male, from the respectable working man upwards, was to earn enough to be able to keep his wife at home to look after house and family. Although there is evidence in all social classes of genuine affection for children, so also is there evidence of a strong belief in their innate tendencies towards evil, and of the need for harsh discipline and violent punishment. The retributive principle dominated the criminal justice system, based on hanging, flogging, birching and penal servitude with hard labour.

In keeping with the perception of man as head of the household and woman as subordinate to him, women did not have the vote in 1914 (only in Norway and Finland, Australia and New Zealand, and a few of the American states, did any women have the vote at this time). It is often pointed out that, while in Republican France men were 'citizens', in Britain they were 'subjects' of the Crown. The essence of the British political system was that it was 'representative'. All of those who had a stake in society, principally in the form of property, were entitled to be represented in decision-making, which, after all, might affect their interests: the vote was something to which you had to have an entitlement, or which you had to earn. A series of Reform Acts in the nineteenth century had greatly extended the franchise: the upshot in the years before 1914 was that a complex set of qualifications, of which the most important was the householder franchise, requiring proof of 12-months' unbroken occupation of the house in question, ensured that while a substantial number of wealthy individuals actually had several votes, two-fifths of adult males had no votes at all.[24] Some of these were unmarried men with, according to the ideology of the time, no real stake in society, but many simply lost their place on the voting register through moving.

Very large landowners, manifestly, had a very large stake in society. Those who were peers could directly represent themselves by taking their seats in the House of Lords, joining the many more recently created peers, successful figures from the worlds of finance, government or industry. The full representative principle was embodied in the House of Commons. The coexistence of the hereditary and the representative principle is a particularly striking instance of the respect for tradition, for hierarchy *and* the belief that there must always be balance in the British way of doing things, together with gradual adaptation to changing economic and social circumstances (all facets of secular Anglicanism): the House of Lords was still very important, but its importance was being diminished in favour of the House of Commons. I am talking of the ideas of people of power and influence (whether or not they were shared by the mass population). And here it is very important to note attitudes and values which came to hold sway in the upper echelons of society, from the early and middle years of Queen Victoria's reign, when older ideas of *noblesse oblige* and patrician responsibilities towards the plebs were intensified and codified, while aristocratic self-indulgence and irresponsibility was condemned. The classic text was the *Northcote and Trevelyan Report* (1852), a blueprint for a civil service which would no longer be the private playground of an idle aristocracy, but would operate to the highest standards of public service; the classical vehicles for propagating the philosophy of public service were the reformed nineteenth-century public schools (i.e. elite private boarding schools). Henceforth, the ethos on which the British prided themselves was to be one of a bribe-free civil service, and in tandem with that, corruption-free elections – with, as I have already said, the vote being gradually extended to all who deserved it.

All labels in historical discourse have their problems: the neatest one for the kind of ideas I am discussing here is 'liberalism'. Liberalism (in this sense – the word has many different uses) also embraced certain fundamental economic principles – basically that state interference in economic and social matters should be kept to a minimum, that markets both international and internal should be unfettered, and that private enterprise was to be encouraged. Yet, with its concern for the deserving, this liberalism could also tolerate modest social reform. The social reform element in the Liberal party, as a political movement, was strengthened in the early years of the century as a new political philosophy stressing the importance of the state, referred to as New Liberalism, began to be propagated. The most obvious outcome was the National Insurance Act introduced by the Liberal government in 1911.

Along with the cleaning up and codifying of administration and politics, went the cleaning up and codifying of popular sports and pastimes. In regard to party politics, as well as more widely, the notions of obedience to the captain, loyalty to the team, and 'playing the game' have great significance. Some imaginative individuals did enter politics as 'Independents', but if you hoped for office you had to be a Liberal or a Conservative (usually labelled Unionist in this period). You had, of course, to believe that your 'team' had certain distinctive principles, and be loyal to these. And within a consensus over most of the values I have already discussed, the two parties did have distinctive differences on certain issues. Though upper-class Liberals (or 'Whigs') were happy Anglicans, and thus never a million miles away from the Conservatives, always strong upholders of the privileges of the Church of England, basic Liberal ideology was pervaded by the ideas and prejudices of nonconformism. Conservatives, in power up until 1905, had introduced economic reforms beneficial to the Irish people, but a Conservative could not possibly support Home Rule for Ireland, or anything which could be seen as weakening the unity of the United Kingdom – hence the taking on of the label 'Unionist'. Conservatives had reacted against the fear that foreign goods were being allowed to enter Britain too easily, and therefore believed in replacing 'Free Trade' with 'Tariff Reform', that is the imposition of import taxes; these would then be relaxed for countries of the British Empire through 'Imperial Preference', which, it was argued, would serve to bind the Empire more closely together. For Liberals, any infringement of Free Trade was abhorrent. The Liberals felt committed to Home Rule, and they looked with favour on the recently-arrived Labour party, seeing it as a laudable example of working-class self-help, and sympathizing with its basic cause: improving the lot of the working man.

That basic policy is best described as 'labourism', the philosophy of most Labour MPs, of whom there were 42 in 1914. What became the Labour party had been created in 1900 as the Labour Representation Committee (LRC), a title highly revealing of what precisely was the fundamental aim of the new organization, by the main trade unions (not including the miners, who joined in 1908, by which time the title had been changed to Labour party), and the Independent Labour Party (ILP), founded in 1893. Apart from the objective of getting working men into parliament, the ILP, which continued an active autonomous existence within the Labour party, espoused the approach which we would now call 'ethical socialism', which had deep roots in nonconformist religion. To join the Labour party it was necessary to belong to a trade union, or to the ILP, or one of the other smaller socialist societies (e.g. the Fabian Society). Marxist ideas of proletarian revolution played no part in Labour party policy. Private coal-owners were seen to be brutally exploitative, so Labour wanted the nationalization of the coal mines; it wanted more limitations on hours of work, and pensions and social insurance. In addition, it put forward the idea of a general wealth tax, the 'Capital Levy', and also of a minimum wage, the 'National Minimum'.

The available varieties of socialism in Britain, if not very profound, were sensible enough as responses to existing circumstances. At least they did not have the futility of the brand of Marxism espoused by French Socialist leaders who believed that there was no point taking any action until the historical moment arrived when capitalist society was ready to be taken over by socialism. A few trade unionists, and intellectuals, in Britain did take up another French philosophy, Syndicalism. According to this theory, the workers should seek to build one giant, unified union which would take over the state and thus lead, as it were, to workers' control from below. An almost opposite view prevailed in the Fabian Society, whose most important figure was Sidney Webb, a civil servant, and, jointly with his wife Beatrice, a historian and social investigator. The Webbs had an optimistic view of the existing state, believing that it was now engaged in extending its powers in ways which would only be beneficial to people as consumers. 'It seems', they wrote in the socialist weekly the *New Statesman* in 1913, 'that the modern function of the State . . . is destined altogether to outweigh, and finally to submerge, the function of the State as a coercive authority . . . The New State, able more and more to take order for granted, devotes its energies to securing progress.' To the Webbs, trade unions were fundamentally self-interested: their socialism was essentially a faith (not fully justified, one might think) in the gradual extension of state power in order to enable people to operate fully and freely as consumers.[25]

Really, in 1914, there was not much in the way of what might be called alternative ideologies. Many working-class families had traditional loyalties to the Liberals or to the Conservatives; there certainly was nothing like a unified working-class adherence to 'labourism', let alone 'socialism'. In parliament, the Liberals tended to treat Labour as a mere adjunct to their party. There was, as we shall see in the next section, a strong 'women's movement', supported also by men, but nowhere was there serious challenge to the ordering of British society, and everywhere there was a faith in monarchy, social hierarchy and the British way of doing things. Still, there *was* a difference. There *was* a party of tradition and the *status quo*, there *was* a party of change. Conservatives were proud to be conservative, Liberals would have been deeply embarrassed at being thought conservative. The Conservatives identified themselves with British institutions exactly as they were; Liberals claimed to be responsive to any perceived needs for change. Professor Duncan Tanner has explained that Conservative success among working-class voters was built 'on cultural affinities with working-class social activities, on attendance to ethnic tensions, and, allied to this, support of British values, British jobs and British international prestige'.[26] The Conservatives, in other words, played on working-class fear and self-interest and on British working-class dislike of Irish and Jewish immigrants.

At times, political disputation could be very bitter. Such sectarianism as there was could sweep down the narrow channels of politics, especially over the funding of education: nonconformists looked to the Liberals to prevent the Conservatives from doing anything which might privilege Church of England schools. Party politics became particularly bitter with Lloyd George's 'People's Budget' of 1909, aiming to raise taxes to finance social reform. The Conservatives exploited their entrenched majority in the House of Lords, which in turn led to the Parliament Act of 1911, which reduced the powers of the Lords to delaying bills for no more than two years, and laid down that the Lords could not interfere with fiscal (i.e. to do with taxation) bills. The angry divide between the parties was intensified by the determination of Conservatives and Ulstermen to resist Home Rule.

### *INSTITUTIONS*

We have moved into the realm of institutions. The word 'institution' can be used in various ways: basically I am thinking of organs or agencies of government, or of special interests, of processes and conventions, all in some sense deliberately created, and, therefore, open to alteration or abolition by deliberate effort of will. Private agencies usually have sets of rules; in most countries the public ones are governed by written constitutions, something, notoriously, Britain did not have. As subjects, the British had no formal statement of their rights. However, the proper working of representative government was, more or less, guaranteed by: elections free of government manipulation and, as far as possible, the bribing of voters; a newspaper press free of government control (obviously the rich men who owned the newspapers had agendas of their own, but generally British newspapers by this time offered a recognized allegiance to one or other of the big political parties – the puny, struggling *Daily Herald* appeared in 1913 as Labour's first national daily); the right of free assembly, that is, the holding of political and protest meetings, etc. (sometimes the police might be there, but unless they could make a case that some law was being broken, they could not act).

Though the notion of balance was a pervasive one, Britain did not have any kind of formally elaborated 'checks and balances' or 'separation of powers', as seen in its most pure form in the United States' system of President, Congress and Supreme Court. Laws enacted by parliament, and given Royal approval (never denied), were supreme. Still, where there was no absolutely unambiguous statute, the courts (there were, and are, two separate and distinct systems, one in England and Wales, another in Scotland: after the partition of Ireland in 1921 Northern Ireland had a variant of the English system under its own Lord Chief Justice, the first one actually being a Catholic) could make decisions of considerable general significance – with regard to trade-union rights, for instance, or the legality of the expenditure of public money on education, or other social services. On the whole, the attitudes of the judiciary operated as a strongly conservative force.

From 1911, general elections had to be held at least every five years (they still spread over several weeks). The Prime Minister could choose the date thought to be most advantageous to himself and his party, advising the monarch when to dissolve parliament, advice which, by convention, the monarch always accepted. Most of the country was divided into single-member constituencies, but in most larger towns historic double-member constituencies had survived. The usual choice was between Liberal and Conservative; as a rule Labour and Liberal candidates did not stand against each other, or shared the 'progressive' platform in double-member constituencies. The system was that which has come to be known as 'first-past-the-post', the candidate or candidates with mere pluralities of the votes being elected. Thus, as is well known, the number of seats a party won in the House of Commons would not usually be an accurate representation of its overall vote. Countries which habitually tore up, and rewrote, constitutions did things differently. In the French Third Republic there was a system of second ballots in circumstances where no candidate secured a clear majority of the votes. After the war this was replaced with a system of multi-member constituencies – a system which in fact gave unfair advantage to parties willing to make electoral alliances, which in France meant parties of the Right. The new German Republic introduced a system of full proportional representation, the system under which Hitler came to power – so maybe the British system wasn't so bad after all (but see the next section for subsequent developments).

In Britain, the members of parliament in the majority party chose their leader who then, by convention, was invited by the monarch to be Prime Minister, and then, as Prime Minister, chose his government, consisting of the Cabinet, which collectively, under the leadership of the Prime Minister, had the responsibility of deciding policy, and the non-Cabinet members, whose responsibility was essentially confined to their own department. All members of the government had also to be members of one or other of the Houses of Parliament, and a certain minimum number had to be from the House of Lords. Civil servants were expected to give the best possible advice to ministers of whatever party was in power and to carry out their instructions, but weak ministers could find themselves dominated by their civil servants. The Treasury, guardian of financial frugality, was a particularly powerful department, and a major obstacle to any minister with high-spending plans. There was no cabinet secretariat: the only record of proceedings and decisions was that jotted down by the Prime Minister himself to enable him to carry out his constitutional duty of keeping the monarch informed. Obviously the balance of power between Prime Minister and Cabinet depended very much on the personality of the Prime Minister, and also, sometimes, on circumstances. The Cabinet was not actually consulted on the ultimatum which led to the formal declaration of war on Germany.

I have mentioned the all-pervasive effects of religious ideas. Church leaders were still very important figures with great influence on both the national, and local, scene; always on the side of conventional morality, and usually on the side of the existing social hierarchy, though there were ministers of religion who played prominent parts in the Labour movement. While social control by the religious bodies was indirect, the main institutional means for controlling the population was the police. By comparison with continental police forces, substantial components of which, at least, had military origins, the British police forces (thought not in Ireland) were relatively restrained in their methods. They did not carry firearms (again Ireland was different), an absolutely crucial factor in the extremely low loss of civilian life accompanying riots and other disturbances, compared with the norm on the continent. But, as seems to be inevitable everywhere, the police to some extent did form a kind of state within the state; generally politicians preferred to leave them to get on with their job in their own way, without inquiring into methods and practices.

The main institution on behalf of ordinary people was the trade-union movement. Adherents of classical liberalism could either see trade unions as acting 'in restraint of trade', as the phrase was, that is to say violating the pure principles of unfettered private enterprise, or they could see them (as John Stuart Mill, the learned philosopher of nineteenth-century liberalism, had done) as manifestations of self-help and responsibility on the part of the workers. At the beginning of the nineteenth century there had been laws against 'combination' (i.e. the formation of unions), but a Liberal government Act of 1870, as expanded by a Conservative Act of 1876, accorded positive legal recognition to unions and their customary form of action – strikes. However, many within the judicial system – judges, lawyers, magistrates – continued to resent what they saw as special privileges; so also did employers, many of whom refused to recognize the union in their own workplace. In an environment in which the balance of power lay very heavily with the employers, and which was deeply coloured by employer hostility, it was not surprising that union leaders themselves tended to be confrontational, deeply possessive over the more esoteric features of their particular trade ('the tricks of the trade', one might say), and resistant to the idea of third-party arbitration. At the opening of the twentieth century, union leaders still felt great insecurity over whether statute law really gave them the full protection they needed.[27] That their fears were justified was shown by a pair of legal decisions in 1901, and 1909.

After an 11-day strike in August 1900, the Taff Vale Railway Company in South Wales sued the local Amalgamated Society of Railway Servants for its losses, taking the case all the way to the House of Lords. The decision there that the union must pay the railway company £23,000 in damages meant that union funds were henceforth at risk every time there was a strike. Securing a new act of parliament that would establish security for the unions became a major aim of the newly founded LRC. Pressure from the LRC (now the Labour party) upon the Liberal government elected in January 1906 resulted in the Trades Disputes Act of that year, which gave the unions what lawyers considered a privileged position: they could not be sued for losses caused by strike action and peaceful picketing. The unions financed the Labour party by paying to it a proportion of the subscriptions they received from their own members. In 1908, W. V. Osborne, Secretary of the Walthamstow Branch of the Railway Servants Union, being a member of the Liberal party, took legal action against the union for paying part of his subscription in this way to the Labour party. Again, the case went right up to the House of Lords (not in fact the entire chamber, but a court of five senior judges who sat in the Lords). Their judgement, in December 1909, ruled that it was illegal for trade unions to finance the Labour party in this way. The Act of 1911, introducing the payment of MPs, did something to help the Labour party, now thrown into a most parlous situation. The Trade Union Act of 1913 authorized unions to set up a separate political levy through which their members could contribute to the Labour party, with, however, individual members being given the right to 'contract out' if they did not wish to support the Labour party. Apart from the basic protection now offered by the law, unions had their own rules and regulations: about apprenticeship, about how jobs should be graded, and about what categories of worker, and what members of which unions, should be responsible for particular jobs – 'restrictive practices', opponents called these.

In the last years before the war, prices continued to rise in what had been a long boom cycle, while wages were static. The unions felt confident enough to take action so that these years have become notorious, not just for the large number of strikes and working days lost, but also for the violence that accompanied encounters between pickets and the police. The number of trade-union members went up during those years, though the total only accounted for about a quarter of all working men; an overwhelming number of unions (mostly very small ones, though) remained unaffiliated to the Trades Union Congress (TUC) which had been founded in 1868. The year 1911 began with the strike by seamen at Southampton who, by holding up the new liner *Olympic*, got a quick pay increase. A strike at London docks forced the employers' organization, the Shipping Federation, to grant recognition to the Sailors' Union. A two-day national railway strike (the first ever) in August also won recognition for the rail unions. On 12 February the Miners' Federation began a national strike, which caused immense disruption throughout the country: although the union did not get the minimum wage it was demanding, the government was forced to rush through a Bill which set up local wages boards. The unions were far from being major powers in the land, but they were becoming forces which governments had to reckon with.

An added source of tension and bitterness in the years before the war was the campaign for votes for women, a campaign which cut across the existing political structures. Most back-bench Liberals were for, but Asquith himself was against. Some Conservative leaders were for, but the mass of the party was against. Labour leaders were generally for, but most ordinary trade unionists were against. Several times there were majorities in the House of Commons in favour of enfranchising women; but there was never the formal government support needed to get any measure through. While the suffragists continued a peaceful campaign, the suffragettes became more and more violent, on the whole alienating many of their former supporters in parliament. No doubt, the militant suffragettes posed an extreme case for the policing and judicial systems, but the record was appalling and glaringly revealed the prejudices behind the systems. The women were harassed, imprisoned, forcibly fed; then the 'cat-and-mouse' tactic was introduced, releasing hunger-striking women when they were on the point of death, then rearresting them when restored to health.[28]

Trade unions, judicial systems and cabinet government are in some sense the deliberate, witting creations of human beings. The same thing cannot exactly be said about classes. But nor, though we do speak of 'class structure', do classes belong to quite the same category as the facts of geography, demography and economics. Too many alleged studies of class do not get to grips with the subject at all, but instead discuss what Marx said, what Weber said, what more recent sociologists have said, and so on. Frankly, we can ignore Marx and Weber. It is abundantly clear from the historical evidence that all industrialized societies divide horizontally, as it were, into a limited number (three or four) of 'strata' (to continue with the metaphor), or, in the language regularly in use in the societies concerned, 'classes'. We can map these classes fairly precisely if we integrate the perceptions of people themselves within the societies studied, with the hard facts of economic and political power.[29] The Marxist rule-book has classes rising up and overthrowing each other. That does not happen. Classes evolve and change as circumstances change: successful middle-class groups do not challenge the class above, they strive to be absorbed into it; workers in Britain, with only individual exceptions, do tend to remain within the working class.

In 1914 classes existed in the United States, in France, in Germany: however, there could be differences in the extent to which distinctions of class were prioritized, of which class governed other facets of society (political, social and cultural) and which class determined decision-making. The key points about British class structure in 1914 (and to a considerable extent today) are the existence of the world's oldest, and most class-aware, working class and the existence of the world's most self-confident and well-organized upper class. I avoid the phrase 'class-conscious' because that has become a technical phrase in Marxism, carrying the meaning that the workers were conscious of the need to fight in the allegedly inevitable struggle with the bourgeoisie. What I am saying is that the British working class was aware of being working class and was in some senses proud of it, aware of being in very different circumstances from the classes above, but also aware of being different from the class below, the complete unfortunates, the 'residuum', or 'people of the abyss' as the Victorians said – the 'underclass' as we would say today.

There are always those on the fringes of one class and another, but that does not invalidate class analysis. Broadly, the working class – contemporaries usually spoke of 'the working classes' (plural), signifying recognition of the range of status groups, and incomes, within the entire working class – are all those in manual occupations, together perhaps with those exclusively serving the working class, such as shopkeepers and bookmakers. The fifth schedule of the Housing Act of 1925, repeated as the eleventh schedule of the 1936 Housing Act, offered a statutory definition:

> the expression 'working class' includes mechanics, artisans, labourers and others working for wages, or working at some trade or handicraft without employing others except members of their own family, and persons other than domestic servants, whose income does not exceed an average of three pounds a week and the families of such persons who may be residing with them.

The upper class is an amalgam of traditional elements from the aristocracy and the squirearchy, who tend to set the general tone and ethos, and the most highly successful elements from finance, industry, the professions and government. The middle classes (and here the plural is fully justified even in the kind of historical analysis I am making) are all those in between. As the agricultural sector was squeezed by industrialization, independent farmers came to be seen as part of the middle class, while landless farm-labourers had low status within the working class. In 1914, the working class made up about 75 per cent of the population; the middle class between 15 and 20 per cent; the upper class 2 or 3 per cent; the residuum up to 5 per cent.[30] Comparisons with France, with Germany, with America, are not easy to make. America had a very positive ideology of mobility and classlessness. France had a substantial, and reasonably prosperous, peasant (or farming) class; the working class was small and isolated: yet, at the same time, French society was pervaded by the notion of citizenship. In Germany, lacking in proper representative institutions, the hostility of the autocracy towards the working class and its organizations was much more overt than that shown by any of the authorities in the other countries; notions of military hierarchy were strong. Neither France nor Germany had such a thoroughly developed and coherent upper class as Britain had. Trying to summarize, and always remembering that what I am trying to do here is to set out the circumstances which governed the potential for change, I would say that an awareness of class played a greater part in a British, and above all, an English person's identity than it did elsewhere, and also a significant part in decision-making.

## The Politics of Total War

### *The Liberal Government, 1914–1915*

Actually, the incumbent Prime Minister, Asquith, as a gentlemanly Liberal, was not the man for waging total war. Fortunately, however, the essential condition for waging total war was there from the outset: political, and, indeed, national, unity. Those who had been most vehement in denouncing Lloyd George's budget, in upholding the full rights of the House of Lords and in opposing Home Rule, were among the most eager to proclaim support for a united national effort. The Conservative leader, Bonar Law, committed his party to 'patriotic opposition', and the parties agreed an 'electoral truce' to last until Christmas when, it was thought, the war would be over; seats falling vacant would simply be filled by the party holding the seat, without a contest. Parliament went into a kind of semi-abeyance: 184 members, 139 of them Conservative, were away much of the time on active service; no vote was taken in parliament until 5 July 1915. The Chairman of the Parliamentary Labour Party (Labour did not at this time recognize a 'leader'), Ramsay MacDonald, one of the very few members of parliament to maintain the position that Britain should have stayed out of the war, resigned his position and was succeeded by Arthur Henderson, trade-union leader and formerly an official of the Iron Founders Union (MacDonald, though from humble origins, can best be described as an 'intellectual'; he had never done manual work). Both Labour in parliament, and the trade-union movement outside, now offered full support to the government. The suffragettes called off their campaign, and becoming *plus militaristes que les militaristes*, entered passionately into the recruiting campaign. The suffragists continued quiet propaganda on behalf of votes for women while encouraging women to demonstrate their mettle by taking on jobs of national importance.[31] Lord Kitchener made a spendid non-party figurehead;

and, indeed, given that it involved a complete reversal of all traditional British ideas about how wars were fought, the raising of the 'New Army' went ahead reasonably effectively.

No more than the wise Suffragists did the wider Labour movement shut up shop for the duration. As early as 5 August Henderson had summoned representatives from all sections of the movement to the conference which established the War Emergency Workers National Committee to safeguard the conditions of workers and their families throughout the war. On 24 August the Liaison Committee of the Labour party, the General Federation of Trade Unions and the Parliamentary Committee of the TUC agreed an 'Industrial Truce'. As prices rose rapidly this was not particularly welcome to ordinary workers. In February 1915 some 10,000 engineering workers on the Clyde went on a fortnight's strike in support of a wage increase to meet the rising cost of living. Because this was in defiance of the official union leaders, the strike was led by the shop stewards, part-time representatives of the unions on the shop floor, of little consequence in pre-war days, and who formed the Central Withdrawal of Labour Committee. The men won their main demands. The Withdrawal of Labour Committee quickly became the Clyde Workers' Committee, whose first manifesto declared:

> The support given to the Munitions Act by the officials was an act of treachery to the working classes. Those of us who have refused to be sold have organised the above Committee.

The basic aim expressed was the extremely pragmatic one of dealing with the infringement of traditional rights felt to be involved in government policy. However, one wider objective was that of 'Workers' Control' – that is, that 'organized labour' should have 'a direct share in the management down through all departments'. Also in February 1915, Treasury civil servant Sir George Askwith concluded the 'Shells and Fuses Agreement' with the engineering and shipbuilding unions. The unions agreed to 'dilution', the introduction of unskilled labour, including that of women, on jobs formerly reserved for skilled men, in return for guarantees by both government and employers that normal trade practices would be restored at the end of the war. Between 17 and 19 March union representatives attended a conference at the Treasury with Lloyd George, as Chancellor of the Exchequer, and Walter Runciman, President of the Board of Trade. Using both his considerable charm, and his passionate sense of urgency, Lloyd George persuaded the union leaders (the Engineers coming in after a slight delay, the Miners not at all) to accept the 'Treasury Agreement' whereby 'present trade practices' would be relaxed in all industries essential to the war effort. An undertaking was given that the extra profits private companies would make out of this arrangement would be taxed. It was confirmed that the traditional situation would be restored at the end of the war; in the meantime the wage rate for a skilled job would be maintained even if the job was being performed by someone the unions did not consider skilled.[32]

So far so good. But the military events I have already described inevitably impacted upon domestic politics, creating the context for the political crisis of

May 1915. In April there was much agitation in press and parliament over Sir John French's complaints that he was being crippled by the shortage of high explosive. At the same time it was becoming clear that the Dardanelles expedition was replicating the pattern of heavy losses and no gains. French turned up the pressure by instigating the military correspondent of *The Times*, Colonel Repington, to publish a piece on the 'shells scandal' in *The Times* of 14 May; this was accompanied by a leading article which declared the shortage of high explosive 'a fatal bar to our military success'. Just as Sir John French played up the shell shortage for his own purposes, the First Sea Lord, Sir John Fisher, sought to use the Dardanelles fiasco to challenge his political boss, Winston Churchill, and create a situation out of which he would emerge with powers over the navy similar to those that Kitchener had over the army. On 15 May he resigned and, to create maximum disarray, disappeared without trace into a London hotel, until the crisis was over.

Because the Liberals, who were the ruling party from 1906 to 1914, with a number of considerable achievements to their credit, came out of the war fatally weakened, it has sometimes been assumed that Asquith was tricked, or forced, into forming a coalition with the Conservatives. But Asquith was not a politician to be tricked or threatened. From a middle-class background, he had used an education at Oxford and a brilliant self-made career as a barrister, to move himself towards the upper class. He listened long and passively and took his time about making up his mind, the better to grasp a problem in all its ramifications, and act accordingly. His perhaps over-used response, 'wait and see', became notorious: but rather than indolence and procrastination, it carried the steelier connotation of 'you'll find out soon enough'. He had total domination over his Cabinet. But he could see that the electoral truce was not going to last. It had been renewed in January 1915, but only on a month-to-month basis; there was still the presumption that, as the law required, a general election would have to be held before the end of 1915. Given this longer-term consideration, along with the growing restlessness and aggressiveness of the Conservative back-benchers, and now the interlocking shell shortage, Dardanelles fiasco and Fisher resignation crisis, Asquith calmly reached the conclusion that the Conservatives must be brought into the Government; the Fisher resignation was not crucial in itself, but Asquith could use it to persuade reluctant members of his own party that there was no alternative to a coalition.

Meanwhile the Conservative leader came to the same conclusion. Bonar Law was a brusque, somewhat graceless, Canadian-born businessman from Glasgow, who had emerged as the compromise candidate in 1911, when the party might have split over the choice between two patricians, Austen Chamberlain and Walter Long: Law at least had the appeal of being the total antithesis of the languid, aristocratic Balfour. Not surprisingly, he found great difficulty in communicating directly with Asquith. Instead he went to Lloyd George, also an 'outsider', who from a modestly comfortable Welsh background had made his way as a successful lawyer and passionate orator on behalf of nonconformity and social reform and against the idle rich. Lloyd George was genuinely convinced, as Asquith was not, that Kitchener was incompetent, that the war effort was being run inefficiently and that something must be done immediately about the munitions crisis. It was Lloyd George who put the proposal for a coalition to Asquith on 17 May; Asquith agreed immediately, though he had not consulted his Cabinet. Parliament was in recess at the time, and simply had the decision announced to it on reassembling.[33]

### *The Asquith Coalition Government, May 1915–December 1916*

There are two opposite forms of political ambition. In one, the political actor perceives that there is a great task which must be carried out, and decides that he (or she) is the person to do it successfully; in the other, the political actor decides to avoid any assignment which could possibly damage his reputation and seeks to consolidate his position quietly. Lloyd George was of the former type. It proved impossible to move Kitchener from the War Office, so munitions supply was removed from its purview, Lloyd George taking on the onerous, and risky, responsibility for setting up an entirely new Ministry of Munitions and getting to work at once on resolving the shell shortage. Bonar Law accepted the post of Colonial Secretary – somewhat far from the central running of the war; perhaps here he betrayed something of the second type of ambition. In general, within the constraints imposed by events, Asquith had, in the formation of this new Cabinet, asserted his authority. As Chancellor of the Exchequer he had the free trade, private enterprise Liberal Reginald McKenna, and he managed to save a Cabinet place, though the modest one of Chancellor of the Duchy of Lancaster, for Churchill.

A former Conservative from an aristocratic family, who had joined the Liberals in 1904, Churchill was detested by members of all parties and positively hated by Bonar Law; and anyway, his Dardanelles policy and rift with Fisher had been part of the crisis. At the end of the year Churchill went off to serve as a battalion commander in France. Balfour came back from the living dead to take over at the Admiralty. A most significant appointment was that of Arthur Henderson, essentially to advise the Cabinet on labour problems, though actually given the title of President of the Board of Education. Two other Labour MPs attained minor office: William Brace, a South Wales miner, became Under-Secretary at the Home Office and G. H. Roberts, a printer, became a Government Whip.

Lloyd George was a passionate orator with the power to sway large crowds, but he could also be immensely persuasive in intricate one-to-one discussions. Among his many soubriquets, the most flattering (which several were not) was the 'Welsh Wizard'. If he were alive today we would probably call him a 'Welsh Windbag' – save that, were he alive today, he would be wise enough to adopt a totally different style. His is the classic case of someone with a very strong immediate identity (in his case with Welsh nationalism and Welsh nonconformity) extending it into a larger identity, in this case that of Britain, or even the British Empire. In the milieu in which Lloyd George grew up, alcohol was, in the language of that milieu, 'an abomination', regarded as the respectable today regard heroin or cocaine. British governments had indeed long recognized that alcoholic liquors did react with human beings in such a way as to make these drinks different from other items of human consumption. Acts regulating alcohol consumption had been passed in 1495, 1551, at the height of the Gin Age in the eighteenth century, and during the burst of Gladstonian piety in the nineteenth century. The cumulative effect was that all premises selling alcohol had to seek a licence year by year from the local magistrates, and that, in 1914, there was in all areas a legally imposed closing time: in London this was half an hour after midnight, the pubs opening again at 5.00 a.m. In other towns the opening hours were 6.00 a.m. to 11.00 p.m. and in country districts 6.00 a.m. to 10.00 p.m. Scotland suffered a harsher regime, the open hours being from 10.00 a.m. to as early as 9.00 p.m. in some areas, 11.00 p.m. in others. On Sundays, pubs in both Scotland and Wales were closed, while in England they were open for a couple of hours in the middle of the day, then closed in the afternoon, to open again at 6.00 for a further four or five hours.

By the terms of the Intoxicating Liquor (Temporary Restriction) Act of 31 August, the Chief Officer of Police in any licensing district was empowered to have restrictions imposed on the hours of sale of alcohol in order to maintain order and suppress drunkenness. Lloyd George was being entirely true to his origins in two speeches of early 1915. On 28 February he declared: 'Drink is doing us more damage in the war than all the German submarines put together.' By 29 March the threat had assumed even more serious proportions: 'We are fighting Germany, Austria and Drink, and, as far as I can see, the greatest of these deadly foes is Drink.' The Coalition Government brought in the Defence of the Realm (Amendment Number Three) Act on 19 May, following it with the establishment of the Central Control Board (Liquor Traffic). The new Board took over direct control of liquor-licensing in those areas where excessive drinking could be held, in some way or another, to be impeding the war effort. In these areas the sale and consumption of alcohol was limited to two-and-a-half hours in the middle of the day, and to three or sometimes two hours in the evening. Early in 1916 pubs in particularly sensitive areas were nationalized: Enfield Lock in London, the Border area embracing Carlisle in England and Gretna in Scotland, the first a historic munitions centre, the second a new one; and Invergordon and Cromarty, where there were important naval establishments. Beer was reduced in strength, and spirits were not to be stronger than 70 proof. Punitive taxation was imposed. From the pain there was much gain: chronic drunkenness disappeared as a major social problem.

The munitions problem was fundamentally a manpower problem. With skilled workers as well as unskilled responding to the Kitchener appeal, the supply of skilled workers in the munitions trades had somehow to be greatly expanded. Actual implementation of the 'Treasury Agreement' only came now that Lloyd George was established as Minister of Munitions and with the passing of the Munitions of War Act (2 July 1915). The Act contained one feature workers found particularly obnoxious: munitions workers were not allowed to leave their jobs unless their employer gave them a 'Leaving Certificate'. Immediately before the war there had been a combined total of 212,000 women working in low-grade occupations in existing arms factories and in other factories (mainly chemicals) which were to become part of the wartime munitions industries. The enrolment of women took time, but by July 1917 there were 520,000; meantime women were beginning to appear in a whole range of occupations, most prominently as railway ticket-collectors, tram conductors and even drivers.[34]

The Munitions Act had only been in force for a few days when the South Wales miners rejected the wage award made by the government arbitrator, Sir George Askwith: Lloyd George at once issued a proclamation under the Act, declaring that any strike would be illegal. When, two days later, 200,000 miners came out, the new Munitions Minister realized that there was nothing for it but to agree to their demands – the war effort simply could not afford the disruption a strike would cause. On Clydeside there were several incidences of resistance to the terms of the Munitions of War Act. Lloyd George himself came to Glasgow to address a mass meeting on Christmas Day. His oratory fell flat – so flat, indeed, that the press was prohibited from publishing any report of the meeting save a small official hand-out. For printing a full and circumstantial account, the Glasgow *Socialist Weekly Forward* was suppressed. The report began:

> The best paid munitions worker in Britain, Mr. Lloyd George (almost £100 a week), visited the Clyde last week in search of adventure. He got it.

Lloyd George was informed that the shop stewards were not opposed to dilution as such, but that 'dilution must be carried out under the control of the workers'. Three Commissioners were despatched to Glasgow and succeeded in working out with the shop stewards a mutually acceptable scheme of dilution. Before the scheme came into operation, however, there was a further Clydeside strike, lasting from 17 March to 4 April 1916. Ten of the leaders were deported to other parts of the country: the main effect was to spread the Clydeside pattern of industrial action to other areas. A nationwide version of the Clyde Workers Committee appeared as the Workers Committee Movement.

All this time more and yet more men were wanted to compensate for the losses on the battle fronts. Thus the Munitions of War Act was followed by an Act instituting National Registration of Manpower to take place on Sunday, 15 August, and involving all persons, male or female, between the ages of 15 and 65. This looked like an exercise of state power over the individual on such a brutal scale that 30 Liberals created the first parliamentary division so far. The statistics revealed by national registration made it starkly clear that without the introduction of women into the war industries the shortfall in munitions production would have become disastrous.[35]

Asquith was a New Liberal, cognizant of the importance of the state, and not therefore a fundamentalist opponent of conscription, as so many in his party were. But, as always, his strategy was to proceed cautiously until a clear solution to the problem (in this case manpower, and in particular, the needs of the army) emerged. In a conference held between the government and unions on 28 September, the latter expressed inflexible opposition to military conscription. This was followed by the appointment on 11 October of Lord Derby in the new office of Director-General of Recruiting. The 'Derby Scheme' was based on the continental practice of dividing the adult males of the country into annual classes, each class in turn to become available for military service with the changing of the calendar. But it stopped short of conscription: men were simply called upon to 'attest', that is to say, undertake to serve if and when called upon to do so. Reasons for exemption were to be noted, such as work of national importance, or severe personal circumstances. The scheme itself was launched in October 1915, and followed in November by the setting-up of tribunals throughout the country, charged with pronouncing on the validity of the claims for exemption. A guarantee was given that married men would not be considered until there were no longer any unmarried men available.

The Derby Scheme had been in operation for only just over a fortnight when Asquith put his finger up to the wind. 'If', he said:

> there should still be found a substantial number of men of military age not required for other purposes, and who, without excuse, hold back from the service of their country, I believe that the very same conditions which made compulsion impossible now – namely the absence of general consent – would force the country to a view that they must consent to supplement, by some form of legal obligation, the failure of the voluntary system.

Six weeks later, in his *Report* on the Scheme, Lord Derby revealed the extent of the 'holding back'. Of 2,179,231 single men shown by the National Register to be of military age, only 1,150,000 had attested; the proportion of married men was not greatly different – 1,152,947 out of 2,832,210. Lord Derby's conclusion was that, in view of the pledge to take single men first,

> it will not be possible to hold married men to their attestation unless and until the services of single men have been obtained by other means, the present system having failed to bring them to the colours.

The 'other means' appeared within days in the Military Service Bill introduced on 5 January 1916 by the Prime Minister. Its main clause declared that all single men (including widowers without children) would be deemed to have enlisted and to have been transferred to the Reserve, whence they could be called up as required. The Liberal newspapers were most unhappy about this, even if it could simply be represented as the necessary redemption of the pledge to married men, but only one Liberal Cabinet minister resigned – Sir John Simon (son of a Congregationalist minister), who thereafter made no further attempt to fight the issue. While Sir John Simon resigned because of his fundamentalist opposition to conscription, the Labour representatives in the government, who believed the provisions of the Bill to be necessary, were expected to resign in order to be free to support it; the TUC had just voted against the Bill by over two million votes to less than half a million. But in the end the Labour members withdrew their resignations, and criticism from the party outside was stayed until a formal conference could meet and thrash out the problem.

The first Military Service Act of January 1916 imposed conscription on unmarried men between the ages of 18 and 41. Fifty Liberals voted against the bill. A new exemption was introduced, that of 'conscientious objection' – with provision for the case to be made to the local tribunals which had been set up under the Derby Scheme. Semi-conscription did not produce the numbers required, yet prominent Liberal members of the government were opposed to universal conscription. So touchy was the issue that the House of Commons went into its first secret session of the war on 25 April to discuss a second Military Service Bill, which still stopped short of universal compulsion. Asquith's weakness was that he wanted to proceed by consensus and compromise. His agonies over this issue (there were worse ones to come) were interrupted by the Dublin Easter Rising, which created a tide of patriotic emotion in parliament ('how dare those damned Irish rock the boat!') which swept through a complete, uncompromising, universal Military Service Act (2 May 1916). The Easter Rising, the apparent stumbles over conscription, and a growing sense among politicians and journalists of a lack of dedicated direction at the top led to mutterings about Asquith's methods, and indeed about the Prime Minister himself. Asquith was continuing to govern in accordance with the conventions of joint Cabinet responsibility, as he had successfully done between 1908 and 1914. Appreciating that the demands of war might require a speedier and more decisive mechanism, he had, as early as November 1914, established a War Council of eight, which included the military and naval leaders. But this remained subordinate to the main Cabinet. After the formation of the first Coalition, the War Council was replaced by what was called the Dardanelles Committee, which discussed strategic matters, particularly the Gallipoli campaign, but was still subordinate to the full Cabinet. On 2 November 1915, Asquith set up a War Committee with himself doubling as War Minister. This was intended, in particular, to take decision-making powers away from Kitchener, in which it was quite successful. A further opportunity to diminish the powers of Kitchener offered itself when the post of Chief of the Imperial General Staff (CIGS) fell vacant. The fact that practically no one has heard of the previous incumbent, Sir James Wolfe-Murray, indicates how unimportant the job actually was. But in taking up Asquith's offer of the post, Sir William Robertson, a highly regarded general who uniquely (he was the son of a tailor) had entered the army as a private, insisted that he should determine strategy and deal directly with officers in the field.

But the creation of the War Committee did not meet the criticisms of those who were increasingly arguing that the war must be run by some small group, free of all other responsibilities, and possessed of executive powers. One such critic was Sir Edward Carson, formerly leader of the Ulster cause, brought into the first Coalition as Attorney-General; another was Bonar Law's adviser, Max Aitken (shortly Lord Beaverbrook), a Scottish-Canadian newspaper millionaire; a third was Lloyd George, who had come closer to the central direction of the war when he took the place at the War Office vacated by Kitchener's drowning, and also closer to what he perceived as Asquith's failure to provide dynamic and decisive leadership. Aitken brought Bonar Law, Carson and Lloyd George together for the first time on 25 November. From this group there emerged the proposal that there should be a small War Council with full executive powers, chaired by Lloyd George. Asquith, in some form or another, would remain formal head of the government, but would not be involved in running the war effort. Asquith at first expressed assent to some such arrangement, but then, assured of the support of the Liberal Cabinet ministers, he repudiated this.[36]

Standing back from the detail of political intrigue, one can, perfectly properly, say that this political crisis of December 1916 was brought about by unhappiness and frustrations over the terrible and apparently fruitless losses on the Western Front and the sense that these were due to a lack of dynamism and decisiveness in the British political leadership. On the evidence, Lloyd George, who had been innovative and energetic, looked a much better war leader than Asquith, who had striven to maintain traditional standards and had shown great political skill, but who seemed unable to rise to challenges of a totally new sort. But there was no neat constitutional mechanism for translating widespread uneasiness and, indeed, anger into actual political change, short, at any rate, of a General Election, and everyone agreed that an election must be avoided. Most Conservatives disliked Lloyd George, and resented Bonar Law's dealings with him, while Asquith had the support of the Liberal grandees. However – a critical development this – a canvass of Liberal MPs by Lloyd George's crony, junior minister Christopher Addison, showed that in certain circumstances Lloyd George would have considerable back-bench Liberal support against Asquith. So the principal players embarked on a high-stake game of resignations and threatened resignations. Lloyd George was first when, on 5 December, he received Asquith's repudiation of the Law–Carson–Lloyd George scheme. Bonar Law was forced to give open support to Lloyd George by threatening his own resignation. Other leading Unionists then decided that they could not serve in an Asquith government from which both Bonar Law and Lloyd George had resigned. So now Asquith resigned; his hope was that Lloyd George, being opposed by the Liberal grandees and disliked by the Conservatives, would not be able to form a government, thus putting Asquith back into the Prime Ministership. But Bonar Law, who had refused the premiership for himself, had undertaken that the Conservatives would serve under Lloyd George – *the* critical development according to Professor John Ramsden.[37] Lloyd George's cunning and charm also played a part. He promised jobs to all the leading Conservatives and to Balfour who had been very much an Asquith supporter. The only Liberal to be offered an important post (the Ministry of Munitions) was Addison. Lloyd George formed his government but had put his fate utterly into the hands of the Conservatives; they insisted that he must keep Haig as British Commander-in-Chief.

### *THE LLOYD GEORGE COALITION*

The circumstances were infinitely more fraught and dangerous, yet it is perhaps not altogether absurd to compare Lloyd George's 'revolution' in government with that of Margaret Thatcher some 70 years later. Lloyd George's innovations were more comprehensive, but he faced more severe constraints, both the imperatives of war and the demands of his new political allies. More: his overriding objective being military victory, his reforms were all directed to that end, and, therefore, were not necessarily intended to be permanent. He created a War Cabinet of five, supported by a proper Cabinet secretariat, headed by Maurice Hankey, a former marine officer who had been Secretary to the Committee of Imperial Defence since 1912. Hankey prepared agendas, kept records and ensured that ministries actually carried out War Cabinet decisions. Only one member of this War Cabinet, Bonar Law as Chancellor of the Exchequer, had departmental responsibilities. The new importance of Labour was signalled by the inclusion of Arthur Henderson. The other two members were both passionate imperialists, the Earl Curzon, Tory grandee, and Viscount Milner, scholar and civil servant – strange bed-fellows for the nonconformist and Liberal pacifist, it would have been thought not many years previously.[38]

Lloyd George brought new sorts of people into government, in particular experts from business and from labour, rather than professional politicians. He created new ministries, directed at the challenges of total war: Shipping, headed by Sir Joseph Maclay, a Glasgow ship owner, who refused to become a member of parliament; Labour, headed by John Hodge, a trade unionist and Labour MP; Food, headed by Lord Devonport, head of a grocery chain; Pensions, headed by another trade unionist and Labour MP, George Barnes; National Service, headed by Neville Chamberlain, a Birmingham businessman and former Lord Mayor as well as Conservative MP; and Reconstruction, headed by Addison after he made way at Munitions for the return to politics of Churchill. An agricultural expert, R. E. Prothero, became head of the Board of Agriculture; a civil engineering contractor, Lord Cowdray, became Chairman of the Air Board; and H. A. L. Fisher, Vice-Chancellor of Sheffield University and a historian (nice to find a historian being regarded as an expert), became President of the Board of Education. Altogether there were eight members of the Labour party in the government, in addition to Arthur Henderson.

Unionists saw the war as an imperial war which would, they hoped, result in the Empire becoming a massive economic monopoly, with Britain at its heart. For his part, Lloyd George hoped that he might be able to enlist the Dominions against the generals. In March 1917 the Dominions' Prime Ministers (or in the case of South Africa the Minister of Defence, General Jan Smuts) came to London for an Imperial War Cabinet. Lloyd George seized the opportunity to introduce another unique development in cabinet government: he persuaded Smuts, who had actually fought against the British in the Boer War (when Lloyd George had been a pacifist and 'pro-Boer') to stay in Britain as a member of the War Cabinet. Smuts was sent to the Front to find the general who could replace Haig, but reported that there simply was no one else.

Lloyd George admired professionals and experts on the domestic scene – all, of course, subordinate to himself. The same did not hold true of the army and navy. As we saw, he did have one important victory over the Admiralty in 1917, one absolutely crucial to Britain's survival – that is, over the introduction of convoys. He was, to say the least, considerably less successful in his hostility towards the generals, specifically Haig and Robertson. Lloyd George was what came to be called an 'Easterner', that is to say he was appalled by the slaughter on the Western Front and believed that Germany could be defeated by attacks on her allies in the East. Haig and Robertson were out-and-out 'Westerners'.

Daring as he was in so many ways, Lloyd George simply could not risk sacking Haig: the Conservatives were totally against it, and the blow to public confidence might have been disastrous. The balance swung slightly towards Lloyd George as the nature and consequences of Haig's Flanders Campaign became clear, and Robertson's insistence that the Palestine Campaign would be unsuccessful without massive reinforcements was disproved by General Allenby's triumphant entry into Jerusalem. In November Lloyd George was successful in having the Supreme War Council established. Instead of appointing Robertson British representative, Lloyd George sent Sir Henry Wilson, a sprig of the Anglo-Irish ascendancy, whom he had been using for some time as an unofficial adviser. Upon this gambit, Lloyd George managed to build a minor victory. When Robertson protested, Lloyd George informed him that he was, after all, to be British representative, but that Wilson had been appointed CIGS in his place, with the powers of that post reduced to what they had been under the unknown Sir James Wolfe-Murray. Then Robertson was given the opportunity to resume as CIGS, but with the curtailed powers. On 16 February 1918 his 'resignation' was formally announced. Lloyd George's idea had been that after getting rid of Robertson, he would be able to get rid of Haig.[39] But the great German offensive rendered that once more out of the question.

Lloyd George was inventive, energetic, and very successful in rushing the troops Haig desperately needed over to France. Thus, the Prime Minister was basically in the right when he was accused of deliberately starving Haig of troops. The charge was made by the recently dismissed Sir Frederick Maurice, who had been Robertson's Director of Military Operations, in a letter to *The Times* on 7 May. The precise accusation was that Lloyd George had lied to the House of Commons on 9 April when he had said that the British army in France on 1 January 1918 was numerically stronger than it had been on 1 January 1917. Maurice was probably right about the situation in January 1918, but since then Lloyd George had done everything possible to rectify it. Thus, Asquith and his supporters were unwise to take the matter up in the House of Commons, where Lloyd George achieved an overwhelming triumph by showing that the figures he had relied on had been supplied from the War Office by Maurice himself (though there is some evidence that Lloyd George was concealing a subsequent correction which Maurice had sent).[40] For the first time in the war, the Opposition, on 9 May, pressed a motion against the government to a division, securing 98 votes, all Liberals.

### *Votes for Women (and Men)*

Meantime the question of the franchise was coming back to the top of domestic political discussion. Expansion of job opportunity was the central phenomenon of women's war experience, with many repercussions, including political ones. Yet the issue which, after decades of suffragist and then suffragette agitation, and 18 months of bloody total war, brought votes for women back into the realm of practical politics was that of votes for men. Because votes for men were based on the antiquated occupational qualification, thousands of men had actually lost their right to vote through going out to serve their country. Thousands of other men who were also serving their country had never had the vote in the first place. Eagle-eyed suffragists perceived that consideration of these problems provided the opportunity to bring the question of votes for women back into open discussion. Rumours about possible changes in the franchise for men began to circulate in late 1915. In January 1916, a number of the suffragist organizations held a private meeting in London which, while showing that there were still strong differences of opinion between those who favoured complete adult suffrage, and those who simply wanted women to be enfranchised on the same terms as men, did produce an agreed resolution that any Bill increasing the number of votes should be so framed as to include the enfranchisement of women. In May, Mrs Millicent Fawcett, leader of the main suffragist organization, the National Union of Women's Suffrage Societies (NUWSS), raised the issue directly in a letter to Asquith:

> When the Government deals with the franchise, an opportunity will present itself of dealing with it on wider lines than by the simple removal of what may be called the accidental disqualification of a large body of the best men in the Country, and we trust that you may include in your Bill clauses which would remove the disability under which women now labour. An agreed Bill on these lines would, we are confident, receive a very wide measure of support throughout the Country. Our movement has received very great accessions of strength during recent months, former opponents now declaring themselves on our side, or at any rate, withdrawing their opposition. The change of tone in the Press is most marked . . . The view has been widely expressed in a great variety of organs of public opinion that the continued exclusion of women from representation will . . . be an impossibility after the war.

Asquith denied that alteration of the Register was being contemplated, but added that if such an alteration should become necessary Mrs Fawcett's points would be 'fully and impartially weighed without any prejudgement from the controversies of the past'.[41]

From inside the Government itself, the officials of the Local Government Board placed before the Cabinet the argument in favour of a comprehensive Bill simplifying the existing system of franchise and registration, and the Labour Cabinet Minister Arthur Henderson put forward a paper calling for universal adult suffrage. However, Henderson wanted the qualifying age for women to be 25, not 21 as for men: this is an important point – even democrats feared seeing women in an overall majority in the country, particularly since they were widely believed to be overwhelmingly supporters of the Conservative party. Questions in the House of Commons about the government's intentions brought the matter back into the headlines and roused the National Union of Women's Suffrage Societies (NUWSS) to action: a joint Suffrage Conference in June agreed that if an extension of the male franchise was intended, then agitation for female suffrage must be resumed. NUWSS deputations were received by Asquith on 25 July, and by Bonar Law and Lord Robert Cecil, a strong Tory supporter of the women's cause within the Cabinet, on 3 August. The main points made by the women, set out in another letter to Asquith on 4 August, were that, provided there were no proposals to alter the basis of the old Register (as distinct from modifications necessary to enable voters who had enlisted to maintain their qualification), they would not resume their agitation: they would, however, force the suffrage issue if the male vote was to be extended, or if it were intended to hold a General Election. It was at this point that Mrs Pankhurst signalled her effective abandonment of the suffrage fight by letting it be known that she was in favour of soldiers and sailors getting the vote whether or not women got it as well.

The government introduced its Special Register Bill in parliament on 14 August, but there were so many other issues, apart from votes for women, including the question of plural voting and the possible introduction of proportional representation, that it was finally decided that all of these problems should be referred to a Committee representing all parties and drawn from both Houses of Parliament, to sit under the Chairmanship of the Speaker. The deliberations of the Speaker's Conference, which held its first meeting on 12 October, were secret, and it refused to hear evidence from the NUWSS. The Speaker, J. W. Lowther, cleverly got all the other contentious issues settled, before turning to that of women's suffrage. A majority of 15 to 6 favoured at least some votes for some women; by 12 votes to 10 it was agreed that there must be restrictions to prevent women voters from being in the majority.

The advent of the Lloyd George Government in December 1916 augured well for the women. The press magnate Lord Northcliffe was a supporter of the women's case, as well as of Lloyd George, and he was able to generate favourable publicity in his newspapers. Reporting on 30 January 1917, the Speaker's Conference unanimously supported three basic propositions and a host of lesser ones. The three proposals were: that the unsatisfactory occupational basis of the existing franchise should be replaced by a simple residential qualification; that there should be a simplification of the Local Government Register; and that proportional representation should be introduced. Section Eight of the Report read as follows:

> The Conference decided by a majority that some measure of women's suffrage should be conferred. A majority of the Conference was also of the opinion that, if Parliament should decide to accept the principle, the most practical form would be to confer the vote in the terms of the following resolution:
>
> 'Any woman on the Local Government Register who has attained the specified age, and the wife of any man who is on that register, if she has attained that age, shall be entitled to be registered and to vote as a Parliamentary elector.'

For the 'specified age' the report suggested 30 or 35. Apart from this projected age-bar, there was an implied property and class qualification: only householders were on the Local Government Register. In the country at large there were over 12 million women aged 21 or over: under 9 million held the necessary household qualification and an age-bar of 30 would reduce that number to under 7 million.

To keep up the pressure on the government, and to affirm that there had been no slackening in women's support for the principle of votes for women, the London Society for Women's Suffrage organized a 'Women Workers' Suffrage Demonstration' at the Queen's Hall on 20 February. It was left to the Executive, and then the National Council, of the NUWSS to grasp the problem of the unequal treatment for women proposed by the Speaker's Conference. Again under Mrs Fawcett's shrewd leadership, the National Council endorsed the Executive's resolution that the NUWSS should, for the moment, drop its older demands for complete equality and go hard for a Bill along the lines recommended by the Speaker's Conference. This caused enormous heart-searching within the suffrage movement, so that a special circular letter had to be sent out explaining that Mrs Fawcett and Mrs Ray Strachey (another suffragist leader) had interviewed two members of the War Council and seven members of the government before concluding that it was vital to support a compromise measure. In particular, the two women had been informed:

> That no bill of any sort will be introduced unless the Government feels assured that there will be practical unanimity in the House and little opposition in the country, the Government preferring an immediate General Election on the old Register to wasting time over controversy in the House of Commons.

Furthermore, moderate anti-suffragists were prepared to accept this as a working compromise for the sake of clearing the decks for reconstruction legislation after the war. On the other hand, argued Mrs Fawcett and Mrs Strachey, supporters of complete adult suffrage should accept it as an instalment which would secure the crucial breaking-down of the sex barrier, and which would inevitably lead to complete equality in the near future.

The next development in parliament was a highly significant one. Asquith, ousted Prime Minister, bastion of the resistance to the women's claims in pre-war days, reluctant conceder of women's value in time of war, now moved a resolution calling for an early Bill to implement the recommendations of the Speakers Conference. 'Some of my friends may think', he said contritely, 'that . . . my eyes, which for years in this matter have been clouded by fallacies and sealed by illusions, at last have been opened to the truth.' The motion was passed by 341 votes to 62.

At 10 Downing Street, the next day, Saturday, 29 March, Lloyd George welcomed a women's suffrage deputation. It was an Imperial as much as a national occasion; but there were no Duchesses, and working-class women at least got a mention, if not exactly a look-in. After Mrs Fawcett had explained their willingness to support an imperfect scheme, the next speaker was HM Chief Lady Factory Inspector, who introduced herself as a 'daughter of Greater Britain', born in Australia, and closely associated with both Australia and New Zealand, 'the homes of enfranchised women'. She followed with some words on the British working woman:

> The last thing I want to do is to make her out a paragon which she is not; but I do maintain that the least thing we have to fear is danger to our Country if the English, Scottish, and Irish women should ever voice their own political, industrial,

> and social needs, which are those of their fathers and husbands, and lovers and brothers, and children also. Anyone who has a thinking mind knows and admits that these women are worthy of better conditions than they have, whether in their dwellings, or their occupations, or their wages. The first step – the urgent step – is to consult them; and the next thing, it seems to me, is to go on consulting them.

The emphasis on women workers was continued in a speech by the leading woman trade-unionist, Mary Macarthur. Then, for obvious reasons, Lloyd George specially requested Mrs Pankhurst to speak. She could not have been more obliging:

> I want to say for members of my organisation, and I think for patriotic women generally, that we recognise that in war-time we cannot ask for perfection in any legislation . . . we want to see this thing done as quickly as possible, with as little dispute and as little difference of opinion as possible . . . I want to assure you that whatever you think can be passed, and can be passed without discussion and debate . . . we are ready to accept (hear hear). We know your democratic feeling, and we leave the matter in your hands.

Lloyd George followed with a long speech of his own. He admitted that an age-bar was 'illogical and unjustifiable'. But, he said, the compromise measure would no doubt lead later to full equal rights. At this point, a member of Sylvia Pankhurst's uncompromising Worker's Suffrage Federation interrupted to make the claim for votes for women under 30. Lloyd George's curt reply was that he had nothing more to say, having already explained the position. On that cue, Mrs Fawcett hastily brought proceedings to a close.[42]

The government's Bill, which settled upon 30 as the minimum voting age for women and gave the vote to all adult males, passed through the House of Commons fairly easily in June 1917: the largest vote against the women's suffrage clause was 55. The House of Lords, which still had the power to delay legislation, might have been a tougher proposition. The debate in the upper chamber took place on 11 January 1918: Lord Curzon spoke against votes for women, but recommended those who agreed with him simply to abstain, in order to avoid a clash with the House of Commons. In fact, the Bill secured a very convincing majority of 136 to 71, and it passed into law on 6 February 1918.

It has been argued that this was a muted victory, and less than women would have got had there been no war. But it seems to me that the United Suffragists got it right. As early as 26 November 1915 the front page of their paper, *Votes for Women*, carried a cartoon headed: 'Votes for Heroines as well as Heroes' (see plate 3). They saw the Act of February 1918 as a mighty victory which would lead quickly and inevitably towards complete women's suffrage; indeed they brought publication of *Votes for Women* to an end. It is perfectly true that a broad, liberal–democratic movement starting in the late nineteenth century, and supported by men as well as women, had come near to achieving votes for women before 1914. Yet the political advance of women in 1914 was still blocked by two great fortresses of prejudice: the vigorous hostility of a majority of men, particularly powerful ones, and the often fearful reluctance and opposition of many women. The war experience brought a new confidence to women, dissipated apathy and silenced the female anti-suffragists. Asquith was only the most prominent of the converts among men. No doubt the actual swing-round among members of the House of Commons was not enormous; but as politicians, whatever their private convictions, most came to feel that it was no longer politically wise to make strong statements against women's suffrage. No

"Votes for Women," November 26, 1915 — Registered at the G.P.O. as a Newspaper.

**The War Paper for Women**

**VOTES FOR WOMEN**

OFFICIAL ORGAN OF THE UNITED SUFFRAGISTS

VOL. IX. (Third Series), No. 403. — FRIDAY, NOVEMBER 26, 1915. — Price 1d. Weekly (Post Free 1½d.)

**VOTES FOR HEROINES AS WELL AS HEROES**

**CHIVALRY: "Men and women protect one another in the hour of death. With the addition of the woman's vote, they would be able to protect one another in life as well."**

*(The Anti-Suffragists used to allege, as one reason for refusing women the protection of the vote, that women were already protected by men's chivalry—as in a shipwreck, when the women are always saved first. When the hospital ship Anglia went down, last week, the women nurses refused life belts, saying, "Wounded men first.")*

**Plate 3** 'Votes for Heroines as well as Heroes': cover from the war-time suffragist paper (on which men were as active as women), *Votes for Women*. Courtesy of Mary Evans/Fawcett Library

doubt many agreed with a member of the Conservative Party Central Office that: 'the granting of a vote to the wives of the duly qualified male electors would as a rule increase the majority of the opinions of the male voters'. The replacement of militant suffragette activity by frantic patriotic endeavour played its part as well.

More than this, the war generated a tremendous mood favourable to change and democratic innovations. An editorial comment on Mrs Pankhurst's first great recruiting speech had hinted at this as early as November 1914:

> After this war many things can never again be as they were before it broke out. Some of the changes, perhaps, may be for the worse; the majority . . . will, we trust, be for the better. Is it too much to hope that the altered position and prospects of the women's movement will be among the national gains?[43]

Such sentiments were repeated over and over again until some people actually began to believe in them. From May 1915 there were Labour members in the government, and although they wanted many other things, no doubt more pressingly, they also supported votes for women. The words of politicians are not usually the most reliable of historical sources. But E. S. Montague, Lloyd George's successor as Minister of Munitions, put the matter well when on 15 August 1916 he said in parliament: 'Women of every station . . . have proved themselves able to undertake work that before the war was regarded as solely the province of men.' The armies, he said, 'had been saved, and victory had been assured, by women'. 'Where', he asked, 'is the man now who would deny woman the civil rights which she has earned by her hard work?'

In October, when the press was full of talk of the imminent collapse of the Germans, an important Bill was rushed through parliament, its single important clause reading:

> A woman shall not be disqualified by sex or marriage from being elected to, or sitting or voting as, a Member of the Commons House of Parliament.

After the General Election of December 1918, which in effect continued Lloyd George's Conservative-dominated Coalition Government, the Sex Disqualification Act was passed, which opened jury service, the magistracy and the legal profession to women, and gave them qualified entry to the upper reaches of the civil service; it was also made clear that there was in law no barrier to their full membership of the ancient universities of Oxford and Cambridge. At the end of 1919, with the establishment of a State Register of Nurses, nursing was for the first time recognized as a full profession. The National Insurance Acts of 1918, 1920 and 1921 made women, as wage-earners, eligible for National Insurance benefits. In 1928 political emancipation was completed when all women over 21 without qualification were given the vote.

The voting qualification for men was six-months' residence (which excluded, as it still does, about 5 per cent of the adult population). Plural voting was not entirely abolished: if you were a university graduate, you could vote, as appropriate, in the Oxford University seat, the Cambridge University seat, the

Combined Universities seat (England and Wales) or the Scottish Universities seat; or if you had business premises in certain city constituencies you could have an extra vote there. A majority in the House of Commons favoured single-member constituencies, with the alternative vote, which, by giving electors second choices, ensures that the candidate elected has a genuine majority behind him or her, rather than simply being 'first past the post'. In the House of Lords there was a strong preference for proportional representation, which meant grouping constituencies together; this was said by opponents to break the historic tie between a member of parliament and his constituency. The compromise eventually worked out provided for the alternative vote in the university constituencies but nowhere else, while provision was made for an experiment in proportional representation to be held in 100 large towns which returned three or four members. What the Representation of the People Act of 6 February 1918 did, apart from the historic granting of votes to women, was create single-member constituencies, of roughly equal size (an electorate of about 70,000), each returning one member on the first-past-the-post principle, the proportional representation experiment never in fact being tried. Ten boroughs, with more than 70,000 voters but not as many as 140,000, remained as two-member constituencies. All elections were to be held on the same day.[44] The argument that participation in the war effort brought votes to women, and also to many men previously disfranchised, gets a little bit of extra support from the provision that conscientious objectors should be denied the vote for five years.

### *Conscientious Objectors*

The ILP (Independent Labour Party) members within the parliamentary Labour party held to the position that Britain should not have become involved in the war. Some of them joined with anti-war Liberals in forming the Union of Democratic Control (UDC) – the implication was that if there was democratic control over foreign policy rather than statesmen forming secret alliances, then wars would never happen. With the threat of the introduction of conscription came the founding of the No-Conscription Fellowship (NCF). These were the main bodies on the anti-war side: a small minority indeed.

To begin with, as conscientious objectors had their applications rejected by the tribunals, they were passed on to the military authorities. Three groups, deemed to have enlisted in the Non-Combatant Corps, were smuggled out to France: there sentence of death was read out to 34 men, commuted (after a pause) to ten years' penal servitude. The information service of the NCF at once alerted its Liberal and ILP friends in parliament, who secured from Asquith, who was undoubtedly appalled by the action of the military, a statement that no executions would be carried out (altogether on the Western Front 313 soldiers were executed for 'desertion' or 'cowardice'). A further triumph for the anti-conscription movement was the issue, on 25 May 1916, of Army Order X, which laid it down that after being court-martialled, conscientious objectors should be handed back to the civilian authorities for incarceration in one of His

Majesty's prisons. In June, the government, to its credit, seriously disturbed by the problem of the conscientious objector, set up the Pelham Committee, which was charged with finding alternative national work for men who were prepared to take it. A Central Appeals Tribunal was to consider all cases of men already in prison held to be 'genuine' and to direct them towards the Pelham Committee. Those who were willing were released from prison and employed under what was called the Home Office Scheme.

Altogether there were about 16,000 conscientious objectors: about 3,300 accepted service in the Non-Combatant Corps, somewhat under 3,000 did various forms of ambulance work or work under the direct supervision of their tribunals, around 4,000 accepted work forthwith from the Pelham Committee, and rather more than 6,000 went to prison at least once. Of these, 3,750 were subsequently employed under the Home Office Scheme, leaving 1,500 intractable absolutists whose challenge to the authority of the State the government simply could not comprehend. In July 1916, Lloyd George delivered himself of a resounding denunciation of the absolutists:

> I do not think they deserve the slightest consideration. With regard to those who object to the shedding of blood it is the traditional policy of this country to respect that view, and we do not propose to depart from it: but in the other case I shall only consider the best means of making the lot of that class a very hard one.[45]

That these sentiments in regard to all types of conscientious objectors were shared by most members of the community, there can be little doubt. There are many reports of ILP or UDC peace demonstrations being broken up, of Quaker meetings being disturbed and of conscientious objectors serving the national interest in such innocuous occupations as felling trees and being molested by local inhabitants. For the absolutists, the authorities (having practised pre-war on the militant suffragettes) provided only a dismal treadmill of arrest, court-martial, imprisonment, release, arrest, court-martial, and so on. Clifford Allen, Chairman of the No-Conscription Fellowship, was imprisoned thrice before becoming so seriously ill that the government, reluctant to have him die on their hands, gave him a conditional – that is, conditional upon his remaining seriously ill – release. Allen's case was typical of many; about 70 men actually died from their prison treatment.

## *What about the workers?*

The year 1917 was one of extreme working-class discontent for reasons which were varied and which differed in emphasis from place to place. Among them were: the Conscription Acts, and the manner in which they were applied by over-zealous military authorities; the Munitions Acts, with 'leaving certificates' still a special grievance; the attempts by private employers to extend dilution; high prices; bad housing; and the resentment of skilled workers who found themselves overtaken in the wage race by unskilled. It was in 1917 that the method of working-class action through shop stewards and unofficial representatives, developed on Clydeside and elsewhere in the earlier years of the war, began to react positively with rapidly growing working-class resentment. First, news of the Russian Revolution in March 1917 caused great excitement in all corners of the Labour movement, but above all to the advocates of workshop organization. Stress and strain of war, and the sight of much affluence, often just out of reach, were other less tangible agents of unrest.

Before its fall the Asquith Government had been negotiating for official trade-union support for the extension of dilution to work other than that connected with the manufacture of war materials, but had failed to win over the Amalgamated Society of Engineers. The desire to maximize national productivity in all commodities was now inextricably bound up with, and overshadowed by, the desire to release as many fit men as possible for service in the armed forces. When, therefore, the new government again proposed dilution for private work in March 1917 it followed this up on 3 April with the withdrawal of the 'trade cards' scheme, which had been a great triumph for the Amalgamated Society of Engineers, in giving them control of the call-up of their own skilled men. In place of the 'trade cards' scheme the new Ministry of National Service operated a 'schedule of protected occupations', and began to accelerate the release of skilled men for military service; greater use was made of the substitution schemes of September 1916, which had established yet another set of special local committees, this time charged with the task of finding unfit substitutes for militarily fit men.[46]

Before any enactment had been made in regard to the dilution issue, a Rochdale engineering firm saw fit to cash in on what it believed to be the government's intention, and began to introduce dilutees into its own private work: a strike followed immediately (3 May). At once the authorities called up some of the strikers for military service, but at the same time the firm was fined, a recognition of the justice of the strikers' case. Meanwhile, national and local grievances throughout the country produced the unofficial 'May strikes' which began on 10 May and lasted for a fortnight. Eight leaders were charged under the Defence of the Realm Acts, but the charges were dropped and the government agreed that all outstanding complaints would be dealt with by negotiation between government and trade-union leadership; again, unofficial action had brought formal gain.

On 13 June the government appointed a series of Commissions of Inquiry into Industrial Unrest in eight separate areas of Great Britain. The task of summarizing the reports was given to one of the Labour ministers, George Barnes. One point Barnes picked out was:

> the feeling that there has been inequality of sacrifice, that the government has broken pledges, that the trade union officials are no longer to be relied upon, and that there is a woeful uncertainty as to the industrial future.[47]

A positive consequence of the Commission of Inquiry was the abolition of the leaving certificate system.

Representatives of trade-union branches attended a June conference in Leeds organized by the leaders of the ILP and of the minuscule British Socialist Party, to celebrate the first Russian Revolution. In the euphoria, the conference actually called for the establishment of Workers' and Soldiers' Councils of the Russian type in Britain. This was pure hot air, though the government at the time, and Marxist commentators since, have thought differently. The Cabinet feared a Russian withdrawal from the war effort, and so sent Arthur Henderson on a mission to Russia to seek out the best means of keeping the new government in the war. Henderson, however, concluded that Britain should join with the new Russian leader, Kerensky, in exploring the possibilities of a negotiated peace with Germany and her allies. He therefore proposed sending delegates from the Labour party to a projected International Socialist Congress in Stockholm, to be attended also by German representatives, and got the support of a special Labour Party Conference for this. The War Cabinet was outraged, and in the celebrated 'doormat incident' Henderson was kept waiting outside the Cabinet door, before being brought in to face a reprimand from Lloyd George. Henderson resigned; but it was agreed that his position in the Cabinet should be taken by George Barnes.

As trade-union leaders began to interest themselves in the question of war aims and a possible negotiated settlement, so the anti-war and pro-war wings of the Labour movement began to come together. In general, there was a surge of confidence throughout all branches of the movement, particularly noticeable, the *Observer* commented, at the TUC Congress of October 1917. Arthur Henderson and Sidney Webb completed their draft of a new constitution for the Labour party, which, while retaining such autonomous components as the ILP, would make it possible for people to join the party directly through local constituency parties, turning the ramshackle structure into the sort of mass electoral machine which would be necessary if Labour were to compete successfully with the other political parties. The new constitution also committed the party to a clear socialist objective, that is to say, wholesale nationalization, embodied in the famous 'Clause Four'. The new constitution came before the Labour Party Conference in January 1918, and, after a second conference, was finally adopted. Labour members were performing reasonably well in government: G. N. Barnes was modestly competent as Minister of Pensions, until he replaced Arthur Henderson in the War Cabinet; J. R. Clynes was praised, first as Under-Secretary at the Food Ministry, then as Food Controller. Before the war the Labour party had been little more than a pressure group, speaking up for working-class interests. Now it was beginning to look like a potential party of government. The *Observer* predicted that in ten years' time Clynes would be Prime Minister of a Labour government;[48] actually there was a Labour government in six years, and Clynes just missed being Prime Minister.

## *Reconstruction and General Election*

With the Ministry of Munitions had come 'National Factories', directly run by the state, and 'Controlled Factories', strictly governed by the terms of the Act. In 1917 and 1918 state interference in the economy was greatly extended; indeed, this was the main purpose behind many of the new ministries. Lloyd

George was nothing of a theorist, very little of a planner; his concern was to get things done, his strength that he would give a hearing and a trial to all suggested means. Most of the direct initiative came from within the civil service. The real pioneers of bulk purchase were the 'whirlwind trio' at the Army Contracts Department, E. M. H. Lloyd, 'the brains behind the throne'; E. F. Wise, 'Director of Offensive and Defensive Operations'; and U. F. Wintour, who instituted the policy of bulk purchase for hides and leather. Up until December 1916 less than half the total of British shipping and practically none of the great liners had been requisitioned by the state; under the new Ministry of Shipping, almost every ship was taken over, so that the Shipping Controller, working in conjunction with a committee of management of the big ship owners, was now able to organize and redistribute the nation's ships in the most economical manner. Early in 1917, the Coal Controller took over the entire coal industry, with financial arrangements similar to those operating in regard to the railways. Lord Devonport, as Food Controller, was not a success. The first successful rationing schemes were in fact introduced by cooperative societies or local authorities. The fear was that any national scheme would damage civilian morale and give encouragement to the enemy. In September, price control was introduced for meat, and, with the assistance of a government subsidy, for bread. At last, in February 1918, rationing of meat was introduced in London. A new word came into everyday language as 'coupons' were to be clipped from the customer's ration card. From 7 April, meat rationing of this type was applied to the whole country. Universal rationing, by registration card, not coupon, followed for tea and butter. As a failure, Lord Devonport was matched by Neville Chamberlain, the first Director-General of National Service. To be fair, it was difficult to see where the functions of National Service differed from those of the recently established Ministry of Labour. Chamberlain shortly resigned, 'because', said the socialist academic R. H. Tawney, many years later, 'he had nothing to do'.[49] Under the direction of Sir Auckland Geddes, the ministry was reorganized and given a general responsibility as 'the War Cabinet's General Staff on Man-Power'.

The War Cabinet committed itself to the principle of 'reconstruction', which, it said, was 'not so much a question of rebuilding society as it was before the war, but of moulding a better world out of the social and economic conditions which have come into being during the war'.[50] Obviously the new Ministry of Pensions was mainly concerned with death and disablement on the military front, but its remit was extended to cover all persons employed in trades relating to the war effort. All through 1917 and 1918 work continued on the most ambitious reconstruction of all, the abolition of the Local Government Board and the creation of a Ministry of Health. A Bill was introduced into the House of Commons four days before the armistice, but then, basically because of resistance from the mandarins of the Local Government Board, was withdrawn. A new Bill finally passed into law in April 1919.

In August 1917, the new President of the Board of Education put his proposals for the first major Education Act since 1902 before the House of Commons. It was, he said, 'prompted by the deficiencies which have been revealed by the War', and by the need 'to repair the intellectual wastage which has been caused by the War', by which he meant the growing pressure for children to work, rather than stay in school. On the positive side he referred to the 'increased feeling of social solidarity which has been created by the War', and remarked that the acceptance of conscription 'means that the boundaries of citizenship are not determined by wealth and that the same logic which leaves us to desire an extension of the franchise points also to an extension of education'. As with the Ministry of Health Bill, so too the Education Bill, faced with the opposition of vested interests, had to be withdrawn. Introduced in a new form in early 1918, it passed its third reading in July. A universal minimum leaving age of fourteen was to be enforced, and there were to be compulsory day continuation schools for those between 14 and 18 not undergoing suitable alternative instruction. All fees in public elementary schools were to be abolished.

With over nine-tenths of the country's imports being bought directly by the state, with 240 national factories in operation and large sectors of economic and social activity under direct state supervision, people by 1918 were becoming acclimatized to the idea of state collectivism. Informed observers tended to the belief that some at least of the socialistic experiments would be worth maintaining after the war; making the best of a bad job, the Anti-Socialist Union changed its name to the Reconstruction Society. The leaders of private industry were remarkably silent while the war lasted, contenting themselves with singing the praises of large-scale industrial organization. Overt hostility to state control did not burst out until October 1918 when the war looked to be all but won:

> Among the business community there is practical unanimity of agreement that there should be as little interference as possible on the part of the state in the future Governance of Industry.

The same writer did recognize 'that the resettlement of the industries of the country on a peace basis is a task so huge that it could not satisfactorily be left to unguided private effort'. Officially the government verdict was that the 'war has brought a transformation of the social and administrative structure of the state, much of which is bound to be permanent'. At the same time, those already inclined towards socialism failed to see that what might be attempted under war conditions might be less appropriate in times of peace.

It was a measure of the new mood in the Labour movement, and the resentment at the government's intolerance of any talk of a negotiated peace, as, for example, the proposal by Lord Lansdowne, that the leaders of the big unions, the Miners, the Railwaymen and the Engineers, called on the Labour ministers to withdraw from the Coalition the moment the war ended.[51] There had been no General Election since 1910; the franchise had been reformed; most of all, Lloyd George wanted to cash in on his reputation as 'the man who won the war'. The General Election of December 1918 is thus often known as the 'khaki' election. The Liberal party, of course, was split between those who had supported the Coalition Government, and those who had gone into opposition with Asquith. But what if Conservatives stood against Lloyd George's Liberals? It was agreed, therefore, that there would be approved Coalition candidates who would not oppose each other. Their letter of endorsement was mockingly termed a 'coupon', thus giving this notorious election its alternative title as the 'coupon' election. Khaki election or not, the arrangements for soldiers to vote were utterly inadequate, so that the turnout of the eligible electorate was only 57 per cent (compared with 82 per cent in December 1910).[52] An imperfect guide, then, to how political opinion had shifted over the war period, yet a stunningly revealing one in many ways.

**Table 1.6** General Election, 14 December 1918

| | *Electorate 21.4 million* | | *Turnout 57 per cent* | | |
|---|---|---|---|---|---|
| | *Coalition parties* | *Other Conservatives and Unionists* | *Labour* | *Liberal* | *Sinn Féin* |
| Total votes | 5,121,359 | 663,097 | 2,385,472 | 1,298,808 | 486,867 |
| Percentage of votes cast | 47.6 | 6.1 | 22.2 | 12.1 | 4.5 |
| Seats | 478 | 48 | 63 | 28 | 73 |

The Coalition, with 65 members returned unopposed, and therefore not included in the total, attained 53.2 per cent of the popular vote. Because of the distorting effects of the first-past-the-post system, this yielded 523 seats, in a House of Commons of 707. The Asquith Liberals got only 13 per cent of the popular vote, giving them 36 seats. All of the ILP members within the Labour party, including MacDonald, were defeated, as punishment for their opposition to the war; as was Arthur Henderson, who had shown himself altogether too keen on the idea of a negotiated peace. Nonetheless, Labour got 20.8 per cent of the vote (compared with only 6.4 per cent in December 1910 – when the Liberals had gained 44.2 per cent), producing a party in parliament which was very much a party of trade unionists, and, in particular, miners: MacDonald contemptuously spoke of 'a party of checkweighmen',[53] and indeed the new Chairman of the Parliamentary Labour Party was the unexceptional Fifeshire miner Willie Adamson.

But where the results were most portentous was in Ireland. Here was the strongest evidence of the advance of the new Sinn Féin (turnout though was low – 47.1 per cent). Twenty-five candidates were unopposed, and 73 were elected in all, while the Irish Nationalists, who had held 84 seats before the war, now had the derisory total of seven. Sinn Féin did not take their seats at Westminster, a tangible and ominous sign that they wished to have nothing to do with the British system of government. Another ominous sign was the powerful contrary vote in Ulster, which returned 25 Unionists. Some general elections really do provide a distillation, however crude, of what has changed over the previous few years and even offer a vision of what is yet to come: in this respect the 1918 election ranks with those of 1945, 1979 and 1997.

## NOTES

Place of publication is London unless stated otherwise.

1 Quoted in R. F. Foster, *Modern Ireland 1600–1972* (1989), p. 466. My account in this paragraph broadly follows Foster, pp. 461–71. See also Dermot Keogh, *Twentieth Century Ireland: Nation and State* (1994).
2 Correlli Barnett, *Britain and Her Army 1509–1970: A Military, Political and Social Survey* (1970), p. 373. For the outbreak of war, see J. M. Bourne, *Britain and the Great War 1914–1918* (1989), pp. 13–19; Peter Simkins, *Kitchener's Army: The Raising of the New Armies, 1914–16* (Manchester, 1988), pp. 34–8; Martin Gilbert, *Winston S. Churchill, vol. III: 1914–1916* (1971), pp. 21–31.
3 Simkins, *Kitchener's Army*, p.49. For this and the next paragraph see Simkins, pp. 49–78; Arthur Marwick, *The Deluge: British Society and the First World War* (1965; new edition, 1991), pp. 69–93.
4 Niall Ferguson, 'The Kaiser's European Union: What if Britain had "Stood Aside" in August 1914?' *Virtual History: Alternatives and Counterfactuals* (1997), pp. 228–80, and again in *The Pity of War* (1998).
5 See Ian F. W. Beckett, 'Total War', in Colin MacInnes and I. D. Sheffield (eds), *War in the Twentieth Century: Theory and Practice* (1988), pp. 1–23. For the war in comparative perspective there are two indispensable collections of essays: Jay Winter and Richard Wall (eds), *The Upheaval of War: Family, Work and Welfare in Europe 1914–1918* (1988); and Hugh Cecil and Peter Liddle (eds), *Facing Armageddon: The First World War Experienced* (1996), p. 466.
6 I have discussed these issues in the Introduction to the new edition of *The Deluge*.
7 In these paragraphs I have relied heavily on the excellent account in Bourne, *Britain and the Great War*, pp. 19–80. The giant work is David French, *British Strategy and War Aims, 1914–1916* (1986). For a complete account of the military war, John Keegan, *The First World War* (1998), is latest and best.
8 Quoted by Donald Richter, 'The Experience of the British Special Brigade in Gas Warfare', in Cecil and Liddle, *Facing Armageddon*, p. 354.
9 Colonel Repington, *The First World War 1914–1918* (1920).
10 Bourne, *Britain and the Great War*, p. 51.
11 A. J. P. Taylor, *English History 1914–1945* (Oxford, 1965), p. 81.
12 Bourne, *Britain and the Great War*, p. 73. The remainder of my account follows Bourne closely. For overall strategy see David French, *The Strategy of the Lloyd George Coalition, 1916–1918* (Oxford, 1995).
13 Foster, *Modern Ireland*, p. 471. The next quotations are from pp. 471 and 474.
14 Alvin Jackson, 'British Ireland: What if Home Rule had been Enacted in 1912', in Ferguson, *Virtual History*, pp. 175–227.
15 P. J. Cain and A. G. Hopkins, *British Imperialism: Crisis and Deconstruction* (1993), passim, and pp. 297–300; W. D. Rubinstein, *Culture, Capitalism and Decline in Britain 1750–1900* (1993), esp. pp. 37–9.
16 Cd 7190 (1914), pp. 6–8, quoted in Marwick, *The Deluge*, pp. 58–9.
17 *Report of the British Association 1919*, pp. 15, 258, quoted in Marwick, *The Deluge*, pp. 273–4.
18 Marwick, *The Deluge*, pp. 269–71.
19 Ibid., p. 147; Taylor, *English History*, p. 165.
20 *Report of British Association 1919*, pp. 18, 165, cited in Marwick, *The Deluge*, p. 275.

21 John Woolff, 'Religion and "Secularization"', in Paul Johnson (ed.), *20th Century Britain: Economic, Social and Cultural Change* (1994), pp. 427–41; Edward Royle, *Modern Britain: A Social History 1750–1985* (1987), pp. 335–42; Arthur Marwick, *British Society since 1945* (1996), pp. 11, 460–2.
22 Compiled from information in: A. D. Gilbert, *Religion and Society in Industrial England: Church, Chapel and Social Change 1740–1914* (1976), p. 31; Woolff, 'Religion'; and Royle, *Modern Britain.*
23 Arthur Marwick, *Women at War 1914–1918* (1977), pp. 19–20.
24 On the franchise, Neal Blewett, *The Peers, the Parties and the People* (1972); see generally Martin Pugh, *The Making of Modern British Politics* (Oxford, 1992), pp. 1–136, 202–20.
25 J. M. Winter, *Socialism and the Challenge of War: Ideas and Politics in Britain, 1912–18* (1974), pp. 35–6.
26 Duncan Tanner, *Political Change and the Labour Party 1900–1918* (Cambridge, 1990), p. 165.
27 There is an excellent summary in Henry Pelling, *A History of British Trade Unionism* (Harmondsworth, 1987), pp. 101–38.
28 See Marwick, *Women at War*, p. 25; in general see Martin Pugh, *Votes for Women in Britain* (Historical Association, 1994).
29 This approach is explained in Arthur Marwick, *Class: Image and Reality in Britain, France and the USA since 1930* (1990), pp. 1–17.
30 The bases for these calculations are in Marwick *The Deluge*, pp. 59–63. For the upper class see David Cannadine, *The Decline and Fall of the Aristocracy* (1990).
31 See Marwick, *The Deluge*, pp. 102–8.
32 Pelling, *Trade Unions*, pp. 140–2.
33 John Turner, *British Politics and the Great War: Coalition and Conflict 1915–1918* (1992), pp. 56–61; John Grigg, *Lloyd George: From Peace to War 1912–1916* (Methuen, 1985), pp. 248–55; Trevor Wilson, *The Downfall of the Liberal Party* (1966, paperback 1968), pp. 56–68; Bourne, *Britain and the Great War*, pp. 107–15.
34 For these and the next paragraphs see Marwick, *The Deluge*, pp. 101–2, 117–19.
35 Turner, *British Politics*, pp. 86–90; Bourne, *Britain and the Great War*, p. 122.
36 For this and the next paragraph, see Turner, *British Politics*, pp. 112–48; Grigg, *Lloyd George*, pp. 446–74; Bourne, pp. 119–27; Wilson, *Downfall*, pp. 92–111.
37 John Ramsden, *An Appetite for Power: A History of the Conservative Party since1830* (1998), p. 231.
38 Grigg, *Lloyd George*, p. 476; Taylor, *English History*, p. 67.
39 French, *Strategy*, pp. 164–8; Turner, *British Politics*, pp. 297–99.
40 Grigg, *Lloyd George*, pp. 481–7; Taylor, *English History*, pp. 69–79.
41 Marwick, *The Deluge*, pp. 140–1.
42 Marwick, *Women at War*, pp. 153–7.
43 Ibid., p. 158; for a different view, persuasively argued, see Pugh, *Votes*.
44 Peter Clarke, *A Question of Leadership: Gladstone to Thatcher* (1991), pp. 103–4. There is a useful summary in Taylor, *English History*, note C, pp. 115–16.
45 Marwick, *The Deluge*, pp. 243–5.
46 Pelling, *Trade Unions*, p. 146; Marwick, *The Deluge*, pp. 246–7.
47 Pelling, *Trade Unions*, p. 148.
48 *Observer*, 30 June 1918, quoted in Marwick, *The Deluge*, p. 250.
49 Marwick, *The Deluge*, pp. 232–6, 293.

50 Ibid., pp. 279–86, 293–4, for this and the next three paragraphs.
51 Pelling, *Trade Unions*, p. 148.
52 Election statistics here and throughout the book are culled from David Butler and Gareth Butler, *British Political Facts 1900–1994* (1994).
53 Pelling, *Trade Unions*, p. 149.

# 2 Between Two Wars, 1919–1939

## The Structural, Ideological and Institutional Context

### *Hard facts*

Words readily associated with the inter-war years are 'depression' and 'recession'. It is a familiar notion that economic activity, and particularly international economic activity, goes in cycles: 'booms' and 'slumps', we say. The nineteenth century can be quite neatly divided up into cycles of rising prices, and cycles of falling prices. Prices had begun falling in 1873, bringing to an end the 'mid-Victorian boom', and deepening in the 1880s into the 'Great Depression'. Prices began to rise again towards the end of the 1890s so that the country (or some of it – workers and their families suffered severely when wages did not keep up with prices) was enjoying the 'Edwardian boom' when the war broke out. Scarcities and destruction of capital drove prices up at accelerated rates; 'boom' conditions continued throughout 1919 and up until the autumn of 1920. There then began the long cycle of falling prices, aggravated by the Wall Street crash of 1929, and the series of crises affecting European banks in the couple of years that followed. At one time, the term 'Great Depression' was reapplied to Britain in the thirties, though recent accounts are more likely to stress the elements of recovery. Once again there is no substitute – though as a tentative start only – for scrutinizing the statistical tables.

The column to concentrate on in table 2.1 first is the middle one. Note that the figures are not in pounds or millions of pounds or anything like that. They are simply relative to the middle of our period (1930), which is taken as being a baseline of 100 for each different set of figures. We can then see that prices continue rising until 1920, then begin dropping in 1921. They get to their lowest point in 1933, then show a slight recovery, though in 1938 they are still below what they had been in 1930. One can see where the notion of the 'Great Depression' came from. Falling prices mean falling profits, rising unemployment, general pessimism, and, of course, falling wages. Employers, naturally, hope to save their businesses by cutting wage bills; but the overall effect on the economy can be to intensify the downward spiral since reduced incomes lead to reduced purchases.

**Table 2.1** Indices of wages, prices and real earnings, Britain, 1913–1938 (1930 = 100)

| | *Weekly wage rates* | *Retail prices* | *Average annual real wage earnings* |
|---|---|---|---|
| 1913 | 52.4 | 63.3 | 82.8 |
| 1919 | – | 136.1 | – |
| 1920 | 143.7 | 157.6 | 92.2 |
| 1921 | 134.6 | 143.0 | 94.1 |
| 1922 | 107.9 | 115.8 | 93.2 |
| 1923 | 100.0 | 110.1 | 90.8 |
| 1924 | 101.5 | 110.8 | 91.6 |
| 1925 | 102.2 | 111.4 | 91.7 |
| 1926 | 99.3 | 108.9 | 91.2 |
| 1927 | 101.5 | 106.0 | 95.8 |
| 1928 | 101.1 | 105.1 | 95.2 |
| 1929 | 100.4 | 103.8 | 96.7 |
| 1930 | 100.0 | 100.0 | 100.0 |
| 1931 | 98.2 | 93.4 | 105.1 |
| 1932 | 96.3 | 91.1 | 105.7 |
| 1933 | 95.3 | 88.6 | 107.6 |
| 1934 | 96.4 | 89.2 | 108.1 |
| 1935 | 98.0 | 90.5 | 108.3 |
| 1936 | 100.2 | 93.0 | 107.7 |
| 1937 | 102.8 | 97.5 | 105.4 |
| 1938 | 106.3 | 98.7 | 107.7 |

*Source:* D. H. Aldcroft, *The Inter-War Economy: Britain 1919–1939* (London: Batsford, 1970), pp. 352, 364.

The first column is an index of weekly wage *rates* (i.e. taking no account of overtime) in actual pounds, shillings, and pence (there were twenty shillings in a pound, twelve pence in a shilling), and so not in any way reflecting changes in the cost of living and the consequent changing value of money, as before expressed in percentages relative to 1930. If we want to chart the movement of wages in real terms (that is to say with respect, not just to overtime, but to changes in the value of money), we should concentrate on column three. For example, column one shows us that in money terms wage rates were nearly three times as high in 1920 as they had been in 1913; column three shows us that in real terms workers had made gains of almost 10 per cent, and by 1921 over 10 per cent. Thereafter, as we can see, real wages start to drop, with slight fluctuations: after 1923, 1926 – the year of the General Strike – is a low year. Real wages are clearly in recovery by 1930, and the recovery continues (with slight fluctuations), real earnings by the thirties being a good 20 per cent and more above their figure in 1913, and 10 per cent and more over where they were in 1920.

Employers, politicians and journalists were very familiar with the notion of the trade cycle and the belief that wages would have to come into balance with prices if there was ever to be recovery and expansion once more. They were reluctant to

**Table 2.2** Percentage distribution of world's manufacturing production, 1913–1938

| | *US* | *Germany* | *UK* | *France* | *Russia* | *Sweden* | *Japan* | *India* | *Rest of the world* |
|---|---|---|---|---|---|---|---|---|---|
| 1913 | 35.8 | 14.3 | 14.1 | 7.0 | 4.4 | 1.0 | 1.2 | 1.1 | 21.1 |
| 1926–9 | 42.2 | 11.6 | 9.4 | 6.6 | 4.3 | 1.0 | 2.5 | 1.2 | 21.2 |
| 1936–8 | 32.2 | 10.7 | 9.2 | 4.5 | 18.5 | 1.3 | 3.5 | 1.4 | 18.7 |

*Source:* A. G. Kenwood and A. L. Lougheed, *The Growth of the International Economy, 1820–1980* (London: Routledge, 1983), p. 183.

see that Britain's structural problems went much deeper than this. Though often paranoiac about foreign competition, they were unwilling to face the fact that international markets, and Britain's place in them, had changed crucially in a number of ways. Germany had always been the bugbear: what was not understood was not only that Britain's eminence as a manufacturing and trading power had gone, but that, without there being any open political manifestations of this, that eminence had been taken over by the United States, and rested on the unshakeable basis that American productivity was high, and costs of production low. Obviously America was going to fulfil its potential before long, and was already showing strong signs of doing so in the years before the war. But, in waging total war, Britain lost markets for both goods and services, and ran down her overseas investments; America, on the other hand, came out of the war as a major creditor. A second development was that there were now many more suppliers, or would-be suppliers, in the market place. India, previously a massive market for British cotton goods, took the opportunity, when supplies were cut off during the war, of developing her own industry; the new nations of post-war Europe were determined to build up their own industries and to shut out imports. In 1913 Clydeside alone built a third of all the world's ships. But, since Britain herself was the biggest trading nation, the bulk of ships built went to British owners, rather than being exported. Lower levels of international trade lowered the demand for new construction, and, anyway, over the war period other countries, particularly the United States and Japan, had established shipping industries of their own. Thirdly, demand had dropped catastrophically for the products which had formed Britain's staple exports, coal and cottons. All of these developments were set within a general situation in which trading between nations no longer functioned with the relative smoothness of the pre-war years, when Britain had been the prime provider of loans, even though her holdings of gold were relatively moderate. Much of what Britain was able to do before the war was based on confidence and trust. These qualities were largely destroyed in the war. In any case, Britain no longer had the same resources, so that the role of principal lender passed to the United States. But whereas Britain's debtor countries could repay their loans, and thus keep the system going, through their exports to Britain, America had no need of such exports. Thus debts piled up, and the international trading mechanism jammed up. Britain was bound to be a particularly serious sufferer. It is fashionable today, in explaining Britain's economic problems (and those of other European countries), to speak of 'globalization'. Britain, of course, had been a pioneer in opening up global markets – on her own terms. Already, in the 1920s, she was being squeezed by changing global realities, almost a kind of de-globalization (see table 2.1).

The obvious remedy – if it were only that simple – would have been to stop producing goods foreigners did not wish to buy, and produce, at much lower prices, goods they did want to buy. There was not very much Britain alone could do about the tariff barriers which were going up all around the world (inhibiting global exchange). Britain's coal, steel, and heavy engineering industries had in fact been developed to their utmost as part of the national effort during the war years; it wasn't easy now to suddenly switch them off. Immediately after the war, during continuing boom conditions, British cotton manufacturers invested heavily in new plant and machinery, believing, not altogether unreasonably, that their dominance of world markets would continue. In fact, apart from the emergence of new competitors, total world trade in cotton textiles contracted by between one-third and a half. In 1920, the last year of the boom, cotton made up 30 per cent of all exports, while coal accounted for 9 per cent.

Much of the ill-judged expansion in the cotton industry was financed by borrowing. This brings us to the first of a number of costs which manufacturers have to bear, and upon the level of which can depend their own success, and therefore the success of the economy as a whole: that is, the cost of borrowing, the interest rate, basically determined by the 'Bank Rate' set by the Bank of England (now known as the Minimum Lending Rate). We will look at the details in the next section, but generally Bank Rate, whatever other needs it may have met, was higher than manufacturers would have desired. The prices charged by manufacturers, allowing margins for profits, distribution to shareholders, future investment and taxes, were computed in sterling; the prices paid by foreign purchasers would depend on sterling's exchange rate with their own currency, determined by sterling's valuation in gold, and its exchange rate with the dollar. A restoration of the pound to its pre-war value, which was something practically all politicians and financiers wanted, would mean a high value on the pound, and therefore a handicap on exports. A third cost to manufacturers is that of wages. Now, the way British society had evolved, it would have been all but impossible to push wages any lower, while, of course, there were plenty of arguments that they should have been considerably higher. The purely economic fact, and the one affecting manufacturers, was, as we have seen, that real wages were outstripping prices.

In a modern society, especially one committed to the sort of 'reconstruction' which was being spoken of at the end of the war, certain levels of taxation will be inevitable. How far taxes can genuinely be seen as a cost on manufacturing potential and cost effectiveness is an uncertain point. Quite possibly higher rates tend to discourage investment; and low levels of investment (as compared, say, with the United States) can be taken as an independent variable adversely affecting British industry. Once again we have to return to the cost of waging total war: the national debt, £620 million in 1914, had risen to about £8,000 million at the end of the war. Just to finance interest charges relatively high taxes (in comparison with the shocking 1s 2d of Lloyd George's People's Budget of 1911) had to be levied; 6s in 1919–22 and 5s in 1923. Anyone making £100 on their investments, had to pay £25 in tax, of which £10 went to interest charges on the National Debt.[1]

Was there something inherently wrong with British entrepreneurs themselves? Had there been, as Martin Wiener claimed in a famous book, a 'decline of the industrial spirit', an ethos hostile to business, and one in which the ablest brains turned away from industry towards the cultured life?[2] The thesis was not altogether new. J. M. Keynes, who had already achieved fame for his condemnation of the harsh terms imposed on Germany at the end of the war, specifically the demand for reparations from Germany for the costs of the war she was alleged to have started, in *The Economic Consequences of the Peace* (1919), made a famous attack on British entrepreneurs in the Liberal weekly paper, *The Nation*:

> The mishandling of currency and credit by the Bank of England since the war, the stiff-neckedness of the co-owners, the apparently suicidal behaviour of the leaders of Lancashire, raised the question of the suitability and adaptability of our Business Men to the modern age of mingled progress and retrogression. What has happened to them – the class in which a generation or two generations ago we could take a just and worthy pride? Are they too old or too obstinate? Or what? Is it that too many of them have risen not on their own legs, but on the shoulders of their fathers and grandfathers?[3]

In fact, there is no record of consistent incompetence. Some entrepreneurs were highly successful, showing great flair and great dedication; others did match the stereotypes drawn by Wiener and Keynes. Actually, it was customary in all countries, including America, for the very successful in business to hope to slip into the cultured world of the aristocracy, but Britain certainly did not have a unified culture hostile to industry. What could be said is that the world of finance tended to attract higher prestige, and provide greater rewards, than the world of industry, with banks being more ready to support the former rather than the latter – wisely, according to the theory, about which I am sceptical, that Britain's best option lay with finance and trade. Old approaches were adhered to most strongly, by labour as well as management, in the older industries, which still overwhelmingly dominated the economy. Productivity matched the best levels in other countries in the new industries, electricity, rayon, motor vehicles, patent foods, luxuries, but having amounted to 6.5 per cent of Britain's total industrial output in 1907, these contributed a mere 12.5 per cent in 1924, and 16.3 in 1928.

Could the new industries have been expanded more rapidly? Could new technologies have been exploited more extensively? Although Britain had been far behind France and the United States before the war, the technological knowledge was now there for the full flowering of a domestic motor car industry, as it was for the production of electrical and other consumer goods. The central problem was that of demand, which indeed was the central problem of the entire economy, and that of all the industrial economies, including America after 1929. World economic conditions seemed to rule out creating overseas markets for these new goods. During the twenties, Britain was a net importer of cars. So, manufacturers concluded, it was to the domestic market that they must cater. Ideas about the nature of that market were a compound of practicality and prejudice. Cars, before the war, had been the prerogative of the upper class. Now they could be targeted at most sections of the middle classes; as also could electrical and other consumer goods. During the debates over reconstruction, and the launching of a massive house-building programme ('homes fit for heroes to live in') at the end of the war, it had been a widespread joke that if you gave the working class baths they would simply keep the coal in them. So, obviously, such luxuries as private cars and domestic appliances were not for the working class; and, naturally, given the absence of any will to make such products widely available, working-class incomes were generally too low to make such purchases possible.

Similar considerations both affected the electricity supply companies in their programmes for connecting up customers, and then determined the nature of demand for electrical goods: if you had no electricity supply – and rural areas were almost totally neglected – you wouldn't be in the market for an electric iron (the cheapest and most popular of the new conveniences), or an electric cooker – sales here really are strikingly low. As for refrigerators, they look to be confined to members of the upper class (see tables 2.3 and 2.4).

The principal use of such tables, obviously, is to tell us about living conditions and lifestyles (the subject of the Modernism and Mass Society section, p. 116). That is still more true of table 2.4; yet it does also show the extent of, and, more critical to my present purpose, the limits upon, growth in some of the new industries.

William Morris, in 1924, made clear his dislike of the methods associated with Henry Ford:

> Let me say at once that our success has not been achieved by what is commonly called 'mass production'. I prefer to spell 'mass' with an 'e'. So far mass production has meant merely *mess* production when applied to motor cars in this country.[4]

**Table 2.3** Percentage of connected homes with certain electrical goods

| | *Percentage of homes connected up to electricity supply* | *Cookers* | *Irons* | *Water heaters* | *Wash boilers* | *Refrigerators* |
|---|---|---|---|---|---|---|
| 1932 | 31.84 | 4.9 | – | – | – | – |
| 1933 | 49.15 | 6.1 | 56.4 | 1.2 | 0.9 | – |
| 1934 | 49.33 | 9.3 | – | 1.9 | 1.4 | – |
| 1935 | 54.54 | 11.3 | – | 3.1 | 2.0 | – |
| 1936 | 57.75 | 13.4 | 70.9 | 3.8 | 2.4 | 2.3 |
| 1937 | 61.77 | 15.4 | – | 4.8 | 2.9 | – |
| 1938 | 65.39 | 16.9 | – | 5.6 | 3.5 | 2.4 |

*Source:* Sue Bowden, 'The New Consumerism'. In Paul Johnson (ed.), *20th Century Britain: Economic, Social and Cultural Change* (London Longman, 1994), p. 245. Blanks indicate figures not available.

**Table 2.4** Statistics relating to new industries

| | *Number of radio licences per 1,000 families* | *Motor cars in use* | *Rentals of telephone services for personal use* |
|---|---|---|---|
| 1922 | 5.8 | – | 176,000 |
| 1923 | 10.7 | – | 204,000 |
| 1924 | 15.4 | 579,800 | 238,000 |
| 1925 | 20.0 | 692,800 | 274,000 |
| 1926 | 21.7 | 800,300 | 321,000 |
| 1927 | 23.4 | 898,900 | 369,000 |
| 1928 | 26.0 | 997,900 | 419,000 |
| 1929 | 29.6 | 1,098,100 | 468,000 |
| 1930 | 37.1 | 1,177,900 | 514,000 |
| 1931 | 44.5 | 1,192,900 | 551,000 |
| 1932 | 50.0 | 1,236,000 | 580,000 |
| 1933 | 56.1 | 1,313,300 | 609,000 |
| 1934 | 60.7 | 1,420,500 | 667,000 |
| 1935 | 64.4 | 1,592,400 | 757,000 |
| 1936 | 68.3 | 1,726,000 | 882,000 |
| 1937 | – | 1,890,400 | 1,024,000 |
| 1938 | – | 2,045,400 | 1,143,000 |

*Source:* Sue Bowden, 'The New Consumerism'. In Paul Johnson (ed.), *20th Century Britain: Economic, Social and Cultural Change* (London: Longman, 1994), p. 246. Blanks indicate figures not available.

While Ford alone was producing nearly two million cars in the United States in 1923, the total UK production was only 182,000 in 1929, 390,000 at its peak in 1937. Morris and Austin had built up a combined market share of 60 per cent in 1929. Ford sales in Britain, which had 24 per cent of the market in 1913, collapsed to 4 per cent in 1929. In the thirties Morris and Austin were put under pressure by several vigorous smaller firms, so that in 1938, together they only had 45 per cent of the market, with Vauxhall, Rootes and Standard, together with Ford, claiming over 10 per cent of the market each. Ford's Manchester operation was almost free of unions. The huge open-field Dagenham site in the East End of London was being developed from 1927 and opened in 1932.

British motor manufacturers in the thirties kept their shareholders happy by distributing substantial dividends rather than retaining profits for investment in any substantial expansion, or reducing prices. Instead of seeking economies of scale, each company produced rather a large variety of models each tailored to the precise social status of potential buyers. Although car-workers were among the country's most fortunate, the employers kept their wages under firm control. When, at Crossley Motors in November 1921, the Amalgamated Engineering Union protested that a wage cut had been made under duress, the company got the workers to sign a document declaring that this had been by mutual agreement.[5] The union presence in the car industry was in fact rather peripheral, generally involving only the craft workers: the AEU was based in skilled heavy engineering, the National Union of Vehicle Builders in woodworking, and the Transport and General Workers Union in docks and transport. In 1928, Percy Keene, Head of the Cost Department at Austin, made it clear: 'We definitely set out to manage as managers and the result is that we have no representation anywhere from the workers' side.'

In 1914 the British electrical engineering industry was small by international standards, with a substantial part owned by the Germans or the Americans. The inter-war period was very much one of catching up.

**Table 2.5** Electrical engineering: percentage of value of gross British output

| | |
|---|---|
| 1907 | 0.7 |
| 1924 | 1.9 |
| 1935 | 3.0 |

*Source:* R. E. Catterall, 'Electrical Engineering'. In Neil K. Buxton and Derek H. Aldcroft (eds), *British Industry Between the Wars: Instability and Industrial Development 1919–1939* (Aldershot: Scolar Press, 1979), p. 241.

By 1938, those employed in electrical engineering amounted to 5 per cent of all employed in manufacturing (the equivalent figure for motor cars was 6.2 per cent).

The most obvious symptom of structural weaknesses in the British economy was unemployment, which both scarred the lives of those who endured it, and, through the expenditure on unemployment insurance benefits, added to the country's financial problems. From table 2.8, it can be seen that Britain, throughout the twenties, was much more seriously affected in this respect than France

**Table 2.6** Estimated number of domestic electrical appliances in use and annual sales, Great Britain, 1939

| | *Estimated number in use, in thousands* | *Number per thousand homes* | *Estimated annual sales in thousands* |
|---|---|---|---|
| Cookers | 1,500 | 195 | 220 |
| Water heaters | 480 | 63 | 100 |
| Washing machines | 150 | 19 | 80 |
| Wash boilers | 288 | 38 | 60 |
| Refrigerators | 200 | 26 | 20 |
| Vacuum cleaners | 2,300 | 300 | 400 |
| Electric irons | 6,500 | 850 | 1,500 |

*Source:* R. E. Catterall, 'Electrical Engineering'. In Neil K. Buxton and Derek H. Aldcroft (eds), *British Industry Between the Wars: Instability and Industrial Development 1919–1939* (Aldershot: Scolar Press, 1979), p. 265.

**Table 2.7** Distribution of employment in electrical engineering trade, UK, 1935

| | *Numbers employed* | *Percentage of total* |
|---|---|---|
| Greater London | 114,439 | 46.2 |
| Midlands | 54,977 | 22.2 |
| Lancashire and Cheshire | 48,542 | 19.6 |
| Scotland | 3,299 | 1.3 |
| Wales | 424 | 0.2 |
| Rest of United Kingdom | 26,267 | 10.5 |
| Total | 247,948 | 100.0 |

*Source:* R. E. Catterall, 'Electrical Engineering'. In Neil K. Buxton and Derek H. Aldcroft (eds), *British Industry Between the Wars: Instability and Industrial Development 1919–1939* (Aldershot: Scolar Press, 1979), p. 270.

or Germany. (French figures, in particular, benefit from the large number of peasant proprietors whose families never appear in the statistics, while unemployed British agricultural workers do.)

It is difficult to discuss structural factors without sometimes bringing in ideological and institutional ones, and it is quite impossible to exclude events altogether (as my occasional references back to the war have shown). It is now essential to bring in the economic events of 1929 to 1931. From table 2.8 it is

**Table 2.8** Unemployment in Britain, Germany and France, 1922–1933

| | *Great Britain* | | *Germany* | | *France* |
|---|---|---|---|---|---|
| | *Number in thousands* | *Percentage of working population* | *Number in thousands* | *Percentage of working population* | *Number in thousands* |
| 1922 | 1,543 | 15.2 | 215 | 1.1 | 13 |
| 1923 | 1,275 | 11.3 | 818 | 4.1 | 10 |
| 1924 | 1,130 | 10.9 | 927 | 4.9 | 10 |
| 1925 | 1,226 | 11.2 | 628 | 3.4 | 12 |
| 1926 | 1,385 | 12.7 | 2,025 | 10.0 | 11 |
| 1927 | 1,088 | 10.6 | 1,312 | 6.2 | 47 |
| 1928 | 1,217 | 11.2 | 1,391 | 6.3 | 16 |
| 1929 | 1,216 | 11.0 | 1,899 | 8.5 | 10 |
| 1930 | 1,917 | 14.6 | 3,076 | 14.0 | 13 |
| 1931 | 2,630 | 21.5 | 4,520 | 21.9 | 64 |
| 1932 | 2,745 | 22.5 | 5,603 | 29.9 | 301 |
| 1933 | 2,521 | 21.3 | 4,804 | 25.9 | 305 |

*Source:* Arthur Marwick and Wendy Simpson (eds), *War, Peace and Social Change: Documents 2, 1925–1959* (Buckingham: Open University Press, 1990), p. 10. The French statistics are particularly unreliable (too low) and do not provide percentages.

clear that, across three countries, not just in Britain, things had got very much worse by 1932. There was, in other words, an international crisis, not just a British one. The crisis, indeed, demonstrated the crucial position America now occupied in the world economy. It had been said in the nineteenth century, when political revolution seemed to spread outwards from France, that 'when Paris sneezes the rest of Europe catches a cold'. Henceforth, it could well be said that 'when Wall Street crashes, the rest of the world crashes with it'. The American economy, in sharp contrast with the British, boomed throughout the twenties. But there were three serious weaknesses. Agriculture, which employed a quarter of the workforce, was already in deep depression. Secondly, the American mass market for cars and consumer goods was beginning to dry up: wages were not high enough to provide the purchasing power to sustain the boom. Thirdly, the boom conditions encouraged a get-rich-quick mentality and a frenzy of speculation.[6] The bubble was bound to burst, and it did in August 1929. Americans immediately began withdrawing their savings from their banks. The American banks then began calling in their debts from Europe. In May 1931 the largest bank in Austria, the Kreditanstalt, became bankrupt. Then the German banks began to collapse. Bankrupt countries could not buy British exports. Unemployment, already high and a drain on the nation's resources, shot up and so also did government expenditure on the unemployed. The great fear was of a withdrawal of funds from London. As it happened a minority Labour government was in office, naturally less capable of commanding foreign confidence than a Conservative government would have been. Yet it desperately needed to raise an American loan. Businesses foundered, mass unemployment mounted still higher. The Gold Standard was abandoned and so was Free Trade: tariffs now protected British industries. Recovery began sooner in Britain than elsewhere, as the unemployment figures and sales of cars and consumer goods indicate. There was expansion in another area also: throughout the twenties at least 200,000 houses were built each year; throughout the thirties, the figure was 360,000. Conditions remained appalling in the 'depressed areas', areas dependent on ship-building, or cotton, or coal, for which new markets were simply not to be found. So in the country as a whole, in 1938, the unemployment figure was 13.3 per cent; average annual real earnings were 7.7 per cent above what they had been in 1930.

## *A DIVIDED COUNTRY*

Just on living standards and life chances alone, Britain was a divided country. Between 1923 and 1930, unemployment in Scotland averaged 14 per cent, compared with 11.4 per cent for the United Kingdom. The difference worsened over the thirties when Scottish unemployment rose to 21.9 per cent, as against 16.4 for the United Kingdom, with a 76 per cent increase in the number of Scots on poor relief, compared with a United Kingdom increase of 13 per cent.[7] Central Scotland was dominated by the heavy industries whose overseas markets had collapsed: ship-building, heavy engineering, coal-mining. Three other factors aggravated the Scottish situation. First there was the high Scottish birth rate: more factory fodder, but fewer factories to feed. Second, productivity in Scotland actually improved at a higher rate than that for the United Kingdom as a whole: 8 per cent between 1931 and 1935, compared with 5.6 per cent. So the Scots were tending to do themselves out of jobs. Thirdly, there was a sharp change in the pattern of emigration, traditionally the high road which led ambitious, or starving, Scots to the Dominion countries. The average figure per decade between 1861 and 1911 had been 147,000. For the next two decades this figure more than doubled, but then between 1931 and 1939, fell to below 100,000.[8] It was the potential earners who had emigrated, leaving the old and the young. In the thirties the potential earners stayed behind, but an awful lot of them weren't earning.

The figures for Wales (and indeed one part of England, as we shall see in a moment) were even worse. What industrial South Wales largely produced was raw materials: coal and metals. The South Wales coalfields were particularly difficult, and therefore expensive, to work: in 1921 the net cost per ton of coal mined in South Wales was 60s 9d, compared with the United Kingdom average of 38s 11d.[9] In Wales, unemployment rose from 13.4 per cent in December 1925 to 23.3 per cent in December 1927; by July 1930, the figure was 27.2 per cent. In December 1930 the unemployment level in the Pontypridd-Mountain Ash-Rhonda coal-mining areas was 30 per cent; in the steel-smelting district of Newport it was 34.7 per cent. In June 1935 the unemployment level in the coal-mining Merthyr-Tydfil area was 47.5 per cent. Of course, there is more to Wales than the coal and iron-smelting areas of South Wales, just as there is more to Scotland than the central industrial belt. And there was more to the new province of Northern Ireland, which steadily became the part of the United Kingdom with the highest unemployment and the lowest wages, than Belfast. Belfast's one major industry was ship-building. Northern Ireland's one other industry was the production of linen: as with cotton in Lancashire, this was also afflicted by a sharp decline in demand. Unemployment in the former actually went as high as 65 per cent, and in the latter as high as 56 per cent. Throughout the thirties, average unemployment in Northern Ireland was 30 per cent.[10]

Almost as bad was the north-east of England, where unemployment was particularly high in the Tyneside shipyards. As also, on the other side of the country, it was bad in the shipyards of Barrow-in-Furness, and only marginally less bad in the coal mines both of the north-east and of Lancashire, and in the Lancashire cotton industry. Tables are again the best way of expressing the sharp differences in the fortunes of different parts of Britain (see table 2.9).

If we look at Germany and the advent of Hitler, and the French crisis of 1934 and the violent struggles which followed, perhaps even at depression America, Roosevelt's New Deal notwithstanding, perhaps Britain did not do so badly. What alternatives were there? The central problem was the general collapse of international trade. Britain might continue to follow the orthodox liberal economic policies upon which her international position had been based in the nineteenth century, Free Trade and adherence to the Gold Standard, but, without international cooperation, these would be ineffective, or perhaps even counter-productive. That is the first point to be made. The second one is that, over the entire inter-war period, the performance of the British economy

**Table 2.9** Unemployed as percentage of insured workers in various regions

| | *1929* | *1932* | *1937* |
|---|---|---|---|
| London and south-east England | 5.6 | 13.7 | 6.4 |
| South-west England | 8.1 | 17.1 | 7.8 |
| Midlands | 9.3 | 20.1 | 7.2 |
| North, north-east, north-west England | 13.5 | 27.1 | 13.8 |
| Wales | 19.3 | 36.5 | 22.3 |
| Scotland | 12.1 | 27.7 | 15.9 |
| Great Britain | 10.5 | 22.5 | 10.8 |
| Northern Ireland | 15.1 | 27.2 | 23.6 |

*Source:* John Stevenson, *British Society 1914–45* (Harmondsworth: Penguin Books, 1984), p. 271.

does not seem to have been notably worse than those of the other industrial countries. The only country which appeared to storm ahead unaffected by the world crisis was the Soviet Union (see table 2.2). But this was from a very low base, and, apart from its many inefficiencies, the Soviet command economy was of such brutality that, fortunately, there was no likelihood of anyone who was anywhere near the levers of power trying to use it as a model (though many left-wing intellectuals praised it). In a world hell-bent on economic nationalism, the economic internationalism of classical liberalism was not going to work. The major alternative proposed from the Right was that of Protectionism – the imposition of tariffs against foreign imports – in order to protect British industries, and, more important, enhance the (increasingly mythical) possibilities of a great British Empire, based on Empire Free Trade. The other major coherent alternative, being proposed mainly by those on the Left in politics, was that based on notions of under-consumption and the need for a living wage: British workers simply didn't earn enough to be able to purchase goods and therefore keep up demand for employment – this was to be remedied by paying all workers a living, or minimum, wage. The idea was most strongly advocated in the 1920s by the ILP within the Labour party, though it never became Labour party policy. Labour was officially committed to nationalization: given that the coal industry was fragmented into a large number of small, separate, ownerships, and given that the coal-owners showed themselves to be stubborn and inflexible, it is possible that nationalization of the coal industry might have had some positive effects. But nationalization, in itself, was scarcely a remedy for Britain's structural problems. There were those who advocated confronting unemployment directly by setting up government-financed public work schemes; but these could scarcely compensate for, say, a complete collapse of the shipbuilding industry. The economist J. M. Keynes did excoriate those actions of the government which made matters worse, but his own comprehensive theories about how demand within the economy must be managed (strong echoes here of under-consumption theories) in order to keep employment levels high, were not expounded until the middle thirties.[11]

There were some employers, and some politicians, who saw the trade unions as the problem: if only wages could fall to their 'natural' level, then British goods would once again be competitive. But it was difficult to portray trade unionists, who, after all, had loyally stood by the national interest during the war, as irresponsible, let alone dangerous or revolutionary. There was no great pressure to remove the privilege unions had at law and to leave the unions, as in America, to take their chances in the courts. The British context was not one in which goon squads and open violence could be employed or starvation wages enforced. It may be noted, on the other side, that the more extreme members of the ILP spoke of unions as regrettable institutions of capitalist society which would wither away under socialism.

## *Political faiths*

The split in the Liberal party, the arrival of a Labour party no longer in any sense an appendage of it, advantaged the Conservative party. On the whole, the first-past-the-post electoral system consolidated that advantage. Dominating politics throughout the inter-war years, Conservatives were unlikely to opt for bold policies going outside existing orthodoxies. There was neither the will nor the way for Liberals and Labour to form an imaginative, progressive Coalition. In the last quarter of the nineteenth century and into the early twentieth century a process had developed whereby two strong, opposing, political parties presented their broad agendas to the electorate; strongly assisted by the electoral system this, with some qualifications, produced a series of alternating strong governments. This process, such as it was, was completely dislocated in the inter-war years, without there being any alterations to the electoral system. But we cannot entirely blame processes, or politicians: electoral results indicated that the profoundest conservatism lay among the British people themselves.

A fundamental of political ideology was loyalty to party. How much say 'the public' or 'the British people' really had is a matter of considerable doubt, but, given that elections tended to be determined at the margins anyway, there was a pervasive sense (perhaps again partly derived from sport) that there ought to be two sides, and that a politician ought to make it clear which side he (it was nearly always a he) was on. In August 1923 a Lloyd George-leaning (but not too far) Liberal wrote in *The Times* that Labour and the Liberals had better 'relearn the old lesson of British politics that parties are two, the "for" and the "against" and that the nation has little use for either so long as it is divided against itself'. He was arguing that the 'true place for Liberalism is the Left'.[12] Labour, however, liked to present the Liberals, as well as the Conservatives, as 'capitalist' parties.

To a great extent, the parties had faiths rather than philosophies. The Liberal faith was in Free Trade. Apart from the Empire and the Union, the Conservatives believed in getting back to the 'normal' working of the system, in leaving things alone, in – the word was Bonar Law's – 'tranquillity'. Labour's faith was in nationalization and the Capital Levy (a general wealth tax). Much of the Labour party was made up of practical trade unionists who wanted better wages, better social services, fairer running of such chaotic industries as coal-mining. But there was also a pervasive faith that it was so obvious that the current system was ridden with evils that there just must be a better system ready to come into existence if only the correct levers were pulled. That was the real divide in political attitudes: between those who believed that the existing system was basically sound, and simply needed to be restored to proper working, and those who thought that somehow a new system could be brought into being. Both, alas, were wrong, and both were inhibited from seeking imaginative solutions to specific problems: certainly the conditions of the inter-war years were new, though there was nothing new about either unemployment or poverty. Both had an unalterable faith either in the British way of doing things, or in British solutions to British problems. Apart from the brief burst of enthusiasm for Russian experiments, there was very little looking for lessons from other countries.

## THE PENDULUM THAT WOULDN'T SWING: HIGH POLITICS, 1919–1939

Lloyd George had been returned to office, in triumph, as 'the man who won the war'. He had the challenges of the Peace Settlement and then successive international crises to wrestle with. He had a transformed Ireland to face. He had promised reconstruction, and did indeed believe in it, as long as the post-war boom lasted, at least. He had the demands of returning soldiers and of a confident Labour movement to respond to, all at a time when there was insurrection and revolution abroad, and fears that British soldiers might hold on to their weapons. He had a peacetime economy to run. He had to stay in power.

Lloyd George had actually talked of a 'Centre Party' during the crisis over the House of Lords in 1910. In 1915 he had been reflecting that 'party politics are gradually vanishing' and had expressed the hope that 'when the hour of reconstruction comes all will be for the State, all will be for the nation'.[13] Conservatives were happy for the time being to cash in on Lloyd George's popularity: but most of their back-benchers disliked and distrusted him, and hoped to have the joys and fruits of power entirely for themselves as quickly as that could be decently achieved. The 'Squiffites' (also known as the 'Wee Frees', after the Free Presbyterian Church in Scotland), Asquith's opposition Liberals, felt they had reason enough to detest Lloyd George. Early in 1920 the Prime Minister addressed himself to the issue of 'the fusion' of Coalition Liberals and Coalition Conservatives into a 'Centre' party. Bonar Law and the Conservative leaders were amenable. But the Coalition Liberals were adamantly opposed, and it was on that traditionalist rock that the idea foundered. The fact was that in the country Liberals continued to see themselves as one party and hankered for reunion between the 'Coalish Liberals' and the 'Wee Frees'.[14] The most notorious of Lloyd George's ploys for securing his position was his 'political fund' created from the sale of peerages, knighthoods, and other honours. There was nothing new about the securing of titles through contributions to party funds: critics in the Edwardian period had spoken scathingly of 'the beerage'. However, Lloyd George was notably graceless: he had a fixed tariff for each level of honour. Worse, he kept the proceeds for himself, rather than sharing with the Conservatives. When he fell from office in 1922, Lloyd George had a dowry of £1 million: all dressed up . . . but who would accept his hand?

The Versailles Treaty and Lloyd George's part in drawing it up have been analysed many times.[15] As a world statesman, it can be fairly said, Lloyd George appeared more realistic than President Wilson, and less pig-headed than Clemenceau and Orlando, respectively the French and Italian premiers. Before the public, the man who won the war was now also the man who was winning the peace. But ordinary Conservatives had their distrust of him boosted even further as they perceived him as being far too soft on Germany. At the same time, the equally mistrustful Labour party, now reinforced by the accession, via the ILP, of many anti-war former Liberals (many had in fact become strongly socialist as well as being internationalist – C. P. Trevelyan is a good example), was outraged at the harsh conditions imposed on Germany, particularly reparations for the costs of the war.

## *IRELAND*

Nearer to home, there was Ireland. As Lloyd George largely conducted his own foreign policy, so he largely conducted his own Irish policy. The immediate pressures on him were those of his Unionist colleagues, but it is not at all clear that even if free of them, he would have acted differently on Ireland. Refusing, as we saw, to take their seats in the Westminster parliament, the 73 Sinn Féin representatives set themselves up in Dublin as the Parliament of Ireland, Dàil Éireann, and, in January 1919, issued a Declaration of Independence proclaiming an independent Irish Republic. Meantime, the government had to prepare for the fact that the Home Rule Act of 1914 would come into effect automatically once the Peace Treaty was signed. Sinn Féin were not interested in Home Rule; the Ulster Unionists were as anxious as ever that they should be excluded from it. Historic Ulster had extended to nine counties, but the Ulster Unionists themselves now wanted to confine themselves to the six counties where there was an assured Protestant majority, two-thirds Protestants to one-third Catholics. Although their profound wish had been to continue to be governed directly from Westminster, they now began to see the need for a parliament of their own in Ulster, to counter-balance what would be set up in Dublin, whether by the enactment of a Home Rule Act or by the independent action of Sinn Féin.

The Government of Ireland Act became law on 23 December 1920, creating a 'Northern Ireland', consisting of the six counties of Antrim, Armagh, Down, Londonderry, Fermanagh, and Tyrone, and a 'Southern Ireland' consisting of the remaining 26 counties. In Northern Ireland there was to be a House of Commons of 52 members, elected by the alternative-vote system (demonstrating that, given the political will, such a system could have been introduced for the whole of Britain), and a Senate of 26 members, 24 to be elected by the

House of Commons, and two, the Lord Mayor of Belfast and the Mayor of Londonderry, sitting *ex officio*. There would be 13 Northern Ireland MPs in the Westminster parliament, which retained powers over imperial and foreign affairs, the armed forces, income tax and customs and excise. The Northern Ireland parliament was to have powers to make laws for the 'peace, order and good government' of Northern Ireland; it was specifically prohibited from making any laws or taking administrative action which violated the principle of equality between Protestants and Catholics. A new Governor of Northern Ireland would represent the Crown. Ireland was not as yet seen as being irrevocably split, so the Act provided for a Council of Ireland, to consist of 20 representatives from each of the northern and southern parliaments, under the Presidency of the new Lieutenant Governor of Southern Ireland appointed in 1920[16] (in what was intended as a conciliatory gesture he was, for the first time ever, a Catholic). The British, and Unionist, aspiration after unity was perfectly genuine, but they conceived of unity as being within a United Kingdom framework. If Nationalist Ireland was determined to secede from that framework, then Protestant Ulstermen were determined that they would secede from that Ireland. The Council never met; but the idea was revived again in the 'peace process' of the seventies, eighties and nineties.

To secure secession, a civil service for the new Northern Ireland (strictly speaking, North-East Ireland), recruited from existing staff at Dublin Castle, was already coming into being before the Act became law. The first general elections for the new parliament took place in May 1921. With an 89 per cent turnout, the Unionists won forty seats, Sinn Féin and the Irish Party six seats each, on 21 per cent of the poll for Sinn Féin as against 19 per cent for the Irish Party. Sinn Féin did not take their seats. Elections also took place for the 'Southern Ireland' parliament. Sinn Féin had no intention of giving credibility to this British-imposed partition, but, just as they had put up candidates in the 1920 local elections held under the old system, in order to demonstrate their popular support, so they did the same in this election. When this new Dublin parliament assembled, only four members, all Unionists, elected for Trinity College, Dublin, took their seats.

While all this was going on, Ireland was in a state of undeclared war. For eight months the Dàil, set up in the Mansion House in Dublin, had been left undisturbed by the British authorities, who perhaps thought it no more than a talking-shop for Irish dreamers. But in September 1919 the British government, having declared Sinn Féin illegal the previous month, followed up with a proscription of the Dàil. Ireland was now bestrewn with bits and pieces of different kinds of authority, the shadowy relics and reinventions of British rule, and various bodies representative of the different tendencies in Irish nationalism. Four men both illuminate these different tendencies and demonstrate the importance of personality in the drama-filled events which followed. Arthur Griffith, physically a little man with pebble-lens glasses, was the founder of the original, non-violent Sinn Féin of pre-war years, but had been an active member of the Irish Volunteers since 1913. A former printer, his *The Resurrection of Hungary: A Parallel for Ireland* (1904) indicated that just as Hungary achieved independence within the Austro-Hungarian Empire, so Ireland should aim for independence within the British Empire. He was Vice President of Sinn Féin in 1918, and Acting President of the Dàil in 1919. Eamon de Valera was born in New York, of a Spanish father and Irish mother, and brought up in County Limerick. A Professor of Mathematics and Physics, he had an austere, courteous, academic manner. He had distinguished himself in the Easter Rising as the last Brigade Commander to surrender. Because of the American citizenship, which he disavowed, he was spared from execution. Elected First President of the Dàil, he almost immediately set out on a successful fund-raising mission to the United States. Griffith and de Valera were scholars and politicians, as well as fighting men.

Cathal Brugha – the insistence on the Irish form of his name (Charles Burgess) was deeply significant – was a fighter and not much else: a little, gingery man, who was permanently crippled in the Easter Rising. When the Volunteers became the Irish Republican Army (IRA) in 1917, Brugha was First Chief of Staff; he also presided over the first meeting of the Dàil in January 1919, and then was Minister of Defence until January 1922. The man with film star quality was Michael Collins, tall and fair-haired, born in County Cork in 1890. He worked as a clerk in London, returning to Ireland in 1915. He was interned for his part in the Easter Rising, and became Adjutant-General on the Executive of the Volunteers. According to colleagues he could be domineering, jolly, silent and mysterious: a true James Bond, in fact.[17] More to the point, he combined the talents of a brilliant soldier and intelligence-gatherer, and, a pragmatic politician. Formally Collins was Minister of Finance in the Dàil government, very successful in securing money and arms. He was also effectively Commander of the IRA, and from mid-1919, President of the Supreme Council of the Irish Republican Brotherhood, a body which claimed a more profound and permanent authority than that of the Dàil.

Had the bloodshed, death, and sadistic brutality of 'The Troubles' (poignantly understated word) been only those of a film set, there would have been something deeply alluring about many of the events of the time. As a biproduct of the alleged 'German Plot', de Valera was imprisoned in Lincoln Jail in early 1919; Collins was the organizer behind his melodramatic escape on 3 February 1919. There was to be a whole monkey-load of escapes and chases and disappearances. But the essence was much grislier. On the day independence was declared, 21 January 1919, an armed guard of police escorting a cart of gelignite in County Tipperary was ambushed and two policemen killed. On 31 January the IRA weekly paper declared that, as a state of war existed, murder and violence were no crimes until the alien invaders had withdrawn from Ireland. There was nothing like unity behind this policy among the various nationalist tendencies, and a good deal of opposition and doubt, but as a policy it certainly was implemented. Police officers were ambushed or openly 'executed' in the streets. 'Atrocity' is the only word which fits; though a point to be remembered is that unlike police on the mainland, the Royal Irish Constabulary were armed. Women, mainly through the organization known as Cumann na mBann, played an important role in moving lethal weapons around, the British forces being too delicate, or simply too contemptuous of women's capabilities, to subject them to street searches.[18] Meantime Sinn Féin built up its control of local authorities and local courts: justice was not necessarily always impartial or disinterested – but then the same could be said of centuries of British rule.

'Atrocity' was a fair word, but nothing could justify the response adopted by the British government in 1920. Frequently there are times when governments feel that they must do something, without being very clear what that something should be, or what it should try to achieve. It was very much in Lloyd George's character to act first and think things out later. Policing Ireland, certainly, was becoming an impossibility as assassinations and resignations depleted the Royal Irish Constabulary (recruited mostly from local people). But to recognize a war situation would, as the government saw it, be to give recognition to the 'Irish Republic' as a legitimate belligerent. Opening negotiations with Sinn Féin and the Dàil was made difficult for the government by virtue of the fact that it had just declared both illegal. In a rational world the terms of the eventual treaty could well have been secured without the mutual killing; but, despite the fact that dirty wars (in particular) create lasting bitterness, it also seems to be a kind of historical truth that it is only through waging war that rebel nationalities gain the status of negotiating parties – this certainly applied to Czechs and Poles fighting in the Great War. That the government knew very well that it was in fact engaged in war is suggested by the decision to transfer General Sir Nevill Macready on 23 March 1920 from being Commissioner of the Metropolitan Police to being Commander-in-Chief of the British Forces in Ireland.

Shortly a Chief Secretary for Ireland of a rather unusual hue was appointed: Sir Hamar Greenwood, born in Canada, worked as a barrister in Australia, became a businessman in Britain and a Liberal MP (from 1906), and served at the Front before moving to a junior post at the War Office, where he displayed a brutal efficiency. He was the ideal front-man for the evil policy in which Lloyd George fully connived, that of responding in kind to Irish terror tactics. To carry out this policy, two sorts of recruits were sought. All European countries in the aftermath of war had pools of disgruntled, rootless ex-soldiers and other men disorientated by the disruptions of war. From Britain's analogue of the pools which provided continental countries with their fascist gangs, reinforcements for the Royal Irish Constabulary (RIC) were recruited, and kitted out with surplus khaki uniforms adorned with the black belts and dark green caps of the RIC. These were the original Black and Tans (the name of a famous hound pack in County Limerick). The Black and Tans, properly so called, were paid 10 shillings a day. The other force, no less viciously-minded, came from a higher class in the same unstable constituency: ex-officers. They were to form a separate Auxiliary Division of the RIC: they had a distinctive dark blue uniform, with Glengarrie caps, and were paid a pound a day. These were the 'auxies', though by the Irish always also called the Black and Tans, or just Tans. Major-General Henry Tudor was appointed Police Adviser to the RIC, and Brigadier-General F. P. Crozier Commandant of the Auxies. By October another special force, confined to the North, had appeared, the Ulster Special Constabulary. Class A were full-time, Class C a reserve force. But the 'B Specials', 16,000 in all, were part-time and paid only a small allowance. They were the Ulster Volunteer Force under cover of an official name, and became associated with the harassment and murder of Catholics. However, it was the Black and Tans and the Auxis who engaged most thoroughly in terror and counter-terror, murder, torture, and hostage-taking, roaring into villages at night, evicting the denizens and setting fire to their cottages. The original 'Bloody Sunday', 21 November 1920, condenses into one day the disgraceful tale of atrocity and counter-atrocity. At nine in the morning IRA members broke into houses and hotels throughout Dublin, hauling from their beds and shooting, in some cases in the presence of their wives, fourteen British officers and civilians. In the afternoon, the Black and Tans carried out the 'massacre' at a football match at Croke Park, Dublin. Soldiers gave orders that all spectators were to file out of the ground to be searched. Meantime Black and Tans arrived in lorries and began firing into the crowd. Twelve people were killed and sixty wounded, many in the ensuing stampede. As always, Ireland was the choice place for the British behaving badly.

By now, the British had about 50,000 men under arms in Ireland (police and army); the IRA had perhaps 15,000. Up to the truce in July 1921, 400 police, and a 160 soldiers, were killed; Irish losses, including civilians as well as IRA men, totalled 752. British policies were condemned in all sections of the press. The Labour party, demonstrating its importance as a national party, sent an investigative delegation to Ireland. Arthur Henderson reported that: 'A state of affairs prevails which is a disgrace to the human race.' The Free Liberals joined the attack. 'Things are being done in Ireland', Asquith thundered, 'which would disgrace the blackest annals of the lowest despotism in Europe.' Intelligent military minds on both sides understood that there would have to be a truce. IRA leaders saw that they could never achieve military victory, in the sense of driving the British out completely; Collins was aware that, in Dublin at least, the IRA might suffer defeat. But, given that they had the general support, or at least acquiescence, of the population, they could never be defeated either. British terror tactics simply drove moderates towards Sinn Féin. A self-styled 'peacefully inclined man' said that what drove him 'into rebellion' was 'the British attitude towards us, the assumption that the whole lot of us were a pack of murdering corner-boys'. On the British side, General Macready was signalling that without massive, and probably politically unacceptable, troop reinforcements, victory could not be envisaged.

There were irreconcilables on both sides, but for the pragmatic a practical basis for negotiation lay in the twin facts of a government-created, and recognized, Southern Ireland parliament (even if ignored and despised) and, more important, of a separate and secure Northern Ireland parliament. As usually transpires to be the case in such matters, secret negotiations took place before the officially acknowledged meeting in London on 8 July, attended by de Valera, Griffith, Macready, Lloyd George and Unionist representatives, which announced that a truce would come into effect from noon on Monday, 11 July. It may be noted that there was no surrender of arms by the IRA, and that indeed the IRA continued its lethal attacks right up until the truce. There followed protracted negotiations, both by letter, and in meetings, over the drawing up of a treaty.

The Anglo-Irish Conference took place in London between 11 October and the night of 5–6 December 1921. The plenary meetings were at Downing Street, but there were also meetings elsewhere between Lloyd George and individual members of the six-man Irish delegation, of which de Valera cunningly refused to be part. So did Brugha, not a man for negotiating with the English. The most important members were Griffith and Collins: Collins hadn't wanted to go either, but was not one to shirk an unpleasant duty. The most important members of the British delegation were Lloyd George, and the two senior Conservatives Austen Chamberlain and Lord Birkenhead, who fortunately took a much more moderate line than most Conservatives would have done. One of the reasons for the conference taking so long was that the Irish delegates frequently had to refer matters to de Valera by letter, or sometimes by making actual visits back to Dublin.[19]

Partition and a separate Ulster parliament already existed. One major question was whether that should continue. The other was a more profoundly ideological one. Sinn Féin was nothing if it was not republican. And while, within the narrow confines of British political philosophy, republicanism merely connotes being against the monarchy, in the European context it means being true to the democratic principles of the French Revolution. On the British side, the Imperial idea, indissolubly associated with the idea of the monarch as its head, was intensely held, certainly by Lloyd George and his Conservative associates. There was no question but that the Irish would get far more than anything that had been envisaged in previous Government of Ireland Acts, including the most recent – if waging a war had had a positive result, this was it. No longer local Home Rule under the Westminster parliament, but Dominion status (like that of Canada) was there for the taking (though most Conservatives remained vehemently opposed). But being part of the Empire, or 'Commonwealth', as from the middle years of the war certain dedicated enthusiasts for Imperial reform were calling it, meant an oath of allegiance to the Crown. For true republicans an oath of allegiance was not something easily swallowed. De Valera felt very strongly about this; he also, pedantically no doubt, but not without vision, wanted an 'association' with the 'British Commonwealth of Nations', not actual membership of it. In addition, there was the practical consideration that Dominion status so near to the home country (compared, say, with Canada) might not turn out to be much different from Home Rule.

The British Empire, it may with some difficulty be recalled today, was at the peak of its power at this time: membership was not without appeal for Collins and Griffith. To try to make the oath slip down as easily as possible it was phrased as follows:

> I do solemnly swear true faith and allegiance to the Constitution of the Irish Free State as by law established, and that I will be faithful to HM King George V, his heirs and successors by law, in virtue of the common citizenship of Ireland with Great Britain and her adherence to and membership of the group of nations forming the British Commonwealth of Nations.

'Irish Free State' was patronizing, recalling the 'Orange Free State' won by the Boers after their war against the British. But given the Ulster problem, 'Ireland' was not possible, though, most interestingly, the product of this conference was to be called 'Articles of Agreement for a Treaty Between Great Britain and Ireland'. The 'Common Citizenship' is an interesting reflection on the constant love/hate relationship between the British and Irish, and has continued to this day. Yet there also remained that sense of racism (as if the Irish were indeed a kind of Boer), revealed in many documents, and, strikingly, in a famous speech by the King on 22 June 1921:

> I speak from a full heart when I pray that my coming to Ireland today may prove to be the first step towards an end of strife amongst her people, whatever their race or creed.[20]

On the matter of the oath and of membership of the Empire, Lloyd George was successful in persuading Griffith and Collins. In any case, Irish independence was a bit like votes for women; the women accepted less than they wanted, because they knew that once the principle was conceded, everything would come their way. However, with Ireland there remained the problem of the six counties. What the British government proposed was that while Northern Ireland should retain its local parliament in Belfast, it would otherwise be subject to the Free State parliament (and not Westminster). If, however, within a month after the ratification of the Anglo-Irish Treaty, Northern Ireland, by an address to both Houses of Parliament, indicated its wish to contract out of the Free State, then it would retain the status already determined by the Government of Ireland Act.

In the negotiations, there were two examples of the kind of trickery for which Lloyd George was famous. To convince Collins to accept the deal on (allegedly temporary) partition, he promised a Boundary Commission, which, he hinted, would make Northern Ireland even smaller, and thus so unviable that it would have to be absorbed into the Free State. Relatively uncontroversial was the stipulation that the British navy should have the use of certain 'treaty ports' in Ireland. The other piece of trickery was the ultimatum which Lloyd George issued once he had pretty well got agreement in principle from Griffith and Collins. He demanded immediate signature without further reference back to the Dàil, or the resumption of all-out war. The necessary signatures were forthcoming at 2.30 a.m. on 6 December.

Thanks to the provisions of the 1920 Act, the British were able to hand over power in a completely constitutional fashion. There were long and bitter debates in the Dàil, with opposition to the treaty being led by Brugha and de Valera himself. In the vote taken on 7 January 1922, 64 voted for the treaty, 57 against. A week later the 'legal' parliament of Southern Ireland elected under the 1920 Act met in the form of the four who had attended its inauguration, together with the 64 pro-treaty members of the Dàil. Due process was fulfilled when this parliament elected a Provisional Government, headed by Collins, to take over the administration of the country from the British authorities until the government of the Irish Free State had been constituted. Evacuation of British troops began at once.

However, a government which was legitimate in the eyes of the British, was unlikely to seem so in the eyes of uncompromising republicans, most of whom, anyway, did not accept the articles of the treaty. By April 1922 civil war, more brutal even than the troubles, broke out between 'the Provisional Government' and 'the Irregulars'. In the renewed troubles of fifty years on, Gerry Adams of Sinn Féin constantly reminded the British government that 'conflict resolution' required understanding and compromise. The very notion of 'conflict resolution', of course, was unknown in the 1920s: even if it had been, it would not have appealed to the Irish of that era. Just as the end of world war had left soldiers on the loose, and only too ready to go on the rampage in the Black and Tans, so the truce had left members of the IRA bereft of what they had become most used to doing. The core split was between the 'old IRA', which became the army of the Free State, with Collins as Commander-in-Chief, and the 'IRA Irregulars', which both Brugha and de Valera joined. The Irregulars issued death threats against all in positions of authority, including members of the Dàil. The Provisional Government made the possession of firearms a capital offence, and promised reprisals for all attempts at murder. Court martials and summary executions were frequent. When a member of the Dàil was murdered on 7 December 1922, four Irregular prisoners in Mount Joy prison were immediately taken from their cells and shot. Brugha was mortally wounded on 5 July and died on 7 July. Collins was shot and mortally wounded on 22 August.

There were, in fact, two other conflicts going on at the same time, apart from that over the treaty (which in fact enveloped all sorts of local and personal squabbles). The worst of these was in Ulster and on the borders of the Free State; an apocalyptic vision of things to come fifty years later. The Protestants, through the B Specials and the Orange organizations, waged a war of intimidation and expulsion against Catholics. Between July 1920 and July 1922, 257 Catholic civilians were killed out of a total civilian death toll of 416 (though Catholics formed only one-quarter of the Belfast population). In the same period around 10,000 Belfast Catholics were driven out of their jobs and 23,000 forced out of their homes, with about 500 Catholic businesses being destroyed. Over the six counties as a whole, 303 Catholics were killed, 172 Protestants, and 82 members of the police and British army. During the civil war both wings of the IRA were very active in assassinating both Protestant civilians and members of the security forces.[21] Altogether, in 1922, 294 persons were killed in Northern Ireland. In a manner which was to become something of a pattern among Northern Ireland leaders, Sir James Craig, the Prime Minister, furiously demanded more British troops, while at the same time denouncing the agreement Lloyd George had made that there would be a Boundary Commission to examine the frontier. The response from Churchill has an enduringly apposite quality to it: 'You ought not to send us a telegram begging for help on the largest possible scale and announce an intention to defy the Imperial Parliament on the same day.'[22] The second conflict was that between workers and employers, and, most of all, between labourers and farmers. The forces of the Free State sometimes took time off to suppress the strikes and protests.

The Provisional Government had majority support, and its ruthless policies brought the civil war to an end with the ceasefire of 24 May 1922, the establishment of the Free State being finally proclaimed on 6 December 1922. The Governor-General (the official representative of the British Crown – there was one in each Dominion) was to be an Irishman, T. M. Healy. In the end, for all the talk of a Boundary Commission, the borders of 1920 were left to stand unchanged. In the press, and before the public, Lloyd George could be presented as the man who had brought peace to Ireland. But Conservatives had yet more reason to hate him; so, for entirely opposite causes, principally the conduct of the Anglo-Irish war, had Labour and many of the Free Liberals.

### *THE GOVERNMENT AND LABOUR*

For Lloyd George's relationships with labour, we have to go back to the end of the war. There are no Laws of History. Revolutions in the western world are exceptions which don't prove a rule which doesn't exist. Societies, of course, are riddled with conflicts of interest, which is not the same thing as being 'ripe for revolution'. Some historians, believing that the First World War ought to have created a revolutionary situation throughout Europe, have developed the notion of 'corporatism', the notion that governments bought off labour and its alleged revolutionary potential by integrating the trade unions, along with big business, in the running of the country; other historians, not necessarily subscribing to the revolutionary thesis, saw this alleged corporatism as a means of stifling competition, and creating a comfortable, complacent regime in which the powerful (including trade union leaders) benefited, while the rest of society suffered.[23] There was no likelihood of revolution in Britain at the end of the First World War (nor, for that matter, in France); a forced corporatism was introduced in Mussolini's Fascist Italy after 1922, and more thoroughly and efficiently in Hitler's Germany after 1933. There was no corporatism in Britain, though it is a concept we will have to keep an eye on.

For employers who imposed on their workers conditions they themselves could never have tolerated, the notion that their workers might rise up against them was not a totally far-fetched one. There was after all the spectre of Bolshevik revolution in Russia, accompanied by the murder of the Tsar and his family, and of attempted risings across Central Europe. There was always the fear that men who had been using rifles and bayonets on the front line might not turn in their weapons, but rather turn them on their bosses. At a Cabinet meeting on 5 August 1919, Lloyd George claimed that the Bolsheviks had captured the trade-union organizations. The government, he said,

> could not take risks with labour. If we did, we should at once create an enemy within our own borders, and one which would be better provided with dangerous weapons than Germany. We had in this country millions of men who had been trained to arms, and there were plenty of guns and ammunition available.[24]

Government fears were intensified by a short police strike in London in August 1918, such an obviously unpropitious time that the anger of the men over rising prices and the stresses of war must have been extreme. August 1919 wasn't really a very good time either since the government still had large forces of undemobilized soldiers at its disposal. The rioting which took place in Liverpool between Friday, 1 August and Sunday, 3 August no doubt showed how willing many ordinary citizens were to take advantage of the absence of the usual law enforcement officers, but they certainly didn't provide any evidence of revolutionary intentions on the part of organized labour. Altogether, 2,600 troops were brought in, with four tanks and HMS *Valiant* and two destroyers, which stood off Liverpool port. After a round of shots one civilian died of wounds, and there were bayonet charges on the Sunday night.

The wartime Clydeside strikes had been spontaneous and broad-based. When the Clydeside workers' leaders called for a general strike on Monday, 27 January, to press their very practical demand for a forty-hour week as a means of absorbing returning servicemen, they were fully supported in all the principal factories: three mass demonstrations followed on 27, 29 and 31 January. The government anticipated the third demonstration by concentrating troops, tanks and machine-guns on the city, though the actual 'Battle of George Square' was fought with policemen's truncheons and lemonade bottles. On 1 February the tanks moved in upon the deserted battlefield, the strike continuing for a further ten days. The press was filled with alarmist tales, though the Red Flag raised by the strikers was a symbol, not of revolution, but of working-class solidarity.

A dozen leaders were arrested, but only against two could a successful charge be made out, and that scarcely implied any deep subversion of the established order: Willie Gallacher and Emmanuel Shinwell were imprisoned for 'inciting to riot'. Looking back ruefully many years later, Gallacher unwittingly exposed the reality of the situation: 'We were carrying on a strike when we ought to have been making a revolution.'[25] The government sent a secret military circular to all commanding officers in Britain asking whether their troops would respond to orders necessary for preserving public peace, and whether they would participate in strike-breaking. A few days later a permanent anti-strike organization, in the form of a Committee of the Cabinet, was established, headed by the tough guy we have already met: Sir Hamar Greenwood.

The miners intended to guard the gains they had made during the war and were determined, in particular, that the mines should not be handed back to the individual coal-owners for them to run them as they pleased. The threat of a strike in January 1919 forced Lloyd George to set up a special Statutory Commission to investigate the industry, to which the miners themselves would nominate half the members, with the chairman being a judge, Sir John Sankey. The Commission was utterly split on the question of nationalization, though Sankey himself did recommend 'that the principle of state ownership of the coal mines be accepted'. On 14 August Lloyd George rejected this recommendation. The Miners' Federation persuaded the TUC and the Labour party to mount a joint political campaign 'The Mines for the Nation', but did not renew the strike threat. Meantime, on the railways, which were still being run by the government, the workers were having a wage cut imposed on them. Not unnaturally, the National Union of Railwaymen called a general strike to begin on 30 September. Before the strike began the government reconstituted the Cabinet Strike Committee, and divided the country into twelve divisional areas, each with a Commissioner and staff. The Defence of the Realm Act still being in force, a state of emergency was declared immediately the strike began. On Friday, 3 October the Home Secretary appealed to all citizens to join in the formation of 'Citizen Guards' in face 'of the menace by which we are confronted today'. However, the railwaymen's case was essentially a reasonable one, and it was reinforced by a deputation of the Transport Workers' Federation led by Arthur Henderson and J. R. Clynes, who were able to assert some of the influence which had accrued to them because of their participation in the political direction of the war. The strike ended on 5 October when the government decided to maintain existing wages for a further year.

There were several other strikes of a similar nature; then, half-way through 1920, there came a series of events which seemed to indicate that labour was prepared to use its industrial power to influence the foreign policy of His Majesty's duly elected government. The object once again was a precise one: to stop Britain being involved in a war on behalf of Poland against Soviet Russia. Unconstitutional perhaps, but a very different thing from aiming at the overthrow of established government. The first event was the refusal on 10 May 1920 of a gang of London dockers to coal the *Jolly George*, believing it to be carrying munitions bound for Poland. The incident does not seem to have disturbed the Cabinet, which was absorbed in other matters. On Sunday, 8 August a series of labour demonstrations against the possibility of British intervention on behalf of Poland was organized, followed on 9 August by the setting-up of a Council of Action to implement a joint Labour party–TUC decision to use 'the whole industrial power of the organized workers' against the war'. There was in fact no British intervention against Russia; and the Cabinet papers make it clear that whatever Labour thought or did the government was by no means hell-bent on supporting Poland.[26] By 10 August any danger of intervention was over as the Cabinet decided that the Russian terms for an armistice with the Poles were reasonable.

Two attempts at the end of the war to improve industrial relations were the establishment of Whitley Councils of employers and employees, in a few industries, and the passing of the Industrial Courts Act, providing for arbitration. This mechanism was agreed to by both sides when the London dockers went on strike in 1920. The dockers' case was put by a pudgy, physically rather unprepossessing, but powerful and resourceful, national organizer, Ernest Bevin, formerly a Bristol mineral-water roundsman. So effective was Bevin that the dockers won most of the rise they claimed, and Bevin achieved a national reputation as 'the dockers' K.C.' (a 'King's Counsel' being a top-flight barrister).

The post-war boom was giving way to depression as the miners and the unemployed both came back into the headlines. To meet the still rising cost of living, the miners went on strike briefly, and successfully, to win a 2 shilling increase per shift. They had secured the revival of the pre-war Triple Alliance between themselves, the railwaymen and the transport workers. Threatened by a strike of the entire Alliance, the government, though refusing permission to the Chief of the Imperial General Staff to move troops into the mining areas, passed an Emergency Powers Act, to provide for the maintenance of essential services. Meantime, the miners got a further wage rise, though only for the six remaining months of government control. The first major post-war incident involving the unemployed (October 1920) became known as the Battle of Downing Street. A deputation of London mayors led by George Lansbury, with the workless marching behind in their thousands, had demanded an interview with Lloyd George to discuss the unemployment problem in their boroughs. A peaceable demonstration erupted into violence when the police suddenly decided to clear Whitehall by means of mounted baton charges, causing many ugly incidents. Throughout 1921 there were further violent scenes associated with the unemployed. Yet although a headship to the agitation was given by the Communist-sponsored National Unemployed Worker's Movement, the demands made were always specific and practical, so that when open conflict with the police did break out it was usually over the elementary right of the unemployed to free assembly.

On 31 March crisis returned to the coal industry. As government control ended, the coal-owners posted new terms, which in most cases involved substantial wage cuts for the miners. The miners, cheated as they believed, of nationalization, argued strongly for a national wages agreement drawing upon a national wages pool, so that the relatively prosperous mines could subsidize the uneconomic ones. Determined upon the total return to unrestricted private enterprise, the owners would have none of this. Declaring that the attack on their standards was merely a prelude to a general attack on working-class living standards, the miners felt justified in again expecting the support of the Triple Alliance. The labour correspondent of the *Daily Express* got things exactly right:

> one thing should be made clear. The issue at present is wholly industrial. The trouble is over wages and nothing else. Questions of political and constitutional policy have not yet entered into the matter. The movement at present is not a 'Red' one – but the manner of its development depends on circumstances.

At a Cabinet presided over by Austen Chamberlain, 'misgivings' were expressed over the way the crises had been brought about by sudden wage cuts:

> During the war the miners had shown that they were immensely patriotic, and it would be a calamity if Labour generally obtained the impression that the Government was siding in this matter with the employers.[27]

What exactly the miners' secretary Frank Hodges meant by a famous remark is far from clear – he was probably not clear himself:

> When the country knew that the Government was adopting such tactics, then the leash which checked revolutionary action would be loosed and there would be upheaval and rebellion.

Immediately upon the commencement of the coal strike, and long before any decisions had been taken on joint action by the Triple Alliance, the government declared a State of Emergency under the terms of the 1920 Act. On Monday, 4 April the Cabinet discussed the disposition and availability of the armed forces, authorized the Secretary of State for War to prepare for the mobilization of the Territorials and the call-up of the Army Reserve, and appointed a sub-committee to consider the idea of creating a special force of 'loyal ex-servicemen and loyal citizens'. Approval for the special Defence Force was given at a conference of ministers on 6 April, though the meeting at which the leaders of the Triple Alliance agreed to sympathetic action on behalf of the miners did not take place until 8 April. Over the succeeding weekend, enrolment of the Defence Units began, encampments being formed in parks, on the outskirts of the main cities, and in disused military camps. The following week there were movements of troops, transports and tanks, while troops equipped with machine-guns moved in on the Fife coalfield. Where managerial staff remained behind in the pit to man the pumps, they were liable to attack from angry strikers; riots broke out in Lanarkshire, Fife and South Wales. The Triple Alliance strike was set for midnight of Tuesday, 12 April, unless, as J. H. Thomas and a deputation of railwaymen and transport workers put it to the Prime Minister, negotiations with the miners were resumed. The Triple Alliance stance was: 'We are not proclaiming a revolution, we are standing shoulder to shoulder for fundamental trade union rights.'

Thus pressured, the government did in fact institute negotiations with the owners and the miners, and the Triple Alliance strike was called off. But there remained a basic stumbling-block on the question of a National Agreement on miners' wages, something for which Lloyd George had by now conceived an almost pathological hatred: 'the national pool', he told his colleagues, 'merely signified control in a most virulent form'.[28] With the breakdown of negotiations on this issue, the Triple Alliance strike was rescheduled for midnight on Friday, 15 April. But on 'Black Friday' the attempt at united action collapsed. Out of the meeting of Coalition MPs on 14 April, attended by Frank Hodges, there had emerged a possible compromise which Lloyd George immediately seized upon: on the fatal Friday he offered the miners a temporary arrangement on wages, provided the National Agreement question was shelved. Essentially moderates, the Triple Alliance leaders urged the miners to discuss this proposal. The miners, who felt that they had been duped once too often by Lloyd George, refused. The Triple Alliance leaders cancelled the strike. The miners fought on alone, finally on 1 July being forced back to work, to local agreements and, in most areas, to substantial cuts in wages.

Given the slump conditions, it is not surprising that strikes in various other industries during 1922 were unsuccessful in resisting wage cuts; it should be remembered, too, that along with wages, the cost of living was dropping from the post-war peak. So the centre of militant working-class activity moved back to the unemployed. On Armistice Day 1922, 25,000 London unemployed tacked themselves on to the official ceremony, carrying at their head a large wreath inscribed: 'From the living victims – the unemployed – to our dead comrades, who died in vain.'[29] At the end of 1922 the first Hunger Marches began, organized by Wall Hannington in the south and by Harry McShane in Scotland. References to unemployed marches in *The Times* were indexed during the twenties under the heading 'Russia: Government Propaganda'. True, members of the National Unemployed Workers Committee Movement took an oath 'to never cease from active strife against this system until capitalism is abolished, and our country and all its resources belong to the people', but in fact Hannington, McShane and their associates concentrated their energies on specific abuses within the Unemployment Insurance Scheme and the Poor Law.

In protest against the heavy burden being imposed on borough rates, and against the attempt of the government to control expenditure on poor relief, George Lansbury and the Poplar Council refused to pay the proportion of the Poplar rate due to the London County Council (the precept). The thirty councillors were imprisoned for over a month, but, as did some of the protests of the unemployed, their gesture brought its reward: an Act was passed spreading the costs of relief more equitably over London as a whole.

## *SOCIAL REFORM AND EXPENDITURE CUTS*

Addison's Housing and Town Planning Act of 1919 was born out of reconstruction and perished in the slump, though its spirit was enduring. It called upon the local authorities to conduct surveys of the housing needs of their areas, to draw up plans for dealing with these needs, and to submit the plans for approval to the Ministry of Health. When these plans had been approved, all losses incurred in carrying them out, save for the tiny contribution yielded by the penny rate which the local authorities were to levy, would be borne by the Exchequer. The State, in other words, was assuming direct financial responsibility for a large sector of the future homes of the working classes. Rents were to be determined by the existing controlled rents of working-class houses, but could be varied according to the amenities of the house and, more important, the tenant's capacity to pay. Though it was expected that by 1928 it would be possible in most cases to charge an economic rent, the principle of subsidized accommodation for those most in need was to be maintained. In that the minister had powers to insist that the new houses should have fitted baths, a modest impetus was given towards the general diffusion of higher material standards. The principle of deficit funding was not a sound one; as costs escalated, there was talk of a 'Housing Scandal'. The subsidies were cut in 1921 and the scheme abandoned altogether in 1922. At least, by that time, 213,800 decent houses had been built, and the principle of a compulsory Act financed by the central government had been established. Poor Addison was abandoned to his fate by Lloyd George, and resigned, subsequently joining the Labour party.

The National Insurance Acts of 1920 and 1921 greatly extended the unemployment insurance provisions of the 1911 Act (though there were no significant changes in the health insurance provisions). Unemployment insurance was now extended to all wage-earners, save for non-manual workers earning more than £250 per annum, farm labourers and domestic servants. A contribution of 10d per week for men, shared, as in the 1911 Act, between employee, employer and state, yielded an unemployment benefit of 15s per week for a maximum of fifteen weeks in any one year, provided that a minimum of twelve contributions had been made, and provided that though capable of work, the applicant had been genuinely unable to find any.[30] The 1921 Act made two crucial amendments. Dependant's allowances were introduced, and 'extended benefit' was granted beyond the original fifteen weeks: an expedient to meet the onset of post-war unemployment, this was theoretically treated as an 'advance' against future contributions; in reality an irreparable hole had been blown in the insurance structure, constantly widened as the irresistible tides of mass unemployment poured in after 1921.

These acts represented the government's commitment to reconstruction. But a much deeper imperative was to cut expenditure and restore the economy to what was thought to be its natural workings. The two contrasting faces can be seen in what happened to the railways. Far-reaching plans for reorganization and electrification had been developed, particularly through the initiatives of the Scottish businessman Sir Eric Geddes. In the end, much to the resentment of Geddes, his ambitious plans were dropped, while the numerous companies of the pre-war years were grouped into four, the London Midland and Scottish, the London and North Eastern, the Great Western, and the Southern (which did go ahead with electrification). The press waged campaigns against alleged prodigality in government expenditure, inventing two feckless civil servants, 'Dilly' and 'Dally', and in June 1921 two by-elections were won by self-styled 'Anti-Waste' candidates. Lloyd George set up a special Economy Committee under Geddes, which proposed drastic economies across the public services, most of which were implemented. Thus Geddes, who would have liked to be associated with reorganization of the railways, became indelibly associated with what the press gleefully called 'the Geddes Axe'. Most seriously affected was education: the programme of building continuation schools was stopped, and the funds available for free places in secondary schools were heavily reduced. In his war budget of 1915 the then Chancellor of the Exchequer, Reginald McKenna, had introduced the McKenna duties on imported luxury items. These continued after the war, and were confirmed in the Safeguarding of Industries Act of 1921. This upset the Coalition Liberals, though, in practice, it represented only the tiniest breach in Free Trade principles.

What, now, was Lloyd George for? His position had been unexpectedly strengthened in one particular. Bonar Law, always a rather detached supporter, had been forced by ill health to withdraw from politics, being succeeded as Conservative leader by the patrician, monocled, Austen Chamberlain, who actually believed that he (and the country) owed a debt of loyalty to Lloyd George, and behaved in accordance with this principle: Austen Chamberlain, as everyone knows, 'always played the game, and always lost' (Beaverbrook's improvement on an original phrase of Churchill's).[31]

## *REVOLT, AND RETURN, OF THE CONSERVATIVES*

Then a tiny after-tremor of the Great War, needlessly, but characteristically, turned into a crisis by Lloyd George, brought the Conservatives to open revolt, and Bonar Law out of retirement. The frontiers between Greece and the defeated enemy, Turkey, now galvanized by the new Nationalist leader, Mustapha Kemal, had still not been finalized. A small British force held a vital point in the neutral zone on the Asian side of the Bosphorus, Chanak (near the site of ancient Troy). Having in August 1922 routed (and massacred) the Greeks in Asia Minor, the Turks were advancing on the Bosphorus. Lloyd George attempted to enlist the support of the Dominions in threatening war against the

Turks. The Dominions refused (incidentally providing Collins and the Irish with evidence that Dominion status could effectively mean independence). The Turks behaved with good sense. The crisis was over, but not before Lloyd George had presented himself as an over-heated war-monger. Yet, wars, and threats of wars, do win elections, so with the support of Austen Chamberlain, Birkenhead, and Churchill, Lloyd George decided, on 10 October, to seek another mandate for his Coalition government. Chamberlain played his part in the game by undertaking to call a meeting of Conservative MPs to defeat any opposition to continuing the Coalition. He lost. At the famous Carlton Club meeting on 19 October Birkenhead praised Lloyd George as 'a dynamic force'. With the kind of low-level astuteness which was to characterize him, the relatively unknown President of the Board of Trade, Stanley Baldwin, picked this up: 'A dynamic force is a very terrible thing; it may crush you, but it is not necessarily right.'[32] With respect to his future career, Baldwin had sounded the vital bite. Far more important for the moment was the fact that Bonar Law, who on 6 October had written to *The Times*, 'We cannot act alone as the policeman of the world,' had been persuaded to come out of retirement and attend the Carlton Club meeting. His was the decisive voice in recommending that the Conservatives withdraw from the Coalition and stand as an independent party. The vote for this was 187 to 87; an auspicious occasion in Conservative party history, celebrated from 1925 onwards when the full Committee of Conservative back-benchers assumed the title 'the 1922 Committee'.

Lloyd George resigned as Prime Minister that very afternoon – but where should he go? He had made it clear that he thought the Liberals finished; and in his zeal to establish a Centre party he had completed his alienation of the Labour party by attacking their 'dangerous' policies of nationalization and the Capital Levy. There was consistency in his decision that he would stand with those Conservatives, led by Austen Chamberlain, Balfour and Birkenhead, who had remained faithful to the Coalition. That made for a rather odd line-up in the election which took place on 15 November: there were Coalition Conservatives; Coalition Liberals; Conservatives now free of, as they saw it, the deadly embrace of Lloyd George, and again led by Bonar Law; Liberals, still led by Asquith; and Labour. Bonar Law fought on the slogan of 'tranquillity'. Lloyd George and his National Liberals were forced back to the sheerest windbaggery, without a hint of 'dynamism', calling for the union of 'all men who believe in the existing fabric of society, who believe in the principles on which our prosperity has been built, free private enterprise – of men who are opposed to revolutionary proposals, and who are equally opposed to reactionary proposals'.[33] The main strength of the Lloyd George Liberals (if we call them 'Coalition Liberals' we have to remember that there actually wasn't a coalition anymore; they became the National Liberals) lay in industrial areas which had once been bastions of traditional Liberalism. Generally Conservatives of both varieties (who wouldn't have had a hope in the industrial constituencies anyway), gave them a free run. Still, many Conservatives were exuberant about attacking Lloyd George Liberals, from whom they took 31 seats. But now, the jingoistic fever of 1918 long since abated, Labour could enter into what was beginning to seem like its natural heritage. One result can perhaps be taken as symptomatic: a Lloyd George Liberal, Winston Churchill lost his seat to Labour in Dundee. Thus, Lloyd George ended up with just 60 supporters in parliament.

The Independent Liberals made a massive effort, spending nearly £127,000. They often did well in seats where there was no Labour candidate, but generally succumbed when there was one: thus, with 57 seats they didn't quite make Lloyd George's total. Labour, still generally not contesting seats where there was no working-class element, polled 29.7 per cent of the vote, and won 142 seats. The Liberals combined, with 28.3 per cent of the popular vote, came very close, as is often pointed out; but then, though more united in the country than at Westminster, the Liberals in fact were *not* combined, and more than that, the majority of Lloyd George Liberals were dependent upon Conservatives not standing against them. The party doing best, as everyone expected, was the Conservatives with 38.5 per cent of the vote, and 344 seats. Turnout was 73 per cent. (I do not print full tabulations for this and the next election because the official figures do not reflect the actual party splits and alliances. It should also be noted that at this time around 50 MPs were returned unopposed.)

In forming his government, Bonar Law was denied the big-name Conservatives, like Austen Chamberlain, who had remained loyal to Lloyd George; another of them, Birkenhead, said the new Cabinet consisted of second-class brains, which gave the aristocratic Tory Lord Robert Cecil the opportunity for a neat dig at Lloyd George (or was it Birkenhead – who had a 22-year-old mistress?), saying that second-class brains were better than second-class characters.[34] Where exactly Stanley Baldwin should stand in such ratings I am not entirely sure: he had donated a portion of the fortune his family iron-works made from the war to the nation, and he was always to present himself as 'honest Stanley Baldwin', the man you could trust. Whatever, Bonar Law reluctantly found that he had no choice but to appoint Baldwin Chancellor of the Exchequer – always a good job to get, at least if you are a Conservative and thus can count on the support of the markets. When Bonar Law succumbed to cancer, Baldwin, on 22 May 1923, succeeded him; he had been reckoned a 'sound' Chancellor. Baldwin had also made a famous speech in which he had said that salvation for the country and the world was to be found in four words: 'Faith, Hope, Love and Work'. The man most obviously qualified to succeed Law was the Foreign Secretary, the Marquess Curzon of Keddleston, who had chaired Cabinet meetings in Law's absence. Lord Salisbury had been Prime Minister at the beginning of the century, and all Cabinets had had a substantial number of peers in them. However, the case was now made that since the Labour Opposition had very few representatives in the Lords, it would not be appropriate for the Prime Minister to be in that House. So Baldwin got the job.

Neville Chamberlain came into the Cabinet in March 1923 as Minister of Health. Although he had lacked the imagination to turn his nothing job as Minister of National Service at the end of the war into something, he was a master of administrative detail, and relentless in argument; in time he was to become the most intimidating figure within Conservative governing circles. He was responsible for the one real achievement of this government of 'tranquillity', the 1923 Housing Act, which maintained the Addison principle of a subsidy from the state to the local authorities to enable them to get houses built (now £6 per year for each house, for twenty years). The distinctive features were: private builders were to be preferred, though local authorities were not prevented from building the houses themselves; the houses were for sale, at an economic price taking the subsidy into account, not for subsidised rent; the houses were to be small, originally limited to a surface area of 850 square feet, though Chamberlain, showing that he was far from being utterly inflexible, raised this to 950 square feet. It was not a question now of baths, but of whether the working class should have parlours. In fact the houses tended to go to the lower-middle class, though, no doubt, with the effect of releasing the rented housing that some of the new purchasers had previously occupied. Chamberlain enhanced his reputation as an administrator and also, with Labour, his reputation for being stingy and an enemy of the working class.

The Chairman of the parliamentary Labour party at the time of the 1922 election had been J. R. Clynes (who had succeeded Adamson). When the greatly expanded parliamentary Labour party met after the election it had two candidates for the leadership, Ramsay MacDonald being put up in opposition to Clynes. Because of MacDonald's later reputation as the man who betrayed the Labour party, this election has attracted a lot of attention. It is true that left-wing MPs, notably those in the Scottish ILP, voted for MacDonald, who had been 'anti-war' when Clynes was 'pro-war'. More important, Clynes had been a poor parliamentary leader, and even to right-wingers MacDonald was much the more impressive figure. He was handsome (a quality which can be critical in certain marginal situations), had considerable intellectual power, and had that kind of Scottish speaking voice which many people find authoritative, while at the same time classless. MacDonald won, and, as the *Manchester Guardian* sharply noted,[35] was declared 'leader' as well as Chairman of the parliamentary party – the first time the Labour party had equipped itself with a leader.

Depression and unemployment were something the government had to make some response to. Bonar Law himself was a convinced believer in Tariff Reform, but felt that to challenge the principle of Free Trade would be to go against the principle of 'tranquillity'. In the later part of 1923 Baldwin came to feel that he must adopt Protection: the iron industry, catering to the domestic market, was one which definitely could benefit; Protection was also a cause which would attract many of the big-name Conservatives still standing aloof from the government. However, Law had given a pledge in 1922 not to introduce tariffs before another General Election had been held. Thus, it was very much consonant with Baldwin's plain-dealing image that when, on 25 October, he announced that he wished to have a free hand to impose tariffs he also announced a General Election for 6 December. 'Suicide in a temporary fit of insanity', has become the hackneyed verdict on this decision. Probably the proper charge to be made against Baldwin (from a Conservative point of view, that is) is that he was too indolent to do the job of trying to prepare the electorate for this switch in policy.

Would the Liberals be reunited at last? On the night of the previous election Independent Liberals had uproariously cheered whenever the news came through of the defeat of a National Liberal.[36] Baldwin's action completely altered the context. Lloyd George was actually in America at the time and rumoured to be contemplating some kind of Tariff Reform programme of his own. But when he returned he committed himself totally to Free Trade. That was a banner under which the two groups of Liberals could unite, more particularly because the Asquith Liberals were now too broke to fight an election, while Lloyd George had his political fund. With respect to the popular vote, the election of 6 December 1923 differed very little from that of 23 October 1922. The turnout was down slightly from 73 per cent to 71 per cent. The squeeze was actually on the smaller parties, so that the Labour vote (4,438,508) went up by exactly one per cent to 30.5 per cent, while the Liberal vote went up by 1.4 per cent to 29.6 per cent. The Conservative vote only fell by one per cent to 38.1 per cent, but with 258 seats, they had manifestly not won their mandate for Tariff Reform. Labour had 191 and the Liberals 158. However, Baldwin did not immediately resign, leaving the outcome of the election to be determined by a vote in the House of Commons. It might have been wise for Labour and the Liberals to work out some kind of joint plan; but MacDonald was both deeply hostile to what he believed the Liberals stood for, representing them as being a less honest 'capitalist' party than the Conservatives, and convinced that Labour must supplant the Liberals, not cooperate with them. Asquith, for his part, believed that without actually doing anything, the Liberals would somehow have a controlling hand over Labour. When the House met, Liberals and Labour voted together to turn the Conservatives out of office, leaving Labour, as the largest party, with the responsibility of forming a government. With his consciously developed sense of playing the game, Baldwin was happy for Labour to take their chance, telling the King that anything other than an immediate resignation might seem 'unsporting'; he could see that a minority government would scarcely be in a position to do anything very radical.

### *The first Labour Government*

Arthur Henderson had managed to lose his seat (only getting back into the House through a by-election), so it was not altogether outrageous that MacDonald passed him over for Foreign Secretary (Henderson in fact got the Home Office), deciding himself to double as both Foreign Secretary and Prime Minister. As these things go, MacDonald had quite a decent record as Foreign Secretary, playing his part in the general lightening of the international atmosphere in this period. There was minor controversy over whether Labour ministers should wear court dress when being sworn in. MacDonald who, perfectly sensibly, wanted to demonstrate that Labour was 'fit to govern', and to increase its appeal among the middle classes, got his way. Apart from foreign affairs, the government's main achievements were in Housing, where the least charismatic but most intellectually able of the Clydeside ILP group, John Wheatley, was the responsible minister; Education, where the minister was a former Liberal, Charles Trevelyan, who had joined the party at the end of the war; and Unemployment Insurance. Faced with strikes, the government showed itself completely ready to use the emergency legislation which had been prepared by its predecessors. Financial policy, in the hands of the austere Philip Snowden, as Chancellor of the Exchequer, was totally orthodox. The McKenna duties and other infringements of Free Trade were removed (this had the enthusiastic support of the Liberals but the opportunity to secure a firm interparty agreement was not exploited). Expenditure on public work schemes for the unemployed, which would have unbalanced the budget, was not to be tolerated.

The Wheatley Housing Act increased the state subsidy to £9 a year for forty years, so that local authorities could themselves build houses for rent, their actual size remaining that finally agreed by Chamberlain. Trevelyan restored the Geddes Axe cuts in secondary education and also set up the Hadow Committee, which eventually produced the most important recommendations on education of the inter-war years. Pending any attempt to reduce unemployment, the Labour Government sought to ease the lot of those claiming unemployment benefit: in particular the irksome condition that claimants had to establish that they were 'genuinely seeking work' was abolished. Unemployment benefits were increased, and 'uncovenanted benefit', which previously claimants had to argue for, was now to be given as a right, despite not being covered by insurance payments. Something was also attempted in respect of that centre of storm and despondency, the coal industry. The government could be congratulated on the careful negotiations it carried out with both coalowners and the miners' union, producing an Act which in its final form reduced the working day to 7½ hours and set up a Committee charged with rationalizing the industry. Lloyd George attacked the proposals as too timid, but his party split over this, further reducing the credibility of the Liberals. Subsequently a policy approaching tacit cooperation with the government was evolved, one clear product being the Agriculture Marketing Act of 1931, where, ironically, the collaboration was with Christopher Addison, now Labour Minister of Agriculture. These Acts have been seen as 'corporatist': certainly they involved agreements between government, capital, and labour, but they scarcely formed part of a grand plan to alter the way in which the country was run. Herbert Morrison, the policeman's son who had become a powerful force on the London County Council, and was now Minister of Transport, began the process of setting up the London Passenger Transport Board, as a public corporation to run London transport, his work being consummated by the succeeding government. Not dissimilar things were happening to air transport.

But the government failed to establish a full working relationship with the Liberals, who became increasingly alienated as they were denied credit for supporting the measures which the government passed. No doubt it was true that in a two-party system Labour needed to supplant the Liberals. But the two-party system wasn't really working, so that, if Labour and Liberals failed to get together, that simply meant that Labour's own voters were going to be left to the mercies of the Conservatives.

The Labour Government fell because of (not unjustified) Liberal resentment; Ramsay MacDonald's sense (alas, to be repeated again by Clement Attlee in 1951) that Labour had put on a brave show, and now could honourably withdraw from the trials and frustrations of government; and, more generally, a paranoia about 'Bolshevism'. One of MacDonald's first acts had been to recognize the legitimacy of the Soviet government. Then, in August, thanks to the initiatives of some left-wing MPs, a complex agreement was arrived at comprising a commercial treaty (which might be useful in helping to reduce unemployment), a further treaty dealing with debts owed to Britain from the time of the Tsarist regime, and then a guaranteed loan to Russia. Against Asquith's better judgement, Lloyd George persuaded the Liberals to attack the government, particularly over the loan, when parliament reassembled after the summer recess. Then a minor event occurred, but one which evoked the Bolshevik menace. A Communist of the local variety, J. R. Campbell, who was also a disabled war hero, published, as editor of the *Worker's Weekly*, a fairly routine article calling on soldiers not to shoot on their working-class comrades during industrial disputes. Campbell was charged under the Incitement to Mutiny Act of 1797. The Attorney-General, Sir Patrick Hastings, a classy recent recruit to the Labour party, pressed both by left-wing back-benchers and MacDonald himself, took the eminently sensible course of dropping the prosecution. The Conservatives, never enthusiastic upholders of the rights of free speech, or at least, left-wing free speech, chose to see this as a case of political interference in judicial processes, and put down a vote of censure for parliament's reassembly at the end of September. Very honourably, Asquith went the last mile to try to let the government off the hook: he both proposed that the matter be referred to a committee of the House of Commons, and then suggested that the Liberal places on that committee could be taken up by Labour members. MacDonald, for reasons I have already indicated, rejected the Liberal proposal. The Conservatives voted for it, and so the government were defeated by 364 to 191. George V was reluctant to grant Labour's request for a dissolution but, having consulted both Baldwin and Asquith, felt he had to comply.[37]

### *A SECOND BALDWIN GOVERNMENT*

In the election results in table 2.10, the first thing to note is the rise in turnout, probably accounted for by middle-class voters brought out by the Bolshevik scare, which was intensified just before the election by the release of a forged

**Table 2.10** General Election, 29 October 1924

| | *Electorate 21.7 million* | | *Turnout 76.6 per cent* |
|---|---|---|---|
| | *Conservative* | *Labour* | *Liberal* |
| Total votes cast | 8,039,598 | 5,489,077 | 2,928,747 |
| Percentage of votes cast | 48.3 | 33.0 | 17.6 |
| Seats | 419 | 151 | 40 |

letter, purporting to be from Zinoviev, President of the Communist International, to the British Communist Party, calling upon it to overthrow the 'bourgeois' Labour Government. The second thing to note is that the Labour popular vote increased by about a million, though their number of seats fell by 40. The third thing to note is that this time the Liberals really did hit the drop. Desperately short of funds, they put up only 346 candidates, 110 less than in 1923. They found that Labour was now everywhere putting up candidates against them, almost always with the consequence that the Conservatives won the seat. So the Liberals won only 40 seats, less, of course, with their 17.6 per cent of the vote, than they would have under a fairer electoral system; even so a drop from 29.7 to 17.6 really did suggest that the terminal phase had now arrived. Only the Conservatives, naturally, could profit from the bitter hostility between Labour and Liberals, and they took 48.3 per cent of the poll, more even than Labour was to get in 1945.

Stanley Baldwin, having lost office through committing himself to Protection, now that he had regained office, disavowed Protection. This meant that his government could be joined by life-long Free Traders, and, most notably, Winston Churchill who, now returned to his original Conservative allegiance, became Chancellor of the Exchequer. As such, he was at the cutting edge of the government's determination to restore all the conditions of the pre-war economy, the first strand of government policy. The others concerned the handling of organized labour and the unemployed, in a period of renewed turbulence, and the important, orderly, reforms carried out by Neville Chamberlain, again Minister of Health. Austen Chamberlain was back as Foreign Secretary.

All expert opinion was clear that, to restore international trade to its buoyancy of pre-war years, the country must return to the Gold Standard (Philip Snowden and the Labour leaders agreed) and that the parity of pound to dollar must be restored to the pre-war rate of $4.86. The Gold Standard, it was said, was the best 'Governor' that could be devised and was 'knave-proof'; with respect to the exchange rate, 'the pound must be able to look the dollar in the face'.[38] To Churchill's credit, he did cross-question his advisers, but they were unshakeable in their faith in gold. The rate in 1920 had been as low as $3.66, but by this time was up to $4.40. In his 1925 budget Churchill announced the return to the Gold Standard with a parity of $4.86. This overvaluation of the pound by 10 per cent, as they saw it, was attacked by the Labour party, and particularly vehemently by a new young upper-class recruit from the Conservative benches, Sir Oswald Mosley. The most famous criticisms of all came from J. M. Keynes in articles subsequently published under the striking, but slightly unfair, title of *The Economic Consequences of Mr. Churchill.* So powerful has become the tide of historical opinion that the problems of the inter-war economy were beyond the writ, or at least the wit, of politicians, many historians now claim that even if a 10 per cent excess was placed on British export prices, 10 per cent is too small a proportion to have had an effect.[39] The simple story that Churchill put 10 per cent on coal prices, which the coal-owners then tried to recover by cutting wages by 10 per cent, which in turn led to the General Strike, has fallen into disrepute. Let us admit that the coal industry was in a mess whatever the government did and that the coal miners (not altogether surprisingly) could not understand why, from belonging to one of the highest paid and most prestigious working-class occupations, they were now being afflicted with unemployment and attempts to drive down their wages. My conclusion would still be this: a more realistic parity might have done some good, which the unrealistic one manifestly did not, while a policy of cheaper money would have given some boost to internal markets. There was no getting away from the gloomy global situation, but a more imaginative, less hide-bound combination, might just have relieved the gloom a little.

## *The General Strike*

Anyway, whether or not the Chancellor's decision has any direct bearing on the matter, events were beginning to fall into the pattern which led to the General Strike and the tragic miners' strike which continued after it. As a consequence of a brief revival of prosperity during the French occupation of the Ruhr, the miners had gained an 'addition' to their standard wage. Now, on the last day of June 1925, the owners announced the abolition of the 'addition'. The miners turned to the TUC General Council, which promised them support in their 'resistance to the degradation of the standard of life of their members', and ordered an embargo on the movement of coal as soon as the miners went on strike at midnight on Friday, 21 July. This was a victorious 'Red Friday' with which to try to expunge memories of the humiliating 'Black Friday'. Baldwin's government intervened, offering a subsidy to maintain existing wages until a Commission of Enquiry under Sir Herbert Samuel could investigate the whole problem of wages and costs.

Without doubt, Baldwin did have some sympathy with the plight of the miners, but he also shared something of continuing upper- and middle-class fear of working-class insurrection:

> I am convinced that if the time should come when the community had to protect itself, with the full strength of the Government behind it, the community will do so, and the responsibility of the community will astonish the forces of anarchy throughout the world. I say it merely as a warning.[40]

To make the warning meaningful the government brought back into working order the anti-strike organization which had originally been conceived in face of the industrial troubles at the end of the war, and which had had a skeleton existence ever since. No special Defence Units were recruited, but the government offered its blessing to the privately-sponsored Organization for the Maintenance of Supplies, which, though it had no military role, was drawn largely from the same groups as had joined the Defence Units. If the government felt it necessary to justify these moves, it had only to turn to the speeches of the fiery miners' leader, A. J. Cook. Of Cook it was once said, unkindly but not altogether unfairly: 'Before he gets up he has no idea what he is going to say; when he's on his feet he has no idea what he is saying; and when he sits down he has no idea what he has just said.' Referring to the government subsidy,

Cook declared: 'Take it from me there would otherwise have been a revolution. I fear there will be trouble next May.' Like other British 'revolutionaries' of the period, Cook combined a mystical faith in the might of the working class with a complete disregard for any kind of revolutionary planning and an even more complete disregard for the necessary role of weapon-power in any successful revolution:

> I don't care hang for any government, or army or navy. They can come along with their bayonets. Bayonets don't cut coal. We have already beaten not only the employers, but the strongest government in modern times.

On 14 October a raid was conducted on the headquarters of the Communist Party and on the houses of twelve of its leading members, all of whom received prison sentences. The General Council, having notched up its initial victory, now sat back in the complacent hope that the Commission would come up with some acceptable solution. The Commission reported in March, giving little joy to either owners or miners. Stressing the parlous economic state of the industry, it recommended a two-stage operation. As an immediate remedy for the 'disaster . . . impending over the industry' the miners must accept cuts in wages; but the long-term problem could only finally be solved by sweeping reorganization.

Four parties were involved in the General Strike. In the forefront were the miners, who were fighting against cuts in wages and for reorganization of the industry and the principle of national wage agreements, and the coal-owners, determined to impose cuts and to resist reorganization and the national wage principle. Behind the miners stood the remainder of the British trade union movement, represented for this purpose by the Industrial Committee of the General Council of the TUC: as in 1921, the members of this Committee could see that the miners' cause was the cause of all British trade unionists, but, also as in 1921, they were chary of action which could be labelled unconstitutional. In a dangerous situation of this sort, responsibility for decisive action lay fairly and squarely with the fourth party, the government. It is true that the Baldwin ministry persevered right up until the last with round after round of discussions with the other three parties, but in so far as it made no attempt to impose the recommendations of the Samuel Commission upon the principals it was favouring the economically stronger party, the owners, and accepting the thesis, of which Lloyd George, formerly, and Baldwin's own right-wing colleagues in 1926, were leading exponents, that a showdown with labour was inevitable and necessary.

On Saturday, 1 May, miners everywhere, refusing to accept the new wage cuts, were out on strike. The executive committees of the various separate unions now met and agreed to hand their powers over to the TUC General Council. This was the first real preparation which the unions made for a National Strike – two days before it began. What, anyway, did the decision mean? Did it entrust to the General Council powers to negotiate on behalf of the miners, or did it mean that the General Council had to fight things out until a settlement acceptable to the miners was reached? The miners believed the latter, the General Council the former. No one noticed at the time, but it was the same difference of interpretation that had caused 'Black Friday'. Satisfied that everything was in train for a National Strike, the miners' representatives left London. This created an unfortunate delay when the General Council, still locked in last-minute conclave with the government, wished to consult the miners on a new compromise proposal. Nonetheless, channels between the government and the TUC Industrial Committee still seemed open late into the night of Sunday, 2 May. Then news reached the Cabinet that the *Daily Mail* printers, acting on their own account, had refused to print an editorial describing the threatened strike as a 'revolutionary movement'. On the pretext that here were trade unionists abusing their power and interfering with free speech, the government broke off the negotiations which the General Council were only too anxious to continue: thus was the General Strike precipitated as an actual event, commencing at midnight on 3 May.

From the trade union point of view, three characteristics stand out from the nine days of General Strike. Since all the classes of workers that the General Council called out did in fact come out, it was a successful demonstration of working-class solidarity in the cause of the miners. Given the complete lack of any advance planning, the relatively successful organization of the strike was a tribute to the improvisational qualities of both national and local trade union leaders. Thirdly, in the minds of the members of the General Council of the TUC there was no question of a direct challenge to the British constitution. As the *British Worker*, the news-sheet brought out to counter-balance the government's *British Gazette,* reiterated, 'The General Council *does not* challenge the constitution'; it was 'engaged solely in an industrial dispute'; 'there is no constitutional crisis'. Left-wing political activists, who were only too keen to participate in the running of the strike, were resolutely kept out. For the community as a whole, the days passed remarkably uneventfully, partly because of the untypically benign weather – but not completely uneventfully – stories of policemen and strikers playing football together have been allowed to obscure the fact that in many places there were repetitions of the Battle of Downing Street type of situation which had been endemic between police and workers in 1920 and 1921.

Successful within its limits, the strike posed the General Council with the fundamental problem: 'What do we do now?' The General Council had hoped all along that it would not become involved in a strike; once in, it hoped that such chaos would be created so quickly that the government would be forced to reopen negotiations. Worried by the drain on trade union funds, and by arguments that their action was unconstitutional (in the House of Commons Sir John Simon, with little more than faith to justify him, announced that under the Trades Disputes Act of 1906 a General Strike was illegal), the moderate trade union leaders were anxious to find some middle man who could reopen negotiations without too much loss of face for the unions. That man was Sir Herbert Samuel. Acting entirely on his own initiative, Samuel prepared, as a possible basis for a settlement, a précis of the Royal Commission Report, usually referred to as the Samuel Memorandum. The government, insisting upon unconditional surrender, would give no undertaking in respect of the Memorandum, and the miners rejected it outright; nonetheless, so anxious were the

TUC leaders to see the strike ended that they unilaterally declared the Memorandum an acceptable basis for bringing the strike to a close. Officially the General Strike ended on 12 May; but realization that no real concessions had been gained on behalf of the miners and bitterness over attempted victimization by employers brought a second spontaneous General Strike on 13 May, involving more men than had the nine days' strike. In the few days of the second strike there were manifestations of bitter class feeling.

The Baldwin Government was entitled to the credit which it claimed in the aftermath of the strike; however, any hope of redeeming the economic chaos and virulent industrial relations rampant in the British coal-mining industry had gone for good. Within the trade union movement disillusionment with the collapse of the strike, combined, in all probability, with pressure from employers, produced a drop in membership, which in 1927 stood at less than five millions for the first time since 1916. Besides these considerations, the Trades Disputes Act enacted by the government after the strike, though a source of political controversy and bitterness to activists in the labour movement, was probably of less significance. The Act declared general strikes illegal (convincing evidence that previously they were *not* illegal) and altered the basis of the trade-union contribution to the finances of the Labour party: the individual trade unionist now had to 'contract in' to payment of the political levy instead of 'contracting out' if he did not want to pay it. Apathy was no longer on the side of the angels, and Labour party income naturally fell.

At the same time there was a movement towards industrial cooperation, associated with talks held between Sir Alfred Mond, for management, and Ben Turner for the TUC. Thus, after the dislocations of the first post-war years, there was something of a resumption of the wartime trend towards social harmony. At the same time Ernest Bevin, who was now clearly emerging as the greatest trade union leader of his generation, reached a decision which could have potential influence in improving the lot of the working class: he decided that, instead of undertaking independent, and futile, industrial action, the TUC must exert a more direct influence on the Labour party.

### *Conservative social reform*

'Our policy', Neville Chamberlain explained during the second reading of his Widows', Orphans' and Old Age Contributory Pensions Bill, 'is to use the great resources of the state, not for the distribution of an indiscriminate largesse, but to help those who have the will and desire to raise themselves to higher and better things.'[41] In getting this legislation through, Chamberlain took on, and vanquished, the vested interests of the private insurance companies. It applied to those already covered by National Health Insurance, whose weekly contributions were now increased, in order to provide a pension of 10s a week at age 65, and also 10s. a week for widows, and 7s 6d a week for orphan children. The old non-contributory old-age pensions at age 70 continued in parallel, having been increased to 10s. a week in 1919. In November 1928, Chamberlain introduced his Local Government Bill, a significant initiative towards both expanding the tasks of local authorities and asserting central control over them (here beginning the long road to Thatcherism). The main local authority tasks were concentrated in the hands of the counties and the county boroughs, and the former tasks of the Poor Law Guardians were transferred to them, to be administered through their Public Assistance Committees. At least as important, new powers were created over roads, public health, maternity and child welfare, and town and country planning. The Act also had substantial fiscal implications. Following the initiative of the Chancellor of the Exchequer, Winston Churchill, Chamberlain sought to stimulate employment by abolishing local taxation ('rates') on industrial property and substantially reducing it on railways ('de-rating'). To make up for the loss of revenue, local authorities were to get 'block grants' from the Treasury. Existing grants for education, police, housing, and road-building and maintenance continued as a separate exercise.

Conservative reform extended into two areas where technological development had been stimulated by the exigencies of war. By January 1920 three British companies were operating in the cross-channel skies, but simply were not profitable, so that the government had to provide temporary state subsidies. In 1923 the Baldwin Government set up a Committee on Civil Aerial Transport (the Hambling Committee). The upshot was the formation in 1924, with Labour in office, of British Imperial Airways, government-subsidized and with several government-appointed directors, and a vigorous and highly successful chairman: Sir Eric Geddes.

The Marconi company had been the first to attempt to exploit the potential of radio communication, and was responsible for the celebrated opera broadcast by Dame Nellie Melba from Chelmsford in June 1920. What Marconi, as well as the British Thomson-Houston Company, the Metropolitan-Vickers Electrical Company, the Western Electric Company, the Radio Communications Company and the General Electric Company all wanted to do was to sell receiving sets. After government intervention, broadcasts of one hour a day began on 11 May 1922 at 2LO – Marconi House in the Strand. The single personality who most influenced 2LO policy and helped to establish some of the basic principles on which British broadcasting subsequently developed was Arthur Burrows, who had been employed during the war by the government to monitor wireless transmissions by the Central Powers. Burrows argued that while there should be a large number of items of 'a really popular character' the attempt should also be made to 'lift' the public above its 'present standards of musical appreciation'. Pressure from the six companies, together with the example of the colossal radio boom which took place in the United States at the beginning of the twenties, brought about the 'treaty' between the companies and the Post Office which established the British Broadcasting Company. This Company began transmissions at the end of 1922 and in April 1923 moved to its famous home at Savoy Hill. Under the direction of Burrows and of a puritanical, dictatorial Scot, John Reith, the company set high standards. The great fear, very strong in Conservative circles, was that Britain would nonetheless succumb to the American example whose crass commercialism was thought to be entirely alien to British traditions, so a Committee under Lord Crawford was set up by the Baldwin Government. Meantime the General Strike afforded the opportunity for the British Broadcasting Company to show its importance as the government's basic means of communication. The Crawford Committee recommended that the company become a public corporation, the British Broadcasting Corporation, and the necessary legislation was passed at the end of 1926. Reith was in charge, determined, as he rationalized it in 1949, to use 'the brute force of public monopoly' to maintain austere standards.[42] It was also in December 1926 that the Act creating the Central Electricity Board, a public board appointed by a government minister, became law. The basic achievement of the Act was a standardized, national electricity distribution system, 'the grid'. Power was bought at cost from selected generating stations, and then sold to the existing private or municipal undertakings for retail distribution. By 1933 power was coming from 130 selected stations and was distributed over 4,000 miles to 630 local plants.

In a *Punch* cartoon of 29 April 1927 (plate 4, p. 102) one sees a cloche-hatted, cigarette-smoking, short-skirted young woman (the skirt being labelled 'flapper'), swanning down Downing Street perusing a piece of paper labelled 'vote'. The shade of a militant old suffragette (the redoubtable 'Bulldog' Drummond) chained to the railings, and carrying a battle-axe, is muttering wrathfully: 'So this is what I fought for!' There had been some suggestion in sections of the press that women under thirty years of age, the 'flappers', had shown themselves to be far too frivolous to merit the vote. However, the most telling feature in this cartoon is an avuncular Stanley Baldwin standing in the doorway of No.10 benevolently puffing on his pipe. In reality, there was no serious opposition to the Act of 1928 which gave all women the vote on exactly the same terms as men. Baldwin could quietly claim the credit (and certainly hoped to claim the young women's votes); the crucial advance had in fact been made at the end of the war. The war had been crucial, too, in the spread of the cigarette-smoking habit, through soldiers being provided with free packs of cigarettes by the tobacco companies.

## *The* Liberal Yellow Book *and the 1929* General Election

There were over eight million first-time voters in the General Election of 30 May 1929 (see table 2.11), in which the Conservatives attempted to combine the notion of modernity with that of tranquillity by adopting the motor transport slogan: 'Safety First'. Since the Conservative vote only went up by 600,000 compared with 1924, while the Liberals gained over two and a quarter million votes, and Labour nearly three million votes, it is quite clear that the 'flapper' vote did not go *en masse* to the Conservatives. The Conservative percentage of the vote was still higher than that of Labour, but Labour got more seats. Although the Liberals had gone up to 23.4 per cent of the votes, they got only 59 seats. Obviously, the Conservatives had lost, dropping from 48.3 per cent of the votes and 419 seats.

The second Labour Government is best known for the mode of its demise, succumbing to economic crisis, giving way to a Conservative-dominated National Government, and going down to heavy defeat in the subsequent General Election. Yet the 1929 election is the one which conclusively demonstrated

SHADE OF OLD MILITANT: "So this is what I fought for!" *April 29th, 1927.*

**Plate 4** Strube cartoon, 29 April 1927. Courtesy of Daily Express/University of Kent

that Labour had decisively supplanted the Liberals as one of the two main parties in the two-party system. Looking ahead to the election, 'whenever it may come', the *Manchester Guardian* had reckoned 'a Liberal majority is not impossible, and a formidable Liberal party in Parliament is almost assured'.[43] Asquith, his health broken, had resigned in October 1926 (and died eighteen months later). Lloyd George not only re-emerged as leader, but used all his energies to ensure that the Liberals would come before the electorate as a party with positive and persuasive policies directed towards the single most worrying issue, unemployment. First a committee of distinguished experts produced a

**Table 2.11** General Election, 30 May 1929

| | *Electorate 28.9 million* | | *Turnout 76.1 per cent* |
|---|---|---|---|
| | *Conservative* | *Labour* | *Liberal* |
| Total votes cast | 8,656,473 | 8,389,512 | 5,308,510 |
| Percentage of votes cast | 38.2 | 37.1 | 23.4 |
| Seats | 260 | 288 | 59 |

report, published early in 1928, *Britain's Industrial Future*, also known, from the colour of its cover, as the *Liberal Yellow Book*. Upon this was based the Liberal electoral appeal, launched on 1 March 1929. Lloyd George declared:

> If the nation entrusts the Liberal party at the next general election with the responsibilities of government, we are ready with schemes of work which we can put immediately into operation . . .
>
> The work . . . will reduce the terrible figures of the workless in the course of a single year to normal proportions, and will . . . enrich the nation and equip it for successfully competing with all its rivals in the business of the world. These plans will not add one penny to the national or local taxation.

There followed the pamphlet *We Can Conquer Unemployment* – the *Little Yellow Book* – which set out how many men would be employed in each scheme, roads and bridges, housing, electrical development, etc.

On the surface, there were good grounds here for the optimism expressed by the *Manchester Guardian*. But, to take the lesser handicap first, large numbers of electors did not trust Lloyd George to deliver; the major handicap was that, whatever people thought of Lloyd George, few really thought the Liberals would end up being in a position to take on 'the responsibilities of government'. They were expected to hold the balance of power, but no more than that. The question pundits concentrated on was what the Liberals would do with their position. Not expected to actually form a government, they suffered from the wasted vote syndrome. Labour, soft-pedalling on anything that sounded too socialistic, simply absorbed Liberal public works proposals into its own programme. Thus, while the Liberals did make considerable gains in the rural areas at the expense of the Conservatives, they lost heavily to Labour in the industrial areas. The challenges of war and the different ways in which, in particular, Lloyd George and Asquith had responded to them, had done heavy damage, intensified by the experience and strength Labour had drawn from the war experience. There were silver linings to be found and corners to turn throughout the twenties: but it all came together, devastatingly, in the 1929 results.

### *The second Labour Government*

Baldwin certainly thought in conventional two-party terms, with Labour now definitively the replacement for the Liberals. Not even considering the possibility of a coalition with the Liberals (which would not, of course, have done them much good in the long term), he resigned immediately after the election and advised the King to send for Ramsay MacDonald. MacDonald could not this time prevent Arthur Henderson from becoming Foreign Secretary, where he performed at least as creditably as MacDonald had done in 1924, with the additional advantage that he was not as strongly anti-French and pro-German as MacDonald had shown himself to be. Snowden was again Chancellor of the Exchequer, with Clynes as Home Secretary.

The government had few domestic successes, and again failed to come to any arrangement with the Liberals, though it did go ahead early in 1931 with a Liberal-friendly proposal to introduce the alternative vote. Approved by the House of Commons, this had not got through the House of Lords by the time the government fell. The Liberals supported the second reading of the Trade Union Bill designed to restore the rights which had existed before the General Strike, but then got into acrimonious dispute with the government over amendments in the Committee Stage. C. P. Trevelyan, again at the Board of Education, sought to make the Hadow Report, a product of his own previous ministerial activity, a reality by raising the school-leaving age to fifteen. He ran into difficulties with those Labour back-benchers from Clydeside and Lancashire, dependent on the working-class Catholic vote, who insisted that more money must be allocated to Catholic schools. When the Conservatives joined with the Labour rebels, the government agreed to the extra allocation of money, the occasion for Churchill's famous description of MacDonald as 'the boneless wonder'.[44] In the end the Bill was defeated in the House of Lords, leading to Trevelyan's resignation. Matters went better in the realm of housing where Arthur Greenwood, the Minister of Health, was able to restore the Wheatley subsidies, and initiate a slum clearance programme which, though temporarily delayed, was of some significance in the second half of the thirties. Labour's left-wing became increasingly disenchanted. Resigning from the party in disgust, the left-wing MP W. J. Brown applied a touch of historical perspective:

> It seems that we have spent twenty years destroying the Liberal Party in order to get a Government whose policy is less radical in relation to the needs of today than that of the Liberals was in relation to the needs of 1906–14.[45]

From the start, J. H. Thomas, as Lord Privy Seal, was the 'minister for unemployment'. Thomas was an ebullient, outgoing type, who got on well with businessmen: he was assisted by the left-winger George Lansbury, the competent Scottish Under-Secretary Tom Johnston, and the hyperactive, but ruthlessly domineering, Conservative convert Sir Oswald Mosley. Though this group did come up with quite a range of job-creation schemes, almost all foundered on the opposition of civil servants, and, indeed, of the Chancellor of the Exchequer himself. They put their proposals directly to the Cabinet, in the name of the most junior, but most aggressive, member – hence the 'Mosley Memorandum'. Some of Mosley's ideas were probably good ones, low interest rates for instance, though this moment when Britain's chronic economic crisis was being swamped in a sudden, massive, international one, may not have been appropriate; his pet idea, imperial autarky – high tariffs and imperial preference – was a bad one. The proposals were rejected, so Mosley resigned. While Lansbury and Johnston soldiered on, Mosley won support at the party conference. But soon he left the party to found his 'New Party' (he might have given it a more original title, such as the 'Mosley Party'). It has been claimed that Mosley was a lost leader, who could have led Britain boldly out of depression.[46] Leaders have, when absolutely necessary, to be able to work with others; they certainly have to have some sense of how they appear to others. Mosley's was a deeply flawed personality, sadistic and xenophobic. He may have been a Führer manqué, but he was no lost leader.

The key circumstance was that Britain could not isolate itself from the rest of the world. The growing indebtedness of the unemployment insurance fund and what was perceived as a high level of government expenditure would lead to a loss of confidence in the pound, a withdrawal of funds from London, a devaluation and an enforced abandonment of the Gold Standard. The collapse of London as an international money market would mean the wiping out of a substantial portion of Britain's vital invisible exports. If the country was forced to seek loans from abroad, then these loans would only be obtainable on terms imposed by the foreign bankers. The final crisis began in May 1931 with the series of bank collapses in Central Europe, resulting both in further withdrawal of funds from London, and the loss of British assets deposited in Central Europe.

Being in a minority, the government was always at risk. Political crisis appeared at hand in February 1931 when the Conservatives moved a vote of censure over government expenditure, particularly that being poured into the unemployment insurance fund. The Liberal amendment calling for the appointment of a special committee to review national expenditure and recommend economies (a Geddes Axe, mark two) offered the government a way out, and was warmly taken up by Snowden. The new axe-wielder was to be Sir George May, recently Secretary of the Prudential Assurance Company; there were four representatives of the business community and two of labour.

The moment parliament rose for the summer recess, the May report was published: it was couched in such gloomy terms that the outflow of funds was greatly accelerated. The Cabinet authorized its chief ministers to enter into discussions with the Opposition leaders over the emergency measures which would have to be introduced. In July the weekly journal of the ILP, whose tiny band of left-wingers in parliament had been more or less constantly at war with what it saw as the compromising policy of the Labour government, carried a front-page article headed 'Towards a National Government'. The final stages of the crisis began when, on 11 August, Ramsay MacDonald made a sudden return to London from holiday in his native Lossiemouth. Within the Cabinet, discussion was centred on the size and nature of the economies which would have to be made to bring about the necessary restoration of confidence. Meanwhile, the Bank of England was endeavouring to raise loans from American and French banks. Provisionally, the Cabinet was prepared to approve economies of £76 million, though there was strong resistance to a suggested cut in unemployment benefits, reinforced when the General Council of the TUC came out strongly against any such attack on those who were already the worst-off members of the community. The Conservative leaders thought that greater economies would be necessary, and in fact, on the evening of Sunday, 23 August, news reached what proved to be the final meeting of the Labour Cabinet that the Federal Reserve Bank in New York would only grant a loan if the government proved its determination to face up to the problem of high government spending by imposing a 10 per cent cut in unemployment benefits. And so, in the words of the formal Cabinet record:

> the Prime Minister warned the Cabinet of the calamitous nature of the consequences which would immediately and inevitably follow from a financial panic and a flight from the pound. No-one would be blind to the great political difficulties in which the giving effect to the proposals as a whole would involve the government. But, when the immediate crisis was over and before parliament met, it would be possible to give the Labour party full explanation of the circumstances which had rendered it necessary for the government to formulate such a drastic scheme . . . The only alternative was a reduction not of 10 per cent, but of at least 20 per cent, and he could not believe that the Labour party would reject the proposals when they knew the true facts of the position . . . In conclusion, the Prime Minister said that it must be admitted that the proposals as a whole represented the negation of everything that the Labour party stood for, and yet he was absolutely satisfied that it was necessary in the national interests to implement them if the country was to be secured. He then pointed out that, if on this question there were any important resignations, the government as a whole must resign.[47]

Eleven members of the Cabinet were prepared to support the cut, with nine against; since several of these nine were prepared to go to the length of resignation, it was clear that the Cabinet could not continue; their collective resignation was put at MacDonald's disposal and he was authorized to advise the King to hold a conference the following morning between himself, Baldwin and Samuel, acting leader of the Liberals, Lloyd George being ill. The King agreed to the meeting between the three party leaders, but apparently also impressed upon MacDonald 'that he was the only man to lead the country through the crisis'. Not surprisingly, MacDonald gave no intimation of this to his Cabinet colleagues when he returned to confirm that their period of office as a united Cabinet was over. MacDonald then had a meeting with Baldwin, Samuel *and* Chamberlain. The good news was that the necessary credits were there for the taking, the bad news, that there no longer existed a Cabinet to take up the offer. MacDonald said that he would, from the opposition benches, help to get the proposals through; Chamberlain tried to persuade him to form or join a National Government. The meeting of the King and the party leaders duly took place at 10 o'clock the next day. The King persuaded MacDonald to stay on as Prime Minister in a National Government supported by the Conservatives and Liberals. Snowden, Thomas and Lord Sankey joined this government; the rest of the Labour party went into opposition.

Although no one as yet had developed a fully coherent alternative to financial orthodoxy, it is possible that in the right political circumstances, that is a strong government open to the most innovative thinking, the economy might have shared some of the more cheering features to be found in other economies, and unemployment might not have been such an unrelenting, and dominating, burden. Any minority government would have been in considerable difficulty, any Labour government was going to find that it did not inspire confidence in the areas where confidence was most essential. In the end, economic collapses in other parts of the world were of critical importance. But the problems were political and ideological as well as economic. Particularly damaging was the way in which the May Committee was set up, the way it operated, and the way in which it presented its conclusions. Snowden too obviously wanted to scare his own back-benchers with an 'objective' demonstration of the gravity of the financial situation; the upshot, the very worst outcome, was that the biggest scare of all was administered to foreign bankers and investors. Governments in deep crisis do not usually do well if they conceal the nature of the crisis; but they do not do well either to overstate it. The May Committee used all the most austere and pessimistic accountancy principles in making its assessments, for example classifying all unemployment relief as a charge on income: even by the standards of the time, its prediction of a budget deficit of £120 million was exaggerated.[48] By openly discussing its figures, and its divisions, with the Opposition leaders, the Labour Government put itself in a position where it had no room for manoeuvre; something again which Snowden probably welcomed. MacDonald, it must be stressed, was not rigid in the manner of Snowden, but open to the more innovative ideas. But in the end, as just remarked, there was no room for manoeuvre to implement these. Although in many respects the crisis has an air of inevitability about it, things need not have accelerated downhill in exactly the way that they did. Unfortunately, political errors kept on interacting with economic imperatives.

### *The National Government*

Snowden brought in his crisis budget on 10 September. The standard rate of income tax was increased from 22½d. to 25d. and there was a 10 per cent increase in surtax; altogether £80 million of new taxes. The Economy Bill presented the following day by MacDonald proposed a range of cuts in public salaries and 10 per cent off all unemployment benefits, reducing government expenditure by £70 million. Unfortunately, even allowing for the fact that cuts hit the poor much harder than they hit the rich, there were other disgraceful inequalities. When, on 15 September, sailors in the Royal Navy at Invergordon heard that they might be in for cuts of 25 per cent, compared with 7 per cent for admirals, they went on strike. This was as bad as the May Committee report. Again there was an accelerated withdrawal of funds from London. Doing the only thing it could do, the Bank of England suspended payments in gold. Britain had gone off the Gold Standard: the pound slipped down to the much more realistic rate of $3.40. No longer having to support an artificial rate, the Bank, by June 1932, was able to reduce Bank Rate to 2 per cent. 'Nobody told us we could do that,' a member of the former Labour Cabinet lamented. But of course a Labour government, unless strongly entrenched and completely self-confident, could not have done *that*. As *The Times* put it on 21 September 1931, 'a suspension of gold payments by a Socialist government would have been one thing. But a suspension by a National Government committed to retrenchment and reform is another'.

It is reasonable to believe that MacDonald expected the formation of a National Government to be a merely temporary expedient to get through the crisis; on the other hand, he made no attempt to maintain contact with the Labour party – neither he nor Snowden attended the meeting of the parliamentary

Labour party on 28 August when they could at least have explained their policies. Notions of loyalty to party are strong in Britain, and in the case of the Labour party become bound up with notions of loyalty to class. Accusations of 'treachery' over the establishment of the National Government were unfair, but, in giving way to Conservative demands that there should be a General Election, and in agreeing to stand with the Conservatives against his former party, MacDonald really did earn the enmity which henceforth his name usually aroused in Labour party circles. The Conservatives not only wanted, as in 1918 and 1922, to be sure of the spoils of office for themselves, but wanted to clear the way ahead for Tariff Reform. Labour put itself forward as the party of Free Trade, and now also spoke boldly of economic planning and deficit financing. Faced with an election, from which it was obvious only the Conservatives could gain, the Liberals, whose own divisions had been particularly apparent in the early stages of the Labour Government, once more split into two main sections, with, in addition, a third one. The official Liberal party, still led by Samuel, himself a member of the National Goverment, perforce supported that government, opposed Labour, but distanced itself from the Conservatives and Tariff Reform. The other main section, led by Sir John Simon, a brilliant, upwardly mobile former lawyer, was prepared to give wholehearted support to the Conservatives in the hope of being spared contests with them in the constituencies. To say that Simon in his day enjoyed something of the same kind of reputation as Michael Howard in ours, would be unfair to both men – Simon was the target for Lloyd George's witticism: 'Simon has sat on the fence so long that the iron has entered into his soul'. Recovering from his prostate operation, Lloyd George put seven 'Independent' candidates into the field. Four were successful, Lloyd George, his son, his daughter, and his son-in-law. Among those defeated was Edgar Wallace, the thriller-writer, whose Conservative opponent, it was said, eclipsed him when it came to chilling the electors' blood with far-fetched stories.[49]

And that was part of the Labour complaint against MacDonald. Snowden and Samuel could not agree to Tariff Reform, so instead of putting a unified programme before the electorate, the National Government simply asked for a 'Doctor's Mandate', while former Labour ministers were not backward in producing scare stories and vicious attacks on the Labour party. MacDonald held up handfuls of worthless German bank notes dating back to the great inflation;

**Table 2.12** General Election, 27 October 1931

| | *Electorate 30 million* | | *Turnout 76 per cent* |
|---|---|---|---|
| | *Conservative and National* | *Labour* | *Samuel Liberal* |
| Total votes cast | 13,129,417 | 6,649,630 | 1,403,102 |
| Percentage of votes cast | 60.5 | 30.6 | 6.5 |
| Seats | 521 | 52 | 33 |

Snowden described Labour policy as 'Bolshevism run mad'; the Samuelite Liberal Runciman suggested that money in post office savings banks was not safe from Labour. Turnout in the General Election of 27 October 1931 (see table 2.12) was almost exactly the same as that in 1929. The Conservatives and the Samuelite Liberals together got 60.5 per cent of the vote – 473 Conservatives, 37 Simonites. Possibly the miserable 6.5 per cent achieved by the Samuelite Liberals (33 seats) should be added to that as well. Labour was reduced to 52 seats, though managing 30.6 per cent of the popular vote. Whether it liked it or not, it had the support of the four Lloyd George Liberals. Labour's established leaders were either on the other side, or defeated in the election, as was one rising star, Herbert Morrison: so the pacifist and left-winger Lansbury was elected leader, with the earnest, unassuming former public school boy, settlement worker, and First World War major, Clement Atlee, being elected as deputy.

In January, the Cabinet decided it would go ahead with protectionist policies. Samuel and his Liberals, as well as Snowden, were persuaded to withdraw their resignations, in accordance with a strange new formulation of the idea of joint Cabinet responsibility: the Cabinet would 'agree to differ'. Neville Chamberlain, now again Chancellor of the Exchequer, brought in his Import Duties Bill in February, emotionally invoking the memory of his father Joseph Chamberlain. There were to be 10 per cent duties on practically all imports, while the question of Imperial Preference was to be referred to a small Advisory Committee under the apparently indispensable Sir George May. While higher tariffs were imposed on certain manufacturers, the details of Imperial Preference were to be worked out at the Imperial Economic Conference in Ottawa. But since the Dominions were not prepared to let British manufacturers in to compete with their own, Imperial Preference tended to mean ready access to Britain for Commonwealth imports, but no noteworthy benefits for British industry.

Once Britain had been the world's greatest trading and banking nation, all transactions being ultimately based on gold. Now Britain was a power only in the parts susequently formalized as the 'sterling area', the Empire minus Canada, together with some other countries heavily dependent on trade with Britain; trade within this area was in sterling. This was all too much for the Samuelite Liberals who now left the government. In fact, as much by accident as by design, the economic policies of the National Government were working tolerably well. The Bank Rate, which had been raised to 6 per cent at the time of the departure from the Gold Standard, came back down, as we saw, to 2 per cent, while Chamberlain astutely seized the opportunity to reduce the heavy burden of National Debt interest charges by carrying out a conversion to lower interest rates.

## *'Secular Anglicanism' and the 'Social Service State'*

Work on building the 'social service state' (as the phrase was in the 1930s) could recommence, with Chamberlain the directing spirit. There were four main areas of concern: the provision of some kind of income whenever ordinary earnings were interrupted or brought to an end, whether because of unemployment, injury, bad health, or old age; health; housing; and education.

Mass unemployment was the great and terrible cause of interruption of earnings. Official figures, as shown in table 2.8, almost certainly underestimated the magnitude of the problem. After the 1931 crisis, the system was that an unemployed man, in good standing as far as contributions were concerned, could claim 'of right' twenty-six weeks of benefit at 17s (85p) a week (with further small sums for dependants); he then went on to 'Transitional Payment' (long christened the 'dole' by the right-wing press), paid through the Public Assistance Committee (PAC) of the local authority, and subject to a stringent Means Test. Men in danger of destitution because they had no unemployment insurance could apply for Poor Law Relief from the PAC. The Means Test investigated all sources of family income and created further stresses between husbands and wives, parents and children, and parents and grandparents.

Chamberlain's 1934 Unemployment Act reasserted the sharp distinction between Unemployment Assistance and Unemployment Insurance. Unemployment Assistance was to be administered by a completely separate Unemployment Assistance Board (UAB) which took over the responsibility for unemployed workers receiving Transitional Payments from the PACs. The UAB in January 1935 announced new uniform rates and a standardized Means Test: there was an immediate outcry since the new uniform rates were below those being paid by some PACs. Such was the outcry that the government retreated and allowed the unemployed to claim either PAC rates or the new rates. Finally, in 1937, new higher uniform rates were established, and the UAB also took over responsibility for those in need due to causes other than unemployment – those who had hitherto applied to the PAC-administered Poor Law. The whole bitter subject of the Means Test and its application has figured prominently in the literature of the thirties, as for example in Walter Brierley's *Means Test Man* (1935). A Depressed Areas (Development and Improvement) Bill was introduced in November 1934, to be supported by a rather tiny grant of £2 million. Reluctant to call a spade a spade, the House of Lords changed the term to Special Areas. They were: South Wales, Tyneside, West Cumberland, and Scotland. Each special area had an unpaid Commissioner. Subsequently (in 1937), obviously aware that something more radical was required, the government appointed a Royal Commission on the Distribution of the Industrial Population, the Barlow Commission.

The Means Test, the hunger marches, the malnutrition endemic in families dependent on the dole, the total blighting of lives caused by long-term unemployment: all of these created great anger, not just among the direct sufferers, but among upper- and middle-class observers. There were marches organized by the Communist-led National Unemployed Workers Movement; there were marches, and deliberate displays of thuggery organized by the British Union of Fascists founded by Oswald Mosley. In the immediate aftermath of the crisis, there was a recrudescence of the type of militant activity that had appeared at the end of the war, involving a number of clashes with the police. On 15 January 1932 the Territorials were called out to guard Rochdale Town Hall, and in October rioting in Belfast resulted in two workers being fatally injured and many others seriously wounded. In this year also, Wal Hannington, the NUWM leader, was arrested 'for attempting to cause disaffection among the Metropolitan Police Force'. The NUWM organized a hunger march on London in February 1934. There were some violent scuffles resulting in about 65 injured, but from the rather confused press accounts it does seem that most of the trouble was caused by a few members of the London riff-raff, armed with staves and railings, rather than by the main body of marchers. The anger and the bitterness should not be glossed over, but overall the salient characteristics exhibited by Britain in the thirties, as in the twenties, are those of stability, moderation, and 'secular Anglicanism'.

Despite the attention attracted by Communist intellectuals and poets, the Communist party was scarcely very popular. Until 1936 its membership remained below 10,000; its highest point was when it rose to 18,000 in the summer of 1939. It had strong support only in certain localized parts of Wales, Scotland and London. The NUWM, in any case, stuck to limited and practical objectives. On the other side, the body which might have provoked conflict, the National Union of Fascists, never had widespread support either. When the thuggery of their methods became only too plain, a middle-class pressure group, the National Council for Civil Liberties, was formed, and the government itself took action with the Public Order Act of 1936, which controlled processions and outlawed paramilitary organizations. As Stevenson and Cook put it, the debate over public order 'helped to articulate a consensus of opinion about what has been called "the threshold of violence" permitted in British society'.[50] Between these extremes, holding the middle ground, and the loyalty of a remarkable sector of the British people, stood the Labour party, which both inspired general idealism and served as a pragmatic force in British society.

There were many rabid imperialists, and indeed racists, in governing circles. Yet during 1934 the government secured the passing of the Government of India Act, which provided for free elections in India, and moved towards internal self-government, with only external issues being reserved to the Viceroy and his administration. Other moves were of the sort which have been described as 'corporatist'. The Milk Marketing Board, set up in 1933, guaranteed farmers a 'pool price', and provided subsidized milk to mothers in the special areas and to children in the state schools. Successive governments were unsuccessful (they did not try very hard) in attempts to reorganize the coal industry. But in 1938 a new Coal Commission was given revised powers of reorganization: it was also given control of the royalties which coal mines had to pay to the owners of the land – these in fact were nationalized, being bought out for the sum of £76.5 millions. In July 1939 a Bill was introduced to merge Imperial Airways and British Airways into a public corporation, British Overseas Airways Corporation, which actually came into being in April 1940, shortly before the Second World War changed from a 'phoney war' to a desperately real one.

Those historians who find the corporatist thesis a fruitful one point also to a number of non-party groups which set themselves up as alternative policy-makers, usually known collectively as 'middle opinion' (I put this term into circulation in an article published in the *English Historical Review* in 1964).[51] Already, in the late twenties, there had been the innovative economic proposals of the Liberal *Yellow Book*, and also of the 'YMCA', a group of young

Conservative survivors of the 'lost generation', including Harold Macmillan, who had published *Industry and the State* in 1927, and Oliver Stanley. And the assumptions of orthodox finance had been ruthlessly questioned by J. M. Keynes and Ernest Bevin during the deliberations of the Treasury Committee on Finance and Industry, which sat under the Chairmanship of Lord Macmillan (not to be confused with Harold) from 1929 to 1931. The first of the middle opinion groups was actually formed on 15 March 1931, shortly before the final political *dénouement* – Political and Economic Planning, originally intended to be pronounced 'PEP', but always subsequently rendered as 'PEE-EE-PEE'. The major group was the Liberty and Democratic Leadership Group, formed in July 1933, which, in July 1935, became the Next Five Years Group. A leading figure was Clifford Allen, formerly Chairman of the ILP, a supporter of MacDonald in 1931, and created by him Lord Allen of Hurtwood; another was Harold Macmillan who, not without a certain ruthlessness, gradually pushed Allen out of the central role. 'Planning' is another of the handful of key words always associated with the thirties. The middle opinion groups hoped to achieve a more rational, and a more compassionate, planning of Britain's resources through 'agreement', or 'consensus' as we would say today. Their importance is significant evidence that, aside from the (limited) violence and justified anger, there was a strong consensual element in thirties politics. It is possible to trace links between middle opinion and the planning policies of wartime and of the post-war Labour government: though, as we shall see, the critical factor was the war experience itself.

To call the exponents of middle opinion corporatists seem to me absurd, though on the fringes, in industry, and in government, there certainly were those of that persuasion. Dr Daniel Ritschel has noted that the Self-Government for Industry Bill of the mid-thirties was sponsored by PEP and the Industrial Reorganisation League and supported by Conservative back-benchers and influential sections of the business community, while also being considered seriously by both the Federation of British Industries and the National Government itself. He has commented:

> Carried to its intended end, the Bill would have established in Britain a variant of a corporatist economy, composed of functionally organised industrial corporations and headed by a representative 'Parliament of Industry', but free of either public controls or the restraints of the competitive market system.[52]

However, it wasn't, and it didn't.

As well as being criticized for being lukewarm about economic planning, inactive in face of high unemployment, and harsh towards the unemployed themselves, the National governments of the thirties have been attacked for a lack of boldness towards a rapidly strengthening Germany, and a failure to support collective security. The issues surrounding appeasement (in itself a highly praiseworthy aim) were not absolutely straightforward. Germany, potentially, was as strong as ever she had been; Britain could not automatically rely on the support of the Dominions. Almost all politicians, and most people everywhere, had a very profound feeling that the awful slaughter of the First

World War must not be repeated: on how that was to be best avoided there were all kinds of opinions, and none. If it can fairly be said that the Conservatives affected to believe in collective security, while being neither terribly keen about the idea, nor totally without admiration for the dictators, it can equally be said that Labour, and most of middle opinion, while in principle strongly in favour of collective security, were less clear in their support for the idea of going to war to enforce it. The indications of 'public opinion' (a slippery concept at the best of times) which used to be cited in the textbooks really do not offer very clear indications. Given the class-based nature of the educational system, the connection between the famous 'King and Country' debate in the Oxford Union in February 1933, and the opinion of any wider public is pretty tenuous. The motion, carried by a substantial majority, that 'this House will not fight for King and Country', in any case did not say 'this House will not fight for collective security under the League of Nations' though, to be strictly accurate, that very notion had scarcely yet been formulated: the vote was *against* what was almost everywhere seen as the horrible mistake of the First World War, and *for* world peace. At the East Fulham by-election in October of the same year, where the Conservatives had a seemingly impregnable majority of 14,521, a fire-eating reactionary, Alderman W. J. Waldron, was defeated by the convincing margin of 4,840 votes by an attractive young Labour candidate, J. C. Wilmot. In his pronouncements on foreign policy, Wilmot stressed disarmament and international cooperation through the League of Nations. But domestic questions, particularly bad housing in Fulham and the general record of the National Government, played a much bigger role. East Fulham was a protest vote against an uninspiring government and its unattractive candidate, and, less certainly, his jingoism. If it was for anything in foreign policy, it was not pure pacifism, but support for the League of Nations; however, Wilmot, like other members of the Labour party, certainly did not spell out the military implications of support for the League of Nations. A similar, though slightly more positive, conclusion emerged from the results of the 'Peace Ballot' of 1935, a protracted house-to-house canvass conducted by an offshoot of the League of Nations Union. Although the *Daily Express* commanded its readers not to participate in 'the Blood Ballot', 11½ million people recorded their votes: 11 million favoured continued British membership of the League of Nations, 6,784,368 (against 2,351,981) were prepared 'if necessary' to support military sanctions against an aggressor. Early in 1936, the new Foreign Secretary, Sir Samuel Hoare, who had taken over from Sir John Simon (himself moved to the Home Office), concluded a shady deal with the French Prime Minister, Pierre Laval, whereby the Italian dictator Mussolini, who was waging an aggressive war against Abyssinia, would be ceded a large slice of Abyssinian territory in return for ending the war. Professor Trevor Lloyd writes that 'the public were furious when they learned what had been planned'.[53] Whether or not that is quite the best way of putting it, Hoare and the Conservatives were attacked by politicians and the press for a clear betrayal of the principle of collective security, and Hoare had to be shunted to the Admiralty.

But although the Labour party might bitterly attack the government over the so-called 'Hoare–Laval' pact, the Labour party itself was a major factor for stability. It had the appearance, in the 1931 election, of having been beaten into impotence – 'Socialists wiped out' was the exultant *Daily Express* headline. But the popular vote had held up quite well, and Labour continued to be of importance in local government, actually winning control of the London County Council in 1934. The ILP, which was becoming an extreme left-wing rump anyway, disaffiliated from the Labour party in 1932, but that simply took it a further massive step towards total oblivion. George Lansbury, as a pacifist, could not give a convincing lead in terms of supporting the League of Nations and collective security, and at the 1935 Labour Party Conference was subjected to a devastating attack by Ernest Bevin, who accused him of 'hawking your conscience round from body to body asking what you ought to do with it'. Lansbury resigned, and was replaced by Attlee. Meantime, in June 1935, MacDonald, now a sad parody of himself, the once fine rhetoric verging on gibberish, gave way to Baldwin, himself taking the latter's post as Lord President of the Council. A general election followed on 14 November.

**Table 2.13** General Election, 14 November 1935

| | *Electorate 31.4 million* | | *Turnout 71 per cent* |
|---|---|---|---|
| | *Conservative* | *Labour* | *Liberal* |
| Total votes cast | 11,810,158 | 8,325,491 | 1,422,116 |
| Percentage of votes cast | 53.7 | 37.9 | 6.4 |
| Seats | 432 | 154 | 20 |

As can be seen, the majority attained by the National Government, among whom Simon and the National Liberals were almost completely assimilated as Conservatives in everything but name, remained formidable. Labour actually polled nearly one per cent more than in 1929 though this scarcely showed in seats. However, since the Liberals not only polled only 6.4 per cent, but won only 20 seats, the two-party system was clearly back in operation, and Labour were indisputably the single Opposition party.

### *JARROW, ABDICATION, AND APPEASEMENT*

Two famous, but utterly different, events stand out in 1936: the Abdication Crisis and the Jarrow March. The Jarrow March, or 'Crusade', of Autumn 1936 used to be taken as merely a symbol of the evils of capitalist rationalization, which had closed down the Jarrow shipyards, and of the consequent plight of the unemployed. In fact, like the rush to the colours in 1914, it is symbolic of British stability. The Labour party had kept aloof from previous unemployed marches, because of their Communist leadership. But the Jarrow Crusade had the official support of the Labour party and that of many other individuals and groups, and indeed – secular Anglicanism at its very best – the local Conservative agent helped in the organization. The final stage from Luton to London was led by Ellen Wilkinson, the local Labour MP, who subsequently produced a classic book, with a classic title, *Jarrow: The Town that was Murdered.*

When George V died early in 1936, it was known in high society circles, and in practically every foreign country, that the heir to the throne, who succeeded as Edward VIII, was besotted with his mistress, a mature, married American woman, Wallis Simpson. Ah such innocent times! The British press breathed not a word, and the British people were left in total ignorance. Foreign newspapers were censored by their distributors before going on sale in Britain. The Church of England, of which the King was nominally the Head, was still resolutely opposed to divorce. As King, Edward could have continued to have a married woman as his mistress, but he could not marry a divorced woman. When, on 27 October, Mrs Simpson obtained a *decree nisi* from Mr Simpson, which would clear her way to marriage with the King, the King's Private Secretary, and the editor of *The Times* raised the alarm. Baldwin told the King (mistrusted anyway in high political circles for his haughty attitudes and pro-German sentiments) he would either have to give up Mrs Simpson, or abdicate. By the time the matter began to be mentioned in the British press on 2 December, everything had been sorted out. On 10 December Baldwin announced Edward's abdication in the House of Commons. It made a great story, and in the telling of it Baldwin came out as the good guy who had done his best to persuade Edward to forsake love for duty.[54]

Baldwin had the good sense to retire in May 1937; there was no serious contender for the succession other than Neville Chamberlain. Sir John Simon continued his progression through the top jobs by becoming Chancellor of the Exchequer. Anthony Eden, who had succeeded Hoare after the Hoare–Laval debacle, continued as Foreign Secretary, resigning in February 1938 because he opposed Chamberlain's appeasing policies towards Italy. This resignation highlights the point that though Chamberlain enthusiastically pursued the moderate reforming policies I have already discussed, the big issues were those of foreign policy, indeed of war and peace, where Chamberlain was not at all at ease, or, perhaps, where he showed a quite unjustified self-confidence. Munich is, of course, yet another of the highly pejorative words associated with the thirties. Chamberlain continued the rearmament policy which had been initiated by Baldwin; and the Labour party had already in 1937 decided to stop voting against defence credits (it had done this as a sign of its disapproval of the government's foreign policy), believing rearmament essential in face of the growing threat of the dictators. As the years go by, the Spanish Civil War, which broke out in 1936, seems of less and less significance. But at the time, it was an issue on which both those on the Left, and democrats of all parties, felt very strongly, giving their support to the legitimate government against the extreme-right Franco rebels. Baldwin, and then Chamberlain, incurred great unpopularity for their policy of 'non-intervention', which greatly favoured Franco, who was being openly supplied by Hitler and Mussolini. Foreign policy issues rather than domestic (though these were not negligible) stimulated ideas of a United

Front, in 1937, to include the Communist party and the Labour Left, and in 1938, a Popular Front, which would involve Labour, Liberals, elements from middle opinion, and dissident Conservatives. The Popular Front actually won a by-election at Bridgwater against the Government. But officially, Labour remained implacably opposed to any such cross-party movements, and such leading figures as Sir Stafford Cripps, Aneurin Bevan, and G. R. Strauss were expelled for their involvement in them.[55]

Formally, Munich (29 September 1938) was a Four Power Conference, involving Germany, Britain, France and Italy, but in the British context it is usually, and rightly, seen as a deal which Chamberlain enthusiastically concluded with Hitler. Czechoslovakia was forced to yield up a vital (mainly German-speaking) part of its territory, including its munitions industries, to Germany. The only possible defence is that, in an era when Britain could no longer count on the automatic support of the Dominions, it bought time for further rearmament. Morally, it was a betrayal, and may not be justifiable even on pragmatic grounds. In March 1939 Czechoslovakia fell apart, with the Germans occupying the remaining Czech part. Britain *was*, in addition to rearmament, preparing for war, drawing particularly on the lessons of the Great War. Thus a 'Shadow' Ministry of Information was in existence from 1937. In the summer of 1939 a Ministry of Supply was created (on the analogue of the earlier Ministry of Munitions). Under an Act passed in August, young male volunteers began to undergo military training. Nothing was done about Czechoslovakia, but Chamberlain issued a limited Treaty of Guarantee to Poland.

At 4.45 a.m. on 1 September the Germans began their invasion of Poland. At once a War Cabinet of nine was established, with Churchill, the man who had warned of the Hitler menace, being invited to join, though only as First Lord of the Admiralty. In one burst, four new ministries came into being: Home Security, Economic Warfare, Food, and a substantive Ministry of Information. A blackout – that is to say all windows had to be covered in material impermeable by light and all vehicles were to keep their lights switched off – was imposed. In the House of Commons on the evening of 2 September, members in all parties were expecting Chamberlain to announce that an ultimatum had been issued to Germany to withdraw its forces from Poland. Chamberlain talked of diplomatic initiatives, but his words were received in silence. When Arthur Greenwood, Acting Labour Leader while Attlee was in hospital, rose to respond, Julian Amery from the Conservative side shouted: 'speak for England, Arthur!' Greenwood declared that every delay was 'imperilling the very foundations of our national honour'. A British ultimatum was finally delivered to the German government at 9.0 a.m. the following day, expiring two hours later.[56] At 11 a.m. on 3 September, Chamberlain made his doleful announcement to the nation on the radio, perhaps the most often repeated, most familiar, radio message ever.

## Modernism and Mass Society

Italy, from the beginning of the twenties, was a Fascist, corporatist, totalitarian dictatorship. Russia was a 'socialist' totalitarian dictatorship. France, Czechoslovakia and Britain were liberal democracies. Germany, until 1933, was a liberal democracy (the Weimar Republic), then a National Socialist, corporatist, totalitarian dictatorship. But all were 'mass societies' in that their rulers all paid lip service to the notion that they governed in the interests of, and were responsible to, ordinary people, 'the masses': all were pervaded by the mass media, press, films, and radio. The war had been the critical experience in bringing fully developed mass society into being.

## *MODERNISM IN THE ARTS*

In the arts, the dominant movement was 'modernism'. The exponents of modernism saw themselves as presenting an art for modern civilization, often harsh and lacking in harmony, in which there was open recognition that the arts are contrived, not representations of reality. Modernism was often influenced by Freud's strictures against sexual repression, and came over, to the conventional and conservative, as overly, and crudely, preoccupied with sex. Few in the inter-war years doubted that, just as the quintessence of popular music was jazz, so the high art and music of the day, even if one hated it, was modernist. Only because it had this status, was it possible for the middle-brow novelist John Galsworthy, to satirize it.[57] The way the 'entertainment' *Façade* came into existence could almost have featured in one of his novels and certainly could have in one by Aldous Huxley (discussed shortly). First we have an upper-class intellectual trio, a baronet, Sir Osbert Sitwell; his brother Sacheverell; and sister Edith. All are consciously modern, but most of all Edith, who published her first volume of poetry in 1915 – quirky, witty, sensuous, rhythmic. Then we have their protégé, the nineteen-year-old musician William Walton. The Sitwells planned the presentation of *Façade*, a recitation (through a megaphone) of recent poems by Edith, with an accompaniment, picking up from the rhythm of the poems, for percussion, saxophone, clarinet, trumpet, flute and cello, by Walton. The first performance took place in the Sitwells' house in Chelsea on 24 January 1922. There was a further private performance, then a single public one at the Aeolian Hall on 12 June 1923 (with some new poems). There was a second public performance at the New Chenil Galleries, Chelsea, on 27 April 1926. Minority art, or what? Few directly experienced *Façade* (jazzy, hints of Stravinsky, but genuinely original), but the press told the public all they needed to know – 'Drivel. They Paid To Hear' was one headline.[58]

The major figures in British music had in fact established themselves before the war: Vaughan Williams, Frederick Delius, Gustav Holst, Arnold Bax, while the man who had created the English musical renaissance at the end of the nineteenth century, Edward Elgar, had produced his last great concert work and elegy for a lost world, the cello concerto of 1919. The most important event in the social history of classical music was the taking over by the BBC of the Henry Wood promenade concerts, thus ensuring their survival: but these performed mainly the great classics of the European tradition, not a lot of contemporary British music.

The sculptor that the press (and, surely, Galsworthy) loved to hate was Jacob

Epstein, whose major innovations in fact dated back to before the war. His bold rendering of primary sexual characteristics confirmed a very British prejudice that all artists are oversexed. Henry Moore and Barbara Hepworth emerge as the leaders of something both new, and distinctively English, 'that moderate and vernacular modernism' as Charles Harrison has called it (see plate 5).[59]

Whatever the ratings in music and art, an English eminence in literature had never been doubted, and the twenties was perhaps the peak decade for modernist innovation in English literature. Epstein (who ended up Sir Jacob) was actually American-born. So were the two leading post-war poets, T. S. Eliot, and Ezra Pound. Eliot's 'The Love Song of J. Alfred Prufrock' appeared in June 1915. After *Prufrock and Other Observations* (1917), there came *Poems* (1919). Eliot 'struck a new note in modern poetry, satiric, allusive, cosmopolitan, at times lyric and elegiac'.[60] In 1922 he founded his own quarterly, *The Criterion*, in the first issue of which he published his *The Waste Land*. Not only allusive, this was often downright obscure, but it carried that very powerful sense of disenchantment which is truly representative of what the sensitive and educated felt in this post-war era. Pound had been a leading figure in the imagist school of poets before the war. He is as important for the encouragement he gave to other modernist writers – Eliot said he was 'more responsible for the

**Plate 5** Barbara Hepworth: *Kneeling Figure*, 1932. Rosewood, height 68.6 cm. Courtesy of Alan Bowness Hepworth Estate/Wakefield Art Gallery

twentieth century revolution in poetry than any other individual' – as for the incredibly rich, incredibly learned, but often obscure *Cantos*, mostly written in Paris, from 1920, and in Italy, from 1925. The trio of great moderns is completed by an Irishman, James Joyce. For most readers who made the effort, the two celebrated novels *Ulysses*, published in Paris in 1922 and in London in 1936, and *Finnegans Wake*, published in London in 1939, came as intensely compelling revelations; for the press they were exactly what was to be expected of a modern novel, obscene and obscure. With *Jacob's Room* (1922), Virginia Woolf launched into a distinguished career as a writer of poetic, indirect novels, experimenting with 'stream of consciousness' techniques – *Mrs Dalloway* (1925), *To the Lighthouse* (1927), and *The Waves* (1931). If we want to tie her even more tightly to her times we would note the uncompromising feminist sensitivity she brought to her writing.

Son of a coal miner, always short of money, D. H. Lawrence had published important novels before and during the war: *The Rainbow* (1915) was seized by the police and declared obscene. *Women in Love* was finished in 1916, but he couldn't find a publisher for it until 1920 in New York, where again it was subject to prosecution. *Lady Chatterley's Lover*, full of basic Anglo-Saxon words, was printed privately in Florence in 1928.

Aldous Huxley came from the famous family of scientists, and we can, if we want to, associate his novels with the interest in (much simplified) science as a characteristic of mass society – best seen in his vision of the future, *Brave New World* (1932). Before this he had written wickedly brilliant satires on the upper-class intellectual society with which he was very familiar. *Crome Yellow* (1921) is perhaps *the* satire of the gay young, and pretentious older, things of the twenties. As Huxley grew more serious, the mantle of satirist of the age fell to a younger man, Evelyn Waugh. From *Decline and Fall* (1928) to *Scoop* (1938) he captured 'the brittle, cynical, determined frivolity of the post-war generation'.

All of these authors went through the elite educational system, save for Lawrence, who was working-class, and Virginia Woolf, who was female. The elite system stood the country in good stead as far as the production of pure science was concerned, though perhaps not from the point of view of its commercial exploitation. The headline discoveries had already been made, but the high level in atomic physics and astronomy was maintained, while in 1924 Cambridge University created an Institute of Biochemistry for Frederick Gowland Hopkins. Two works of popular exposition enjoyed great success: *Stars and Atoms* (1927) by Sir Arthur Eddington and *The Mysterious Universe* (1930) by Sir James Jeans.

British architecture was nothing to write abroad about. The most influential figures were Charles Voysey who at the turn of the century had been producing the light, uncluttered style which became utterly characteristic of the English suburbs, and Sir Edward Lutyens who had built private houses in many styles before the war. What is best described as the 'brutalist' style can be seen in the headquarters designed for the newly formed Imperial Chemical Industries designed in 1927 for Millbank, London, by Sir Frank Baines. Perhaps more important than company headquarters, were the new cinemas where, in the 1930s, 'the popular fantasy of the Edwardian theatre was carried still further; and period styles were mixed with new jazz expressionist details and other motifs of the modern movement without scruple'.[61] This is the style known as Art Deco, which also pervaded interior design and furniture. The most famous single Art Deco building, and one which integrates neatly with developments in contemporary consumerism, is the Hoover Factory (1932) at Perivale in West London, designed by the architects Wallis, Gilbert and Partners (see plate 6). Most prized by the critics are the private residences High Point One and High Point Two, at Highgate, in North London, designed by Lubetken and Tecton. Among the most daring was the *Daily Express* head office in Fleet Street, by Herbert Ellis and Clarke and Sir Owen Williams, with its black glass curtain wall.

Film was *the* entertainment of mass society. The first 4,000-seat cinemas dated from 1925, in Glasgow, and from 1928, in Croydon, with admissions running at twenty million a week. Most of the films seen were American, and in the international ratings British films did pretty poorly, though there is some evidence that British audiences welcomed the touches of comfortable familiarity British films, such as comedies featuring the working-class protagonists Gracie Fields and George Formby, provided. One film which did enjoy international success was *The Private Lives of Henry VIII* (1933) by the Hungarian expatriate Alexander Korda, who was the dominant influence on British films in the thirties. Several newspapers, however, commented on the unique realism of Victor Saville's *South Riding* (1938) from the novel by Winifred Holtby, published in February 1936: a 'scrupulous, authentic picture of English life for the first time on any screen', said the *Daily Mirror*.[62] Anything too authentic would fall foul of the British Board of Film Censors, a body which had been set up by the film industry itself in 1912 with the basic purpose of making sure that films did not draw any unwanted attention to themselves through being in any way morally

**Plate 6** The Hoover Factory, Western Avenue, London, *c.*1935. Courtesy of Hoover Ltd

or politically controversial. The novels of A. J. Cronin and Graham Greene were popular with film makers. The most 'authentic' film by the end of the decade was *The Stars Look Down* (1939) from the novel by Cronin, set in a South Wales mining community, directed by a man who was to emerge as one of Britain's few truly great film directors, Carol Reed. The mine-owners are presented as vicious and greedy, and indeed responsible for a pit accident in which five miners are killed, while the whole ethos of the film evokes intense sympathy for the ordinary miners.[63] However, a number of production companies were warned off filming Walter Greenwood's *Love on the Dole* (1933), set in Salford, which describes the sufferings, material, moral and psychological, of a local family when depression hits the local engineering works. One consequence of the outbreak of war, and the new mood it engendered, was that John Baxter (a director whose work repays close attention) was able to make the film in 1940, and a mighty condemnation it was of pre-war politics and economics.

With respect to the popularity of films about the British Empire, Jeffrey Richards has some salutary words, which take in also popular literature, and the treatment of public schools its:

> for most people – those for whom literature meant Edgar Wallace, Warwick Deeping and P. C. Wren – the public schools were not represented by those tormented, repressed public school boys who figure in the works of Graham Greene and E. M. Forster. They looked instead to the idealized Greyfriars of Frank Richards . . . to the world of Harry Wharton, Billy Bunter and Mr. Chips. Similarly, the Empire was not the arrogant, hollow, hypocritical sham of George Orwell. It was the mythic landscape of romance and adventure . . .[64]

As well as the 'big picture' and the 'B Movie', audiences saw a newsreel. These contained only a small proportion of hard news, and that was always presented in a bland way which did not run any risk of going against government policy. There were items on arms build-ups in various countries but never any attempt at analysis of what was going on in foreign affairs.

### *Aspects of Mass Society*

Cinema was entertainment for all ages, and both sexes. The other mass leisure activity, spectating at football matches, was still almost exclusively a masculine preserve. Attendances were huge: 60,000 watched Arsenal beat Chelsea four–one at Highbury on 10 December 1932. The professional footballer was simply a working-class man who had escaped to something precarious and not necessarily a great deal better, in which both the maximum wage and strict control of transfers were rigidly enforced.

Much nonsense is talked about how, with the mass production of fashion, all classes came to dress alike. There can be no question but that people still continued to wear their affluence, or their poverty, on their backs. At the same time the advent of stylish, but cheap women's wear did enhance the lives of young women and enable them to have a decent shot at emulating the film stars they flocked to see in the cinemas. Also increasingly on sale were gramophone records, which at 1s 3d cost almost two-thirds as much as a pair of overalls (1s 11d), catering to the boom in popular music, fostered by the dance halls, by musical films and, to a lesser degree, by the BBC. Only by the end of the decade had the number of licences to hold a wireless set risen to nine million, not quite one for every family.

New housing estates, both public and private, provided better housing for the upper-working class, and the lower-middle class, but it was in housing, and in urban geography, that the boundaries of class were most obvious. So too in health (a central issue in many of the novels of A. J. Cronin, himself a former doctor). Health provision was patchy and anomalous. Health insurance was not administered directly by the government, but through private companies, the 'approved societies', because of prevailing sentiments in support of private enterprise and because these companies constituted powerful pressure groups. All of the companies had to provide the standard benefit and also pay a capitation fee to a doctor, so that the insured person then became a 'panel patient', as distinct from a private fee-paying patient, of that doctor. There was no national hospital service: instead an absurd and damaging rivalry between voluntary hospitals, and hospitals run since 1929 by the local authorities. In both, the practice was to charge patients fees in accordance with their means.

The workers (if lucky) had weekly wage packets. Most of the lower-middle and middle-middle classes had annual salaries, paid monthly which meant that, though they would have deprecated the vulgar phrase, they 'had holidays with pay'. The Act of 1938 giving a legal entitlement to one week's holiday with pay to most wage-earners was in keeping with the ideology of mass society; but it is evident from this and other social legislation that there was what elsewhere I have termed the 'statutory working class', distinct from the middle classes above.[65]

Until the early fifties, women continued (in some areas) to be employed at coal mines, working on the surface sorting out the coal on a screening-belt. This just drives home the point that some of the dirtiest, lowest-status jobs were done by working-class women. 'Charring' was a widespread occupation for women. And trying to manage a household, keep children fed, keep house and family clean, on the dole, or on low wages, was a profoundly wearing task, which often involved a woman starving herself to keep her husband and children fed. Yet it is true that women of all classes went through something of the same kind of experience during the war, raising their consciousness, giving them a new sense of self-worth. In his account of life in a shop-keeper's family in a working-class area, *The Classic Slum*, Robert Roberts speaks of the new assertiveness of women, even if activated only within the family circle.[66]

The marriage rate had taken an upward leap in 1915, and this was sustained until the seventies. There was new provision for child nurture and childcare – the Care of Mothers and Young Children Act of 1915 is one of these crucial social documents which the older textbooks never mentioned. For determined women in the middle class and upwards, there were totally new professional opportunities. And, lower down the social scale, the women who returned from the war factories to domestic service insisted, as the abundant evidence shows, on less degrading conditions; many no longer lived in. The same was true among shop assistants – where, anyway, 'living in' had disappeared amid the food shortages of war. Many of the effects were concealed by the depression – which did force women back into the still harsh conditions of domestic service. In 1931 nearly one in every five households still had at least one full-time domestic servant living in, while many more employed a 'daily' to do most of the cleaning and cooking. Women continued to be largely excluded from positions of real power, in both business and politics (Margaret Bondfield, in the 1929 Labour Government, was the first woman Cabinet minister), and women's wage rates remained much lower than those of men.

It is difficult to pin down the exact nature of changes in sexual attitudes and even more difficult to pin down those in actual sexual behaviour; it is also very difficult to be sure whether 'sexual liberation' operates equally for both sexes, or whether sometimes it increases the pressures on, or exploitation of, women. Social surveys and statistics suggest that sexual behaviour was more daring and venturesome, less totally subject to traditional moral and religious codes, than before the war. Technology played its part. To more effective, and more aesthetic, contraceptive methods, we should also add the arrival from America of the tampon in the early 1930s. Marie Stopes became the great publicist for contraception – within a loving marriage. But her film, *Maisy's Marriage*, can have done little to dispel confusion and ignorance. However, word-of-mouth can be a more potent medium of mass communication than any film. And when people start talking, as every Catholic priest and moral counsellor knows, they may start acting; and there were plenty of new developments to talk about in the twenties and thirties. Overall, prudishness ruled. Sex in novels was romantically purple, where it was not simply prim; it hardly existed at all in films. Sir Roy Harrod narrates how a hearty Cambridge undergraduate in 1922 found 'unseemly and immoral' a reference to contraceptives made by Keynes when delivering a paper on Malthus.[67]

Many of the issues which feminists, rightly, have brought into public debate today, simply were not thought of in the inter-war years. So too, race was an issue scarcely mentioned. There were race riots in May and June 1919, all in seaport areas. White mobs carried out violent attacks on blacks, mainly West Indian seamen recruited into the merchant marines during the war, in Cardiff and Liverpool (where altogether three people were killed), and in Glasgow, Tyneside, Newport, and London's Dockland. What the natural supporters of middle opinion and secular Anglicanism would have wished the British outlook to be is made interestingly clear in Michael Balcon's film (completed in 1939 after the outbreak of war), *Proud Valley*. Black merchant seaman Paul Robeson meets some prejudice at first, but then comes the message that all men are black down the pit.

## *NATIONAL IDENTITIES*

In the perceptions of the Welsh held by non-Welsh parts of Great Britain, choirs, nonconformity, sabatarianism, temperance, an accent usually thought to be slightly comic, and rugby football were the strongest images. Obviously to the Welsh, as to any nationality or community, it was the accents of others that seemed strange, comic, or threatening. Accent, in that sense, was a defining part of Welsh national identity. So, most certainly, were the practices and attitudes associated with nonconformist religion. The 1881 Sunday Closing Act was still seen as a triumph for independent Welsh political action, and the closure of pubs on Sundays as an integral part of Welsh culture. That remained the public face, even though there were drinking clubs for those who did want to drink on the Sabbath. There was a distinctive Welsh language, though actual speakers tended to be concentrated in the North and the West. The Welsh themselves, in fact, were much more aware than outsiders of the divide between rural Wales and the industrialized South, the fear of domination by Cardiff and the South actually became stronger than any sense of a united Welsh nationalism. As a working-class sport, rugby football was confined to South Wales, where enormous pride was taken in the open, running game developed there and the regular victories of Welsh national teams over the English, Scots and Irish. The rest of Wales took pride in its football stars, though they all played for English clubs.[68]

The battle for the disestablishment of the (Anglican) Church of Wales had been won by the outbreak of war, and the necessary legislation was enacted immediately the war ended. This, together with the decline of the Liberal party, took the strength out of many of the traditional issues which created a Welsh political identity. There was now really very little support for Welsh independence, or even for home rule. When the party which was to become Plaid Cymru was founded in August 1925, four of the most significant things about it were: first, it was founded in a temperance hotel; secondly, it was established during the Pwllheli *eisteddfod*; thirdly, it was not actually committed to self-government for Wales, but to protection of the Welsh language, including making Welsh the only official language, recognizing it as an obligatory medium in official business and government administration, and using it as a medium of instruction at every level from primary schools to the universities; fourthly, even by 1930, its membership was only five hundred. Chapel congregations diminished, and many famous choirs disappeared. The Welsh seemed to have accepted being not just ruled, but administered, from England. The Welsh Board of Health could not even appoint a cleaning lady without the approval of Whitehall. The Poor Law was administered from Staffordshire. Factory inspection was administered from Liverpool for North Wales and Bristol for South Wales. As Kenneth Morgan puts it:

> the overall picture was a depressing one for nationalists – an institutionalising of the division between North and South Wales, and a failure to achieve either autonomy or the recognition of separate identity in the organs of government.

One might expect the development of the features of mass society to erode any sense of separate national identity. Certainly the growth of broadcasting was a matter of concern to those who were committed nationalists. Unlike Scotland and Northern Ireland, Wales was not at first granted a broadcasting service of its own. From 1935 the regional transmitter at Washford Cross was devoted entirely to a Welsh service, with a relay station at Bangor carrying the programmes to the North. Finally on 4 July 1937 a separate Welsh home service was created, with a full output of programmes from studios in Cardiff, Swansea and Bangor. The BBC Welsh Orchestra, originally founded in 1928, was re-established in 1935. The Welsh in the inter-war years were free of English landlords and the English church, but they were only in the process of finding new causes and new forms of expression. They were certainly not English, but they were perhaps more a distinctive strand of Britishness, than securely and separately Welsh. We come to the mournful conclusion that the single most distinctive characteristic of Wales in the inter-war years was poverty: 'a whole society was crucified by mass unemployment and near-starvation'. As a result, 430,000 Welsh people emigrated between 1921 and 1940, mostly to various parts of England.

Scotland had distinctive institutions of its own, the law, banking, schools and universities, and thus there was a widely felt sense of Scottish nationhood. Scots who thought about these things, held, above all, that they had never been conquered by the English (as the Welsh had), that they had had a continuous history as a separate nation, and that they had entered voluntarily into the Union; when the English banks had failed in the early nineteenth century their note-issuing rights had been taken over by the Bank of England – all of the Scottish banks still proudly issued their own colourful and beautifully designed notes. The fact that, compared with Wales, Scotland was larger and more culturally and geographically various (there being obvious differences between Highlands and Lowlands), also contributed to a stronger sense of a separate nationhood. By the same irony, so did the fact that Scotland had a more carefully articulated class structure. Though public education in Scotland was generally better than in England (or so most Scots believed), there were both 'public schools' of the English type, and, more important, fee-paying day schools for the upper-middle class and aspiring members of the lesser regions of the middle class. Presbyterianism, which had the status of being the established religion, was still associated with temperance and austere lifestyles, but there was also a strong tradition of bibulousness. There was pride in both the beer and whisky industries. Among the leading breweries were William Younger in Edinburgh, George Younger in Alloa, and Tennant's in Glasgow. Cooperative Societies, with their 'divvi' (dividend) and credit facilities, each local one being known as 'the store' (the credit book being 'the store book'), were prominent throughout Scotland. Gaelic was spoken only in the Highlands and could not in any way be represented as the native language of the majority of Scots. English was spoken in a number of different accents, though all unmistakably Scottish and quite different from English. East Coast speech, and that of the educated in the Glasgow area, tended to sound authoritative, while that of working-class Glasgow could be nearly incomprehensible to those unfamiliar with it. Some Scots did attempt to speak with cultivated English accents, but again, in general, it was an English accent which seemed 'different' to most Scots. Football was very much the game, and spectator sport, of the Scottish working class; but the middle-class schools played rugby. (Following) football was a passion, intensified by the fact that certain major clubs still had intense religious affiliations. In Glasgow, Rangers were Protestant, Celtic Catholic; the same was true, though less intensely, of Hearts and Hibernian in Edinburgh. But, once again, such differences intensified the sense of Scotland as a complete nation in all its variety. The Scots enthusiastically supported their own national football and rugby teams, but when it came to cricket, those who were interested in that game practically became Englishmen and supported the MCC (Marylebone Cricket Club, the elite club in London which, selecting players from the English County teams, still took upon itself the role of representing all England in its games against Australia, India etc.). Although Scotland was designated a 'special area', much of Scotland escaped the worst effects of industrial depression. Edinburgh had the genuine attributes of a capital city, and was a city of brewing, printing, and the professions. Its lawyers sat at the head of a system of law courts totally distinct from that of England. Most important of all – a boost to national pride, yet a qualification upon separate national identity – ambitious Scots could feel that they played a disproportionate part in running the United Kingdom. Wales was dominated by England, yet Welsh figures did not obviously play a big part in the running of the United Kingdom. Lloyd George seemed much more of an outsider figure in British public life than did such Scots as Ramsay MacDonald, John Reith, Eric Geddes or Lord Weir.

It was a French critic, Dennis Saurat, who discovered the 'Scottish Renaissance'. As with similar, but less pronounced, stirrings in Wales, this was at first literary and cultural, and represented most strongly by the poetry of Hugh MacDiarmid, the novels of Neil Gunn and Lewis Grassic Gibbon, and the plays of James Bridie. MacDiarmid tried to reconstruct the old Scots tongue as 'Lallans' (language of 'the Lowlands'). In 1925 the National Party of Scotland was founded; it never had more than 5,000 members, and never polled more than 10 per cent of the vote.[69]

The two Irelands were born in violence, and remained disturbed places throughout the twenties and thirties. Independent Ireland seemed priest-ridden, right-wing, and anti-labour. Northern Ireland was dominated by Protestant bigots. To the non-specialist there was little to choose between the accents of Dublin and those of Belfast, or between Belfast Protestants and Belfast Catholics. But the hatred between the religious communities had the intensity of earlier centuries. Above all, Northern Ireland, though not declared a special area, was a sink of poverty in the way that Wales was, mitigated only by the benefits of the British unemployment insurance system and the other scraps of welfare legislation. Catholics in the North, even if the Irish Free State may not always have seemed too tempting, could at least be unequivocal in their sense of Irish identity. The Protestants were desperate to identify themselves as British; they had allies among extreme Orange (i.e. Protestant, after William of Orange) groups on the mainland, particularly in Lowland Scotland, but most Scots, English and Welsh, if they thought of the Ulster Protestants at all, thought of them as extremist and bigoted in a way which was not truly British.

The working class in Ulster, both Protestant and Catholic, played, or at least watched, football. So did the working class in the Irish Free State. Both North and South had their own separate national football teams. One of the most striking symbols of the complex and ironic relationship between the British and the Irish is that there was one national rugby team for the whole of Ireland, rugby being particularly the game of the middle and upper classes in the Free State. The home of rugby was in Dublin and, nicest irony of all, at Lansdowne Road, the Lansdownes being one of the great aristocratic families of the English ascendancy in Ireland.

Strong regional differences were to be found throughout the population of England. Yorkshiremen had their own pride, and a distinctive rivalry with Lancashire. Both looked down on 'effete' southerners, but the point was that they were really imagining themselves as truer and better Englishmen. This holds true of 'Geordies' of the North-East, of Devonians, of Scousers from Liverpool. That said, Scotland, and even Wales, *were* more than regions in this sense. One could, without bathos, speak of Welsh 'language and culture' or of a 'Scottish Renaissance'. These were genuine attributes of nationality: there were no true analogues in the English regions.

There is a collection of feminist essays where, if you look for any trace of Scotland or Wales in the index, all you will find is: 'for Britain see England'.[70] The authors, of course, would be furious if one printed an entry: 'for women see men'. Yet, for all that I have just said, both entries would have held a certain truth for the British Isles in the inter-war years. When they expressed themselves, women still tended to use masculine terms. The male was represented as the normal. And, in Britain too, England was the norm, England set the standards; even Scots often said 'English' when they should have said 'British'. The articulations of a clear sense of Welshness or of Scottishness were in the hands of small minorities. In Ireland, because of the brutality of events, self-ascribed identities were much more clear-cut. But those most certain of their Britishness could not be certain that they would be taken as such by the mainland majority.

## NOTES

1 Peter Clarke, *Hope and Glory: Britain 1900–1990* (1996), p. 128.
2 Martin Wiener, *English Culture and the Decline of the Industrial Spirit, 1850–1980* (Cambridge, 1981). The issues are discussed in Bruce Collins and Keith Robbins (eds), *British Culture and Economic Decline* (1990).
3 *The Nation*, 13 November 1926.
4 Quoted by Steven Tolliday, 'Management and Labour in Britain 1896–1939'. In Steven Tolliday and Jonathan Zeitlin, *The Automobile Industry and its Workers: Between Fordism and Flexibility* (Cambridge, 1986), p. 31.
5 Ibid., p. 47.
6 Peter Fearon, *The Origins and Nature of the Great Slump 1929–1932* (1979), pp. 33ff.
7 C. T. Harvie, *No Gods and Precious Few Heroes: Scotland since 1914* (Edinburgh, 1993), p. 47.
8 Ibid., p. 48. In general see Peter L. Payne, 'The Economy'. In T. M. Devine and R. J. Finlay, *Scotland in the Twentieth Century* (Edinburgh, 1996).
9 Kenneth O. Morgan, *Rebirth of a Nation: A History of Modern Wales* (Oxford, 1982).
10 Thomas Hennessy, *A History of Northern Ireland 1920–1996* (1997), p. 56.

11 Peter Clarke, *The Keynesian Revolution in the Making* (Oxford, 1988), esp. pp. 313–30.
12 Quoted in Trevor Wilson, *The Downfall of the Liberal Party* (1966; paperback, 1968), p. 262. This is a model of scholarship which has reigned supreme for over thirty years.
13 Peter Clarke, *A Question of Leadership: Gladstone to Thatcher* (1991), p. 102.
14 Kenneth O. Morgan, *Consensus and Disunity: The Lloyd George Coalition Government 1918–1922* (Oxford, 1979), pp. 180–90; Clarke, *Hope and Glory*, pp. 98–9.
15 Antony Lentin, *Guilt at Versailles: Lloyd George and the Pre-history of Appeasement* (1985); Alan Sharp, *The Versailles Settlement: Peacemaking in Paris, 1919* (1991).
16 Hennessy, *A History of Northern Ireland*, pp. 4–10.
17 The contemporary descriptions of these four important figures are well summarized by Charles Loch Mowat, *Britain Between the Wars* (London, 1955) pp. 58–61.
18 Charles Townshend, *Ireland: The 20th Century* (1998), pp. 89, 98.
19 Morgan, *Consensus*, pp. 262–4.
20 The full text of the speech (though not, of course, my interpretation of it!) can be found in Harold Nicolson, *King George the Fifth: His Life and Reign* (1952).
21 R. F. Foster, *Modern Ireland 1600–1972* (1984), p. 512.
22 Mowat, *Britain Between the Wars*, p. 101.
23 The corporatist thesis is impressively set out in Keith Middlemass, *Politics in Industrial Society: The Experience of the British System since 1911* (1979); see also James E. Cronin, 'Coping with Labour, 1918–1926', chapter 6 in James E. Cronin and Jonathan Schneer (eds), *Social Conflict and the Political Order in Modern Britain* (1982). For a rebuttal see Forrest Capie, *Depression and Protectionism: Britain Between the Wars* (1994), pp. 64–120.
24 PRO CAB 23/15, 606.
25 William Gallacher, *Revolt on the Clyde* (1936), p. 221.
26 PRO, CAB 23/22.
27 CAB 23/25, 18 (21).
28 CAB 23/25, 19 (21).
29 Wal Hannington, *Unemployed Struggles 1919–1936* (1935), p. 16; *The Times*, 19–20 October 1920.
30 Pat Thane, *Foundations of the Welfare State* (1982), pp. 206–7.
31 Clarke, *Leadership*, p. 108.
32 Clarke, *Hope and Glory*, p. 110. On the Chanak crisis see Morgan, *Consensus*, pp. 318–26.
33 Wilson, *Downfall*, p. 246.
34 T. O. Lloyd, *Empire, Welfare State, Europe: England 1880–1990* (Oxford, 1994), p. 120.
35 *Manchester Guardian*, 21 November 1922.
36 Wilson, *Downfall*, p. 261.
37 Nicolson, *George V*, p. 400.
38 Clarke, *Hope and Glory*, p. 132.
39 Dudley Baines, 'The Onset of Depression'. In Paul Johnson (ed.), *20th Century Britain: Economic, Social and Cultural Change* (1994), p. 179.
40 *House of Commons Debates*, vol.187, col.1592, 6 August 1925. For the General Strike, see Keith Laybourn, *The General Strike 1926* (1993); G. A. Phillips, *The General Strike: The Politics of Industrial Conflict* (1976); John Ramsden, *The Age of Balfour and Baldwin* (1978), pp. 278–85.
41 Mowat, p. 338. See David Dilkes, *Neville Chamberlain*, vol.1: *Pioneering and Reform, 1869–1929* (Cambridge, 1984), pp. 426–9, 431–5.

42 Asa Briggs, *The History of Broadcasting in the United Kingdom*, vol.1: *The Birth of Broadcasting* (1995), p. 217.
43 This and the next quotation are in Wilson, *Downfall*, pp. 363, 372.
44 Quoted in Taylor, *English History*, p. 280.
45 Wilson, *Downfall*, p. 387.
46 Notably by Robert Skidelsky, *Oswald Mosley* (1975; third edn, 1990).
47 Quoted in David Marquand, *Ramsay MacDonald* (1977), p. 634. I have depended heavily on Marquand.
48 Clarke, *Hope and Glory*, p. 157.
49 Wilson, *Downfall*, p. 402.
50 John Stevenson and Chris Cook, *The Slump: Society and Politics During the Depression* (1977), p. 204.
51 Arthur Marwick, 'Middle Opinion in the Thirties: Planning, Progress and Political "Agreement"', *English Historical Review*, 1964. There is a very thorough recent analysis in Daniel Ritschel, *The Politics of Planning, the Debate on Economic Planning in Britain in the 1930s* (Oxford, 1997).
52 Ritschel, *Planning*, p. 183.
53 Lloyd, *Empire, Welfare State*, p. 192.
54 Ramsden, *Age of Balfour*, pp. 350–1.
55 See Ben Pimlott, *Labour and the Left in the 1930s* (1986).
56 Maurice Cowling, *The Impact of Hitler: British Politics and British Policy 1933–1940* (Cambridge, 1975), pp. 344–53.
57 John Galsworthy, *A Modern Comedy* (1920), p. 21.
58 See the fourth volume of Osbert Sitwell's autobiography, *Laughter in the Next Room* (1949), and entries for Edith Sitwell and William Walton in Margaret Drabble, *The Oxford Companion to Literature* (Oxford, 1985). There is an Academy Sound and Vision CD of *Façade*, performed by the London Mozart Players with Prunella Scales and Timothy West (CD DCA679); the helpful notes are by Robin Golding.
59 Charles Harrison, *English Art and Modernism 1900–1939* (1981), p. 226.
60 This, and the following quotations, including the one on Waugh, are from Drabble.
61 Peter Kidson, Peter Murray and Paul Thompson, *A History of English Architecture* (Harmondsworth, 1979), p. 321.
62 Jeffrey Richards and Anthony Aldgate, *The Best of British: Cinema and Society 1930–1970* (Oxford, 1983), p. 32.
63 Peter Miles and Malcolm Smith, *Cinema, Literature and Society* (Beckenham, 1987), pp. 31–3.
64 In Richards and Aldgate, *Best of British*, pp. 13–14.
65 Arthur Marwick, *Class: Image and Reality in Britain, France and the USA since 1930* (1990), pp. 57–65.
66 Robert Roberts, *The Classic Slum* (1971), p. 174.
67 Sir Roy Harrod, *The Life of John Maynard Keynes* (1951; paperback, 1982), p. 328.
68 I have drawn heavily on K. O. Morgan, *Rebirth of Wales*, pp. 242–69.
69 Harvie, *No Gods*, pp. 65–87, 99, 119–139.
70 Margaret Randolph Higonnet, Jane Jenson, Sonya Michel, and Margaret Collins Weitz (eds), *Behind the Lines: Gender and the Two World Wars* (New Haven, CT, 1987).

# 3 War and Aftermath, 1939–1955

## World War

### *The Phoney War*

Was it a second, more immense, world war which began in September 1939? Was it simply the renewal of a 'Thirty Years War' between Britain and Germany, or, in a more sophisticated phrasing, another episode in European Civil War? Was there a merely European war until December 1941, which was then subsumed within the separate truly global engagement between America and Japan? Britain, though, in the shrewd phrase of F. S. Northedge, a 'Troubled Giant',[1] with an inner strength greater than appeasing Conservative politicians fearful of mass society understood, but an external strength considerably less than that suggested by the colourings on the world map, *was* still a world power. She could no longer, it was true, declare war on behalf of the white Dominions, though she did do so on behalf of India and the widespread territories of the Colonial Empire. But the two rising powers of the northern and southern hemispheres, Canada and Australia, *did* declare war side by side with the 'mother country' (then, subsequently, the experience of war transformed the colonial territories into nations well advanced towards independence). Germany, under Hitler, was again seeking parity as a world power with Britain, whom the Führer greatly admired. The Soviet Union, allied to Germany in the 'Nazi–Soviet Pact' of 23 August 1939, while seeming in a sorry state to Western strategists, already had the potential to become a world super-power. The economic problems of the twenties and thirties were, we have seen, global. British imperialists had hoped that victory in the previous war would give Britain a massive economic arena to exploit. Imperialists in Japan were harbouring similar ambitions. American sentiment was isolationist, but American imperialists, from the beginning of the century, had always perceived Germany as a potential threat to American economic interests; now Japan was emerging as a much more immediate and threatening one.

War need not have come in September 1939. But it did. The war which came in September 1939 need not have become submerged in the still mightier conflict between America and Japan. But it did. Wars, once started, are not easily stopped. British politicians and planners, too, feared the threat posed by

Japan to the British Empire. It is one of the many ironies, as well as one of the many instances of the inter-relationship between 'mere' European war and world war, that it was because of a wish to be ready to resist Japan, that British strategists did not wish to become involved in a war with Germany, thus encouraging Germany to take the actions which eventually led to Britain becoming involved with her, and, eventually, with Japan also.

What had happened in the First World War was both the model, and the nightmare, for British military planners. Technology, it was expected, would be an even more dominating force, and, therefore, the war would be even more horrific. Yet, it was felt, some form of trench warfare in the Low Countries and in France would be inevitable; and, it was remembered, to go on the offensive was to court appalling casualties. The French had constructed what was intended to be an impregnable barrier against a German invasion on the 1914 pattern, the Maginot Line. But there were no plans for how a British expeditionary force would operate in concert with the French, nor had a Commander-in-Chief been designated for such a force. For British planners, the ultimate wonder, and therefore ultimate horror, was the aeroplane: Britain had an airforce, independent of both army and navy: it was expected that a central feature of the war would be the bombing of civilians, German and British. Much investment throughout the war, indeed, was directed towards faster and bigger aircraft, to bombs and rockets, to systems for locating enemy aircraft, and to guns for shooting them down. Much pre-war planning in Britain was directed towards air-raid precautions, towards moving civilians out of vulnerable cities, towards coping with the destruction of life and limb it was thought air attacks would necessarily cause. First evacuations to the countryside of mothers and children had actually been carried out at the time of Munich.

On the very day that Britain declared war, Sunday, 3 September, everyone's worst expectations seemed to be fulfilled. Almost immediately after Chamberlain's sad radio address, the air-raid sirens in London began to sound. Incredibly, but most aptly, the alarm had been set off by a French military attaché flying back to Britain as part of the unfocused discusions taking place between the British and French military authorities. There were no public demonstrations of enthusiasm for war. The crowds in Downing Street were serious-faced, and people grasped hold of each other as the declaration of war was made. 'My friend, my sister and I, all under thirty,' a young woman wrote, 'agreed we would almost welcome the war. We turned on the radio, and heard Chamberlain's speech. I felt slightly sick, and yet half relieved.' An older housewife wrote: 'It has happened! My first feeling was one of tremendous relief, that the awful waiting and uncertainty is over.'[2] The popular mood, in so far as one can talk of such a thing, was of release from unbearable tension, of slightly fearful determination and of grim resignation. During the following week at the London railway stations there took place the scenes we are all familiar with from photographs and newsreels of children, brave-faced and tearful, neatly labelled, being packed off to the countryside. The Regulars were ready for active service, the Territorials immediately rejoined their units. Full conscription was brought in by the National Service (Armed Forces) Act of 3 September; work was begun on the compilation of a comprehensive National Register.

Command of the British Expeditionary Force was given to the Chief of the Imperial General Staff, the Sixth Viscount Gort, his position being taken by General Sir Edmund Ironside. The five divisions of the regular army, including the third division under Major-General Bernard Montgomery, were efficiently transferred to France. Between January and April 1940 they were joined by five Territorial Army divisions, trained, as the regulars were, in trench warfare; all but one of these contained the 'stiffening' of a battalion of regulars. In addition there were three Territorial support divisions, not equipped or trained for fighting.[3]

Reluctant to go to war, the Chamberlain Government now appeared reluctant to wage war. As well as the army, the navy and the RAF were mobilized. But postures were essentially defensive, reactive not proactive, with the Government putting great faith in the idea that ultimately economic blockade would bring about German defeat. Supplementary to that was the idea that what Britain most needed was time to build up her armaments. Any notions of the airforce going on bombing raids over Germany were firmly vetoed by the Cabinet: leaflets were dropped, and a few ineffective attacks on German shipping carried out. Hitler, mounting devastating attacks on the civilian population in the rapid conquest of Poland, while the Soviet Union took over East Poland and then the Baltic States, colluded in this 'bore war', as it was called, before the universal adoption (with spelling altered) of an Americanism: well before the end of September, Senator William E. Borah of Idaho had remarked that there was 'something phoney about this war',[4] implicitly criticizing the British and the French for not attacking the Germans in the west while Germany and Russia were still busy 'cleaning up' in the east. Hitler made the first of his proposals for a peace conference, including both Britain and France, on 6 October. At this time Lloyd George, and others, were strong supporters of peace negotiations to avert the carnage associated with the previous war.[5]

The burden of imposing the blockade, of course, fell on the navy; something of what was in store at sea was signalled at once on 3 September when the passenger ship *Athenia* was torpedoed off the coast of Scotland with heavy loss of life. Eventually, aircraft carriers were to prove one of the most critical technological innovations of the war; one of the first British ones, *Courageous*, was sunk in the Channel a couple of weeks later. In October the battleship *Royal Oak* was sunk while at anchor in what proved to be the false security of Scapa Flow. As well as advanced submarines, and skilled and daring officers to man them, the Germans deployed devastatingly destructive magnetic mines. However, in a classic case of technological counter-thrust, the British had within weeks met the threat by equipping ships with 'de-gaussing girdles' which neutralized the magnetic pull. Continuing from the previous war, convoys were used effectively, greatly assisted by the asdic system of sonic location of submarines. A more spectacular victory was achieved in the Battle of the River Plate, off the coast of South America, when three light cruisers, though heavily outgunned, destroyed the German pocket battleship *Graf Spee*.

In this war the Scandinavian countries took on an importance they had not had in the previous one: Germany was heavily dependent on high quality Swedish iron-ore; Stalin perceived his frontier with Finland as a very vulnerable one. In pursuit of security, specifically for Leningrad, Soviet forces invaded Finland, being expelled from the League of Nations, and meeting with brave resistance. Churchill, a spurting geyser in a cabinet of dripping icebergs, proposed a scheme for mining the Norwegian 'leads' or coastal waters, following this up with a plan to join Finland in their war against the Soviet Union by sending troops through the Norwegian port of Narvik. After Churchill's coup of sending a British destroyer into Norwegian waters to release several hundred captured British seamen from the German merchant ship the *Altmark,* Finland's surrender on 13 March rendered the expedition pointless. Mining of the Norwegian leads, however, went ahead on 8 April. The following day German troops occupied Denmark, and began their own invasion of Norway, transporting troops by both sea and air, taking control of towns in the South, as well as Narvik in the North. Churchill's belief was that Hitler had overstretched himself, a view which gained some confirmation with the sinking of ten German destroyers off Narvik, against the loss of two British ones. The aborted plan to route British troops to Finland through Narvik was revised as a plan to land a full army brigade to recapture that town. Then the Norwegians appealed for landings in central Norway, in the vicinity of Trondheim and Namsos, to help them in the fight they were still putting up against the Germans. But, while the Germans had air cover, the British attempt to establish an airfield was unsuccessful, and the British forces were evacuated on the nights of 1 and 2 May, with all efforts being concentrated on Narvik.[6]

On 4 April Chamberlain had told a Conservative meeting that he was ten times as confident of victory as at the beginning of the war, and that Hitler had 'missed the bus'.[7] Chamberlain was neither supremely incompetent nor supremely unpopular. A Ministry of Shipping had been established in October, and the Ministry of Labour had become the Ministry of Labour and National Service. Petrol rationing was introduced: though opposed by Churchill, rationing of butter, bacon and sugar came into effect on 8 January 1940. However, Chamberlain appeared to view the Ministry of Information as a sort of royal commision rather than an executive arm of government and instead of putting a politician in charge, appointed a distinguished Judge, Lord Macmillan. Macmillan, as he himself admitted, was utterly unsuited to the job, and the ministry made a hash of practically everything it touched, though its first poster '*Your* Courage *Your* Cheerfulness *Your* Resolution will bring us victory', was perhaps less snobbish and divisive, and more cognizant of the need to involve the entire population, than the chorus of condemnation ever since allowed for.[8] There were some unsettling reshuffles. The popular Leslie Hore-Belisha, who certainly lacked military experience, and who, it happened, was Jewish, was removed from the War Office in January, being replaced by Oliver Stanley; Sir John Reith replaced Lord Macmillan. Admiral of the Fleet, Baron Chatfield, Minister for Coordination of Defence, chaired a special Military Coordination Committee, advised by the Chiefs of Staff. When he resigned in April, his ministerial post was unfilled, but Churchill took on the Chairmanship. As the Norwegian episode demonstrated, the Committee certainly failed to coordinate. In March, Home Secretary Sir Samuel Hoare swapped places with Air Minister Kingsley Wood. Against these negative features, agreement had been secured in November 1939 that American companies would supply armaments, provided that they were paid for at once and conveyed in Allied shipping, that is on a 'cash and carry' basis. British aircraft production, which had been at the rate of 650 a month in 1939, reached over 1,000 a month in April 1940; though very much the opposite was thought to be true at the time, this figure was actually slightly greater than the German one. In late January, 56 per cent of those participating in an opinion poll (National Opinion Polls – NOP) expressed approval of Chamberlain's leadership. Yet, despite the inclusion of Churchill in the government, the Prime Minister had influential Conservative critics, led by Leopold Amery. Also hostile were an All-Party Action Group chaired by the nominal National Liberal, but increasingly Liberal *tout court*, Clement Davies, and the 'Watching Committee' of leading Conservatives in both Houses, formed by Lord Salisbury.

The Norway events were small-scale ones, with British land casualties amounting to about 2,400, but they had taken war into the era of combined operations – concerted attack by sea, air and land. The ill-executed British effort made clear that combined operations would require higher levels than ever before of planning and coordination. Meantime the British soldiers in France and Belgium were still in the era of trench warfare.[9] Priority was given to digging and fortifying a defensive line along the British sector of the Franco-Belgian frontier. According to the historians of the Coldstream Guards this was 'a dreary period of digging and wiring (in a dismal industrial area of France), interspersed with route marches, weapon-training and battlefield tours'. There was plenty of weapons drill, but no firing. The memoirs of Private George Andow, a Matilda tank crew member in the Fourth Royal Tank Regiment, described many days of idleness in cafes, with very little training in tanks. Living conditions were poor, with men billeted in barns, and even, in one case, a factory. From the beginning of the year the weather was atrociously cold. Diversions were of the most basic sort, discipline severe. General Montgomery nearly secured his own dismissal by advocating the setting-up of licensed brothels for soldiers in need of what he termed 'horizontal refreshment'. There was an obsession with spies – five hundred suspects a day, many being shot with scant attention to the canons of justice. There were occasional exchanges of, sometimes lethal, fire, but not much sight of the enemy on the ground. In the air, the Luftwaffe were very much in evidence, their strafing and dive-bombing causing panic and 'almost universal grumbling and bitterness about the RAF's minimal role'. Suddenly the German invasion began: now numbering 400,000, the British Expeditionary Force joined with the French in moving forward to assist the Belgians and Dutch.

## *The Churchill Coalition*

The Norway fiasco was to have the historical significance of May 1915 and December 1916 combined. In contrast with the two previous political crises this one centred openly on a truly dramatic debate in the House of Commons. Yet it unrolled with a strange ponderousness and some irony. The succession to the premiership of Winston Churchill soon seemed inevitable, but at the time it was not the outcome most principal actors expected. As the military historian Liddell Hart later put it:

> It was the irony, or fatality, of history that Churchill should have gained his opportunity of supreme power as the result of a fiasco to which he had been the main contributor.[10]

The Norwegian campaign was down for debate in parliament on 7 May. The day before, the *Daily Mail* demanded a change of government, with an anonymous politician, who was, in fact, the left-wing Labour MP Sir Stafford Cripps, nominating Lord Halifax, the Foreign Secretary, as Prime Minister. The *Manchester Guardian* (6 May) presented a wider-ranging analysis:

> If we look back over these eight months, with problem after problem mismanaged or neglected, with speech after speech revealing the same lack of grasp and imagination, we are driven to the conclusion that we are facing the greatest crisis in our history with a government weaker than any government that has made war since Addington faced Napoleon . . .
>
> What is needed is a government that can organise the nation's strength, touch its imagination, command its spirit of self-sacrifice, impose burdens fearlessly on all classes.

The Labour leaders were at first very hesitant about pressing their motion to a vote. It was Clement Davies who, after discussing matters with Amory and other Conservatives, urged Attlee to demand a division. Attlee's deputy, Herbert Morrison, sent a message to Lloyd George asking him to attend the debate. Chamberlain sent his Parliamentary Private Secretary, Lord Dunglass (much later, Sir Alec Douglas-Home) round the different Conservative groups with the bribe of a reconstructed government; however, he got the brush-off from the Watching Committee.

During the two-day parliamentary debate the limelight was shared by Sir Roger Keyes, resplendent in the uniform of an Admiral of the Fleet, and Amery, who quoted Cromwell's puissant words to the Long Parliament: 'Depart, I say, and let us have done with you. In the name of God, go!' Despite advice to the contrary from almost the entire press, Labour announced on the second day that it would indeed force a division. Chamberlain's reply to the challenge was not impressive:

> I do not seek to evade criticism but I say this to my friends in the House – and I have friends in the house . . . At least we shall see who is with us and who is against us, and I call on my friends to support us in the Lobby tonight.

Lloyd George delivered the telling rejoinder:

> It is not a question of who are the Prime Minister's friends . . . He has appealed for sacrifice . . . I say solemnly that the Prime Minister should give an example of sacrifice, because there is nothing which can contribute more to victory in this war than that he should sacrifice the seals of office.

When the division came, 41 government MPs voted with the Opposition; a further 60 odd did not vote at all. A government with a normal majority of well over 200 now had a majority of 81.

The argument that Chamberlain was an able peace-time minister reluctantly forced to be a war minister is somewhat weakened by the fact that his first action the next day (9 May) was to see if Attlee and Greenwood would support a coalition under his continuing premiership. Meantime the former solicitor Kingsley Wood had been attracted out of Chamberlain's ambit into Churchill's, and was advising him on how to ensure that he, not Halifax, got the job when it definitively became vacant. The Labour leaders told Chamberlain that they could not give him any decision without consulting the party's National Executive, which was at Bournemouth with the Labour party's annual conference. If Chamberlain could not cling to office, then he preferred to cede it to Halifax who, to be fair, remained Labour's own first choice – they had no reason to like Churchill. In a meeting between Chamberlain, Halifax, and Churchill, the last-named maintained a fine strategic silence, while it became clear that Halifax scarcely really wanted the job – the thought, he confessed, gave him 'a bad stomach-ache', and when, next day (10 May), he still had a chance, he took care to be at his dentist's. The message from Bournemouth came through at 5.00 p.m.: Labour would serve in a National Government, but only under a new Prime Minister. After all the muddles of the thirties, Labour had twice in three days acted with decisive effect. Chamberlain went straight to the King with his resignation. The latter still hankered after Halifax, but Chamberlain made it clear that it must be Churchill.[11] Next day no national newspaper carried Churchill's accession as the main news story: he had been chased from the headlines by Hitler's invasion of the Low Countries.

Churchill immediately formed a small War Cabinet. Chamberlain, still leader of the Conservative party, was Lord President of the Council and Halifax continued as Foreign Secretary. Attlee and Greenwood came in as Ministers without Portfolio. Churchill took on the new title of Minister of Defence, and also appointed himself Leader of the House of Commons. The Liberals were too insignificant numerically to gain a place, though Churchill had hopes of, at some stage, bringing in Lloyd George. The service ministers, kept out of the War Cabinet, were Anthony Eden, Secretary of State for War, A. V. Alexander, of the Labour party, First Lord of the Admiralty, and Liberal leader Archibald Sinclair, Air Minister. (Sinclair had been Churchill's second-in-command in France in the First World War.) Kingsley Wood, the Addison of this crisis, got his reward as Chancellor of the Exchequer. The eternal Simon became Lord Chancellor. The anti-Chamberlainites, Leopold Amery and Duff Cooper, became respectively, Secretary for India and Minister of Information. Sir John Anderson, the former civil servant Chamberlain had brought into government, remained as Home Secretary, while another non-politician, the former chain-store manager Lord Woolton, stayed at the increasingly important Ministry of Food. From the Labour party, Herbert Morrison became Minister of Supply, and Hugh Dalton, Minister for Economic Warfare; though not a member of parliament, trade union leader Ernest Bevin became Minister of Labour and National Service. Newspaper magnate Lord Beaverbrook was coaxed into becoming Minister of Aircraft Production. This was an uncompromising government, which on 22 May took to itself, through the Emergency Powers Act, almost limitless powers over persons and property; at the same time it announced a 100 per cent Excess Profits Tax.

When the German attack in the west began on 10 May, the British forces advanced in good order, as planned, to take up positions on the River Dyle on 12 May. But a couple of days later, the Dutch, well to their left, had capitulated; worse, far to the right, the Germans had broken through the wooded hills of the Ardennes, which the French had thought to be unsuitable terrain for a rapid advance. Now the British had to retreat. Professor Bond sketches out the disaster scenario:

> Only a static or slow-moving campaign had been planned and communications (in all senses) soon collapsed under the unexpected strain. There had been sufficient motor transport for a planned advance but not for an improvised retreat on roads congested with refugees. There was soon an acute shortage of fuel. The British had relied almost entirely on the Belgian public telephone system, which now collapsed. Radio communications had been restricted for security reasons, and now proved useless, as did field telephones. Thus orders could not be transmitted with any confidence and, in effect, confusion reigned.[12]

It was very hot. If information was in disorientingly short supply, so also was sleep, together with food and water. There were a number of German atrocities, and two notorious massacres of prisoners, the first on 27 May, when, after surrendering, about ninety men of the Norfolk Regiment were mown down by machine guns, the second the following day when a similar number of prisoners from the Second Royal Warwickshire were shot or blown up with hand grenades. It was on 26 May that Gort decided that he must seek to evacuate his troops, the decision being approved by the Cabinet. That same day the Germans captured Boulogne and Calais, and on the next the Belgian army capitulated. Evacuation would have to be from within the Dunkirk perimeter, the area from just south of Dunkirk to just north of La Panne, bounded by a rectangular canal.

## *Dunkirk and the Fall of France*

'Operation Torpedo', the evacuation from this area, under the direction of the Vice-Admiral (Dover) Bertram Ramsay, took place between 27 May and 4 June. Altogether 198,315 British soldiers, and 139,911 French soldiers made it to Britain. The events which preceded Dunkirk amounted to a severe indictment of the British Government and British military leaders, and it has become usual to stress that Dunkirk itself was the culmination of a great defeat and to wax cynical about the 'Dunkirk spirit'. Actually, Dunkirk *was* a victory, for a number of reasons; as such, more attention is needed to the geography and logistics of the situation (see map 3), and indeed to the chronology of events, than is usual in textbooks.

The conventional wisdom is well represented by Nicholas Harman's *Dunkirk: The Necessary Myth* published in 1980. It makes the banal point that not

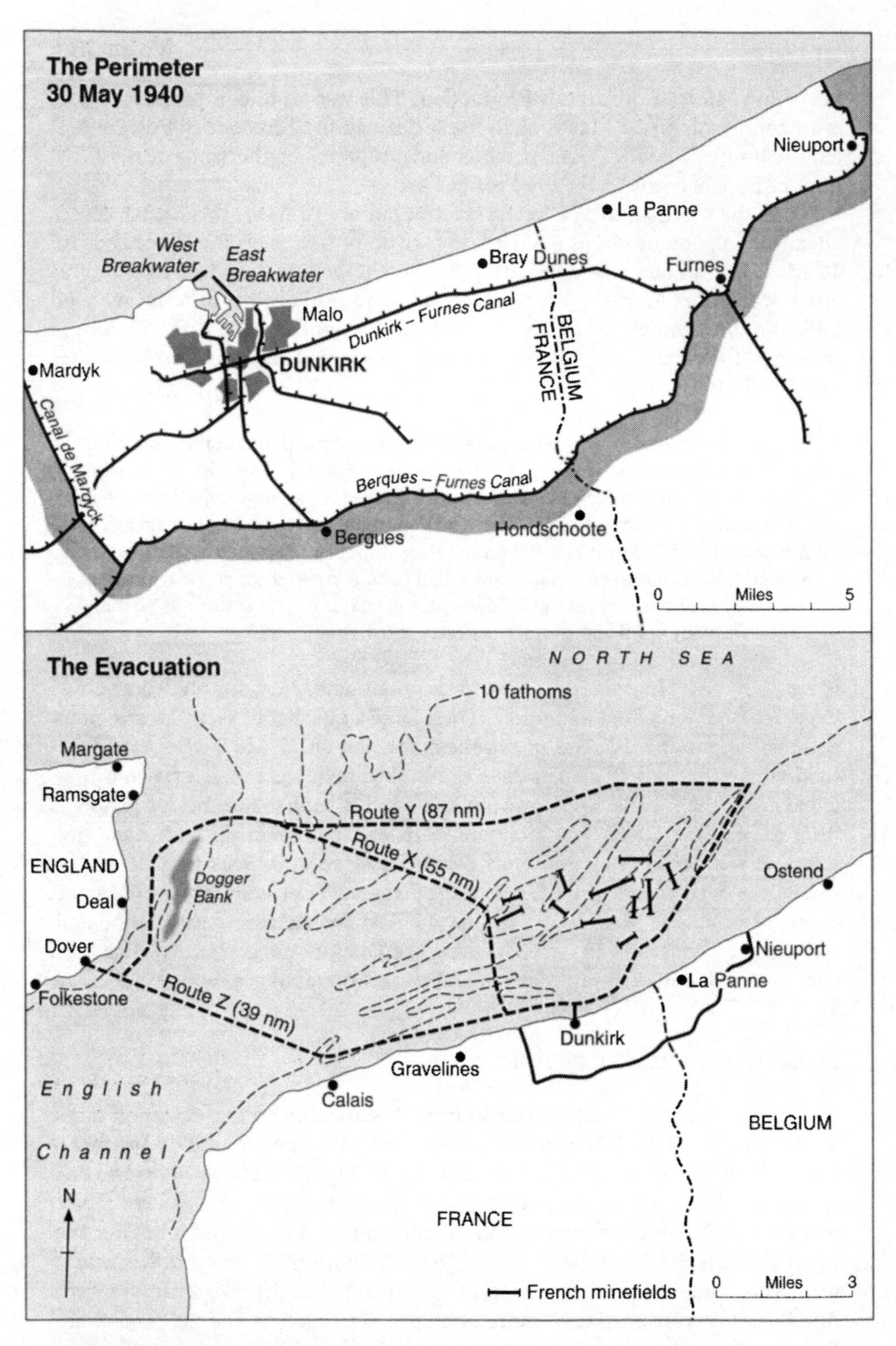


**Map 3** The Dunkirk Perimeter and Evacuation. The two maps are based on three sources: the end paper to Norman Gelb, *Dunkirk: The Incredible Escape*, London: Michael Joseph, 1990); A. J. Barker, *Dunkirk: The Great Escape*, London: Dent, 1977, p. 86; and Robert Johnson, *Dunkirk: The British Evaluation 1940*, London: Arthur Barker, 1976, p. 201.

all involved behaved heroically. Against the myth of the significance of the civilian-owned and civilian-manned 'little ships', Harman declares: 'the little ships operated only on the last two days of the British evacuation, and then to very little effect'.[13] Even accepting that ideas will differ as to what constitutes 'a big effect' and what 'a little effect', this downgrading of civilian involvement is simply wrong. In this most total of wars, with both a Ministry of Shipping and an Admiralty empowered to requisition ships and bring men under military orders, and with naval personnel as well as soldiers who had themselves been civilians only a few months earlier, the lines between the 'civilian' and the 'military' were, in certain situations, less firm than ever before. In fact, Dunkirk, and this was its greatest significance, was the first example in this war of a very close and very effective involvement between civilians and military, first in the boats, and then in the way civilians ministered to the shattered soldiers arriving back in the Kent ports and then travelling on by train.

There need be no denying that the British enjoyed rare luck with the weather. The seas were quite strangely calm; yet there was a great deal of haze, fog, and cloud which just made it significantly more difficult for German planes to attack what were otherwise sitting targets. That said, the odds against a successful evacuation were enormous. The Channel itself, with its many dangerous shoals, is always difficult to navigate. Additionally, there were minefields, laid by the French, in the approaches to the continental ports. Embarking men in channel ferries from a properly equipped port is one thing; embarking them from flat beaches where large vessels have to stand well out to sea, and where even the smallest craft cannot reach right up to the shore, is another. Along the shoreline, apart only from the area within the perimeter, German artillery overlooked the main sea routes to the Kent coast. With regard to the situation in the air, one Luftwaffe pilot declared: 'I hated Dunkirk. It was just unadulterated killing.'[14] The posts and buoys which indicated safe passages round the sand banks were shattered. As is almost too well-known, had Hitler sent in his tanks the perimeter and its inhabitants would have been destroyed before any attempt at evacuation. It may be that Hitler's 'magnificent forbearance' was due to his wish to keep open the prospect of concluding peace with Britain. Or it may be that paying full heed to on-the-spot advice that the retreating soldiers would be finished off anyway, he wanted to keep the tanks and their crews fresh for the final onslaught on France, and avoid the risk of their becoming bogged down in the low-lying land round Dunkirk.[15] If the Germans did think the Allies had no hope of escape, that would only bring out the more sharply how great an achievement Dunkirk was.

Certain crucial technological developments have already been mentioned. In this war of civilian involvement the significance of radio broadcasting should never be forgotten. At 9 a.m. on 14 May the BBC news bulletin included an Admiralty order instructing owners of all self-propelled pleasure craft of between 30 and 100 feet whose craft had not already been offered or requisitioned, to register particulars with the Admiralty's Small Vessels Pool. Though the final crisis came well before the fortnight was up, this was *not* advance planning for the Dunkirk evacuation, which, as yet, had not been dreamt of. These boats were intended for harbour work, mine sweeping, and other auxiliary duties. But the fact that they were already registered was an inestimable boon when the Dunkirk crisis intensified. On 19 May, as the Allied retreat continued, the Admiralty began to draw up broad plans for evacuating 'useless mouths' – support troops and non-combatants of all kinds. It was at first envisaged that embarkation would be from Boulogne, Calais and Dunkirk, using sea ferries. Then, the next day (20 May) it was decided that the Sea Transport Officers in the various ports from Weymouth to Poole, and round the Thames estuary and up the east coast to Harwich, should compile lists of all small craft up to 1,000 tonnes and send details to Dover. Also included were a large number of Dutch coastal motor vessels now in British waters – *schuits*, or, as the British renamed them, 'skoots'.

**Table 3.1** Allied troops evacuated from Dunkirk

| | *From Dunkirk Harbour* | *From beaches* | *Daily total* | *Sum total* |
|---|---|---|---|---|
| Monday, 27 May | 7,669 | Nil | 7,669 | 7,669 |
| Tuesday, 28 May | 11,874 | 5,930 | 17,804 | 25,473 |
| Wednesday, 29 May | 33,558 | 13,752 | 47,310 | 72,783 |
| Thursday, 30 May | 24,311 | 29,512 | 53,823 | 126,606 |
| Friday, 31 May | 45,072 | 22,942 | 68,014 | 194,620 |
| Saturday, 1 June | 47,081 | 17,348 | 64,429 | 259,049 |
| Sunday, 2 June | 19,561 | 6,695 | 26,256 | 285,305 |
| Monday, 3 June | 24,876 | 1,870 | 26,746 | 312,051 |
| Tuesday, 4 June | 25,553 | 622 | 26,175 | 338,226 |
| Totals | 239,555 | 98,671 | 338,226 | – |

*Sources:* Arthur J. Barker, *Dunkirk: The Great Escape* (London: Dent, 1977), p. 236; Russell Plummer, *The Ships that Saved an Army: A Comprehensive Record of the 1,300 'Little Ships' of Dunkirk* (1990), p. 19.

**Table 3.2** French troops evacuated from Dunkirk

| | *By French vessels* | *By British vessels* | *Totals* |
|---|---|---|---|
| 29 May | 655 | – | 655 |
| 30 May | 5,444 | 3,272 | 8,716 |
| 31 May | 4,032 | 10,842 | 14,874 |
| 1 June | 2,765 | 32,248 | 35,013 |
| 2 June | 905 | 15,144 | 16,049 |
| 3 June | 4,235 | 15,568 | 19,803 |
| 4 June | 2,349 | 24,640 | 26,989 |
| 9 June | 140 | 956 | 1,096 |

*Source:* Arthur J. Barker, *Dunkirk: The Great Escape* (London: Dent, 1977), p. 236.

**Table 3.3** Types of British ships in the evacuation

| *Type* | *Number* | *Troops lifted out* | *Losses* | | *Damaged* |
|---|---|---|---|---|---|
| | | | *By enemy action* | *Other causes* | |
| Anti-aircraft cruiser | 1 | 1,865 | 0 | 0 | 1 |
| Destroyers | 56 | 102,843 | 9 | 0 | 19 |
| Sloops | 6 | 1,436 | 0 | 0 | 1 |
| Patrol vessels | 7 | 2,504 | 0 | 0 | 0 |
| Pinnaces | 2 | 3,512 | 1 | 0 | 0 |
| Corvettes | 11 | 1,303 | 0 | 0 | 0 |
| Minesweepers | 38 | 48,472 | 5 | 1 | 7 |
| Trawlers and the like | 230 | 28,709 | 23 | 6 | 2 |
| Naval transports | 3 | 4,408 | 0 | 0 | 0 |
| Armed merchant men | 3 | 4,848 | 1 | 0 | 2 |
| Torpedo boats | 15 | 99 | 0 | 0 | 0 |
| Skoots | 40 | 22,698 | 1 | 3 | 0 |
| Yachts | 27 | 4,895 | 1 | 2 | 0 |
| Ferries | 45 | 87,810 | 9 | 0 | 8 |
| Hospital ships | 8 | 3,006 | 1 | 0 | 5 |
| Cargo vessels | 13 | 5,790 | 3 | 0 | 0 |
| Tugs | 40 | 3,164 | 6 | 1 | 0 |
| Landing craft | 13 | 118 | 1 | 7 | 0 |
| Barges | 48 | 4,726 | 4 | 8 | 0 |
| Little Boats: | | | | | |
| Motor vessels | 12 | 96 | 0 | 0 | 0 |
| Royal Navy launches | 8 | 579 | 0 | 0 | 0 |
| Private motor boats | 203 | 5,031 | 7 | 135 | Not known |
| RNLI lifeboats | 19 | 323 | 0 | 0 | 0 |
| Totals | 848 | 338,235 | 72 | 163 | 45 |

*Source:* Arthur J. Barker, *Dunkirk: The Great Escape* (London: Dent, 1977), p. 235.

The preliminary evacuation began just before 7 p.m. on Sunday, 26 May, when personnel carriers were already loading at Dunkirk as part of the earlier plan to take out non-combatants. By midnight on Sunday almost 28,000 had been landed at Dover – numbers excluded from the official totals for Dynamo (as the evacuation was called), which only went into formal operation on the Monday. Already by that Monday most of the port of Dunkirk had been destroyed, so that less than 8,000 men were evacuated that day: thus the focus moved to trying to evacuate men from the beaches, lifeboats being used to transfer them from the beach to the sea ferries. This was very slow and the results, as table 3.1 shows, were disappointing. It was already becoming clear just how valuable little boats could be: from the Monday evening onwards their owners were being contacted, and some small craft actually began their movement down the Thames. Through various improvisations, the numbers lifted from Dunkirk harbour were greatly increased, though the crossing became even more hazardous as the Admiralty felt it could no longer leave any of its modern destroyers at risk. On Thursday, 30 May the totals embarked from the beaches (basically Malo-les-Bains, Bray Dunes, and La Panne) exceeded those embarked from Dunkirk harbour. For actual transfer across the Channel, the requisitioned sea ferries and other larger ships carried the largest numbers; but the little ships were already playing their part in transferring men from the beaches to the bigger ships and also, in what often gets forgotten, bringing desperately-needed food and water to the waiting men.

Still, the main flotilla of little ships, setting out from Ramsgate, and making up a continuous line of ships stretching for over five miles, did not depart until 1 p.m. on Friday, 31 May. As a result of French expressions of resentment, Admiralty instructions now explicitly gave equal priority to the evacuation of French troops and 31 May was the day on which the largest number of soldiers were saved. Acting under orders, Lord Gort was among those evacuated that Friday evening, his command being passed to General Alexander. Saturday, 1 June was also a good day with respect to numbers, but three of the remaining older destroyers were sunk, and the aerial attack became devastatingly intense. After 3 a.m. on Sunday, 2 June daylight sailings from the beaches were suspended. Numbers consequently dropped, but by 11.30 p.m. on Monday, 3 June all British forces had been evacuated; with the perimeter defences crumbling, evacuation of French soldiers continued into the night, up until the departure of the destroyer Shikari at 3.40 a.m. Some exhausted French soldiers preferred to remain behind.

The scope for individual initiative was small; practically all craft were under the control of the Navy, though very many were crewed by civilians, who often found themselves setting out to the discouraging sight of battered craft full of seriously wounded men coming in to dock. Large numbers of those involved were merchant seamen. One little story neatly encapsulates the relationship between a seasoned merchant seaman (Captain Bennett) and a young officer on a motor torpedo boat wearing a peaked cap, vivid striped pyjamas and carrying a megaphone:

> After asking the names of our two ships, he ordered us to the Owers Lightship until sunrise. This may have been fair enough but he added that gauche remark 'Don't you know there is a war on?' Bennett, who was leaning on his port bridge rail, removed his pipe from his mouth, picked up a megaphone and shouted 'You won't win it in your fucking pyjamas, will you?'

Even for professionals conditions were practically unbearable:

> Men could go on for just so long, and then they reached a point where nature's defence mechanisms came into play . . . engine-room staff, deafened by the peels of fearful thuds caused by exploding bombs compressing the water against the sides of the hull, were no longer able to cope with signals from the bridge; men were badly scalded when steam pipes ruptured; stokers with loaded shovels poised in front of an open furnace, were pitched forward and burned when a ship bucked and gyrated during an air attack . . . The sight of so many men blown to pieces or drowning, and of mutilated corpses and horrific wounds, was too much for them.[16]

On land, a massive job of improvisation and round-the-clock hard labour produced sandwiches and tea, served out of tin cans which had to be used over and over again, for the returning troops, who were given 48 hours' leave, and ordered to return to their units. The BEF had lost all of its transport and much of its weaponry – though not all, rifles being in frequent use in attempts to bring down attacking German aircraft. Two hundred thousand men, the 'whole root and core and brain of the British army', in Churchill's words, had been saved. For the time being there was nowhere for Britain to fight on land, so it is possible that even had these men been lost, the war might have continued. But that seems unlikely: the blow to morale would have been even greater than the loss of the men. So the importance of Dunkirk was that it meant defeat had been averted; and a potential morale-buster became a powerful morale-booster. More, the nightmare of fighting on another Western Front had been banished. It is true that the war was only won with the German invasion of Russia, and the entry of America, provider of almost unlimited resources. But without Dunkirk there would probably have been no war for America to enter.

Cut off from Dunkirk, about 140,000 British troops, including the 51st Highland Division and the 1st Armoured Division, were left behind in France. The 51st was forced to surrender, but other British (and also Polish) troops managed to escape from Cherbourg and other French ports. All in all, in the Battle of France 11,000 British were killed, 14,000 wounded, with 41,000 missing or prisoners of war. On 16 June the British War Cabinet put forward to Reynaud's government a plan for an indissoluble union between the two countries; but it failed to win the acceptance of his colleagues. Reynaud resigned, being succeeded by Pétain. The French government was now at Bordeaux.

Evacuated Belgian and Dutch soldiers, for the time being, remained in Britain. But the French troops were transported first to Bournemouth, and then on to Plymouth, from whence they were shipped back to France, arriving just in time for the French capitulation on 22 June. Northern and western France was occupied by the Germans; the spa town of Vichy, in the south-west, became the capital of what was nominally unoccupied France. Dunkirk is sometimes presented as the culmination of a process whereby the British betrayed the French. It is true that as the retreat began, the British Government refused to station British aircraft in France and, in retreating towards Dunkirk, deliberately misled the French as to their intentions; when in the last desperate days Churchill made his offer of union with France, this could be seen as merely a device for getting his hands on the French navy. But the French were themselves appallingly badly prepared for war, and, in some quarters, highly uncertain as to how far it was worth trying to resist Hitler. The French Commander-in-Chief, Gamelin, was taken by surprise; his replacement, Weygand, somewhat out of touch with reality. Prime Minister Daladier was inclined to defeatism; his replacement, Reynaud, was determined, but Reynaud gave way to Pétain, who was ready to come to an accommodation with Hitler. For sure, Baldwin and Chamberlain had failed to forge a strong alliance with France, and should be blamed for that. But previous turpitude cannot sully Dunkirk. After all, 123,195 French troops were evacuated; only, of course, to be thrown away almost immediately.

A few civilians had been in the front line at Dunkirk. For a brief period

Britain's war was to be fought by the airmen of the RAF in the Battle of Britain, Hitler's attempt to secure air supremacy as a prelude to invasion. Then civilians, particularly in London, but also in most of the major cities, came into the front line as Hitler concentrated on bombing raids designed to destroy morale on the home front.

There was another offer from Hitler to discuss peace terms. The idea that Britain should have made a deal with Hitler, held on to her Empire and left the Germans and the Russians to slog it out, has had its supporters from time to time, and most recently from the ultra-conservative historian John Charmley.[17] Whether a deal could have been done with Hitler which was not, in the long term if not the short, total surrender is open to considerable doubt. Of course, Britain was greatly impoverished by the war, but any idea that she could somehow have held on to the Empire is nonsense. In the upshot, peaceful coexistence with the Soviet Union proved possible for almost fifty years until, in fact, the Soviet regime itself collapsed.

A famous cartoon by left-winger David Low represented a defiant, fist-brandishing Britain on the cliffs of Dover, as 'Alone', protected only by the Channel. Actually, Britain did have the white Dominions, who could not, however, do much to prevent invasion, though there were Dominions recruits in the RAF. Parachutists, aiming to capture key points, were seen as the most immediate danger. That threat, and the threat of seaborne invasion could be (and was) intensified by the existence of Nazi sympathizers and fifth columnists. Already, Norway had a government under the Nazi collaborator Vidkun Quisling, whose name then entered the English language (the British had finally captured Narvik on 28 May, but it was then evacuated almost immediately). On 10 May the order was issued that all male enemy aliens living in coastal areas liable to invasion were to be interned, and on 16 May this was extended to all male enemy aliens. Plans for recruiting a local part-time militia to counteract parachute troops were already being developed: on 14 May, War Secretary Anthony Eden broadcast an appeal for men between 17 and 65 to join the Local Defence Volunteers (LDV). The same day that the Emergency Powers Act was passed (22 May) it was decided to intern all suspected fascist sympathizers, including Sir Oswald Mosley. In mid-June the complete round-up of aliens was carried out, many Jewish refugees and other anti-Nazis being caught in the trawl. In all the circumstances of the time, that was probably understandable.[18]

Another immediate worry was that of the naval forces of defeated France being taken over by the Germans, who already, from 10 June, had Italy as a fellow belligerent. Churchill ordered Admiral Sir James Somerville, Commander of the British Fleet at Gibraltar, to issue an ultimatum to the French Naval Commander at the North African base of Oran to put his ships under British control or despatch them to a neutral port. The ultimatum being rejected, the French fleet was bombarded (3 July) and more than 1,200 French sailors killed. This was a horrible and tragic manifestation of total war in its purely military dimension. General de Gaulle, on 18 June, had broadcast an appeal from London for Frenchmen to continue to serve under his leadership. Oran, though no doubt preferable to the fleet falling into German hands, was not helpful to this cause.

At the beginning of July the German armed forces started reorganizing for an invasion of Britain. Hitler then did two things: he made a final offer of peace; and on 16 July he issued the directive that, if necessary, the invasion of Britain, Operation Sea Lion, would take place not earlier than mid-August. In Britain, the Minister of Aircraft Production, Beaverbrook, acted energetically to increase Britain's air strength: the total number of Spitfires and Hurricanes, down to 331 after Dunkirk, rose to 620; fighter aircraft in reserve rose from 36 to 289. Destroyers were diverted from convoy duties to Channel patrols. The Navy organized forces to attack any troop transporters attempting to cross the North Sea or the Channel, and sowed mines on invasion paths. Production of tanks was rapidly increased (only 25 of the 700 sent to France had been saved), and Sir Alan Brooke organized mobile defence forces designed to attack invaders in strength at any point of landing. Signposts were removed and objects were placed in open fields which might otherwise be used as landing grounds.

### *The Battle of Britain, the Blitz and the Battle of the Atlantic*

The German air offensive began on 12 August. What the Germans most needed to do was to destroy command posts, radar stations, airfields and any aircraft on them, and also, obviously, the pilots and planes of RAF Fighter Command mounting the defence in the skies above the south of England. These pilots amounted to not much over 1,000, men who adopted the distinctive, casual, upper-class manner of the RAF, but who were, in fact, drawn from all social classes; against them they had almost double that number. Their heroism and dedication fully merited Churchill's encomium pronounced in the House of Commons on 20 August: 'Never in the field of human conflict was so much owed by so many to so few.' Their lives were impossible: flying as many as half-a-dozen sorties a day, they often had to go back into the skies totally exhausted or even wounded. A freshly trained squadron of men could be shattered after ten days' active service. Of course, 'the few' were dependent on their ground crews, the women of the WAAF (Women's Auxiliary Air Force), the civilian repair units and the workers in the aircraft factories. Yet, as British resources approached breaking point, defeat might have come during the following two weeks. Meantime, Bomber Command had been doing what it was always intended to do, carrying out bombing attacks on what were supposed to be military targets, particularly synthetic oil plants, in German cities. Some German bombs did fall in London (an unintended by-product of the raids on airfields), and it was decided that Bomber Command should extend its raids to Berlin. This provoked Hitler into making the deliberate decision to switch his attacks away from the airfields and onto Britain's cities. Dreadful for civilians, but a welcome release from pressure on Britain's air defences.

Liverpool was bombed on the nights of 28, 29, 30 and 31 August, with serious fires being started in its commercial centre on the last night. At 5 o'clock on the afternoon of Saturday, 7 September, a glorious summer day, the deliberate mass attack on the East End of London began. Civilians were now right in the middle of the war. The bombs poured down on the dock areas of West Ham and Bermondsey, and adjoining Poplar, Shoreditch, Whitechapel and Stepney. Firemen, and the various auxiliary and voluntary services, fought untiringly, but the authorities simply were not prepared for anything like this. Firemen were filthy, weary, red-eyed, choked and, sometimes, trapped and burnt to death. ARP (air-raid precaution) workers struggled to clear away rubble and bring out the dazed and half-suffocated occupants buried beneath. WVS (Women's Voluntary Service) workers sought to get families away from the stricken streets. Thousands of homes were destroyed; 430 civilians were killed and 1,600 were seriously injured. The bombers returned at 8 o'clock on the Sunday evening; another 400 civilians were killed.

Just as London was beginning in October to adapt to its front-line situation, the air attacks on the provinces expanded and intensified. There was a heavy raid on Birmingham on 25 October, but then on 14 November a new phase began with the total destruction of the whole of the centre of Coventry. Meantime the raids on London, broadening out to cover the West End and the suburbs, as well as the East End, continued for seventy-six consecutive nights, save for 2 November when bad weather kept the raiders at bay. There were daytime raids as well, which were dangerous and disruptive, but it was the night raids which brought terror and devastation. On 29 December came the famous attack on the City of London, when the Thames was at low ebb so that there was a great shortage of water, and when St Paul's itself somehow managed to stand unscathed among the flames all around it. Some of the worst disasters were caused by bombs falling on crowded tube stations. The heaviest raids of all, both on London and on other great centres of population, took place throughout the spring of 1941 – the West Midlands, including Coventry again, suffered raids on 8, 9 and 10 April, and Merseyside had a terrible eight nights, its 'May week', at the beginning of that month. In March 1941 it was the turn of Clydeside: almost every house in the ship-building town of Clydebank was damaged. Northern Ireland (see plate 7) took its share on the nights of 7 and 15 April, and 4 and 5 May: 100,000 people were rendered temporarily homeless as more than half of the city's houses were damaged; 1,100 people were killed. In Wales, Cardiff was attacked on 2 January (death toll 165), while the town centre of Swansea was destroyed in the fire-bomb raids of 19–21 February. The death toll here was 387; throughout 1941, 985 Welsh civilians were killed.

So different parts of the United Kingdom went through similar experiences; and different classes too. But although there is considerable evidence of upper- and middle-class praise for the stoicism and bravery of working-class families, there is very little hard evidence of genuine mixing of the social classes. On the whole, middle-class observers were horrified by the squalor they saw in the early days of families resorting for shelter to the tube stations, and in the large public shelters, some of which, indeed, acquired an unpleasant reputation for their sordid, insanitary state. Many of the very rich continued to lead very segregated existences. The first shelter census of November 1940 showed that, of the 40 per cent who resorted to shelters, 27 per cent used their own domestic shelters and that only 9 per cent used public shelters; 4 per cent resorted to the tubes. Originally the main public shelters provided were surface brick build-

**Plate 7** World War Two: Bomb damage in Belfast. Courtesy of Imperial War Museum

ings which were quite spectacularly useless and dangerous. For private householders the corrugated-iron Anderson shelter was available, but it was only of use for those who had gardens. Although liable to flooding, it was remarkably effective. Then the Morrison shelter, suitable for putting inside working-class homes, was developed.

As opinion polls showed, a substantial majority of the British people were in favour of reprisal raids being carried out on the Germans. In fact the authorities preferred the self-image wherein the British were portrayed as stoically heroic and solidly good-humoured. A series of Pathe newsreel post-Blitz interviews in which the popular will comes through strongly as in favour of immediate and massive reprisals – 'wicked old bugger like 'e is', says one interviewee of Hitler – were never shown, since they were too much at odds with the preferred image. The first evacuation in September 1939 had faded out as bombing raids failed to materialize. The onset of the Blitz reactivated the evacuation movement. Whether evacuation is to be seen as a social experiment which in the long run had beneficial consequences, or whether it is to be seen as a profoundly disturbing experience for the children involved, is still a matter of controversy.[19] Altogether, at the height of the second government scheme, 1,340,000 people were evacuated. By 1942 almost half of these had drifted home again;

the worst of the Blitz was over, though, as we shall see, there were still to be many terrifying raids. Up until the end of 1942, war deaths among civilians were considerably higher than those among the armed forces.

It was not immediately apparent that by his switch in strategy Hitler was losing the chance of mounting his invasion. The alarm, the ringing of church bells, was actually given on the night of 7 September. But in fact, by 15 September, Hitler had decided to postpone Sea Lion indefinitely. Fears of invasion revived in 1941, and the leaflet *Beating the Invader* was issued on 13 March; by August, however, the government had recognized that there was now little likelihood of an invasion actually taking place.

What was looming over the country's survival was what Churchill called the Battle of the Atlantic. In the first nine months of the war, British, Allied and neutral shipping losses had averaged less than 100,000 tonnes per month, but from June 1940 onwards they were running at 250,000. To the submarine menace had been added that of air attack, now that Hitler had bases in both Norway and western France. Attack from the sea seemed a much lesser threat. Then the newly completed battleship *Bismarck* slipped through Norwegian waters and out into the North Atlantic, where it sank the state-of-the-art battle-cruiser *Hood*. The pursuit of the elusive *Bismarck* did indeed make an exciting story, finally ending off the West Coast of France when a naval task force backed by aircraft combined in launching torpedoes, gunfire, and bombs. Destroyers diverted to duties in the Channel were returned to the Atlantic, and American technology helped further: convoys began to be supplied with catapult fighter aircraft and sometimes auxiliary aircraft carriers. But the battle to keep British supply lines open took its toll of another class of civilians: sailors in the Merchant Navy, whose losses amounted to 35,000. In 1941 rationing was extended, and weekly entitlements to such basics as meat, cheese, bacon, and fats were reduced. Household management became still more harassing, and required ever greater ingenuity.

## *North Africa, the Far East, Italy*

The main battlefields for British troops were to be in North Africa, Italy, and, in the last year of war, northern France; and then through the Low Countries and into western Germany. Some, particularly cursed by fate, had to engage with the Japanese in the Far East. Two circumstances made North Africa a possible terrain upon which British troops could continue to fight: Italian entry into the war on 10 June 1940; and the existence of territories, particularly Algeria, belonging to Britain's now defeated ally, France. There were also engagements in the eastern Mediterranean and the Balkans. Basically Mussolini intended to use the cover of German victories to expand from the territories he had conquered before the war, in Africa, and Albania in the Balkans. Then the ill-equipped Italian forces got into trouble, causing Hitler to feel that, to uphold the Axis, he must intervene. The Italians invaded Greece on 28 October 1940; in response to the Greek appeal for help Britain sent troops and aircraft to Crete. Meantime, the Italians were bundled back into Albania with heavy losses. Hitler therefore prepared to attack Greece from his bases in southern Romania. Britain, in turn, felt bound to respond to a further Greek appeal and send an expeditionary corps to the Greek mainland. The Germans invaded both Yugoslavia and Greece. At the end of April 1941 the small British force had to be evacuated from the Greek mainland to Crete and to Egypt. In Africa the Italians over-ran British Somaliland and began to move against Egypt. But in December slightly more than two divisions of troops under General Wavell crushed an Italian army of seven divisions, driving the Italians out of Egypt and occupying the whole of Cyrenaica, the eastern province of the Italian colony of Libya. The Germans both landed in Libya and, on 20 May, began a devastating attack on Crete, forcing a humiliating British surrender and retreat. Fearing a German advance into Syria, controlled by the Vichy French, the War Cabinet instructed Wavell to make a pre-emptive strike in that country. The operation was unsuccessful, as was a new offensive in the Western Desert launched on 15 June. Wavell, British Commander in the Middle East, was sacked, and replaced by Auchinleck.[20]

The British had been thrown out of the Balkans and the Middle East, but retained a reasonable position in North Africa, provided the island of Malta remained a viable part of their communications system. Hitler was not greatly interested in the Balkans or North Africa: on 22 June he began what had always been a major element in his grand plan, Operation Barbarossa, the invasion of Russia. In April, Churchill had sent Stalin a personal message warning him that this was likely to happen, but Stalin made few real preparations, with the result that the German armies made massive advances in the first days of their invasion. As events unfolded in ways no one expected, the pressure eased on Britain, in particular with a sharp diminution in bombing raids; but for the moment there was a new invasion scare, the fear being that after knocking Russia out, Hitler would be able to turn all his forces against Britain. Russian losses were to be enormous (and deeply coloured Soviet foreign policy after 1945); but Hitler's invasion of Russia and the immense resistance he encountered was one of the two sets of epochal events which ensured his own defeat.

The other was the Japanese attack, on 7 December 1941, on the American Pacific Fleet at Pearl Harbor, which destroyed four battleships and crippled two others, and the events which ensued. On 11 December Germany and Italy followed up this Japanese act of war by themselves declaring war on the United States. At the time, things did not look good. The Japanese also invaded British Malaya, and soon were to run up a list of stunning conquests in the Far East.

The Japanese had begun their incursion upon the North of Malaya, the rubber-rich British colony, a few hours before their raid on Pearl Harbor. Within the next 24 hours, Japanese forces in Thailand invaded Burma. Well established on the Chinese mainland itself, they also menaced Hong Kong. In its confusion and incompetence, British Imperial Rule in these countries suggests comparisons with the Tsarist regime at the time of the First World War. The Japanese were numerically inferior to the mainly Indian and Australian forces in Malaya. Singapore, the island at the tip of Malaya, was among the Empire's most vital and most heavily defended naval bases – save that the defences all faced the sea. Making the same mistake that the French had made with respect to the Ardennes, the British failed to see that tanks and mobile artillery would be able to break through the forests on mainland Malaya. Churchill did not even realize that there were no defensive works north of Singapore; he left Malaya itself with less than a third of the aircraft the Chiefs of Staff determined were needed. Hong Kong fell on Christmas Day, 1941. All of Malaya was conquered by the end of January. Singapore surrendered on 15 February. By the end of April the British had been expelled from Burma – save for the thousands of prisoners of war, who, as also in Malaya and Singapore, fell into Japanese hands. Wherever there were Chinese, the Japanese systematically exterminated them. British prisoners, as is well known, were held under conditions of the most appalling brutality and deprivation.

Singapore, Churchill said, was 'the worst disaster and largest capitulation in British history'. There were other setbacks. As the British, with their allies the Americans, were planning to go back onto the offensive in North Africa, the German General Rommel launched an attack of his own on 26 May. On 20 June he attacked the Port of Tobruk and captured it within a day. Churchill declared this a disgrace second only to the loss of Singapore. For many in Britain there had been a greater humiliation earlier in the year when the German battle-cruisers *Scharnhorst* and *Gneisenau* and the cruiser *Prinz Eugen* managed to dodge their way through the English Channel from Brest back to German waters. In June the convoy PQ17, on the Arctic supply route to Russia, lost 23 of its 34 merchant ships to German torpedoes. These reverses touched off two political crises in Britain. Following a three-day confidence debate at the end of January, with only one ILP member (and two tellers) dividing against the government, a Ministry of Production was established under the Conservative businessman Oliver Lyttleton to coordinate all supply matters; Sir Stafford Cripps, who had been expelled from the Labour party in 1939 for supporting the Popular Front, replaced the incompetent Arthur Greenwood in the Cabinet; another Labour man, Hugh Dalton, was promoted to the Board of Trade; and civil servant Sir James Grigg became War Secretary. The second crisis took place at the end of June and beginning of July. On 25 June, four days after the fall of Tobruk, back-benchers of all parties signed a motion expressing 'no confidence in the central direction of the war'. That very day a by-election taking place in the Conservative seat of Maldon in Essex was lost to *Daily Express* journalist Tom Driberg, standing as an Independent. The dissidents, however, made a poor job of their attack, with Ernest Bevin contemptuously rejecting a suggestion that he might run as an alternative Prime Minister, and the former Welsh coal miner and Labour back-bencher Aneurin Bevan making a bitterly idiosyncratic speech. The government won by 475 to 25.[21]

With the Japanese having dragged the Americans into the war, Churchill had gone to Washington on 22 December 1941. While control of strategy remained with the President of the United States and, supported by his War Cabinet, the Prime Minister of Great Britain, it was agreed that advice was to be supplied by a unique new body called the Combined Chiefs of Staff, sitting in Washington (the British Chiefs, in practice, often being represented by deputies). In addition, the policy began to be developed of appointing a Supreme Commander for each particular theatre of war, with staffs drawn from the national forces involved. Reluctantly the Americans agreed to Operation Torch, the invasion of French North Africa: Supreme Command was placed in the hands of the American General Dwight D. Eisenhower. In Britain from July to September the news was mainly of the Russians' desperate defence of Stalingrad. By the beginning of February a Russian counter-offensive resulted in the complete destruction of the German army, with a loss of a quarter of a million men.[22] Also, before Torch, it was important that the British reverse their defeat in Egypt. Showing a willingness to sack generals which had evaded Lloyd George, Churchill replaced Auchinleck with General Sir Harold Alexander, who was thought to have conducted a skilful retreat from Burma; the new Army Commander was to be General W. H. E. Gott, but since his plane was shot down, that role fell to the General Montgomery we last met, with the BEF, in France. In good time for the set-piece battle of El Alamein on 23 October, Montgomery's army received the bonus from President Roosevelt of 300 Sherman tanks and 100 self-propelled guns. Montgomery prepared meticulously, devising a brilliantly elaborate deception plan, and also making himself, and his preparations, known throughout his army: when battle commenced, the Germans and Italians, taken completely by surprise, were outnumbered by almost two to one in practically every department.

In addition, Montgomery had highly superior intelligence about enemy dispositions, plans, problems – increasingly the Allies' most effective secret weapon. To encode and decode their messages the Germans, since the 1920s, had used the 'Enigma' machine, constantly changing the 'key' and adding new complexities. The Poles, aided by the French, had obtained a machine shortly before the war, and made it available to the British. At Bletchley Park (in what is now Milton Keynes) intelligence officers and cryptographers (mainly academics) steadily built up a mastery in decoding some of the most vital German messages, making a small contribution to the Battle of Britain, and a large one to the winning of the Battle of the Atlantic by the end of 1942; and also to the Battle of El Alamein. Individual Americans had already served bravely in the RAF; El Alamein was the first battle in which complete formations of American fighters and heavy and medium bombers took part. Victory was won within a week, though with Rommel managing to retreat with most of his army intact.

Now, on 8 November, the landings in French North Africa could begin. By the middle of November the whole territory had been conquered, save for Tunisia, where Rommel's army and the Italians had now ensconced themselves. At the Lord Mayor's Banquet on 11 November, Churchill offered two of his most glittering sentences. Triumphantly: 'The bright gleam of victory has caught the helmets of our soldiers and warmed and cheered all our hearts.' Warningly (particularly towards the Americans): 'I have not become the King's First Minister in order to preside over the liquidation of the British Empire.'

Hitler's response to French surrender in North Africa was to order the occupation of the whole of France. The Vichy Admiral, Darlan, who happened to be in North Africa at the time, ordered the French naval forces at Toulon to make their escape to North Africa: a few submarines did so, the remaining ships being scuttled. Darlan was shortly assassinated. Churchill and Roosevelt met at Casablanca in January, where the Americans reluctantly agreed that the time was not yet ripe for opening a second front in France, and that priority should be given to the capture of Sicily; so that there could be no German claims, as after 1918, of a 'stab in the back', 'unconditional surrender' was declared the aim of the Allies. After unexpected difficulties, the British Eighth Army forced the Germans and the Italians onto the defensive at the Battle of Mareth in late March, and on 12 and 13 May secured their surrender, yielding a quarter of a million prisoners, more than half of them German. From the start of operations in North Africa, civilian casualties, of course, were very rapidly outstripped by military ones.

The Allies landed on Sicily on 10 July 1943, and made such good progress that Eisenhower agreed to the early invasion of the Italian mainland (something Churchill was very keen on, whereas the Americans had always wished to proceed with 'Overlord', the invasion of northern France, as quickly as possible). Shortly after landing, a British intelligence officer borrowed a motor bike: 'I rode north in the gathering light, with a tremendous feeling of exhilaration: we were out of Africa, and back in Europe!'[23] Then, what should have been good news, wasn't really from the immediate military point of view. On 25 July the Italian King dismissed Mussolini, replacing him with Marshal Badoglio, whose government was prepared to seek an armistice. While the Allies planned landings for early September, the new Italian government began armistice negotiations on 15 August. Terms were signed on 3 September, but kept secret from fear of provoking a German reaction. But the Germans were already primed for an Italian collapse, so the Allies met with heavy resistance. Movement up through Italy was painful and bloody.

In November, Stalin, terrified of flying, agreed to travel as far as Teheran, capital of Persia, to have the first of the 'Big Three' meetings with Churchill and Roosevelt. The Russian dictator supported the Americans in their wish to accelerate the accumulation of forces and supplies in Britain in readiness for Overlord. With his own supplies being curtailed, Alexander tried to unclog the Italian campaign by effecting a sea landing at Anzio, south of Rome. Instead of moving rapidly ahead from his largely unopposed landing, the American General Mark Clark dug in, waiting for the Germans.

Battle conditions in the Second World War were every bit as terrible as those in the First. Inland from Anzio, on the route to Rome, was an area of deep, muddy ravines which became known to the Allies as the Gullies. The area was ringed by German tanks and artillery, and sown with anti-personnel devices, including the deadly miniature *schuh* mine:

> isolated by day and erratically supplied by night, soaked to the skin and stupefied by exhaustion and bombardment, surrounded by new and old corpses yet persistently cheerful, the Guardsmen dug trenches and manned them until they were blown in and then dug new ones, beat off attacks, changed their positions, launched local attacks, stalked snipers, broke up patrols, evacuated the wounded, buried the dead and carried supplies.[24]

Alexander's main thrust was held up at the Monte Cassino Monastery. Although this beautiful, historic, religious house was destroyed by heavy Allied bombing on 15 February, the Germans' ability to hold this natural defensive position was not materially affected. Only at the end of May 1944 were Alexander's troops able to go on the offensive again. Rome was liberated on 4 June. With troops being switched from Italy to take part in the Normandy landings, further progress was extremely slow, with much costly fighting to come. The Germans installed Mussolini as a puppet dictator in the so-called Republic of Salò in Northern Italy. The Italian Partisans fought courageously on the Allied side. On 28 April 1945 they captured Mussolini: he was shot, and hung upside down with his mistress outside a petrol station. A day later, the Germans in Italy unconditionally surrendered, this to take effect on 2 May.

### *The bombing of Germany*

One theatre of war – the one which has aroused the most intense controversy – was especially shattering for combatants. Air warfare was the site of the most concentrated application of rapidly changing technology. New and more sophisticated models were coming into service every few months, flying faster, higher, capable of longer ranges, and of carrying heavier payloads, imposing ever heavier demands and putting airmen at greater risk for longer periods of time. In both fighters (as in the Battle of Britain) and bombers, constant vigilance was required in a confined space, affected by noise, vibration, gravitational forces and the vagaries of the weather. Classic, one-to-one dog fights were, in reality, infrequent. As a fighter pilot, you had to get the enemy by surprise, but he was just as likely to get you. Reactions had to be instantaneous. Getting into an effective firing zone was extremely difficult: the pilot could at once be subjected to several times the force of gravity.[25]

It had always been assumed that bombing raids would be a key part of the war. In the aftermath of Dunkirk, such raids seemed the only way of keeping the war going and of demonstrating, in particular to British civilians and to the Americans, the British will to fight. As it steadily became clear that accurate bombing simply was not possible, rationalizations emerged for the destruction wrought on civilians: 'whilst we should adhere to the rule that our objectives should be military targets,' the War Cabinet minuted in early 1941, 'at the same time the civilian population around the target areas must be made to feel the weight of the war'; Bomber Command was instructed to start 'harassing the enemy's main industrial towns and communications'.[26] As it became clear that only from one-tenth to one-third of bombers got within five miles of their official targets, the policy widened further. In February 1942 Sir Archibald Sinclair, the Air Minister, declared that the 'primary object' should be 'the morale of the enemy civilian population and in particular of the industrial workers'. A series of massive raids on German towns was organized by Air Chief Marshal Sir Arthur Harris of Bomber Command, culminating in the thousand-bomber raid on Cologne in May 1942.

A principal decision at the Casablanca conference in January 1943 was that, in a cosmic new version of the stereotyped strategy of the First World War, British and American bombers together should, as it were, 'soften up' Germany in the months before the Overlord invasion. Using an elite 'pathfinder' force to identify targets, Harris intensified his policy of heavy area bombing of German industrial towns by night. There were also rare, and extremely difficult, precision attacks on, for example, the Moehne and Eder dams in May 1943. The American Eighth Air Force, based in England, followed the perhaps more 'moral' policy of daytime attacks on selected industrial targets; until long-range fighter cover was provided, these produced disastrously high losses. Everybody loves a hate figure. It has been easy to pillory 'Bomber Harris' as solely responsible for the horrendous destruction of German cities and the civilians in them. In fact, responsibility has to be shared with Churchill himself, his scientific adviser Lord Cherwell, Air Chief Marshal Sir Charles Portal, Chief of the Air Staff, and, indeed, the War Cabinet and responsible ministers. Bishop Bell of Chichester raised the question in the House of Lords, calling for bombing to be limited to purely military targets. On behalf of the government, Lord Cranborne, replied:

> The great centres of administration, of production, and of communication are themselves targets in a total war. You cannot escape that fact . . . It may well be . . . that those great German war industries can only be paralysed by bringing the whole life of the cities in which they are situated to a standstill, making it quite impossible for the workmen to carry on their work.[27]

Criticisms from the military chiefs were that air power could have been much more effectively deployed assisting the navy in defending shipping, and giving support in the various land theatres. The waste of resources and of men is certainly a charge which can be levied against Churchill; but, in a total war, the reasons for carrying out bombing raids were not altogether negligible. In July and August 1943 the most awful raids so far took place on Hamburg, when devastating fires and firestorms were set off:

> The scenes of terror which took place in the firestorm area are indescribable. Children were torn away from their parents hands by the force of the hurricane and whirled into the fire. People who thought they had escaped fell down, overcome by the devouring force of the heat and died in an instant.[28]

Apart from the not overly impressive raids of 1940 and 1941, Bomber Command between 1942 and 1945 flew more than 300,000 operational sorties, with about 8,000 aircraft being lost, and a further 1,500 being written off because of battle damage. Over the entire war, practically half of the air crew who served in Bomber Command (this is the truly horrifying statistic) were killed – 56,000 out of 125,000, with 8,400 injured and 11,000 missing or taken prisoner.

### *DOMESTIC POLICIES*

If there had to be a war, Churchill was the best person to run it. He was indomitable, inventive, and the Victorian cadences of his speeches, usually delivered first in the House of Commons, then repeated on radio, were exactly framed to bring the best out of a people proud of their traditional ways. Many of the changes which came about within Britain were against Churchill's volition, brought about by Labour ministers, or by newly-recruited, or newly-promoted, civil servants and non-party ministers, but above all by the ineluctable pressures of war. Attlee, designated Deputy Prime Minister in February 1942, but designated by Dr Paul Addison 'no heavyweight', was notably uninfluential; but Ernest Bevin and Herbert Morrison, bound together in a bond of mutual hatred, were important figures in the cause of social reform; also important were Sir John Anderson, Chairman of the Reconstruction Committee in 1942, and Lord Woolton, Minister of Reconstruction from November 1943.[29] The presence of its politicians as equal partners in the government brought great prestige to Labour. Within the working class, irritation and war weariness were clearly shown in the growth in the number of days lost due to strikes, which rose throughout 1942, 1943 and 1944, dropping slightly in 1945, when it was still double what it had been in 1939. But this militancy also reflected the consciousness of the working class of its strong bargaining position: government and indeed employers preferred to concede higher wages, rather than risk a serious disruption of the national war effort, or to the high profits to be made in the war industries.

It was because of direct pressure from the official TUC that an inter-departmental committee of civil servants under the Chairmanship of Sir William Beveridge was appointed to 'undertake . . . a survey of the existing national schemes of social insurance and allied services . . . and to make recommendations'. Beginning life as a journalist, Beveridge had been associated as a civil servant with the Edwardian Social Insurance reforms; he had been a top civil servant in the First World War, an academic administrator in the inter-war years and Chairman of a number of important committees. Yet his new commission did not immediately please him (he was a very unpopular man, and it is probable the government wished to side-track him away from other work more obviously central to the war effort); as he wrote to his sister on 29 July 1941: 'I'm chairman also of a Reconstruction Committee on the Social Services: but I'm not doing much about that while I can do anything about the war.'[30] It was fortunate that the Secretary to the Committee, D. M. Chester, was a temporary wartime civil servant from a working-class background who had been a lecturer in Public Administration at Manchester University.

Strictly speaking, the deliberations of the Beveridge Committee should have been mainly confined to the technical aspects of social insurance. But all aspects of social policy were now a matter of general debate. Shortly after the members of the Beveridge Committee were appointed, the Minister of Health, Ernest Brown, referred in the House of Commons (9 October 1941) to future health policy:

> The question of post-war hospital policy and reorganisation, more particularly in relation to the Emergency Hospital Scheme has for some time been engaging the attention of the government . . . It is the objective of the government as soon as may be after the war to ensure that by means of a comprehensive hospital service appropriate treatment shall be readily available to every person in need of it . . .

The bulk of the report was indeed concerned with the 'Social Insurance and Allied Services' of the terms of reference. The major innovations were that the insurance scheme should apply to all classes in society, cover all possible contingencies, and provide uniform benefits which would guarantee minimum subsistence; as a good Liberal, Beveridge believed that it should be left to the individual to make additional provision through private insurance. What transformed the report into a truly historic document was the insistence that, 'Organisation of social insurance should be treated as one part only of a comprehensive policy of social progress.' Simultaneously, the report declared that there must be attacks on ill health, inadequate education, bad housing and unemployment. The successful implementation of his social security proposals, Beveridge decreed, depended on three assumptions: the institution of children's allowances, a comprehensive health service, and 'maintenance of employment, that is to say avoidance of mass unemployment'.

Churchill was unenthusiastic about the Beveridge Report: it was not published until 2 December 1942, and not debated in parliament until 16 February 1943. In that debate two government spokesmen, Sir Kingsley Wood and Oliver Lyttleton (both Conservatives), were so feeble and hesitant in their support of the report that they aroused the justifiable suspicion that the government had no serious intention of implementing it. From the records we can see the enormous efforts which were made by the Labour party, particularly acting through its General Secretary G. S. Middleton, by Attlee who drafted a most pungent memorandum on the subject to Churchill, and by D. N. Chester to ensure that the Beveridge Report would indeed be implemented.[31] In fact, in 1943 and 1944 the government issued a series of White Papers which committed it to the main lines of the Beveridge proposals, and to a general policy of social planning and reform.

Two other issues illustrate the divide over social reform which existed among Britain's rulers, and the manner in which the various pressures engendered or strengthened by the war gave at least a qualified victory to the reformers. The first issue was that of Town and Country Planning, brought up originally by the publication in 1940 of the report of the Barlow Commission, then more forcibly by the destruction wrought by bomb attacks. As sequels to the Barlow Report two further committees were appointed to investigate specific aspects of planning: a Committee under Mr Justice Uthwatt on 'payment of compensation and recovery of betterment in respect to public control of the use of the land', and one under Lord Justice Scott on 'land utilisation in rural areas'. Reporting in 1942, the Uthwatt Committee, while dismissing land nationalization as impractical, recommended that the state, on payment of fair compensation, should be vested with the development rights in all lands outside built-up areas, and that local planning authorities should have the power of compulsory purchase over properties in built-up areas needing redevelopment. The most important single contribution of the Scott Report, issued in August 1942, was its adoption and definition of an idea originated by Sir Raymond Unwin and developed experimentally in the 1930s, the 'Green Belt', a ring of open land for agricultural and recreational use to be preserved around the major conurbations. Again resentment was aroused when the government seemed even less enthusiastic about these reports than it had been about Beveridge: in November 1943 there was almost another revolt by Labour back-benchers together with members of the Tory Reform Group. Open revolt did come on the other big social issue of 1942; Ernest Bevin's plan to reform the wages structure of the catering industry – only this time the revolt was from the Right. On 12 November and 17 December 1942 individual Conservative MPs issued threats of large-scale disaffection if the War Cabinet let Bevin have his way. But Bevin was a strong man, and, as the leading representative of organized labour, a valuable one: his proposals were duly carried by the House of Commons on 9 February 1943, when, however, 116 Conservatives voted against them.

In the months that followed, the demands of newspaper publicists and Labour party conferences mounted. In the autumn of 1943 Sir Richard Acland founded the Common Wealth Party, which, combining the aspirations of middle-class social reformers with the solid voting power of the Labour rank-and-file, succeeded in winning a number of by-elections from the government.[32] In its 'White Paper chase' the government published *Employment Policy* (Beveridge had already published his own *Full Employment in a Free Society*), *Educational Reconstruction*, and *A National Health Service*. The Conservative minister R. A. Butler, after long negotiations, particularly with the churches (still, at this time, closely involved with education), introduced his Education Bill in December 1943. Passed in August 1944, this aimed at providing 'secondary education for all' up to the age of 15. Scholarships to maintained grammar schools were to be abolished and instead all places were to be free. Secondary schools run by the churches were to be subject to control of standards by the state, in return for higher grants. Since there was no provision for increasing the number of grammar schools, there was no guarantee that secondary education (ultimately to be extended to the age of 16) would be of a high quality. Fee-paying direct grant schools and the exclusive public schools were left untouched.[33] Labour backbenchers and Tory Reformers united to defeat the government on an amendment calling for equal pay for women teachers, defeating the government by 117 to 116. Next day, Churchill demanded a reversal of this vote, and secured it by a huge majority. The much argued-over question of the war's effect, if any, on the status of women will be discussed in the final section of this chapter.

### *The invasion of France and the end of the War*

Operation Overlord was preceded by what were intended to be precision bombing attacks on French ports and communication systems; altogether the Allies killed 60,000 French civilians. Through their near-mastery of German intelligence, the Allies were able to feed the Germans the false information that the invasion would take place in the Pas de Calais. In fact the landings were to be in Normandy, with 'D-day' fixed for 5 June. Bad weather forced postponement to 6 June. Shortly after midnight parachute troops, followed by gliders, began to land at key points. As first light approached, German coastal defences were bombarded by warships. Then, covered by fighter and fighter-bomber attacks, infantry, tanks and engineers began to land on the various beaches. In the ultimate scheme of things, the Normandy landings were astonishingly successful, with 156,000 Allied troops advancing between four and six miles into Normandy by the end of D-day. But while losses at Passchendaele had run at

2,121 a day, the Normandy campaign cost 2,354 a day, 70 per cent of those in the infantry rifle companies. German losses, too, were very high, particularly from Allied air attacks. But the superior fire power of German tanks meant that many Allied crews were simply burnt to death in their 'Tommy cookers'.[34]

Progress was being made in Normandy when late on the evening of 15 June 1944, an air-raid warning siren sounded again over London and the south-east. The 'all clear' did not go until after 10 o'clock the following morning. To begin with, the BBC simply referred to 'activity over southern England'. The government admitted that an attack by 'pilotless planes' had begun; subsequently the description 'flying bombs' was adopted. The new weapon, the V1, was suitably fiendish. A small plane without a pilot, but carrying a heavy charge of high explosive, it landed whenever its fuel ran out, or sometimes simply dived straight into the ground. Even if shot down, it would still explode. The blast was enormous, and since many came over during the day, when it was impossible for most people to take shelter, the casualties were high. There were various descriptions of the sinister grating sounds made by the V1s, which rose in a most menacing fashion: because of their characteristic, but indefinable sound, the new weapons were christened 'doodle bugs' or 'buzz bombs'.

Moving the anti-aircraft defences out towards the coast helped to contain the V1 threat, and in August their launching pads in northern France were overrun by the invading Allied forces. Already nearly 6,000 civilians had been killed, and 16,000 more severely injured by the V1s. The Germans could still fire V1s from piloted planes, and the attacks continued, more sporadically, but spread over a wider geographical area. For example, 27 people were killed in Oldham on Christmas Eve, 1944. Meantime, a second weapon, the V2, had been brought into service. The first shattering V2 explosion was heard all over London on 8 September. Not until 10 November was it officially admitted that the country was being attacked by rockets. Nearly 3,000 people were killed and over twice that number badly injured in the V2 attacks. By March 1945 the successful advances on the continent of Europe brought the V1 and V2 menace finally to an end.

American and French armies landed in the South of France on 15 August. Two days later the American General Patton's forces, having moved from Normandy through Brittany, arrived on the Seine north-west and south-east of Paris. On 19 August the Paris Liberation Committee led a rising against the Germans and their collaborators. Hitler ordered the destruction of Paris, orders which were fortunately disregarded by General Dietrich von Choltitz. General Leclerc's Second French Division entered Paris on 25 August. De Gaulle arrived on 30 August and proclaimed a Provisional Government of France. Montgomery wanted a rapid thrust against the Germans, Eisenhower preferred an advance on a broad front. There was a long and death-strewn way to go. By September Montgomery's forces were in the Netherlands, poised for a crossing of the Rhine. But the dropping of a British division at Arnhem to cover the Rhine bridge there, was a disaster. In mid-December Field-Marshal von Rundstedt attempted a counter-offensive in the Ardennes, achieving a dangerous breakthrough. But by Christmas it was clear that the Allies had won this 'Battle of the Bulge'. On 13 February 1945, the Allies carried out intensely destructive bombing attacks on the beautiful city of Dresden, which was full of refugees fleeing from the Russian advances in the east: 135,000 civilians were blown to pieces, choked, or burned to death. Dresden was a communications centre; the Allies wished to impress Stalin, whom they were soon to meet at Yalta, with their determination to fight the war with all vigour. Yet Dresden was perhaps an act of total war too far. More heroic engagements were being fought in the Rhineland, and by the end of the month the bridgehead across the Rhine at Remagen had been secured.

By 22 April the Russians were fighting in the streets of Berlin. To the German request on 1 May for an armistice, they replied demanding unconditional surrender. The Berlin garrison surrendered on 2 May. Hitler had committed suicide on 30 April, naming Admiral Doenitz as his successor. On 4 May the German forces in north-western Europe surrendered to General Montgomery at Lüneburg Heath, near Hamburg. On 7 May General Jodl, on behalf of the German Supreme Command, surrendered unconditionally at Eisenhower's headquarters at Rheims. The following day the formal surrender was repeated at the Russian headquarters in Berlin. Already, the British Government had designated 8 May as VE Day – Victory in Europe Day (the war against the Japanese still continued).

It is impossible to generalize about reactions to VE Day. Naturally, there was rejoicing. For the first time for six weary years there was floodlighting of public buildings and statues; restaurants and cinemas and theatres were fully lit up. Indeed, it was said that some children were terrified by the unexpected amount of light. The most powerful source for the nature of the VE Day celebrations is to be found in the Ministry of Information: *War Pictorial News*, Issue 213, item 2b, of May 1945. The scenes are of great patriotic jubilation, together with impressive shots of Churchill, the Royal Family, and other political leaders appearing on the balcony at Buckingham Palace. Yet the enormous emotional impact of this piece of source material derives very largely from the very effective use on the sound-track of Elgar's Pomp and Circumstance March No. 1.

Victory had been expected for some time, and there was frustration over the delays in issuing the final announcement, which did not come until twenty minutes to eight on the night of 7 May. But whatever deeper feelings people may have had, there could be no doubt that 8 May was a day in which almost everyone gave full rein to the immediate feelings of relief and national triumph. It was a mixture of festival, fair, wakes week and rag. For many children it was the first ever opportunity to savour the delights of bonfires and fireworks. For many adults much of the movement was basically aimless, but there were bands, music, flags and a moderate amount of drinking. For the bereaved, as always, much of the rejoicing must have been especially painful: 360,000 combatants had been killed; 60,000 civilians, and 35,000 merchant seamen.

Yet the celebrations were real. A level-headed civil servant, now returned to suburban Surrey after his wartime evacuation to Lancashire, seems, in a matter-of-fact sort of way, to have got it right:

> We went to London on VE night and joined the singing and shouting crowds in the West End. We put a Union Jack on the top gable of our house and strung coloured lights around the edge of the roof. All the houses were decorated and there was dancing round the island in Claygate Lane. Everyone was very happy.[35]

And Churchill got it as right as anyone could in a few sentences, when he told the crowd outside Buckingham Palace:

> This is your victory. It is the victory of the cause of freedom in every land. In all our long history we have never seen a greater day than this. Everyone, man or woman, has done their best.

## THE CONTEXT OF CHANGE

### *DEMOGRAPHICS OF WAR*

If the Second World War had demographic effects, they were slightly surprising ones. Britain, in common with other western countries – most notably, France, which had been particularly severely affected by a declining birth rate in the inter-war years – had a 'baby boom' during, and in greater degree, immediately after, the war. It does seem to be a truism that amid the excitements and horrors of war sexual activity increases. It is not hard to understand that with men going out to face the sort of conditions I described in the previous section, couples should want to make the most of every precious moment and, perhaps, ensure that there would be a child for the father to be remembered by. Illegitimate births, naturally, increased as well as legitimate ones. And while many women enjoyed their wartime activities, or at least felt proud to be doing their bit for their country and their menfolk, many also expressed a wish at the end of the war to get on and build homes and families. That men returning from the war should seek the solace of domesticity is not in any way surprising. On the downside, the war also had very serious economic consequences: everything had to be sacrificed to the war effort – productive resources, export potential, overseas assets, domestic investment. As ever, I'll let the tables carry the tale.

Given the colourful phrases that we are all used to, such as 'baby boom' (for the 1940s), and 'teenage revolution' (for the 1960s), the figures in tables 3.6, 3.7 and 3.8 are perhaps not as striking as one might expect. The problem is that, as is often the case with statistical tables of this sort, sometimes a number

**Table 3.4** Annual average percentage growth rates of population per decade in Great Britain, 1931–1991

| | |
|---|---|
| 1931–9 | 0.47 |
| 1939–51 | 0.43 |
| 1951–61 | 0.50 |
| 1961–71 | 0.53 |
| 1971–81 | 0.03 |
| 1981–91 | –.04 |

*Source:* N. L. Tranter, *British Population in the Twentieth Century* (Basingstoke: Macmillan Press, 1996), p. 4.

**Table 3.5** Total populations in millions, Great Britain and United Kingdom, 1931–1991

| | *Great Britain* | *United Kingdom* |
|---|---|---|
| 1931 | 44.80 | 46.03 |
| 1939 | 46.47 | – |
| 1951 | 48.85 | 50.23 |
| 1961 | 51.28 | 52.70 |
| 1971 | 53.98 | 55.52 |
| 1981 | 54.15 | 55.85 |
| 1991 | 53.91 | 56.47 |

*Source:* Government Census Statistics.

**Table 3.6** Total population of Great Britain by age, sex and (females only) marital status, 1931–1973 (thousands)

| *Age, sex and marital status* | *1931* | *1951* | *1961* | *1966* | *1973* |
|---|---|---|---|---|---|
| Males: | | | | | |
| 0–14 | 5,466 | 5,588 | 6,109 | 6,314 | 6,634 |
| 15–24 | 3,834 | 3,108 | 3,403 | 3,852 | 3,887 |
| 25–64 | 10,733 | 12,567 | 12,958 | 12,944 | 13,037 |
| 65 and over | 1,425 | 2,187 | 2,317 | 2,480 | 2,862 |
| Total | 21,458 | 23,450 | 24,787 | 25,590 | 26,420 |
| Married females: | | | | | |
| 15–24 | 546 | 863 | 1,038 | 1,175 | 1,266 |
| 25–64 | 8,310 | 10,275 | 10,771 | 10,906 | 10,928 |
| 65 and over | 636 | 1,093 | 1,261 | 1,388 | 1,620 |
| Total | 9,492 | 12,231 | 13,070 | 13,469 | 13,814 |
| Unmarried females: | | | | | |
| 0–14 | 5,359 | 5,359 | 5,814 | 6,001 | 6,294 |
| 15–24 | 3,410 | 2,387 | 2,345 | 2,611 | 2,493 |
| 25–64 | 3,820 | 3,376 | 2,801 | 2,559 | 2,425 |
| 65 and over | 1,256 | 2,053 | 2,468 | 2,646 | 2,940 |
| Total | 13,845 | 13,175 | 13,428 | 13,817 | 14,152 |
| Total females | 23,337 | 25,406 | 26,498 | 27,286 | 27,966 |

*Source:* R. C. O. Matthews, C. H. Feinstein and J. C. Odling-Smee, *British Economic Growth, 1856–1973* (Oxford: Clarendon Press, 1982), p. 562.

**Table 3.7** Average family size, 1935–1955

| *Date of marriage* | *Average family size* |
|---|---|
| 1935 | 2.0 |
| 1940 | 2.0 |
| 1945 | 2.2 |
| 1950 | 2.3 |
| 1955 | 2.4 |

*Source:* R. C. O. Matthews, C. H. Feinstein and J. C. Odling-Smee, *British Economic Growth, 1856–1973* (Oxford: Clarendon Press, 1982), pp. 46–7.

**Table 3.8** Growth of UK youth population, 1939–1966

| | *Total UK population (in thousands)* | *Under 20s (in thousands)* | *Under 20s as a percentage of total population* |
|---|---|---|---|
| 1951 | 37,908 | 3,066 | 8 |
| 1961 | 39,360 | 3,575 | 9 |
| 1966 | 40,041 | 4,088 | 10 |

*Source:* Department of Employment, *British Labour Statistics Historical Abstract 1886–1968* (1971), pp. 206–7.

of different trends are involved which, as it were, neutralize each other. You can see the growth in numbers of those under fifteen and of those under twenty-five; you can see the growth of the percentage of young people in the population. The problem here is that because of the continual fall in death rates, leading to a rise in the numbers of old people, the rise in the number of young people does not show up strongly in *percentage* terms, though a 1 per cent rise from a baseline of 8 per cent, is a rise of more than 10 per cent. There is always something slightly ludicrous about a figure indicating '2.4 children', but be aware that a 0.2 rise on a baseline of 2.0 is a ten per cent rise. The culmination of the 'baby boom' came in 1947 with a birth-rate of 20.7 per thousand (1947 and 1964 were the only two years in British history in which over one million births were recorded; generally the figure was fairly steady at around three-quarters of a million).

### *Economic costs of war*

Right. More children being brought into the world, more mouths to feed, more joy for more people – one presumes, provided, of course, that economic circumstances were right. We must look at some more tables.

**Table 3.9** Growth of Gross Domestic Product per man-year: international comparison of annual percentage growth rates

| | *UK* | *US* | *Sweden* | *France* | *Germany* | *Italy* | *Japan* |
|---|---|---|---|---|---|---|---|
| 1937–51 | 1.0 | 2.3 | 2.6 | 1.7 | 1.0 | 1.4 | –1.3 |
| 1951–64 | 2.3 | 2.5 | 3.3 | 4.3 | 5.1 | 5.6 | 7.6 |
| 1964–73 | 2.6 | 1.6 | 2.7 | 4.6 | 4.4 | 5.0 | 8.4 |

*Source:* R. C. O. Matthews, C. H. Feinstein and J. C. Odling-Smee, *British Economic Growth, 1856–1973* (Oxford: Clarendon Press, 1982), p. 31.

**Table 3.10** World exports of manufactured goods (percentage shares)

| | *UK* | *US* | *Germany* | *France* | *Japan* |
|---|---|---|---|---|---|
| 1937 | 20.9 | 19.2 | 21.8 | 5.8 | 6.9 |
| 1950 | 25.5 | 27.3 | 7.3 | 9.9 | 3.4 |
| 1960 | 16.5 | 21.6 | 19.3 | 9.6 | 6.9 |
| 1970 | 10.8 | 18.6 | 19.8 | 8.7 | 11.7 |
| 1979 | 9.1 | 16.0 | 20.9 | 10.5 | 13.7 |
| 1990 | 8.6 | 16.0 | 20.2 | 9.7 | 15.9 |

*Source:* Maurice W. Kirby and Mary B. Rose (eds), *Business Enterprise in Modern Britain: From the Eighteenth to the Twentieth Century* (1994), p. 19.

**Table 3.11** Annual percentage growth rates in real income per man-year

| | |
|---|---|
| 1924–37 | 1.2 |
| 1937–51 | 0.8 |
| 1951–73 | 2.5 |

*Source:* R. C. Matthews, C. H. Feinstein and J. C. Odling-Smee, *British Economic Growth, 1856–1973* (Oxford: Clarendon Press, 1982), p. 171.

In waging war Britain had acquired debts of £3,000 million, had allowed domestic capital to deteriorate by around the same amount, had used up overseas investments to the extent of £1,000 million, and had had to let exports fall to one-third of their pre-war level. But countries which had been invaded, whether by the Germans or the Allies, and countries which had suffered 'strategic' or 'area' bombing (one can pick one's euphemism) suffered much more; only America, as in the previous war, came out with an enhanced balance sheet. Have a look at my tables of international comparisons (3.9 and 3.10) and draw out your own conclusions. The two major questions to address are: the effects of the war on the individual countries; and how well each country adapted to post-war circumstances. If we look at the exports of manufactured goods (table 3.10) we see that, of the countries listed, Germany suffered most from the war; but then achieved a phenomenal adaptation to the new circumstances so that by 1970 she has overtaken the United States. Starting from a much lower baseline, Japan also suffered heavily, but also shows a strong recovery by 1970. Now, we are dealing with percentage shares, not with absolute totals – if some countries take an increasing share others necessarily take a diminishing one, without this necessarily being a sign of failure. Nonetheless, the relativities are interesting. America has considerably increased her share by 1950, and though the share inevitably then falls slightly, it remains substantial, and second only to that of Germany. France has made a good recovery by 1950, and then pretty well holds its position. Britain has made a good recovery by 1950: clearly the war has not been as damaging to her as it was to Germany and Japan. But the rather sharp decline thereafter at least *suggests* that Britain was not adapting so well to the post-war world.

Somewhat similar conclusions are suggested by the table of annual percentage growth rates in GDP per man-year (3.9). Japan, subject to two atomic bomb attacks at the end of the war, actually suffers a decline in GDP over the war and immediate post-war period. Germany's growth rate over the same period is relatively low, but then, at an identical figure, so is Britain's. The highest growth rate is that in Sweden, which had remained neutral during the war, followed by the United States, relatively unscathed by the direct effects of war, as we have noted. Both France and Italy do reasonably well. But then in the next phase, the period of what are known as the 'economic miracles' in France, Germany and Italy, these three countries, together with, to an even greater degree, Japan, undergo substantial increases in their growth rates. Generally speaking, the lower the starting point the greater the possibility of high growth rates, and to a great extent this is what we are seeing in the defeated countries. The higher the GDP the lower possibility, usually, there is for high growth rates. And we see that, while France and Japan continue to grow at much reduced rates, growth tails off in Germany and Italy. It does so also in the United States, the country with by far the greatest GDP. Britain seems to be doing reasonably well but the growth rates are modest compared with those in the countries I have already discussed. Again this might seem to suggest poor adaptation to post-war conditions. Table 3.11 indicates the severe effects on income growth during the war and immediate post-war period, and the rise in incomes during the fifties and sixties.

## *Ideological and Institutional Repercussions of War*

When it comes to ideological and institutional circumstances one is struck by how far the war experience, instead of instituting radical change, confirmed existing ways. Without doubt, among all sections of society – politicians, businessmen, the electorate as a whole – there was a movement towards the Left, towards support for welfare legislation and collectivist intervention.[36] Keynesian ideas were now in the ascendancy, though, as Peter Clarke and others have pointed out, within very strict limits of maintaining conventional financial prudence.[37] Conventional prudence was a facet too of the socialism of the incoming Labour government, a socialism which combined Attlee's ethical outlook with Herbert Morrison's faith in the public corporation. What almost everybody shared was a faith in Britain's continuing role as a world power, possessed of an Empire and Commonwealth, which was thought to confer economic benefits. The truth was that, while individuals had benefited immensely from Imperial investments and activities, the upkeep of the Empire had long been a burden on the Treasury, and continuing to keep up a world role was to impose unaffordable costs on the country. The widespread belief, too, was that, apart from the wartime changes which led to the setting-up of the National Health Service and the Welfare State, British institutions and the economic infrastructure had passed the test of war trailing clouds of glory. While continental countries invested in completely new transport systems, experimenting with new approaches to make them as appealing as possible to the public, Britain, while taking the railways into national ownership, did very little to modernize them. With Germany prostrate, and divided up among the victors, Britain had the pick of the spoils from its occupation zone in Germany. British manufacturers had the opportunity to take over the know-how and technology of Volkswagen. Amazingly, but also typically, they declined on the grounds that British car manufacture, being in a different class, could manage perfectly without.[38] British car manufacture after the war was to be a sorry business, with far too many models, and a kind of perverted pride in the long waiting lists which built up for British luxury models. The soft option was taken, selling to the starved domestic market, while redesigned European factories filled the continental markets that the British manufacturers spurned. The figures speak for themselves: relative to previous eras, the British economy, and the British people, did well; but relatively speaking both were all the time slipping behind renewed and re-energized foreign competitors.

Throughout this book I have stressed the critical importance of global developments. In two respects, they were extremely favourable in the years after 1945. First, massive and successful attempts were made to avoid the distrust, insecurity, and instability which had marred the inter-war years. The international monetary system formulated under American auspices at Bretton Woods was both stable and flexible, while the General Agreement on Tariffs and Trade of 1947 produced a reduction in tariffs on manufactured goods. On the whole the Americans, in contrast with what had happened after the First World War, acted in a constructive spirit, accepting that in the initial stages after the war Britain and the other Europeans would have to discriminate against suppliers requiring payment in dollars and, above all, after 1948, making available Marshall Aid for the reconstruction of the European (including British) economies. Against that, all European countries suffered from a sharp rise in raw material prices. Although pre-war initiatives, and the necessities of war, resulted in great improvements in the productivity of British agriculture, Britain remained a country with hefty import requirements. Failure at the end of the war to remedy Britain's competitive weaknesses, 'including higher prices, less innovative design, inferior quality and reliability, and longer delivery dates', resulted, as the relevant statistical tables suggest, in a consistently precarious balance of payments situation: 'there was generally a surplus on current account, but it was too small and too uncertain to prevent recurrent sterling crises and fears that the currency would be devalued . . . '.[39] To conserve dollars, the Sterling Area had been formerly defined during the war: the 'sterling balances' were the debts Britain incurred during the war to countries in the Sterling Area. While the Empire was generally a liability to Britain, the substantial earnings made from raw material exports from the colonies to the dollar area were of considerable value in building up the positive side of the sterling balances. Against this, the continuing role of sterling as an international currency second to the dollar, was no great asset, and possibly a liability.[40]

The disruptions of war had some effect on class and class relationships. The most important single development was the change in status and bargaining power of the working class. Resorting at times to strikes, the workers were able to exploit the very high demand for labour engendered by the necessities of war to push their real earnings up by well over 50 per cent. The much vaunted 'mixing' of social classes during the war was more in spirit than substance, but undoubtedly there was a new upper-class and middle-class concern that, having played so crucial a role in the war effort, the workers should not be plunged back into the depressed conditions of the inter-war years. The egalitarian policies mooted during the war, and in large degree carried out by the Labour Government after the war, did not, as many hoped (or feared), alter the basic social structure; but in general they favoured the working class. Yet, strengthened in solidarity and self-awareness, the working class was not encouraged to share, nor did it show great enthusiasm for sharing, in the running of the country, or participating in the solving of its problems. High taxation during and after the war hit the upper-middle class hardest, lowering the barriers between it and the rest of the middle class. The upper class survived remarkably unaffected. The Labour Government did nothing to interfere with its traditional educational institutions, and the main obvious change took the form of the entry of upper-class figures into the newer, high-paying, professions: property development, advertising and public relations, entertainment and communications, not to mention holding high office in a Labour Government. Of Labour Cabinet ministers, Hugh Dalton, Sir Stafford Cripps and John Strachey could scarcely be described as anything other than upper-class; Clement Attlee, the new Prime Minister, undoubtedly thought of himself as middle-class and was usually perceived as such by political opponents, but as the product of a prosperous family of solicitors, who had been educated at a fairly prestigious public school, Haileybury, and at Oxford, he could more reasonably be placed as first-generation upper-class. The Haileybury school magazine in November 1945 was able to congratulate itself on the election of only one Conservative old boy, but of four Labour old boys and its first ever Prime Minister, to whom it extended congratulations, 'proud that he is a son of Haileybury, and confident that he will not fail his high trust'.[41] Top civil servants, top economic advisers, and top people in finance and industry continued to be recruited disproportionately from the upper class, whose education, compared with that, say, provided by the system of *grandes écoles* in France, was not adequate for the tasks in hand. There was much talk of 'planning' after 1945, but in fact there was never any rigorous analysis of the country's fundamental problems and never any effective planning to cope with them.

Correlli Barnett, whose excoriation of British governments for their economic policies both during and after the war has met with powerful criticism from professional historians,[42] has declared that the war exposed Britain's deplorable technological dependence on America, particularly with respect to machine-tools. However, Professor Sidney Pollard has maintained that Britain by the end of the war 'had acquired great strength in some of the most promising sectors like vehicles, aircraft and electronics', and even in machine-tools there was an extension to the domestic base.[43] Against the Barnett thesis that expenditure on social welfare had debilitating consequences for the British economy, many economists now argue that such expenditure is absolutely essential to the maintenance of a high-productivity economy, and that the relative failure of Britain in this respect may have been due to under- rather than over-expenditure on welfare.[44]

Was the dominant ideology after 1945 that of consensus? If so, was that a good thing? If not, was *that* a bad thing? The two-party system was back in working order. The pendulum swung so far in 1945 that Labour was returned with a massive majority. In 1951 it swung again, so that the Conservatives were back in office with a comfortable majority. Professor Ben Pimlott has taken a leading position in denying the validity of the label 'consensus' for the post-war period.[45] Undoubtedly there are plenty of signs of bitter adversarial politics. The Conservatives took their defeat in 1945 very badly. Sir David Maxwell Fyfe (later Lord Kilmuir) reported on 'one old Tory MP' as describing the Labour MPs as 'just like a crowd of damned constituents'.[46] Conservative opposition in the first years of Labour government was factious and bitter, Churchill setting the tone:

> I believe profoundly that the attempt to turn Great Britain into a Socialist State will, as it develops, produce widespread political strife, misery and ruin at home . . .[47]

The popular press, with the exception of the failing *Daily Herald* (Labour), the struggling *News Chronicle* (Liberal), and the ebullient *Daily Mirror*, was universally hostile and echoed Churchill in always referring to the Labour Government as 'the socialists'. The Conservatives voted against the Act of 1946 introducing the National Health Service.[48] But, thanks in particular to the activities of the Tory Reform Group, most of the Conservative party gradually became reconciled to the Welfare State, though not, on the whole, to Labour's nationalization policies ('socialist grabs' in the language of the press). The case for using the term 'consensus' rests on the arguments, first, that some of the new unity created in the war did endure, and secondly, that it is essentially a relative term, pointing up a contrast with the highly divisive politics of the mid-seventies, when Margaret Thatcher became leader of the Conservative party and the extreme Left became more and more powerful in the Labour party. On these bases, the term, in my view, does have validity. (Brian Harrison has recently claimed that consensus is a perennial feature, manifesting itself in the inter-war and Thatcher years as 'indirect consensus': I think he is confusing a social phenomenon, best described as 'secular Anglicanism', with a purely political one (well described as 'consensus').[49])

The case against the actuality of consensus (made very forcefully by Margaret Thatcher) is that it led to complacency and a shirking of difficult, but necessary, decisions. The case against the adversarial politics which, quite certainly, make consensus no more than a relative term, is that they led to damaging discontinuities and changes of direction in British policies. It is hoped that the detailed political narrative which follows in the next section will help readers to puzzle out these riddles for themselves.

## Labour Takes Power and Hands it Back to the Conservatives

### *General Elections, 1945–55*

Let us start with facts and outcomes. As a consequence of the General Election held on 5 July 1945, the results being delayed to allow for the counting of the servicemen's votes, a Labour government was formed with a majority over all other parties of 146 seats – in the standard terminology, a 'landslide' victory. The war experience had sharpened the desire, and intensified the solidarity, of the working class, which voted Labour more consistently than ever before; the war experience, too, turned many of the middle classes towards Labour, to the extent of about one-third of all middle-class adults, it has been reckoned.[50] In the General Election of 23 February 1950 the 'landslide' majority very nearly vanished: Labour continued in office, but with an overall majority of only five. A further General Election followed on 25 October 1951: this time the Conservatives secured an overall majority of 17, and once more formed a government. The General Election of 26 May 1955 produced nothing like a landslide, but yielded a comfortable Conservative majority of 60. After securing an apparently impregnable position in 1945, Labour, it seemed, had, in the next two elections, held within a space of nineteen months, handed power back to the Conservatives.

The comprehensive picture is an intriguing one.

Look first of all at what happens to the Labour vote, checking it against the size of the electorate, then look also at the turnout figures. Look at the percentages of the total vote won by Labour and by the Conservatives. Absorb all that before again considering the actual seats won in parliament. How far would it be true to speak of the pendulum swinging against Labour, or of Labour losing the support of the voters?

**Table 3.12** General Election, 5 July 1945

| | *Electorate 33.2 million* | | *Turnout 72.7 per cent* | |
|---|---|---|---|---|
| | *Conservative* | *Labour* | *Liberal* | *Others* |
| Total votes cast | 9,988,306 | 11,995,152 | 2,248,226 | 854,294 |
| Percentage of votes cast | 39.8 | 47.8 | 9.0 | 2.8 |
| Seats | 213 | 393 | 12 | 22 |

**Table 3.13** General Election, 23 February 1950

| | *Electorate 33.3 million* | | *Turnout 84 per cent* | |
|---|---|---|---|---|
| | *Conservative* | *Labour* | *Liberal* | *Others* |
| Total votes cast | 12,502,567 | 13,266,592 | 2,621,548 | 381,964 |
| Percentage of votes cast | 43.5 | 46.1 | 9.1 | 1.3 |
| Seats | 298 | 315 | 9 | 3 |

**Table 3.14** General Election, 25 October 1951

| | *Electorate 34.6 million* | | *Turnout 82.5 per cent* | |
|---|---|---|---|---|
| | *Conservative* | *Labour* | *Liberal* | *Others* |
| Total votes cast | 13,717,538 | 13,948,605 | 730,556 | – |
| Percentage of votes cast | 48.0 | 48.8 | 2.5 | 0.7 |
| Seats | 321 | 295 | 6 | 3 |

**Table 3.15** General Election, 26 May 1955

| | *Electorate 34.9 million* | | *Turnout 76.7 per cent* | |
|---|---|---|---|---|
| | *Conservative* | *Labour* | *Liberal* | *Others* |
| Total votes cast | 13,286,569 | 12,404,970 | 722,405 | – |
| Percentage of votes cast | 49.7 | 46.4 | 2.7 | 1.2 |
| Seats | 344 | 277 | 6 | 3 |

What we actually see is that the Labour vote goes up in 1950, by over 270,000 votes, then in 1951 goes up again, but by a much more substantial figure of over 680,000 votes. The electorate has increased in size by 1950, and by a tiny bit more in 1951. More important, the turnout of voters is exceptionally high in 1950 and 1951. If the Conservatives were getting the larger share of votes of those who had reached voting age for the first time and those creating the increased turnout, that would not appear to be the case for 1951. Though the margin is a fine, and sharply decreasing, one, Labour in both cases has a larger percentage of the total vote. So we can't really speak of the pendulum swinging against Labour, or of the voters turning away. If we then look at the seats won, we can see how the single-member, first-past-the-post system is benefiting the Conservatives. On a proportional system, Labour would have had a larger majority in 1950, and would not have been in a minority in 1951. Labour's tally of seats in 1945 had been boosted by the fact that many of them, being industrial areas, had relatively low populations. But the redistribution of seats, which, in fairness, had to take place, swung too far the other way and facilitated Conservative gains disproportionate to their actual vote. In 1950 the Liberals once more made a bid to regain their former status by putting up 475 candidates. This magnificent piece of *folie de grandeur* bankrupted the party (two-thirds of the candidates lost their deposits): in 1951 large swathes of Liberal voters had no candidate and, where in similar circumstances they might have voted Labour in 1945, they now became another factor in swelling the number of Conservative seats.[51]

By 1955 the size of the electorate had not significantly altered, but the turnout had gone down. So also had the Conservative vote, though by under half-a-million, while the Labour vote had gone down by nearly one-and-a-half million. The Conservative percentage of the votes cast is almost as high as Labour's in 1945, but because the Liberals, once again, have been squeezed, Labour in 1955 has a much better percentage than the Conservatives had in 1945. Could Labour in 1950–1 have held on to the power gained in 1945? Did it, whatever the vagaries of the system, deserve, on its record, to lose power? What did the Conservatives do to turn the minority position in the country and a narrow base in the House of Commons into a majority in the country and a secure position in parliament?

## *Policies of the Labour Government*

The first responsibilities of any government are the defence of the realm and the prosperity of the nation. The Labour Government was also committed to policies which would result in the establishment of what came to be known as 'the welfare state'. The leading Labour ministers had proved themselves as members of the wartime coalition. If this was in some ways least true of Attlee, he certainly set about the job of Prime Minister with brisk efficiency and appealing common-sense. Morrison, who took over as deputy leader from the fading Greenwood, had, as Lord President of the Council, overall responsibility for domestic policy. To avert friction on the home front, Bevin went to the Foreign Office, the post coveted by upper-class Hugh Dalton, who instead became Chancellor of the Exchequer. Austere, Christian, but wine-drinking and heavy-smoking, Sir Stafford Cripps became President of the Board of Trade. Upper-class, former Marxist, John Strachey was Minister of Food, and London-born Emmanuel Shinwell, Red Clydesider of the First World War who had ousted Ramsay MacDonald from his coal-mining Seaham constituency in Northumberland, became Minister of Fuel and Power, and responsible for coal nationalization. The most daring appointment was that of the former miner of patrician tastes, Aneurin Bevan, who had frequently performed during the war as a one-man left-wing opposition to the Churchill coalition, as Minister of Health, with the responsibility for setting up the National Health Service.

Inevitably national security and issues arising from the war were dominant. There were many good reasons for wanting to bring the continuing war against Japan to a speedy conclusion. Attlee did not demur from Truman's decision to use the atomic bomb, in the construction of which British scientists had participated. On 6 August 1945 Hiroshima was devastated; Nagasaki was bombed a few days later. Nuclear disarmament campaigners have been scathing about the 'secretive' way in which the Attlee Government embarked on the building of the British bomb. The moral issues can only be adjudged by individual readers. But it is important to be clear exactly what the members of the Attlee Government did do, why they did it, and the context in which they did it.

Attlee's wish was that collaboration with the Americans in the production of atomic weapons should continue, and that their actual use should be controlled through a proposed UN Commission on Atomic Energy. The Americans were resolutely opposed to both, and shortly the McMahon Act enshrined a legal embargo which prevented the Americans from sharing atomic secrets with any other country. These American decisions, together with the attitudes towards Britain which they represented, formed the primary motivation for the decision to build a British bomb. It is true that the military chiefs, the Foreign Office, and Bevin himself were the strongest proponents of developing atomic weapons: Foreign Office civil servants, particularly Sir Orme Sargent, soon to become Permanent Secretary, already feared that the Soviet Union would expand into the vacuum left by Germany's total defeat, while Bevin had the right-wing trade union leader's distrust of Communists everywhere. The military also greatly feared Russian expansion into the Middle East and east Mediterranean; by April 1946, before a formal decision had yet been taken to build the bomb, they had a detailed plan for atomic attacks on 67 Soviet cities.[52] Nonetheless, Russia was still seen as a wartime ally, albeit a difficult one, a country which had borne much of the brunt of the war. The Cold War had not yet begun, so the decision on the bomb was not in essence a Cold War one.

So far, atomic energy had been put to only one use, bombing Japan. It was perceived that there could be peaceful purposes as well: no strong distinction was made between the two uses, making concealment of military purposes easier, though that was not the original intention. Simply, atomic power was an inescapable issue, and from the start there was a Cabinet Committee on atomic energy. In December 1945 the Chiefs of Staff persuaded the special Cabinet Committee GEN75 to authorize the construction of a plant at Windscale (much later renamed Sellafield) in Cumbria for the manufacture of plutonium. At the same meeting it was agreed that the Chiefs of Staff 'would submit a report' on their 'requirements for atomic bombs'. At the GEN75 meeting on 25 October 1946 the Chiefs wanted more money (£30 million–£40 million over four to five years) for a gaseous diffusion plant to improve the supply of fissile material for the bomb. Dalton and Cripps, convincing Attlee, were successfully leading opposition to this expenditure, when Bevin, arriving late, made his famous declaration that we must have a bomb with 'a bloody Union Jack flying on top of it'. In support, Bevin cited the contemptuous attitudes of the Americans, and particularly those of Secretary of State Byrnes towards himself. The Union Jack bomb was needed to establish independence from America; Bevin made no mention of the Soviets.

GEN75 was the normal Cabinet Committee on atomic matters. But for the formal decision to build the bomb, Attlee created another one, GEN163, which met only once, on the afternoon of 8 January 1947. Dalton and Cripps were kept out; but the Defence Minister, A. V. Alexander, and the Minister of Supply, John Wilmot, were there, together with Bevin, Morrison, and delightful historical twist! – Lloyd George's one-time crony, Lord Addison, now Attlee's revered mentor. Also, of course, the Chiefs of Staff, and Lord Portal, Chief of the Air Staff during the war, but now in the crucial new post of Atomic Controller at the Ministry of Supply. The initiative for a final, formal, decision came from Portal, who told the meeting that the Chiefs of Staff 'were naturally anxious that we should not be without this weapon if others possess it'. Again, Bevin invoked the United States:

> We could not afford to acquiesce in an American monopoly of this new development. Other countries also might well develop atomic weapons. Unless therefore an effective international system could be developed under which the production and use of the weapon would be prohibited, we must develop it ourselves.

'Not,' as Peter Hennessy puts it, 'a whisper of the Soviet threat'. Three days earlier Attlee had sent Bevin a memorandum expressing his own hostility to any policy of committing British forces to the east Mediterranean and Middle East, against any putative Soviet expansionism there, and to any policy of using atomic bombs against Soviet cities.

Attlee was an internationalist, not an incipient cold warrior. But without doubt he deliberately concealed the decision to go ahead with the bomb from the majority of his Cabinet colleagues, and, of course, from parliament, where the only mention came during Question Time on 12 May 1948, sandwiched between questions on House of Lords reform (something which always cropped up when Labour governments came into office) and the quality of Danish beef:

> MR GEORGE JEGER asked the Minister of Defence whether he is satisfied that adequate progress is being made in the development of the most modern types of weapon.
>
> THE MINISTER OF DEFENCE (MR A. V. ALEXANDER): Yes, Sir. As was made clear in the Statement Relating to Defence, 1948 (Command 7327), research and developments continue to receive the highest priority in the defence field, and all types of modern weapons, including atomic weapons, are being developed.
>
> MR JEGER: Can the Minister give any further information on the development of atomic weapons?
>
> MR ALEXANDER: No. I do not think it would be in the public interest to do that.

The Danish beef question projects us right back into the post-war world of grim austerity: beef which the Danes thought only fit for manufacture of meat products was apparently being slipped into the people's meat ration.[53]

By 1951 the bomb-making programme had cost £100 million, but clever laundering made that sum disappear from public scrutiny. In the Cabinet there would have been opposition, on financial grounds, from Dalton and Cripps, and, on grounds of principle, from Bevan and Shinwell. That is how Prime Ministers (advised by their military experts) behave, particularly when matters of national security are felt to be at stake. How 'unconstitutional' it was is hard to say, since the 'constitution' largely consists of a series of precedents, and we saw in chapter 1 how little part parliament played in the crucial changes in government during the First World War. What is certain is that if Attlee had consulted the Cabinet, he would have won, and if he had gone before parliament he would have secured a substantial majority and the overwhelming support of the public. From hindsight we could argue that the British bomb was an irrelevance in world politics (though the debate on that is still an open one), and we could certainly argue that 'atomic energy' has proved to be dirty and dangerous, while the diversion of resources imposed another burden on the British economy: however, in the context of the time, Attlee's decision was, at the very least, understandable.

A powerful part of that context was the argument, made by the Foreign Office, made by the military chiefs, and firmly adopted by Bevin, that never again must there be appeasement of a potential enemy. It was by such arguments that Attlee's internationalism and opposition to an anti-Soviet stance was overcome, while, as the years passed, Soviet intransigence, in Germany, in the take-over of Czechoslovakia, in the 1948 blockade of West Berlin (circumnavigated by the magnificent 'Berlin Airlift'), and in the crude rebuffs of Molotov and Vyshinsky of all attempts at constructive dialogue, became clearer and clearer. Faced with threats of resignation from all three Chiefs of Staff, Attlee finally acceded to the view, firmly expressed by Montgomery, that Britain must hold the Middle East 'in peace and fight for it in war'. Britain, in other words, must maintain a world role, entailing military expenditure out of all proportion to her true economic situation, and must reintroduce conscription.

The government's original National Service Bill proposed military service for eighteen months; however, substantial opposition from within the Labour party resulted in the period of service being reduced to twelve months. Young British conscripts might find themselves serving in Malaya, Borneo, Aden, Suez, Cyprus or various parts of Africa. But not in India, where Britain bowed to the inevitable and left the independent Commonwealth countries of India and Pakistan to emerge from appalling bloodshed between Hindus and Muslims. British forces were withdrawn from Palestine in 1948, also the year in which the government admitted to the Americans that it no longer had the resources to resist the Communists in the Greek civil war. While making clear that it did not itself intend to become involved, the British Government expressed support for the moves being made on the continent towards European cooperation. It did enthusiastically join with the United States in setting up the Western military riposte to the perceived Russian threat, the North Atlantic Treaty Organization (NATO), in 1949. This was accompanied by a programme of rearmament and the increase of the period of conscription to that originally proposed, eighteen months. Again these were not policies helpful to British economic recovery, to which I now turn.

### *The economy under Labour*

What constitutes a healthy economy? What are sound economic policies? There are few supporters now for the view that, allegedly returned on a revolutionary tide (there was, of course, no such tide), the Attlee Government should have introduced a complete socialist state, with workers' control and the expropriation of the rich. Certain recent writers have suggested that while it may be appropriate to talk of relative failure, wrong decisions and missed opportunities, it is inaccurate and simplistic to talk of a British economic decline. They have also suggested that successful economies require prosperous societies with high levels of social welfare. The ultra-Thatcherite views of Correlli Barnett, attributing a woeful profligacy to the social welfare policies of post-war governments, have, we have seen, carried little credibility. We must both keep in touch with the longer perspective and be aware of the difficulties, even with hindsight, in making judgements over policy-making in the aftermath of a devastating war. In the words of Catherine R. Schenk, the British economy in 1945 was 'in a shambles'.[54] A war economy would have to be speedily turned into a peace economy. Exports, it was calculated, would have to rise to 70 per cent over the 1939 level and, though exports depended heavily on imported raw materials, imports would have to be kept under strict control. Along the way conditions were often grim, and sometimes frightening: 1947 and 1949 were years of crises, but by 1950 the export target had been achieved, the economy seemed on the brink of high and sustained growth, and, apart from a few months in 1947, unemployment had been consistently below 2 per cent. If there had been crises, there must have been some skill in crisis management, or at least crisis recuperation. Interest rates had been held at 2 per cent, inflation about the same. Immediately the war with Japan was over, America terminated the Lend-Lease arrangement, and demanded that materials already on the way to Britain be paid for in dollars. What Britain desperately needed was a dollar loan. A negotiating team, led by J. M. Keynes, went to Washington. After three exhausting months, the Americans agreed to a loan of $3,750 million, with an additional $650 million in final settlement of Lend-Lease obligations. Canada added a further $1,250 million. Repayment, to stretch over fifty years, was to begin in five years, at 2 per cent interest. But the Americans, hostile to what they saw as the continuance of British imperialism in the form of the Sterling Area, insisted that within one year sterling should be convertible into dollars. Congress did not ratify the American loan until July 1946.

Meantime it had become clear that the most survival-threatening problem on the domestic front was the appalling condition of the coal industry, run-down, out-dated, and manned by reluctant and resentful miners whose productivity per shift had now fallen below that of 1939. Labour's stated policy, for which it could claim an overwhelming mandate, was that of nationalization of all the major industries. Whereas, in the 1990s, privatization was advocated as a means of raising necessary investment, in the 1940s nationalization and an influx of taxpayers' money was the only means of securing desperately-needed investment in the two most vital industries, coal and the railways. For carrying out coal nationalization, Labour had no advance plans at all. Emmanuel Shinwell, the minister responsible, was long on unreflecting optimism, but very short on administrative skill. Frequently warned in 1946 of an impending fuel crisis, he issued jaunty denials. The coal industry became a national property in January 1947, just as the worst winter in a hundred years began to bite. The country was blanketed in snow. Trains and coastal shipping were immobilized. The demand for coal rose sharply, supplies petered out. The people shivered, industries closed down, throwing 800,000 out of work. Partly because of the obligation to feed the heavily-populated British occupation zone in Germany, bread rationing, never imposed during the war, had been introduced in the summer of 1946. To the vocabulary of 'socialist grab' and 'socialist snoopers', the press could now add, 'Shiver with Shinwell and starve with Strachey'.

The railway amalgamation begun after the previous war was completed with the establishment of British Railways (1946). Theoretically the Transport Act of that same year aimed at integration of rail and road. All forms of road transport, save for municipal bus companies, short-distance road haulage lorries and lorries used by companies for their own products, were nationalized, and integration was to be realized through the British Transport Commission (January 1948). Typically of Labour 'planning', overall coordination never came about.

The icy winter was followed by severe flooding, though the summer was warm. But in July the pound had to be made convertible. Holders of sterling leapt at the opportunity to sell. In just over a month convertibility had to be suspended. The sense of crisis, recalling 1931, was heightened by Dalton's special autumn budget. In the kind of cheerful indiscretion which characterized him, Dalton told a reporter of some of his tax increases as he was about to enter the House of Commons. For this crime of crimes he had to go; so it was by clear chance that Cripps took over as Chancellor of the Exchequer. Ironically, Dalton's last, and emergency, budget has generally been praised as his first to fully employ 'the Keynesian demand management techniques that had been instigated during the war'.[55] Demand, and therefore the risk of inflation, was curtailed through rises in indirect taxation and the abolition of subsidies on clothing and footwear, as well as an increased company profits tax.

There is no simple way of assessing economic performance; Kenneth Morgan sees the years that followed as a time of democratic socialism on 'the defensive', of 'collectivist retreat', while other commentators see the economy as beginning 'to turn the corner from austerity to growth'.[56] Undoubtedly 1948 was a year of marked rise in exports. Nonetheless another crisis was on the way. A slight recession in America in early 1949 dented the British export recovery, sharply affecting the balance of payments. It was clear to some treasury officials that the fixed exchange rate of $4.03 to the pound gave the latter an unrealistically high value. Rumours that devaluation was likely began to spread, not necessarily stemmed by Cripps's vehement denials: there was yet another accelerating run on sterling. Cripps was taken ill and had to retreat to a sanatorium in Switzerland. Treasury officials travelled to Washington in the summer, where it was made clear that the Americans felt that the British ought to devalue. In the Cabinet the young economist Hugh Gaitskell, who had replaced Shinwell as Minister of Fuel and Power, became a strong advocate of devaluation. Cripps, returning from Switzerland for a specially summoned Cabinet on 29 August, reluctantly acquiesced.

By this time an altogether different financial initiative was reaching maturity. The American Secretary of State, General George Marshall, had tentatively put forward the idea of making American aid available for general European recovery. Ernest Bevin responded immediately, helping to make the plan a reality, while at the same time resisting pressure from the Americans to use what became known as the Marshall Plan to force closer British integration with Europe, through the Organization for European Economic Cooperation (OEEC), the main agency for dispensing Marshall Aid funds. British attitudes to Europe may have been short-sighted but one must bear in mind that at this time half of Britain's trade was with the Commonwealth, only a quarter with continental Europe (proportions, much later, to be reversed). Marshall Aid was offered to Russia and her East European satellites, but with the deliberate intention of securing her refusal. Russia's withdrawal from Marshall Aid negotiations definitively marks the beginning of the Cold War.

The British Government's belief in its 'special relationship' with America is clearly seen in the fact that while no discussions over devaluation were held with Britain's European partners in OEEC, Cripps and Bevin arrived in Washington on 7 September to discuss the projected British devaluation. In return for agreeing to a devaluation of the pound to $2.80, Bevin secured some reductions in US tariffs, and an increased share of Marshall Aid. Devaluation was announced to the British public on Sunday, 18 September. There was a further 5 per cent increase in profits tax, and subsequently some reductions in government expenditure. On the whole, the measures were successful in re-establishing growth and putting the British economy in a relatively strong position by 1950. Marshall Aid itself, of course, was a crucial factor, being worth £700 million up to the end of 1950, when it was stopped, the British economy now appearing to be in such good shape.[57]

Crises and crisis management apart, the government did present the appearance of great activity. Nationalization of the Bank of England (March 1946) was little more than a formality. Cable and Wireless Limited became a public corporation in January 1947. Nationalized British European Airways and British South American Airways joined with BOAC in running British civil aviation. For the two major public utilities two separate Acts, with a year's interval between, were passed, establishing the British Electricity Authority in April 1948, and the British Gas Council in May 1949, each with an infrastructure of area boards. To all of these measures the Conservatives could put no more than token resistance. But nationalization of the iron and steel industry, still prosperous, was a different matter. The Labour Government was itself divided on the matter, and delayed so long that the House of Lords was able to hold up the proposal to beyond 1950.

The government maintained the controls of wartime and tried to deploy them in a manner which would maximize exports and minimize domestic consumption. During 1948, the President of the Board of Trade, Harold Wilson, announced a 'bonfire of controls' to coincide with Guy Fawkes night, 5 November, of that year. To Morgan this was part of Labour's loss of confidence, while other commentators have associated the policy with the strong economic growth perceptible after 1948. The government declared its faith in planning, but what *is* quite certain is that no real planning was carried out. This can basically be attributed to complacency about how well British institutions had served the country in wartime, faith in British pragmatism, and the absence of specialist training among British civil servants. The model we have to use for comparative purposes is that of France. Jean Monnet's *Commissariat du Plan* was allied with 'modernization commissions' explicitly aiming at increasing productivity; whatever happened (and France had a bewildering series of changes of government and frequent crises) investment was protected, and investment was directed to, in Peter Hennessy's words, 'sustained, long-term, technology- and productivity-driven economic growth' rather than towards immediate satisfaction. In Britain, the fuel crisis of 1947 (that sad memorial to non-planning) provoked the government to move half a step forward from 'co-ordination through Cabinet committees': a new Central Economic Planning Staff of higher civil servants and economists was formed under the direction of a Chief Planning Officer, Sir Edwin Plowden, who, as Hennessy puts it, was determined 'that it should be nothing more than a small, advisory co-ordinating body'. The convertibility crisis, which was accompanied by a spell when Morrison was thrown out of action by illness, led to the creation of a Ministry of Economic Affairs under Cripps, to which this new planning staff was transferred, and the abolition of the Lord President's Committee, which was replaced by an Economic Planning Board, an example, again in Hennessy's words, of 'British machinery-of-government ad hocery at its worst. Nobody – not Government, then industry, trade unions, or Whitehall – ever knew what it was *for*'. In a word which was coming to have the same hollow ring as planning itself, Attlee explained that Cripps's position was 'one of co-ordination'. When Cripps became Chancellor upon Dalton's resignation, he took with him all the apparatus of his short-lived ministry. The high taxation levels to which the war had accustomed people were maintained; so also was rationing, as well as subsidies, for foodstuffs and other basic items.

The workers, naturally, were determined to hold on to the gains made during the war, and build on them. Strikes continued to be a regular feature of the industrial scene: dockers' strikes were obviously menacing to the government's overall aims, and the Attlee Government did not hesitate to bring in troops to undertake the hard, but essential, labour. On the whole the government, particularly after Cripps, who carried a great aura of moral integrity about him (others saw this as priggishness – 'There but for the grace of God, goes God', said Churchill), became Chancellor, was successful in its appeal to the trade unions for 'wage restraint'. One of the government's very first pieces of legislation in 1946 had been a new Trade Union Act which restored the situation as it had been before 1927, meaning that workers had again to deliberately 'contract out' of paying the levy which went to support the Labour party. That was in itself not of great significance. What was, was the lack of any attempt to deal with trade union restrictive practices, or to encourage workers to take an interest in the running, and success, of their companies. Equally, while there were exceptions in the newer industries, management continued its own casual ways, over-concerned for its rights and privileges. Labour's nationalization policies were supposed to take over the most important 20 per cent of industry, the so-called 'commanding heights'. Apart from the controls and quotas, which frequently caused irritation, little serious attention was devoted to the other 80 per cent, and it could reasonably be said that the government showed little sympathy for the problems, and possibilities, of small business.

During early 1949 Monnet tried to persuade the British of the desirability of economic cooperation between their two countries – there was, he said, a vacuum between Russian communism and American capitalism, which should be filled by some form of European cooperation. He concluded, rightly, that the British, still putting great faith in the value of the Commonwealth, in the 'special relationship' with America, in British sovereignty and Britain's role in the world, would have nothing to do with this. When Monnet, the French Foreign Minister Robert Schuman, the German Chancellor Konrad Adenauer, and his adviser Walter Hallstein mooted the very substantial project of the European Coal and Steel Community (which eventually became the European Economic Community and European Union) the British, in May 1950, were given a deliberately limited period in which to decide whether or not to join. British outrage was factitious, but then so were subsequent claims that Britain had too casually passed up a golden opportunity. Such were the ideological imperatives of the time that the British Government would have to have had superhuman vision to perceive the future development of Europe. With respect to the question of Labour's continuing to hold power, entering into European commitments would certainly have won no plaudits from the electorate. What counted for most with the electorate, as opinion polls made clear, was the setting-up of the welfare state.

### *The welfare state*

The welfare state legislation was intended to mark a break with the past, but was also both constrained by the legislative framework evolved in the past, and coloured by memories of that same past. Labour aimed at a 'universal' welfare state, embracing rich and poor, as distinct from a 'selective' one aimed only at the latter. Every Labour politician knew of the bitterness of the unemployed man thrown off unemployment insurance once his claim on the system was exhausted, and he had to undergo the 'Means Test'. There was humiliation, too, over the way in which 'panel patients' got one standard of service from their doctors, while the private patients got another. The rationale, then, for 'universality' was twofold: only by making the state services open to all could it be ensured that the highest standards would be available to all; only by having a universal service could the stigma be removed from those who had to make use of the state services. 'Universality' was the appropriate principle in 1945. Today, when the poor have been getting poorer, and the well-off more affluent, it has become necessary to reintroduce 'selectivity' whereby resources are directed towards those who most need them.

The first piece of new social security legislation was actually carried out by the Conservative 'caretaker' government which held office between the resignation of the wartime coalition and the assumption of office by the newly elected Labour Government. The most significant point about Family Allowances, payable in respect of second and later children in all income groups, was that they were payable to the mother, thus recognizing women's role as child-rearers, and making sure that husbands would not spend the money on drink or horses. Family Allowances came from general taxation, but when Labour came to the central Act in its social security policy the insurance principle was, in theory at least, maintained. As a consequence of the National Insurance Act, passed in 1946, effective from 1948, 'every person who on or after the appointed day, being over school-leaving age and under pensionable age, is in Great Britain, and fulfils such conditions as may be prescribed as to residence in Great Britain' would have a national insurance card upon which national insurance stamps would have to be stuck, giving an entitlement to 42 shillings (£2.10, and not enough to live on) a week, whenever a regular income was interrupted by sickness or unemployment. Since old-age pensions were to be paid immediately at full rate, there was no possibility of the scheme ever becoming an authentic piece of self-financing insurance. But still there had to be a further means of providing for those who, in one way or another, failed to meet the qualification conditions. Hence the National Assistance Act of 1948 which, though finally abolishing the old Poor Law, required that National Assistance would only be paid out after a personal means test.[58]

In planning the National Health Service, Aneurin Bevan had the benefit of the Emergency Hospital Scheme which had operated during the war. His major problems were the shortage of resources, the (real or perceived) conflicts of interest within the medical profession, and between the profession and the local authorities, and the antiquated condition of British local government. The National Health Service Act passed into law in the autumn of 1946; but the new NHS was not to come into being until 'the appointed day', 5 July 1948. In between, many tense battles had still to be fought out. In broad outline the proposed service was an embodiment of the principle of universality. Although a proportion of the income from National Insurance stamps was to be devoted to it, treatment in no way depended upon insurance contributions and it was, at the point of service, entirely free. No one was to be forced to join, whether as doctor or patient. Private pay beds would be allowed to exist within the hospitals, and general practitioners would be able to carry on their own private practice if they so wished. The senior consultants knew that they would be able to go on earning large fees. And they also had the satisfaction of knowing that the special position of the big teaching hospitals would be safeguarded; junior hospital doctors were quite happy to settle for a salaried service, but how the general practitioners were to be paid was not defined in the Act. In fact, these doctors resisted the infringement of their traditional professional status, which they believed to be involved in the acceptance of a completely salaried service, and held out for a scheme resembling that of the old panel system whereby they received a capitation fee for each patient on their list. Thus, though industrious or popular doctors might be particularly well rewarded, there was no real incentive to good practice.

The most effective reorganization took place with respect to the hospitals. In England and Wales there were fourteen regional hospital boards, each centred on the medical faculty of a university, and appointed by the Minister of Health. Management committees for the 388 hospitals within the system were to be appointed by the regional boards, but the 36 teaching hospitals were given a special autonomy in that their boards of governors were to be appointed directly by the Minister. In Scotland, five regional hospital boards were established, four based at universities, and the fifth at Inverness, and 84 hospital boards of management. There would have been greater efficiency and less waste if this model could have been deployed for all aspects of the service. In fact, historical circumstances and vested interest were too strong, so the health service ended up with its famous 'tripartite' structure. Many of the better services upon which the poor had been able to draw in the past were those provided by the local authorities. So it was not altogether unreasonable that important community health services should be left firmly in the hands of the larger local authorities: these services included midwifery, maternity and child welfare, health visiting, home nursing, domestic help, vaccination and immunization, local mental health services, ambulance transport, and the provision of health centres (though in Scotland the last two were the responsibility of the Secretary of State for Scotland). The smaller authorities were deprived of their health functions. The bulk of the medical profession, however, was determined not to be placed under the authority of local government when, after all, matters of specialized professional judgement would be involved. So, separate structures were set up for the family doctors: in England and Wales, 138 executive councils (in all but eight cases responsible for areas coterminous with counties or county boroughs), on which 12 out of 25 members were to be representatives of local professional interests, were established; while in Scotland, 25 executive councils were established on the same broad principles, though they generally covered areas larger than those of any local authority. These executive councils administered family doctor services, pharmaceutical services, dental services, and ophthalmic services. In Northern Ireland similar arrangements were made for, on the one hand, the hospitals, and, on the other, local authority services. General medical, dental, pharmaceutical and ophthalmic services were to be administered by a new Northern Ireland General Health Service Board.

Public opinion polls revealed that housing was the issue on which people felt most strongly in 1945. Existing housing legislation was quite explicitly selective: it provided housing 'for the working classes'. Formally, housing legislation of 1945 (Northern Ireland) and 1946 (England and Wales and Scotland) made no departure from established principles, though it was explained that the phrase 'working classes' would be interpreted as meaning 'all sections of the working population'.[59] Housing was basically financed through subsidies from the central government to the local authorities. These were particularly generous in Northern Ireland where a 'new Northern Ireland Housing Authority was established to build houses at the British Exchequer's expense'.[60] No support whatsoever was given to private house building, and the balance between private landlord and tenant was kept firmly in favour of the latter by the Rent Control Acts of 1946 and 1949. The Housing Act of 1949 did, at last, drop the phrase 'for the working classes', and at the same time made subsidies available for conversions and renovations. Given the problems of setting up the National Health Service it was probably a mistake for housing to be kept within the ambit of the Minister of Health: apart from insisting that all public housing should be of a high standard, Bevan devoted little attention to the subject, though it is also true that the building industry was in disarray, and necessary materials in very short supply. It was a failure of the Labour Government that only 806,000 houses were built between 1945 and 1950; in addition there were the 157,000 'pre-fabs' erected in the same period.

Educational policy in the post-war era was governed by the Act passed in 1944, and, at times more important, the *interpretations* placed upon it. The great strength of the Act was that it ensured that all pupils would, around the age of 11 or 12, move on to a form of secondary education which would, at the least, be continued till the age of 15. As implemented by almost all local authorities this entailed an 'eleven-plus' examination whose results would determine whether the pupil went on to a grammar school or to a secondary modern school. The route to better jobs and to higher education was through the grammar schools; the secondary modern school was the route to traditional working-class occupations. It also became apparent that middle-class children were far more likely to do well in the eleven-plus than working-class ones who came from a background where academic pursuits were not encouraged. Apart from the non-fee-paying state schools, there continued in existence an older and higher class of grammar schools charging fees, but also supported by a direct grant from the government (as distinct from a subsidy paid through the local authority). And the expensive and exclusive public schools remained untouched. Thus, although the potential for mobility through the educational system was greater than it had been in the 1930s – rather more working-class children did now get through the eleven-plus into grammar schools – the whole system very much replicated the division of the social structure into working, lower-middle, upper-middle, and upper classes.

Where significant developments did take place, though affecting only small sections of the population, was in university education. The Labour Government adumbrated the new policy by extending the terms of reference of the University Grants Committee in 1946; the Conservatives after 1951 carried it out by raising the central grants payable to the universities. By 1956–7 almost 70 per cent of university income was coming direct from the state. Owing to the presence of ex-servicemen, the university population reached an immediate post-war peak of 85,421 in 1949; by 1956–7 it was up to 89,833. At this time over three-quarters of all students in England were receiving public grants, with the proportion rather higher in Scotland, Wales and Northern Ireland. Thus the proportion of students drawn from 'the lower occupational categories' was higher than ever before; but the odds were still heavily weighted against a university education for a working-class child.

While welfare measures did have a significant effect on the living standards of the very poorest sections of the community – this must be borne in mind against the over-repeated and over-stated refrain that the welfare state basically benefited the middle classes – what was most important for living standards and security was the maintenance of full employment. This was an openly declared government objective, and should be seen as a vital component of the welfare state. Just what exactly government policy contributed to full employment, however, as against the general conditions of high demand after the war, is difficult to say. Turning again to the question of Labour's electoral popularity, whatever the irritations of rationing, controls, too frequent crises, and small helpings of suspect beef, the social security provisions, together with the NHS and full employment, undoubtedly gave good cause for many voters, new and old, to support continuance of Labour in office.

## *Ageing Labour and the Korean War*

Labour made the most elementary of mistakes in choosing the date for the election which, by law, would have to be held by July 1950. It seems that the main responsibility lay with Cripps: he refused to present another budget without having a renewed mandate from the electorate, and certainly would not contemplate introducing a budget which might seem to be offering bribes to that electorate.[61] Absurdly prissy, really, since with the combined effects of devaluation, Marshall Aid, and decent management of the economy, things were moving into excellent shape, and a few concessions would not only have been justifiable, but desirable. Attlee opted for 23 February. It may be conjectured that, in the wintry conditions, the bulk of the 16 per cent who did not make the effort to vote were working class; and wintry conditions do not make those who do vote entertain warm feelings towards the government of the day. In addition, the government had been touched by a whiff of scandal through the association between a junior minister at the Board of Trade, the former railway clerk John Belcher, and a notorious black marketeer, Sidney Stanley, whose nefarious dealings were brought out by the Tribunal of Inquiry under Mr Justice Lynskey in November to December 1948. Labour's manifesto, *Let Us Win Through Together*, had nothing like the appeal of *Let Us Face the Future*. Nationalization of iron and steel was still to be completed, sugar, cement and industrial assurance were to be added. One thinks of John Major 40 odd years later with nothing better to offer but more and yet more privatization. The sugar company Tate and Lyle put 'Mr. Cube' on every packet of sugar to warn against nationalization. The Conservative manifesto, *This Is The Road*, was the very embodiment of that consensus which some historians claim did not exist. While against nationalization and 'socialist waste', it endorsed the welfare state and full employment. But, as already noted, in an election in which more people than every before voted Labour, what did most damage was the alteration in electoral boundaries. And it remains hard to believe that Labour, who had not lost a single by-election during its period of office, would have been confined to an overall majority of five, had the election been postponed until June.

The government and its back-benchers were not so much old men, they were sick men. Bevin had to leave the Foreign Office and shortly died, being replaced by Morrison, who was also terminally ill. Cripps had to be replaced by Gaitskell. Attlee had bouts of illness. Worst of all, to ensure its majority, the government had to ship in back-benchers in wheel-chairs or on stretchers. Once more, no thought was given to reaching an accommodation with the Liberals. Attlee projected the sense that he felt that he had had his moment in history and done what he had set out to do. There appeared to be no drive towards establishing Labour as a natural party of government; certainly no sense of using Labour's continuing position in office to build up a more comfortable majority next time, as Harold Wilson was to do when elected on a similar knife-edge in 1964. Then came the Korean War; yet that, as the Falklands War later did for Margaret Thatcher, could have offered a vigorous and self-confident government just the opportunity it needed. The Korean War disrupted economic growth and imposed new burdens on the British people (it may even have disrupted a basis which was being laid for long-term sustained growth, though there is not really sufficient evidence to be sure about that). It also provided the occasion for a natural proclivity among those on the Left, who very definitely do not see themselves as a natural governing party, for shooting themselves in the foot.

As part of the post-war settlement in the Far East, the former Japanese colony of Korea had been partitioned between North Korea, within the Russian sphere, and South Korea, under what proved to be the highly corrupt regime of Syngman Rhee, in the American. Neither Russia, nor her new ally China, which fell to the Communists in the summer of 1949, were looking for war, but they were ever-ready to push their own interests wherever they thought they could do so without opposition. During the night of 25 June, North Korea invaded South Korea. Since Russia, who as a Security Council member had a veto, was boycotting the United Nations at this time in protest at the continued representation of the ousted Chinese regime, that of Chiang Kai Chek, now confined to the Island of Taiwan, the Americans were successful in securing a resolution calling for United Nations action against North Korea. Meeting on 27 June the Cabinet agreed to recognize its obligations to the United Nations. On 26 July the decision was taken to send British troops to Korea, and, most critically, on 3 August, the decision was taken to treble British defence expenditure with, on 15 September, National Service being extended to two years. In December Attlee flew to Washington to secure an assurance from Truman that the atom bomb would not be used against the North Koreans; there was relief for the British when, in the summer of 1951, the bomb-happy American General McArthur was sacked.

The burden was more than Britain could bear: the government's not unreasonable hope was that the Americans would defray the additional military expenditure, most of it in fact devoted to strengthening NATO in Europe, but they never did so. The Treasury sought for savings from the NHS and it was these that Gaitskell proposed to implement in his 1951 budget. Bevan was already furious that the younger man, Gaitskell, had been preferred to him as Cripps's successor, but as the creator of the free NHS it was natural that he should oppose the proposed prescription charges on false teeth and spectacles. Attlee was in hospital with ulcers, Morrison, in addition to being Foreign Secretary, was Acting Prime Minister. Bevan resigned from the government on 21 April; the next day he was followed by Harold Wilson, who made it clear that the substantive issue was the totally unrealistically high level of the new defence figures. He was absolutely right, save that the split in the Labour party was very nearly absolutely disastrous for Labour as a party of government (the 'Bevanites' just might have resigned in silence and remained resigned to silence, but, of course, they didn't). Just (as it must have seemed) to help things along for this star-crossed government, in May, two British diplomats in Washington (Burgess and Maclean), who had been spying for Russia, thought it wise to disappear to that country. Meantime (in April) the new Iranian Prime Minister, Dr Mossadeq, had nationalized the oil refinery built by the Anglo-Iranian company at Abadan. Morrison, not to mention the Conservative Opposition, made belligerent noises, but Attlee's cooler counsel prevailed. The upshot was to make the government appear both vacillating and weak. It was the joker in the constitutional pack, the King, who finally forced the issue of an election: he felt he could not go on his planned Commonwealth tour with the political situation so uncertain at home. The election date was fixed for 25 October.

Churchill, and much of the press, had portrayed Labour policies towards Persia, and also towards the new radical movement in Egypt, as 'socialist scuttle'. The Labour-supporting newspaper, *The Daily Mirror*, responded during the election by posing the question, 'Whose Finger on the Trigger?' Possibly the attempt to portray Churchill and the Conservatives as 'war-mongers' turned some wavering votes back towards Labour. The Conservatives promised to 'set the people free', build 300,000 houses a year, and feed the people on 'good red meat' in place of the miserable eight-pence meat ration of the time. The prime example of the government's belief that the Empire could be made to yield a profit had been the attempt to secure vegetable oil from the Ground Nuts scheme in Tanganyika. The scheme came to a very public and humiliating conclusion in good time for the election. Churchill, during the war, had said to the Americans: 'Give us the Tools and We'll finish the Job.' The scheme was a failure because the intractable terrain simply destroyed the tractors specially supplied for the job. So the mocking cry was: 'Give us the Job and We'll Finish the Tools.' Labour increased its vote and came out 0.8 per cent ahead of the Conservatives, but, as we saw, with fewer seats. Some potential Labour votes went to the Liberals, who secured nine seats.

### *The second Churchill Government*

However, with a majority of only 17, and an economy thrown into crisis by heavy military expenditure, the new Conservative Government might well not have lasted, there being a reasonable expectation that if Labour could regenerate itself and present a united front it might regain power quickly. The Conservatives had two immediate concerns: the first was the massive balance of payments crisis created by Korean rearmament; the second was the image they feared they had of being desirous of returning to the 'bad old days' of the twenties and thirties. These four years of the first post-war Conservative government are fascinating ones, in many ways central to many of the more contradictory, and indeed dismal, aspects of subsequent British history.

First, under this second Churchill Government, it became clear that Britain was definitively embarked on a period of consensus politics, in the limited and comparative sense in which I have already defined the term. The government did not wish to risk undoing those achievements of Labour policy which were clearly popular with the electorate; more than that, leading figures in the government, and others throughout the party, did genuinely believe in a 'one nation' Conservatism which would maintain the welfare and full employment policies of their predecessors. Secondly, it was in these five years that it was decisively demonstrated that Labour had lost its chances of becoming the natural party of government, the Conservatives once more taking over that role. Much of the Conservative success in this respect was due to good fortune. The Korean War ended in 1953 (leaving the situation there as it had been before the Soviets had tried their luck), and, because of a world-wide fall in raw material prices, Britain began to enjoy a particularly favourable trading situation. Of course, to enjoy good fortune, you have to be in power.

If Labour had in some degree given up on the struggle to maintain power, it now went on to behave in such a fashion as to render the expected early return highly unlikely. Short of truly dynamic and charismatic leadership (which neither a weary Attlee nor an ageing and fractious Morrison could provide) the institutional and ideological problems of the party were well-nigh insoluble. The party activists, who kept the local Labour parties going (themselves vital if Labour was to win elections), espoused left-wing policies, and could ensure that like-minded representatives were elected to the constituency section of the National Executive. To get its way, the party leadership needed to exploit the power wielded within the party by right-wing trade union leaders. The constituency parties could plausibly represent this as being deeply undemocratic, and thus fought their left-wing causes with all the more fervour. Few there were to suggest that perhaps Labour's true democratic duty lay towards the mass of its ordinary voters, still less to suggest that a Labour government in office ought to pay heed to the distribution of opinion throughout the country. As Korean rearmament faded away as a left-wing issue, it was replaced by that of German rearmament, and more generally, by Attlee's insistence that the Labour Opposition must support the government in its involvement in various American-sponsored security arrangements, most notably the South East Asia Treaty Organization (SEATO). Indeed, anti-Americanism, not balanced by any noteworthy pro-Europeanism, was a prominent component of left-wing attitudes. Left-wing discontents are an inevitable, and entirely comprehensible, accompaniment to Labour or Social Democratic politics, but they became disastrous at this time because of the potent presence of Bevan, which meant that the party was very publicly divided between the powerful Bevanite faction and the nominal leadership.

The Conservatives, on the other hand, ably established for themselves an identity with which, arguably, a large majority of voters, including many continuing to vote Labour, were very comfortable; while at the same time, greatly assisted by Labour's own squabbling, they gleefully represented Labour as believing in controls and 'snooping' and opposed to initiative and enterprise. Such figures as Harold Macmillan, with long-standing one-nation credentials, joyfully entered into the rumbustious name-calling of party politics,[62] quite compatible, in my view, with a general ethos of consensus. His success as Minister of Housing in building over 300,000 houses a year in each year from 1953 gave substance to the Conservative advocacy of a 'property-owning democracy'. Food rationing was brought to an end in 1954 and, thanks to the favourable terms of trade, food became more plentiful in the shops. At the same time, the Conservatives could make persuasive appeals to imperial and monarchical sentiment. Churchill, at 77, was manifestly a figure of world stature, and he was perfectly genuine in his belief that only if he could reactivate the wartime coalition of Britain, Russia and America, could the great divide in the world be bridged. In 1953 the Coronation took place of Queen Elizabeth II: if this great popular spectacle (as seen on television) paid any political bonuses, they all went to the Conservative party.

Britain went fully public as a nuclear power, with atomic rockets being tested at Woomera in Northern Australia in 1952; the government then proceeded with the development of the hydrogen bomb. The Imperial posture was maintained, more than 300,000 troops being deployed across the world. Soldiers, including young national servicemen, fought and died in British Guyana, Kenya, Malaya and Cyprus. Simultaneously there was a very definite further stage in withdrawal from Empire, independence being conceded to Ghana, Nigeria and Malaya. In what was in some ways the most crucial move, British troops were withdrawn from the Suez Canal zone. There was a small Conservative rebellion, led by two possessors of comic-book names, Lord Hinchingbrooke and Captain Waterhouse, but, largely because there was not the same kind of ideological *hatred* that left-wing politics tended to generate, the Conservatives were able to contain their rebels in a way that Labour could not. Overwhelmingly, this government fostered the delusions of Britain as a world power, and, correspondingly, took what can only be called a furiously hostile attitude to Europe. In the summer of 1955 the six countries participating in the Schuman Plan – France, Western Germany, Italy and the three Benelux countries – began decisive moves towards the establishment of a European Common Market. There followed the Messina (Sicily) conference of November 1955. The Dutch and the Belgians, in particular, made strenuous efforts to secure British involvement. The Labour party, we should be clear, was just as hostile as the government, as indeed – opinion polls make this very clear – was the British public as a whole. Britain was on the sidelines, jeering, but deeply anxious, when the following year the Treaty of Rome created the Common Market.[63] The British rejection of Europe in 1945–50 is fully comprehensible; arguably, by 1955, truly clear-sighted statesmen (Harold Macmillan, in this respect, was one of them) should have been directing the British public away from an illusory world role towards the 'third force' offered by a United Europe.

A less debatable criticism which can be made of this Conservative government is that it was the definitive begetter of the Stop–Go economic policy, so inimical to steady growth, and the ratifier in full measure of the policy, of which Labour had not been entirely innocent, of encouraging consumption at the expense of investment. The new Chancellor of the Exchequer was R. A. Butler, widely admired then and since as a reforming, one-nation Conservative, and the architect of the 1944 Education Act. Undoubtedly Butler was a leading figure in reconciling the Conservative party to the welfare state; he was not, perhaps, the best Chancellor of the Exchequer the country has ever had. His first reaction to the crisis he inherited was a very sensible one (indeed, ironically, it was the one advocated by Bevan): he cut the unrealistic arms programme. Three officials, Leslie Rowan (Treasury Second Secretary), George Bolton (Deputy Governor of the Bank of England) and 'Otto' Clarke in the Treasury came up with a secret plan (code-named, from an amalgamation of their names, ROBO) to relieve the balance of payments problem. The fixed exchange rate of the pound, which constantly entailed using up the reserves to support the pound, would be abandoned, and instead the pound would be allowed to float.[64] Butler enthusiastically put the proposal to the Cabinet: it would conserve precious gold and dollar reserves, though, he admitted, the consequent fall in the value of the pound would result in higher import prices and, probably, considerable unemployment. Latter-day Thatcherites have argued that this is the monetarist policy which Britain should have adopted. However, it was attacked by Churchill's special adviser, Lord Cherwell, and, most angrily, by Eden (who had been away on a mission to America). The government, in the end, was not prepared to contemplate the risk to full employment and, possibly, to other aspects of the welfare state as well. What was agreed, in a sharp break from Labour monetary policy, was a rise in interest rates to 4 per cent. High interest rates (for the time; 4 per cent seems appealingly low in 1999) restrained demand. But Butler also cut taxes ('setting the people free'), thus encouraging consumption (without doing anything to secure investment). In his 1955 budget he reduced the standard rate of income tax to 8s 6d (42½ pence). In the consequent mini-boom, the Conservatives won another election, and imports were sucked in to a potentially disastrous extent. Butler was forced to introduce a second budget in October which increased purchase-tax all round, and imposed it on certain household goods. A direct tax of this sort falls heavily on the poor; more critically, by sharply reducing demand, it imposes a 'stop' on manufacturers. Butler was shunted to the post of Lord Privy Seal, being replaced as Chancellor by Macmillan.

Churchill himself coined the perception that the trade unions were now 'an estate of the realm', and his government was particularly careful not to do anything to alienate this powerful force. The Minister of Labour, Sir Walter Monckton, was notably conciliatory, usually responding to industrial disputes with commissions of inquiry which tended to report in favour of the unions. The consequence was a gentle upwards drift in wages, a slight but steady inflationary pressure, and an unimpeded continuation of trade union restrictive practices. Technically, iron and steel and road haulage were denationalized: with respect to running the economy there was little real change, Labour never having achieved effective planning, the Conservatives retaining some controls. There was a continuation of the sort of nationalization which had first appeared in the 1920s in the form of the setting-up of the Atomic Energy Commission. *The Economist* (13 February 1954), its tongue at least partially in its cheek, invented the term 'Butskellism', suggesting a continuity of economic policy as between Gaitskell and Butler. Butler was more monetarist, and then erratic in sponsoring boom and slump. Gaitskell, referring to the second 1955 budget, said of Butler that he 'began in folly, he continued in deceit, and he has ended in reaction'. But, as a label for broadly consensual politics, *The Economist's* coinage will serve. This is most obviously so in regard to Conservative policies towards the welfare state. Although the charges introduced by Gaitskell were extended, the basic trend under the new Minister of Health, Iain Macleod, was, as the economy grew, to put more resources into the NHS. Macleod did appoint the Guillebaud Committee to investigate the efficiency of the service, but that committee had on it two pro-Labour supporters of the health service, Richard Titmuss and Brian Abel-Smith. More money, also, was put into the state education system. Several local authorities, where Labour continued to rule, began, very tentatively, to convert grammar schools into comprehensive schools: there was no friction with the Conservative Government over this. The most obvious, and the saddest, continuity between Labour and Conservatives was a continuity in complacency: Labour had failed to bring about the fundamental changes that the continental countries felt forced to implement; the Conservatives concentrated too much on confirming what Labour had done and on expanding consumption rather than devoting the newly available resources to structural reforms.

## SOCIETY IN THE AFTERMATH OF WAR[65]

### *SCIENCE AND TECHNOLOGY*

The Second World War is sometimes called 'The Physicists' War', and many of the developments inspired by purely military objectives were to have social repercussions, often rather unexpected ones. The adaptation of nuclear power to the generation of energy for civilian purposes was obvious enough, as was the application of radar to commercial air transport; but radio isotopes, a by-product of the nuclear industry, proved to have important applications in medicine, while the infra-red devices developed during the war for detecting the enemy in the hours of darkness proved invaluable in the scanning techniques developed in medical physics. Penicillin was a pre-war discovery, but it was only exploited in wartime. The successful search for new antibiotics (mainly carried out by American scientists) revolutionized medicine in the post-war years. Within chemicals generally there was a whole range of important developments, including plastics, artificial fibres, fertilizers, and pesticides. There was also a broad shift from 'light' chemicals to 'heavy' – detergents are an important example. Out of the war experience came two new, or almost new, science-based industries: electronics and optics; at the same time an older industry, engineering, was expanded and transformed. For even more traditional industries, new possibilities opened up: the use of oxygen in the continuous strip mill made possible the rapid production of high-quality thin steel sheets.

In contrast to the lack of investment in both infrastructure and manufacturing, Britain spent far more on research and development than any of the other European countries. The heaviest spending was chanelled into aircraft manufacture, telecommunications, precision engineering, and chemicals. By the early fifties a considerable reorientation of Britain's exports had taken place, so that two-thirds were drawn from the new science-based and technological industries. But scientific discovery and technological innovation, by their very nature, are international in their consequences. Britain derived much from American pioneering; but other countries took much from Britain. Scientific and technological innovation alone would not keep Britain in the position which, precariously, she still occupied in Europe in the middle fifties.

## *IRELAND, SCOTLAND AND WALES*

In Northern Ireland, where Unionist objections to 'socialist' measures, and even proposals that the province should escape the socialist embrace through seeking Dominion status, were repulsed, there were considerable gains, but they did not prove durable.[66] The wartime boom for heavy industry, and, in particular, the massive Harland and Wolff shipyards, lasted until 1951; thereafter there was a sharp decline. Throughout the period 1950 to 1960 unemployment never fell below 5 per cent and averaged 7 per cent, the highest figure for anywhere in the United Kingdom. The Industrial Development Act (Northern Ireland) and the Capital Grants to Industry Act (Northern Ireland), respectively, offered new enterprises factory premises and equipment with the necessary infrastructure, and grants of up to a quarter of the cost for any investment in plant, machinery, and buildings. But though these initiatives created perhaps 2,500 new jobs each year in Northern Ireland, this did not match the job losses in the staple industries – linen as well as shipbuilding and engineering. *The Economic Survey of Northern Ireland*, commissioned in 1947, indicted the small companies which dominated the linen industry as being more interested in profit-taking than investment. Even agriculture contracted, with employment there falling by nearly one-third between 1950 and 1960. Government investment in education and health did increase employment in the service sector, but the overall increase in the post-war period of 18,500 could not compensate for the heavy losses elsewhere.

During the war, the wide spaces and sheltered inlets of the Highlands of Scotland were exploited for military training grounds, airfields and port facilities. New roads were built in the Orkneys, the Shetlands, and on the islands of Lewis, Benbecula, and South Uist. New piers were constructed at such shipping ports as Wick, Thurso, Tarbert, and Ullapool. Furthermore, a new hospital for 640 patients was built at Raigmore, Inverness. More important was the government's campaign to increase home-produced food. Highland farmers benefited, and even prospered moderately, from grants under the Marginal Agricultural Production Scheme and from subsidies for hill sheep and hill cattle. Following the establishment of the North of Scotland Hydro-Electricity Board, thanks to the energetic policies of Scotland's socialist Secretary of State in the wartime coalition, Tom Johnston, the building of new hydro-electric schemes continued at a rapid pace in the post-war years. The Highland economy was not saved, and not all of the changes were welcome ones. But a stop had been put to the absolute decline of pre-war years. In the Southern Uplands, both arable and pasture farming prospered in meeting new demands.

Something of a revival in industrial Central Scotland seemed to be heralded by the locating of a number of Royal Ordnance factories, as well as other industrial developments, in this area. A Ministry of Supply clothing depot at Motherwell became, in the post-war years, a Metropolitan Vickers engineering factory. A wartime Rolls-Royce factory at Hillington, just outside Glasgow, was the precursor of other factories in what, in the post-war years, became a new industrial estate. Garelochhead acquired a Metal Industries Limited depot, Falkirk an aluminium rolling mill, and Edinburgh an important Ferranti Electronics complex. Government policy deliberately aimed to bring industry to Scotland; and until the early fifties, at least, a new level of prosperity was attained, even if, from the point of view of the United Kingdom economy, Scotland was not always the most sensible place in which to site new industry.

Central and North Wales met with fewer direct incursions from the war than did the Highlands and Islands of Scotland. Again there was a drive to bring marginal land under cultivation, and on the whole the farming communities of North Wales did well. But for industrial South Wales the legacy was mixed. Munitions factories were built at Bridgend, Hirwaun, Glasoed and Penbury, together with servicing and stores depots. A new aluminium works was also established. The Treforest Industrial Estate, near Pontypridd, was a brave, if tiny, thirties initiative: after war broke out new factories were set up to produce a range of strategic goods from optical lenses to parachutes. During the war, and immediately after, a number of amalgamations took place within the steel industry, so that by the late forties it was largely dominated by Richard Thomas and Baldwins (formed in 1944), and the Steel Company of Wales (formed in 1946).

The great symbol of the post-war reconstruction of the iron and steel industry was the building, between 1947 and 1951, of the Port Talbot works at a total of £73 million. Its importance is encapsulated in the local nickname given to it of 'Treasure Island'. Wartime factories were there to hand for eager industrialists. The Labour Government encouraged the building of the new type of one-storey factories located in open fields outside the towns, and sponsored 112 of the 179 new factories (or substantial factory extensions) which were built in South Wales between the end of the war and 1949. Unemployment dropped to 2.8 per cent compared with 20 per cent in the thirties. Prosperity continued right through to the later fifties so that, not unnaturally, the development area policies were relaxed. But, in the longer term, they were not as satisfactory as they appeared: there was insufficient diversification and insufficient attention to the requirements of world, and even national, markets.

## *The regions of England*

Similar mixed stories apply for the main industrial areas of England. As in Scotland, war factories in the north-east provided the bases for the development of post-war industrial estates, and, for example, the new town of Newton Aycliffe. The largest post-war developments took place on Teeside, with the establishment of a vast new ICI nylon polymer plant at Wilton and the building of Lackenby steel smelting shop, which came into production in 1953. The Labour Government located its new Ministry of National Insurance in Newcastle. While there was to be no long-term recovery for the Lancashire cotton industry, Liverpool prospered in the post-war production drive. New industries, based mainly on synthetics, had been fostered during the war, and the county had been given an injection of metropolitan middle-class lifestyles by the settlement of certain civil service departments in the resort towns of Lytham St Anne's and Blackpool. The big changes in the chemicals industry brought a new prosperity to Warrington, Widnes, and their vicinity. Although West Yorkshire was on the way to becoming a museum, rather than a hive, of industry, with no real recovery for the Yorkshire woollen mills, the coalfields of South Yorkshire were doing well. These practically merged into the coalfields of the East Midlands, which also did very well in the post-war years. In both Nottingham and Derby there was considerable growth of light industry. Nottingham had its famous Raleigh bicycle works, and Derby had its Rolls-Royce, Midland Railway and British Celanese factories. Where the Pennines come to an end in Derbyshire is one of the most famous and popular beauty areas in Britain: in 1949 the Peak District was designated Britain's first National Park.

The most striking success story of the war and post-war years was that of the West Midlands. The Black Country, to the north and west of Birmingham, original home of the Midlands coal mines and iron works, certainly had a somewhat desolate air at the end of the war. But Coventry, to the south-east of Birmingham, although blitzed in November 1940, already by the end of the war stood out for its prosperity resulting from the boom in engineering, motor manufacturing, and other light industry; it was to benefit further from the deliberate attempts to stimulate technological innovation after 1945, as also from the pent-up demand for cars. The West Midlands conurbation can be taken as the most successful example of post-war suburban growth. The potteries of North Staffordshire, to the north, were always of a rather different character. During the war, 37,000 pottery jobs disappeared; on the other hand two important Royal Ordnance factories were established which continued, though on a reduced scale, after 1945, and wartime shadow factories located in the potteries were taken up by Rists, AEI and Simplex. Furthermore accumulated demand, and the general terms of trade, did bring something of a revival in both pottery and coal mining, and by 1951 both industries were re-established at almost pre-war employment levels. Development policies seem to have benefited the West Midlands more than strict assessment of need might have suggested: one-eighth of the area was declared to be 'development land' and was steadily built on and filled in. When the Stop–Go came in the early fifties it had only relatively mild effects on this region, and unemployment always remained at around half the national level.

In the south-west, Bristol did well: out of the war experience burst the growth industries of light engineering, aviation, and electronics, and a new boom in the age-encrusted tobacco trade (again the tobacco companies had distributed cheerfully – women in the war industries being particularly prone to take up the habit). The historic port of Plymouth, its town centre blitzed to the ground, had to embark immediately on an intensive rebuilding programme.

Evacuation had focused attention on the noisome nature of London's slums, while the Blitz had destroyed numbers of them. Overspill, rehousing and the establishment of the green belt were key notions. At the same time, the Labour Government sought to restrict office building in central London. The overall picture was of a movement outwards to new suburban estates, and further afield to the new towns of which London's periphery had a disproportionate number: Basildon, Bracknell, Hemel Hempstead, Hatfield, Stevenage, Harlow and Crawley, together with the older Welwyn Garden City. By 1956 each of these was expanding at a rate of 9,000 houses per year. Overspill could go yet further afield and in 1952 the first Londoners arrived in Bletchley, a town lying on the frontiers of the Home Counties and the South Midlands, which had itself undergone some transformations during the war due largely to the siting there of large numbers of civil servants and the establishment of the Military Intelligence unit in Bletchley Park. Whatever the planners' intentions, the Greater London conurbation expanded at a rate comparable with that of the West Midlands. The unique wash of brick-built terrace houses, brightened by the little high street shopping centres, which spread across such inner London suburbs as Kentish Town, Islington, Leyton, Hackney, Fulham and Camberwell, asserted a special charm. It was already clear by the early fifties that there was no rush to leave these terraces, and that, indeed, they were rising in value as London continued to parade its age-old attractions.

### *Transport and Ordinary Life*

Agricultural areas generally continued to prosper from the wartime policies of bringing 'marginal' land into use. The heights of south-west Shropshire were reclaimed for pasture farming and in the post-war years, through the exploitation of advanced agricultural technology, these continued to yield good profits as a centre of cattle-rearing. The West Country and the Thames Valley profited greatly from the expansion in arable land brought about by the needs of war. The Thames Valley in particular achieved new levels of prosperity both in dairy farming and in the fast developing industry of market gardening. In East Anglia revivals took place in both arable and livestock farming, while in the early fifties trading estates were established at Haverhill and Thetford; more crucially, modest prosperity elsewhere, particularly in London, spilled over into tourism on the Broads and around the coast.

There was a slightly archaic quality to transport and communications. The expanding sector was that of road transport, that is transport by bus and coach, but not private car. While rail passenger transport remained static, by 1950 passenger mileage by bus and coach had risen to 50.2 thousand million passenger miles, as against 19.4 in 1938, now accounting for nearly one-half of the total market compared with less than one-third before the war; road transport as a whole now accounted for about 75 per cent of all mileage travelled. In the towns, buses were taking over from trolleybuses and trams: by 1952 bus passenger miles within the cities and towns amounted to 14.5 thousand million as against 2.9 thousand million by trolleybuses, and 1.8 thousand million by trams.

The great expansion in private car ownership began only in the very last years of the period under review. In 1938 there had been just under 2 million private cars and vans on the roads; in 1948 there were just over 2 million, and in 1950 between 2.25 million and 2.5 million. In 1955 the figure rose steeply to over 3.6 million. Roads were poor, and still served local needs rather than those of national travel. Although dual carriageways had been built near large towns, trunk roads on the whole were narrow and winding. It took a whole day to drive from London to Edinburgh; if going further north, you went upriver to the Kincardine Bridge, or queued for a ferry as medieval citizens had done in the days when Queensferry got its name. To get to South Wales it was necessary to go through Gloucester. Only in 1955 was it announced that Britain's first motorway (planned in the forties) would be built; the word itself was as yet scarcely known to the wider public.

The war had, in many instances, disrupted marriages and family life. Divorces reached a peak of 60,000 in 1947, ten times the pre-war figure. The passing of the Legal Aid Act two years later opened the possibility of divorce to many who had previously been deterred by the expense. By the middle fifties there were about 25,000 divorces a year. Yet there could be absolutely no doubt as to the continued popularity of marriage. Even of those divorced, three-quarters remarried. The more important historical trend can be seen in the figures relating to women in the 20–39 age group: in 1911 only 552 out of every thousand women in this age group were married; in 1951 the figure was 731. Of all children born in 1955, 5 per cent were illegitimate.

The most thorough study of British attitudes to marriage, courtship, and sex was contained in the survey conducted by Geoffrey Gorer in January 1951 through the *People* newspaper, and, after some delay, published in book form as *Exploring English Character* (1960). Just over half the men and nearly two-thirds of the women interviewed by Gorer expressed disapproval of sex before marriage; 43 per cent of his total sample admitted to having had a sexual relationship before or outside of marriage, while 47 per cent gave an emphatic denial. It seemed that men and women differed both in attitudes and in actual experience (or enjoyment) of sex. It was mainly men who declared sex to be 'very important' in marriage, and mainly women who disagreed with the statement that 'women really enjoy the physical side of sex just as much as men'; 65 per cent of men *agreed* with this statement, and 51 per cent of women.

As the war ended, there was a great and immediate resurgence of the leisure activities characteristic of the inter-war years. Blackpool, Scarborough, the Isle of Man boomed. Cinema attendances reached a peak in 1946 (when one-third of the population were going once a week, 13 per cent twice a week) and remained high; football enjoyed a golden age of large crowds. Slowly, from being a lower middle-class preserve, the holiday camps were taken over by working-class holiday makers. The war had given children certain freedoms; economic conditions after the war fostered their independence. Gangs of adolescent, and even younger children, were nothing new, but, with the sanctions of war removed, they certainly flourished. In the forties the grown-up generation provided the semi-outcast figure who shocked the respectable and outwitted the sluggish government: the spiv. With the early 1950s there came the first national and recognized figure representative of youth's detachment from the rest of society and representative also of the fact that for the first time working-class youth could take the initiative: the teddy boy. The name derives from the Edwardian form of dress which, actually, had briefly been assumed by some bright young men of the upper class in the late forties.

### *Media and the arts*

In the cinemas, what audiences saw were largely American films, mainly musicals and romances; there were serious films of social realism, but the issues, race, gangsterism, civic corruption, were all rather remote from British experience. The quota system, introduced in 1927 and strengthened by the Labour Government, was intended to ensure that 30 per cent of feature films were British. The British film industry was an interlinked and overlapping network of production companies, distribution companies and chains of exhibitors, overwhelmingly dominated by one British figure, J. Arthur Rank, and otherwise by the various American companies. Two government-sponsored sources of funding proved to be of only minor assistance to independent producers: the 'Eady Levy' on cinema receipts (voluntary in 1950, compulsory after 1957) tended in practice to be distributed more to the rich than to the poor; funding from the National Film Finance Corporation (established 1949) was in the form of loans not grants. The more important British films can be grouped under five headings: (1) Films of the great classics of English literature – Laurence Olivier's Shakespeare, David Lean's Dickens. (2) Films derived from successful West End plays, sometimes containing some elements of social comment, the well-made, witty plays of Terence Rattigan being almost automatically converted into films. (3) The romantic dramas produced by Gainsborough Films, including *The Wicked Lady* (1945), featuring two of the three top British box-office attractions of the time, James Mason and Margaret Lockwood (the third was Stewart Grainger). (4) The films of Ealing Studios, the production company which had come to prominence during the war for its carefully delineated, and gently understated, celebrations of patriotic Britishness – brilliant post-war cameos were *Passport to Pimlico* (directed by South African-born Henry Cornelius), and *Kind Hearts and Coronets* (directed by Cambridge graduate Robert Hamer, 1949), which is set in the late nineteenth century. (5) And the handful of truly ambitious and challenging films, including *The Red Shoes* (1948), about the tragic romance between a ballet-dancer and an opera-composer, and Carol Reed's masterpiece, *The Third Man* (1949). In addition, a large number of films of variable quality testified to the nation's continuing obsession with its achievements in the Second World War.

The war consolidated the advance of radio, making a radio set a necessity which practically every household had to have. At the war's end, the radio services still monopolized by the BBC were reorganized into three 'Programmes': the Light, the Home Service and the Third. BBC audience research treated the audiences for these three services as synonymous with working-class, middle-class, and upper-middle/upper-class, respectively. The most successful radio soap opera of all time was *Mrs Dale's Diary*, set in a distinctly upper middle-class milieu. The Third Programme played an important part in the musical renaissance after 1945; but much of its output was characterized by mannered pedantry and academic parochialism. The most significant phenomenon was the success of *Saturday Night Theatre* on the Home Service, with an audience at the end of the forties equivalent to one-third of the entire adult population. Television broadcasting, only just beginning at the end of the thirties, had been brought to a stop by the war; it grew again only slowly in the post-war years, though by the early fifties there were five million television viewers. In order that television might not become an addiction or distract children from their studies nor adults from their duties, it was confined to a limited number of hours per day – very much in keeping with the BBC ethic. The first debate over the BBC's position took place in 1954 when, against the convictions of senior Conservatives, the Act was passed which led to the setting-up of a separate commercial television channel.

That small, but potentially influential, group of people who think about these things at all, thought it important to show that in fighting Nazism, Britain was fighting for the finest in European and British cultural traditions. Against the hostility of reactionaries and 'realists', the Council for the Encouragement of Music and the Arts (CEMA) was established as an agency for subsidizing the arts. Myra Hess, the distinguished concert pianist, put on her famous lunch-time recitals in the National Gallery in London; the Sadlers Wells Opera Company, driven out of that same London by the bombing of its theatre, carried opera and ballet round the provinces. Civil servants evacuated from London created new local demands for high-, or at least middle-brow culture. Benjamin Britten, the composer, and Peter Pears, the tenor, willingly returning to Britain in the spring of 1942, were not alone in feeling that Britain in wartime was undergoing a cultural renaissance. In 1946 CEMA was established on a long-term basis as the Arts Council. A number of local theatres were established very much as a direct reaction to the war experience. Yet, in the immediate post-war years a rather self-conscious, overly exclusive, upper-class-leaning bohemia seemed to dominate over any more popular impulses released by the war.

The neo-romantic, rhetorical tendency was abundantly clear in the poetry of the Welsh poet Dylan Thomas. He achieved a wider than usual reputation for a poet when his first play, specially written for radio, *Under Milk Wood*, was broadcast in 1954 and subsequently given in the form both of solo readings by the author and of full-dress stage presentations. But, as best-known poet, Thomas was shortly eclipsed by John Betjeman, whose cunning blend of nostalgia and the kind of idiosyncratic humour that the British love to salute (as for instance in the Ealing Studios films of the time) nicely met the new post-war appetite for poetry: his *Selected Poems* (1948) turned him from minor to best-selling poet. Not, of course, that either of these came close in stature to T. S. Eliot, whose poetry attained its highest reputation at this time.

Evelyn Waugh, while still brilliantly witty, became one of the most extreme critics of the trends towards social and economic democracy of the war and post-war period – he lamented, when the Conservatives returned to power in

1951, that they did not put the clock back by one minute. In 1952 came the first of the *Sword of Honour* trilogy, *Men at Arms*; there followed *Officers and Gentlemen* (1955) and *Unconditional Surrender* (1961). The regimentation, cynicism and muddle of war is presented as a betrayal of high conservative principles. Graham Greene developed an incredible nose for public affairs, a gift for setting his novels in troubled parts of the world almost before they hit the headlines. *The Heart of the Matter* (1948) is set in a West African colony as British colonialism is coming to an end; *The End of The Affair* (1951) evokes the Blitz and wartime London in a far more direct way than Waugh's trilogy. The two most internationally famous novels of the period came from the scion of an impoverished upper-class family who had deliberately not used his education at Eton to regain social status. George Orwell (pseudonym of Eric Blair, 1903–50) was a socialist and ruthless, common sense, critic of left-wing excesses. His *Animal Farm* (1945) was a comparatively light satire on totalitarianism, but it was followed by the nightmare vision of Fascist dictatorship merged with Stalinist oppression, *Nineteen Eighty-Four* (1949).

Writers in what became known as 'The Movement' (early 1950s) were educated at Oxford or Cambridge, but came from the lower ranges of the middle class, having moved upwards via grammar schools and scholarships. They deliberately eschewed big modernist and international issues: Kingsley Amis's *Lucky Jim* (1954) was a novel of the absurdities of provincial university life.

The artists who had already achieved fame before the war were joined by Francis Bacon (b.1909), whose malignant, ominous, twisted figures, part-human, part-animal at first aroused outrage and ridicule from critics. Wide acclaim soon followed: Frances Spalding suggests that, 'to a post-war audience, these goulish celebrants of murderous acts were a horrific reminder of human bestiality'.[67] Reacting against internationalism, modernism, and the London bohemia in rather the manner of 'The Movement', were the artists who in 1954 were given the name the 'Kitchen Sink School' by the art critic David Sylvester: John Bratby, Jack Smith (both born 1928) and Edward Middleditch (b. 1923) all belonged to the English provinces. The question of a distinctive 'Scottishness' comes up in interesting form with Joan Eardley (1912 to 1965), whose English father, an officer, met her Scottish mother in Glasgow during the First World War. She was born in Sussex, but studied at the Glasgow Art School, thereafter being thoroughly identified with the Scottish art world, and its 'colourist' and 'expressionist' traditions, well represented by Anne Redpath and Henderson Blyth. Another Scot, Alan Davie (b. 1920), became a leading figure in the British version of abstract expressionism.

At the end of the war the Sadlers Wells Theatre was reopened as the home exclusively of English-language opera, while the Sadlers Wells Ballet (becoming the Royal Ballet) transferred to the Royal Opera House, Covent Garden, which from being a commercial venue playing host to visits by the top international operatic companies, was re-established, with Arts Council support, as a national home for opera and ballet. Bombs destroyed the Queen's Hall in London forever: the Free Trade Hall, home of Manchester's famous Hallé Orchestra, was not fit for reoccupation until 1951. The Royal Liverpool Philharmonic and the Hallé became full-time permanent orchestras for the first time in 1942 and 1943 respectively. Developments in the post-war years were the reorganization of the Scottish Orchestra into the permanent Scottish National Orchestra in 1950, and the expansion under Charles Groves of the Bournemouth Symphony Orchestra in 1954. But without doubt the major force in British music was the BBC – through its own symphony orchestra, through its regional orchestras, through its broadcasts on the new post-war Third Programme, through its sponsorship each summer of the Royal Albert Hall Promenade Concerts (the Proms), and through the valuable subventions it offered each time it broadcast a concert or music festival.

When Britten and Pears, both pacifists, returned to Britain in early 1942 they were given exemption from military service on condition that they gave recitals for CEMA. Much of Britten's creative energies were devoted to composing an opera based on a poem by George Crabbe: as conscientious objectors, and therefore to a degree outsiders, Britten and Pears identified with the strangely independent and stubborn character of Peter Grimes. If the founding of the Edinburgh International Festival of Music and Drama in 1947 is one impressive testimonial to the new spirit of internationalism, sanity, and reconciliation released by the war, the fact that it was Britten's opera, *Peter Grimes*, which was chosen to reopen the Sadlers Wells Theatre on 7 June 1945 was another.

## *Architecture and the Festival of Britain*

The new houses built, slowly under Labour, more rapidly under the Conservatives were traditional in style. The first generation of new towns, started in the forties, also catered to the traditional taste for low-rise housing set in a reasonable space, while at the same time adopting some of the tenets of the international functionalist style. Harlow (planned by an active modernist of the thirties, Frederick Gibberd) has been widely praised, though it also quickly manifested a problem which became endemic in post-war architecture: the smart white terraces in the international style by two other young modernists, Maxwell Fry and Jane Drew, simply wore much less well than some of their more traditional brick-built neighbours. Industrial techniques for building schools were pioneered in Hertfordshire, then, in 1948, taken up by the Ministry of Education. Several of these schools won international reputations. For the out-and-out modernists more scope seemed to offer itself as the local authorities in the big cities decided that lengthy housing lists and shortages of urban land could only be overcome through building multi-storey housing estates. Important examples were Quarry Hill in Leeds, and Churchill Gardens in Pimlico and the Wholefield Estate in Paddington, both in London.

The first great break from the needs of home, family and children towards the need for public spectacle came with the preparation of the bombed-out Southbank site for the 1951 Festival of Britain.[68] Appointed Director of Architecture, Hugh Casson designed the entire exhibition area in the modernist idiom of a single concept linking together spaces and buildings: the major temporary constructions were the Dome of Discovery, designed by Ralph Tubbs, and the

Skylon, designed by J. H. Moya. The Royal Festival Hall was actually a London County Council project, designed by their chief architect, Robert Matthew, and would have been built anyway, festival or no festival. Though there was a travelling Festival Exhibition which visited Manchester, Leeds, Birmingham and Nottingham, and quite a number of smaller individual Festival efforts, as well as some larger ones such as the Exhibition of Industrial Power in Glasgow, the Festival of Britain in reality, if not intention, came over as very much a metropolitan affair.

Both of those upper-class socialists Hugh Dalton and Sir Stafford Cripps were enthusiastic supporters of good design. Wartime necessity had led to the creation of 'utility' furniture – one nationwide economical style; wartime aspiration had led to the creation of the Council for Industrial Design. Cripps played an important part in the presentation of the 1946 Design Exhibition at the Victoria and Albert Museum: 'Britain can make it'. A million-and-a-half people visited this exhibition of simple, unfussy, rational products, each a tribute to the best in modern functionalism. Unfortunately, few were available for general sale, so that the exhibition was quickly nicknamed 'Britain can't have it'. In 1956 the Design Centre was opened in Haymarket, London, and a year later the Design Centre Awards began. Yet, as Fiona MacCarthy has remarked – and how typical this is of the entire British cultural scene – 'Design was still in many ways an amiable clique. Identical Professors seemed forever giving prizes to their own RCA students, identical designers were forever smiling thanks to the Duke of Edinburgh.'[69]

## NOTES

1 F. S. Northedge, *The Troubled Giant: Britain Among the Great Powers, 1916–1939* (1966).
2 Letters in Imperial War Museum quoted in Arthur Marwick, *The Home Front: The British and the Second World War* (1976), p. 21.
3 Correlli Barnett, *Britain and Her Army: 1509–1970: A Military, Political and Social Survey* (1970), pp. 426–7; Brian Bond, 'The British Field Force in France and Belgium, 1939–40'. In Paul Addison and Angus Calder (eds), *Time to Kill: The Soldier's Experience of War in the West 1939–1945* (1977), pp. 40–1.
4 Quoted in Henry Pelling, *Britain and the Second World War* (1970), p. 55.
5 Paul Addison, 'Lloyd George and Compromise Peace in the Second World War'. In A. J. P. Taylor (ed.), *Lloyd George: Twelve Essays* (1971), pp. 361–74; Anthony Lentin, 'A Conference *Now*: Lloyd George and Peacemaking, 1939: Sidelights from the Unpublished Letters of A. J. Sylvester', in *Diplomacy and Statecraft* (November 1996), pp. 563–88.
6 Peter Calvocoressi, Guy Wint and John Pritchard, *Total War: The Causes and Courses of the Second World War* (revised second edition, 1989 and 1995), pp. 115–23.
7 Pelling, *Second World War*, p. 70.
8 Ian McLean, *Ministry of Morale: Home Front Morale and the Ministry of Information in World War II* (1979), p. 31.
9 Pioneering work on this unjustly neglected aspect of the Second World War experience has been carried out by Professor Brian Bond and published in his chapter in Addison and Calder, *Time to Kill*, pp. 40–9. The remainder of my paragraph

is based on Bond, who gives full references.

10 Quoted by Pelling, *Second World War*, p. 75.

11 There is a good summary in ibid., pp. 70–5.

12 Bond, 'British Field Force', p. 44, to whose chapter I am also indebted for the rest of this paragraph.

13 Nicholas Harman, *Dunkirk: The Necessary Myth* (1980), pp. 11–12; see also Angus Calder, *The Myth of Dunkirk* (1994).

14 Quoted by A. J. Barker, *Dunkirk: The Great Escape* (1977), p. 108.

15 Russell Plummer, *The Ships That Saved An Army: A Comprehensive Record of the 1,300 'Little Ships' of Dunkirk* (1990), p. 14. The next two paragraphs are based on Plummer.

16 Quotation from Barker, *Dunkirk*, pp. 105, 119.

17 John Charmley, *Churchill: The End of Glory: A Political Biography* (1993), esp. pp. 398 ff, pp. 431 ff. See also John Charmley, *Chamberlain and the Lost Peace* (1988).

18 Colin Holmes, '"British Justice at Work": Internment in the Second World War'. In Panikos Panayi, *Minorities in Wartime: National and Racial Groupings in Europe, North America and Australia During the Two World Wars* (1993), pp. 150–65.

19 John Macnicol, 'The effect of the evacuation of school-children on official attitudes to state intervention'. In Harold L. Smith (ed.), *War and Social Change: British Society and the Second World War* (1986), pp. 3–31.

20 Calvocoressi, Wint, Pritchard, *Total War*, pp. 164–79.

21 Pelling, *Second World War*, pp. 144–57.

22 For the appalling horror of this battle, see Anthony Beevor, *Stalingrad* (1998).

23 Hamish Henderson, in '"Puir Bluidy Swaddies are Weary": Sicily 1943'. In Addison and Calder, *Time to Kill*, pp. 319–20.

24 Ian S. Wood, '"'Twas England Bade Our Wild Geese Go": Soldiers of Ireland in the Second World War'. In Addison and Calder, *Time to Kill*, p. 87.

25 Mark K. Wells, *Courage and Air Warfare* (1995), pp. 27–35, 60–7.

26 Pelling, *Second World War*, p. 153; R. J. Overy, *The Air War, 1939–1945* (1980), pp. 103–8, 115–19.

27 Pelling, *Second World War*, p. 192.

28 Report of Police President of Hamburg on the Raids of July and August 1943, quoted in Sir Charles K. Webster and Noble Frankland, *The Strategic Air Offensive Against Germany, 1939–1945*, vol. 4 (1984).

29 Paul Addison, *The Road to 1945: British Politics in the Second World War* (1975), esp. pp. 113, 280.

30 Letter in Beveridge papers, quoted in Arthur Marwick, *The Home Front: The British and the Second World War* (1996), p. 128. In general see José Harris, *William Beveridge: A Biography* (1977).

31 See Arthur Marwick, 'People's War and Top People's Peace? British Society and the Second World War'. In Alan Sked and Chris Cook (eds), *Crisis and Controversy: Essays in Honour of A. J. P. Taylor* (1976), pp. 148–64.

32 Angus Calder, *The People's War: Britain 1939–45* (1969), pp. 546–50; Stephen Brooke, *Labour's War: The Labour Party During the Second World War* (Oxford, 1992), p. 69.

33 P. H. J. H. Gosden, *Education in the Second World War: A Study in Policy and Administration* (1976).

34 Wood, ''Twas England Bade', p. 91.

35 Letter in Imperial War Museum, quoted in Marwick, *Home Front*, p. 166.

36 This is very fully documented in Addison, *Road to 1945*. For changes of outlook among 'ordinary people', see Marwick, *Home Front*, pp. 123–62. See also Harris,

*William Beveridge*, pp. 380–1.

37 Peter Clarke, 'Keynes, New Jerusalem, and British Decline'. In Peter Clarke and Clive Trebilcock, *Understanding Decline: Perceptions and Realities of British Economic Performance* (1997), pp. 145–65.

38 Peter Hennessy, *Never Again: Britain 1945–51* (1993), pp. 106–7.

39 Charles H. Feinstein, 'The end of empire and the golden age'. In Clarke and Trebilcock, *Decline*, p. 214.

40 Bernard Alford, '1945–51: Years of recovery or a stage in economic decline?'. In ibid., p. 191.

41 Quoted in Marwick, *Home Front*, p. 169.

42 Correlli Barnett, *The Lost Victory: British Dreams, British Realities, 1945–50* (1995). A leading critic of Barnett has been Peter Howlett – see his 'The wartime economy, 1939–1945', in R. Floud and D. McCloskey (eds), *The Economic History of Britain since 1700*, vol. 3 (Cambridge, 1994). Again, Peter Clarke provides a brilliant summary in his 'Keynes, New Jerusalem and British Decline', in Clarke and Trebilcock, *Decline*.

43 Sidney Pollard, *The Wasting of the British Economy: British Economic Policy 1945 to the Present* (1982), p. 2.

44 This is a theme throughout Clarke and Trebilcock, *Decline*. See especially José Harris, 'Social policy, saving and sound money: budgeting for the New Jerusalem in the Second World War', pp. 167, 181–2, 185; see also Alan S. Milward, *The European Rescue of the Nation-State* (1992).

45 Ben Pimlott, 'Is the postwar consensus a myth?', *Contemporary Record* 2 (Summer 1989). See Harriet Jones and Michael Kandiak (eds), *The Myth of Consensus: New Views on British History, 1945–64* (1996).

46 Lord Kilmuir, *Political Adventure* (1964), p. 138.

47 W. S. Churchill, *The Sinews of Peace* (postwar speeches, 1948), p. 60.

48 *House of Commons Debates*, vol. 425, cols. 1690–1843, 1886–2014, 22–3 July 1946.

49 Brian Harrison, 'The Rise, Fall and Rise of Political Consensus in Britain since 1940', in *History*, vol. 84, April 1999, pp. 301–24.

50 John Bonham, *The Middle Class Vote* (1954), p. 163.

51 See H. G. Nichols, *The British General Election of 1950* (1951).

52 Hennessy, *Never Again*, p. 262. The next paragraphs are based on pp. 266–71.

53 *House of Commons Debates*, vol. 450, col. 2117, 12 May 1948.

54 Catherine R. Schenk, 'Austerity and Boom'. In Paul Johnson (ed.), *20th Century Britain: Economic, Social and Cultural Change* (1994), p. 300.

55 Ibid., p. 309.

56 Morgan, *People's Peace*, ch 3; Schenk, 'Austerity', p. 309.

57 Hennessy, *Never Again*, p. 100. The next paragraphs are based on Hennessy, pp. 101, 378–81; Morgan, *People's Peace*, ch. 3, and Schenk, 'Austerity', p. 309.

58 For this subsection see: Rodney Lowe, *The Welfare State in Britain since 1945* (1993); Nicholas Timmins, *The Five Giants: A Biography of the Welfare State* (1995); Charles Webster, *The National Health Service: A political History* (1998).

59 *House of Commons Debates*, vol. 421, cols. 231–5, 26 March 1946.

60 Thomas Hennessy, *A History of Northern Ireland 1920–1996* (1997), p. 96.

61 Hennessy, *Never Again*, p. 387.

62 Harold Macmillan, career and attitudes, is admirably summarized in John Turner, *Harold Macmillan* (1994).

63 Morgan, *People's Peace*, p. 136. See Hugo Young, *This Blessed Plot: Britain and Europe from Churchill to Blair* (1998).

64 ROBO is well summarized by Schenk, 'Austerity', pp. 313–14. For a powerful

indictment of Conservative policies see Nick Tiratsoo and Jim Tomlinson, *The Conservatives and Industrial Efficiency 1951–64: Thirteen Wasted Years?* (1998).

65 This entire section draws heavily on my *British Society since 1945* (1996), chs 1–6.

66 T. Hennessy, *History of Northern Ireland*, pp. 93–5.

67 Frances Spalding, *British Art since 1900* (1986), p. 146; for these paragraphs see Marwick, *Culture in Britain since 1945* (1991), pp. 15–64.

68 Mary Banham and Bevis Hillier (eds), *A Tonic to the Nation: The Festival of Britain* (1976).

69 Fiona MacCarthy, *A History of British Design* (1979), pp. 94–5.

# 4 Affluent Britain, 1955–1974

## STRUCTURAL, IDEOLOGICAL AND INSTITUTIONAL IMPERATIVES

In that excellent collection *Twentieth-Century Britain: Economic, Social and Cultural Change* edited by Paul Johnson, the chapter by Peter Howlett on the economy 1955–73 is entitled 'The "Golden Age"', while in the indispensable Clarke and Trebilcock's, *Understanding Decline*, Charles H. Feinstein has a chapter on 'The End of Empire and the Golden Age'. Dealing with the entire world economy from 1945 to 1973 Eric Hobsbawm, too, called upon the golden words 'golden age'.[1] Let us look at the golden statistics.

Given all the doom and gloom there has been in talking down Britain's economic performance, economic historians today tend to play up the impressive side of the growth rate figures up to 1973 (table 4.1). Never in the past, not even in the first stages of industrialization, nor at the height of Victorian prosperity, had Britain enjoyed growth rates anything like these. Compared with America, the figures look pretty good too. Of course, with high productivity rates already, America had less scope for continuous improvement; at the same time, America in the second half of the sixties, what with the Vietnam War and civil rights movement, was a rather disturbed society. Where the performance seems less golden, is in comparisons with other competitors: we can see how

**Table 4.1** Growth of Gross Domestic Product per man-year (annual percentage growth rates)

| | *UK* | *US* | *France* | *Germany* | *Italy* | *Japan* |
|---|---|---|---|---|---|---|
| 1873–99 | 1.2 | 1.9 | 1.3 | 1.5 | 0.3 | 1.1 |
| 1899–1913 | 0.5 | 1.3 | 1.6 | 1.5 | 2.5 | 1.8 |
| 1873–1951 | 0.9 | 1.7 | 1.4 | 1.3 | 1.3 | 1.4 |
| 1951–64 | 2.3 | 2.5 | 4.3 | 5.1 | 5.6 | 7.6 |
| 1964–73 | 2.6 | 1.6 | 4.6 | 4.4 | 5.0 | 8.4 |

*Source:* R. C. O. Matthews, C. H. Feinstein and J. C. Odling-Smee, *British Economic Growth, 1856–1973* (Oxford: Clarendon Press, 1982), p. 31.

**Table 4.2** UK balance of payments (£ millions). Annual averages for selected period

| | *Visible balance* | *Invisible balance* | *Overall balance* |
|---|---|---|---|
| 1955–60 | –94 | +230 | 136 |
| 1961–4 | –226 | +218 | –8 |
| 1965–7 | –322 | +266 | –56 |
| 1968–71 | –191 | +743 | +552 |
| 1972–6 | –3,189 | +1,908 | –1,281 |
| 1977–80 | –2,077 | +2,337 | +814 |

*Source:* Adapted from A. R. Prest and D. J. Coppock (eds), *The UK Economy: A Manual of Applied Economics* (London: Weidenfeld and Nicolson, 1982), p. 135.

**Table 4.3** Annual average balance of payments, 1960–1968: various countries

| *UK* | *US* | *Japan* | *West Germany* |
|---|---|---|---|
| –$0.38 billion | $3.6 billion | $0.1 billion | $0.1 billion |

*Source*: Adapted from B. R. Mitchell, *European Historical Statistics 1750–1975* (London: Macmillan, 1981), pp. 929–41.

**Table 4.4** Unemployment rates (in percentages)

| | *1952–1964* | *1965–1973* |
|---|---|---|
| UK | 2.5 | 3.2 |
| US | 5.0 | 4.5 |
| France | 1.7 | 2.4 |
| Germany | 2.7 | 0.8 |
| Italy | 5.9 | 3.4 |
| Japan | 1.9 | 1.3 |

*Source:* R. C. O. Matthews, C. H. Feinstein and J. C. Odling-Smee, *British Economic Growth, 1856–1973* (Oxford: Clarendon Press, 1982), p. 94.

well France, Italy, West Germany, and above all Japan, are doing. Although there was never any great security over the British balance of payments, the figures (table 4.2) look reasonable for the period 1955–60 (though not as good as those of the other countries in table 4.3). As ever, Britain was importing more than she was exporting, but a good performance on invisible exports gives an overall positive balance. From 1961 to 1967 there is an overall adverse balance, with recovery till 1971, then real cause for doom and gloom.

Since the war the Bretton Woods system of fixed exchange rates had served the international economy well, but in 1971, with new players rapidly entering the international scene, and with the American economy itself extremely

**Table 4.5** Cost of living indices (1953 = 100)

| | *UK* | *France* | *Germany* | *Italy* |
|---|---|---|---|---|
| 1955 | 106 | 101 | 102 | 106 |
| 1956 | 110 | 106 | 104 | 111 |
| 1957 | 114 | 109 | 107 | 113 |
| 1958 | 117 | 125 | 109 | 118 |
| 1959 | 118 | 133 | 110 | 118 |
| 1960 | 119 | 138 | 112 | 121 |
| 1961 | 123 | 142 | 114 | 125 |
| 1962 | 128 | 149 | 118 | 131 |
| 1963 | 131 | 156 | 121 | 141 |
| 1964 | 135 | 161 | 124 | 149 |
| 1965 | 141 | 166 | 128 | 156 |
| 1966 | 147 | 171 | 133 | 159 |
| 1967 | 151 | 175 | 134 | 162 |
| 1968 | 159 | 182 | 136 | 164 |
| 1969 | 166 | 194 | 140 | 169 |
| 1970 | 177 | 204 | 145 | 177 |
| 1971 | 193 | 215 | 153 | 186 |
| 1972 | 207 | 229 | 161 | 197 |
| 1973 | 226 | 245 | 172 | 217 |
| 1974 | 262 | 279 | 184 | 259 |
| 1975 | 326 | 312 | 195 | 304 |

*Source:* B. R. Mitchell, *European Historical Statistics 1750–1975* (Basingstoke: Macmillan, 1981), pp. 781–3.

**Table 4.6** Average annual earnings (in pounds sterling)

| | *Wage earners* | *Salary earners* |
|---|---|---|
| 1951 | 322 | 523 |
| 1961 | 585 | 821 |
| 1971 | 1193 | 1650 |

*Source:* R. C. O. Matthews, C. H. Feinstein and J. C. Odling-Smee, *British Economic Growth, 1856–1973* (Oxford: Clarendon Press, 1982), p. 167.

unstable, America went off the Gold Standard, and the fixed exchange rate system collapsed. In June 1972 the pound was allowed to 'float'; a cartoon at the time portrays a very sick elderly man in bed, with the doctor reporting to an anxious relative: 'he's floating fast'. For Britain, the golden age was already waning, and for the entire industrialized world it collapsed in 1973, the year of the international oil crisis and the doubling of oil prices.

**Table 4.7** Growth of real wages per man-hour (in percentages)

| | |
|---|---|
| 1951–5 | 2.2 |
| 1955–60 | 2.9 |
| 1960–4 | 4.0 |
| 1964–8 | 4.4 |
| 1968–73 | 3.8 |

*Source:* R. C. O. Mathews, C. H. Feinstein and J. C. Odling-Smee, *British Economic Growth, 1856–1973* (Oxford: Clarendon Press, 1982), p. 171.

We saw that unemployment remained (by inter-war standards) very low throughout the forties and early fifties. The figures remained good until 1964, there being something of a worsening thereafter (table 4.4). Once more, however, most other countries do rather better than Britain, with Germany moving into a truly booming employment situation after 1964. Italy, with its constant problem of a depressed South, puts in a notably worse performance than the other European countries, though not that much worse than Britain in the latter part of the period. The United States, the country with the least economic management and the most capitalist freedom and mobility, has consistently high rates. The world in the inter-war years had suffered from deflation. The great danger in a full employment economy is that of inflation: when demand for labour is high, wages tend to go up, and when most people have jobs and money in their pockets, so do prices. The inflation figures up until 1967 were probably just about tolerable, though less than impressive (table 4.5). There was always a worry about their becoming seriously worse, as they did between 1968 and 1973; then, after 1973, with the devastating effect of the doubling of oil prices, they became truly critical, threatening to get out of control. From tables 4.6 and 4.7 we can see that up to 1973 the workers were doing very well indeed. Taking inflation into account real wages doubled between 1950 and 1973. Golden age or not, we are certainly entitled to talk of 'affluent Britain, 1955 to 1974'.

Technological advances very quickly become international. Important examples were: television (including Telstar, the first transatlantic transmission being made in 1962); extended and long-play records, transistor radios, electronic synthesizers, modernized telephone systems; a remarkable expansion in jet travel, as well as the complete substitution of quickly accelerating electric and diesel locomotives for steam ones; advanced consumer products such as refrigerators and washing-machines; synthetic fabrics, such as Dacron and Lycra; aerosol sprays, disinfectants and detergents; frozen foods, new plastics and polishes. Both the United States and Russia were spending 3 per cent of GNP on scientific research; Britain, which continued to have a distinguished record in the winning of Nobel Prizes for science, was spending 2.3 per cent, which compares very favourably with the 1.8 per cent in West Germany, and 1.5 in France.

In Britain, the expansion of car ownership began in the fifties, but accelerated rapidly in the early sixties: 2,307,000 cars and vans in 1950; 3,609,000 in 1955; 5,650,000 in 1960; 9,131,000 in 1965; 11,802,000 in 1970. In November 1959 the first short stretch of the M1 motorway was opened. In 1961 Dr Richard Beeching, first of a new breed of scientist-industrialists, was appointed Chairman of the British Transport Commission. A couple of years later, the Beeching Report on the railways recommended the axing of all branch lines, reducing the railway network from 13,000 to 8,000 miles with a concentration on freight and inter-city services. In the upshot, the system was stabilized at 11,000 miles, but many small towns lost their railway connection nonetheless. At the other end of the scale, domestic air travel doubled between 1961 and 1971 from 1,000 million to 2,000 million passenger kilometres. Hopes were not yet gone that the growth of the fifties and sixties, channelled and shaped by the planning ideas of the forties, could yet create a genuine and better environment, though perceptive commentators noted that such great environmental planners of the war years as Barlow and Abercrombie had scarcely bargained for the new technological civilization of the sixties. In 1963 the Ministry of Transport (Buchanan) Report, *Traffic in Towns*, recommended urban motorways as the remedy for traffic congestion in towns.[2] Planners and developers came together in a clouded vision of brave new architectural concepts, a wish to set up concrete symbols of progress, a need to accommodate to the motor car, and a desire to make affluence yield a decent profit. So the guts were torn out of such cities as Newcastle, Glasgow and Birmingham and replaced with an ugly jungle of urban motorways and high-rise buildings.

The sense of rapidly accelerating science and technology, leaving those educated in the humanities far behind, was expressed in a lecture on 'The Two Cultures' given by C. P. Snow at the University of Cambridge in 1959, and published the same year. During the General Election of 1964 Harold Wilson, now leader of the Labour party, spoke of harnessing 'the white heat of technological revolution'. Achieving office, he established a Ministry of Technology with the powerful trade-union leader Frank Cousins as its head, and with Snow as Parliamentary Under-Secretary; at the same time Dr B. V. Bowden, Principal of the University of Manchester Institute of Science and Technology, was appointed Minister of State in the Department of Education and Science. Like Snow, he was given a peerage.[3] Technology linked to consensus produced an ideology of affluence, whose clearest early expression was in the pronouncement of R. A. Butler, Chancellor of the Exchequer, to the October 1954 Conservative Party Conference that the British standard of living could be 'doubled in the next twenty-five years'.[4]

The ideology of consensus continued to be consistent with the practice of two-party politics, of strongly contrasting programmes being put before the electorate, and of Her Majesty needing an Opposition as well as a government. Many Conservatives remained deeply suspicious of what they regarded as 'socialist' policy, and of the wage demands of the unions, which they saw as a prime cause of inflation. On 30 April 1957, Peter Thorneycroft, Conservative Chancellor of the Exchequer, forcefully pointed out that while incomes had risen by 75 per cent between 1948 and 1956, output had only risen by 28 per cent. The Cabinet, however, showing how strong was the spirit of consensus and acceptance of the need to carry the support of the unions, opposed any limitation on the amount available for wage increases. By the summer there was yet another run on sterling and on 17 September Thorneycroft, again unavailingly, proposed direct limits on the money supply. Bank rate was raised from 5 to 7 per cent and the clearing banks were instructed to restrict advances to the level of the previous year. But Thorneycroft wanted more, using a line of argument which was to become familiar twenty years later:

> With relatively few assets and large debts, we continue to live upon the scale of a great power. We have the most expensive defence forces within Europe. We have joined the nuclear 'club'. We crave at the same time a very high standard of life. We seek to lead the world in the social services we provide.[5]

Pressing for further drastic economies, but failing to carry the Cabinet with him, Thorneycroft resigned on 6 January, together with his junior ministers Enoch Powell and Nigel Birch. Later Thorneycroft was to be represented as a hero who failed in his attempt to get Macmillan to accept the disciplines of monetarism. Macmillan passed the matter off as 'a little local difficulty' and won general approval in referring to Thorneycroft's 'rigidity of thought'. Thorneycroft, replaced by Derick Heathcoat-Amory, did not attempt to fight, and a couple of years later both he and Powell returned to the Cabinet. In the hope of securing expert support for his belief that there must be control of the money supply, Thorneycroft in 1957 had set up the Radcliffe Committee on the Working of the Monetary System. Reporting in 1959 the Committee decisively rejected monetarism, thus confirming the existing consensual economics and placing an emphasis on 'the liquidity of the economy'. The government, accordingly, continued to rely heavily on interest rate manipulation, and, therefore, 'Stop–Go', though in an effort to imitate the indicative planning which was proving so successful in France, it did, in 1962, set up the National Economic Development Council. High growth rates were the objective but 'Neddy' was never very specific as to how these were to be attained.

With an election approaching in October 1964 a massive 'Go' was shamelessly engineered. Coming into office on the narrowest of margins, Labour felt impelled to drastic action, placing a 15 per cent surcharge on manufactured imports. In a further push towards planning, the Department of Economic Affairs was set up in 1964 and, in 1965, a National Plan was promulgated. Inflation, it was hoped, would be controlled by the National Board for Prices and Incomes, also established in 1965. But the wish was still not the father to success: Treasury views continued to predominate, the basic problems in British manufacturing and the infrastructure were not resolved. The trade balance was a growing matter of concern, while Labour's social policies – increasing pensions, abolishing prescription charges, introducing a capital gains tax – all served to alarm the financial world and encourage the selling of sterling. With another balance-of-payments crisis in July 1966, the Treasury insisted upon another 'Stop'. The National Plan was abandoned, while, as Peter Howlett puts it:

> The DEA limped on before final abolition in 1969. Its planning responsibilities passed to the Treasury whilst the Department of Employment and Productivity inherited price and incomes policy.[6]

The Conservative Government under Edward Heath, returning to office in 1970, at first emphasized its differences from Labour's 'socialism' by abandoning attempts at an incomes policy, but then in September 1972 introduced a Statutory Policy which showed some signs of working reasonably well up until the oil crisis of 1973.

Consensus lay in the general wish to protect the welfare state and living standards. Politics were paramount, economics too much the plaything of politics. On the surface Britain's parliamentary democracy sparkled compared with France, where the Fourth Republic collapsed in 1958, being replaced by the presidential government of de Gaulle; Italy, where street demonstrations were necessary in 1960 to prevent the neo-fascist Tambroni from holding power; or the America of the assassinations of two Kennedys and Martin Luther King; but in France (and West Germany) high quality central administrations maintained consistent and successful economic policies, while even Italy had its 'economic miracle'. On the continent manufacturers and trade unions managed to work together in maintaining high levels of productivity.

## THE POLITICS OF CONSENSUS

### *SUEZ*

The title of this section may seem particularly inappropriate since the first major event to confront Eden's re-elected Conservative administration was the one which produced the bitterest divides throughout British society since the Second World War: the Suez crisis of October–November 1956 (see plate 8). Actually, in domestic politics, the most significant feature of Suez is that, utterly disgraceful and inexcusable as the episode was, and one which fully revealed Britain's helplessness as a world power when not supported by the United States, it had no long-lasting effects whatsoever, the divisions it created soon being swallowed up again in general complacency and consensus.[7]

Anthony Eden, as heir-apparent, had long been in the shadow of Winston Churchill, and only succeeded to the supreme office in 1954, gaining full personal legitimacy with his election victory in 1955. Prior to the election Harold Macmillan, glowing with his success at Housing, had moved to Defence; after the election he received the Foreign Office, and it was only with reluctance that he subsequently replaced Butler as Chancellor of the Exchequer, the latter moving to the Home Office. A former Minister of State at the Foreign Office, Selwyn Lloyd became Foreign Secretary. Eden, as Prime Minister, saw himself as *the* expert on foreign affairs, and fully intended to operate as such. The principal roles had been filled for the Suez crisis.

British influence in Egypt had been practically obliterated by the 'Revolution of the Colonels' earlier in the fifties, which eventually left the determined

**Plate 8** Suez, 1956: 'Edinburgh University students demonstration over government's action in the Middle East. Women students carrying protest banners are surrounded by government backers.' *Glasgow Herald*, 4 November 1956. Courtesy of Scottish Media Newspapers

modernizer Colonel Nasser in power. A central element in Nasser's programme was the building of the Aswan Dam, which he hoped would be mainly financed by the Americans. It was the refusal of the Americans to come up with the cash which provoked the momentous step that set the Suez crisis in motion. The Suez Canal runs through Egyptian territory, but most of the profits went to the original shareholders, the British and French governments. There were good nationalist arguments for Egypt to nationalize the Canal: Nasser's action of 26 July 1956, however, was basically motivated by the desire to put the profits towards the building of the dam. The British (as well as the French) government clearly had to react. What turned a problem into a crisis was the overreaction of the British, particularly Eden and Macmillan. Both had been beneficiaries of their opposition to the Munich settlement, and of their important roles in the war against Nazism. Both made an entirely false equation between the current situation and Munich, and between the small-time dictator of a small country trying to cast off the last influence of colonialism, and Adolf Hitler. Both thought, again quite mistakenly, that the rest of the developed world would share their sense of outrage. When, next day, Eden set up a special committee of the Cabinet, the Suez Committee, Macmillan was a member of it, as he remained right through to the end. Shortly, the full Cabinet resolved to act together with the French in regaining the Canal by force, and overthrowing the Nasser regime.

The problem was that President Eisenhower and his Secretary of State, John Foster Dulles (increasingly preoccupied anyway with the American presidential election), would not endorse such action, while the Russians were showing signs that they might violently oppose it. A way round seemed to be opened up by discussions the French were having with Israel. On 14 October the French proposed to the British the 'Challe Plan': Israel would invade Sinai and then move on into Egypt, giving Britain and France a pretext to exercise their treaty rights to protect the Canal by occupying the Canal Zone. On 16 October Eden received the support of the Suez Committee for this devious scheme. That afternoon he and Selwyn Lloyd flew to France to work out a preliminary agreement. Just under a week later, on 22 October, Lloyd joined the French and the Israelis in a conference at Sèvres. Two days later two British officials signed the Treaty of Sèvres. The Israelis undertook to attack on 29 October, creating the opportunity for France and Britain, separately, to issue ultimatums calling upon both Israel and Egypt to disengage; in the expectation that this would be rejected, France and Britain would attack Egypt in the early hours of 31 October. The British negotiators knew that they were falling well below the moral standards expected of British governments, and all British copies of the Treaty were destroyed; the French had no such qualms.

What followed was a bit like one of those cops-and-robbers films where first we see the ideal crime carried out in the imaginations of the criminals, then the cock-up which actually occurs when imagination encounters reality. The Israeli invasion went ahead as planned, but then the United States and the Soviet Union, on 30 October, both put resolutions to the United Nations Security Council calling for Israel to withdraw. Britain, ignobly, had to resort to its veto. Air attacks on Egypt began on 30 and 31 October together with naval attacks on Egyptian vessels at sea. Parachute troops landed at Port Said on 5 November, with a seaborne invasion force arriving the next day. As a combined military operation the whole venture was not unsuccessful, but as a costly and unpopular one it provoked a severe financial crisis. There was a disastrous run on the pound with the Americans refusing to offer any support. Macmillan, as Chancellor of the Exchequer, had earlier ignored the risks on the (unfounded) basis that he could always get American support; now he knew that the losses were unsustainable. He was thus the first to argue that Britain must accede to American demands, withdrawing unconditionally, and give place to a United Nations force. Anthony Nutting, Under-Secretary at the Foreign Office, had resigned rather than support the invasion, but neither Macmillan, nor any other member of the government, ever admitted that collusion had taken place with France and Israel. The relevant parts of Macmillan's own diary were destroyed at the time, and the government papers are either heavily weeded or unavailable. Government statements, inevitably, were clumsy and contorted; the condemnations of the government were powerful enough, though made without knowledge of the full extent of its wrongdoing. In one of the most explosive House of Commons debates in modern times on 12 November, Macmillan passionately expounded his opposition to 'appeasement': 'It is because I have seen it all happen before.' Macmillan's version was that the ceasefire had been declared, not because of American pressure and the run on the pound, but because the 'job was finished'.

Macmillan was principal aider and abettor in the Suez folly, but the fundamental responsibility lay with Eden who had overruled his Foreign Secretary (who would have preferred action through the United Nations) and his Foreign Office advisers. Eden was a sick man and the stresses of covering up collusion and then collapsing in ignominy were too much for him. He went into hospital, leaving Butler to explain an episode he had always been unenthusiastic about and on which he had never been fully informed (he was not a member of the Suez Committee). Macmillan was very aware that a successor to Eden was going to be needed sooner rather than later: during this 'interregnum' he made a point of staying away from the House of Commons, speaking only once and then on purely economic matters. Commentors have generally mingled admiration for the brilliance with which Macmillan maintained an air of enthusiastic conviction and calm confidence, with distaste for the brutality with which he demeaned Butler as his principal rival for the succession. His leading role in the Suez operation can reasonably be termed 'criminal' and his initial taking for granted American support and subsequent failure to spot that the manifest lack of that support would be financially disastrous, must be accounted crass incompetence brought on by serious wishful thinking. But his besting of Butler (not a good Chancellor of the Exchequer, as we saw) was merely part of the political game.

## *Macmillan as Prime Minister*

A crucial date is 22 November, when both Butler and Macmillan addressed the 1922 Committee. Butler made a feeble and boring speech on Conservative party propaganda (Macmillan could hardly be blamed for that), while his rival gave a rousing oration, again playing the old Munich card. Eden, a broken man, returned briefly. At 3.00 p.m. on 9 January 1957 Macmillan was called to 10 Downing Street: Eden told him that he had already informed the Queen of his intention to resign on the grounds of ill health. Lord Salisbury, a senior Cabinet minister, announced that he would summon Cabinet ministers one by one to his room in the nearby Privy Council Offices, where he was assisted by Lord Kilmuir, to get their views on the succession. As the famous story has it, Salisbury, with a grandee's disrespect for the letter 'r', asked each minister in turn: 'Well, who is it, Wab or Hawold?' Salisbury also interviewed the Chief Whip, Edward Heath, and the Chairman of the party Oliver Poole. Kilmuir took a telephone call from John Morrison, Chairman of the 1922 Committee. It seems that there was practical unanimity in favour of Macmillan; Eden was not consulted. Macmillan was summoned to the Palace for 2.00 p.m. the next day; his sixty-fourth birthday was only days away. When the new Prime Minister decided to hold a General Election on 8 October 1959, Suez was scarcely an issue in that election campaign. The statistics are set out in table 4.8.

**Table 4.8** General Election, 8 October 1959

| | *Electorate 35.4 million* | | *Turnout 78.8 per cent* | |
|---|---|---|---|---|
| | *Conservative* | *Labour* | *Liberal* | *Others* |
| Votes | 13,749,830 | 12,215,538 | 1,638,571 | |
| Percentage of votes casts | 49.4 | 43.8 | 5.9 | 0.9 |
| Seats | 365 | 258 | 6 | 1 |

In parliamentary terms this was a magnificent victory for Macmillan, winning him the soubriquets of: 'Supermac' (even if intended ironically, actually pregnant with genuine admiration), and 'The Actor Manager' (less flattering, but still containing a strong element of admiration). If we judge Macmillan by what he tried to achieve, then his record in foreign policy, which was what he himself prized most, is a reasonable one, though in the area which really mattered, Britain's relationship with Europe, he failed. He did appreciate that Britain's days as an imperial power were over, but continued to believe it proper for Britain to spend far more on defence than any of the continental European countries. In social policy and economic policy, he represented, respectively, the best and worst of consensus politics: he safeguarded the welfare state, but did nothing about Britain's fundamental economic problems.

'Appeasement' (hostility to) had been the talisman explaining the major events to date; now the talisman was the fancy that Britain should play Greece (repository of brains and culture) to America's militarily powerful and economically strong Rome. Whatever the scars left by Suez, there can be no doubt that Eisenhower and Dulles were far happier with Macmillan than they would have been with Butler, and so the American President was persuaded to visit Britain, the two appearing on television as world statesmen together. From Eisenhower, Macmillan obtained the Blue Streak Nuclear Missile (which, however, was quickly obsolete). At the beginning of 1958 he set out on a tour of the Commonwealth, a famous speech in South Africa signalling that, while no radical upholder of black African rights, he recognized that white supremacists would have to yield to changing circumstances: he detected, he said, 'a wind of change'. On Macmillan's own terms, his outstanding achievement came in the Nassau Agreement of December 1962 when pertinacious lobbying persuaded President J. F. Kennedy that it was politically expedient to grant Britain Polaris submarines, though, in Kennedy's view, 'a piece of military foolishness'. In February 1959 Macmillan presented himself as someone who could speak to the Russians, going on a famous (though also much-jeered-at) trip to Moscow. At the end of the same year he took part in something very close to his heart, his summit conference in Paris. Macmillan's pertinacity paid off in another event. Neither Kennedy nor the rest of the British Government were particularly enthusiastic about the signing of a treaty banning the testing of nuclear weapons; yet Macmillan succeeded in bringing this about in 1963. But his vaunting of his ties (real and imagined) with America was the last thing to endear his bid (launched in August 1961) to join the European Common Market to General de Gaulle: Macmillan was genuine in his belief in Europe, but his lack of total commitment helped to bring upon himself de Gaulle's decisive veto of January 1963.

After the 1959 election Derick Heathcoat-Amory was replaced as Chancellor of the Exchequer by the docile, and broadly expansionist, Selwyn Lloyd. The arrival of affluence is always associated with Macmillan – and he is endlessly misquoted as mindlessly exulting in this. That he did have worries about inflation comes through strongly in his most famous speech of all, actually made in a football stadium in Bedford as early as 20 July 1957 – *not* during the 1959 election campaign, though the famous phrase extracted from the speech was much quoted in that campaign:

> Let's be frank about it; most of our people have never had it so good. Go around the country, go to the industrial towns, go to the farms, and you will see a state of prosperity, such as we have never had in my lifetime – nor indeed ever in the history of this country. What is beginning to worry some of us is 'Is it too good to be true?' Or perhaps I should say 'Is it too good to last?' For, amidst all this prosperity, there is one problem that has troubled us – in one way or another – ever since the war. It's the problem of rising prices. Our constant concern today is – can prices be steadied while at the same time we maintain full employment in an expanding economy? Can we control inflation? This is the problem of our time.[8]

Important though it is to be absolutely accurate about what Macmillan said and where, he did not actually do anything about inflation. Heathcoat-Amory's (pre-election) 1959 budget was later to be stigmatized as contributing greatly to subsequent economic problems, particularly 'stagflation', inflation without growth (i.e. stagnation). In March 1962 manifest failure to address fundamental economic problems led to Macmillan sacking one-third of his Cabinet, including Selwyn Lloyd, in the 'Night of the Long Knives'. Harold Wilson, now leader of the Labour Opposition, joked, with understandable exaggeration, that half the Cabinet had been fired – 'the wrong half, as it happened'.

By 1963 there was something of a boom in critical analyses of the weaknesses of British society, and also the more famous 'satire boom' – led by the Cambridge undergraduate show 'Beyond the Fringe' – for which, in many ways, Macmillan was a perfect target. He was getting old, and, worse, was feeling old. He nevertheless behaved with decency, as well as with the fastidiousness and fear of sexuality which had been a characteristic throughout his life, in dealing with the 'Profumo' case. John Profumo, a junior minister at the War Office, had consorted sexually with a high-class prostitute, Christine Keeler, who also had a liaison with Captain Ivanov of the Russian Embassy. Security risk was joined to sexual truancy. When Profumo denied what was called 'impropriety' Macmillan believed him. When the full scandal came out, Macmillan was placed in a cruelly embarrassing position. He was in fact suffering from prostate trouble, and had to be suddenly hospitalized on 10 October 1963. Yet one more ruthless act lay within his power. On 9 October he wrote to the

Queen that he would have to resign – but he did not formally do so till, from his hospital bed, he had successfully done his damnedest to ensure that his Foreign Secretary, Lord Home, who gave up his peerage and entered the Commons as Sir Alec Douglas-Home, should inherit the prime ministership, not Butler. Macmillan's favoured candidate had been the Second Viscount Hailsham, a vigorous polemicist on behalf of the Conservative party, and, sign of the times, first ever Minister of Science. In 1960, the Labour MP Anthony Wedgwood Benn had refused to accept his succession to the title of his father, Lord Stansgate, overwhelmingly winning the by-election for the vacancy created by his elevation: thus an Act was speedily passed making it possible for peerages to be renounced, provided the deed was done within twelve months. Hailsham announced his intention of taking advantage of this provision, but so vociferously, and so obviously with his eye on the prime ministership, that he alienated many supporters, including Macmillan. Macmillan hated Butler, and was not enthusiastic about the other potential candidate Reginald Maudling, the relatively young Chancellor of the Exchequer, and beneficiary of the 'Night of the Long Knives'. Macmillan did organize an elaborate consultation process of members of the Cabinet and senior Conservatives, while himself representing Home as the compromise candidate who could maintain party unity; it was Home he recommended to the Queen.

### *The Labour Opposition*

Peter Clarke has said that the 'twelve-month premiership of Sir Alec Douglas-Home . . . was dominated by Harold Wilson'.[9] Back in November 1955, when Attlee had at last resigned as Labour leader, his own favourite as successor was Gaitskell who, in fact, easily won the poll of the Parliamentary Labour Party against the other two candidates, Morrison and Bevan. Although Bevan was appointed Shadow Colonial Secretary in 1956, the division between Right and Left remained as sharp as ever, and became particularly bitter as the government went ahead with the manufacture of the hydrogen bomb. The opponents of Britain's retention of the hydrogen bomb made the case that to hold, and threaten to use, a weapon of mass destruction which threatened the survival of the human race itself, was immoral, but they shared in the general overestimation of Britain's position as a world power when they declared that Britain's giving up of the bomb would give a lead towards universal nuclear disarmament. They failed to appreciate, too, that from the start Britain had gone into the nuclear business in order to try to assert independence from America, not, as they believed, as part of an American conspiracy against Russia. They felt betrayed when, on 3 October 1957, Bevan argued that Britain must retain the bomb, asking the Labour Party Conference 'not to send the British Foreign Secretary naked into the conference chamber'.[10] What nobody understood very well was that simply having the bomb (not too outrageously expensive) was of little use without the intercontinental ballistic systems (quite outrageously expensive) being developed in the United States and the Soviet Union. Nor was it understood that a design flaw could easily wipe out massive sums of money already spent, nor how quickly delivery systems could become obsolete. The attempt to build Britain's own rocket, Blue Streak, was cancelled in 1960 because of the impossible expense. It was then decided to buy Skybolt from America; it was after the Americans abandoned Skybolt that Macmillan did his deal over Polaris. At the 1960 Labour Party Conference a resolution calling upon the party to adopt the policy of nuclear disarmament was passed: in opposing this, Gaitskell vowed to 'fight, fight, and fight again'. In that same year Wilson stood (though unsuccessfully) against Gaitskell for the party leadership. In 1961 Gaitskell and his right-wing allies succeeded in getting the previous year's conference resolution reversed.

The other great issue of the time was that of Britain's putative membership of the European Economic Community. While Macmillan, with the negotiations being led by Edward Heath, made his not altogether wholehearted, and ultimately, unsuccessful effort, Gaitskell in October 1962 effectively committed the Labour party against, with a rather factitious invocation of 'a thousand years of history'. Butler got in a neat one with his 'For us, the future' at the succeeding Conservative Party Conference. That pointed out the fact, earlier driven home by the 1959 election, that as long as the Conservatives could claim the credit for an affluent society, Labour (which a decade before might have put itself in the position of reaping the benefits of affluence) was severely handicapped. However, the sun does sometimes set on the Conservatives; the winter of 1962–3 was almost as bad as that of 1946–7, with the result that unemployment went up to nearly 800,000. The terrifying world crisis of November 1962, when President Kennedy succeeded in persuading the Soviet Union to withdraw the missiles it had set up in Cuba, demonstrated how little Macmillan really counted in world councils. The point was driven home a month later when the former American Secretary of State, Dean Acheson, being cruel to be kind, declared that 'Britain has lost an Empire and not yet found a role.'[11]

The position of the Labour party, and of its leader, Hugh Gaitskell, was manifestly strengthening, when Gaitskell himself in January 1963 succumbed to a deadly virus. Harold Wilson had previously stood against George Brown, a volatile former trade union leader, for the deputy leadership of the party, and had lost. Perhaps Brown should have succeeded to the leadership, but with another figure on the right of the party, James Callaghan, standing as well, Wilson, though thought to be on the left, succeeded fairly easily. It quickly appeared, as the remark of Peter Clarke quoted earlier suggested, to be an inspired choice. Labour moved well ahead in the opinion polls, as the Conservatives were helped neither by the Profumo affair, nor by the advent to the prime ministership of Douglas-Home. But the sun shone throughout the summer of 1964 and right through to the election in October. The Labour manifesto promised planning of the economy, higher welfare benefits, and the ending of selection for secondary education. The Conservatives referred to their own moves towards modernizing the running of the economy, and warned of the cost of Labour's programme. Douglas-Home himself stressed the importance of retaining the nuclear deterrent, no doubt partly in the hope of directing attention to Labour's divisions on this matter.[12] The results were close.

**Table 4.9** General Election, 15 October 1964

| | Electorate 35.9 million | | Turnout 77.1 per cent | |
|---|---|---|---|---|
| | *Labour* | *Conservative* | *Liberal* | *Others* |
| Total votes | 12,205,814 | 12,001,396 | 3,092,878 | |
| Percentage of | 44.1 | 43.4 | 11.2 | 1.3 |
| Seats | 317 | 304 | 9 | 0 |

### *WILSON IN OFFICE*

Clearly, Douglas-Home had been defeated, however narrowly, and he resigned immediately. Before the election the Liberals had said that if they held the balance of power they would support Labour, but once again there was no agreement between the parties. Certainly, Wilson acted with great coolness, and every show of confidence, in his not very enviable situation – an overall majority of five. Attempting to get his choice as Foreign Secretary, Patrick Gordon-Walker, who had been defeated in the election, back into the House of Commons, he in fact threw away a precious seat, when the voters in Walthamstow objected to being used as pawns in this way. Gordon-Walker, 'a dowdy Gaitskellite', was replaced with a figure 'with equal lack of charisma', Michael Stewart.[13] The new Ministry of Economic Affairs went to Brown, while Callaghan became Chancellor of the Exchequer. The biggest problem, inevitably, was the economy. Wilson, in his election promises, had put forward some of the right ideas. In all the circumstances, it would have taken a more far-seeing and single-minded man than he to carry them out. That said, there were decisions which were very largely personal to Wilson (particularly with regard to shirking immediate devaluation) which were positively harmful. He can be criticized too for his policies towards Central Africa and towards America and the Vietnam War. Though he perceived the need to curtail the power of the unions, he retreated from reform. Yet, by 1970 the economy, temporarily at least, seemed to be in quite sound shape; had Roy Jenkins (Jenkins had been a notably successful Home Secretary; Callaghan, at the Exchequer, less so; in 1968 a typical Wilsonian job-swap took place) remained Chancellor of the Exchequer that soundness might have been maintained. And the Wilson Government did carry through some important reforms with respect both to the welfare state and to what Jenkins, while still Home Secretary, called 'The Civilized Society'. The first Wilson Government aroused expectations which it failed to satisfy. Left-wingers were to attack him bitterly. The radical Right associated him with the 'permissive society' and the subversion of moral values. Many moderate reformers declared him 'unprincipled', too preoccupied with the short term and the quick fix.

One way of dealing with the balance of payments crisis which greeted the new government would have been to devalue, but Wilson was convinced that

Labour must avoid having itself tagged as the party of devaluation. Apart from the bank rate rise and the temporary surcharge on imports, income tax was raised to 8s 3d (41.25 per cent). Assurances were secured from the Americans that they would support sterling at its current exchange rate, on the understanding that the government's policies would be aimed in the same direction. Brown went ahead with intensive work on his National Plan, whose target of sustained growth at 4 per cent per annum, was not entirely compatible with the government's deflationary steps.

In July 1965, Douglas-Home resigned from the Conservative leadership, leading to the ballot of MPs which had been agreed upon in the aftermath of Douglas-Home's somewhat dubious 'emergence'. Wilson sparkled, while Edward Heath, who defeated Reginald Maudling, seemed dull and lacking in charisma: the Hull by-election in January 1966 showed a strong swing to the government. Wilson skilfully gave the impression that with a secure majority behind it, his Government really would carry through the reform of Britain: 31 March was his chosen day, a one hundred seat majority over the Conservatives his prize.

The renewed government's new economic device, designed to discourage employment in the service sector and encourage employment in manufacturing, was the Selective Employment Tax, the bright idea of economist Nicholas Kaldor (one of the 'Hungarians' said by the right-wing press to be misadvising the government). Little more than a bit of academic game-playing, the tax was mildly deflationary, then sank without trace. On 16 May the National Union of Seamen went on strike, seriously interfering with exports. Added to all the usual underlying causes this produced the almost equally usual balance of payments crisis in July. Many important members of the Cabinet, including the Chancellor Callaghan, now thought devaluation definitely necessary, but Wilson remained resolutely opposed. Despite the Prime Minister's reference to the leaders of the National Union of Seamen as a 'tightly knit group of politically-motivated men', the government did eventually have to concede their wage demand. Immediately afterwards the Prices and Incomes Act set up the Prices and Incomes Board, which could delay wage increases until the Board had assessed them. Frank Cousins, committed as a trade unionist to the principle of free collective bargaining, resigned from his post as Minister of Technology,

**Table 4.10** General Election, 31 March 1966

| | *Electorate 35.96 million* | | *Turnout 75.8 per cent* | |
|---|---|---|---|---|
| | *Labour* | *Conservative* | *Liberal* | *Others* |
| Total votes | 13,064,951 | 11,418,433 | 2,327,533 | |
| Percentage of votes cast | 47.9 | 41.9 | 8.5 | 1.2 |
| Seats | 363 | 253 | 12 | 2 |

while a small group of MPs kept alive Labour's reputation as a disunited party by consistently voting against all prices and incomes decisions.

With his National Plan in ruins, Brown swapped places with Michael Stewart. In late 1966 the tough-minded Minister of Defence, Denis Healey, began a review designed to secure cuts, especially in overseas military expenditure. This was not something that would appeal to America, not best pleased at the way Wilson had insisted in keeping British troops out of Vietnam. When Wilson tried to use the visit to Britain in February 1967 of the Soviet leader Kosygin as an opportunity to stimulate negotiations for peace in Vietnam, he was snubbed by Washington. He did go ahead both with a phased withdrawal East of Suez, and with a new attempt to enter the EEC. On the latter initiative, put before parliament in May, the government had the support of the Conservatives and Liberals, while 36 Labour MPs voted against. By November devaluation was unavoidable: Wilson blamed the Six-Day Arab-Israeli War, and the closure of the Suez Canal, and in his broadcast on both TV channels on the evening of Sunday, 19 November declared that 'devaluation . . . does not mean that the pound in the pocket is worth 14 per cent less'. Wilson was trying to reassure the elderly that each pound saved had *not* been reduced to 17 shillings.[14]

The Conservatives were now riding high in the opinion polls and Labour was losing by-elections, most notably at Hamilton on 2 November when the charismatic, or at any rate voluble, Mrs Winnie Ewing turned a 16,000 Labour majority into an SNP one of 1,799. Yet 1967 was the *annus mirabilis* of 'civilized society' legislation. As a back-bencher, Roy Jenkins had, with government support, been responsible for the Liberal Obscene Publications Act of 1959. As Home Secretary in 1967, he used the same procedure in introducing two pieces of 'permissive', and therefore controversial, legislation. When the young Liberal MP David Steel won the private members' ballot, Jenkins wanted him to put forward a Bill legalizing homosexual acts between consenting adults in private, as had been recommended by the Wolfenden Committee ten years earlier. Steel, however, preferred to put forward another much-needed reform, the liberalization of the abortion law. The new Act made an abortion available if two doctors were satisfied that it was necessary on medical or psychological grounds. Another Labour back-bencher, Leo Abse, sponsored the Sexual Offences Act, which rendered adult homosexuals relatively immune to persecution and blackmail. The National Health Service (Family Planning) Act, also of 1967, and sponsored by the Minister of Health, Hilary Marquand, authorized the local authorities to provide contraceptives and contraceptive advice. In 1968 the Family Law Reform and the Representation of the People Acts, respectively, lowered the age of legal majority and the voting age to eighteen. In 1969 there came the Divorce Reform Act which laid it down that: 'the sole ground on which a petition for divorce may be presented to the court by either party to a marriage shall be that the marriage has broken down irretrievably'. The Matrimonial Property Act of 1970 established that a wife's work, whether as a housewife within the home, or as money-earner outside it, should be considered as a valid contribution towards creating the family home if, as a result of divorce, that had to be divided. In the same year the Equal Pay Act was passed: this laid down the principle, for both sexes, of equal pay for equal work, though there were many exceptions and loopholes, and the Act was not to come fully into law for another five years. Theatre censorship by the Lord Chamberlain was abolished in 1968.[15] Taken together, this legislation put Britain ahead of the rest of the western world with regard to freedoms of ordinary people; not a bad achievement for a government otherwise so much maligned.

By the late fifties it was clear that while flat-rate contributions to National Insurance were quite burdensome for the lowest-paid, the flat-rate benefits themselves were falling far behind the sort of income expected within an affluent society. Thus, in 1959 the Conservatives introduced a new scheme whereby better-off employees paid an additional graduated contribution which in return qualified for an additional earnings-related pension. The new principle was extended by the Labour Government in 1966 when it introduced earnings-related contributions and benefits to cover the first six months of loss of earnings from other causes than retirement. The Redundancy Payments Act of 1965 provided for lump-sum payments, financed partly by the employer and partly by compulsory contributions from all insured employees, payable to employees with over two years' service dismissed simply because of a change in the employer's requirements or circumstances.[16]

Labour' s major piece of welfare legislation was the Ministry of Social Security Act of 1966 which, among other things, sought to remove the stigma still attaching to National Assistance by replacing it with Supplementary Benefits. The growing view of official Labour, as well as Conservative circles, was that applying the universalist principle of 1945 wasted scarce resources. Thus Supplementary Benefits both depended upon a Means Test, and were administered in a flexible way, with much depending upon the discretion of local officials. Humane and sensitive in many respects (greater efforts were made to bring to the attention of the deprived the benefits to which they were entitled), the scheme unfortunately included the bureaucratic device of the 'wages-stop' designed to ensure that Supplementary Benefits did not act as an encouragement to the work-shy. Those who, when in employment, earned less than the income normally supplied by supplementary benefits were deliberately, when out of work, paid a level of benefits slightly below their potential earnings when in work. Thus such people were placed in a poverty trap from which, short of a miraculous change in their employment prospects, there was no prospect of escape.

A major problem of the Health Service in its first dozen years was the desperate shortage of hospitals. To this, because of government miscalculation, was added, by the late fifties, a shortage of doctors. In the sixties genuine attempts were made to deal with both problems. A ten-year hospital-building programme was announced by the Conservatives in 1962; and in 1966 the introduction of special additional allowances secured an even spread of doctors across the country. In 1970 came one of the most civilized pieces of legislation, the Chronic Sick and Disabled Persons Act, which symbolized and ratified a new openness towards, and a new concern for, the problems of the disabled.

By 1964 a powerful consensus, including the progressive Conservative Minister for Education, Sir Edward Boyle, had developed against the eleven-plus examination. In July 1965 the Labour Government issued Circular 10/65 calling upon all local authorities to submit proposals for establishing comprehensive schools. Published in 1963, both the Robbins Report on Higher Education and the Newsome Report on Secondary Education advocated expansion and envisaged greater social mobility and a society appreciative of the values of education. The Plowden Report of 1967 supported the growth of pupil-centred teaching in primary education, as well as the abolition of corporal punishment in all schools. Many colleges, particularly in the spheres of art and design, were upgraded, as were teacher-training colleges; quasi-university status was given to leading colleges of technology – re-christened Polytechnics, their degrees were awarded by one national body, the Council for National Academic Awards (CNAA), founded in 1964. Certain colleges of higher technology became full universities, and totally new universities were created: Sussex, York, Kent, Warwick, Lancaster, East Anglia, Essex and Stirling. More controversial was the 'University of the Air' proposed by sociologist Michael Young, drawing upon extension college experiments in America, Russia, and some Commonwealth countries. The idea was taken up in government by Jennie Lee and then Harold Wilson himself: The Open University, aiming to take its first students in 1971, was fully established in 1969. Many influential Conservatives strongly opposed it.

## *From Wilson to Heath*

In the wake of Macmillan's 'winds of change' speech both Conservative and Labour governments were committed to the principle of independence within the Commonwealth for former African colonies, provided that majority (i.e. black) rule had first been secured. The trouble with Southern Rhodesia (simply Rhodesia after Northern Rhodesia became independent as Zambia) was that the white rulers, under Ian Smith, were firmly determined to retain white supremacy. After Smith made a Unilateral Declaration of Independence (UDI) in November 1965, Wilson carried out some highly publicized negotiations with him, first on HMS *Tiger,* in December 1966, and then on HMS *Fearless,* in October 1968, the ships both times being anchored off Gibraltar. Pressed by the Commonwealth and the United Nations, Britain officially imposed an economic embargo on Rhodesia, but shrank from the confrontation with South Africa necessary to making the sanctions effective. In December 1968, and again in October 1969, certain Cabinet members wanted to institute sales of military aircraft to the apartheid regime in South Africa: Wilson, it should be noted, brought both attempts to an end. Shortly after the first of these attempts, Brown put in one of his petulant resignation letters. This time Wilson accepted. Jenkins insisted on the withdrawal from East of Suez being accelerated, and a cut of one-third in defence spending within seven years. The target of building 500,000 new houses was to be abandoned and the raising of the school-leaving age to sixteen postponed. Already in his budget of March 1968 Jenkins had imposed a one-off tax on high incomes, and increased duties on petrol, alcohol and tobacco.

The government at least seemed genuinely embarked on some tough decision-taking. Wilson's long-time associate Barbara Castle, as Minister for Overseas Development, had, in increasing overseas aid, exemplified Labour's civilized policies. As Minister of Transport she fitted well the general configuration of government weakness in failing to carry through genuine integration of transport, but she did show strongly on such issues as the compulsory wearing of seat belts and the introduction of the breathalyser. In April 1968 she became First Secretary of State at the Department of Employment and Productivity, entrusted with the task of producing trade union reform. Reform of the House of Lords was also mooted, but rather quickly withdrawn.

**Table 4.11** Strikes: some international comparisons

| *Countries* | *Stoppages per 100,000 employees* | | *Striking days per 1,000 employees* | |
|---|---|---|---|---|
| | *1965–9* | *1970–4* | *1965–9* | *1970–4* |
| United Kingdom | 9.5 | 12.0 | 156,585 | |
| Australia | 31.4 | 45.2 | 217,581 | |
| Belgium | 1.9 | 5.1 | 73,242 | |
| France | 9.6* | 17.7 | 126* | 166 |
| German Federal Republic | | | 649 | |
| Italy | 16.3 | 25.6 | 8,171,070 | |
| Japan | 3.0 | 6.2 | 68,115 | |
| United States | 6.4 | 6.7 | 4,925,311 | |

* 1968 excluded from the average.
*Source:* International Labour Office, *Year Book of Labour Statistics* (Geneva, 1976).

As can be seen, Britain's strike record was not particularly bad in comparison with other countries, though the record in some countries was certainly much better. Industrial relations, restrictive practices, low productivity, disruption of exports caused by strikes, inflationary pressure generated by trade union demands: these interlinked issues had been central in Britain's post-1945 history. At the same time the ideologies of both consensus and class accepted, and indeed welcomed, the position unions had established. That workers should have decent wages and should have unions to protect them were commonplaces. Union leaders, in any case, were generally forces for moderation and restraint. What caused most immediate concern was the number of unofficial or 'wildcat' strikes contained within the formal figures. The insecure Labour Government of 1965 had no particular agenda in mind when it appointed the Donovan Commission to investigate the condition of British trade unions. Representing the orthodoxy of the time, the commission, reporting in July 1968, came down against the introduction of any laws to regulate or constrain trade union activities. The Conservatives, under Heath, however, were now taking the view that some regulation was required and in *Fair Deal at Work*, published in April 1968, they addressed, in particular, the problem of wildcat strikes, proposing a 60-day cooling-off period.

Castle belonged to a left-wing tradition which saw unions as facets of unregulated capitalist society, as selfish, rather than socialist. Encouraged by Wilson and Jenkins, but quite blatantly challenging the convictions of almost all members of the Labour party, she came out in January 1969 with the White Paper *In Place of Strife*. She took up the cooling-off idea (limited to 28 days and officially termed a 'conciliation pause') and proposed powers for the minister both to order strike ballots, and to impose settlements in inter-union disputes. These powers could lead to the prosecution of individual trade unionists before a new Industrial Relations Court. While public support was registered in opinion polls, opposition from trade unionists, led in particular by Jack Jones of the Transport Workers and Hugh Scanlon of the Engineers, across the Labour party, and within the government, where the most influential leader was James Callaghan, was solid. Wilson has often been accused of cowardly retreat from essential reform; but in face of the profound opposition of his own side, there was really nothing he could do, even if on 1 June 1969 he conjured up a sinister image in urging Scanlon to 'get his tanks off my lawn'.[17] The upshot was the Downing Street Declaration of 18 June in which, in words which were immediately subjected to well-deserved mockery, the TUC gave a 'solemn and binding agreement' to undertake the monitoring of strikes and labour disputes.

Wilson was actually not unsuccessful in presenting the Downing Street Declaration as a triumph on his part (and, realistically, it *was* about the best he could have achieved), while, at the same time, the unmistakable signs of economic recovery began to appear, partly the delayed consequences of devaluation, partly the result of Jenkins's rigorous economic management. From performing disastrously in by-elections and opinion polls, Labour began to look like potential winners of the forthcoming election. The Conservatives, in January 1970, took a very public step towards establishing themselves as a party which wished to cut state spending and regulation, free up economic forces, and control the unions, promulgating such policies at a conference at Selsdon Park in Surrey. The mockery inspired by the notion of 'Selsdon Man' further suggested that Labour could be on the road to electoral victory. Wilson, after wide consultation, decided to go for it while the going seemed good, and scheduled the election for June; Jenkins insisted on a responsible budget, refusing to offer bribes to the electorate.

**Table 4.12** General Election, 18 June 1970

| | *Electorate 39.3 million* | | *Turnout 72 per cent* | |
|---|---|---|---|---|
| | *Conservative* | *Labour* | *Liberal* | *Others* |
| Votes | 13,145,123 | 12,179,341 | 2,117,035 | 906,345 |
| Percentage of votes cast | 46.4 | 43.0 | 7.5 | 2.1 |
| Seats | 330 | 287 | 6 | 7 |

Perhaps the most critical figure in table 4.12 is that for turnout. It seems that the bulk of those who stayed at home were Labour voters,[18] feeling no doubt that Wilson had betrayed the high hopes of 1966. Since a Labour victory had been widely expected, Edward Heath gained considerable credit for the way in which he had doggedly worked for victory. But his achievements as Prime Minister were not, on the whole, to be highly rated. It could be said that the phrase 'U-turn' was invented to deal with the sharp changes of policy he was involved in. Or, it could be said that his period of office marked a bridge between the consensual collectivism of earlier governments, and the monetarist and free-market policies which came fully into existence under Margaret Thatcher in the 1980s; and that, indeed, Heath was the perfect pragmatist.[19] His greatest achievement was not a popular one, and, indeed, almost got lost in the welter of other problems and difficulties. Nonetheless, Britain's relationship with Europe is one of the great transcending issues of the second half of the twentieth century, and Heath it was who finally succeeded in taking Britain into the EEC in 1973 – the year also of the introduction, at a rate of 10 per cent, of the EEC-style in direct tax, VAT. Unpopular over big issue number one, it was Heath's misfortune to be overwhelmed, and very publicly, by the two other big issues: Ireland, and the control of wage inflation. While he just happened to be in office on 15 February 1971 when the long-planned decimalization of the currency came about, Heath, and, in particular, his Minister for Local Government, Peter Walker, were very proactive in carrying through the Local Government Acts (England and Wales, 1972; Scotland, 1973) which during 1974 and 1975 recognized the great conurbations (e.g. Merseyside, Strathclyde) as metropolitan counties, abolished historic Rutland, and redesignated the City and Royal Burgh of Edinburgh a mere District.

## *Northern Ireland, c.1963–75*

Elsewhere I have argued that where the 'cultural revolution' of the sixties had some of its most profound effects was in the most backward areas of the West – southern Italy, rural Brittany, the American South.[20] Very much was this true of Northern Ireland. Some of the warming rays of affluence began touching the province in the early sixties, when life became a little less cramped, aspirations a little less confined. Thanks to the Education Act of 1944 a new educated Catholic middle class was emerging which was not particularly attracted by traditional Republicanism. Catholics were 22 per cent of the student body at Queen's University Belfast in 1963, and 32 per cent in 1971. As in France and Italy, young married women, more perhaps than students and teenagers, began to voice new demands. News filtered in of black civil rights demonstrations in America. Catholics as well as Protestants were benefiting from post-war welfare policies, and strong new initiatives were announced by the Wilson Government. But at the same time relative discrimination against Catholics became more obvious. A number of devices ensured an unjustified Protestant dominance of the local authorities: the local franchise was a rate-payer's one, denying votes to poorer Catholics; ward boundaries were deliberately drawn to ensure that Protestant voting power had maximum effect. Part of the discrimination practised by the local authorities in the allocation of subsidized housing was designed to ensure that Catholic voters would not outnumber Protestant ones in key areas. The investment brought by the Wilson Government tended to go to the industrial east (where for instance the new town of Craigavon was built), which was predominantly Protestant, rather than to the rural and Catholic west.

In my discussions of the 'cultural revolution' (see next section) I have stressed the importance of tolerant, liberal-minded figures within the establishment who practised 'measured judgement'. In 1963 the ultra-conservative Lord Brookeborough was succeeded as Prime Minister of Northern Ireland by Captain Terence O'Neill, an Old Etonian army officer who was in many ways a model practitioner of measured judgement, going far beyond his predecessors in making a positive appeal to the Catholic minority. Unfortunately his appeal, though admirable in so many ways, was too obviously that of a British patriot, who thought Catholics should be 'proud to be part of a nation' characterized by 'magnanimity' and 'a fuller, richer life'.[21] With his Commerce Minister Brian Faulkner, O'Neill enthusiastically put into practice the Wilson Plan of December 1964, involving an initial investment of £450 million, followed up by further grants. In January 1965, without consulting or informing anyone else, he had a meeting at Stormont with the Taoiseach of the Irish Republic, Seán Lemass, and in his 1965 Stormont election campaign, he declared in favour of economic cooperation with the Irish government.

But legitimate grievances over housing and jobs were not going to be so easily resolved; and people were increasingly prepared, in both senses of the term, to take reasoned and organized action themselves. In early 1963 a group of housewives presented a petition to Dungannon Urban District Council protesting that while they were stuck in overcrowded insanitary accommodation, Protestants coming in from outside the area were being given new houses. Out of this in May 1963 came the Homeless Citizens' League. On 17 January 1964 the Campaign for Social Justice (CSJ) was founded in Belfast. In the 1966 General Election, Gerry Fitt, standing as a Labour candidate, won West Belfast from the Unionists, and was able to join up with the back-bench Labour group Campaign for Democracy in Ulster, founded the previous year. The CSJ, republican clubs in both Dublin and Belfast, trade unionists, the Northern Ireland Labour Party, the Communist Party, and the Ulster Liberal Party came together at the end of January 1967 to found the body which came into formal existence on 9 April 1967 as the Northern Ireland Civil Rights Association (NICRA); the Chairman of Queen's University Conservative and Unionist Association was subsequently co-opted onto the committee. On 24 July 1968 two thousand NICRA protestors marched into Dungannon. The episode passed off peacefully, though the protesters were faced by 1,500 counter-demonstrators led by the Reverend Ian Paisley.

In all western societies the sixties was an era of the founding of groups and movements of all types, many of which may have been on the side of the angels but not necessarily that of human progress – Christian Fundamentalism, creationism, oriental mysticism, all had their activists. The Reverend Ian

Paisley was born in April 1926, son of a Baptist minister. Strong in Wales, the Baptists were almost negligible in Ireland, where the O'Neills and Brookeboroughs were Anglican, and almost all the other Protestants were Presbyterian. Studying first at the South Wales Bible College, Paisley then returned to the Reformed Presbyterian Theological College, Belfast, being ordained in 1946; in 1951 he identified himself with Ulster history by founding his own Free Presbyterian Church of Ulster. Paisley was the voice and face of that bigotry and irreconcilability which was to be one of the forces making the Irish problem, now that it was springing back into life, so difficult to resolve. His Ulster Constitution Defence Committee, and his Ulster Protestant Volunteers, were vociferous opponents of O'Neill. Support for Paisley was particularly strong among the Belfast working class, but was quite evenly spread across the whole of Northern Ireland: 32 per cent of Protestants in 1967 said that they usually agreed with him, while 58 per cent usually disagreed.[22]

A number of marches and demonstrations in the spring and summer of 1968 passed off without serious incident. But the Minister of Home Affairs, William Craig, an uncompromising Protestant unsympathetic to O'Neill's moderate policies, banned an NICRA civil rights march to be held on Londonderry (or Derry as Nationalists called it) on 5 October 1968. The march went ahead and there were violent confrontations with the RUC. Television coverage, featuring the free and ferocious wielding of batons by the RUC, did the Unionist cause no good at all with the British public. O'Neill, Craig and Faulkner were summoned to London. O'Neill accepted Wilson's insistence that there should be an impartial inquiry into the events of 5 October, what became the Cameron Commission. A reform programme was instituted, aimed, it could be said, at making Northern Ireland a part of the United Kingdom of which the British need not feel ashamed. In a special television broadcast on 9 December 1968 O'Neill warned that 'Ulster is at the crossroads.' Referring to the Paisleyites he said:

> These people are not merely extremists. They are lunatics who would set a course along a road which could only lead at the end into an all-Ireland Republic. They are not loyalists but *disloyalists*: disloyal to Britain, disloyal to the Constitution, disloyal to the Crown, disloyal – if they are in public life – to the solemn oaths they have sworn to Her Majesty the Queen.[23]

Two days later O'Neill ejected Craig from the Cabinet. Nationalists and civil rights leaders were impressed, but unfortunately a new organization, People's Democracy (PD), the first big manifestation of activism on the part of students from Queen's University, was not. Explicitly imitating the 1966 civil rights march from Selma to Montgomery in Alabama, PD organized a four-day march from Belfast to Londonderry, starting on 1 January 1969. The avowed aim of the march, generally condemned by civil rights leaders and nationalists, was to arouse class, rather than sectarian consciousness; ironically the extremely violent confrontations it provoked swamped both the increasingly fruitful civil rights movement and the moderate reforms of O'Neill and brought sectarianism, red in tooth and claw, right into the front line. At Burntollet Bridge, just short of Londonderry, the marchers were attacked by about two hundred loyalists, including off-duty B-Specials. This was followed by violence involving the RUC in the Catholic Bogside area of Londonderry. Later in January there was rioting in Newry and again in Londonderry, just as the Cameron Commission, which now had plenty of material to chew over, was being established.

The Commission reckoned that, while the IRA had infiltrated marches and demonstrations, it was not responsible for organizing them. The RUC had been 'ill-co-ordinated and inept' and had used unnecessary force on 5 October. While critical of Paisley's 'extremists' and 'lunatics', Cameron did recognize, as we should too, the real basis to Protestant fears. The Protestant population in the Irish Republic had declined cataclysmically, while the Catholic population in the North was constantly expanding; largely these were products of the ban by the Catholic Church on birth control and its insistence that in mixed marriages all children should be brought up as Catholics. The Irish constitution laid claim to all 32 counties of the island of Ireland; the right of Northern Ireland to exist was not recognized. Living standards were low in the Republic, which seemed a priest-ridden country with ludicrous censorship laws, bans on birth control and divorce, and considerable restrictions on individual freedom. In those local authority areas in the North which were dominated by Catholics, such as Newry, discrimination was practised against non-Catholics.

Cameron, like O'Neill, could not see that it was quite unreasonable to expect the Catholic minority in the North to forswear its sense of Irishness for a sense of Britishness. Unfortunately, the new Irish Prime Minister, Jack Lynch, leader of the ultra-Republican Fianna Fáil party, made pronouncements of such an unhelpful nature as to push still further over the horizon any prospect of even moderate Protestants recognizing the Irish dimension to the Northern Ireland crisis. The problem with politics in Northern Ireland was that there was no politics in Northern Ireland, no way of representing the new ideas, no way of voting for profound change *within* the existing constitution. In the Stormont election of 24 February 1969 the Unionist monolith cracked, with Paisley putting forward his own Protestant Unionist party, and with many official Unionists openly opposing O'Neill; the failure of the Nationalists to represent the new currents was also drastically exposed. As a consequence of the upsets of the election, two new parties, ultimately to be vital to the peace process, came into being.

The turnout was 72 per cent, good by Northern Ireland standards. Of the 39 Unionists returned, 24 were 'official' Unionists who supported O'Neill, three were 'unofficial' Unionists who also supported the Prime Minister, and a dozen were 'official Unionists' who did not support O'Neill – the pro-O'Neill vote amounted to 44 per cent of the electorate, the anti-O'Neill Unionist vote to 13 per cent. The Nationalists held six seats, but lost three to Civil Rights candidates. The Northern Ireland Labour Party and Republican Labour each won two seats in Belfast. Most portentous was the return of Catholic school teacher and socialist from Londonderry, John Hume who fought his campaign in Foyle on a need for the creation of a new social democratic party on the European model. He played a leading role along with Gerry Fitt in launching just such a party early in 1970, the Social Democratic and Labour Party (SDLP). Among its aims were: 'To promote the cause of Irish unity based on the consent of a majority of people in Northern Ireland.' It also aimed 'to contest elections in Northern Ireland with a view to forming a government' which, among other things, would implement: 'the abolition of all forms of religious, political or class discrimination'. Soon after, in April 1970, the Alliance Party was formed, mainly from people who had not previously been active in party politics. It drew in people both from the O'Neill Unionists and from the Northern Ireland Labour Party; a couple of years later three sitting MPs joined it, two Unionists and one Nationalist. A thinkers' party, the Alliance never enjoyed great electoral success, but it was an important presence in the cause of non-sectarianism.

On 23 April 1969 there were bomb attacks on public buildings and utilities. Inevitably the IRA were blamed, though in fact the bombings were the work of the Ulster Defence Force, aiming a blow at O'Neill's government. Five days later O'Neill did resign, and was replaced by Captain James Chichester-Clark. In August, the new, most violent phase yet of confrontation between Catholic and Protestant communities began – the phase which brought in British troops and initiated the Thirty Years War of horrific maiming and killing. Several factors turned a disturbed situation in which positive elements of hope were actually emerging, into an era of hopelessness and continual carnage. The first was the greatly intensified sense within the Protestant community that it must go out of its way to assert itself in the face of the claims, and gains, being made by Catholics; that explained the events of August. What came second was a reorganization within the IRA at the end of 1969, leading to the emergence of the Provisional IRA, ready to wage war, not so much on Protestant Northern Ireland, but on Britain itself. Then a series of criminal misjudgements by the British army, originally welcomed by most in the Catholic community, meant that they could soon be represented as the violent upholders of illegitimate British rule. Finally, the Irish Taoiseach, in a television broadcast of almost fathomless irresponsibility, delivered on 13 August, declared the August crisis to be of Stormont's making, the Stormont government to be no longer in control, the RUC to be aggressors against innocent Catholic people, any intervention of the British army to be unacceptable, and called for a peace-keeping force to be sent by the United Nations, while the Irish army would provide field-hospitals along the border to succour Catholic victims of British aggression. He concluded that the British Government must enter into early negotiations over creating a united Ireland. If Protestant phobias were previously unjustified, with one bound Lynch had turned them into reality.

The traditional way for Protestants to make a public spectacle of their hegemony in Northern Ireland was through the Orange marches held in July and August: this year there was a determination to make them more triumphalist than ever. Orange marches on 12 July provoked aggressive Catholic responses in Londonderry, Dungiven, and various parts of Belfast. The Derry Citizens' Defence Association took upon itself the defence of the Bogside by whatever means might prove necessary. In early August there was Protestant rioting on the Shankhill Road in Belfast. Then came the 12 August march by the Apprentice Boys of Derry, which was met with a hail of stones as it passed the Bogside.

Riots in Londonderry, which lasted three days, spread to Coal Island, Dungannon, Belfast, Newry and Armagh. Partly, this was a deliberate ploy on the part of the Catholics to stretch the RUC to breaking point. In fact, the RUC were unable to cope in Londonderry, and in the late afternoon of 14 August the authorities there had to ask the army for assistance. Chichester-Clark flew to London, where Harold Wilson issued yet another Downing Street Declaration: this one, of 20 August 1969, affirmed that 'the Border is not an issue', and that Northern Ireland would not cease to be a part of the United Kingdom without the consent of the people and parliament of Northern Ireland. The deployment of troops was stated to be only a temporary expedient until the restoration of law and order. The momentum of reform had to be maintained and equal rights guaranteed to all citizens in Northern Ireland 'as obtains in the rest of the United Kingdom'. The B-Specials were to be replaced by the British-controlled Ulster Defence Regiment. The Paisleyites chose to interpret all this as capitulation to Catholic threats: thus the Protestants went on winding themselves up.

Now came the deadly developments on the other side. There was dissatisfaction with the IRA's apparent failure to protect Catholics from Protestant mob violence – 'IRA – I Ran Away' said slogans on Belfast walls. A number of younger figures, including Gerry Adams, came to feel that there simply would be no justice for Catholics while there was a British presence in Ireland, and that that presence would only be removed by force. The split within the IRA came at an extraordinary army convention in December 1969. A group led by Seàn MacStriofàin held their own convention, establishing the Provisional IRA and Provisional Sinn Féin. Provisional Sinn Féin denied the legitimacy of both the Northern Ireland government and the Irish Republic, and pledged allegiance to the 32-county republic proclaimed in 1916 and established in 1919. In the first days of January 1970 the Provisional Army Council met to decide a three-stage military policy: the first stage would be one of defending Catholic communities from the loyalists and the British army; the second stage would be one of 'combined defence and retaliation'; the third stage would be an all-out offensive against the 'British occupation system'.

### *Enter the Provisional IRA*

The scene was being set for the murderous mayhem which was to follow. The Wilson Government saw its initiatives as being designed to restrain Northern Ireland Protestants and to create new opportunities for Catholics. But greater British involvement was simply taken by the IRA as supporting their case that the fundamental problem was the British presence; unfortunately British errors of both omission and commission gave further substance to that view. That is not to deny that there was a manifest bloodlust and love of violence for its own sake among elements on the other side (characteristics also to be found among some Protestants). Probably the only policy which could have preserved a kind of peace would have been that of sending in a massive British force determined to enforce British standards of tolerance and respect for civil rights, involving the banning of all Orange marches. The Orange march down the Crumlin Road in Belfast went ahead on 3 June 1970, but then, in recognition of Catholic sensibilities, was diverted near the Ardoyne. That inflamed Protestant sensibilities and two nights of rioting followed in which firearms were used. Further Orange marches on 27 June provoked Catholic rioting and the first 'defensive' actions by Provisional IRA snipers. The balance of deaths is important to record: five Protestants and one Catholic; twenty-six people were wounded.

The Provisionals had the guns, but ordinary working-class Protestants had brute majority power. Next day the Protestant workers in the Harland and Wolff shipyards in East Belfast ejected about five hundred Catholic workers from their jobs. At this point it was absolutely vital for the British troops to be seen still to be absolutely neutral and as ready to defend Catholics as Protestants, not easy, of course, when the IRA (both wings were united on this) openly declared British soldiers to be legitimate targets. It was announced that the British army would shoot on sight anyone carrying a gun, not as reasonable a policy as it sounds since in practice it is easy to imagine weapons that are not actually there or to mistake the direction from which fire is coming. There then followed an action which was tantamount to identifying the Catholic Lower Falls area of Belfast as hostile territory. A thirty-four-hour curfew – though with a two-hour shopping break – was imposed, and a house-to-house search carried out by British troops. Gun battles took place between British soldiers and both wings of the IRA: five local people, two of them snipers, were killed, and forty-five injured: fifteen soldiers were injured. Justification for the policy could be found in the army haul of 100 firearms, 100 home-made bombs, 250 pounds of explosives, 21,000 rounds of ammunition, and eight two-way radios. But the behaviour of the British troops, fearful and ignorant, conceiving the entire local population as 'the enemy', was such as to give an immense, and critical, boost to the Provisionals. As Paddy Devlin, member of the Northern Ireland Labour Party and hostile to the Provisionals, put it:

> The military, cock-a-hoop with their illegal takeover of the Falls, proceeded to put the boot in with a vengeance . . . even as an MP, I was subject to constant harassment and suspicion by the military. Overnight the population turned from neutral or even sympathetic support for the military to outright hatred of everything related to the security forces . . . Gerry Fitt and I witnessed voters and workers . . . turn against us to join the Provisionals.

With some active and much tacit support from the local Catholic population the Provisionals both carried out devastating bomb attacks on 'economic targets', and picked off soldiers and RUC officers. The brief prospect of Northern Ireland as a normal part of the United Kingdom had completely evaporated: once again the RUC were given guns, and also bullet-proof vests. Also in March 1971, there was a gun battle between the two wings of the IRA: the following year the Officials declared a ceasefire, leaving the Provisional campaign to escalate ever higher. Whatever the mental set of some gunfighters and bombers (on both sides) the Provisionals did have a policy with which they hoped to appeal to Northern Ireland Protestants, which insisted on 'British Imperialism' as the only true enemy. The trouble was that the absolute core of Protestant hostility was the determination to continue to be British, and a deep fear of any 32-county Ireland. In the SDLP John Hume was stressing that the old romantic republican notion of the inviolable unity of the *land* of Ireland should be replaced by a focus on the *people* of Ireland: the crucial divide was not in territory, but among the people, and that was the divide which had to be resolved. But that was a notion buried beneath burnt-out buildings and shattered bodies. Two by-elections in April 1970 brought Ian Paisley and William Beattie into Stormont as Protestant Unionists. And after 18 June there was a Conservative government, organically associated with Unionism, in London.

The reform programme, it should be stressed, did continue, rapidly increasing Chichester-Clarke's unpopularity with his own followers. There was to be local government reform and reform in the drawing of electoral districts. Responsibility for prosecutions was removed from the RUC and put in the hands of the Director of Public Prosecutions (May 1971). On 18 March 1971 Chichester-Clarke flew to London to seek a large increase in the British army presence; he got only another 1,300 troops. Arguing that there was no immediate hope of defeating the Provisional IRA, Chichester-Clarke resigned a couple of days later. If the events I described earlier definitively marked the beginning of a war waged by the Provisionals with much local support, the advent to the prime ministership of Brian Faulkner, combined with the fact of a Conservative government at Westminster, definitively marked a switch in British policy from 'minimum force' and 'peace-keeping' to something approaching aggressive war. Faulkner pressed the need for this switch upon the Commander of the British Army in Northern Ireland, General Tuzo, and then, on 1 April 1971 in London, on Heath, who was very receptive. Faulkner also came up with proposals for some SDLP participation in government, but then his further warlike moves alienated the SDLP. There was a case for greatly strengthening the number of British soldiers in Ireland – the army was not able to prevent the formation of 'no-go' Republican areas which the British army simply could not enter – though the problem with that was that it would simply intensify Provisional and IRA irreconcilability.

For four nights in the first week of July 1971 British soldiers, trying to cope with Catholic rioting in Londonderry, faced stones, petrol bombs and gunfire. First a local civilian was shot by a soldier, later dying from loss of blood. The rioting intensified, and another civilian, Desmond Beattie, was shot. Local people said both men had been unarmed. The SDLP withdrew from Stormont. They pointed out the futility of the British Government's intervening militarily, if it was not at the same time prepared to propose a political solution. The government in fact responded with what, with hindsight, can be seen as its greatest mistake so far, 'internment', the arrest and detention of those 'known' to be members of the IRA. If internment was to have any success at all, it would depend on very high quality RUC intelligence; in fact, particularly because of the rise of the no-go areas, RUC intelligence was highly defective. Using a list of 452 men, the British army carried out a series of dawn raids on 9 August: they managed to pick up 342, of whom 103 had to be released a couple of days later. The actual search operation could only cause great anger among Catholic householders; and rumours quickly spread of ill-treatment of those who were interned. Recruitment to the Provisionals accelerated, as did violent acts on the part of ordinary Catholics. The SDLP called upon all Catholics to withdraw from participation in public office, and they organized rent strikes and civil disobedience campaigns. The SDLP felt it had to take such actions to prevent its support from being entirely sucked away by the Provisionals; to Unionists such actions made the SDLP seem little better than the Provisionals. Faulkner had to talk to someone. The chance came with the Chequers talks of September 1971, between him, Heath, and Lynch. Faulkner wanted Lynch to act against the Provisionals in the Republic, who could constantly re-equip and reinforce the gunmen and bombers in the North. It was clear that the British Government really had only one policy, military defeat of the IRA. Home Secretary Maudling, appallingly, spoke of 'acceptable levels of violence'.[24] Harold Wilson, for the Labour Opposition, did in November 1971 put forward his '15-point plan' with a United Ireland as the ultimate objective. Unfortunately this just intensified Unionist fears, and, of course, their hostility to Labour. With escalating Provisional action, many Protestants regretted the disappearance of the B-Specials, feeling that the Ulster Defence Regiment was no adequate substitute. Thus, in September 1971, a new paramilitary organization, overwhelmingly working class, the Ulster Defence Association came into being in addition to the older Ulster Volunteer Force (UVF): these organizations applied to themselves the term 'loyalist'. The commencement of systematic loyalist violence was signalled by the UVF bombing of McGurk's Bar, Belfast, on 14 December 1971, killing 15 people, including three women and two children, and by the shooting dead on the Crumlin Road on 8 February 1972 of Bernard Rice, a 60-year-old member of the Catholic Ex-Servicemen's Association. Over 200 such murders followed in the next eighteen months.

And there was Bloody Sunday. Orange marches, we have noted, were not banned. But a civil rights march planned for 30 January 1972 in Londonderry was. An idiotic move, since the march took place anyway, with almost ten thousand people participating. When part of the crowd attempted to climb over a barrier erected by the security forces, the army forced them back with rubber bullets and water cannon. Stones and iron bars were thrown at the troops by young demonstrators. Then shooting began. Exactly how, or even whether there was any fire from the Catholic side, has never been securely established, though later television investigations certainly brought out the disgraceful inadequacy of the official investigation at the time. What is beyond question is that the British Parachute Regiment did open up heavy fire, killing thirteen unarmed civilians immediately, with another dying subsequently, and seventeen being wounded. The event was appalling, the bluster and cover-up of the Heath Government equally so. The IRA had been handed its biggest propaganda victory. In Dublin, the British Embassy was burned to the ground. In February 1972 the official IRA exploded a car bomb at the 16th Parachute Regiment's barracks at Aldershot in England, killing seven civilians. The Provisionals bombed the Abercorn Restaurant in Belfast on 4 March, killing two and maiming and injuring 130. Six people died and more than a hundred were injured by a Provisional car bomb in Lower Donegall Street, Belfast, on

20 March. In this case a deliberately misleading phone call was used to bring people into the danger area.

Four days later Heath announced the measure which the Labour Government had been contemplating, the suspension of the Stormont parliament and the imposition of direct rule from London, achieved through the Northern Ireland (Temporary Provisions) Act 1972, and implemented through a newly created Secretary of State for Northern Ireland. The Provisionals rejoiced. Ulster Unionists trembled, and William Craig, now Leader of Ulster Vanguard, a fringe organization within the Unionist party, threatened a Northern Ireland loyal to the Crown, but independent of the British parliament. The Provisionals, on 22 June 1972, announced a ceasefire, provided the British forces publicly reciprocated, with a view to there being direct talks between themselves and the British. As the first Northern Ireland Secretary, Heath had chosen the very distinctively upper-class, but genuinely conciliatory William Whitelaw. Whitelaw acceded to Provisional demands that Republican prisoners should be allocated 'special-category status', treating them, in Republican eyes, as prisoners of war not common criminals. On 7 July in London, Whitelaw and other British ministers met a Provisional IRA delegation, consisting of Mac Stiofáin and other older leaders, as well as the younger figure, Gerry Adams (specially released from internment) and Martin McGuinness. Could this secret meeting have brought peace? Revealing the meeting to the House of Commons a week later, Whitelaw described the IRA as having issued 'absurd' ultimatums. The Provisionals wanted the future of Ireland to be determined by the people of all Ireland voting as a unit; they wanted total withdrawal of British forces by 1 January 1976. Whitelaw could not withdraw from the British commitment that the future of Northern Ireland would be settled only with the consent of a majority there. Whitelaw had probably fooled himself into believing that the British army was a neutral force (and, of course, he saw the IRA and civil rights protestors as the aggressors, the enemy). He blindly insisted that British troops did not fire on unarmed civilians when the Provisionals had very good grounds for believing otherwise. The mismatch of beliefs and assumptions was probably just too great. The two-week ceasefire came to an end on 13 July when three soldiers and one civilian were killed, the figure for the following day being one soldier and four civilians. Within the week the hundredth soldier in this war had been killed. And then came Bloody Friday. A Provisional bomb at a bus station on 21 July, one of the 26 set off that day, blasted eleven people into fragments, injuring a further 130.

Internment had not been successful in getting the men of violence locked up, while the normal processes of law were vitiated by intimidation of witnesses and juries, and perverse jury verdicts. As a result of the Diplock Report of December 1972, 'Diplock courts' were set up, dispensing with juries in the case of terrorist offences, and putting all powers in the hands of a single judge.

Direct secret negotiations with the Provisionals having achieved nothing, the government did proceed to a number of highly laudable initiatives. Principally it sought to recognize the Irish dimension, to recognize, as the SDLP urged, that there must be scope for all sections of Northern Ireland to participate in decision-making ('power-sharing'). A White Paper, *Northern Ireland*

*Constitutional Proposals,* was promulgated on 20 March 1973. The proposals were:

1 A Northern Ireland Assembly of about 80 members, elected by proportional representation;
2 The Assembly's Executive must draw upon the Catholic community as well as the Protestant;
3 In recognition of the 'Irish dimension', the British Government, after elections to the Assembly, would convene a conference with the Irish Government and representatives from Northern Ireland to discuss effective North–South cooperation.[25]

These proposals were embodied in the Northern Ireland Assembly Act and the Northern Ireland Constitution Act (1973). Unionists irreconcilably opposed to the proposals, resigned to form the Vanguard Unionist Progressive Party.

The elections for the new Northern Ireland Assembly, held on 28 June 1973, revealed that Faulkner was in fact in a considerable minority among Unionists as a whole. Again there was a 72 per cent turnout. Faulkner's Unionists won 24 seats, on 29 per cent of valid first-preference votes. The anti-Faulkner Unionists totalled 26 seats, made up of eight non-Faulkner Unionists with 9 per cent of first-preference votes, eight members of Ian Paisley's Democratic Unionist Party (as it was now calling itself) with 11 per cent of the first-preference votes, seven Vanguard members with 11 per cent, and three West Belfast Loyalists with 2 per cent. The SDLP won nineteen seats, with 22 per cent of first-preference votes, the Alliance Party eight seats with 9 per cent, and the Northern Ireland Labour Party one seat with 3 per cent. The Ulster Unionist Council endorsed Faulkner's participation in a power-sharing executive by just 379 votes to 369. On the formation of the Executive (22 November 1973) Faulkner was Chief Executive, and Gerry Fitt, Leader of the SDLP, Deputy Chief Executive (thus foreshadowing the composition of the Executive of 1998). There were six other Unionist members, five SDLP members, and two Alliance Party members.

To fulfil the third proposal of the White Paper, talks were convened at Sunningdale, Berkshire, the following month, with representatives of the British Government, each of the three parties in the power-sharing Executive, and of the Irish Government. Faulkner, a wealthy and shrewd textile manufacturer, and committed Orangeman, had in the end shown himself to be the most imaginative and least bigoted of Unionist leaders. But, basically for that very reason, the ground was crumbling beneath his feet. On 5 December 1973 five of the Ulster Unionists' seven Westminster MPs decided to ally themselves with Faulkner's principal critic, Harry West. On 6 December disaffected Unionist delegates, Vanguard, the Democratic Unionist party and the Orange Order formed a joint organization, the United Ulster Unionist Council, to oppose the Sunningdale Agreement. The Orange Order described its differences from Faulkner and Sunningdale as 'irreconcilable'. Most menacing of all was a new organization of loyalist workers, the Ulster Workers' Council (UWC). First, civil disobedience was threatened if the newly-elected Assembly was not dissolved and new elections called. Then, from 15 May 1974 the UWC began a general strike which brought power cuts and factory and shipyard closures. Though the strength of the UWC was that it was working class, all the usual suspects appeared on the Co-ordinating Committee which ran the strike: Paisley, West, Craig, the heads of the UDA and the UVF, respectively, Andy Tyrre and Ken Gibson, with the Chair being Glen Barr of both the UDA and Vanguard. With the Loyalist paramilitaries at their disposal, the strike leaders could ensure that the strike was joined even by otherwise unwilling workers. So this was not really simply a non-violent strike. On 17 May three car bombs exploded in Dublin, killing 22 people and injuring over a 100, while another car bomb killed five and injured 20 in Monaghan. It was twenty years before responsibility was admitted by the UVF.

Harold Wilson had been back in office since 4 March. His television and radio broadcast on the strike may well have told the truth, may well have shown that his heart was in the right place, but it was singularly ill-judged. After describing the strike as a 'deliberate and calculated attempt to use every undemocratic and unparliamentary means', he subsequently referred to many in Northern Ireland as 'sponging on Westminster and British democracy'. Conservative governments had always been unwilling to act against Unionists; despite Wilson's harsh words, the new Irish Secretary, Merlyn Rees, was not prepared to act against workers. With Northern Ireland paralysed, Faulkner, on 28 May, resigned as Chief Executive, making the unassailable point that the degree of consent needed to support the Executive simply did not exist. Rees reassumed direct powers, with the Assembly being prorogued, and then finally dissolved in March 1975.

Meantime, as a result of talks between Protestant churchmen and members of the Provisional IRA Army Council, which took place on 10 December 1974 at Feakle, County Clare, the IRA called a temporary truce to last from 20 December to 2 January 1975. This led to talks between British government officials and provisional Sinn Féin from 22 December to 17 January, leading in turn to the IRA extending its ceasefire until 17 January. Bomb outrages in London and Manchester marked the end of that short ceasefire, but then another indefinite ceasefire was announced to begin on 10 February. Serious negotiations now took place between British officials and Provisional IRA representatives, with the British deliberately scaling down army patrols and house-to-house searches. The basic IRA offer was of a permanent ceasefire if Britain would make a public declaration of an intention to withdraw from Ireland. The British could contemplate the steady withdrawal of the British army from internal security functions, but not total disengagement from Northern Ireland. Such a disengagement was not, in any case, acceptable to the government of the Irish Republic. Unionist death squads played their part in sabotaging the talks by intensifying their murderous campaign against ordinary Catholics. The truce broke down on 22 September 1975, and was shortly followed by some of the most brutal of Provisional attacks, including the murder on 5 January 1967 at Kingsmill, County Armagh, of ten Protestant workers returning home in a mini-bus.

## *Economic and industrial policies of the Heath government*

Ted Heath, and his Chancellor of the Exchequer, Anthony Barber, very self-consciously set out on a programme of deregulation and curbing trade union power. The intended keynote was struck early.[26] Labour's Industrial Reorganisation Corporation was abolished, along with the Prices and Incomes Board and the Land Commission, and subventions to failing industries were cut. The new Minister of Technology, John Davies, head of the Confederation of British Industries, famously remarked that the government would not subsidize 'lame ducks'. Faced with yet another dock strike, the Minister of Labour, Robert Carr, ostentatiously eschewed intervention: the dockers and their employers must fight it out. Barber's first budget in April 1971 made large cuts in taxation, including a reduction in the standard rate of income tax by 6d in the pound. There were substantial cuts in public expenditure, amounting to £330 million in 1971–2 and including reductions in subsidies for council housing and school milk – the responsibility for the implementation of the latter falling upon Heath's only woman minister, Margaret Thatcher at Education.

Non-intervention in industrial conflicts was intended to keep wage inflation down. In fact, the unions in such vital spheres as the docks and the motor industry ensured that wages went up. There was a postal workers' strike at the beginning of 1971, just, incidentally, when the new Open University was about to deliver its first materials (by post!) to its first students (the Open University had been threatened with suffocation at birth by the Conservatives' most prestigious figure Ian McLeod who, however, died soon after the formation of the government, his place, most inadequately, being taken by Barber; this tragic blow for the Conservatives and McLeod's very many admirers, was a blessing for the Open University, which, on the whole, had the support of Thatcher).[27] Two gigantic 'lame ducks' loomed on the horizon. The first was Rolls-Royce, manufacturer of luxury cars, but much more significantly, also of aero-engines. Despite having a valuable American contract to build the engines for the Lockheed Tri-star RB211 it was suffering from cash-flow and management problems. Rolls-Royce was nationalized – to the sound of mocking laughter. The second firm was Upper Clyde Shipbuilders. With the management ready to close down with the loss of 4,000 jobs, the employees staged a 'work-in' led by two lively Communist shop-stewards, Jimmy Reid and Jimmy Airlie. Not only job losses, but serious violence could be expected if the yard did close. It was kept going with a government subsidy of £35 million.

The curbing of trade-union powers was to have been achieved through Robert Carr's Industrial Relations Act (1971). Few would disagree today that some regulation of the unions was required – after all, Wilson and Castle had made their own attempt. The great flaw in the Heath Act was that to come within the jurisdiction of the law, unions first had to register, and this they simply refused to do. Then there was reluctance over actually sending union officials or members to prison. The imprisonment of certain dock workers involved in an unofficial strike, the 'Pentonville Five', caused embarrassment; fortunately the Official Solicitor came up with the solution that the action should have been taken against the union rather than the 'Five'. In calling a strike in May 1972 the National Union of Railwaymen had failed to go through the new procedures, but then frustrated government action by winning massive membership support in a strike ballot.

As public servants, the postal workers had not done well out of their strike.

The government put heavy pressure on the National Coal Board to try to ensure that it would not concede a substantial wage increase to the miners, very moderate in their claims for many years, but now beginning to feel that they were falling far behind other industries. Rejecting an 8 per cent offer, the miners began a national strike on 9 January 1972. Coal, for the generation of electricity, was still absolutely vital to British industry. Cessation of the cutting of coal would not have had an immediate impact; but the left-wing Yorkshire leader, Arthur Scargill, organized a system of 'flying pickets' which prevented access to stocks already above ground. Most notoriously, a solid mass of up to 15,000 pickets at the Saltley coke depot in the Midlands prevented any movement of supplies. On the whole, miners retained public sympathy, while the government was forced to impose a three-day week on industry; during the frequent power cuts, homes, and pubs, resorted to the use of candles. After a month, the government set up a Committee of Inquiry under a High Court Judge, Lord Wilberforce. Reporting quickly, Wilberforce recommended substantial wage increases, but the miners held out for even more: better holidays, better pensions, the Saturday 'bonus' shift incorporated into normal shift rates. Miners' earnings went up by 16 per cent, adding nearly £117 million to the cost of coal. What Heath had been seeking was the dynamism of the continental economies. What they had also, were forms of industrial partnership, 'co-determination' in West Germany, where workers played a part in management. Heath now went hard for cooperation between industry, unions, and government, very much like the policies of the Wilson governments in fact – what critics were beginning to term 'corporatism'. What Heath wanted to do was to negotiate a voluntary, but firm, prices and incomes policy with the TUC. But a powerful trade union leadership, much to the left of those of the forties, fifties and sixties, was set on getting what it could for its members, and quite unwilling to help a Conservative government. So, in November 1972, a statutory prices-and-incomes policy was announced. During the first six months there was to be a complete freeze on wage increases. During Phase II there was to be a Pay Board to decide on all putative wage increases. Phase III, introduced towards the end of 1973, sought to limit all increases in wages or salaries to £350 a year.

With the miners declaring an overtime ban and putting in a further substantial wage claim, Heath, on 13 November, declared a State of Emergency, enabling him to call in the armed forces if necessary to keep essential supplies moving. Talks with the Executive of the National Union of Mineworkers broke down on 28 November; on 13 December Heath, for a second time, introduced a three-day week. Whitelaw, who appeared to be having success with his Irish policy, was moved to the Department of Employment, but failed to charm the miners, and his promise of extra payments to cover the time miners spent in the showers was rejected by the government's own Pay Board. Obviously, when on 9 January the miners declared another national strike, they were going for what they could get. The new General Secretary of the TUC, Len Murray, came up with the proposal that if the miners were granted their demands the TUC would use its authority to stop other unions from taking advantage of this 'special case', but having earlier sought cooperation with union leaders, the government now brusquely rejected this approach. Heath had his emergency powers; Carr, at the Home Office, had mobile squads of police ready to counteract flying pickets. The country was suffused in candle-lit gloom.[28]

The annual growth rate, in the previous four years stuck around 2 per cent, actually went up to 7.4 per cent in 1973. But the crazy situation had been reached whereby interest rates were lower than inflation rates. Not a lot of point in lending money; the thing to do was to hold on to your assets. The 'Barber boom' became a horrific example for later governments. The British balance of payments deficit for 1973 was the highest ever, £1.5 billion. High inflation, a balance of payments crisis, confrontation with the miners, bomb attacks (rather harmless) by the self-styled Angry Brigade, devastating ones by the IRA, there was much talk of 'extremism' and questioning about 'Who Governs Britain?' Fortified by an 80 per cent membership ballot in favour, the miners were due to go on full strike on 9 February. A possible way out for Heath was to seek a renewed mandate from the people: he opted for an election on 28 February. At least he could boast of having taken Britain into the Common Market; Labour said it would try to amend the conditions of membership, and then submit the results to a referendum. On the credit side too, Heath had secured the resignation in mid-1972 of Maudling for being too closely associated with the corrupt architect John Poulson; more, on 15 May 1973, he had castigated the grasping directors of Lonrho for revealing 'the unpleasant and unacceptable face of capitalism'.

**Table 4.13** General Election, 28 February 1974

| | *Electorate 39.8 million* | | *Turnout 78.7 per cent* | | |
|---|---|---|---|---|---|
| | *Conservative* | *Labour* | *Liberal* | *Nationalist* | *Others* |
| Votes | 11,868,906 | 11,639,243 | 6,063,470 | 803,396 | |
| Percentage of votes cast | 37.9 | 37.1 | 19.3 | 2.6 | 3.1 |
| Seats | 297 | 301 | 14 | 9 | 14 |

At first Heath hoped that he might be able to form a coalition with the Liberals who, in terms of votes, had done very well under the leadership of Jeremy Thorpe. However, the Liberals (though not necessarily their voters) saw themselves as definitely a leftward looking party, while all of the Nationalists (seven SNP, two PC) and the one SDLP member among the 'others', looked to Labour rather than to the Conservatives (who could not necessarily count on all of the seven Ulster Unionists, three Vanguard and one DUP). Thus Harold Wilson, rather to his surprise, and in circumstances which seemed much less favourable than those of 1970, again formed a government.

## THE CULTURAL REVOLUTION

### *THE BASICS OF CULTURAL TRANSFORMATION*

Within society a unique conjunction of circumstances brought about changes which greatly affected the lives of ordinary people: there was no political revolution, no economic revolution, but there was, in the sense in which I am using the term, a 'cultural revolution'. These changes began to assume critical mass around 1958–9, though the lifestyles and forms of popular culture which are most readily associated with the sixties only came to full prominence in the 'high sixties' from 1964 onwards (see plate 9). Britain did not in 1968 and 1969 go through the upheavals which affected all other western countries; still, after 1969 there was an ultra-extremist phase, and also one in which more remote areas caught up with the styles of the high sixties. The cultural revolution, in three phases, then, takes place over the 'long sixties', roughly 1958 to 1974. One interesting phenomenon is the way in which aspects of British popular culture attained the kind of international primacy long associated with the United States.

**Plate 9** 19 May 1967. The Beatles at a press conference following the completion of *Sergeant Pepper's Lonely Hearts Club Band.* Clothes, and haircuts, like these could now be obtained in boutiques and hair-dressing salons in all Britain's major cities. Left to right: Paul, Ringo, John, George. Courtesy of Hulton Getty.

Some of the ideas, movements, or subcultures, distinctive of the sixties, could be seen in earlier decades. But there were increasingly more of them after 1958, and they expanded and interacted with each other in such a way as to create a condition of rapid change and ever-developing innovation. All were characterized by the spirit of criticism of, or opposition to, one or more aspects of established society. While some of the new clubs, galleries and magazines were subsidized by local or national government, very many of them exhibited a strong entrepreneurial spirit; many, too, were very much part of youth subculture. As already noted, there were many technological advances and refinements coming closely together in this period: they pervaded almost all aspects of society (some of the oppositional movements claimed to be anti-technology).[29]

The sixties, partly because of the almost universal presence of television, was an era of 'spectacle' as an integral part of the interface between life and leisure. The most rebellious action, the most obscure theories, the wildest cultural extremism, the very 'underground' itself: all operated as publicly as possible, and all, thanks to the complex interaction with commercial interests and the media, attracted the maximum publicity. Thus one extreme gesture accelerated into the next; each spectacle had to be more extreme than the previous one. In the past the flow of both technology and popular culture had very much been from America to Britain, and to the rest of Europe (though the continental countries were more successful in preserving traditions of their own). Now, a recovered Europe was participating in unprecedented international cultural exchange: from Italy to Britain came espresso machines, from France discos; from America, intriguingly, there came experimental theatre.

It is a mistake to believe that there was one unified 'counter-culture' aimed at overthrowing 'mainstream' or 'bourgeois' culture, in some dialectical process. In fact, there was a whole variety of different subcultures, most challenged existing society in some ways, but were also implicated in it, sometimes through the acceptance of national or local subsidies, mainly through entrepreneurialism and commercialism. The new subcultures *permeated* and eventually transformed society, encouraged by 'measured judgement', consisting of secular Anglicanism in high places, a genuine liberal tolerance and willingness to accommodate to the new developments (but see plate 10). Examples are: the Albemarle Committee, which reported so perceptively on young people in 1959; the authors of such progressive documents as the *Robbins Report on Higher Education* (1963) and the Plowden Report on Primary Education (1967); Sir Hugh Carlton-Greene, who became Director-General of the BBC in 1960, and who made possible the presentation of the satirical programme, quite revolutionary at the time, *That Was The Week That Was*, in 1962–3; John Trevelyan, Secretary to the British Board of Film Censors from 1958, and fully sensitive to the changes taking place in society; journalists such as William Rees-Mogg, the editor of *The Times*, who spoke out against the imprisonment of Rolling Stone Mick Jagger for possession of four amphetamine tables, in his famous leading article, 'Who Breaks a Butterfly on the Wheel?', and the members of the higher judiciary, such as the Appeal Court which conditionally released Jagger, and quashed the sentence against his colleague, Keith Richards (magistrates and judges in the lower courts could often be bigoted and vicious).

"Bad Luck, Sir! Never mind — if I catch the scoundrels, I'll give them a sharp tap on the head with this report!"

**Plate 10** Cummings cartoon, *Daily Express,* 16 November 1960. The Commitee on Children and Young Persons reporting in October 1960 came out very strongly against the restoration of judicial flogging and birching (abolished in 1948). The escaping youths on the right have Italian haircuts, winkle-picker shoes, a cosh, chain and open razor. The police constable is R. A. Butler, the reforming Home Secretary in the Macmillan government. The cartoon is a salutory reminder that however appropriate it is to stress liberalization and change, the punitive viciousness of the Victorian era still had strong roots in British society. Courtesy of Daily Express/University of Kent.

The sixties was not a golden age. There are no golden ages. Some activities were downright stupid, particularly those fuelled by the notion that somehow demonstrations (or dropping out) would bring the revolution and the alternative society just waiting around the corner. The belief that drugs would bring enlightenment was misguided and self-indulgent. Up until the sixties drugs were under control in Britain, with registered addicts receiving prescriptions on the National Health Service. The sixties' fantasies drove that policy to destruction. Drugs went out of control, and the situation has continued to get ever worse ever since.

### *CONSUMERISM AND YOUTH*

In explicating these points and making some further ones, I must start with the transformation in material conditions and availability of consumer goods, which lies at the base of the cultural revolution. In 1956 only about 8 per cent of households had refrigerators; this rose to 33 per cent in 1962 and 69 per cent

**Table 4.14** Disposable income and consumer expenditure at constant 1970 prices in pounds sterling

| | *1951* | *1961* | *1971* | *1972* | *1973* | *1974* |
|---|---|---|---|---|---|---|
| Personal disposal income | 390 | 532 | 638 | 680 | 719 | 724 |
| Consumer expenditure | 385 | 486 | 578 | 611 | 638 | 637 |

*Source:* Central Statistical Office, *National Income and Expenditure* (1975).

by 1971. Television sets had been a rarity in the 1950s; but by 1961, 75 per cent of families had one, and by 1971 it was 91 per cent. By 1971, also, 64 per cent of families had a washing machine. Although technological developments elsewhere were matched in the realm of telecommunications, there was not quite the same expansion in households having a telephone. Subscriber trunk dialling was introduced in Bristol in 1958, in London in 1961, and thereafter was slowly extended to other parts of the United Kingdom. In 1951, 1.5 million householders had a private telephone; by 1966 this figure had risen to 4.2 million: nevertheless at the end of the decade more than half of all households, as yet, had no telephone.

Youth, an elastic term, sometimes confined to teenagers, sometimes stretched to include all those under thirty, is certainly central to the sixties cultural revolution, partly because many of the new modes and styles originally were developed exclusively by, or for, young people. However, dazzled by 'the teenage revolution', too many commentators have ignored the importance of married couples as protagonists of the general spread of consumerism. Youth subculture is most obviously characterized by its dress and its music. Distinctive voices are apparent in the fifties, by the early sixties we have a full chorus. Mary Quant, student at Goldsmiths Design College, was 21 in 1955 when, together with her husband to be, Alexander Plunket-Green, she established Bazaar on the Kings Road, Chelsea, as the first of what were to become known as 'boutiques', selling clothes which deliberately defied the conventions of established fashion (see plate 11). In 1958, John Stephen, aged 21, set up 'His Clothes' in Carnaby Street, selling sharp, but not particularly original, continental suits. Others joined him in Carnaby Street, particularly dress designers Sally Tuffin and Marion Foale, who declared their belief in the 'ridiculous'. Mary Quant was absolutely right in declaring:

> London led the way in the changing focus of fashion from the Establishment to the young. As a country, we were aware of the great potential of this change long before the Americans or the French. We were one step ahead from the start . . . [30]

Chronologically, jazz was the first black American musical form to make a significant impact on fifties Britain, mainly among middle-class, left-wing intellectuals. But among young people, and particularly working-class young people, a kind of do-it-yourself version developed in the form of 'skiffle',

**Plate 11** A composed publicity photograph, labelled 'not available until June 1965', of Mary Quant at home with husband Alexander Plunkett-Greene, and model Celia Hammond in 'a green dress of silk twill popping with polka dots'. Courtesy of Camera Press, Hayes Davidson/John Maclean

employing such humble 'instruments' as broom handles and washing-boards. Then came the much more trenchant influence of rock'n'roll, through imported records and through the film *Rock Around the Clock*, exhibited in Britain in 1956, and through the tour of Bill Hayley and his Comets in 1957. The new sounds pervaded the technical colleges, art colleges (critically important in pioneering all of the new forms of popular culture), universities, and even public schools, as well as the milieu of young workers. In Liverpool, John Lennon (lower middle-class) and Paul McCartney (upper working-class) were captivated both by rock'n'roll and by some of the black vocalists; in 1956 they became part of the local group, The Quarrymen.[31]

Of a number of groups which moved from jazz to skiffle and then to rock, the most widely known was The Shadows (with Hank Marvin) who subsequently teamed up with Cliff Richard, one of a number of young performers who adapted a kind of cheeky, music-hall presentation to skiffle and then rock. Much in the same mould were Lonnie Donegan, Tommy Steele, and Joe Brown and the Bruvvers. In brief, the music evolving in the British working-class clubs had more complexity than rock 'n' roll and more beat than rhythm-and-blues. Old-style popular music had been aimed at adults, and was intended to create a mood of elegant sophistication; by the fifties, instead, the mood was becoming one of sickly sentimentality. Still, at its best, big-band swing had required rather demanding woodwind and brass playing. The new music was, usually, simpler to play. More important, it was played by a small group of named individuals with whom young fans could identify personally. And the subtleties and sonorous sentimentalities of the saxophone gave way to the intoxicating strumming of the electric guitar. Full transformation in Britain was not achieved until the end of 1963.

In 1960 Lennon and McCartney, together with George Harrison and Pete Best, had formed The Silver Beatles to play in such Liverpool clubs as The Cavern and The Jacaranda. Though starting in frank imitation, the group was already beginning to evolve a distinctive style, partly imposed by the line-up of three guitars and drums. That style was 'beat'. During a visit to Hamburg (venue for a number of British bands) the group were persuaded by their German impresario to introduce an element of dramatic performance into their show; they also adopted mop-top haircuts and collarless suits. But in rock/pop you were nothing if you were not selling on disc. Thoroughly deserved but utterly unpredictable good fortune arrived in the form of the 27-year-old gay Jewish manager of the local record shop in his father's chain, Brian Epstein, who put himself forward as manager for the group. Five record companies turned the Beatles down before Epstein persuaded the Parlophone subsidiary of EMI, where staff man George Martin recognized the genuine musical skills of the group, to take them on. *Love Me Do*, with Ringo Starr replacing Best as drummer, was recorded and released in October 1962. It was a hit in the sense of making the lower reaches of the top twenty. *Please, Please Me*, which followed, reached second place. By this time, all records aimed at the mass market were subject to the wonders of double and multiple-track recording. The Beatles brought with them the directness of their live performances. Theirs were truly group songs, the sentimentality cut with high spirits, songs to involve an entire age group, but actually much more than one age group. The quality of 'youthfulness' is to some extent self-chosen. At the beginning of January 1964 a young Cambridge don just returned from America expressed his enthusiasm for The Beatles: 'it is a relief to lose one's-self in the unconscious hypnotic euphoria of the music'. Speaking of the twist, which arrived in Britain in 1962, via Paris and Milan, an over-forty remarked: 'the older folks like it because you move quite separately and therefore don't have to worry about your partner's feet'.[32]

## *INTERNATIONAL SUCCESS OF BRITISH POPULAR CULTURE*

The growing hegemony of British youth-based popular culture was widely recognized abroad. In May 1966 the French news magazine *L'Express* declared that Great Britain is the country 'where the wind of today blows most strongly'. Just over a year later the same publication remarked: 'Thanks to The Beatles, to The Rolling Stones, England rules over international Pop Music; their young actors are the best in the world.' The American magazine *Time* brought out a special issue in April 1966 devoted to 'swinging London', that city being described by the Italian colour magazine *Epoca* as 'the happiest and the most electric city in Europe, and the most nonconformist'. 'Today it's the British hour,' declared the same Italian magazine in a survey of the international film scene: 'for two years, in the international market, they have had success after success'. But if we are talking about *market* success should we not be looking at where the film investment came from? As long ago as 1974 the distinguished film critic Alexander Walker, in his *Hollywood England*, mocked British pretensions on the ground that the most famous British films of the sixties were almost entirely financed from the United States. But perhaps it would be more logical to praise the achievements of British films, given the grudging environment in which they were made, and to argue that these achievements would have been still greater had there been internal financing on a rational and organized basis. In fact, the early films which themselves played a part in launching the cultural revolution *were* largely British-financed. *Room At the Top* (made in 1958, released in January 1959), *Saturday Night and Sunday Morning* (1960), *A Taste of Honey* (1961) and *A Kind of Loving* (1962) were all permitted scenes which previously would have been censored, because, the censor argued, society itself had changed; at the same time these films legitimated changing sexual values and behaviour, especially among young people. They also demonstrated the new visibility of the working class in British life. This is most specifically true of Lindsay Anderson's masterpiece *This Sporting Life* (1963), with Richard Harris and Rachel Roberts giving unsurpassable performances as tragic working-class hero and heroine.

The 'successes' identified by *Epoca*, which show the range of genres now replacing the 'New Wave' social comment films I have just mentioned, were: *A Taste of Honey*, *Billy Liar* (both 'New Wave'), *The Servant* (1963, directed by American immigrant Joseph Losey, with a screenplay by the new master of menacing experimental theatre, Harold Pinter), *Tom Jones* (1963), *The Ipcress File* (1965) and *Darling* (1965). *Tom Jones*, directed by 'New Wave' director Tony Richardson and financed by the American United Artists, being based on Henry Fielding's picaresque eighteenth-century novel, was redolent of the rumbustious, hedonistic, sexually liberated spirit then breaking out in British society. Heading the all-British cast was the new working-class star of *Saturday Night and Sunday Morning*, Albert Finney. *The Ipcress File* is a slice-of-life spy story, the spy being perky, working-class Harry Palmer, played authentically by working-class Michael Caine, struggling to make a not very glamorous living and done down by his upper-class bosses.

An altogether more glamorous fictional figure was the upper-class Commander James Bond, Secret Agent 007 ('licensed to kill'), the invention of novelist Ian Fleming. Bond was to be played by Sean Connery, a former milk delivery man in Edinburgh, whose native accent was slow and easy to follow. Such a riotous international success were these films, that the Italian word today for secret agent is '007' (pronounced *'zayro zayro setty'*). Peter Sellers, essentially a character actor, also became an international star. The Hollywood director Stanley Kubrick came to London to make two films with Sellers, *Lolita* (1962) and an incisive satire on those American leaders who cheerfully contemplated nuclear engagement, *Doctor Strangelove or, How I Learned to Stop Worrying and Love the Bomb* (1964). The third new-style British international star was Julie Christie, who seemed the embodiment of the independent, swinging, short-skirted, knee-booted young English female. After *Billy Liar* she was the unscrupulous, success-seeking young woman in *Darling*, and then the spirited Bathsheba in *Far From the Madding Crowd* (1967) from the Thomas Hardy novel, all three of these films being directed by John Schlesinger. Britain, it could be said, was ready for *the* film of the London-centred international cultural revolution of the sixties: American-financed, Italian-directed *Blow-Up* (Antonioni, 1967) featuring the prospering celebrity photographer Thomas, played by working-class David Hemmings. The blow-up of a photograph Thomas has taken in a deserted park seems to reveal a murder; an elegant young lady (Vanessa Redgrave) attempts to retrieve the photograph. Within a visually rich series of images operating on many levels, the dialogue itself is very effective, and very British: it was largely written by another playwright making his name on the London stage, Edward Bond

As well as film, British theatre was enjoying a very high reputation. Under the headline 'English theater tries everything – and becomes the finest in the world', a correspondent for the American magazine *Life* (20 May 1966) singled out *Saved* by Edward Bond, *The Homecoming* by Harold Pinter, Peter Brook's *Marat/Sade*, and *The Killing of Sister George*, a play about lesbianism by Frank Marcus. *Life* spoke also of the high quality of the plays televised by the BBC and ITV. The main showcase, and also an opening onto the consummating cultural revolution of the high sixties, was the BBC's Wednesday Night Play. Nell Dunn's *Up The Junction* (1965) caused an outcry for its abortion scene. Another important Wednesday Play author was the working-class but Oxford-educated Dennis Potter, whose *Vote, Vote, Vote for Nigel Barton* took a working-class lad through Oxford into Labour politics. However, the sensation was *Cathy Come Home* (November 1966), written by Jeremy Sandford and directed by Ken Loach, the story of a young mother moving from one squalid lodging to another, then into a hostel for the homeless before finally being evicted and having her children taken away from her. Fortuitously the broadcasting of this play coincided with the founding, mainly by young people, of the voluntary organization on behalf of the homeless, Shelter.

Under the aegis of BBC Director-General Sir Hugh Greene, several comedy series with an unconventional, disturbing edge to their social comment were broadcast. The ultimate came in 1966 in the form of *Till Death Us Do Part*, written by working-class Johnny Speight and featuring the ultra-conservative working man, Alf Garnett (played by Warren Mitchell). *Till Death Us Do Part* dared to portray Alf Garnett openly, and shockingly, as the racist too many British people actually were. It had a regular audience of over 17 million, and was enthusiastically commented on by the critics. What brought the almost mystic status of British television internationally was the BBC's last black-and-white drama series, *The Forsyte Saga* (1967), fashioned from the distinctly lower-middle-brow novels of John Galsworthy, set between the late Victorian period and the 1920s, but with a brilliant cast of actors.

## *FAMILY, PERMISSIVENESS, FRANKNESS*

The heart of the cultural revolution lay in the transformation in human relationships, between parents and children, between men and women. Not least of the new freedoms was the freedom to be honest, to speak frankly, to be free of the old conventions and circumlocutions. Before the sixties, what were widely referred to as 'dirty books' had to be imported surreptitiously from France. Most notorious was D. H. Lawrence's 1920s novel *Lady Chatterley's Lover*. In 1955 a shopkeeper in a lower-class part of London was sentenced to two months in prison for having this book in stock. It was in the latter half of 1959 that the ultra-respectable paperback publishers Penguin Books decided to mark the 30th anniversary (falling in the following year) of Lawrence's death, and the 25th of Penguin's birth, with eight Lawrence titles, including an unexpurgated *Lady Chatterley's Lover*. Of this, 200,000 copies were printed, but held back while a dozen copies were sent to the Director of Public Prosecutions. Thus it came to pass that the most celebrated and illuminating show trial of this critical time of change was held at the Old Bailey during five days in November 1960.

Some of the statements of the expert defence witnesses read comically today: they were at pains to stress that *Lady Chatterley's Lover* is 'hygienic' and 'wholesome'; it was a book 'Christians ought to read', 'a guide to young people about to get married', with, according to the bishop of Woolwich, the adultery between Lady Chatterley and her gamekeeper being 'an act of holy communion'. But such comedy was nothing to the ludicrous opening address to the jury by prosecution barrister Mervyn Griffith-Jones, which aroused great hilarity at the time and has continued to do so ever since:

> You may think that one of the ways in which you can read this book, and test it from the most Liberal outlook, is to ask yourselves the question, when you have read it through, would you approve of your young sons, young daughters – because girls can read as well as boys – reading this book. Is it a book that you would have lying around in your own house? Is it a book that you would even wish your wife or your servants to read?[33]

Unwittingly, poor, befuddled Griffith-Jones had stumbled on the fact that, while formally proceedings were about how far explicit descriptions of sexual acts could be published, and therefore discussed, this trial also had a class dimension. The defence stressed the extent to which Penguin Books had pioneered the supply to the working classes of classic books; their star expert witness, Richard Hoggart, spoke very much as a son of the working class. The jury (five of whom had had difficulty in just reading the oath) acquitted *Lady Chatterley* of obscenity; printing hundreds of thousands of new copies (two million were sold within the year), Penguin added a blurb referring triumphantly to the trial: 'it was not just a legal tussle, but a conflict of generation and class'.

Changes in sexual attitudes and behaviour affected large sections of society, but were most striking among young people. The first really systematic survey ever of *The Sexual Behaviour of Young People* – the title of the book by Michael Schofield, Research Director of the Central Council for Health Education and organizer of the survey, published in 1965, concluded that while some teenagers (mostly boys) certainly were sexually active, any idea of teenagers being generally promiscuous was quite incorrect. Government statistics did show that in 1960, 31 per cent of girls who married in their teens were already pregnant. Girls were becoming more independent-minded. An inquiry conducted in the industrial city of Sheffield reported (1963):

> signs that some girls are tending towards more independence in their dealings with men, and that they will not be content to sign over their lives to their husbands on marriage . . . they are determined to remain smart and in control of events after they have married; they are not prepared to be bowed down with lots of children, and they will expect their husbands to take a fuller share than their fathers in the running of the home.[34]

Guides to etiquette are valuable sources: important changes can be tracked as between the 1956 and 1969 editions of the popular publication *Lady Behave*, written by Anne Edwards and Drusilla Beyfus. The rather hesitant 1956 section on 'the New Frankness in Speech' was replaced in 1969 by the direct 'Frankness in Speech':

> One of the significant changes in manners over the past few years has been the liberalisation of attitudes towards what can be said in mixed company. Candour, frankness and honesty in conversation have become admired attributes . . . Particularly this relates to the old inadmissibles, intimate sexual experiences, detailed descriptions of violence and every kind of physical expression and emotion.

In 1968 Hannah Gavron published her *The Captive Wife: Conflicts of House-bound Mothers*. Both working-class and middle-class wives were asked whether they felt that their marriages were more equal than those of their parents. Of the middle-class wives, 64 per cent said that they were, by which they meant that they had more independence within the marriage than their mothers had. Among the working-class wives, 56 per cent replied affirmatively, but what they meant was that they felt closer to their husbands than they felt their mothers had been to their fathers. In general, fathers in both social classes seemed to be taking on more family responsibilities. The changing position of children within the family is fully documented. In a survey of 48 working-class wives from Kentish Town in London and 48 middle-class wives from West Hampstead in north London, it emerged that 62 per cent of the middle-class wives felt that they gave their children much greater freedom than their mothers had given them, while 69 per cent of the working-class mothers felt they were bringing up their children differently from the way in which they had been brought up, which in 80 per cent of cases meant 'less restriction and more understanding'. Some of the working-class wives drew attention to the ways in which they were more relaxed than their parents:

> 'My parents were always on at me. In fact my father used to really knock me about. I certainly hope not to be like that', said the wife of a sheet-metal worker. 'My Dad was a really hard man', said a labourer's wife. 'There was no affection in him. We are not like that at all.'[35]

## *Protest*

There were demonstrations against government policy in the Suez crisis, based in the universities, but mainly along conventional party-political lines. The first sustained protest movement was the Campaign for Nuclear Disarmament (CND), inaugurated at a well-attended meeting in the Central Hall, Westminster, on 17 February 1958. The first march took place that Easter, from central London to the nuclear missile site at Aldermaston in Berkshire; thereafter there were annual marches from Aldermaston to London. Most active between 1958 and 1964, CND had a very British, rather fiftyish, somewhat scruffy old-Left image; yet during this period at least half the marchers and demonstrators were always young people under twenty. CND leaders took a key role in planning the first anti-Vietnam War demonstration in 1965, from which sprang the Vietnam Solidarity Campaign which had considerable support among students – there were teach-ins on Vietnam at the London School of Economics and Oxford University in the summer of 1965. The Vietnam Ad-Hoc Committee was an elite, militant group, responsible for organizing the mass demonstrations of 1968. The ageing, but increasingly radical, British aristocratic philosopher Bertrand Russell, in November 1966 launched his Vietnam War Crimes Tribunal, in cooperation with French existentialist philosopher Jean-Paul Sartre. It finally convened in Stockholm in May 1967, with, to no one's surprise, America being condemned on all counts.

Many of the new movements and subcultures of the sixties, and much individual action, showed new concerns for civil and personal rights, and a new willingness to become involved in often risky action on behalf of these. The wish of certain young people to turn idealism into action is apparent in the founding of Shelter, the Child Poverty Action Group, and Release (aimed at helping young people arrested for drug offences). In everyone's minds, rightly, the sixties is associated with disgraceful urban redevelopment schemes, and the building of ugly, unloved, high-rise domestic dwellings. However, it was also in the sixties that protest movements against 'urban renewal' and in favour of conservation began to mobilize and that, indeed, official conservation agencies and local pedestrianization schemes began to be put in place. At government level the Civic Amenities Act of 1967 was followed by the revised Town and Country Planning Act of 1968, the basis for expanding environmental initiatives at the end of the decade.

British secondary schools were notably untroubled by the activism apparent in France and Italy. Probably British young people of school age were less mature, and also less prone to political commitment and direct action; perhaps also they had less to complain about – while the secondary moderns, which ditched their pupils at the age of 15, were often pretty appalling, the grammar schools, catering for pupils up to the age of 18, were generally quite well equipped; and British schools, unlike those in France and Italy, still employed the sanction of corporal punishment which almost certainly dissuaded too much adventurous nonconformity. The new university campuses were richer in facilities and far better designed than places like Nanterre, on the outskirts of Paris. Most students, and practically all academics, considered that with respect to curriculum, teaching methods, and the organization and running of the university, there was no place for student opinion or student influence. Founded in 1966, the Radical Students' Alliance never amounted to anything in terms of numbers, but did proselytize actively on behalf of student power and student commitment on such issues as Vietnam.

Britain's only major student disturbances before 1968 came at the London School of Economics (a component college of the University of London) in the autumn of 1966 as a consequence of the announcement that Dr Walter Adams, previously Principal of University College, Rhodesia, had been appointed the next Director of the college. Rhodesia had recently declared itself independent of Britain, and its regime, in the eyes of leftists and liberals, represented all the evils of white supremacism and racial segregation; Adams was seen as standing for these evils.

After an attempted 'Stop Adams' meeting (31 January 1967), at which a 64-year-old porter had a lethal heart attack, two students were suspended. From 13 March there was a nine-day student occupation of the college, with another attempted occupation being foiled by the police. On Friday, 17 March the student 'Daffodil march' took place down Fleet Street: accompanied in the usual British way by an escort of police, it was completely peaceful. Although Britain never endured the sustained and horrifying violence of Rome and Milan, the Paris Left Bank, Berkeley and Columbia, the British disturbances of 1968 and 1969 did have distinctive colourings. The British Empire remained an issue in a way the French Empire no long was in France, and racism, closely bound up with Empire, had a salience it did not possess in either France or Italy. The notion of free speech stirred resonances which were different from those of Berkeley in 1964, and almost non-existent in France and Italy. Student representation and student rights of various sorts *were* the central matters which linked together the rather isolated and sporadic outbreaks.

Following the earlier troubles at the LSE the first event in the new phase of more widespread disruption, punctuated by the occasional bout of violence in the streets, was the anti-Vietnam War demonstration of 22 October 1967, originally conceived by the traditional Left as a 'peace' demonstration, but which the Vietnam Solidarity Campaign (VSC) consciously tried to turn into a 'Victory to the NLF' (the Vietnamese National Liberation Front) campaign. Some VSC militants just about managed to fight their way through the police to reach the steps of the American Embassy in Grosvenor Square. A leading figure was Tariq Ali, wealthy Pakistani, Trotskyite, and former President of the Oxford Union, much given to spouting the then fashionable nonsense about the imminent collapse of capitalism.[36]

In almost all universities and colleges, discussions were now under way over securing some form of student representation on the main governing bodies, usually called senates and councils ('courts' in Scotland). In Aston University in Birmingham, then Leicester University, there were small demonstrations. However, more attention was attracted by the more or less violent attempts to prevent unpopular speakers from gaining a hearing. At the University of Sussex a speaker on Vietnam from the American Embassy was covered in red paint. At the University of Essex two Conservative MPs, including Enoch Powell, who was now beginning to take an extreme white racist line, were attacked. The Labour Secretary of State for Education and Science, Patrick Gordon-Walker, was shouted down at Manchester, while Labour Defence Secretary Denis Healey almost had his car overturned by Cambridge students, and Home Secretary James Callaghan ran into similar threats at Oxford. Two of the students involved at Manchester were suspended. In the working-class district of Shoreditch, somewhat to the east of the LSE, there was a sort of Anti-University, substantially the work of the American Allen Krebs, following the example of the Free School of New York: a mixture of left-wing academics and figures from experimental theatre provided rather fragmented educational experiences which petered out by the summer of 1968.

But all developments were eclipsed by the Vietnam demonstration on 17 March, in which 25,000 participated. This time the VSC was better prepared, and the scenes broadcast from Grosvenor Square were the most violent yet seen on British television. The main offensive weapons of the demonstrators were firecrackers aimed at police horses, with marbles rolled under their hooves, and the poles of banners, which were hurled at the police. A mounted police charge caused much screaming, and the use of truncheons many injuries, but tear-gas was not used. In fact, only 45 demonstrators received medical treatment, as against 177 police; charges were brought against 246 people. Most sloganizing inevitably has its mindless quality: 'Ho-Ho-Ho Chi Minh!' had exactly the right exultant and triumphalist sound. Another demonstration was held the following week, this time, though still dominated by young people, kept largely under the control of CND. CND then had its not very spectacular Easter March

At Essex, a scientist from the Ministry of Defence's chemical warfare establishment at Porton Down was prevented from giving a lecture. The Vice-Chancellor, Sir Alfred Sloman, took immediate and drastic action, expelling three students, on the grounds that while there were no designated disciplinary proceedings for dealing with this offence, to deny free speech was to destroy the whole basis on which a university existed. It was an argument which many students, and quite a number of staff, did not find persuasive. A sit-in, supported by members of staff, resulted in the students being reinstated. With its self-contained campus, a large number of innovative practices, and young staff, strong in the social sciences, Essex became Britain's model centre of protest, with a 'Free University' attracting 1,000 staff and students. Plans were made for a completely new government structure, new kinds of degrees, the abolition of exams. At Hornsey Art School, in north-east London, a student movement for total reform, rather on the model of the Beaux-Arts in Paris, took over the college, with the support of most of the staff. The Hornsey episode has the honour of producing one of the best known of counter-revolutionary, bourgeois, silent majority or common-sense documents of the time, an editorial in the local paper, the *Wood Green, Southgate and Palmers Green Weekly Herald*:

> a bunch of crackpots, here in Haringey, or in Grosvenor Square, or Paris, or Berlin, or Mexico, can never overthrow an established system . . . They may dislike having to conform to a system in which they are required to study, and follow set programmes, and take examinations or their equivalents; and acknowledge that in doing so they are through the indulgence of others, preparing themselves for a lifetime of earning . . . The system is ours. We are the ordinary people, the nine-to-five, Monday-to-Friday semi-detached, suburban wage-earners, who are the system. We are not victims of it. We are not slaves to it. We are it, and we like it. Does any bunch of twopenny-halfpenny kids think they can turn us upside down? They'll learn.[37]

Occupations followed at Croydon College of Art in south London and Guildford School of Art to the south-west of London. At Hornsey, the local authority used security guards and dogs to chase out the small number of students still maintaining the occupation, shortly before the summer vacation. Although the principal was keen to make some accommodation with the students, the local authority locked the college at the beginning of the autumn term, dismissing all students and part-time staff who had been involved in the revolt. At Guildford the college was also closed, with students expelled, and nearly 50 staff dismissed.

Meantime, at the LSE, plans for student involvement in college government were due to be announced in October; however, the next Vietnam demonstration, scheduled for that month, was a much greater source of excitement, and a further occupation formed a part of that demonstration. This time, the police took the precaution of searching marchers for weapons, but nothing very sinister was discovered. The march split, with only about 3,000 once again making for the American Embassy. There had been one Battle of Grosvenor Square in March, but there was scarcely a second one; an observer commented sadly: 'The whole of swinging London seems to be here.'[38] The visual record we have of this demonstration is enhanced by the fact that since the previous one in March, colour television had arrived.

The LSE, throughout the weekend, presented a festive appearance, particularly with its perky banner: 'Adams Closed It, We Opened It'. But at a January teach-in on South Africa and Rhodesia, things turned nasty, and militant students used pickaxes, crowbars, and a sledgehammer to attack 'the Gates', iron gates recently installed by the administration at strategic points. There were arrests, a four-week closure of the college (till 19 February), another occupation. In the end two lecturers were dismissed, harsh and untoward action for a British university. With the summer vacation, the main spasm of turbulence in the British universities faded somewhat, though over the next few years there were to be incidents of a sort which a few years previously would have been thought entirely alien to British higher education.

In listing the agonies of the Heath Government I mentioned the Angry Brigade, which was modelled on the American terror organization the Weathermen. During 1970, this minuscule organization exploded several bombs, though always with the apparent intention of avoiding any loss of life or limb – most notably two outside the house of the Home Secretary, Robert Carr, and one at the cathedral of innovatory sixties fashion and consumer enjoyment, Biba. Unrest continued sporadically at universities, and even reached some schools. The most noteworthy episode involving students was in Cambridge, where, at the end of a 'Greek Week' designed to confer respectability on the shabby and cruel dictatorship of the colonels, some 400 students picketed the reception at the Garden House Hotel on Friday, 13 February. The arrival of the police, combined with the presence of some socialist militants, produced a flurry of flying bricks and an unplanned invasion of the hotel; among those injured were a university proctor and a policeman. Six students were arrested at the time, followed, on information received from university authorities, by a further thirteen members (including one don) of the University Socialist Society. At the end of June twelve were put on trial at Hertford and found guilty of 'unlawful assembly' and 'riot'. Judge Melford Stevenson was no representative of measured judgement: handing down sentences ranging from several months in Borstal to eighteen months in prison, he made it clear that his anger was not directed at the younger generation alone; the sentences, he said, would have been even more severe were he not aware that the defendants had been exposed to 'the evil influence of some senior members of your university'. Reforms of university procedures were taking place piecemeal, but in many places of learning comfortable relations between administration, academics, and students were still not fully established. There were troubles in 1972, then again in 1974, most notably at the University of Essex.

### *Women's liberation and Gay liberation*

What really were important were the movements for women's liberation, and, somewhat in the rear, gay liberation. As with the new British popular culture of the sixties, women's liberation in Britain had its own unique history, while also owing something to American influences – distant in that there was a vague general knowledge of the early feminist initiatives in the United States, and contingent in that certain American women in theVietnam Solidarity Campaign in London founded one of the first British Women's Liberation groups in 1968. Much of the impetus, as in America, came from left-wing and radical groups, such as the International Socialists, the International Marxist Group, the Vietnam Solidarity Campaign, and CND. Specifically British were the contributions of a more traditionalist group of pacifists and moderate feminists who, in February 1968, organized celebrations for the fiftieth anniversary of a most important event in British history, the granting of the vote to women, and of a handful of highly practical women trade unionists. In Hull, in the spring of 1968, Lil Bilocca led a campaign of fishermen's wives for improved safety at sea. In June, Rose Boland led the sewing machinists at the Ford Dagenham plant in east London in a three-week strike for the right to undertake higher-grade work on equal terms with men. At around the same time a group of London bus conductresses demanded the right to become bus drivers. We are here at the very heart of what was truly significant in the changes in consciousness brought about by sixties developments: action not just by gilded youth, but by ordinary, underprivileged working-class women. The upshot was the establishment at top trade union level of the National Joint Action Campaign for Women's Equal Rights (NJACWER), which was both successful in pressuring for the 1970 Equal Pay Act and a stimulus to the budding women's liberation movement.

Sheila Rowbotham, who in 1969 produced a crucial statement about the need for socialists to understand and internalize the concrete realities of the cultural oppression of women, *Women's Liberation and the New Politics*, has given a sharp insight into the way many women felt *before* the convergence of circumstances in 1968–9 got things moving:

> In the diary I kept during 1967 there are persistent references to incidents I'd seen and books I'd read from a women's liberation point of view. I can remember odd conversations with women who were friends of mine, and particularly very intense movements when I was hurt and made angry by the attitudes of men on the left. But it was still at an intellectual level. We didn't think of meeting consciously as a group, far less of forming a movement. We were floundering around. The organisational initiative came from elsewhere.[39]

Many of the 'floundering' feminists of the time turned to Marxism for inspiration. Tariq Ali's 'underground' journal *Black Dwarf* obliged in January 1969 with an entire issue offering Marxist interpretations of the oppression of women. To the group formed in Tufnell Park, north London, by the American expatriates were added groups at Essex University and in Peckham, south London. In May 1969 a first newsletter was issued. That British 'women's libbers' had a sense of humour was made clear in the title chosen for the second issue, 'Harpies Bizarre'; thereafter the publication settled down as *Shrew*. By the end of 1969 there were about seventy groups spread across Great Britain.

One important intellectual development of the sixties was the sponsorship of 'democratic' history, best seen in the 'history workshops' (discussing the history of ordinary working people) held at Ruskin, the 'workers' college', at Oxford. It was at a history workshop there in September 1969 that the idea was mooted of having a women's liberation conference at the same venue in February 1970. This was attended by 600 delegates, and out of it came the Women's National Co-ordinating Committee, putting forward the following four not unreasonable demands: equal pay; equal educational and work opportunities; free contraception and abortion on request; free 24-hour child care for working mothers.

This was the moderate, practical tone of *The Female Eunuch*, a book which, at the same time, presented a very individualistic (some were later to say idiosyncratic) version of feminism. Germaine Greer was a graduate in English from Australia who had come to Cambridge to do a PhD, and who subsequently obtained an academic appointment at the University of Warwick. Tall, good-looking and intellectually brilliant, she was the embodiment of the emancipated female, enjoying the permissive society to the full, associating with the underground and turning her talents to earning fame and fortune. Contemptuous of the sexual prowess of British males, she wrote a series for *Oz* on 'In Bed with the English'; she had her own 'alternative' comedy show, *Nice Time*, on Granada TV. The more usual kind of feminist, deriving from the New Left and Marxism, was represented in Britain by the psychoanalyst Juliet Mitchell. In 'Women: The Longest Revolution' published in *New Left Review* in November 1966, Mitchell had identified the family as a key institution of capitalism, through which women reproduce and maintain the workforce, while they are fooled into believing that these are their natural tasks in which they find fulfilment. Where Greer was rumbustious and in touch with life as it was lived at the end of the sixties, Mitchell was erudite and theoretical: she developed her views in the weighty book *Women's Estate* (1971).

Rather more than two years after their American counterparts, British radical feminists took direct action against a beauty contest, this time against the Miss World competition taking place at the Royal Albert Hall on 20 November 1970. A fluoride bomb was exploded outside the hall; but the demonstrators also managed to get inside and, witnessed by millions of television viewers, created a great din with whistles and rattles while throwing flour, smoke-bombs and stink-bombs at the ageing American comedian Bob Hope, who was presenting the show. They also displayed placards referring to the event as a 'cattle market degrading to women'. Meantime, in the summer of 1970, the Women's Street Theatre Group was formed. On the following 11 March, Women's Day marches were held; as an offshoot of the massive London one, the Women's Street Theatre Group produced in Trafalgar Square one of the most spectacular shows ever, *Sugar and Spice*, featuring huge models of a deodorant, a sanitary towel, and a gigantic red, white and blue penis. Tight police security meant that the group's attempt at a second Miss World demonstration (also attended by the newly formed Gay Street Theatre Group) was confined to a parade outside the Albert Hall. The contest was parodied in 'The Flashing Nipple Show', in which the actresses had flashing lights at breasts and crotch. These were minority but highly dramatic activities. Of more enduring significance was the founding in 1972 of the monthly journal *Spare Rib*. Following behind, and drawing more direct inspiration from the United States, came the movement for Gay Liberation.

### *Innovation in the Arts*

In painting, the first completely innovative *collective* development was the emergence of Pop Art in the middle fifties. British Pop Art sprang from two very different sources, the one organized and intellectual, the other personal and inspirational. The intellectual element came from a coterie of artists and critics, including Eduardo Paolozzi (b. 1924 to an Edinburgh–Italian family), Reyner Banham (architectural historian, critic and journalist), Lawrence Alloway (art critic), and Peter and Alison Smithson (both architects), who, calling themselves the Independent Group, were from 1952 holding meetings at the recently formed Institute of Contemporary Art (ICA). The preoccupation of the Independent Group was with the consumer goods, mass communications and urban lifestyles so manifest in the America of the time, though scarcely yet present in Britain. In 1956 the group organized an exhibition at the Whitechapel Art Gallery (henceforth an important venue for introducing new art) entitled 'This Is Tomorrow', an exhibition as much about the artefacts of American urban culture (which is what the organizers meant by 'pop') as it was about representations of, or artistic references to, that culture (what came to be known as Pop Art). The spontaneous, and much more youthful, element came from a group of students at the Royal College of Art. At the time of the 'This Is Tomorrow' exhibition, Peter Blake (b. 1932) was in the final year of his postgraduate studies when he painted *Children Reading Comics.* Meantime, older fellow-student Joe Tillson (b. 1928) was beginning to produce his distinctive toy-like painted constructions. A third RCA student, Richard Smith (b. 1931), shared a studio with Blake during 1957–9. Smith embodied international cultural exchange, and the elements of still-enduring American cultural hegemony. He went to America in 1959, thus coming directly into contact with such artists as Jasper Johns

As a force in the world art scene, London and Britain still came well behind both Paris and the United States. But now developments began to take place analogous to those in rock/pop music: American influences of various sorts were still definitely present, but more and more receding into the background, while specifically British – and, to a considerable degree, provincial British – innovation came more and more into the foreground. The dominant note was of furious experimentation, of several different 'isms' being pursued simultaneously and of the merging of styles: colour–field abstraction, for instance, moved into what had formerly been thought of as 'sculpture'; figurative elements began to show themselves in what appeared to be abstract painting. Special exhibitions succeeded each other with almost bewildering rapidity, accompanied by what, for Britain, was unusual media attention to avant-garde art, and by policy statements often incomprehensible and sometimes meaningless (as artists using words to be reflexive about visual works frequently are). Most genuinely innovative was the 'Young Contemporaries' exhibition of student art held early in 1961, which introduced what must really be called post-Pop Art, much more varied than the original Pop Art and much more open to influences outside Pop strictly defined. Among the artists were Derek Boshier and David Hockney, both born in 1937, and Patrick Caulfield, born in 1936 – all on average just under 25 years old at this time. Hockney's freshly playful paintings, combining abstract and figurative elements, frankly reminiscent of Dubuffet, contain strongly personal and autobiographical elements, his own homosexuality being strongly hinted at in *Going to Be a Queen Tonight* (1960), *Bertha Alias Bernie* (1961) and *We Two Boys Together Clinging* (1961). Hockney with 'his dyed blond hair, owlish glasses, and gold lamé jacket' became a symbol of the new, more approachable art, as the Beatles were the symbol of the new popular music. More purely Pop works (though generally of a complex and sophisticated type) continued, principally from the hands of Richard Hamilton and Peter Blake.

In 1963 the Whitechapel Gallery held the first public exhibition of the brightly painted welded metal constructions of Anthony Caro, followed in Battersea

Park by the exhibition, 'Sculpture: Open Air Exhibition of Contemporary British and American Works'. The Battersea exhibition featured most notably the American David Smith, as well as Caro and some of those British sculptors who were soon to be known as the 'New Generation' group (Barry Flanagan, Richard Long and Tony Cragg). Caro (b. 1924) had a two-day-a-week teaching post at St Martin's School of Art, where he exerted a very powerful influence, though sometimes as much by reaction as by example. In 1962 and 1963 the private Gallery One held exhibitions of the black-and-white optical work of Bridget Riley (b. 1931). American-born R. B. Kitaj, quite definitely cerebral in his wish to bring into his painting the quality of modern poetry, is a fine example of pure sixties individualism, his reputation steadily growing in later decades.

In Genoa in 1967 the Italian art critic Germano Celant organized an international exhibition of what he called 'Art Povera'. Among British artists, Celant included Barry Flanagan (b. 1941 in Wales), and Richard Long (b. 1945 in Bristol), both members of the 'New Generation' of sculptors profoundly influenced by Anthony Caro – the title came from the group exhibition held at the Whitechapel Art Gallery in east London in 1965. Flanagan's work is always immediately recognizable, basically consisting of coloured hessian sacks filled with paper, foam, or sand: before Celant tried to bring everything together as Art Povera, this was variously described as Process Art, Anti-form, or Post-minimalist. Flanagan then moved into Temporal Art, constructions which are dismantled after being viewed. Long was an Earth Art man: he presented maps and photographs of landscape as well as arrangements of stones.

If we wanted to look at early seventies art as representing sixties innovations overstated and then made banal, an appropriate place to start would be with the English artists Gilbert and George. Gilbert (b. 1943) and George (b. 1942) were still sculpture students at the St Martin's School of Art when they attracted international attention for a peculiar and highly personal twist on the notion of art as 'performance' and as being 'temporal': in what was first called 'Our New Sculpture', then 'Underneath the Arches' and finally 'The Singing Sculpture', they themselves posed as their own 'sculptures'. The next stage was to seek a permanent form for these 'living sculptures': they began to use the traditional media of painting and drawing in a novel and witty way, creating numerous 'drawing pieces', 'charcoal on paper sculptures' and one 'painting sculpture', in all of which the posed image of the artists appeared life-size. In 1971 Gilbert and George turned to photography, creating the 'photo-piece' which henceforth was to be the basic form of their art, which many critics saw as simplistic and meretricious. The 'Life of People' seemed, in their paintings of the middle and later seventies, to be the life of the lavatory wall: titles ran from 'Prostitute Poof', 'Shag Stiff' and 'Wanker' to the less and less printable, the photo-pieces incorporating graffiti, photographs (sometimes of male sex organs), and red paint.

The fifties beat tradition of poetry readings and poetry and jazz, developing into poetry and light shows, poetry and happenings, expanded greatly in the high sixties. Underground poetry could scarcely have found a more visible venue than the massive Albert Hall in London for the 1965 'International Poetry Incarnation', seen as the grand climax of underground poetry by its anthologist, Michael Horovitz. Some poetry was openly political (American racism and American policy in Vietnam being frequent targets), some was ferociously savage (in Britain, George McBeth represented the former and Ted Hughes the latter). Poetry became international and cosmopolitan as never before.

The 'rise' of the provinces, of remote regions and minor nationalities, involving the emergence of new purchasers and new, insistent voices, was an important force behind the turbulent interactions between the new intellectual and cultural movements of the sixties. It is instructive to look at what was happening to poetry in Scotland. The 'Scottish Literary Renaissance' began in the 1920s, paralleling the not utterly dissimilar black 'Harlem Renaissance'; in the post-war years a high critical reputation was enjoyed by Hugh MacDiarmid (1892–1978), Robert Garrioch (b. 1909), Norman MacCaig (b. 1910) and Edwin Morgan (b. 1920), all active figures in a clearly visible Scottish bohemia. What happened in the sixties was that the wider Scottish society (traditionally governed by strongly puritan tenets), or at least parts of it, was brought into a closer alignment with this bohemia, while the poets themselves developed a new self-awareness and confidence. George Mackay Brown (1921–96) emerged into a more public light, being joined by Alan Jackson and, later, by Alan Bold (b. 1942) who in his early works at least was a conscious carrier of MacDiarmid's Marxist torch. Analogous developments, involving such poets as Dannie Abse, took place in Wales. Writing in the poetry magazine *Agenda*, the English poet Kathleen Raine stated: 'much fine verse is being written in Scotland and for a like density of good poets one would have to go to Wales'. Poetry magazines proliferated throughout the provinces and nationalities of the British Isles. In 1967 one of these, *Phoenix*, moved to Belfast in Northern Ireland: among the local poets published by *Phoenix*, one was very quickly to rise to international fame, Seamus Heaney (b. 1939).

Britain offered a paradigm of the way in which theatrical innovation advanced across a broad front, in the new civic theatres which were essentially a legacy of the war, in the slightly older proscenium-arch experimental theatres (Royal Court, Arts, Hampstead), in certain of the big subsidized companies (especially Peter Brook's Royal Shakespeare Company) and in the new spaces: the Traverse in Edinburgh (part-founded by American Jim Haynes), the Open Space (founded by the American sponsor of Theatre of Cruelty, Charles Marowitz), The Arts Lab. Theatre Workshop, very much in the older agitpop tradition, achieved a permanent home in a traditional suburban theatre in working-class east London: The Theatre Royal, Stratford East. *Oh! What a Lovely War* (1963) brought music-hall techniques to a bitterly satirical critique of the inefficiency and corruption of generals and politicians in the First World War. Before his final break with Edinburgh, Jim Haynes, with the help of the secretary of the Arts Council, Arnold Goodman, established a second Traverse in the Jeanetta Cochrane Theatre in London. He was also (May 1966) awarded the Whitbread Prize for outstanding service to British theatre – richly deserved, but not exactly the appropriate accolade for an enemy of society – which, of course, Haynes never was. Haynes was involved in the founding of *IT* (*International Times*), which can be described as an underground newspaper – it was concerned with the preoccupations of the protest movement as well as with sex and drugs – and in the founding of the multimedia Arts Lab. Brook mounted a 'theatre of cruelty' season in 1964, then a play about the Vietnam War, *US*, in February 1968. The Lord Chamberlain had wanted to ban *US*, but, as one member of the establishment talking to another, the Chairman of the RSC Board of Governors, George Farmer, persuaded him that *US* was in fact a responsible production. Experimental theatre was often highly effective in putting the feminist case, and such plays as Colin Spencer's *Spitting Image*, premiered at the Hampstead Theatre Club as early as 9 September 1968, that for gay liberation. The crossover with popular music was strongly represented in the rock musical *Tommy* (1969) by Pete Townshend and the Who. Experimental theatre represented a direct and personal response to the totalizing pressures of a multinational commercialism operating through the electronic media.

By the beginning of the sixties a new novel by Kingsley Amis was treated by the posh Sunday papers as a major literary event: as social structure and sexual morality shifted so did Amis's witty chronicles of his time; the sexual revolution to which I have referred is well represented in the contrast between *Take a Girl Like You* (1960), wherein Jenny Bunn preserves her virginity throughout almost all of the novel, and *I Want It Now* (1968), the unambiguous sentiment of the leading, and very youthful, female character. At the beginning of the decade, the working-class experience was incorporated in the novels which formed the basis for the 'New Wave' films I have already discussed. Rapidly there followed an emphasis on the experience of women, increasingly explicit in the discussion of sexual relationships. There arrived Edna O'Brien (b. 1936) with *The Country Girls* (1960), *The Lonely Girls* (1962), *Girls in their Married Bliss* (1964) and *August is a Wicked Month* (1965) – all banned in her native Ireland; Penelope Mortimer (b. 1918) with *The Pumpkin Eater* (1962); and Margaret Drabble with *A Summer Bird-cage* (1963), *The Millstone* (1965) and *The Waterfall* (1969), all related to the role of women in contemporary society. *The Golden Notebook* (1962) by Doris Lessing (b. 1919) was both modernist and strongly feminist; another strongly feminist novel, *The Snow Ball* (1964), came from Bridget Brophy (b. 1929), who had already made her name in the fifties. Full middle-brow (at the very least) status was now accorded to the novels (by Brian Aldiss, J. G. Ballard, and Ray Bradbury) making up the 'new wave' of science fiction, a most important sixties phenomenon. So also to the high-quality spy thrillers of John Le Carré (pseudonym of D. J. M. Cornwell, b. 1931), author of, *inter alia*, *The Spy Who Came In from the Cold* (1963)), Len Deighton and Dick Francis.

In the world of classical music – embracing concert hall, radio (in 1964 a daytime Music Programme was adjoined to the evening Third Programme, the two in 1970 becoming Radio 3, supreme purveyor of classical music), and records – non-British works continuing overwhelmingly to dominate the market, with the most notable alteration in taste being a swing towards 'early music' (including performance on 'early' instruments). Recording companies, of course, were engaged on a constant search for new products; still, the (relative) turning away from the Romantic classics of the later nineteenth century and the search for authenticity in performance can reasonably be linked to the spirit of dissent and innovation apparent in other spheres. The native giants continued to be Britten, whose *War Requiem,* given its first performance at the opening of the new Coventry Cathedral (1962), enjoyed a remarkable success for a piece of contemporary classical music, and Tippett, in all senses a more radical figure, who in the early sixties began to receive the recognition which had previously eluded him, while around 1970 there was a positive upsurge of enthusiasm. Mainly, Tippett's political commitment and his sheer energy and inventiveness in incorporating a massive range of influences (crossover) in his powerful music, caught the predilections of a changing audience; partly he was helped (as certainly younger composers were helped) by sponsorship of modern (as well as early) music by William Glock, BBC's Controller of Music, 1959–72.

Younger radicals looked in a firmly modern direction, influenced by the continuing innovations abroad of Karlheinz Stockhausen, Olivier Messiaen, and of Pierre Boulez, who conducted the BBC Symphony Orchestra in the early sixties. The London Sinfonietta was an important force in the playing of contemporary music. In all this, parallels with, say, the 'New Generation' sculptors are very clear, though for once the musical avant-garde actually appeared a decade earlier, in fact in mid-fifties Manchester, where Harrison Birtwhistle, Peter Maxwell Davies and Alexander Goehr (son of a German refugee) were all pupils at the Royal Manchester College of Music. These three, in common with other modernists such as Richard Rodney Bennett and Nicholas Maw, all had periods of study in continental Europe; Peter Racine Fricker and Iain Hamilton both moved, early in the sixties, to permanent jobs in the United States: all of which was entirely in keeping with the cosmopolitanism and ferment of cultural exchange of this new era in the arts.

### *Multiculturalism*

It has to be admitted that the main story of race relations in Britain in the sixties is of increasing tension and increasing racism; yet there were, too, the first positive signs of multiculturalism.[40] Immigration from the colonies and new commonwealth, fairly steady during the fifties, accelerated at the beginning of the sixties (see table 4.15).

Two places where blacks from the West Indies settled were Notting Hill in west London and St Ann's in Nottingham, where, in the few weeks before August 1958 at least a dozen black men were beaten up and robbed by Teddy boys, with the police apparently showing little inclination to try to catch the culprits. On Friday, 22 August an Afro-Caribbean got into an argument with his white woman friend and hit her. A limited scuffle spread to the whole pub, in which there was an overwhelming preponderance of whites. The few blacks were badly beaten up. The following evening a group of Afro-Caribbeans armed with knives and razors turned up at the pub. They went into the attack at closing time and injured six whites. As always in such circumstances word spread quickly, no doubt being embellished along the way. A mob of 1,500 whites launched a counter-attack with razors, knives, palings and bottles. Eight

**Table 4.15** Net immigration from colonies and New Commonwealth, 1 January 1948 to 30 June 1962

| | *West Indies* | *India* | *Pakistan* | *Others* | *Total* |
|---|---|---|---|---|---|
| 1948–53 | 14,000 | 2,500 | 1,500 | 10,000 | 28,000 |
| 1954 | 11,000 | 800 | 500 | 6,000 | 18,300 |
| 1955 | 27,550 | 5,800 | 1,850 | 7,500 | 42,700 |
| 1956 | 29,800 | 5,600 | 2,050 | 9,400 | 46,850 |
| 1957 | 23,000 | 6,600 | 5,200 | 7,600 | 42,400 |
| 1958 | 15,000 | 6,200 | 4,700 | 3,950 | 29,850 |
| 1959 | 16,400 | 2,950 | 850 | 1,400 | 21,600 |
| 1960 | 49,650 | 5,900 | 2,500 | –350 | 57,700 |
| 1961 | 66,300 | 23,750 | 25,100 | 21,250 | 136,400 |

*Source:* Dilip Hiro, *Black British White British: A History of Race Relations in Britain* (Grafton, 1991), p. 331.

people, including policemen, were badly enough injured to need hospital treatment.

Already there had been incidents in Notting Hill. In a way which was to quickly become very familiar, the news conveyed by radio and television of events in St Ann's, Nottingham, acted as an incitement in Notting Hill and the surrounding districts, collectively known as North Kensington. Certain extreme right-wing groups already had offices in the area and had been organizing meetings, as well as distributing leaflets and scrawling slogans, all to the basic refrain of 'Keep Britain White'. The news from Nottingham set a gang of Teddy boys off on a violent spree of seeking out and assaulting blacks, using a variety of offensive weapons, with the result that at least five blacks were left unconscious on the pavements. The following Saturday, 30 August, was the peak day of combined violence in both Nottingham and Notting Hill. However, when a crowd of 3,000–4,000 whites gathered at the junction of St Ann's Well Road, Pease Hill Road and Pym Street in Nottingham, there were no blacks in sight; their leaders had instructed them to stay indoors throughout the weekend. Then the white mob turned on the police, blaming them for having protected blacks the previous Saturday. Anything that happened in Nottingham was totally eclipsed by the widespread and vicious violence against black persons and property in Notting Hill. Shortly before midnight a gang of about 200 whites attacked blacks in the vicinity of Bramley Road; one property was set on fire. The following day, Sunday, a mob of 600 or so broke into black houses, assaulting the inhabitants with a fearsome array of weapons and shouting particularly offensive slogans, most notably, 'Lynch the blacks'. The assaults and skirmishes spread far beyond Notting Hill itself and to the furthest extremities of North Kensington. Firm action was taken against the main perpetrators of the violence, nine white ringleaders being sentenced, in mid-September, to four years in prison.

A year after the riots, on Saturday, 16 May 1959, Kelso Cochrane, a carpenter from Antigua who had been in Britain for five years, was stabbed to death by six white youths. Most whites were profoundly shocked. Nonetheless, at Cochrane's funeral, racist slogans were shouted. While the Institute of Race Relations was set up in 1958 to seek solutions, the Conservatives talked of bringing in controls on immigration. As with so many other aspects of British life in 1958, a new era had begun. The British had become conscious that they too had a race relations problem; and West Indians had become conscious that they formed an embattled community.

The announcement in 1960 that immigration definitely would be restricted, led to a rush to gain entry, particularly from India and Pakistan. The Immigration Bill proposed a quota system for ordinary immigrants, with vouchers for those who actually had jobs or who were possessed of special skills; it was hotly attacked by the Labour Opposition, but eventually became law on 27 February 1962. An opinion poll at the end of the previous year indicated 90 per cent support for the new legislation. Many Labour members abstained in the February vote, and steadily, as complaints arose from working-class areas, Labour moved towards support for controls. In February 1965 the Wilson Government introduced stricter restrictions on the number of unskilled workers entering the country. But it also set out positively to legislate against discrimination. Britain's first-ever Race Relations Act set up, in 1966, a Race Relations Board aiming at conciliation in cases of proven discrimination on grounds of race or colour. Roy Jenkins, as Labour Home Secretary and protagonist of the civilized society, was one of the few politicians with a genuine vision of multiculturalism, defining integration 'not as a flattening process of assimilation but as equal opportunity, accompanied by cultural diversity, in an atmosphere of mutual tolerance'. But Jenkins's successor, Callaghan, had a more traditionalist working-class vision. The two-pronged policy was continued in 1968 when new legislation against racism was coupled with a rather more substantial Act to control entry.

Respectable parliamentarians, Labour, Conservative and Liberal, were agreed in trying to prevent race from becoming a national political issue. Yet race as a political issue led to the establishment, through a fusion of existing groups, of the National Front, as a minority right-wing party, in 1966. Then on 20 April 1968, while parliament was discussing the new stronger Race Relations Bill, the Conservative front-bench spokesman for Defence, Enoch Powell, delivered a speech in Birmingham in which he envisaged a staggering growth of the non-white population: 'like the Romans, I seem to see "the River Tiber flowing with much blood"'. Apart from a Gallup poll showing 75 per cent of the population broadly sympathetic to the sentiments expressed by Powell, there were also a number of working-class demonstrations in his support. But Powell was instantly dismissed by Edward Heath from his position in the Conservative Shadow Cabinet. Nonetheless, the Conservative Immigration Act of 1971 was the most overt yet in discriminating against non-whites.

Multiculturalism was a clear aspiration in the Institute of Race Relations report, *Colour and Citizenship* (1969), but it could hardly be said that the aspiration was widely held among politicians. The real heart lay in that universal popular language of the sixties, rock/pop. Jimi Hendrix's partners in his group the Jimi Hendrix Experience were both white. Blind black prodigy Stevie Wonder (b. 1950, Detroit) had many hits in the United Kingdom, including his version of Bob Dylan's anti-war song *Blowing In the Wind* (1966), and emerged as a classic exponent of the multiculturalism inherent in rock/pop, his *A Place in the Sun* (1966) being influenced by the Beatles as well as Dylan. The experimental rock musical *Hair*, which opened in London in November 1968 on the very day after theatrical censorship ended, encompasses some of the key themes of the cultural revolution: youth, anti-war protest, permissiveness and multiculturalism. In one split-level scene, three black girls, above, sing the praises of white boys, while three white girls, below, praise black ones. Whatever their weaknesses, the counter-cultural and movement groups are very important for their genuine celebration of the colour, the variety, and the mutual stimulus to be found in multicultural communities.

## NOTES

1 Eric Hobsbawm, *The Age of Extremes: The Short Twentieth Century 1914–1989* (1995), part 2.
2 British Railways Board, *The Reshaping of British Railways* (1968), aka 'The Beeching Report'; Derek H. Aldcroft, *British Transport since 1914: An Economic History* (1975), pp. 143–158, 262–9.
3 C. P. Snow, *The Two Cultures and the Scientific Revolution. The Rede Lecture, 1959* (1959); Kenneth O. Morgan, *The People's Peace: Britain 1945–1990* (1991) pp. 144–5, 233.
4 Lord Butler, *The Art of the Possible: Memoirs of Lord Butler* (1971), p. 175; T. O. Lloyd, *Empire, Welfare State, Europe: England 1880–1992* (1994), p. 328.
5 Quoted in Kenneth Morgan, *The People's Peace: Britain 1945–1990*, pp. 173–4.
6 Peter Howlett, 'The "Golden Age", 1955–1973'. In Paul Johnson (ed.), *20th Century Britain* (1984), p. 330.
7 My sources for this account of Suez will be found in my 'Macmillan' in *Biographical Dictionary of British Prime Ministers*, ed. Robert Eccleshall and Graham Walker (1998), pp. 320–9. See David Carlton, *Britain and the Suez Crisis* (1988).
8 Quoted in John Turner, *Macmillan: A Political Biography* (1994), p. 228.
9 Peter Clarke, *Hope and Glory: Britain, 1914–1990*, p. 293.
10 *Labour Party Annual Conference Report, 1957*, pp. 179–183; Morgan, *People's Peace*, p. 182.
11 T. O. Lloyd, *Empire, Welfare State, Europe*, pp. 381–3.
12 D. E. Butler and Anthony King, *The British General Election of 1964* (1965), pp. 93, 129–131.
13 These typically witty soubriquets are Peter Clarke's – *Hope and Glory*, p. 296.
14 Harold Wilson, *The Labour Government 1964–1970: A Personal Record* (1971), pp. 463–4.
15 Arthur Marwick, *The Sixties: Cultural Revolution in Britain, France, Italy and the United States, c.1958–c.1974*, (1998), p. 351; Ben Pimlott, *The Queen: A Biography of Elizabeth II* (1996), pp. 374–5.
16 The best up-to-date accounts of welfare state developments are Rodney Lowe, *The Welfare State in Britain since 1945* (1993); Nicholas Timmins, *The Five Giants: A*

*Biography of the Welfare State* (1995); Charles Webster, *The National Health Service: A Political History* (1997).

17 Morgan, *People's Peace*, p. 302.

18 Michael Steed, 'An Analogue of the Results'. In David Butler and Michael Pinto-Duschinsky, *The British General Election of 1970* (1971), pp. 386–394.

19 See the balanced assessment, 'The Heath government in history' by Anthony Seldon, in Stuart Ball and Anthony Seldon, *The Heath Government 1970–1974: A Reappraisal* (1996), pp. 1–19. Also John Campbell, *Edward Heath*, pp. 289–619, and Dennis Kavanagh, 'The Heath Government 1970–1974', in Peter Hennessy and Anthony Seldon, *Ruling Performance: British Government from Attlee to Thatcher* (1989, paperback), pp. 216–240.

20 Marwick, *The Sixties*, esp. ch. 8.

21 T. Hennessy, *A History of Northern Ireland 1920–1996* (1997), p. 123. For an excellent summary of 'The Thirty Years' crisis, 1968–1998' in Northern Ireland, see Charles Townshend, *Ireland: The 20th Century* (1998), pp. 203–34.

22 T. Hennessy, *Northern Ireland*, pp. 126–39; for Paisley and Paisleyism see Steve Bruce, *The Edge of the Union: The Ulster Loyalist Political Vision* (1994).

23 Quoted by T. Hennessy, *Northern Ireland*, p. 147. For the following paragraphs, including quotations, I am indebted to Hennessy, esp. pp. 152–6, 182–3, 126–9, 186, 175.

24 Foster, *Modern Ireland*, p. 591.

25 T. Hennessy, *Northern Ireland*, pp. 200–18; the rest of this subsection is based heavily on Hennessy, pp. 219–21, 222–30, 255–6.

26 Robert Taylor, 'The Heath Government, Industrial Policy and the "New Capitalism"'. In Stuart Ball and Anthony Seldon (eds), *The Heath Government, 1970–1974: A Reappraisal* (1996), pp. 148ff.

27 Rodney Lowe, 'The Social Policy of the Heath Government'. In Ball and Seldon, p. 211.

28 For this and the remainder of this section, see Morgan, *People's Peace*, pp. 347–9, 351.

29 This section is based on the relevant parts of my *The Sixties*. Anthony Aldgate, *Censorship and the Permissive Society: British Cinema and Theatre, 1955–1965* (Oxford, 1995) is a classic of historical method applied to a topic too often subject to 'theoretical' speculation.

30 Mary Quant, *Quant by Quant* (1966), p. 111.

31 See Barry Miles, *Paul McCartney: Many Years From Now* (1997).

32 The first quotation is from a letter in the Bancroft Library, California; the second is from Frances Rust, *Dance in Society* (1969).

33 C. H. Rolf, *The Trial of Lady Chatterley* (1961).

34 M. P. Carter, *Education, Enjoyment and Leisure* (1963), p. 155.

35 Hannah Gavron, *The Captive Wife: Conflicts of Housebound Mothers* (1964; paperback 1968), p. 34.

36 Tariq Ali, 'The Extra-parliamentary opposition' in Tariq Ali (ed.), *The New Revolutionaries: A Handbook of the International Radical Left* (1969), p. 67.

37 Quoted in Students and Staff of Hornsey College, *The Hornsey Affair* (1969), p. 207.

38 Report in *New Society*, 31 October 1968.

39 Sheila Rowbotham, 'The Beginnings of Women's Liberation in Britain'. In Micheline Wandor, *The Body Politic: Women's Liberation in Britain* (1972), p. 91.

40 Mike Phillips and Trevor Phillips, *Windrush: The Irresistible Rise of Multi-Racial Britain* (1998), pp. 182–8.

# 5 The Ending of Consensus and the Thatcherite Revolution, 1975–1990

## Ideology, Economy and the Advent of Thatcherism

### *Key circumstances*

Decline and fluctuations in international trade following the oil crisis, together with the structural weaknesses in the British economy, as ever, continued to affect what happened inside Britain. In addition, it was during the 1970s that the globalization of the money markets came to assume its contemporary potency: fundamental was what Sir Douglas Wass, Permanent Secretary to the Treasury, described as 'the increased integration of the world economy'.[1] Contributory factors were the replacement of fixed exchange rates by floating ones, and the rapid development of the unregulated London-based Eurodollar market. But now ideology, too, became red in tooth and claw. What was new in the middle and later seventies was the growth both of the extreme Left, widely known as the 'loony left', and of the extreme Right, more politely known as the 'radical right'.

Britain's Labour party had long been a force for stability in British society. The most the extreme Left had ever been able to achieve was to create strife within the party, and render it unappealing to voters. The growth of left-wing groups, factions, and 'tendencies' inside and outside the Labour party, in the trade unions, in schools, in higher education, and among intellectuals had diverse origins. Most significant was the failure of the sixties Labour government to bring about any fundamental change in the economic and political organization of society. Frustration and anger were intensified under the unheroic ministries of Wilson and Callaghan between 1974 and 1979. In intellectual circles there had been the 'New Left' revival of Marxism way back in the late fifties, which had helped to sustain the protest movements of the sixties, which in turn experienced grave disappointment when the years 1968/69 turned out to be no more revolutionary years than any other years in contemporary society are ever likely to be. From the Left Bank in Paris came the post-structuralist, Marxist doctrines that to achieve a genuine revolution, 'bourgeois' language, ideology, and education would have to be obliterated. Since it was impossible to have anything but contempt for Soviet Communism, some declared allegiance to the original Russian revolutionary who had been hunted down and killed by Stalin's agents, Leon Trotsky. In keeping with the sixties' changes, many of the leadership figures in the various areas of left-wing activism were notably youthful. Ken Livingstone, who came from a family of working-class Tories, joined the Labour party in 1968 at the age of 23; he became a full-time GLC councillor in 1974. That was the year in which Derek Hatton, a former fire-fighter, now a social worker, joined the Liverpool Labour Party. Hatton has written:

> I had always known that Socialism was correct but I didn't want to know about fringe organisations like the Communist Party or the Socialist Workers' Party. As far as I was concerned they were Mickey Mouse outfits. At the same time I didn't know whether I could exist within the Labour Party itself.

In fact, the following year Hatton joined the Militant Tendency, associated with the fundamentalist Liverpool paper *Militant*. Hatton's ideology was that of the zealot:

> When I talk about Marxism, or Militant, I am talking about an exact political science, not what someone would or would not like to do . . .
>
> It is a question of what can, and cannot, exist.

To that he added: 'the working classes can and will win. That victory is inevitable.'[2]

These were very much the sentiments of Arthur Scargill, elected Yorkshire Area President of the National Union of Mineworkers in 1973, who believed in the power of the working class to overthrow existing society, and envisaged the miners as the revolutionary vanguard, who had the right to call upon the loyalty of all other sections of the working class. Also in 1973 the Campaign for Labour Party Democracy was set up within the party[3] – 'democracy', not as in 'heeding the voice of the majority of the electorate', but as in 'heeding the voice of the socialist activists who dominated the local Labour Parties'. Among front-bench Labour politicians the voice of extreme socialism was that of the former Viscount Stansfield, now Anthony Wedgwood-Benn, soon to be plain Tony Benn. Also on the front bench was Michael Foot, later seen as spokesperson for what was to be termed the 'soft left', as distinct from the 'hard left' of Benn, Scargill, Hatton, and (in the early stages at least before the distinction had been recognized in so many words) Livingstone. The Labour party machine, usually supported by the older right-wing trade union leaders, exerted a tight control over left-wing elements, but left-wing pressure, often of a most unscrupulous kind, was increasingly applied in the constituencies, steadily taking its effect on back-bench MPs. Where Labour did often have real power was in the big cities and in the working-class parts of London, though challenged now, in particular, by the Liberals, who though still weak in the country at large, had become quite a powerful force in city politics, partly through their exposure of Labour incompetence in local government. Generally the leading Labour figures on the local authorities had been of the same moderate, 'labourist', character as was to be found in the party nationally, and in the big trade unions. But now the fundamentalist Left was set on practising the Trotskyite tactic of 'entryism' in Labour-dominated local government. Where the Left did control local councils, they acquired a reputation among most middle-class voters, and many respectable, hard-working working-class ones, for lowering educational standards (scorning good English and sound mathematics as merely 'bourgeois' values), extravagance, inefficiency and corruption in public services, and excessive rates (i.e. local taxation).

The situation worsened after the Conservatives returned to power in 1979, as Labour councils resisted the Conservative Government's war on high local government expenditure. In 1981, Ken Livingstone, rather than the moderate Andrew McIntosh, became Leader of the GLC. The old-style moderate leader in Liverpool, John Hamilton, continued in office only by permission of Militant; his deputy, Hatton, being effectively in control. The latter has remarked that by 1983 'the Labour Party which John had supported in Liverpool was dead and buried'.[4] Livingstone's 'Fare's Fair' subsidized transport policy was a brave effort to interfere with the process by which London was becoming one of the most expensive cities in the world, but had little hope of long-term success in a world where Thatcherism held the ultimate power. Less appealing was the way in which Livingstone attempted to put together a coalition of outsider groups: blacks, gays, members of the underclass. In 1983, Labour took power in Liverpool for the first time in ten years. Among a number of London councils to fall under 'loony left' influence was Lambeth under 'Red Ted' Knight. In the parliamentary Labour party it was not just the shift to the left, but the fear of the Left among moderate elements, which was signalled in the election to the leadership (November 1980) of Michael Foot, by the admittedly narrow margin of 139 to 129 over Denis Healey – the one major Labour party figure the Conservatives feared. Soft left members wanted Foot, middle-of-the-road members feared that Healey would alienate the Left, and hard Left members wanted a weak leader,[5] which Foot manifestly was. In their last opportunity to determine the Labour party leadership, the parliamentary Labour party had condemned itself to impotence. They fully merited their replacement by a wider electoral college, as proposed by the Campaign for Labour Party Democracy, which now also secured the mandatory reselection of Labour MPs (designed to enable the activist constituency parties to threaten MPs thought to be too right-wing). Former junior minister Roy Hattersley, now arriving on the front bench, declared that while on the right himself, he had to recognize that the party had moved left. Distinguished historian Royden Harrison wrote to *The Times* that at last Labour had ceased to be labourist, and had become genuinely socialist: with supporters like that, it is no wonder that Labour remained in the wilderness until 1997.

## *EARLY THATCHERISM*

Dominant ideologies – I use the term in a neutral, descriptive, sense, not in the loaded, technical one developed by the Italian Marxist intellectual Gramsci – are as much about what it is thought politic to express, as about deeper, more atavistic instincts. During the years of consensus (as I have explained that term) there were those who spoke out for the older principles of strict control of government expenditure, 'discipline' for the working class, strict control of the money supply, 'freedom' for entrepreneurs. There were many others who instinctively hankered after such policies but either had no party to hand ready to implement them, or, if politically ambitious themselves, felt it best to remain within the accepted perimeters of consensus. The Institute of Economic Affairs had been set up in the 1950s as a free-market pressure group. Advocates of the free market looked towards America, and derived intellectual fodder from, in particular, the monetarism of the American economist Milton Friedman. The case for limiting the powers of trade unions was most vociferously argued by the National Association for Freedom. There had always been academic economists arguing for the principles of classical political economy: a younger one now coming to the fore, was Professor Alan Walters at the London School of Economics. More important were certain financial journalists, Samuel Brittan, Douglas Jay, Nigel Lawson, and Alfred Sherman, who also set himself up as a political consultant.

Before its notorious U-turn the Heath Government had attempted more aggressively right-wing, market-oriented, policies. In that government, Sir Keith Joseph, rich businessman, and self-torturing intellectual with a penchant for picking up, then often discarding, the newest intellectual fads, proponent of the theory of selectivity in the welfare state, was already convincing himself of not just the virtues, but the necessity, of monetarism. The collapse of the Heath Government, and the failure of the Conservatives in the first 1974 election, gave a great stimulus to radical right criticisms of the policies of all governments since 1945, including the Heath one. When Joseph, with Alfred Sherman, proposed a research group for the investigation of free-market policies, this won the approval of Heath. But only one Conservative front-bencher joined this new Centre for Policy Studies, Margaret Thatcher, the former Education Secretary. Probably deep down, Thatcher, the daughter of a Grantham shopkeeper and Alderman, who had taken a chemistry degree at Oxford, become a barrister, and married a very rich businessman, felt drawn to fundamentalist Conservative policies, though while in office she had shown no signs of disagreeing with Heath's basically consensual ones. But through the run of political fortune and the support and advice of her own close circle, among whom John Hoskyns (a businessman associate of Sherman) became increasingly important, she became the leader of the new radical right.[6] Another front-bencher who had seemed a good consensus man in Heath's government, but who found it easy to slip into atavistic, radical conservatism, was Sir Geoffrey Howe. Just as the Labour Government in office from 1974 to 1979 was essentially moderate in outlook, the Conservative Opposition led by Margaret Thatcher from

February 1975 had powerful, consensual figures in it, with the difference, of course, that the leader herself was inclined towards extremism. She was a person of belief and conviction in a way that Wilson and Callaghan were not – simple Conservative convictions, the beliefs of a lower-middle-class person made good, convictions still mixed with some of the caution which had become political nature during the years of consensus, convictions that yet lacked a full monetarist and free-market philosophy.

The essential launching pad for Thatcherism was the apparent failure of previous governments and previous policies. Fundamental weaknesses in the British economy had not been remedied, while globalization and the power of the money markets intensified the need for strict control of public expenditure. Leading moderates on the Labour side were beginning to perceive this, and Healey's budget of 1976 has often been described as the first monetarist budget.[7] Whether enthusiastically or not, he was forced to go along with the cuts imposed by the International Monetary Fund. Leading trade unionist, Hugh Scanlon came to believe that high public spending was starving industry of funds and thus creating unemployment.[8] At the 1976 Labour Party Conference Prime Minister Callaghan himself delivered a speech which had been written by his son-in-law, the monetarist journalist, Peter Jay:

> We used to think you could spend your way out of recession and increase employment by cutting taxes and boosting government spending. I will tell you in all candour that that option no longer exists, and that in so far as it ever did exist, it only worked on each occasion since the war by injecting a bigger dose of inflation into the economy, followed by a higher level of unemployment as the next stage.[9]

Of course, such sentiments from the Labour leadership simply intensified the determination and sense of righteousness of the extreme Left.

What really happened in the economy must, naturally, be distinguished from theories about what was happening in the economy. Monetarist and free-market policies were very much approved of by the powerful global interests, but were not necessarily of benefit to the 'real' economy. Denis Healey, as Chancellor, found that his 'experts' exaggerated the extent of the deficit being run up by the government.[10] But forecasts and rhetoric influenced the international markets: there was often to be a sharp disjunction between Thatcherite pronouncements and actual out-turns.

Margaret Thatcher had been returned as Conservative member for Finchley, in north London, in 1959. In October 1961 she took junior office as Joint Parliamentary Secretary at the Ministry of Pensions and National Insurance. Between 1964 and 1967, she was Opposition front-bench spokesperson for, respectively, Pensions and National Insurance, Housing and Land, and Treasury matters. In October 1967 she entered Heath's Shadow Cabinet with the Power portfolio. A speech she delivered at a fringe meeting organized by the Conservative Political Centre at the Blackpool Party Conference on 10 October 1968 was expressive of the views of many ordinary members generally to the right of the leadership. The 'great mistake', exclaimed the first heavily leaded heading in the printed version, is 'too much government'; and, she implied, there was too much emphasis on 'growth' as 'the key political word':

> the way to get the personal involvement and participation is not for people to take part in more and more government decisions but to make the government reduce the area of decision over which it presides and consequently leave the private citizen to 'participate', if that be the fashionable word, by making more of his own decisions.

In denouncing prices and incomes policies she touches on what, within ten years, were familiar themes (though she was still enough of a Keynesian to speak of demand management):

> We now put so much emphasis on the control of incomes that we have too little regard for the essential role of government which is the control of money supply and management of demand . . . there is nothing wrong in people wanting larger incomes . . . The point is that even the Good Samaritan had to have the money to help, otherwise he too would have had to pass on the other side.

The Good Samaritan became a stock figure in future Thatcher speeches, as did the Victorian economic liberal J. S. Mill, who is here quoted approvingly:

> The only freedom which deserves the name is that of pursuing our own good in our own way so long as we do not deprive others of theirs, or impede their efforts to obtain it . . . Mankind are greater gainers by suffering each other to live as seems good to themselves than by compelling each to live as seems good to the rest.

Thatcher had begun her speech by claiming that people voted, not for specific manifesto commitments, but for broad political principles, declaring – the emphasis on principle was to be more important than that on tolerance: 'There is, and has to be room for a variety of opinions on certain topics within the broad general principles on which each party is based.' Now she attacked the notion of consensus across the two sets of political principles, defining 'the essential character' of the British party-political system as follows:

> There is an alternative policy and a whole alternative Government ready to take office. As a result we have always had an Opposition to act as a focus of criticism against the Government. We have therefore not suffered the fate of countries which have had a 'consensus' or central government, without an official opposition . . .
>
> There are dangers in consensus; it could be an attempt to satisfy people holding no particular views about anything. It seems more important to have a philosophy and policy which because they are good appeal to sufficient people to secure a majority.

Was she consciously recognizing, one wonders, that this 'majority' might be well short of one in the country as a whole? Thatcher then claimed that members of an undergraduate audience she had addressed found her views much more challenging 'than expecting government to solve all problems'. She quoted one student as saying to her: 'I had no idea there was such a clear alternative.'[11] Above all, Thatcherism was offering a clear alternative to all policies promoted since the war, and, in the same breath, insisting that her alternative was the only alternative. Half-way through the Thatcher Government of the 1980s that message was being driven home by her acolyte, Nigel Lawson, Vice-Chairman of the Conservative political centre, 1972–5, and now, 6 July 1983, her Chancellor of the Exchequer:

> the approach we pioneered when we came to office in 1979 does run counter to conventional post-war wisdom. Many interpreters of the economic scene, many so-called opinion formers, are still anchored in the old way of thinking. But I have to tell them that our approach is now internationally accepted throughout the world.[12]

A major part of conventional post-war wisdom had been that aggregate demand within the economy must always be kept high enough to avoid unemployment, demand being 'damped down' when there was a risk of 'over-heating'. As Thatcher paid more and more attention to anti-Keynesian economists, she began to embrace the idea that, instead of attempting to manipulate demand, government should concentrate on the 'supply side', improving the (admittedly poor) performance of the productive sectors in the British economy. If unemployment rose, that was regrettable, though it did have the bonus of imposing discipline and wage restraint on the workers; certainly, avoidance of unemployment was no longer to be a central government objective.

How strong consensualism still was in the later seventies, however, is apparent in one of the great 'lost political programmes' (rather than 'lost leaders'!) of recent British history. *The Right Approach to the Economy: Outline of an Economic Strategy for the Next Conservative Government* (October 1977), by Geoffrey Howe, James Prior, Keith Joseph, David Howell, and edited by Angus Maude, is Tony Blair's 'Third Way' *avant la lettre*. Had it been implemented Britain would have been a happier, and less divided, society throughout the 1980s and 1990s. Thatcher hated it, and, in the event, none of its distinguished signatories stood up for it.[13] It calls for (of course!) a 'more stable economic climate'; 'strict control by the Government of the rate of growth of the money supply'; 'firm management of government expenditure'; 'lower taxation'; 'the removal of unnecessary restrictions on business expansion' (p. 6). The 'over-riding objective is to unwind the inflationary coils which have gripped our economy' (p. 8); 'state ownership' must be reduced (p. 47). So far, so Thatcherite. But the authors are firm supporters of manufacturing industry (pp. 39–42) – savaged by Thatcher and Howe during their first two years in office. More, the document is quite stunningly consensual and opposed to political tribalism. It is recognized that the then Labour Government was 'now belatedly trying to pursue' correct policies (p. 8), and, 'urged on by the Conservative Party, has taken the first steps' in the right direction – 'we intend to build on its work' (p. 12); 'the need for control of the money supply and of government expenditure has been accepted . . . on both sides of the House of Commons'. At the same time the authors explicitly disavow any belief that 'one has only to follow the right money supply path and everything in the economy will become right'. Britain should learn lessons from Germany and our other competitors (pp. 9, 17 – Thatcher was particularly contemptuous of this): there should be both a 'more independent role for the Bank of England' (p. 9) and joint discussions (pp. 9, 17) between the Bank, *both* sides of industry *and* then parliament, through the National Economic Development Council (which Thatcher at first ignored, then dismantled in 1987, final abolition being carried out by Norman Lamont in July 1992).

Monetary discipline would be extended *gradually* (p. 8), not as 'a prescription for poorer social provision', but as 'a recipe for better housekeeping in all public services'; there would not be 'savage and indiscriminate cuts in public programmes' (p. 10). The attitude towards trade unions was a million miles away from that which came to be associated with Thatcherism:

> We see the trade unions as a very important economic interest group whose co-operation and understanding we must work constantly to win and keep, as we have done in the past. We see no need for confrontation and have no wish for it!

Calling for 'fuller participation at work' (p. 50) the document sounded far distant from Thatcherism, but very close to Blairite 'inclusiveness':

> we are looking at ways in which people at work can be given the right to information about the big decisions affecting them. And we shall encourage the development in a variety of ways and means for employers to influence these decisions. (p. 51)

Finally, the document taunted those in the Labour party still evincing 'blatant hostility' to the EEC (pp. 52–3) – 'blatant enthusiasm' was not to be one of Thatcher's salient characteristics!

But, once Thatcher had come to power, and particularly after she won a second general election in 1983, radical right-wing policies accelerated and spread (Prior himself coming to accept Thatcherism, and to recant the criticisms of it he was making within the Cabinet in the early eighties). In this connection, one must again bring in the institutional factor – the British electoral system. Margaret Thatcher never achieved more than 44 per cent of the popular vote, and as attitude surveys demonstrated, Thatcherite ideology never gained the support of a majority of the British people. Such considerations, however, were unimportant compared with the fact that the first-past-the-post system gave Thatcher power and substantial parliamentary majorities, and Thatcher was to exploit that power more ruthlessly than any previous Prime Minister. Indeed, perhaps even more important than the economic implications, Thatcherism entailed showing no respect for the 'give-and-take' spirit, the respect for those who, in parliamentary terms, were in opposition, which had previously been held to be a vital part of the British two-party system.

## *NATIONALISM*

If there was anything of a consensus beginning to form in favour of paying heed to nationalist aspirations, Thatcher was firmly against that, too. The sixties growth in support for Scottish Nationalism had been demonstrated at the Hamilton by-election of 2 November 1967. Both voters and activists overwhelmingly came from people, particularly working-class people, who had not previously been involved in politics. And devolutionist sentiment was growing strongly in such non-political bodies as the Church of Scotland, to the extent that the Scottish Conservatives stopped calling themselves Unionists, and persuaded Edward Heath to set up a Committee which in March 1970 reported in favour of devolution.[14] Reporting in November 1972 the Kilbrandon Commission, appointed by Wilson in December 1968, asked for, by a majority of thirteen to two, a devolved Parliament in Scotland and a local Assembly for Wales. Labour in Scotland expressed hostility, and immediately lost a by-election in Govan to the SNP. In the first General Election of 1974, the SNP won a further seven seats with its votes going up from 11.4 to 21.9 per cent. Meantime the beginnings of exploration for North Sea gas and then North Sea oil strengthened views about the economic viability of an independent Scotland, while also creating some resentment that almost all of the massive equipment required was being constructed outside of Scotland. 'It's Scotland's oil' was the slogan of an effective campaign initiated by the SNP in September 1972. In the second 1974 election the SNP won a further four seats and its vote rose to over 30 per cent. The Labour leadership was tending towards devolution, while much of the Scottish Labour party, which did pretty well out of the existing situation, was hotly opposed to it. Early in 1976, Jim Sillars, a recent convert, broke from Labour to create the devolutionist Scottish Labour Party. There was sufficient growth in Welsh Nationalism (Plaid Cymru won three seats in the October 1974 election) to make it impossible to detach the issue of Welsh devolution from that of Scottish devolution, though hostility in traditional Welsh Labour circles to devolution was even stronger than that in Scotland.

## *KEY STATISTICS*

Again, before we turn to the detailed political battles, we must look at some of the key statistics. The tables of economic statistics presented here are a measure of the problems facing the country and its politicians; they are also, of course, indications of the success, or failure, of politicians in dealing with these problems. The hope of the Thatcher Government from 1979 onwards was that by implementing the ideology already described there would be a great turnaround in Britain's fortunes. The tables show that some things stayed much the same (being perhaps beyond the power of governments), some things improved, some things got worse; and they also show that the Thatcher Government benefited from a colossal windfall – first the coming ashore of North Sea oil and then the second great rise in oil prices at the beginning of the eighties which, unlike the rise of 1973, was very much to Britain's advantage. However – nothing ever being that simple – this second rise in oil prices did provoke a world-wide recession, and from that Britain inevitably suffered. Consider the following tables, and work out how they relate to the points I have just been making.

**Table 5.1** Percentage shares of world trade in manufacturing, 1960–1990

| *Country* | *1960* | *1970* | *1979* | *1990* |
|---|---|---|---|---|
| France | 9.6 | 8.7 | 10.5 | 9.7 |
| Germany | 19.3 | 19.8 | 20.9 | 20.2 |
| Japan | 6.9 | 11.7 | 13.7 | 15.9 |
| United Kingdom | 16.5 | 10.8 | 9.1 | 8.6 |
| United States | 21.6 | 18.6 | 16.0 | 16.0 |

*Source:* N. F. R. Crafts, *Can De-Industrialization Seriously Damage Your Wealth? A Review of Why Growth Rates Differ and How to Improve Economic Performance* (Institute of Economic Affairs, 1993), p. 20.

**Table 5.2** North Sea oil: output, trade and revenues, 1979–1990

| | *Production in million tonnes* | *Consumption in million tonnes* | *Petroleum and petroleum product exports less imports £ billion* | *Taxes and royalties for North Sea oil and gas £ billion* |
|---|---|---|---|---|
| 1979 | 77.9 | 84.6 | −1.1 | 0.6 |
| 1980 | 80.5 | 71.2 | +0.1 | 2.3 |
| 1981 | 89.5 | 66.3 | +2.9 | 3.7 |
| 1982 | 103.2 | 67.2 | +4.4 | 6.5 |
| 1983 | 115.0 | 64.5 | +6.8 | 7.8 |
| 1984 | 126.1 | 81.4 | +6.6 | 8.8 |
| 1985 | 127.6 | 69.8 | +7.8 | 12.0 |
| 1986 | 127.1 | 69.2 | +3.7 | 11.5 |
| 1987 | 123.3 | 67.7 | +4.0 | 4.8 |
| 1988 | 114.4 | 71.6 | +2.1 | 3.2 |
| 1989 | 91.8 | 73.0 | | 3.2 |
| 1990 | 92.1+ | 74.9+ | | 2.3 |

*Source:* S. Pollard, *The Development of the British Economy 1914–1990* (Aldershot: Edward Arnold, 1992), p. 403.

It will be noted that the figures do not rise continuously. Two factors are involved here: the fall in domestic demand because of the decline in size of major industries such as iron and steel; and a fall in oil prices from the high at the beginning of the decade.

**Table 5.3** UK balance of payments, 1979–1990, $ billion

| | *Exports* | *Imports* | *Visible balance* | *Services balance* |
|---|---|---|---|---|
| 1979 | 40.5 | 43.8 | –3.3 | +3.8 |
| 1980 | 47.1 | 45.8 | +1.4 | +3.7 |
| 1981 | 50.7 | 47.4 | +3.3 | +3.8 |
| 1982 | 55.3 | 53.4 | +1.9 | +3.0 |
| 1983 | 60.7 | 62.2 | –1.5 | +4.1 |
| 1984 | 70.3 | 75.6 | –5.3 | +4.5 |
| 1985 | 78.0 | 81.3 | –3.3 | +6.7 |
| 1986 | 72.7 | 82.1 | –9.5 | +6.7 |
| 1987 | 79.4 | 90.7 | –11.2 | +6.6 |
| 1988 | 80.8 | 101.9 | –21.1 | +4.5 |
| 1989 | 99.8 | 116.6 | –23.8 | +4.7 |
| 1990 | 102.7 | 120.7 | –17.9 | +4.4 |

*Source:* S. Pollard, *The Development of the British Economy 1914–1990* (Aldershot: Edward Arnold, 1992), p. 422.

**Table 5.4** Changes in industrial levels 1973 and 1989

| *Country* | *1973* | | *1989* | |
|---|---|---|---|---|
| | *Percentage employed in industry* | *Percentage value added from industry* | *Percentage employed in industry* | *Percentage value added from industry* |
| France | 39.7 | 38.1 | 30.1 | 28.9 |
| Germany | 47.5 | 47.0 | 39.8 | 39.3 |
| Italy | 39.2 | 42.2 | 32.4 | 33.8 |
| Japan | 37.2 | 46.3 | 34.3 | 41.6 |
| Sweden | 36.8 | 34.8 | 29.4 | 30.8 |
| UK | 42.6 | 38.4 | 29.4 | 29.5 |
| US | 33.2 | 34.1 | 26.7 | 29.2 |

*Source:* N. F. R. Crafts, *Can De-Industrialization Seriously Damage Your Wealth? A Review of Why Growth Rates Differ and How to Improve Economic Performance* (Institute of Economic Affairs, 1993), p. 21.

Scrutinize this table very carefully: several different points can be read off from it.

**Table 5.5** Percentage growth in GDP

(a) UK

| | | | |
|---|---|---|---|
| 1970 | 2.0 | 1980 | –2.0 |
| 1971 | 1.7 | 1981 | –1.2 |
| 1972 | 2.8 | 1982 | 1.7 |
| 1973 | 7.4 | 1983 | 3.8 |
| 1974 | –1.5 | 1984 | 1.8 |
| 1975 | –0.8 | 1985 | 3.8 |
| 1976 | 2.6 | 1986 | 3.6 |
| 1977 | 2.6 | 1987 | 4.4 |
| 1978 | 2.9 | 1988 | 4.7 |
| 1979 | 2.8 | 1989 | 2.1 |

*Source:* C. Johnson, *The Economy Under Mrs Thatcher 1979–1990* (Harmondsworth: Penguin, 1991), p. 265.

(b) Other countries

| | *France* | *Germany* | *Italy* | *Japan* | *US* | *EEC* | *OECD* |
|---|---|---|---|---|---|---|---|
| 1980 | 1.6 | 1.5 | 4.2 | 4.3 | –0.2 | 1.5 | 1.5 |
| 1981 | 1.2 | 0.0 | 1.0 | 3.7 | 1.9 | 0.1 | 1.7 |
| 1982 | 2.5 | –1.0 | 0.3 | 3.1 | –2.5 | 0.8 | –0.1 |
| 1983 | 0.7 | 1.9 | 1.1 | 3.2 | 3.6 | 1.6 | 2.7 |
| 1984 | 1.3 | 3.3 | 3.0 | 5.1 | 6.8 | 2.5 | 4.8 |
| 1985 | 1.9 | 1.9 | 2.6 | 4.8 | 3.4 | 2.4 | 3.4 |
| 1986 | 2.3 | 2.3 | 2.5 | 2.6 | 2.7 | 2.6 | 2.7 |
| 1987 | 2.4 | 1.7 | 3.0 | 4.6 | 3.7 | 2.8 | 3.5 |
| 1988 | 3.8 | 3.6 | 4.2 | 5.7 | 4.4 | 3.9 | 4.4 |
| 1989 | 3.7 | 4.0 | 3.2 | 4.9 | 3.0 | 3.5 | 3.6 |

*Source:* C. Johnson, *The Economy Under Mrs Thatcher 1979–1990* (Harmondsworth: Penguin, 1991), p. 266.

**Table 5.6** Productivity

(a) Annual average productivity growth rates in manufacturing

| | *US* | *Japan* | *Europe* | *UK* |
|---|---|---|---|---|
| 1960–73 | 3.3 | 10.3 | 6.1 | 4.2 |
| 1973–9 | 1.4 | 5.5 | 4.0 | 1.7 |
| 1979–89 | 3.6 | 5.5 | 3.1 | 4.7 |

*Source:* OECD.

**Table 5.6** Productivity *cont'd*

(b) Increase in labour productivity per employee

| | *EEC* | *US* | *Japan* | *Germany* | *France* | *Italy* | *UK* |
|---|---|---|---|---|---|---|---|
| 1974–9 | 2.6 | 0.9 | 5.0 | 3.1 | 3.7 | 5.3 | 0.6 |
| 1980–8 | 3.3 | 3.3 | 5.8 | 2.9 | 2.2 | 4.0 | 4.2 |

*Source:* C. Johnson, *The Economy Under Mrs Thatcher 1979–1990* (Harmondsworth: Penguin, 1991), p. 314.

**Table 5.7** UK output per person-hour in manufacturing (1985 = 100)

| | |
|---|---|
| 1980 | 78.1 |
| 1981 | 82.2 |
| 1982 | 86.7 |
| 1983 | 92.1 |
| 1984 | 97.5 |
| 1985 | 100.0 |
| 1986 | 103.8 |
| 1987 | 109.6 |
| 1988 | 115.5 |
| 1989 | 120.8 |
| 1990 | 121.1 |

*Source:* OECD.

**Table 5.8** Annual inflation rates

(a) UK

| *Dates* | *Retail price index* | *Dates* | *Retail price index* |
|---|---|---|---|
| 1970 | 6.5 | 1980 | 18.0 |
| 1971 | 9.2 | 1981 | 11.9 |
| 1972 | 7.5 | 1982 | 8.6 |
| 1973 | 9.1 | 1983 | 4.5 |
| 1974 | 15.9 | 1984 | 5.0 |
| 1975 | 24.1 | 1985 | 6.0 |
| 1976 | 16.6 | 1986 | 3.4 |
| 1977 | 15.9 | 1987 | 4.2 |
| 1978 | 8.2 | 1988 | 4.9 |
| 1979 | 13.4 | 1989 | 7.8 |

*Source:* C. Johnson, *The Economy Under Mrs Thatcher 1979–1990* (Harmondsworth: Penguin, 1991), p. 280.

**Table 5.8** Annual inflation rates *cont'd*

(b) Several countries: inflation measured by Consumer Expenditure Deflator

| | *UK* | *France* | *Germany* | *Italy* | *Japan* | *US* | *EEC* | *OECD* |
|---|---|---|---|---|---|---|---|---|
| 1980 | 16.3 | 13.3 | 5.8 | 20.5 | 7.1 | 10.8 | 12.9 | 11.3 |
| 1981 | 11.2 | 13.0 | 6.2 | 18.1 | 4.4 | 9.2 | 11.6 | 9.5 |
| 1982 | 8.7 | 11.5 | 4.8 | 16.9 | 2.6 | 5.7 | 10.2 | 7.2 |
| 1983 | 4.8 | 9.7 | 3.2 | 15.2 | 1.9 | 4.1 | 8.1 | 5.5 |
| 1984 | 5.1 | 7.7 | 2.5 | 11.8 | 2.1 | 3.8 | 6.8 | 4.9 |
| 1985 | 5.4 | 5.8 | 2.1 | 9.0 | 2.2 | 3.3 | 5.5 | 4.3 |
| 1986 | 4.4 | 2.7 | –0.5 | 5.8 | 0.6 | 2.4 | 3.2 | 2.7 |
| 1987 | 4.3 | 3.1 | 0.6 | 4.9 | –0.2 | 4.7 | 3.1 | 3.4 |
| 1988 | 4.9 | 2.7 | 1.2 | 5.3 | –0.1 | 3.9 | 3.3 | 3.3 |
| 1989 | 5.9 | 3.3 | 3.1 | 6.0 | 1.7 | 4.4 | 4.4 | 4.3 |

*Source:* C. Johnson, *The Economy Under Mrs Thatcher 1979–1990* (Harmondsworth: Penguin, 1991), p. 281.

**Table 5.9** UK real earnings (1913 = 100.0)

| | *Money earnings* | *Cost of living* | *Real earnings* |
|---|---|---|---|
| 1970 | 1840.3 | 636.6 | 289.1 |
| 1971 | 2029.3 | 695.1 | 291.9 |
| 1972 | 2350.1 | 747.1 | 314.6 |
| 1973 | 2684.7 | 782.8 | 343.0 |
| 1974 | 3190.6 | 945.2 | 337.6 |
| 1975 | 3902.2 | 1172.6 | 333.4 |
| 1976 | 4393.8 | 1367.5 | 321.3 |
| 1977 | 4787.4 | 1585.1 | 302.2 |
| 1978 | 5401.8 | 1755.0 | 315.0 |
| 1979 | 6236.4 | 1945.6 | 320.5 |
| 1980 | 7534.7 | 2296.4 | 328.1 |
| 1981 | 8508.6 | 2569.3 | 331.2 |
| 1982 | 9306.8 | 2790.1 | 336.6 |
| 1983 | 10091.3 | 2916.8 | 346.0 |
| 1984 | 10706.8 | 3063.0 | 349.6 |
| 1985 | 11613.2 | 3248.1 | 357.5 |
| 1986 | 12533.0 | 3358.4 | 373.2 |
| 1987 | 13508.7 | 3498.2 | 386.2 |
| 1988 | 14681.9 | 3669.9 | 400.1 |
| 1989 | 16017.9 | 3954.8 | 405.0 |
| 1990 | 17574.2 | 4329.0 | 406.0 |

*Source:* P. Scholliers and V. Zamagni, *Labour's Reward: Real Wages and Economic Change in 19th- and 20th-Century Europe* (Aldershot: Edward Elgar, 1995) p. 266.

**Table 5.10** UK trade-union membership

| | *Membership in millions* | *Percentage of employees* |
|---|---|---|
| 1979 | 13.3 | 57.4 |
| 1980 | 12.9 | 56.4 |
| 1981 | 12.1 | 55.3 |
| 1982 | 11.6 | 54.2 |
| 1983 | 11.2 | 53.4 |
| 1984 | 11.0 | 51.8 |
| 1985 | 10.8 | 50.5 |
| 1986 | 10.5 | 49.3 |
| 1987 | 10.5 | 48.5 |
| 1988 | 10.2 | 46.0 |

*Source:* C. Johnson, *The Economy Under Mrs Thatcher 1979–1990* (Penguin, 1991), p. 312.

**Table 5.11** Working days lost through stoppages, per thousand employees

| | *UK* | *US* | *France* | *Italy* | *Australia* |
|---|---|---|---|---|---|
| 1979 | 1,270 | 230 | 180 | 1,920 | 780 |
| 1980 | 520 | 230 | 90 | 1,140 | 630 |
| 1981 | 190 | 190 | 80 | 730 | 780 |
| 1982 | 250 | 100 | 130 | 1,280 | 370 |
| 1983 | 180 | 190 | 70 | 980 | 310 |
| 1984 | 1,280 | 90 | 70 | 610 | 240 |
| 1985 | 300 | 70 | 40 | 270 | 230 |
| 1986 | 90 | 120 | 30 | 390 | 240 |
| 1987 | 160 | 40 | 30 | 320 | 220 |
| 1988 | 166 | | | | |
| 1989 | 182 | | | | |

*Source:* C. Johnson, *The Economy Under Mrs Thatcher 1979–1990* (Harmondsworth: Penguin, 1991), p. 312.

Two sets of statistics, often seen as being closely interrelated, and often used, along with one of the tables I have given here, to measure a government's performance, I am holding over until the next section. Have you noticed what they are? I'll return to them in a moment, but first let us work through the tables in turn, summarizing the information we can derive from them. Britain's share of world trade in manufacturing continues to decline, but has been slowed over the 1980s. The biggest decline was in the 1960s, and France had already overtaken Britain by 1979. With Japan continuing to carry all before it, Germany's share has declined slightly over the eighties, though still higher than it had been throughout the sixties. The second table shows the immense, though ultimately diminishing, benefits Britain is deriving from North Sea oil. Despite that, the balance of payments situation by the end of the eighties is as bad as ever. Invisible exports (financial services, etc.) are still playing a valuable part. In all developed countries the industrial sector is diminishing, though the biggest drop is in Britain (13.2 per cent of employees between 1973 and 1989, compared with 9.6 per cent in France). If you looked closely as I suggested, you will have noted a measure here of Britain's industrial inefficiency. In 1973 the percentage of value added was considerably lower than the percentage of employees; as a sign of increase in industrial efficiency these figures have been reversed by 1989, though only just. Growth figures are very erratic in the 1970s, but by the late eighties are coming through relatively strongly, even in comparison with major competitors. This, naturally, is related to growth in productivity: table 5.6 brings out clearly the poor performance from 1973 to the end of the seventies, and the relatively good one in the 1980s. Table 5.7 confirms the improving performance in the later eighties.

Inflation was one of the endemic British economic diseases which Thatcher openly set out to conquer and is one of the indicators by which governments tend to be judged. The terrible record of the mid- and later seventies, as also that of the early Thatcher era, is apparent. Because of the world-wide slump there are quite bad figures for most countries at the beginning of the eighties; Britain is doing better in the later eighties, but does not come near to matching the figures in Japan and Germany. For all that, real wages, with some small fluctuations, continued to advance, with the peak in 1974, not being matched again until 1983. These figures tell us nothing about how those not in steady employment were faring. The other indicators of government performance which will fit better into the next section are unemployment statistics, and, generally seen as closely related to them, interest rates. Trade-union membership, we can see, was in steady decline throughout the Thatcher years. There were two particularly bad years for strikes, 1979 (the last year of Labour government) and 1984 (the year of the miners' strike); but clearly the basic trend under Thatcher is for the number of days lost to strike action to be substantially reduced. These conclusions are broadly confirmed by table 5.6 (b).

## THE COLLAPSE OF LABOUR AND THE TRIUMPH OF THATCHER

### *THE THIRD WILSON GOVERNMENT*

Wilson had faced this situation before; in the sixties he'd been given great credit for the way in which he had played his hand through 1964 and 1965 to ensure a substantial majority in the election of 1966. This time, the trick Wilson pulled, holding another election within eight months in October 1974, was a very weak reprise of the original effort. Barely favourable electoral arithmetic meant that much time and thought had to be given to keeping the government afloat in parliament, particularly when by-election losses began to mount. More immediate even than that was the need to neutralize left-wing influences on the government, while trying to avoid the total alienation of gathering left-wing sentiment. The new government's first task was to appease the miners and bring an end to the three-day week. Then it had somehow to pursue the complex, interrelated policies of maintaining the support of the unions, demonstrating a concern for social justice, and keeping wages and prices under control. And in a world environment more hostile, and more apt to expose long-term economic weaknesses, than ever before, the government had to battle to secure economic survival. From Heath it had inherited membership of the European Economic Community, to which a majority of the Labour party was opposed on principle, with the economic terms negotiated by Heath being criticized by Wilson and other leading figures. Right-wingers in the government, apart from Wilson himself, were Denis Healey as Chancellor of the Exchequer, James Callaghan as Foreign Secretary, and Roy Jenkins as Home Secretary. Tony Benn, at Trade and Industry, was the most extreme left-winger, with Michael Foot, Secretary for Employment, representative of the moderate Left; other left-wingers were Barbara Castle and Peter Shore. The miners were bought off; the Heath Industrial Relations Act and statutory pay policy were dropped. Healey introduced two budgets, one in March, one in July: the first raised both pensions and taxes on the rich; the second put spending power back into the economy. In July the government announced that it would be activating the 'Social Contract' which Wilson and Vic Feather had concluded in 1972: the unions would operate voluntary pay restraint, while the government would improve social benefits, allow the nationalized industries to run up deficits, and guarantee not to interfere with collective bargaining.

In the October election the turnout fell by nearly 7 per cent, and the votes of Conservatives, Labour and Liberals all dropped, but the Conservatives by the most significant amount. The 2 per cent swing to Labour gave that party the narrowest of majorities.

What was the government to do about British membership of the EEC? As recently as 1972 the party had formally expressed its outright opposition. In its election manifestos it had promised substantial renegotiation of the terms of membership. But a process had begun which has continued to develop ever since. Most British people were extremely ill-informed about the EEC, and

**Table 5.12** General Election, 10 October 1974

| | *Electorate 40 million* | | *Turnout 72.8 per cent* | | |
|---|---|---|---|---|---|
| | *Labour* | *Conservative* | *Liberal* | *Nationalist* | *Northern Ireland* |
| Votes | 11,457,079 | 10,464,817 | 5,346,754 | | |
| Percentage of votes cast | 39.2 | 35.8 | 18.3 | 3.5 | 2.4 |
| Seats | 319 | 277 | 13 | 14 | 12 |

most were affected by a fundamental xenophobia and chauvinism. Yet a feeling was developing that, perhaps, like it or not, Britain's future was bound up with Europe, and that perhaps association with Europe could bring some of the economic success which the continental countries were enjoying.[15]

Callaghan, who led the British negotiations, shared these sentiments; with him he had Peter Shore, who remained an unreconstructed anti-European, and Roy Hattersley, who was a genuine enthusiast. On the European side much warmth towards Britain was expressed by the German Social Democratic leader Willy Brandt and by the French President, Giscard d'Estaing, right-wing, but relatively youthful, forward-looking and Anglophile. With respect to payments, some concessions were made in the light of Britain's chronic balance of payments problems, it being recognized that Britain's situation might improve greatly once the North Sea oil started flowing in the eighties. Negotiations were completed at a meeting in Dublin in March 1975. Tony Benn, hotly opposed to the EEC on the socialist grounds that it was simply 'a rich man's club', had succeeded in getting Labour to promise that once renegotiations had been carried out a referendum (a completely new device in British politics) would be held on whether or not Britain should stay in, or come out of, the EEC. This was duly held on 5 June. The government voted £125,000 to enable both sides to finance their campaigns. Government ministers were left free to speak for or against. Ironically in this time of the break-up of consensus, something akin to coalition politics emerged in the way in which Heath, Jenkins, and Thorpe stood together on the same pro-Europe platform. The big money went to the pro-Europe campaign, which as a public relations exercise was by far the more impressive. Although most Labour members remained opposed, use of the big union votes, where minds had changed remarkably quickly, facilitated a pro-Europe Labour Conference vote of 3,724,000 to 1,986,000. In the actual referendum, with a turnout of about 65 per cent, the pro-Europe vote was 17,378,581 to 8,470,073.

As we have seen from table 5.8 (a), inflation by the end of 1974 was running at over 28 per cent. As the unions chased each other in celebrating the return of a Labour government, wage rates had risen by well over a quarter. Inflation did then, as the table shows, begin to come down steadily. The major implementation of the government side of the 'contract' was the Employment Protection Act of 1975, whose provisions covered the right not to be unfairly dismissed, to written statements of terms and conditions of employment, guaranteed pay, time off work for trade-union duties, redundancy pay, minimum periods of notice, and maternity leave. Cash limits on the nationalized industries were relaxed, while the Industry Act (1975) established the National Enterprise Board to pursue interventionist policies in industry. In rescuing the last remaining motor car company, British Leyland, the government in effect nationalized it, at the same time pouring in public funds. Aircraft and shipbuilding were also nationalized. At the same time, the government tried to implement anti-inflationary measures while ministers raged publicly about the folly of inflationary wage increases – all, that is, save Tony Benn who continued to encourage workers to demand everything they could get, provoking Wilson, in June 1975, into moving him from the Department of Trade and Industry to the

Department of Energy. Declaring 'the party' to be 'over', Anthony Crosland, Secretary of the Environment, imposed controls on local authority spending.[16] In January 1975 Healey announced that limits must be imposed on public expenditure and that wage inflation was causing unemployment. True to his words, his budget of April 1975, his fourth since Labour's confirmation in power, raised old taxes, invented new ones, and steeply increased a recent one, VAT, while cutting public spending by over a billion pounds. Meantime, the big union leaders were themselves becoming worried by the unprecedented levels of inflation. The left-wing leader of the massive Transport Workers' Union proposed that there should be a voluntary agreement that wage rises for everyone should be limited to £6 a week. That trade unions had a greater sense of responsibility than the Right was now attributing to them, was shown by the acceptance by the General Council (in June) and the TUC Conference (in September) of this wage-restraint policy. Symbolic of the facts that both inflation and strike action were significantly easing off, there was now, miraculously, a full twelve-month interval before Healey's next budget: in a flat reversal of the agreement to recognize free collective bargaining, his budget of April 1976 put a legal limit of 3 per cent on wage increases. What everyone most feared was rising unemployment.

Right at the heart of this time of troubles, within the space of one year and one month, both parties underwent a leadership change. The advent to the Conservative leadership of Margaret Thatcher can be squarely blamed on her predecessor, Edward Heath. Had Heath resigned, as by obvious standards of political behaviour he should have done, immediately after his second electoral defeat, he would most certainly have been succeeded by another figure in the traditional, consensual, one-nation mould, probably William Whitelaw. As it was, Heath's self-centred obstinacy in continuing as leader provoked the fateful challenge from Thatcher – ironically, Heath himself had been the first beneficiary of the Conservatives' post-Douglas-Home system for electing the leader, one which also required the leader to submit to annual re-election. Instead of giving way gracefully to one of his like-minded associates, Heath demanded their loyalty. The obvious challenger, therefore, would have been Sir Keith Joseph. Would have been . . . ! First, Sir Keith let it be known that he was indeed a candidate, then within a week placed his foot firmly in his mouth: quite possibly many of Sir Keith's audience of Birmingham Conservatives agreed with the view that ignorant, lower-class women were having too many children, but the press publicity for this idiosyncratic insight into the Victorian values of which Margaret Thatcher herself was often to speak, totally sunk his credibility as a leadership candidate.[17] Joseph withdrew. Thatcher, who would not have dreamed of standing against him, and indeed had not yet dreamt of ever rising higher than the post of Chancellor of the Exchequer, but already hating Heath and everything she thought he stood for, put her name forward. For a time, Edward DuCann, the classic back-bencher's hero, apparently perennial Chairman of the 1922 Committee, seemed a likely candidate for those categorically opposed to Heath. But DuCann, who never perceived a bet without hedging it, withdrew. It was Thatcher against Heath, with independent-minded back-bencher Hugh Fraser as third candidate. The rules decreed that if no candidate got an absolute majority on the first ballot, a second ballot should be held. Whitelaw and the others told themselves that if Heath failed to jump this hurdle they could always come into the second ballot. Heath did fail, but more disastrously than expected. Thatcher was first with 130 votes, Heath had 119, and Fraser 16. Just possibly if Whitelaw had stood alone against Thatcher he might still have won, though the figures suggest the contrary. But, having shirked the first ballot, others now also dived in. The result was: Thatcher 146, Whitelaw 79, Howe 19, Prior 19, Peyton 11. The old Tory system of leaders emerging from smoke-filled rooms had condemned itself when it presented the country with Sir Alec Douglas-Home as Prime Minister; it might have redeemed itself by giving the country William Whitelaw. The new system, combined with the obstinacy of Heath and the flabbiness of his former colleagues, gave the country Margaret Thatcher.

### *The Callaghan Government*

Even more astonishing, save for a tiny group in the know, was the announcement by Wilson on 16 March 1976 that he was retiring from office. The parliamentary Labour party needed three ballots, but eventually James Callaghan emerged as victor, the growing strength of the Left in the parliamentary Labour party being indicated by the fact that Callaghan's strongest opponent was Foot, whom in the end he defeated by 176 votes to 137. It was widely surmised that Wilson must know something appalling about Britain's economic prospects. But in fact Wilson, with a self-knowing wisdom he had not always shown, had long planned to retire at the time of his sixtieth birthday; he did not wish to risk being caught in office while entering his dotage. Callaghan had established a decent reputation for himself as Foreign Secretary. If he, wisely, did not do very much with respect to the Turkish invasion of Cyprus, or the fishing dispute (the 'cod war') with Iceland, he did it rather well. Britain's relationship with the United States was warmer than it had been under Heath; and, as we saw, he had secured some concessions over Britain's financial contributions to the EEC. As Prime Minister, Callaghan seemed open and straightforward, where Wilson had often seemed devious. However, discussion of the continuing obsession with maintaining an alleged independent nuclear deterrent was a matter for discussion only by an inner group of the Prime Minister himself, Healey, the Foreign Secretary David Owen, and Fred Mulley, the Defence Secretary. This group approved the exorbitant expenditure on the latest generation of nuclear warheads, Chevaline. The promotion to the Foreign Office of the young, personable, former Under-Secretary was something of a surprise; it certainly further promoted the latter's overweening confidence in his own abilities.

The Callaghan Government persevered with some of the features of the Social Contract, but was mainly preoccupied with inflation and the balance of payments. It became demonstrably less Keynesian, and aimed at ever tighter control over wages. But it did take up the cause of industrial democracy, partly in the interests of social justice, partly because of a belief that Germany's economic successes owed something to the way in which unions there cooperated with management. Though there was still great resistance to the whole concept from within the trade union movement itself, worker participation schemes, on government directions, were introduced into the British Steel Corporation, British Leyland, and Chrysler, and in December 1975, a Committee of Inquiry under the Chairmanship of Lord Bullock was appointed.

The Bullock majority proposed that workers' representation on management should be controlled by the trade unions. The minority argued that representation should be directly from the workforce as a whole, not through the unions.[18] Though worker cooperation in management was something Britain desperately needed, the government produced a cowardly scheme whereby workers would serve only on 'Policy Boards', not 'Management Boards'. The scheme then died, to be buried deep by Thatcher.

The April 1976 budget had its social justice element: both 'Family Income Supplement' (from July) and Pensions (from November) were to be increased. It had its pay restraint element, the rather odd one of tax cuts being offered conditional upon the unions agreeing to a 3 per cent limit on pay increases. In the end, a new agreement was made with the TUC in May 1976, whereby average wage increases were to be kept to 4½ per cent. Inflation was actually being brought down, but as yet this was very far from apparent. The international markets were naturally less trusting of a Labour government than they would have been of a Conservative one. And this government, after a series of disastrous by-election results, and without the support of the minority parties, including the break-away Scottish Labour Party, had no majority. By all the principles which had obtained since 1945 it had an appalling unemployment problem (see table 5.13); and also once more, a rapidly increasing balance of payments deficit (see table 4.2). Sterling was pouring out of London and the pound slid down from over $2.00 to $1.56, a greater loss of value than in the planned devaluation of 1967. The government was under pressure from its own left-wingers. An all-out strike was called by the National Union of Seamen. Bank rate was raised to 15 per cent.[19]

**Table 5.13** Unemployment in the 1970s

| | *Unemployment percentage* |
|---|---|
| 1970 | 2.6 |
| 1971 | 3.5 |
| 1972 | 3.8 |
| 1973 | 2.7 |
| 1974 | 2.6 |
| 1975 | 4.1 |
| 1976 | 5.7 |
| 1977 | 6.2 |
| 1978 | 6.1 |
| 1979 | 5.7 |

*Source:* Arthur Marwick, *British Society since 1945* (Harmondsworth: Penguin, 1996), p. 185.

In July Healey announced massive cuts in public spending for the following year. But there was no alternative to seeking a loan from the IMF. The peak of the crisis lasted between October and December 1976, as the Cabinet held a long series of meetings arguing over the terms on which the IMF was insisting if the necessary loans were to be forthcoming. Already in the previous year Healey had set cash limits on public spending, suggesting a sensitivity to the monetarist argument that the money supply must be controlled; and in July 1976 this was followed up by the government's own declaration that the Borrowing Requirement would be held down to £9 billion a year. The Left saw the crisis as a capitalist one with right-wing Labour leaders complicit in it. In all sections there was a fear of a 1931-style collapse. In fact, Callaghan and Healey, in their negotiations with the IMF, showed great skill and patience: the eventual expenditure cuts of £2 billion were considerably less than the draconian figures put forward at the height of the (somewhat factitious) panic. Overall, public spending estimates for 1977/78 were to be cut by £1 billion, and for 1978/79 by a further £1.5 billion. In return a loan of $3 billion would be made available in three instalments, the first coming early in 1977. Certainly, the government was fully in retreat from its policies of subsidizing industry; and actually moved in the direction of privatization, raising £500 million through the sale of shares in British Petroleum.

All the main indicators now suggested an economy in recovery. The parliamentary situation was a difficult one, but if Labour could only continue to govern with confidence, there was the prize of North Sea oil soon to be grasped. Of course, first, another General Election would have to be faced and won. What in fact happened was the 'Winter of Discontent' of 1978–9, and defeat by the Conservatives in the General Election of 4 May 1979. Callaghan later explained this as being the product of 'a sea change' in public opinion. Was Labour defeat inevitable? Or did Labour once again throw its chances away as it had done at the beginning of the fifties? The greater the challenges of 1976, you could say, the greater the credit to the Labour government for coming through them. But there were other issues, too, still to come to the ultimate crisis point, in particular those relating to Irish, Scottish and Welsh nationalism. There was also the gathering problem that increased welfare benefits (the 'social wage') didn't do much for the well-organized workers on reasonably high wages who, at the same time, found wage restraint particularly irksome. Also, formerly unorganized general workers, including women, were now being efficiently organized through the National Union of Public Employees (NUPE) putting forward claims of their own.

## *NORTHERN IRELAND*

Northern Ireland, in this period of Labour government, went from faint hope to utter hopelessness, the first phase coinciding roughly with the time in office as Irish Secretary of the energetic Merlyn Rees (he moved to the Home Office) and the Fine Gael/Labour government in the Republic under Liam Cosgrave, the second with the tenure at the Irish Office of the dour, security-obsessed ex-miner, Roy Mason, and the return of Fianna Fáil and the uncompromising Jack Lynch. There were a number of appalling IRA atrocities on mainland Britain while in Northern Ireland itself, apart from some brief interludes, there seemed to be nothing but pointless killing. Amidst the display of Protestant triumphalism following the collapse of the Sunningdale Agreement and the power-sharing executive, the violent Ulster Defence Association was formed. Labour now tried to create a Constitutional Convention which, it said, must involve 'some form of power-sharing and partnership because no political system will survive . . . unless there is a widespread acceptance of it within the community'. Still more, the relationship with the Republic must be acknowledged, so that any political arrangements 'must recognise and provide for this special relationship. There is an Irish dimension.'[20] Reintroducing direct rule (temporarily it was hoped), the Northern Ireland Act 1974 set out the arrangements for this Constitutional Convention. Turnout for the elections, held on 1 May 1975, was, at 66 per cent, quite encouraging, save, of course, that some of those most eager to turn out were also those most eager to defend their traditional communal interests. The results were as follows:

**Table 5.14** Northern Ireland Constitutional Convention, election 1 May 1975

| *Party* | *First-preference votes* | *Seats* |
|---|---|---|
| United Ulster Unionist Council (UUC) | 55% | 47 |
| SDLP | 24% | 17 |
| Alliance Party | 10% | 8 |
| Unionist Party of Northern Ireland (led by Brian Faulkner) | 8% | 5 |
| Northern Ireland Labour Party | 1% | 1 |

No sooner had the Convention met than the UUC made it clear that it wanted a return to the situation as established by the Government of Ireland Act 1920; it was opposed to any kind of association or constitutional arrangement with the Republic. The backward-looking obduracy of this position was sharply illuminated by the imaginative responses of the SDLP, which argued that a 'normal political society' could only be arrived at through the 'path of partnership' between both traditions and both parts of Ireland, while accepting that there was a 'British dimension' and that it was the declared wish of a majority in Northern Ireland to remain within the United Kingdom. Most strikingly, with reference to issues of identity and Britishness, the SDLP pointed out to the Unionists that if they wished to be British they had to behave in a British way, following this up, in talks with the UUC leadership on 27 August 1975, with the remark that it was part of the British tradition that the opposition could always expect to become the government; as that was simply not a possibility in Northern Ireland, there had to be power-sharing instead. Only William Craig of the Vanguard Party within the UUC was responsive, arguing that it would now be feasible to form a coalition government in Northern Ireland which would include the SDLP. But, within the UUC, Ian Paisley had a resolution carried against 'Republicans taking part in any future cabinet in Northern Ireland': only Craig voted against, with the result that he and his three supporters in the Convention were thrown out of the UUC. The Convention now endorsed the unyielding UUC position by 42 votes to 31. Having got from square one to square one in fairly rapid order, the British Government dissolved the Convention. There had been a brief Provisional IRA truce in February 1975; in the summer of 1976 Betty Williams and Mairead Corrigan, two women from Catholic Belfast, initiated the 'Peace Movement' which both dramatized the deep longing for peace, and demonstrated that without political initiatives of a completely new sort, there would be no progress. As the army became more uncompromising and as power, including fire-power, drifted back to the RUC and the Ulster Defence Regiment, the Provisional IRA became ever more provocative, and ordinary Catholics ever more resentful. No credit accrued to the Callaghan Government, and Labour's general credibility with the electorate was not enhanced by the way in which some of its left-wingers vociferously identified themselves with the Republican cause and even the Provisional IRA.

### *THE END OF THE CALLAGHAN GOVERNMENT*

Constitutional reform (introducing proportional representation, abolishing the House of Lords, creating a Scottish Parliament) always in the end seems more trouble than it's worth. Plans for Scotland and Wales were announced by the Wilson Government in *Changing Democracy: Devolution in Scotland and Wales* (November 1975). Getting the legislation through was left to the Callaghan administration, and a messy business it proved. Mordantly analysing the Scottish provisions of the White Paper, Christopher Harvie describes it as 'essentially a Whitehall creation' showing 'a successful resistance by ministers and civil servants to the concession of any significant degree of autonomy' to the proposed Scottish Assembly.

> The Secretary of State still retained substantial powers: over agriculture, fisheries, most of law and order, electricity, large areas of economic policy. He stayed in the Cabinet, but also had quasi-Viceregal powers *vis-à-vis* the 142-seat Assembly. He would appoint its Executive and adjudicate on whether its enactments were within its 'vires' or not. Scotland would continue to send 71 MPs to Westminster.[21]

The Assembly had no revenue-raising powers. The Welsh Assembly would be an even more modest institution. As Kenneth Morgan puts it: 'Its powers would be confined largely to the executive aspects of social policy, with a block grant of £850 million provided by the Treasury for expenditure on local administration.'[22] The Scotland and Wales Bill was tabled by Michael Foot on 13 December 1976; when in February 1977 its progress came to a complete halt during the committee stage, the Nationalists no longer had any reason to support the government. Thus Callaghan looked towards the Liberals. Jeremy Thorpe had come to a sad end in a trial – for attempted murder, no less (he was acquitted) – in which the principal witness and alleged victim was a former gay lover. His successor, David Steel, of Abortion Law fame and a genuine progressive, was sympathetic towards Callaghan's moderate policies, and, above all, had no wish to see his party face an immediate General Election. Hence the 'Lib–Lab Pact' whereby, in effect, the Liberals kept the government in office and the government avoided all contentious legislation, save for the reintroduction of the devolution proposals, which the Liberals supported, this time in the form of two separate Bills, one for each country. It was during the parliamentary debates on the new proposals that George Cunningham, a Scot, but MP for Islington in London, succeeded in introducing the clause which declared that in the referendum to be held in Scotland once the Bill was passed, 40 per cent of the total Scottish electorate, not just a simple majority of those voting, must support devolution for it to come into effect. The gloom lightened: in a by-election in May 1978 Labour actually won back the Hamilton seat; and by the summer, even the opinion polls were beginning to look almost favourable. Wise men then and since have said that Callaghan should have called an election for the autumn of that year. Had he done so, there is a possibility that Labour might have won; there is a certainty that Labour would not have lost as heavily as it did in May 1979. Callaghan had his agreement with the Liberals, and had the Scottish and Welsh referendums coming up on 1 March 1979; he really wasn't doing at all badly. If the Conservative lead in the polls was disappearing might not Labour build up a substantial one of its own as the months passed? But then the roof fell in.

The government had become too complacent over its incomes policies, and too ambitious. In July 1978 it announced its intention of limiting pay settlements to 5 per cent. At the Labour Party Conference in September, the pay limit was rejected and support given to NUPE (National Union of Public Employees) in its campaign for a national minimum wage of £60 per week. In the same month Ford workers embarked on a nine-week strike, which ended in their winning a 17 per cent pay rise. Soon after, the Transport and General Workers Union (TGWU) claimed a 22 per cent rise on behalf of the road haulage drivers, turning down an offer of 13 per cent. Early in January 1979 the drivers came out on strike, marking what is usually taken as the beginning of the Winter of Discontent. There followed a day of action on 22 January when 1.5 million public service workers came out on strike, as a prelude to the series of selective strikes, which had the much publicized results of denying children school meals, of rubbish piling up in festering mounds, and, in Lancashire, of the dead not being buried; all this amid the snows of a particularly cold winter.

After years of high inflation there was genuine desperation among many workers; there was pride among the low-paid (very many of them women) that at last they were taking positive action. But there was also, as a TGWU official in South Wales put it, 'not bloody mindedness' but 'bloody mindlessness'. The number of working days lost was higher than that of 1926, the year of the General Strike, though day-to-day conditions were not nearly as bad as those in 1974. However, in the invented stories of the right-wing press it sounded bad, on television it looked bad, and for millions of discomfited citizens it felt bad. The phrase 'Winter of Discontent', apparently first used by Peter Jenkins in the *Guardian*, probably had an unusually high recognition factor among the British public because of the virtuoso performance by Laurence Olivier in the fifties film *Richard III*, and particularly the distilled venom in the rendering of the opening words 'Now is the winter of our discontent . . . '. It was a phrase which could readily be used against Labour for years to come. Another phrase was held particularly against Callaghan. Returning on 10 January 1979 from a meeting of European leaders in the French West Indies, Callaghan, looking relaxed and sun-tanned, was pressed by reporters on the industrial chaos. What Callaghan said was: 'I don't think that other people in the world would share the view that there is mounting chaos.' This, for journalistic purposes, was turned into: 'Crisis – what crisis?'[23]

The day of the referendums, 1 March 1979, arrived. In Scotland, the turnout was 63.63 per cent. Of those voting, 51.6 per cent supported devolution, 48.4 opposed it; the 40 per cent hurdle had not been jumped. In Wales devolution was overwhelmingly defeated, 46.5 per cent of the electorate being against, to only 11.8 per cent for. The Scottish Nationalist members at Westminster were angry. They refused the all-party talks which Callaghan proposed. On 28 March they tabled a motion of no confidence in the government's handling of the industrial situation. The Celtic fringe struck with a vengeance – Gerry Fitt of the SDLP (Social Democratic and Labour Party), angry about a proposal to increase the number of MPs returned from Northern Ireland (which would have favoured the Unionists), broke with his usual habit and voted against the government. One Labour MP was too ill to vote. The government fell by 311 votes to 310.

Throughout the election, opinion polls gave Callaghan a higher personal rating than Thatcher, again a hint that in better circumstances all might not have been lost for him. The Conservatives, promising to cut taxes, reduce the role of government, and, above all, to introduce legislation to curb the power of the unions, spent £2.3 million as compared with Labour's £1.6 million, on a well-produced campaign. The PR firm Saatchi & Saatchi stole the show with a poster presenting an endless queue of unemployed, captioned with: 'Labour isn't working'. Thatcher was persuaded to change her image, and lower her voice. The *Sun* newspaper waged the first of its powerful and persuasive campaigns against Labour.

**Table 5.15** General Election, 3 May 1979

| | *Electorate 41 million* | | | *Turnout 76 per cent* | | | |
|---|---|---|---|---|---|---|---|
| | *Conservative* | *Labour* | *Liberal* | *Scottish Nationalist* | *Plaid Cymru* | *Ulster Unionist* | *Others* |
| Total votes cast | 13,697,690 | 11,523,148 | 4,313,811 | 504,529 | 132,544 | 410,419 | 630,107 |
| Percentage of votes cast | 43.9 | 36.9 | 13.8 | 1.6 | 0.4 | 1.3 | 2.0 |
| Seats | 339 | 269 | 11 | 2 | 2 | 10 | 2 |

Working-class voters who were, or who wanted to be, upwardly mobile, had switched to Thatcher's Conservatives. Losing nine seats, the Scottish Nationalists had done themselves no good at all.

Evidence for the sea-change theory is most strongly represented in the deficit in the Labour popular vote compared with that of the Conservatives: at over two million it was the biggest such deficit since that between victorious Labour in 1945 and defeated Conservative. Leaving aside the question of the timing of the election, it was clear that Labour's total image simply did not appeal to large numbers of ordinary voters. Unfortunately, practically everything the party did thereafter further reduced its credit. Crucially, Foot, not Healey, succeeded Callaghan. All that said, some of the early policies of the new government were so unpopular that for several years it was perfectly reasonable to believe that Thatcher herself might not last the full term, and the Conservative Government beyond it.

### *THATCHER IN POWER*

Whether, after her election to the leadership, Margaret Thatcher continued to believe that a party must represent a broad range of views seems unlikely, but it was simply not possible for her to exclude major figures whose views still leaned towards consensus politics. When Thatcher formed her first government the introduction of the new economic policy was to be led by Sir Geoffrey Howe, appointed Chancellor of the Exchequer, with John Biffen, who had derived his form of Thatcherism from Enoch Powell, as Chief Secretary. Joseph became Industry Minister, while the despised Prices and Consumer Protection function was joined to Trade, this ministry being headed by a convinced monetarist, John Nott. Howell was Minister for Energy, outside of the Cabinet. An older post, carrying no specific responsibilities, Paymaster General, was re-established and allocated to Angus Maude, who had been speaking up for radical-right dogma long before it became fashionable to do so. Whitelaw (Home Secretary) was undoubtedly in the older tradition, yet had shown himself eager to identify with Thatcher. More detached as upholders of that tradition were Lord Carrington (Foreign Secretary), Francis Pym (Defence), Prior (Employment), Sir Ian Gilmore (Lord Privy Seal with responsibility for foreign affairs), Peter Walker (Agriculture) and Michael Heseltine (Environment).

The Thatcherite agenda was first and foremost an economic one, a shopkeeping one, a housekeeping one. Anyone who did not take it seriously was due for enlightenment within three weeks of the new government taking office, when Howe introduced his budget of 14 June. In the name of improving the supply side, income tax was cut to 30 per cent, where it had been between 1970 and 1974 (the highest rate was reduced from 80p to 60p with corresponding cuts in other rates of surtax), the short-fall being made up through a swingeing increase in VAT, a universal rise from 8 per cent and 12½ per cent to 15 per cent. Big cuts in public spending were announced, and the monetarism sketched by Healey was formalized in a commitment to control the borrowing requirement at £8 billion a year. This was part of the 'medium-term financial strategy': target figures were set for 'the money supply', 'M3'. As a further counter-inflationary measure, pensions were no longer to be kept in line with changes in standards of living, but merely with price increases. There was, compared with Healey's initiative, a more significant sale of government petroleum assets. Altogether, the overwhelming thrust of economic policy was towards defeating inflation, with maintenance of employment no longer a primary objective. Controlling money supply was not in practice as easy as textbook theory might suggest – apart from anything else, there were various ways in which money could creep in from outside. Thus, in abolishing exchange controls, the government shot its monetarist policy in the foot. In a more traditional move to make money scarce, minimum lending rate was set in the budget at 14 per cent: unprecedentedly, this was shortly pushed up above 16 per cent.

**Table 5.16** Minimum lending rates

| | |
|---|---|
| 1979 | 13.7 |
| 1980 | 16.3 |
| 1981 | 13.3 |
| 1982 | 11.9 |
| 1983 | 9.8 |
| 1984 | 9.7 |
| 1985 | 12.2 |
| 1986 | 10.9 |
| 1987 | 9.7 |
| 1988 | 10.1 |
| 1989 | 13.9 |

*Source:* C. Johnson, *The Economy Under Mrs Thatcher 1979–1990* (Harmondsworth: Penguin, 1991), p. 279.

**Table 5.17** Unemployment, percentages – OECD standard basis

| | *UK* | *US* | *Japan* | *Germany* | *France* | *Italy* | *EEC* |
|---|---|---|---|---|---|---|---|
| 1980 | 6.4 | 7.0 | 2.0 | 3.0 | 6.3 | 7.5 | 6.4 |
| 1981 | 9.8 | 7.5 | 2.2 | 4.4 | 7.4 | 7.8 | 8.2 |
| 1982 | 11.3 | 9.5 | 2.4 | 6.1 | 8.1 | 8.4 | 9.5 |
| 1983 | 12.4 | 9.5 | 2.6 | 8.0 | 8.3 | 8.8 | 10.4 |
| 1984 | 11.7 | 7.4 | 2.7 | 7.1 | 9.7 | 9.4 | 10.7 |
| 1985 | 11.2 | 7.1 | 2.6 | 7.2 | 10.2 | 9.6 | 10.8 |
| 1986 | 11.2 | 6.9 | 2.8 | 6.4 | 10.4 | 10.5 | 10.8 |
| 1987 | 10.3 | 6.1 | 2.8 | 6.2 | 10.5 | 10 9 | 10.5 |
| 1988 | 8.5 | 5.4 | 2.5 | 6.2 | 10.0 | 11.0 | 9.8 |
| 1989 | 6.9 | 5.2 | 2.3 | 5.5 | 9.6 | 10.9 | 8.9 |
| Mean | 10.0 | 7.2 | 2.5 | 6.0 | 9.1 | 9.5 | 9.6 |

*Source:* C. Johnson, *The Economy Under Mrs Thatcher 1979–1990* (Harmondsworth: Penguin, 1991), p. 315.

**Table 5.18** Monetary targets and out-turns, 1979–1987 – percentage annual rate of increase of M3

| | *Target* | *Out-turn* |
|---|---|---|
| 1979–80 | 7–11 | 12 |
| 1980–1 | 7–11 | 19 |
| 1981–2 | 6–10 | 13 |
| 1982–3 | 8–12 | 11 |
| 1983–4 | 7–11 | 10 |
| 1984–5 | 6–10 | 13.5 |
| 1985–6 | 5–9 | 15.3 |
| 1986–7 | 11–15 | 20 |

*Source:* S. Pollard, *The Development of the British Economy 1914–1990* (Aldershot: Edward Arnold, 1992), p. 384.

**Table 5.19** PSBR: targets and out-turns, 1979–1988

| | *Target, percentage GDP* | *Out-turn, percentage GDP* |
|---|---|---|
| 1979–80 | | 4.75 |
| 1980–1 | 3.75 | 5.25 |
| 1981–2 | 4.25 | 3.25 |
| 1982–3 | 3.50 | 3.25 |
| 1983–4 | 3.25 | 3.25 |
| 1984–5 | 2.5 | 3.0 |
| 1985–6 | 2.25 | 1.50 |
| 1986–7 | | 1.0 |
| 1987–8 | | –0.75 |
| 1988–9 | | –0.75 |

*Source:* S. Pollard, *The Development of the British Economy 1914–1990* (Aldershot: Edward Arnold, 1992), p. 385.

Unluckily for its anti-inflation agenda, the government had inherited the Clegg Commission report on public sector pay, and felt it had to implement the quite substantial awards recommended there. Once-bitten, the government thereafter set out to maintain draconian controls on public sector pay. The second great rise in oil prices pushed the world into recession, with serious consequences for British manufacturing, though with benefits to the balance of payments as North Sea oil began to flow copiously. The combination of international recession and Thatcherite policies took a devastating toll of British industry, reflected in the substantial rise in unemployment (table 5.17), and the contraction in GDP (table 5.5), even while European countries continued to expand. A bitter and violent strike in the steel industry failed to stop closures and job losses (the government, however, for the time being avoided any confrontation with the miners). The West Midlands joined with Scotland, the North and Wales as areas in which manufacturing industry was drastically shrinking, the queues for unemployment benefit lengthening. The March 1980 budget recognized both a drop of 2 per cent in real national income and rising unemployment, which, in turn, entailed rising government expenditure on social security benefits, one of the very things the government was supposed to be controlling.

During the public-spending round in the autumn of 1980 the non-Thatcherite ministers argued for the maintenance of public expenditure and investment, while at the party conference Thatcher declared: 'U-turn if you want . . . the lady's not for turning' (the reference to the post-war Christopher Fry play *The Lady's Not For Burning* being provided by her highly literate scriptwriter Ronald Millar). 'Wet' minister Francis Pym was replaced at Defence by 'dry' John Nott (the epithets were Thatcher's, signifying, respectively, wishy-washy liberal, and tough monetarist). The budget of March 1981 was savage. It was a key moment in the rise of Thatcherism. It, and the developments which followed, marked the establishment of her full control over her government; at the same time, in revealing a government of apparently unheeding extremism and no compassion, it suggested to most observers a government which could not survive the next election, if meantime it managed to survive internal revolt. The non-Thatcherite ministers had been successful in warding off the heavy cuts proposed in the autumn round. Professor Alan Walters, now acting as a personal adviser to the Prime Minister, insisted that there must be no slackening in the 'reform' policies, stressing the need to maintain the confidence of world financial markets: the Public Sector Borrowing Requirement (PSBR) must be reduced by £4,000 million, with substantial rises in taxes (particularly in direct taxes) to take yet more money out of circulation. The rebels of the autumn were aghast, and even Howe resisted. Then, rather than lose his job, Howe proposed cuts of £3,500 million, recognizing that these would further reduce output by one per cent and cause unemployment to rise above three million until at least the next General Election. He also proposed substantial tax increases: apart from indirect taxes, personal allowances would be left unadjusted despite inflation. This was the most deflationary budget in modern history, aiming further blows at British industry. Prior and Gilmour contemplated resigning, but then joined with the others in going along with the budget. Thatcher publicly attacked her own colleagues saying that having failed to support proposed savings in the autumn they now had to accept the consequential tax rises.[24] With Gross Domestic Product dropping by 6¼ per cent and unemployment indeed rising remorselessly above three million, reaching its highest-ever figure of 3,190,621 at the end of 1982 (*Conservatism* certainly wasn't working), the country was undergoing the worst recession of the twentieth century.

With recession came a horrific new kind of urban rioting, first appearing in April 1981. The location was Brixton in south London, over the long weekend 9–13 April. Seventy-six shops and homes were seriously damaged, as well as many police and private motor-vehicles; 143 policemen were taken to hospital, one seriously ill with a fractured skull; at least 30 civilians were treated in hospital; 199 people were arrested. The government immediately announced that a public inquiry would be undertaken by Lord Scarman. A week later, on 20 April, there was another riot in London, this time at Finsbury Park in the north-east: 32 members of the public were injured, 60 police, and there were 91 arrests. The Scarman Inquiry was still sitting when, on Saturday, 4 July, there was a violent confrontation between skinheads and Asians in Southall, west London, fought with bricks and then petrol bombs. That same day in Toxteth, central Liverpool, there were clashes between police and young blacks, who complained of police harassment; white youths, suffering all the frustrations of unemployment, were also involved. On 6 July, *The Times* reported:

> For the second successive night the Toxteth district of Liverpool became a battlefield last night as mobs of young rioters fought police. Buildings blazed as the rioters, some little more than children, attacked police lines with barrages of missiles, driving hijacked milk-floats and a concrete-mixer into their midst.

Rioting continued over several weeks. The police took heavy punishment, but were themselves accused of brutality, particularly in the use of vehicles to charge rioters: one 22-year-old white man, disabled since childhood, was run down and killed. A week after the beginning of the Southall and Toxteth rioting, there was a further outbreak in Brixton, and also in Moss Side, Manchester, as well as in Bristol, Leicester and Wood Green in north London. In the press and on television, the images of burned-out streets and of police dressed in riot gear, aggressively wielding their truncheons, were stark ones. Published in December, the Scarman Report indicated the extent to which insensitivity and, indeed, provocation on the part of the police had contributed to riots, which, however, were largely borne out of frustration in an economic recession that weighed most heavily on black youth. In the spread of the riots there was a copycat element; there was also an element of premeditation – both reacting with a volatile mix of unemployment, frustration and over-intensive policing.

The publication of the Report was the perfect background for Howe to tell the Cabinet, on 23 July, the last meeting before the summer recess, that he was proposing cuts of £5,000 million in next year's spending. There was almost universal opposition. Heseltine referred to the rioting in the cities, Biffen and Nott defected from the monetarist side, upheld only by Joseph and Brittan, apart of course from Howe and Thatcher. Thatcher used the summer to plan the removal of her opponents. In August it became known to Prior that he was to be moved to the Northern Ireland Office: at first he intended to resist, but then, being a man of decency and honour, he felt he couldn't refuse. The announcements were made on 14 September: Gilmour, Lord Soames, who had performed respectably in handling both a civil service strike and another of the several African crises (over Zimbabwe), and Mark Carlisle, the Education Secretary, were all sacked; hard man Norman Tebbit replaced Prior as Employment Secretary, Lawson took Energy, Nicholas Ridley, driest of drys, became Financial Secretary to the Treasury, and Cecil Parkinson replaced Thorneycroft as Party Chairman. He was the sort of good-looking young man Thatcher liked;

similar considerations may have played a part in saving the posts of both Heseltine and Walker. In terminology coined by Thatcher herself, some of the worst 'wets' were out, the government now strongly 'dry' in composition.

Meantime, a still more damaging split had opened in the Labour party. Labour's standing in the Callaghan years had been weakened by the departure of Roy Jenkins, disillusioned both by what he saw as the incipient corporatism of Wilson and Callaghan, and by the antics of the Left, to become President of the European Commission. In his Dimbleby Lecture in 1979 he put forward the idea of a new political movement between the extremes of Labour and Conservative. In 1980 three members of the previous Labour Cabinet, David Owen, Shirley Williams and William Rodgers, emerged as strong opponents of Labour's leftward shift, seen particularly in policies of unilateralism and withdrawal from the European Community. They took up the cry of 'one member, one vote' as against trade union domination of conference decisions, a policy which the Left defeated at a special conference at Wembley in January 1981, the exact month in which Jenkins returned from his European job. From David Owen's posh house in east London, there was issued the 'Limehouse Declaration', which foreshadowed the formation of a new party which would 'break the mould' of British politics, that is to say replace the allegedly destructive, though also often sham, conflict between the two major parties that monopolized power. Jenkins had joined with the other three to form 'the gang of four' – an ironic echo from Chinese totalitarian politics – and in March the new party, the Social Democrats, was launched.[25] Twenty-nine Labour MPs, and one Conservative, joined the new party. With both Conservatives and Labour displaying the ultimate in extremism, the SDP had a series of stunning by-election successes. At Crosby in Liverpool, in November 1981, Shirley Williams converted a Conservative majority of 19,000 into an SDP majority of 5,000. A humbler party member then won the Conservative seat of Croydon in south London before, in March 1982, Jenkins won Glasgow Hillhead from Labour. In early 1983 the SDP formed the Alliance with the Liberals. Opinion polls put the SDP in the lead, with the Conservatives struggling to avoid third place.

In implementing its promises on trade union legislation the government did have considerable popular support, but then it also, in the main, had the support of the Alliance parties. Prior had been responsible for the first 'Employment Act' of 1980: secondary picketing was outlawed, and ballots on strike action, funded by public money, were made compulsory. Tebbit's Act of 1982 was much more drastic in that it opened the unions to severe financial penalties, for, in particular, financial loss caused by strikes; there were to be heavier penalties for secondary picketing, and compensation was to be provided to those dismissed as a result of closed-shop agreements (that all workers must belong to a union). The TUC 'day of action' against this legislation in 1982 was a flop. As the world recession began to ease in 1983, so the basic economic indicators began to improve. However, many influential Conservatives still felt the policies of the Thatcher Government not only to be electorally disastrous, but to be utterly wrong in both practical and moral terms. There was every reason to believe that there was a solid political basis upon which older policies of managing the economy so as to maintain employment, of acknowledging full state responsibility for looking after those unable to look after themselves, and of fostering the unity of the nation, would be re-established, perhaps in a Conservative government without Thatcher perhaps, after a General Election, in a government in which the new Alliance would play a crucial role. Despite the defects of Michael Foot as a national leader, Labour looked secure in its traditional strongholds and appeared to be regaining some of the ground lost at the General Election.

But, as has been repeatedly emphasized in this book, events in themselves can often have important consequences. The news of the Argentine occupation of the Falkland Islands (2 April 1982), if anything, further lowered the standing of the government, which, through its own defence cuts, had gravely weakened its ability to defend such remote outposts, and indeed had seemed to imply that it had no will to defend them: it failed to give a contrary signal to Argentina whose ambitions in the area were long-standing. Most honourably, the Foreign Secretary, Lord Carrington, resigned – incidentally removing another respected non-Thatcherite from the Cabinet. But Thatcher, at her best in a crisis of this sort, acted with great decisiveness in mustering and despatching a military task-force. While there were very proper doubts about the government's own responsibility for this situation, and about the appropriateness in the late twentieth century of resort to military solutions, it was virtually impossible for the Opposition to mount an effective critique, particularly once the lives of British servicemen were at stake; Argentina had violated international law, was denying basic rights to the Falkland Islanders, and was ruled by a particularly vicious military dictatorship.

National pride, loyalty to the community, and its symbols and surrogates (songs, flags, football teams, etc.), remain a potent force (too often mistaken for, and therefore written off as, something slightly different – imperialism). On 14 June, after feats of great heroism and military skill, the British forces secured the surrender of the occupying Argentine force.[26] In the intervening months the government had commanded the political stage. In May it jumped into the lead in the opinion polls with a figure of 50 per cent. In the succeeding weeks all major ships, including the main troop-carrier, *Canberra*, returned to home base, to scenes of great patriotic jubilation and pride. Thereafter, the government continued to have a commanding lead in the opinion polls. The breakthrough had been made: not the Conservative party, but the Thatcher Conservative Government was in the ascendant; many, probably a majority in the electorate, remained opposed to much of her philosophy, but she not only offered, but was now palpably perceived to be offering, a toughness and leadership that could not be matched anywhere else in the political spectrum – save perhaps by Healey, but he still stood second to Foot.

Then, with almost a year of her mandate still to run, Thatcher decided to cash in on what were beginning to look like very favourable circumstances: she now had an air of authority, the demeanour of an established and confident leader. The Opposition was divided between Labour and Alliance; many electors shrank from Labour's association with left-wing policies and high taxation; Michael Foot hardly seemed credible as a possible Prime Minister. He addressed enthusiastic meetings of the party faithful, still seemingly blissfully unaware that to win an election he had to appeal to a majority of the people, not just a majority of Labour people. The Labour election manifesto reflected the policies adopted at left-dominated party conferences; party moderate, Gerald Kaufman, was apparently responsible for describing it as the 'longest suicide note in history'.

**Table 5.20** General Election, 9 June 1983

| | *Electorate 42.2 million* | | *Turnout 72.7 per cent* | | | |
|---|---|---|---|---|---|---|
| | *Conservative* | *Labour* | *Alliance* | *Scottish Nationalist* | *Plaid Cymru* | *Northern Ireland* |
| Total votes cast | 13,012,315 | 8,456,934 | 7,780,949 | 331,975 | 125,309 | 764,925 |
| Percentage of votes cast | 42.4 | 27.6 | 25.4 | 1.1 | 0.4 | 3.1 |
| Seats | 397 | 209 | Liberal 17<br>SDP 6 | 2 | 2 | 17 |

The first things to note are the drop in turnout and the fall in both the votes cast for the Conservatives (by nearly 700,000) and the Conservative share of the total vote (by 1.5 per cent). The next things to notice are the collapse in Labour support (by over three million votes), and the closeness between the Labour vote and that of the Alliance. If the Conservatives were not loved, Labour was not trusted. If there was no majority for the Conservatives in the country, there certainly wasn't one for socialism. It could not be concluded that the SDP split in itself had denied Labour votes; rather that there needed to be a genuine centre-left association between Labour and the Alliance, or that Labour itself would have to assume Alliance policies. No chance, of course. Too much of the Labour party was still under the sway of the fallacies of Marxism – and those who might have fought this had gone to the SDLP, or felt themselves totally powerless as the Left increased its grip on the constituencies. The Alliance, of course, in terms of seats, won only a miserable travesty of its popular vote. Under the current system, a third party would always have the greatest difficulty, not just in breaking the mould, but in breaking into Westminster politics. That again suggested that what was really needed, if Thatcherism were to be defeated, was a reformed Labour party.

Foot resigned immediately. It can be conjectured that he could have done his party an immense service by resigning before the election, and letting Healey, the one Labour politician the Conservatives truly feared, take over. Healey showed his desire to be free of party in-fighting, and to be free to concentrate on one of his true interests: he did not stand for the leadership, but remained Shadow Foreign Secretary. There were no commanding figures. A group of trade union leaders gave their support, and two-thirds of Labour's electoral college their votes, to youth, and soft-left enthusiasm, in the shape of 41-year-old Welshman Neil Kinnock. Kinnock's main defeated opponent, Roy Hattersley, on the right of the party, was then elected Deputy. In a momentary return of optimism this was referred to as the 'dream ticket'. But it was a dream ticket only with reference to a fatally divided Labour party (as commentators were wont to point out, the different factions hated each other more than they hated the Conservative enemy). Both Kinnock and Hattersley had considerable personal qualities. But physical attributes, genetic inheritance, aura, these count for more in all aspects of life than fashionable theories about the cultural construction of reality allow. Just as Foot and Benn, with their posh accents, seemed to speak for the sectarian faithful, rather than the nation as a whole, so also did Kinnock with his working-class Welsh accent. Like William Hague later, Kinnock scarcely projected youthfulness and hope of a break with the past, but seemed rather an ageing schoolboy debater; as with Hague, he had a voice which many found extremely irritating. Hattersley just *seemed* a bumbler. Francis Pym had suggested during the election that it might not be a good thing if Thatcher won too big a majority. He was now sacked from the government as a number of younger Thatcherites moved forward. Howe moved to the Foreign Office to make way for Lawson as Chancellor of the Exchequer. Brittan became Home Secretary. Parkinson became Trade and Industry Secretary, but had to resign when his jilted mistress, whom he had treated shamefully, put the spotlight on him. Tebbit took over.

### *THE MINERS' STRIKE AND RISING LEVELS OF VIOLENCE*

The occasional violence of the seventies, repeated in stronger form during the 1980 steel workers' strike, manifested itself in a more concentrated form than ever before: first in a relatively small strike in 1983, then in the epic miners' strike of 1984 to 1985. Consider this report of happenings on 29 November 1983 at the Stockport plant of a provincial proprietor and enthusiastic proponent of the new information technology, Eddie Shah, and note both the invocation of Northern Ireland and the reference to one of the special police groups – in this case the Tactical Aid Group, Manchester's equivalent of London's Special Patrol Squad:

> The Tactical Aid Group were finally sent in, and cut through the crowd with their batons flailing. Soon the road round the back of the plant looked like an Ulster riot – with burning barricades, felled telegraph poles and groups of riot police with clubs chasing after pickets. There were excesses on both sides.[27]

The National Graphical Association (NGA) was battling to maintain its closed shop in the Shah Group. It had steadily increased its picketing throughout the autumn, and members of other unions, including in particular Scottish miners, had become involved. But 'most of the pickets were stunned by the efficiency and ruthlessness of the police-clearing operation and started to hurry away'. An ominous wind was blowing: the police had also called in Police Support Units (thirty men, three sergeants and an inspector); more, they had blocked off exits on the M62 motorway to prevent pickets reaching the plant.

In the coal industry there was declining demand, competition from oil, nuclear energy, and cheap coal imports. The broad implications had not been contested by Joe Gormley, President of the National Union of Mineworkers until 1982, who had accepted a carefully paced contraction, with good redundancy terms and high wages for remaining miners. The incoming Conservative Government of 1979 sought a drastic reduction of production and accelerated closures, with a view to making the coal industry self-supporting by 1983–4. Gormley threatened to ballot all mineworkers in the certainty of securing support for an all-out strike; the government, in February 1981, backed down.[28] Gormley had to retire the following year, and was succeeded by Arthur Scargill.

The appointment of Ian MacGregor to the Chairmanship of the Coal Board in September 1983 was an earnest indication that cost-effectiveness and the right to manage were to be the cornerstones of government and Coal Board attitudes; if, from the miners' side, there was a capitalist enemy, MacGregor perfectly embodied it. The preparations of Scargill and his closest associates (though no one was very close) aimed at instigating a strike. The preparations of the government were more open-ended but much more effective: the buying-in of extra coal stocks for the power stations was actually seen by Scargill as a concession to the miners' power – thus do the purveyors of crazy theory and wild rhetoric delude themselves – when, of course, it was designed to ensure that even if there were a strike there would be no power cuts. That the strike would be long, and that it would be bitter and violent, was made certain by the government's determination to make a very public show of not intervening in any way, leaving the Coal Board, and of course the police, to fight it out with the miners.[29]

Since becoming miners' President, Scargill had already called for industrial action on the issues of wages and pit closures, but in October 1982 he was defeated in a national ballot. Throughout 1983, however, there were a number of industrial disputes in different coal-mining areas. In November 1983 a special conference was called to impose an overtime ban. The most fateful development, however, had come in March 1983 when Scargill indicated that (since he was unlikely to get a majority under union rule 43, which required first a national ballot and then a majority of 55 per cent in favour of a strike) he might make use of rule 41, under which the different mining areas could call out their own men on strike, as their own area rules dictated. Such a proposal was put to the union executive on 4 March, but the moderates insisted that there should be a ballot of the membership, and this resulted in Scargill's second defeat, 61 per cent of the membership voting against strike action. On 1 March 1984 the Director of the South Yorkshire area, on instructions from the Coal Board head office, announced that Corton Wood colliery was to be closed, despite the fact that not long before, miners had been assured that it would be kept open for another five years. The Coal Board and its local director had made an unutterable blunder, which Energy Secretary Peter Walker, despite his best efforts, was unable to recoup. Not surprisingly, the Yorkshire area went on strike from 9 March. Meantime, Scargill, very properly, had insisted on a meeting with the Board, held on 6 March, to discuss exactly what was intended in the way of closures – Scargill spoke dramatically, but not altogether unjustifiably, of MacGregor's 'hit list'. It appeared from the meeting that the Board were planning the closure of twenty pits. Scotland immediately joined Yorkshire in deciding to go on strike. The national executive now crushed any attempt at having a national ballot, and gave advance approval to any other areas that decided on strike action. When a further call was made for a national ballot at the executive meeting on 12 April, Scargill ruled it out of order on the grounds that a decision had already been made on 8 March. The 'rolling' national strike was already well under way, that is to say a strike in which areas came in without necessarily balloting their own members and without, of course, any national ballot.

Immediately the strike started in Yorkshire, pickets streamed down into the Nottinghamshire coalfield, where, as a ballot subsequently showed, majority opinion was against the strike. The police went quickly into action in a manner quite alien to the traditions of British policing, the establishment of a National Reporting Centre at Scotland Yard being a large step towards the establishment of a nationally coordinated police force. Unprecedented methods were adopted to prevent pickets travelling to Nottinghamshire, where at such pits as Harworth, Ollerton, Thoresby and Welbeck, the first stone throwing, barricade building and damaging of cars was taking place. On 14 March a 24-year-old Yorkshire picket, David Jones, was crushed to death in a mêlée between local people and the pickets. The first phase came to a kind of culminating point when, on 2 May, a record total of 8,000 pickets turned out at Harworth.

Phase two was dominated by the mass picketing at the Orgreave coking plant on the outskirts of Sheffield, a supplier of coke to the big steel plant at Scunthorpe. Scargill's attitude towards other unions was a mixture of contempt for the official leadership of the TUC and of several other unions, an assumption that other unions ought unquestioningly to support the miners, and a supreme faith in the potency of the miners' own picketing. There was supposed to be a triple alliance involving the steel workers (whom the miners had supported in 1980) and the railwaymen. Action on the part of the steel workers was constrained by the slimming down process in their own industry, the fear that the Ravenscraig complex had received only a temporary reprieve in 1982, and the insurmountable fact that blast furnaces not kept in commission would be permanently damaged. More support was forthcoming from the railwaymen, but British Rail craftily avoided any victimization of rail men who refused to move coal or steel, and thus kept their own system in almost full operation. Tension was very high at Ravenscraig early in May when convoys of lorries were bringing in the coal necessary to ensure the safety and survival of the works. The words of local union spokesman Tom Brennan (*The Times*, 3 May 1984) speak worlds for both the class solidarity that genuinely existed, and the intolerable strains that were being put upon it:

> Today we have failed to impress upon the miners our need for the extra coal. It is a very sad and daunting position that faces us now because we do not want to go outside the fraternity of the trade union movement.

However, it was Orgreave that established the images, relayed on television, indelibly associated with the coal strike. Controversially, police were for the first time wearing riot gear; even more open to criticism was the way in which mounted police were deployed. At times, however, the police were under enormous provocation. The worst abuse on the police side was the repeated indiscriminate use of truncheoning, a particularly horrific example being caught by ITN cameraman Frank Harding; Harding, however, was clear that when the four mounted police were sent in to charge the crowd, police had undergone a long spell of stone throwing, protected only by one long line of riot shields. The first convoys at Orgreave began on 23 May, with the real violence starting on 29 May, just when secret talks were due to take place between the mine workers' leaders and the National Coal Board. Police claimed that the new level of violence was connected with the arrival of Scargill himself.

A *Times* report (30 May) noted that the two hundred full-time coke workers at the Orgreave plant had tried unsuccessfully to persuade the lorry drivers and contract loaders not to move the coke. Sixty-four people were injured and 84 people arrested. Next day Scargill was arrested, together with 35 others; 16 were injured, most of them policemen. When the miners dispersed, police said they left behind 'barricades, a telegraph-pole "battering-ram", barbed wire, a burning Portakabin and a wire stretched across the road intended to bring down police horses'.[30] Among missiles the police said had been found were '2 lb hammer, an 18" cast iron pipe, a steel coach-bolt and steel nuts with nails'. Some police officers regretted the police violence, many protested that the police were being left to do the government's and the Coal Board's work. Some miners showed obvious disgust at the violence on their own side. The government never condemned police violence, as Scargill never condemned the pickets' violence. When asked to do so, he repeatedly produced the irrationally glib response (which alienated much potential support), 'I have always condemned police violence.' The final mass picket, 10,000 strong, came on 18 June. The coke had run out, but Scunthorpe was being supplied from elsewhere in any case; the miners had achieved nothing.

The third phase began quietly in the coalfields, then the violence of Orgreave transferred itself there in the autumn, as more and more men tried to go back to work. Briefly in July, when the dock workers had a dispute of their own over the Dock Labour Scheme, but were also sympathetic to the miners, it looked as though a kind of working-class solidarity was putting real pressure on the government: for a time workers at Dover, not affected by the Dock Labour Scheme, joined in. Newspapers spoke of the country's economic and industrial crisis: minimum lending rates were put up by 2 per cent. But the crisis passed; vigorous action by lorry drivers (again!) broke through the bottleneck at Dover.

Attention shifted back to Yorkshire, where some of the most notorious incidents took place around Arnthorpe, after three working miners had been bussed through into Markham Main colliery; things got worse as local people stoned a convoy of police support units. It was at this period that the police introduced the intimidatory tactics (very quickly dropped again) of beating rhythmically on their riot shields; it was also at this time that, in pursuit of pickets, they smashed their way into private houses. In South Wales, all through the first phase of the strike, there had been sporadic attempts to stop coal convoys moving along the M4 motorway. Then a concrete block was dropped on a taxi bringing a working miner to the Merthyr Vale colliery: taxi driver David Wilkie was killed.

From December, matters quietened down as it was widely realized that the strike had been utterly futile and that there was no prospect of substantial concessions for the miners. Behind-the-scenes negotiations intensified, particularly involving Norman Willis, General Secretary of the TUC; but the miners' executive were not open to any agreement acceptable to the Coal Board. On 3 March 1985 a miners' special delegate conference agreed to a return to work, but without any agreement at all having been made. For the Labour party, the strike was a massive embarrassment; Labour leaders continuously disowned picket-line violence. As the men returned to work there was a sullen fatalism in the coalfields. Closures, flexible working, the six-day week followed. Those miners, centred in Nottingham, who had strongly opposed the strike, formed a separate Union of Democratic Mineworkers. Though now a much subdued figure, Scargill still commanded sufficient loyalty to secure re-election to the Presidency of the NUM by a two-thirds majority over a moderate opponent.

Militancy was on retreat throughout the trade union world, but it seemed that the new bitterness and violence, the openly confrontational tactics of the police, had come to stay. Economic and technological imperatives affected industries other than coal, notably newspaper publishing and cross-Channel ferries. The move of News International to Wapping, together with the refusal of staff to accommodate to the new technology, resulted, early in 1986, in picketing at Wapping of the type now indelibly associated with Orgreave. Picketing and clashes continued well into 1986. Then on 24 January 1987, 7,000 pickets and demonstrators gathered in a forceful commemoration of the anniversary of the move to Wapping. They were confronted by 1,000 police officers; clashes were violent, and about 300 people were injured, including 162 police officers. Many allegations of police brutality were made, and after an independent investigation of more than 440 allegations by a senior member of the Northamptonshire Police Force, 26 summonses were issued, with fourteen Metropolitan police officers being suspended from duty. The Seamen's strike of 1987 did little more than demonstrate the helplessness of a small union facing adverse economic circumstances, ruthless employers and a determined government.

Catastrophic violence, nonetheless, had struck again well before the end of 1985; the root cause this time was again urban deprivation and racial tension; once more confrontational police methods were sharply exposed. The first area to be put to the torch was Handsworth in Birmingham, an area of high unemployment, bad housing and drug peddling, where 60 per cent of the population consisted of a mix of Afro-Caribbeans and a variety of Asians, several of whom were relatively prosperous shop-owners. Police attempts to crack down on drug dealing over the previous months had created resentment, particularly among young blacks who depended on it for their only source of income. Monday 9 September was the night of rampaging mobs, terror, and arson; two Asians died in the burnt-out wreck of their shop. Within three weeks similarly horrific events were taking place in Brixton. Here there was a background of armed police raids on targeted suspects. Early on the morning of 28 September such a raid went badly wrong when armed police shot and seriously wounded Mrs Cherry Groce in a search for her son. A riot of firebombing broke out immediately.

During the morning of Tuesday, 1 October rioting reappeared in Toxteth. The dreadful role-call reached its appalling climax at the Broadwater Farm housing estate in Tottenham, north-east London. Again the trigger issue was a badly bungled police raid in which a sick black woman (Mrs Cynthia Jarrett) died, having been knocked to the floor and refused any medical assistance. The next day at noon, police and community leaders met at Tottenham police station. But a riotous mob was already assembling, clearly determined to inflict as much damage on the police as possible. Three policemen and two journalists received shotgun wounds, and in a total of 200 police casualties, several others were very seriously wounded. Most horrific of all, PC Keith Blakelock was savagely done to death with knives and a machete. For their part, in their own major coordinated counter-offensive the police returned to the intimidatory tactic of the rhythmic beating of their shields first tried out in the miners' strike. They succeeded in pinning down the rioters in the centre of the estate, but did not retake this area until 4.35 a.m. the next morning.[31]

The first evidence of a new level of destructive violence in British society had appeared in the early seventies. Just as one ingredient then had been IRA terrorism, so it was an important factor in the violence of the middle eighties. On 12 October 1984, while the miners' strike was at its height, the IRA made its most direct and daring attack on British authority, when it attempted to wipe out the British Government by placing a bomb under the sixth floor of the Grand Hotel, Brighton, where Mrs Thatcher and other senior delegates to the Conservative Party Annual Conference were staying. The hotel was wrecked, four people were killed (a fifth died a month later), and there were many extremely serious injuries. Norman Tebbit, now Industry Secretary, was dug out of the rubble after being entombed for four hours; his wife was permanently paralysed. The Prime Minister's bathroom was destroyed, though she herself was unhurt. As always, atrocity in Northern Ireland itself aroused less concern; however, two incidents produced reactions that suggested that the Irish issue was lodged more firmly in the British consciousness than at any time since the era of the Black and Tans. First, on Remembrance Sunday 1987, when the ordinary people of Enniskillen had gathered to commemorate the dead of both world wars, an IRA bomb placed nearby exploded, killing 11 people. Only a few months later, on 19 March 1988, two British soldiers who blundered into a Republican funeral were beaten up and then murdered (the whole episode being all the more nightmarish because parts of it, captured on army helicopters, were relayed on television). Terror returned to England when in August 1988 an explosion at Inglis Barracks in North London killed one soldier and injured nine; miraculously there were no casualties in the bombing of Clive Barracks, Shropshire, in February 1989.

### *PROSPERITY, PRIVATIZATION AND A THIRD ELECTION VICTORY*

There was division and violence in British society, but there was also, for those in decent employment, considerable prosperity. As tables 5.18 and 5.19 show, the government was not successful in attaining its monetary targets, and as the economy recovered, overt targets were in fact abandoned; unemployment remained high; and inflation though reduced, appeared not to be under secure control. The Conservatives boasted of an average growth rate of 3.5 per cent per year, but this figure was obtained by calculating from the depths of the recession in 1981; a more legitimate calculation from one peak, in 1979, to the next, in 1989, yielded a figure of 2.2 per cent.[32] Productivity rates in such manufacturing as had survived, greatly improved. But Britain, since 1983, had for the first time since the industrial revolution, become a net importer of manufactured products. The workshop of the world had become the big spender of Europe: as table 5.3 shows, the new good times were linked to a constantly threatening balance of payments situation.

Since Thatcher acquired a reputation of sweeping all before her, it is important to stress that she continued to face considerable opposition both outside and inside the Conservative party even after the post-Falklands election. Thatcher liked to project an image of bluff, no-nonsense honesty. Some doubts were cast on this characterization, first by the *General Belgrano* case, and then by the Westland Affair of January 1986. During the Falklands War, Britain had declared an 'Exclusion Zone' around the islands, warning Argentine shipping to keep clear. On 2 May 1982, the Argentine ship *General Belgrano* was sunk by the British submarine *Conqueror*, with the loss of 368 Argentine lives. The government version at the time was that the *General Belgrano* was inside the Exclusion Zone and that the decision had been made on the spot by the submarine commander.[33] In fact, the Argentine ship was well outside the Exclusion Zone and sailing away from it; the decision to sink it had been authorized by Thatcher herself. Labour MP Tam Dalyell alleged that the sinking had been deliberately ordered in order to sabotage peace proposals then being put forward by the Peruvian President, which would, in Dalyell's view, have denied Thatcher her glorious military victory. There may, in military terms, have been more of a case for this ruthless action than critics allowed; the problem was that Thatcher continued to prevaricate about the precise circumstances long after the event, including the lie that at the time of the sinking the government was not aware of the Peruvian proposals. Continuing attempts at cover-up in 1984 so offended a senior civil servant in the Ministry of Defence, Clive Ponting, that he leaked incriminating documents to Dalyell. Just how high-handed, and how determined to cover its tracks, this government had become was made clear when Ponting was put on trial, with the judge taking it upon himself to make the case for the government: 'The policies of the state were the policies of the government then in power.' For once in modern times a jury showed sublime contempt for such a doctrine, the satirical journal *Private Eye* brilliantly catching the essence of the affair in having the judge ask of the jury foreman 'And is that the verdict of you all?' as the foreman raises two fingers to him.

The Westland Helicopter Company of Yeovil was in difficulties and looking forward to being taken over by its American rival Sikorsky, with the general approval of Brittan at the Department of Trade and Industry (DTI), and Thatcher herself. Heseltine, Minister of the Environment, however, wished the company to be taken over by a European Consortium. He let it be known by means of a letter to Lloyds Merchant Bank, who were acting for the European Consortium, that if the company became American all European orders would be lost (a not altogether accurate statement). On being consulted, the Solicitor-General, Sir Patrick Mayhew, gave it as his view that the Heseltine letter contained 'material inaccuracies', and was prevailed upon by Thatcher to write to Heseltine saying this. Thatcher made it known to her intimates that she really needed to have this correction in 'the public domain'. At the DTI Brittan expressed a similar view, but only 'subject to the agreement of No. 10'.[34] And so it came to pass that selected parts of the Solicitor-General's letter were leaked to the press, the *Sun* responding magnificently (Monday, 6 January) with a front-page photograph of Heseltine and the headline 'You Liar!' At the next Cabinet meeting on 9 January Thatcher produced a ruling that all future statements about Westland would have to be cleared with the Cabinet Office: Heseltine walked out. The smokescreen was put up of an inquiry by the Cabinet Secretary, Robert Armstrong; Brittan, whose office had certainly been responsible for the actual physical act of leaking a Law Officer's confidential letter without his approval, was made the 'sacrificial victim'. Labour called an emergency debate for Monday, 27 January. As she left for the House Mrs Thatcher told one associate: 'I may not be Prime Minister by 6 o'clock tonight.' Kinnock put on an appalling display of Welsh wind-baggery, totally failing to pin down precisely what Thatcher was being accused of. She still had to make what, for her, was a remarkably contrite speech, but the chance to force her resignation was gone. Once again Labour had demonstrated only abysmal incompetence.

The (by now) historic overspend on defence continued. As a product of the very close relationship Thatcher enjoyed with President Reagan, Britain was to be supplied, at almost unimaginable expense, with Trident missiles to replace Polaris, while allowing the Americans to base their Cruise missiles in Britain. The Campaign for Nuclear Disarmament underwent a phenomenal resurgence. A most impressive testimony to guts and endurance was provided by the feminists who camped out year after year at the American Cruise missile base on Greenham Common in Berkshire.

One Thatcherite reform that achieved a mythic status out of all proportion to its effects on ordinary people was 'Big Bang': this referred to the Stock Exchange where on 27 October 1986 traditional restrictive practices came to an end and the old, frantic, entertaining scene of gesticulating brokers and esoteric hand signals gave way to the cool world of electronic work stations. This was all of a piece with the government's privatization programme, save that, rather than having a programme, the government appeared to be making up policy as it went along. There were some fundamental principles: a commitment to rolling back the state, and to going beyond a property-owning democracy to a share-owning democracy, the need for ready cash to keep the PSBR down. But there were no clear principles over what should go, and in what order. Privatization on a substantial scale had never been carried out before; there were considerable technical difficulties in unloading large numbers of shares and making sure that they were successfully taken up. What was sold depended on the portfolio of companies, apart from the big utilities, which happened to be in the government's possession. Pricing would be aimed more at having a successful launch than at getting a fair price for the tax payer.[35]

**Table 5.21** Privatization

| *Company and date of privatization* | *Proceeds £ million* | *Costs of issue (percentage of proceeds)* | *Times subscribed* | *Underpricing (end of first week, percentage)* |
|---|---|---|---|---|
| British Petroleum (1979) | 290 | 4.8 | 1.5 | 6 |
| British Aerospace (1981) | 149 | 3.8 | 3.5 | 15 |
| Cable and Wireless (1981) | 224 | 3.1 | 5.6 | 17 |
| Amersham International radio-chemical centre (1983) | 71 | 4.4 | 24.0 | 35 |
| Associated British Ports (1983) | 22 | 11.8 | 34.0 | 28 |
| Jaguar (1984) | 294 | 1.9 | 8.3 | 7 |
| British Telecom(1984) | 3,916 | 3.9 | 3.0 | 33 |
| British Gas (1986) | 5,434 | 3.2 | 4.0 | 10 |
| Rolls-Royce (1987) | 1,363 | | 9.4 | 35 |
| British Airports Authority (1987) | 1,225 | | 8.1 | 16 |
| British Airways (1987) | 900 | | | 32 |
| British Steel (1988) | 2,500 | | 3.3 | −1 |
| Ten Water Companies (1989) | 5,240 | | 3.4 | 22 |
| Twelve Regional Electricity Companies (1990) | 5,100 | 3.7 | 11.5 | 21 |

*Source:* Mathew Bishop, John Kay, Colin Mayer (eds), *Privatization and Economic Performance* (Oxford: Oxford University Press, 1994), p. 294.

It may be noted that the privatization programme in France, carried out in the second half of the 1980s, also involved similar losses to the public purse.[36] Whether, in the long run, the public gained from greater efficiency in the privatized services has scarcely yet been conclusively settled. The British Government also mounted a massive campaign to persuade people to transfer to private pensions, almost all of which proved to be extremely bad value, with, in particular, far too much money going into the pockets of agents: this scandal had not fully been settled, and participants fully compensated, a decade later, and along with a number of other scandals forms part of a severe indictment of the Thatcher Government's naive belief in unrestricted private enterprise.

Sometimes Thatcher gave the impression that she did not consider herself part of government, but that she had joined with the people in the fight to release them from control by the state. It was part of her atavistic faith that the size and the power of the civil service must be cut down. In fact, as has often been pointed out, the upshot of Thatcher's policies, despite privatization, was to increase centralized control – control, of course, being centralized in the hands of herself and her cronies; most especially this was a result of her battle to control expenditure by local authorities, ending in a very drastic reduction in their powers.[37]

The Conservative leader found herself in a condition of war against high-spending Labour local authorities, but then so did the Labour leader. When he found he could no longer overspend, Derek Hatton adopted the ploy of making government-imposed cuts, including those resulting in sacking public employees, as public as possible. In perhaps his most effective speech as Leader of the Opposition (there weren't too many), Kinnock attacked Hatton at the 1985 Labour Party Conference, referring effectively to Hatton's use of taxis to issue redundancy notices to council employees. Thatcher rid herself of turbulent local authorities in one fell swoop: the Local Government Act of 1986 (characteristic of Thatcher in doing things which previous politicians would not have dared to do) garrotted the Metropolitan Authorities – the GLC (Greater London Council), Merseyside, etc. and castrated the smaller authorities.

With most people doing well, and with, contrary to serious monetarist principles, money freely available, Thatcher once again held an election with nearly a year of her legal term still to go.

**Table 5.22** General Election, 11 June 1987

| | *Electorate 43.1 million* | | | *Turnout 75.3 per cent* | | |
|---|---|---|---|---|---|---|
| | *Conservative* | *Labour* | *Alliance* | *Scottish Nationalist* | *Plaid Cymru* | *Northern Ireland* |
| Votes | 13,736,066 | 10,029,778 | 7,341,290 | 416,473 | 123,599 | 730,152 |
| Percentage of votes cast | 42.2 | 30.8 | 22.6 | 1.3 | 0.4 | 2.2 |
| Seats | 376 | 229 | 22 | 3 | 3 | 17 |

This was the triumph of Thatcher and Thatcherism indeed: an unprecedented hat trick of election victories. The Conservative vote had gone up by over half-a-million. Twenty-two seats had been lost, mainly because of the continuing trend whereby the Conservatives were being reduced to a mere rump in Scotland and Wales. The Labour vote had gone up by about 1.5 million. It rather looked as though the Alliance, with the loss of 400,000 votes and one seat, had peaked. The presentation of 'the two Davids', Owen and Steel, as joint leaders of the Alliance had provoked adverse comment and even laughter; in the work of canvassing and getting the vote out the Alliance, or particularly the Social Democratic part of it, seemed to lack energy and enthusiasm.

To keep themselves in power, political leaders needed support in the country (42 per cent of the 70-odd per cent actually bothering to vote was the going rate), the support of their party, as demonstrated by whatever voting mechanisms were in operation, and, critically important, the support of their most important parliamentary colleagues. Thatcher offered strong government, in contrast with the weakness and division of her Labour opponents, and she seemed in command of the economy, with low direct taxes, prosperity for the majority and prospects of upward mobility. While we move towards considering why she fell from power in November 1990, we must also keep in mind that the Conservatives, largely continuing to follow her policies, won a fourth election victory in 1992.

### *THATCHER AND IRELAND*

The tough policies of Roy Mason had involved both increasing the size, and the paramilitary functions of the RUC and the UDR, with the latter, which had originally been conceived as largely a part-time force, becoming very nearly 50 per cent full-time by 1988. Although the formal aim of the IRA was withdrawal of British soldiers, their replacement by Ulster Protestants only intensified the communal divide even further. Tougher policies did push the Provisionals onto the defensive, turning them, however, still further away from any inclination towards negotiations, towards the acceptance of a 'Long Term Armed Struggle'. At the same time a more audacious paramilitary organization, the Irish National Liberation Army, emerged. Meantime Loyalist violence declined somewhat. The relative failure of an attempt in May 1977 to mount a strike which would repeat the success of 1974, suggested that the mass of Unionists no longer felt themselves as threatened as they had at the earlier date. Tougher RUC methods led to controversies over the use of plastic bullets, and still more over the alleged 'shoot-to-kill' policy in 1982. Eventually, disciplinary proceedings were taken against more than 20 officers.

Thatcher's first major political initiative was a meeting with Charles Haughey, the Taoiseach, in May 1980. This proposed 'closer political cooperation' and 'regular meetings', the first of which was held in December 1980. However, the prospect of further developments was soured by the IRA hunger strikes of 1981. One important element in the 'get tough' policy had been the ending of special-category status after March 1976 for prisoners guilty of terrorist offences. The first campaign by Republican prisoners for restoration of their political status had taken the form of the 'dirty' protests of the late seventies, most notorious for the smearing of cells with their own excrement. A hunger strike begun by seven Republicans at the Maze prison, on 27 October 1980, came to an end on 18 December 1980, when it appeared that the new Secretary of

State for Northern Ireland, Humphrey Atkins, was prepared to consider their demands. However, on 1 March 1981, the fifth anniversary of the ending of political status, Bobby Sands, serving a 14-year sentence for firearms offences, began his own hunger strike. Almost immediately the seat at Fermanagh–South Tyrone fell vacant: Sands was elected. In the end, Sands was the first of ten hunger-strikers to die, on 5 May 1981; the last died on 20 August. Thatcher's reaction was uncompromising: 'Mr Sands was a convicted criminal. He chose to take his own life. It was a choice that his organization did not allow to many of its victims.'[38] But whether by commission, or omission, the creation of martyrs is never a wise policy. Catholic sentiment hardened, Sinn Féin gained in credibility as a political, as well as a military organization. Danny Morrison enunciated the notorious policy in October 1981: 'Who here really believes we can win the war through the ballot box? But will anyone here object if, with a ballot paper in one hand and the armalite in the other, we take power in Ireland?'[39] Sinn Féin now set out to wrest the support of Catholic voters away from the SDLP. In the 1983 General Election Gerry Adams, soon to become the new younger-generation President of Sinn Féin, won the West Belfast seat by a majority of 5,445 over the SDLP candidate (though he had broken with Sinn Féin tradition in standing, he did not break with the tradition of not actually taking his seat in the House of Commons).

The government moved away from trying to develop the Irish dimension, towards trying to re-create a devolved government for Northern Ireland. The White Paper *Northern Ireland: A Framework for Devolution*, of April 1982, was followed by the Northern Ireland Act of the same year, which brought into being a 78-member single-chamber assembly, to be elected by proportional representation, but limited to 'scrutinizing' and 'consultative' functions, without legislative or administrative ones: however, these might be added later through 'rolling devolution'. The Assembly would not be able to submit proposals unless they clearly had the support of the Catholic community as well as the Protestant one. Once more elections took place, but the new Assembly foundered on the refusal of the SDLP, which, as Hume replaced Fitt as leader, was moving away from socialism further towards nationalism, to participate. The SDLP now fostered the discussions held during 1983 and 1984 with the main parties in the Irish Republic, known as the New Ireland Forum. The Forum did recognize that nationalists had 'hitherto in their public expression tended to under-estimate the full dimension of the Unionist identity and ethos'. The fall of Haughey's Fianna Fáil Government and its replacement by a Fine Gael–Labour coalition, under Dr Garret FitzGerald, provided the opportunity for a new Anglo-Irish summit held in November 1984. Immediately after the summit Thatcher seemed to do her best to destroy the good relations just established. At a press conference she reduced the document produced by the new Ireland Forum, which FitzGerald had supported, to its three suggested alternative outcomes for Northern Ireland: unification, confederation or a joint authority. Of each, she repeated: 'That's out . . . that's out . . . that's out'.[40]

Anglo-Irish talks continued. They were supposed to be secret, but soon, in August 1985, the new leader of the Ulster Unionist Party, James Molyneaux, and the rather old leader of the extremists, Ian Paisley, expressed concern both about the secrecy and about the direction of the talks. They made clear that there were two points they could never accept (two points, in fact, that would have to be accepted if ever there were to be peace): no Nationalist participation in any Northern Ireland government; no British–Irish machinery as any part of Northern Ireland government. However, this very point was violated in the Anglo-Irish Agreement concluded on 15 November 1985: there was to be an inter-governmental conference which was to deal with political matters, security and related matters, legal questions, the promotion of cross-border cooperation, and was to form 'a framework within which the Irish Government may, where the interests of the minority community are significantly or especially affected, put forward views on proposals for major legislation and on major policy issues, which are on the purview of the Northern Ireland departments'. The Agreement was vociferously opposed by the mass of Unionists in Northern Ireland, with their MPs resigning their seats in order to fight them again: although one seat was lost to Séamus Mallon of the SDLP, the others were overwhelmingly re-won, with the Alliance Party collapsing. There was a Unionist 'day of action' on 3 March 1986, and then, after the banning of the Apprentice Boy's Parade in Portadown later in the month, tensions between Loyalists and the RUC, leading to Loyalist attacks on RUC families. Against Unionist opposition the Anglo-Irish Agreement was ineffectual. A totally new initiative launched by Hume in 1988 was not at first attended by any success either. Although the memory of Enniskillen was still reverberating, Hume entered into discussions with Provisional Sinn Féin. Sinn Féin rejected SDLP concern for Unionist rights and argued that before any conference could take place the British must announce their intention to withdraw from Ireland. For all that, the Thatcher Government did in the late eighties take positive action to improve community relations and employment prospects for Catholics. In 1987 the Central Community Relations Unit was established, followed by the Northern Ireland Community Relations Council in 1990. The Labour Government's Fair Employment Act of 1976, had established the Fair Employment Agency. The Standing Advisory Commission on Human Rights reported on the failure of this to achieve its purpose and in 1989 the Conservatives passed a new Fair Employment Act which obliged all employers with more than 25 employees to ensure that they were providing equal employment opportunities.

These were gleams of hope, but there was no getting away from the fact that between 1969 and June 1989 political violence had claimed 2,761 lives, of which 55 per cent were civilian, 31 per cent army or police, and 13 per cent paramilitary. The IRA groups were responsible for about 70 per cent of the deaths.

### *The fall of Thatcher*

The main source of division and disaffection on the mainland was the handling of the economy, the introduction of the community charge (universally known as the 'poll tax'), the direction taken by privatization and the introduction of market principles into the NHS; within the Conservative hierarchy it was policy towards Europe. Privatization of the water and electricity supply, both natural monopolies, seemed to owe more to ideology than to any practical benefits for consumers. The National Health Service Act of 1989, introduced by the Minister of Health, Kenneth Clark, had scarcely had time to take effect before Thatcher was ousted, but its proposals to introduce an 'internal market', encouraging general practitioners to become 'fundholders', and large hospitals to become self-governing trusts, aroused much distrust as a kind of creeping privatization, and were attacked by doctors.

Thatcher objected to the way the local taxes (rates) spent so freely by Labour local authorities were paid for only by those well enough off to own property (the grander the house the higher its rateable value), while much of the spending was for the benefit of those who did not pay rates at all. If everybody, poor as well as rich, had to pay the same community charge, that might make local authorities less profligate. Those who refused to pay the new tax would be deprived of their right to vote. The poll tax was introduced, creating enormous resistance, in Scotland in 1989, and then in England in 1990, provoking rioting at the end of March. Lawson, as Chancellor of the Exchequer, had had the good sense to oppose the poll tax, but, though he oozed enormous self-confidence, he was really something of a charlatan; even when the evidence was against him, he continued to believe that earlier reforms had produced a sound basis for continued expansion. The first major warning was 'Black Monday', 19 October 1987, when there was a collapse in share values. Lawson represented this as a temporary setback, and went ahead in his budget of March 1988 with enormous cuts in income tax: for income between £2,600 and £21,900 there was to be a single rate of 25 per cent, with everything above that being taxed at 40 per cent. The Chancellor was encouraging a glorious boom, which would surely lead to an inglorious bust. The only means of control he was prepared to use was the resort once again to extremely high interest rates. As house prices escalated, so did the cost of mortgage repayments, to the distress of many.

Lawson was probably right to argue from 1985 that (in the current economic situation) it would be wise to join the Exchange Rate Mechanism (ERM), by which the other EEC countries undertook to prevent the value of their own currencies against that of other currencies from fluctuating outside a certain narrow band (if necessary, they could make a one-off adjustment to their declared exchange value). Lawson believed that joining the ERM would bring a useful stability to the exchange value of the pound. Thatcher, however, was opposed to this, so Lawson adopted the policy of ensuring that the pound 'shadowed' the Deutschmark.[41] As the economy seemed to be going wildly out of control, Lawson argued more insistently for joining the ERM. In order to resist this, Thatcher turned again for private advice to Sir Alan Walters. Lawson was undoubtedly right to object to this demonstration of lack of trust in him. No doubt he also realized that this was a good time to jump ship, so in October 1989, at a time when he himself had put the minimum lending rate to 15 per cent, he resigned. He was succeeded by the relatively unknown John Major, whose main policy was to use high interest rates to induce deflation. In an economic situation which was now much less propitious, Major took the pound into the ERM early in October 1990, at what was the dangerously overvalued rate of DM 2.95. Thatcher had treated her former close supporter Sir Geoffrey Howe very badly, first pushing him into the meaningless post of Deputy Prime Minister, and now affronting his pro-European views through her violently expressed opposition to monetary union and what she saw as the drift towards federalism. On 1 November Howe resigned; his subsequent resignation speech, especially coming from one so sheep-like, was devastating.[42]

On 14 November Heseltine announced he would challenge her for the leadership. Under the rules, Thatcher needed to secure 208 votes for outright victory, although, of course, if that was all she got, that would demonstrate how far she had lost the support of MPs now perceiving her as a liability. In fact she secured 204 votes to Heseltine's 152. Immediately Thatcher announced that she would stand in the second round, but several colleagues advised against this. She decided to give up. In the second round, held on 27 November, 197 votes would be needed for outright victory. In fact, John Major, Thatcher's own favoured candidate, got 185 against 131 for Heseltine, and 56 for Hurd. Heseltine withdrew to leave Major as new leader of the Conservative party and Prime Minister.[43]

## THE PEOPLE VERSUS THEIR RULERS

### *A FRACTURED SOCIETY*

'The government has no more right to call itself the state,' said George Bernard Shaw, 'than the smoke over London has the right to call itself the weather.' Margaret Thatcher aimed to establish more centralized control over the state than any other Prime Minister in peace time. In common with all but utterly totalitarian governments, hers could not control society. But then she herself asserted: 'there's no such thing as society'.[44] A silly statement, but true to the extent that different sections of society, different families and individuals, believe different things and behave in different ways. Many people idolized Thatcher, many others voted for her because they believed she was good for the country, or at least better than the alternatives. Obviously, it is not a case of 'Society *v.* Thatcher'. My major points are: that while Thatcher preached the virtues of 'family' or 'Victorian' values, and excoriated the 'decadence' she attributed to the sixties, while also extolling self-help and work rather than welfare, large sections of the population embraced with ever-increasing enthusiasm the libertarian trends of the sixties and a generally collectivist approach towards the poor and underprivileged; that authority figures and representatives of the state fell into disrepute on a scale quite different from the dissidence of the sixties; and that in many different spheres British society was fractured in a way in which it had not been since before 1914. Many changes were for the good rather than the bad, many of them products of long-term forces. Many changes were due to new technologies and globalization, rather than to Thatcherism. Bitter divides, polarization, confrontation, riots *and* tranquil progress: but the first four characterize the Thatcher years. Britain, largely through Thatcher's energetic prodding, was becoming more American, with some of the achievements of that society, and many of the failings. Here follow seven topics illustrative of these points.

### *ECONOMY AND GEOGRAPHY*

Everywhere there was a chasm between the main body of society, and the poorest 10 per cent, on the way to becoming the poorest 15 per cent, and constantly, in real terms, getting poorer.[45] Geographically there was a divide between the

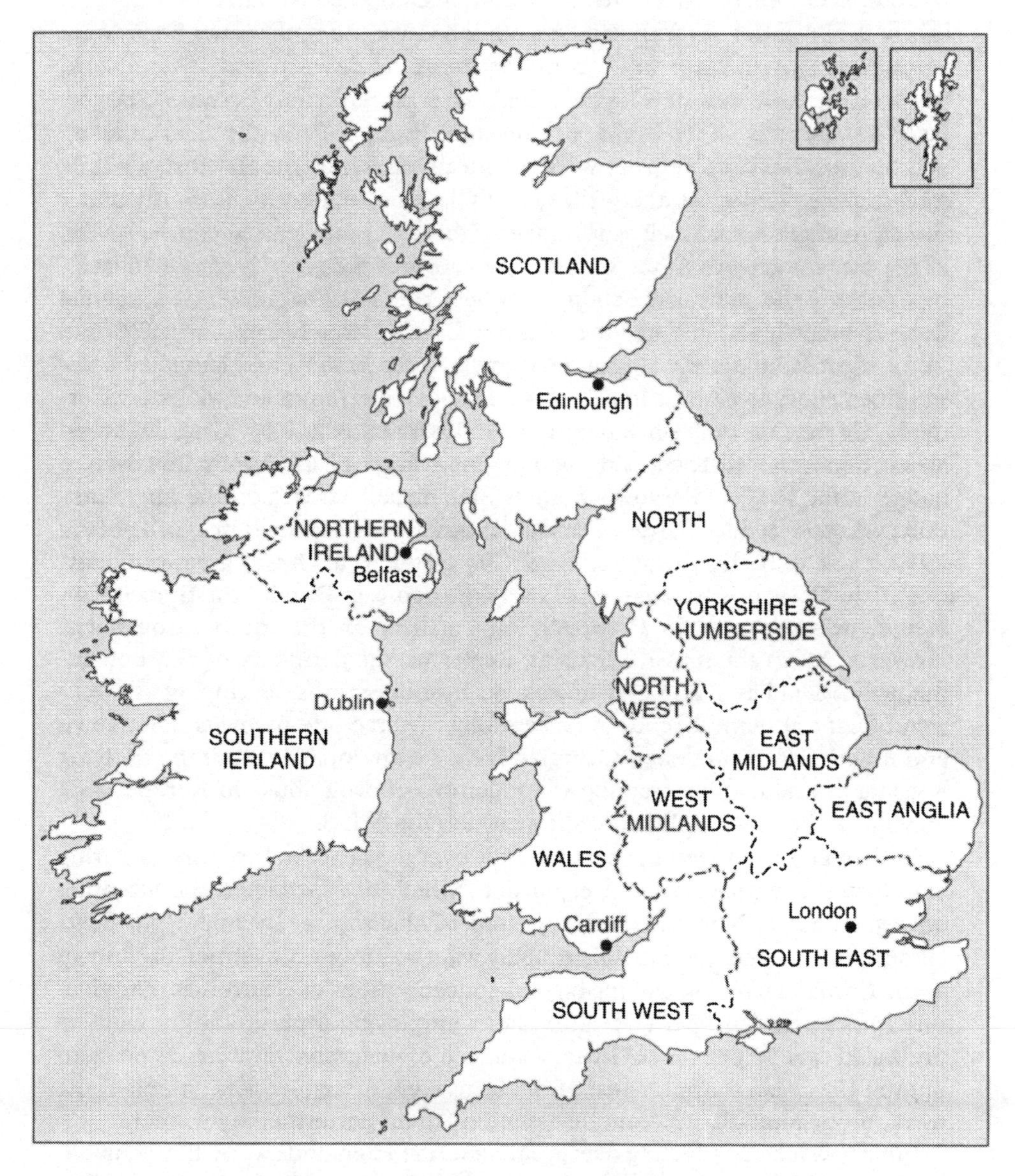


**Map 4** Regions and nations of the United Kingdom (adapted from Paul Johnson, ed., *20th Century Britain*, Harlow: Longman, 1994, p. 48).

north, including Scotland, Wales and Northern Ireland, where industries were being closed down, and the south where new service industries were developing (see map 4). Within cities, there was a divide between localities which were being gentrified, and outer suburbs of crumbling sixties housing estates, generally even worse than such deprived central areas as Toxteth in Liverpool. The population of Scotland continued to decline, to 5,112,000 in 1987, while unemployment continued to rise, to 13.7 per cent in 1986, easing marginally to 13.3 per cent in 1987.[46] Glasgow provides an excellent focal point for the debates going on about what was really happening around Britain. Population was still in decline but at a much reduced rate compared with that of the sixties and of the seventies. As with Britain's other historic ports, the inner docks were completely closed; there was a container terminal downstream at Greenock, but no large-scale new development had taken place, mainly because Glasgow faced towards the wider world, not towards Europe. Both the steel industry and the ship-building industry were practically finished (the Ravenscraig bulk steel-making plant at Motherwell, east of Glasgow, had been constantly under threat, to which it eventually succumbed); there was only partial compensation in the way the growth of the oil industry had brought some business in steel-pipe making and the construction of oil rigs. Yet Glasgow, under its perennial Labour council, had initiated the Glasgow Eastern Area Renewal in 1976, and in the eighties, under the slogan 'Glasgow's Miles Better', had launched a determined effort to alter its image as a centre of deprivation and violence. Certainly, for the first time since before the industrial revolution, Glasgow looked clean. Pedestrian districts had been an innovation of the 1960s, but were a badge of the 1980s; Glasgow's famous Sauchiehall Street became one, naturally; Glasgow had its Garden Festival (another badge of the times) in 1988; in 1990 it was to be European Cultural City of the Year. Amid great publicity, one of the finest privately assembled art collections in Britain, the Burrell Collection, was rehoused in a specially built gallery on the southern outskirts. However, life in the massive housing estates on the periphery of Glasgow remained as awful as ever. Forty miles east, Edinburgh was developing as a centre of financial services, and, in its carefully restored late-medieval Old Town and immaculately preserved Georgian New Town, looked it; but the outlying housing estates had become the worst centres of drug abuse in Europe, and, inevitably, the most prolific breeding ground for AIDS.

In Scotland, engineering accounted for over a quarter of the manufacturing workforce. The major area of expansion, which now attracted the attention once focused on North Sea oil, was that of electronics. By mid-1986 Scotland's 'Silicon Glen' (comprising roughly what was more conventionally known as the Lowlands) had one of the biggest concentrations of electronics manufacture in Western Europe. Over 250 plants employing around 43,000 workers produced over 50 per cent of Britain's output of integrated circuits, 15 per cent of total European output. Most of the firms were foreign-owned; much of the work, though not all, was routine assembly, often performed by women.

Four new factors affecting development in the Highlands were: the availability from 1982 of funds from the EEC channelled through the Integrated Development Programme for the Western Isles; the Thatcherite emphasis on small business; the production of luxury primary food products based on fish farming and red-deer estates; and the advent of a more systematized approach to tourism, with centres for skiing, angling, climbing, and hillwalking, as well as craft shops. The traditional whisky industry had suffered in the recession, but in the mid-eighties revived under the stimulus of higher consumer demand. Tree-planting was being subsidized by the government through tax concessions, much to the anger of environmentalists, who claimed that natural wild beauty was being ruined by afforestation.

The north continued to suffer the highest rates of unemployment on mainland Britain, though it did share with the West Midlands the distinction of a slight decline in 1986 (unemployment eased in the West Midlands in both 1985 and 1986). The problem of the North was that it failed to attract light manufacturing industries such as electronics, computers, and consumer goods. Yet again there could be seen, in the region's largest city, Newcastle, the Janus-face of 'post-industrial' Britain. Operating as a service centre for the whole area, Newcastle had attracted commercial enterprises and much new office building. In the city centre was a modern leisure complex and the fashionable Eldon Square Shopping Centre. In Cumbria there remained the now no longer glamorous nuclear power stations, together with reprocessing facilities. In the rural areas sheep farming and forestry predominated; fishing was undergoing a slight revival. Population in the north was in steady decline until 1986, when it stood at 4,899,000; there was a tiny shift to 4,900,000 in 1987.

The north-west came second only to the north for high unemployment levels, just displacing Wales in this dismal league table in 1983. The reduced motor-vehicle industry was showing some signs of recovery in the Ford plant at Halewood and the Vauxhall one at Ellesmere Port. Oil refining was taking place at Eastham and Stanlow, with large tankers off-loading at the Tranmere Oil Terminal. Most buoyancy was to be found in the food-processing and food-manufacturing industries. Manchester had become an important centre for computer manufacture, which seemed to be on the upturn in the second half of the decade. 'Post-industrial' development on the American model was most obviously to be seen in the establishment of the Wirral Science Park, and the Birchwood Science Park near Warrington, factory estates designed to attract electronics and other high-tech enterprises.

In the aftermath of the Toxteth riots much attention was focused on Liverpool, a civil service task-force was established, and highly publicized efforts were made to attract private capital into urban-renewal developments. The most famous of the new initiatives, a classic instance of what came to be termed the 'heritage industry', was the conversion of the Albert Dock, the largest group of Grade I listed buildings in the United Kingdom, into a complex of shops, offices, pubs, restaurants, private residences, a maritime museum and the Granada TV News Centre. With the opening of a Liverpool Tate Gallery, occupying the largest warehouse in the dock, the project was complete. The militant Labour council that had ruled Liverpool in the early eighties had energetically built council houses, but on borrowed money due for repayment to Japanese banks in 1989; for lack of maintenance, much of this housing rapidly turned into slums.

In Wales, the most striking development was in electronics: an influx of over 200 overseas-owned, or overseas-associated, firms brought employment to around 45,000 people in South Wales, though, even more than in Scotland, the work was mainly of the routine assembly kind. In a manner characteristic of the eighties, Cardiff benefited from the expansion in financial business services. Milford Haven, surrounded by a prosperous refinery complex, remained one of Britain's major oil ports. Systemized tourism advanced in such coastal resorts as Tenby, Rhyl, and Colwyn Bay, and in the National Parks of Snowdonia, the Brecon Beacons and the Pembrokeshire Coast.

In part the attractiveness of South Wales to foreign electronic firms lay in its position at the subsidized end of the famous 'M4 corridor', the M4 being the motorway linking London with South Wales. The three main towns of what has been called 'England's new industrial axis' were, going east, Swindon, Newbury and Reading. In general, this was an area of government military and research establishments, classically a stimulus to electronics technology. While the towns just mentioned were expanding in population, Bristol to the west was declining, though by the later eighties, showing many signs of prosperity, particularly as a result of aerospace, as well as electronics, developments.

We are now well ensconced in the 'prosperous' south. Yet unemployment in the south-east reached levels that once would have been considered shocking, rising from 7 per cent in 1982 to 8.4 per cent in 1986, easing to 7.2 per cent in 1987. But, on the whole, London and the south-east were well suited to profit from the characteristic developments of the post-industrial age; 75 per cent of all employees were in the service sector. In 1980 part of London's derelict docklands was designated an enterprise zone and a year later handed over to the London Docklands Development Corporation, funded by the government. Much of central London itself was assuming the aspect and noise of a permanent building site, so long known to denizens of North American cities. East Anglia generally prospered, and recorded the highest car ownership throughout Britain: 66 per cent of all homes had a car. The plight of those in remote areas without access to cars was becoming ever more serious.

Northern Ireland really did seem an awful place. Conditions in housing estates segregated by religion were worse than anywhere else in Europe. Unemployment was the highest in the United Kingdom, and, with the highest number of people drawing benefits of some sort, this was the classic case of a 'dependency culture'. Catholics continued to be disadvantaged in the job market, for a number of reasons, including the 'chill factor':

> the impact of inter-communal hostility and fear, where members of one community are often reluctant to take up work in a work-place dominated by the other community or to travel to work through territory dominated by the other community.[47]

The Troubles helped nobody. However, it was believed that the Provisional IRA particularly singled out for assassination the eldest sons in border families who were the managers or principal wage-earners. The newest economic developments were in synthetic rubber, vehicle components, oil-well equipment, electronics, telecommunications equipment, carpets, food processing and packaging. The discovery of lignite around Lough Neagh offered possibilities; experiments were actually taking place in once again cultivating flax. It could be said that the British Government had not done much to help Northern Ireland when it might have counted; industry continued to depend on expensively produced energy from oil-fired power stations. Yet Britain was pouring in considerable financial support, with building grants, machinery grants, start-up grants, free factory rentals for five years, loans, help for transferred workers, training grants, tax allowances, and research and development grants. Enterprise zones were established in Belfast and Londonderry; Aldergrove Airport was declared a 'free port'. In 1986–7 the United Kingdom Government pumped nearly £1,700 million into Northern Ireland.

The province did have some remarkable achievements. The annual Belfast Festival at Queen's University was the second largest international festival in Britain. Pianist Barry Douglas won the International Tchaikovsky Competition in Moscow in 1986; the flautist James Galway and soprano Heather Harper were already famous. In popular sport, the boxer Barry McGuigan and the snooker player Dennis Taylor were true local heroes.

### *SERVICE, SECURITY AND SAFETY*

Some of the gains from the enterprise economy which Thatcher was striving to create have been detailed above. And while there are other gains still to be recounted, my second topic concerns the connection between enterprise and the decline in services, security and safety.[48] An independent variable, fostered by the enterprise economy, was New Technology, or Information Technology (IT – computers and electronic office machinery, telecommunications and electronic video and satellite equipment). IT created new opportunities and new sources of prosperity, but it also brought redundancies and new insecure contracts of employment. Most important of all, with respect to the main themes of this section, it polarized working skills, and condemned former manual workers who could not acquire the new skills to the outer darkness. IT was also important in that it brought into being, often almost randomly, banks of information, sometimes quite inaccurate, on private citizens. Legislation giving every individual rights of access to such information, which came into effect in 1988, was a necessary, if perhaps inadequate, safeguard. The new technology did help break the dead hand which the printing unions had too long laid on innovation and enterprise in the newspaper industry. But the emergence of Rupert Murdoch, Australian-born and an American citizen, fully endorsed by Margaret Thatcher, to a position of near-monopoly in the British media, was another sign of the fracturing of British society.

A rather similar comment could be made about the rise of big-money sports sponsorship. The most significant feature of the eighties, when the total sum devoted to sports sponsorship rose to over £60 million, was the way in which sponsorship, still rather low-key and isolated in the 1960s, had become part of the basic fabric of the nation's spectator sport, association football. According to the 1983 Howell Report for the Central Council of Physical Recreation, football was attracting £12 million in sponsorship, second only to motor sports with £19 million.

Enterprising shop-owners were now keeping their shops open for much longer hours: a boon to shoppers, but also a source of exploitation of the workforce, increasingly being hired on short contracts of less than 16 hours, which was an effective way of evading most of the legislation governing the conditions of shop workers. The Health and Safety Executive reported at the beginning of December 1988 that 'many of the 19,000 new work-places visited were found to be working in ignorance of legal requirements and basic standards for occupational health, safety and welfare'. This issue was glaringly highlighted by an unprecedented series of tragic disasters running through 1987, 1988 and into 1989. On 6 March 1987 the Townsend Thoresen cross-Channel ferry *Herald of Free Enterprise* capsized while leaving Zeebrugge Harbour in Belgium, killing 193 passengers and crew; on 18 November 1987, in the early evening, just as the rush-hour was coming to an end, fire swept through a section of Kings Cross underground station in London, killing 31 people; on 6 July 1988 the Piper Alpha North Sea platform exploded, killing 167; on the morning of 12 December 1988 three trains were involved in a crash near Clapham Junction in London, killing 35; on 20 December 1988 a Pan-Am jumbo jet blew up over the borders of Scotland and crashed down on the town of Lockerbie (a bomb was the cause; questions were raised about safety precautions – the announcement early in January 1989 that additional checks were to be imposed on air passengers together with the screening of cargo effectively confirmed that previous safety procedures had been inadequate); early in March there were rail accidents at Purley, South London (five killed), and Glasgow (two killed). During the early hours of Sunday, 20 August 1989 the cruise boat *Marchioness*, carrying over 100 party revellers, was in collision on the River Thames with the dredger *Bow Belle*; 26 young people lost their lives. Appalling luck played a part each time; yet each case (save perhaps the Lockerbie disaster) did reveal clear signs of economy and profits being higher concerns than safety.

In the world of food production and marketing, a sad little drama was played out in the early months of 1989 that neatly expressed the perilous relationship between enterprise, safety and government authoritarianism and secrecy: a confused public learned of the unquantified dangers of eggs, chicken, soft cheeses and apparently many other foodstuffs as well, without the help of clear pronouncements or reassuring action from a government for whom protection of consumers was apparently a very low priority. The policy and spirit of deregulation had already (as we shall see in the next chapter) permitted 'mad cow disease' to enter the human food chain.

### *WELFARE 'REFORM'*

The new spirit that was to inform social security provision was made clear in the 1985 White Paper *Reform of Social Security: Programme for Action*, which spoke of giving 'greater responsibility and greater independence to the individual'. The new spirit, and a new structure, were embodied in the Social Security Act of 1986, whose main provisions came into effect in April 1988. Administratively Social Security was again separated from Health, as it had been in the original welfare state. One purpose of the new legislation was to simplify and systematize the quite extensive, and arguably confusing, list of benefits and allowances – for clothing, housing, furniture, etc. – that had grown up since the 1960s. Critics claimed that the upshot was an overall reduction in what those in need could claim. Means tests were made more rigorous; applicants for unemployment benefit had to demonstrate that they were genuinely available for work. Supplementary benefit was replaced by income support, which, in the interests of targeting benefits where they were felt to be most needed, was divided into two components: a personal allowance, and then additional premiums for families, single parents, pensioners, and long-term sick and disabled people. The new housing benefit scheme operated on a similar basis to that of income support: both schemes denied benefits to persons with more than the most modest amount of capital, thus dealing harshly with pensioners possessing a house, whose saleability, in reality, might be pretty well nil. On the other hand, the new family credit scheme did appear to be benefiting many more families than the old family income supplement; maternity and widows' benefits were also improved. Sickness and disablement benefits remained much as before. One remnant of the old universalist policies of the 1940s continued: child benefit, costing the state £5 billion a year. In place of the former single payments to cover various eventualities there was now a social fund, which offered loans not grants: the cruel irony was that the poorest and neediest, being in no position to pay back loans, were denied the resource they needed (to visit a sick child in hospital, to buy a pram, etc.). Family credit, paid to the those on low incomes, because of the 'poverty trap' (as income rose, benefits decreased) almost seemed designed to cage people in the worst-paid jobs.

National Health Service reform, outlined in the DHSS report *NHS Management Inquiry*, of October 1983 ('the Griffiths Report'), consisted of: introducing outside managerial skills into the various levels of the service; the privatization of many ancillary services; the encouragement of the private sector; and the advocacy of contracting out of services on a competitive basis, even within the National Health Service. By the later eighties it was absolutely clear that the National Health Service was failing. The government had made a concerted effort to reduce waiting-lists, and had deliberately diverted resources from London to the less well-served regions. But from all quarters came well-authenticated stories of units closing, of beds standing empty, of postponements and delays in vital operations. Protests rained in from distinguished doctors and surgeons. In November and December 1987 there was a crescendo of protests from patients, heart surgeons, health districts and from the Presidents of the medical Royal Colleges. Already the result of government policies was the development of two very different systems: a hard-pressed public service with long waiting-lists; and a luxurious private system catering to a small minority, yet parasitical upon the public service. At the end of 1987 the government announced charges for eye-tests, and the abolition of free medical check-ups. The right to sell spectacles was extended to those without ophthalmic qualifications. There remained much validity in the universalist argument that if the rich opted out into private medicine, there would be no influential customers to complain about second-rate service in public medicine.[49]

Back in 1945, when housing had been the single issue on which most members of the electorate felt most strongly, the problem had been an absolute shortage of housing. Since that was no longer *the* problem, it was reasonable that policies on housing should have shifted. The new elements of the eighties were the encouragement of private ownership, the encouragement of private building, and the attempt to make the renting of accommodation a purely market-place transaction. The governing legislation was contained in the main Housing Act of 1980 and the consolidating one of 1985. In many respects these acts gave new rights to council tenants (to exchange homes or take in lodgers, for instance), in response to the numerous complaints about the petty despotisms exercised by many local authorities over their housing estates; moves were in hand to enable public-sector tenants to change their landlord if dissatisfied with the local authority. Most important was the provision that council tenants of at least two years' standing could buy their house or flat at a discount. By the end of 1987, 1.1 million council, housing association and new town homes had been purchased in this way. At this same date 64 per cent of all dwellings in the country were owner-occupied. Officially, the number of families identified as homeless was 128,345. However, the housing pressure group set up in the 1960s, Shelter, in its *Christmas Report on Homelessness 1988*, declared that the real figure was probably far higher, going, if individuals were counted, into the millions. One fundamental part of the problem was that households were splitting up much earlier than formerly, with large numbers of single young people looking for accommodation. More immediate causes were the virtual cessation of local-authority house-building and the sharp price rises in the now predominating private market. Private landlords were unwilling to rent to unemployed young people, many of whom were adversely affected by the social security changes I have just discussed. As the Shelter report put it:

> Without somewhere to live they can't get on a Youth Training Scheme. Without YTS they get no income support. Many young people are literally being forced on to the streets.[50]

But by the last year of the decade it was clear that disaster was also striking those rather higher up the social scale. In 1987 one in a hundred house-buyers were losing their homes through failing to keep up their mortgage payments, and the figure was rising. House prices had gone up by 14.6 per cent in 1986–7, though were levelling off by 1989. However, by this time the much more serious problem of continually rising interest rates, which meant a frequent upwards adjustment of mortgage payments, was striking hard. Redundancy, too, could affect business and professional families.

Education in the United Kingdom continued to be ruled by the genuine, though flawed, 'secondary education for all' principles of the 1944 Butler Education Act (there were always separate Acts to meet the particular structures of

Scotland and Northern Ireland, respectively), as applied and interpreted by the different local authorities. International comparisons and the chronic poor performance of the British economy suggested that there was something rotten throughout the educational system; 'loony-left' local authorities, I have already suggested, had much to answer for. Thus there was something to be said for the introduction, by the Education Act (No. 2) of 1986, of performance appraisal for teachers. And something also for the introduction, in the Education Reform Act of July 1988, of a national curriculum (in England and Wales – guidance along similar lines was to be issued by the Scottish Education Department) containing the 'core subjects' of Mathematics, English and Science, as well as the 'foundation subjects' of History, Geography, Technology, Music, Art, Physical Education, and for secondary pupils, a modern foreign language. More dubious were the rigid assessment procedures to be applied at the ages of seven, eleven, fourteen and sixteen. The Education Reform Act, introduced by the self-promoting Education Secretary, Kenneth Baker, was Thatcherite in that it sought to reduce local authority control over schools, to encourage schools to go independent and take direct funding from Whitehall, to give greater power to parents, to link funding to the number of pupils schools attracted, and to make governors and head masters responsible for managing schools as if they were commercial businesses. Freedom for parents in effect meant freedom for better-off parents who could, for instance, afford to send their children considerable distances to attend the more successful schools. 'Sink' schools in the areas where poorer parents and children were stuck, sunk still further. As with the National Health Service, the sums put into education continued to rise, but, as with the National Health Service, that did not prevent publicly funded schools (which still catered for 93 per cent of the country's children) being starved of essential books and other educational materials.

The nation's universities felt themselves to be in a condition of war with the government. Throughout the eighties government policies of 'level funding', of refusing to accept the real implications of inflation in educational costs, of salary increases, etc. meant that all universities were suffering from cuts in posts and facilities, and some were in desperately dire straits. The Education Reform Act replaced the University Grants Committee, once the symbol of expansionism in higher education and of freedom and independence for universities, by the Universities Funding Council, which was clearly intended to take a more business-oriented line. Security of tenure for academics was to be phased out as new appointments, or promotions, were made. Open government encouragement of technology and business studies (sensible enough in itself) seemed to menace the standing, not just of the arts and humanities, but of pure science. Maintenance grants for students were already being severely squeezed, with the aim of putting the onus back on parents. Subsequently it was revealed that the government intended to move to the American system of loans, rather than grants; at the beginning of 1989 the American model of mixed funding was being openly extolled.

### *CLASS, RACE, GENDER, RELIGION*

Fourthly, I come to the historic divisions of class, race, gender and religion.[51] With regard to gender, a vital statistic is that by 1988 there were 212,000 more males than females in the sixteen to thirty-five age group, and 59,000 more in the peak marriage years of 20–24. In class structure, there were changes, though not fundamental ones. There was an acceleration in the breaking up of the rigid frontiers of the working class (a process long talked about, but less readily perceivable as an actual reality), and more abrupt openings to positions of power and influence for people who had not taken the trouble to absorb the traditional upper-class lifestyle. The much talked-of 'yuppie', though over publicized, did have corporeal existence. In this era of buying and selling (in information services, shares, land for development – in one notorious case the Westminster Council sold off, for practically nothing, cemeteries in its care – and goods of all kinds) there were large incomes and commissions to be earned in finance, accountancy, law, in agencies and consultancies of all kinds, as well as in commerce. That, combined with vigorous propaganda on behalf of the notion that success was far more important than social origins, was the basis for the yuppie phenomenon. Working-class and lower middle-class forms of speech, and provincial accents, were being heard as never before in the world of finance and the commercially oriented professions.

Evidently the number of manual workers employed in manufacturing industry was shrinking drastically, while the numbers of those performing the tasks of the skilled manual worker, but as self-employed entrepreneurs, were increasing. However, a reduction in the size of the working class did not necessarily mean that the boundary between working class and lower middle-class was any less solid, or that a sense of working-class awareness had diminished. Fortunately we have the carefully presented results of a well-conceived survey carried through in the period 1 March to 3 July 1984 (published in 1988 as *Social Class in Britain Today,* by Gordon Marshall, Howard Newby, David Rose and Carolyn Vogler). Of a final sample of 1,770, over 90 per cent were readily able to place themselves in a specific class category. Adjusting the responses to exclude refusals and don't-knows, the authors come up with the figure of 58 per cent working class and 42 per cent middle class (the authors, wrongly in my view, make no allowance for an upper class: since the upper class tend to be concentrated in particular areas, and since there is a polite convention that one does not call oneself upper class, surveys tend anyway to underestimate this element). The authors made a particular point of drawing attention to the inequalities with regard to mobility, earnings, etc. suffered by women. And, of course, they recognized the salience of race, the disadvantages and the political significance (a strong likelihood of voting Labour) of being non-white.[52]

In November 1988 a demonstration held at Westminster by 16,000 students, against government proposals to introduce student loans, was marred by the Trotskyite element who hurled missiles at the police, to which the police responded by mounting terrifying charges on otherwise peaceful students. At the end of March 1990 there was a massive demonstration in London against the poll tax. On 1 April 1990 the *Observer* front page carried a photograph of a shirtless demonstrator in front of a blazing building, with the headline: 'Scores Hurt, Buildings Blaze in Poll Tax Riot'. Inside were stunning photographs of mounted riot police charging fleeing demonstrators, a demonstrator lying unconscious on the street, and riot police making an arrest (pictures, of course, duplicated in all the papers).

Here, race was not a prime factor, though it had been in a number of other riots already discussed. The Scarman Report, and survey material from the late seventies, brought out clearly the inequalities suffered by black people: racism on the part of the police, hostility from many whites, appalling housing and lack of job opportunities. Harassment by the police was more usually directed at young Afro-Caribbeans. But Asians, generally industrious, often quite prosperous, and frequently high achievers at school, were frequently attacked by xenophobic Britons. On 23 April 1979 the National Front deliberately held a meeting in the Town Hall of Southall, a predominantly Asian community in west London. Four thousand policemen were drafted in to confront 3,000 anti-National Front demonstrators. A large number of these were Asians, but there were also many whites; and it was a white teacher, Blair Peach, who was killed that day, quite possibly at the hands of a member of the Metropolitan Special Patrol Group. Already, the Callaghan Labour Government had introduced a new Race Relations Act which declared all forms of discrimination illegal, and had set up a Commission for Racial Equality with powers of enforcement. Both the economic trends and the social policy changes of the eighties were adverse in their effects on the underprivileged, among whom racial minorities formed a disproportionate number. More and more women were coming in to the job market, many, however, as part-timers. It is right to record that the enterprise culture did offer opportunities to women wishing to run their own businesses, and their number greatly increased, so that by 1994 more than 740,000 women were running their own businesses, nearly double the number in 1980. With the loss of male manufacturing jobs, in many places women were the sole or major wage-earners. But women's earnings generally ran at less than 75 per cent of those of men. In 1987, 3,430,000 part-time women workers were earning less than what the Council of Europe regarded as a 'decent' wage.

A quick scrutiny of table 5.23 shows some obvious conclusions. With a plethora of minority religions, Britain was now indisputably a multiracial society, while white Britain was overwhelmingly a secular one. The figure of 6.08 million members of the traditional churches in 1995 amounts to no more than 15 per cent of the UK adult population, the lowest church membership figure in western Europe. The highest level of church membership in the European Union is in the Republic of Ireland, with church membership also being high in Northern Ireland: here is a very critical difference between mainland Britishness, and Irishness of either variety. On the mainland, 11.7 per cent of adults were attending church once a week or more. If we turn away from actual church membership, and regular church attendance, we find that slightly over 70 per cent of adults in the UK claimed to have some religious affiliation – just about the same proportion as in 1970; that is to say, though not practising church-

**Table 5.23** Membership of religious organizations of persons aged 16 and over, in millions

| *Organization* | *1970* | *1980* | *1990* | *1995* |
|---|---|---|---|---|
| Traditional British Christian | | | | |
| Anglican | 2.99 | 2.18 | 1.73 | 1.79 |
| Presbyterian | 1.66 | 1.43 | 1.21 | 1.10 |
| Methodist | 0.64 | 0.52 | 0.45 | 0.40 |
| Baptist | 0.27 | 0.24 | 0.23 | 0.22 |
| Other Free Churches | 0.65 | 0.52 | 0.60 | 0.65 |
| Roman Catholic | 2.71 | 2.46 | 2.20 | 1.92 |
| Total | 8.92 | 7.35 | 6.42 | 6.08 |
| Greek Orthodox | 0.19 | 0.20 | 0.27 | 0.29 |
| Non-Traditional | | | | |
| Mormon | 0.09 | 0.11 | 0.16 | 0.17 |
| Jehovah's Witnesses | 0.06 | 0.08 | 0.12 | 0.13 |
| Others | 0.14 | 0.15 | 0.18 | 0.22 |
| Total | 0.29 | 0.34 | 0.46 | 0.52 |
| Non-Christian | | | | |
| Muslims | 0.13 | 0.31 | 0.52 | 0.58 |
| Sikhs | 0.10 | 0.15 | 0.27 | 0.35 |
| Hindus | 0.08 | 0.,12 | 0.14 | 0.16 |
| Jews | 0.12 | 0.11 | 0.11 | 0.09 |
| Others | 0.02 | 0.05 | 0.08 | 0.12 |
| Total | 0.45 | 0.74 | 1.07 | 1.30 |

*Source:* (Adapted from) *Social Trends 29* (1999), p. 220.

goers, a substantial majority of British people retained some attachment to religion (and used the churches for life's major ceremonies, particularly marriage and burial).

## *DRUGS AND CRIME*

In the 1970s there had been an alarming rise in heroin abuse, with its potential for social violence and disruption. In fact, cocaine was the preferred drug of the eighties, the highly purified form, crack, being the staple of one facet of yuppie lifestyle, used in a highly controlled way, its supporters claimed, while less pure forms (together, of course, with other hard drugs) were widely diffused.[53] In a 1986 report, *Danger: Drugs at Work*, the Confederation of British Industry warned that drug abuse was a threat from shop-floor to board room. A Scotland Yard Assistant Commissioner (Specialist Operations) reckoned that UK drug trafficking amounted to £400 million in 1984, and £500 million in 1985. In 1987 the Customs and Excise did have an unprecedented success when they made a single haul of 208 kilos of cocaine. But, discounting that exceptional seizure, the figure for cocaine seizures increased by, to use the word of the Chief Investigation Officer, a 'sinister' figure of 80 per cent. Apart from drugs coming in from South America and the Indian sub-continent, often via the United States or European countries, there was manufacture within Britain itself of the second most widely used drug, amphetamine sulphate. The first-ever coordinated government strategy against drugs was initiated in 1984, with a major publicity campaign in 1985; in 1987 this merged into the campaign over AIDS.

Right down the age scale there was a cheap, do-it-yourself, but scarcely less pernicious, version of the drug habit – solvent-sniffing among young children, which was sometimes fatal. The growth in the problem can be charted by government reactions: voluntary guidelines were drawn up in 1983 for retailers to curb the sale of solvents (glue, lighter-fuel, etc.), while legislation passed in Scotland added solvent misuse to the list of grounds on which a child might be considered to need compulsory care; in 1985 there was English legislation making it an offence to supply such substances to children; a further campaign aimed at retailers was launched in 1987.

How rising crime rates affected individuals depended a great deal upon where you lived, what class and race you belonged to, how old you were, or whether you were male or female. Between 1981 and 1987, the number of notifiable offences recorded by the police in England and Wales rose by 5.5 per cent per year; in a single year 1986–7 crimes against the person increased by 12 per cent. Recorded cases of violent and sexual crimes rose again in 1988 (partly because allegations of rape were now recorded, although the total number of convictions actually declined). Old people in run-down housing estates felt greatly at risk, many speaking of their total fear of going out at all. Women's 'Right to the Night' campaigns had begun in the seventies. Many of the danger spots were located in the abysmal redevelopment projects of the 1960s, but the government of the eighties showed great reluctance to follow up simple remedies, such as the provision of better street lighting. The fear of crime was reflected in the proliferation of neighbourhood watch schemes.

In the mid-eighties society became aware of another group at risk, partly because of the highly publicized developments in Cleveland, where large numbers of alleged child abuse victims were identified. No doubt child abuse there had a long, subterranean history; no doubt also the numbers of cases in Cleveland were exaggerated by the over-zealous paediatrician Dr Marietta Higgs and her colleague Dr Geoffrey Wyatt, both criticized by the official Butler-Sloss Report 'for the certainty and over-confidence with which they pursued the detection of sexual abuse in children referred to them' and for failing to consider whether their practice 'was in the best interests of the children, their patients'; but such expert bodies as the National Society for the Prevention of Cruelty to Children were clear that the actual number of cases was on the increase.

### *LIFE AND LEISURE*

Developments in ordinary life, leisure activities and in the arts and entertainments, my sixth topic, largely have a momentum of their own, but were certainly not untouched by the new emphasis on business sponsorship, the desirability of profit-making and arguments over whether Thatcherism in effect could be equated with philistinism.[54] In ordinary life, the most significant changes were the advent of the video recorder (the number of households possessing these more than doubled between 1983 and 1986, and had reached 47 per cent of homes by 1987), home computers (17 per cent of households in 1986), microwave ovens (23 per cent of households in 1986) and the great expansion in the use of the telephone (83 per cent of households in 1986). The amount of time spent watching television had risen quite significantly to 25.5 hours per week on average. Going out for a drink remained for all men and for younger women the most popular extramural activity, with going out for a meal now actually coming fairly close. An existing trend towards the drinking of wine (in pubs and wine bars) was overtaken by another one for drinking exclusive foreign beers, genuinely imported in bottle. Drinking and driving was now coming to be positively frowned upon, as smoking also was becoming increasingly socially unacceptable, many public buildings and many sectors of public transport being declared no-smoking areas.

There was a Thatcherite policy towards the arts, signalled in the appointment in 1983 of Luke Rittner, a former Conservative councillor in Bath and organizer of the Association for Business Sponsorship of the Arts, as Secretary-General of the Arts Council; in the launching in 1984 of the Business Sponsorship Incentive Scheme; and in the National Heritage Act of 1983, which removed the responsibility for historical buildings from the Department of Environment, giving them to the new body known as English Heritage. A highly interventionist policy towards television was inaugurated. In 1987 the government sought to persuade the ITA to ban a Thames Television programme, *Death On the Rock*, which was an attempt to investigate what actually had happened when members of the SAS (Special Air Services) shot three IRA terrorists as they were entering Gibraltar. Lord Thomson, Chairman of the ITA, refused to give way to government pressure, and the programme was duly broadcast. Government ministers, and the government-supporting press, made many wild accusations against the programme, and against individuals who appeared on it (one secured libel damages). The programme was finally vindicated through an independent inquiry, reporting early in 1989, conducted by Lord Windlesham, a widely respected hereditary peer and former Conservative minister, and Richard Rampton QC.

Three internationally-renowned figures dominated British architecture: James Stirling, Richard Rogers and Norman Foster. *The* architectural event was the completion in 1986 of the new Lloyds of London, to the design of Richard Rogers, who had earlier been partly responsible for the Beaubourg in Paris. Both buildings were built on what has been called the Meccano set principle, with the service ducts and pipes on the outside. The most publicized artists of the time, bitterly disliked by many for their apparent admiration of Thatcher and overt commercialism, were Gilbert and George. A Gilbert and George exhibition, 'Pictures 1982–86', sponsored, it may be noted, by Beck's Beer, had toured Brussels, Basle, Madrid and Munich, before coming to the Hayward Gallery, London, in July 1987.

Opera seemed to enjoy a genuine rise in popularity, but to many was too closely associated with business sponsorship and the commandeering of excessively expensive seats for business entertainment. Yet, in addition to the marvellously inventive productions of the experimental Opera Factory, Scottish Opera, Welsh Opera, the English National Opera and, indeed, the Royal Opera House were all putting on innovative productions of most of the great classical and romantic operas. That opera was not an archaic art was demonstrated by the productions of Harrison Birtwhistle's *The Masque of Orpheus* (English National Opera, 1986) and Nigel Osborne's *The Electrification of the Soviet Union* (Royal Opera House, 1987).

It would be difficult indeed to maintain that British theatre betrayed a conformist trend. Leading left-wing writers such as Howard Brenton, David Hare and David Edgar did not suddenly go into retirement. Indeed, Brenton and Hare collaborated on the runaway success at the National Theatre *Pravda*, a satire whose target was quite manifestly Thatcherite newspaper magnate Rupert Murdoch. The target of Caryl Churchill's *Serious Money* was the stock market of eighties yuppiedom. A staple attraction for tourists continued to be classical plays imaginatively staged, the sensation of 1984 being Antony Sher's portrayal of *Richard III* at Stratford-upon-Avon as a 'bottled spider', an embittered cripple on crutches.

Modernism touched some of the novels of the 1980s, in the form of 'magic realism' in the case of Salman Rushdie, who in 1989 gained a peculiar and unwanted fame when, after his *The Satanic Verses* had been burned – terrible sign of the times! – by incensed Muslims in Bradford, a death sentence was pronounced on him by Iran's Ayatollah Khomeini. But in the main, British novels continued to be accounts – often highly inventive – of the manners and morals of the age. Fay Weldon remained an exuberant guide to post-feminist sensibilities: *Leader of the Band* (1988) portrays the sex-pot musician for whom, out of lust, the narrator Starlady Sandra has given up her work as a brilliant astronomer. David Lodge, whilst still offering a nice commentary on contemporary intellectual fashion, entered the world of industry in post-industrial Birmingham: *Nice Work* (1988) could well be *the* novel of life in Thatcherite Britain – the year 1986 is 'Industry Year'; universities are encouraged to appoint one 'industry year shadow', who, by following a local industrialist around, will learn about the vital importance of making money.

The up-and-down story of the British film industry, so repeatedly undercapitalized and confused as to its objectives, was generally on an 'up' in the later eighties. Richard Attenborough secured international commercial success with his *Gandhi* (directed by David Lean); *The Last Emperor* was another successful block-buster. But consistent success was to be found among the low-budget films sponsored by television's Channel 4. Particularly relevant to social themes were *My Beautiful Launderette* (involving British Asians and non-heterosexual relationships), *Mona Lisa* (in which the dominant figure is a beautiful black woman), and *Wish You Were Here* (featuring a liberated young woman, Lynda, in 1940s Britain).

There was, of course, no way of reinventing the pop revolution of the sixties. But in March 1984 the *Observer* was reporting that 'Britain has returned to its customary position as the world leader in pop music.' The groups singled out were Culture Club, the Police and Duran Duran. Late in the eighties the popular music scene was noteworthy for the strong Irish influence: in March 1985 *Rolling Stone* nominated the Dublin group U2 as 'band of the eighties'. The point to bring out at the end of this inevitably hasty catalogue is that U2 songs were distinguished by a strong element of social criticism and political protest.

British science had much to be proud of, but there was a well justified worry that scientific funding was now seriously inadequate, a point almost inadvertently touched on in passing is the most famous work of scientific popularization of the decade, *A Brief History of Time: From the Big Bang to Black Holes* (1988) by the Lucasian Professor of Mathematics at Cambridge University, Stephen W. Hawking. Hawking explained and summarized the latest developments in our understanding of the universe, many the product of his own researches.

### *THE PERSISTENCE OF PERMISSIVENESS*

Finally, the point with which I started, the disjunction between Thatcherite policies and values, and the actual attitudes and behaviour of a majority of people in society. There was a good deal of clever talk about 'the new piety', but this, as such talk often does, missed the realities of actual attitudes and behaviour. AIDS was a worry, but its impact was curiously double-headed: in a most ironic way the government educational campaigns of 1986 and 1988 brought to British television screens an anatomical explicitness, and an open acceptance of the sexual urges of young females as well as males, that would not have been contemplated in the sixties. The most illuminating figure yielded up by the official statistics was the numbers of people of opposite sexes living

**Table 5.24** Growing permissiveness

| 'A single mother can bring up her child as well as a married couple' | |
|---|---|
| Agree | Disagree |
| 48 (30)% | 41 (51)% |

| 'People who want children ought to get married' | |
|---|---|
| Agree | Disagree |
| 52 (70)% | 35 (17)% |

together without bothering about the ritual of marriage. This may perhaps be seen as a sign of emancipation among women; at any rate, the figures are given in the form of 'percentages of women cohabiting'. In the age group 18–49 the figure more than doubled from 2.7 per cent in 1979 to 6.4 per cent in 1987; for those in the age group 18–24 the respective figures were 4.5 per cent and 11.5 per cent. In 1988, 79 per cent of those aged 18–24 regarded 'premarital sex' as 'rarely wrong' or 'not wrong at all'. Opinion surveys conducted in the early nineties strongly suggested a steady advance in libertarian attitudes among society as a whole. Table 5.24 shows the National Opinion Poll figures from December 1993, giving responses to a couple of propositions, in comparison with responses to the same propositions in 1987 (in brackets).

Whatever the government might wish, there were influential agencies much more in tune with public sentiment. Early in 1989 the British Board of Film Classification proposed that in addition to the 15 category (suitable for showing to those over fifteen) and the PG category (parental guidance required) there should be a new 12 category. As reported in the *Independent* on 27 January 1989, James Ferman, Director of the Board, stated:

> *Crocodile Dundee* is the best example of all. We had to give that a 15 on the single word 'fucking'. It's lunatic that 12, 13 and 14-year-olds should be stopped seeing such an otherwise suitable film because of one word that they probably hear every day.

The report continued:

> The Board has recently stopped giving films a PG certificate which include 'shitting' and 'arse-hole', but which are unobjectionable in other ways. However, it feels that putting such movies into the 15 class is unduly restrictive.

The British were generally resistant to Thatcherite economic philosophy as well. A Gallup Poll carried out for London Weekend Television in August 1986 revealed that they were nothing like as interested in getting rich as the Japanese or the Americans. Only 9 per cent of Britons said that their main goal in life was to get rich, whereas 38 per cent gave this answer in Japan, and 15 per cent in the United States. The great majority of British respondents said that their main aim in life was 'to live as I like' (77 per cent). The majority

**Table 5.25** Higher welfare spending versus lower taxes (per cent of those interviewed)

| | *1983* | *1986* | *1990* | *1993* |
|---|---|---|---|---|
| If the government had to choose it should . . . | | | | |
| Reduce taxes and spend less on health, education and social benefits | 9 | 5 | 3 | 4 |
| Keep taxes and spending at the same levels as now | 54 | 44 | 37 | 29 |
| Increase taxes and spend more on health, education and social benefits | 32 | 46 | 54 | 63 |

disagreed, too, on Thatcherite views on welfare spending and taxes, and the disagreement got ever stronger (table 5.25).

Against all this, of course, one does have to remember that people continued to vote Conservative. No doubt there was an element of double-think, particularly when it came to the crunch in the voting booth. But probably also a not unjustified fear that Labour could not be trusted to implement these desirable policies, without also following totally disastrous ones.

## NOTES

1 Quoted in Kathleen Burke and Alex Cairncross, *Goodbye, Great Britain: The 1976 IMF Crisis* (1992), p. 165.
2 Derek Hatton, *Inside Left: The Story So Far . . .* (1988), pp. xiv, 27–8.
3 Eric Shaw, *The Labour Party since 1945. Old Labour: New Labour* (1996), p. 163.
4 Hatton, *Inside Left*, p. 68.
5 Shaw, *Labour Party*, p. 163.
6 Hugo Young, *One of Us: A Biography of Margaret Thatcher* (1989), pp. 83–8, 113ff.
7 T. R. Lloyd, *Empire, Welfare State, Europe: England 1880–1990* (Oxford, 1994), p. 464; Morgan, *The People's Peace, Britain 1945–1990* (Oxford, 1994), p. 385. But see also Clarke, *Hope and Glory, Britain 1900–1990* (1996), p. 351.
8 Shaw, *Labour Party*, p. 141.
9 James Callaghan, *Time and Change* (1987), pp. 426–7; G. C. Peden, *British Economic and Social Policy: Lloyd George to Margaret Thatcher* (Oxford, 1991), p. 210; Morgan, *People's Peace*, p. 382.
10 Denis Healey, *The Time of My Life* (1989), pp. 391–406, 428–37; but see also Joel Barnett, *Inside the Treasury* (1982), pp. 97ff.
11 Margaret Thatcher, *What's Wrong with Politics?* (1968), pp. 6–14.
12 Nigel Lawson, *Britain's Economy: A Mid-Term Report* (1985), p. 6.
13 Margaret Thatcher, *The Path to Power* (1995), p. 404; Conservative Central Office, *The Right Approach to the Economy* (1977) – the only copy I have found is in the Conservative Party Archives, Bodleian Library; I am grateful to James Walsh and Jill Davidson for facilitating access.
14 This paragraph is based on Christopher Harvie, *No Gods and Precious Few Heroes: Scotland since 1914* (Edinburgh, 1993), pp. 148–9, 159–62.
15 See Hugo Young, *This Blessed Plot: Britain and Europe from Churchill to Blair* (1998), pp. 286–99.
16 Morgan, *People's Peace*, p. 378.
17 Hugo Young, *One of Us*, p. 93. This paragraph is based on Young, pp. 93–9.
18 *Report of the Committee of Inquiry on Industrial Democracy*, Cmnd 6706 (1977).
19 Peden, *Economic and Social Policy*, p. 208; Morgan, *People's Peace*, p. 383.
20 Thomas Hennessy, *A History of Northern Ireland 1920–1996* (1997), pp. 230–4.
21 Harvie, *No Gods*, p. 162.
22 Morgan, *People's Peace*, p. 370.
23 Kenneth O. Morgan, *Callaghan: A Life* (Oxford, 1997), p. 662.
24 Young, *One of Us*, pp. 212–17.
25 See Ivor Crewe and Anthony King, *SDP: The Birth, Life and Death of the Social Democratic Party* (1995).
26 Max Hastings and Simon Jenkins, *The Battle for the Falklands* (1983, 1997).
27 D. Goodhart and P. Wintower, *Eddie Shah and the Newspaper Revolution* (1986), pp. 12–13.

28 Joe Gormley, *Battered Cherub: The Autobiography of Joe Gormley* (1982), pp. 173–9.
29 Martin Adeney and John Lloyd, *The Miners' Strike, 1984–5: Loss Without Limit* (1986).
30 Arthur Marwick, *British Society since 1945* (1996), p. 339.
31 Ibid., pp. 344–5. On violence see Charles Townshend, *Making the Peace: Public Order and Security in Modern Britain* (Oxford, 1993).
32 Peden, *Economic and Social Policy*, p. 227.
33 Young, *One of Us*, pp. 276–7, 285–7.
34 Ibid., pp. 431–2, 435–57.
35 Christopher Johnson, *The Economy Under Mrs Thatcher, 1979–1990* (1991).
36 Tim Jenkinson and Colin Mayer, 'The Costs of Privatization in the UK and France'. In Mathew Bishop, John Kay and Colin Mayer (eds), *Privatization and Economic Performance* (1994), p. 293.
37 Morgan, *People's Peace*, p. 476; Clarke, *Hope and Glory*, p. 379.
38 Young, *One of Us*, p. 467.
39 T. Hennessy, *Nortern Ireland*, p. 263.
40 Young, *One of Us*, p. 469.
41 Bruce R. Jewell, *The UK Economy and Europe* (1993), pp. 277–8.
42 Clarke, *Hope and Glory*, p. 399; Morgan, *People's Peace*, p. 505; Geoffrey Howe, *Conflict of Loyalty* (1994), pp. 645–68.
43 Anthony Seldon, *John Major: A Political Life* (paperback 1998), p. 127.
44 In an interview with *Woman's Own* in October 1987, subsequently publicized on the front page of the *Guardian*. See Hugo Young, *Thatcherism: Did Society Survive?* (1992), p. 2.
45 See especially Joseph Rowntree Foundation, *Income and Wealth* (1995).
46 The geographical survey is drawn from Marwick, *British Society*, pp. 287–307.
47 T. Hennessy, *Northern Ireland*, p. 239.
48 For this subsection see Marwick, *British Society*, pp. 319–23.
49 See Rodney Lowe, *The Welfare State since 1945* (1993); Nicholas Timmins, *The Five Giants: A Biography of the Welfare State* (1993); and Charles Webster, *The National Health Service: A Political History* (1997).
50 Shelter, *Christmas Report on Homelessness 1988* (1989).
51 Marwick, *British Society*, pp. 325–30.
52 Gordon Marshall, Howard Newby, David Rose and Carolyn Vogler, *Social Class in Britain Today* (1988).
53 *Social Trends 29* (1999), pp. 15–28.
54 A view vigorously advanced by Robert Hewison, *The Heritage Industry: Britain in a Climate of Decline* (1987) and *Culture and Consensus: England, Art and Politics since 1940* (revised edn, 1997).

# 6 The Nineties: Nasty, Then Nice?

## Recession, Recovery – and Continuing Crisis in Manufacture?

Through twice declaring war on Germany in the half-century of total war, Britain became involved in world events which then impinged upon Britain's own historical development. The two world wars were tragedies caused by human folly and human evil. But the events of 1989 suggested that rationality and respect for human rights had grown in the most unexpected places: in one of history's few truly joyful and inspiring episodes the Soviet Empire collapsed. Britain played no part, though it shared with the other western powers in the mindless encouragement of the free-market extremism which shortly brought a new brand of misery and criminality to Russia, and was complicit in the indecisiveness and cowardice which permitted the Serbs to wage genocidal war in the former Yugoslavia, particularly against the Bosnians. The world events which actually affected Britain's destiny in the nineties were the usual ones of global economic crises and recession.

Nigel Lawson had claimed to have set Britain on the path of steady econ-omic expansion. He then resigned and left others to clear up the mess he had done so much to create. Unshameable, he declared in a lecture on 20 June 1994:

> The plain fact is that the economic cycle is endemic – which means, incidentally, that all the current talk of no return to 'boom and bust' is somewhat premature to say the least. As experience throughout the world makes clear, abolition of the economic cycle is simply not within the power of any government to deliver.[1]

In 1990 and 1991 Britain moved into a depression much deeper than that suffered by the other European countries (though Germany did shortly begin to suffer severely from the costs of union with the clapped-out, inefficient former Soviet-dominated East Germany). From 1995 Britain appeared to be ahead of the other European countries in beginning to move out of recession: however, many economic indicators remained unfavourable and there was a general ab-sence of the business and consumer confidence which the government might have expected on the basis of the economic cycle alone. By 1998, with a series of crises in the Far East, the onset of further recession was being widely pre-

**Table 6.1** Some economic indicators

| | *Year on year inflation* | *Unemployment* | *GDP (1990 = 100)* | *Balance of payments in £ million* | *Interest rates* |
|---|---|---|---|---|---|
| 1988 | 3.5 | 9.1 | | –3257 | |
| | 4.3 | 8.3 | 96.5 | –3099 | |
| | 5.5 | 7.9 | 97.9 | –3331 | |
| | 6.5 | 7.0 | 99.6 | –5833 | |
| 1989 | 7.7 | 7.0 | 99.1 | –4778 | |
| | 8.2 | 6.5 | 99.3 | –4989 | |
| | 7.7 | 6.2 | 99.5 | –6065 | |
| | 7.6 | 5.9 | 99.8 | –4572 | |
| 1990 | 7.8 | 5.7 | 100.4 | –5349 | |
| | 9.6 | 5.7 | 100.7 | –5217 | |
| | 10.4 | 5.7 | 99.8 | –2619 | |
| | 10.0 | 6.0 | 98.1 | –2261 | |
| 1991 | 8.7 | 6.7 | 98.1 | –2303 | |
| | 6.0 | 7.6 | 97.6 | –208 | |
| | 5.3 | 8.3 | 97.5 | –1240 | |
| | 4.2 | 8.7 | 97.5 | –642 | |
| 1992 | 4.1 | 9.1 | 96.8 | –2025 | 10.5 |
| | 4.1 | 9.5 | 96.9 | –2325 | 10.2 |
| | 3.6 | 9.7 | 97.3 | –2492 | 9.7 |
| | 3.0 | 10.1 | 97.6 | –3291 | 7.3 |
| 1993 | 1.8 | 10.5 | 98.2 | –3114 | 6.0 |
| | 1.3 | 10.4 | 98.6 | –2327 | 6.0 |
| | 1.7 | 10.3 | 99.4 | –2411 | 6.0 |
| | 1.6 | 10.1 | 100.0 | –2443 | 5.7 |
| 1994 | 2.4 | 9.9 | 101.8 | –1140 | 5.3 |
| | 2.6 | 9.6 | 103.1 | –519 | 5.3 |
| | 2.3 | 9.3 | 104.1 | –106 | 5.4 |
| | 2.6 | 8.9 | 105.0 | 110 | 5.9 |
| 1995 | 3.4 | 8.6 | 105.4 | 587 | 6.6 |
| | 3.5 | 8.3 | 105.8 | –1653 | 6.8 |
| | 3.7 | 8.2 | 106.4 | –1354 | 6.8 |
| | 3.2 | 8.1 | 107.0 | –1252 | 6.7 |
| 1996 | 2.8 | 7.9 | 107.6 | –1206 | 6.2 |
| | 2.2 | 7.8 | 108.2 | 689 | 5.9 |
| | 2.1 | 7.6 | 108.9 | –426 | 5.8 |
| | 2.6 | 7.2 | 109.7 | 508 | 6.0 |
| 1997 | 2.7 | 6.5 | 110.8 | 1459 | 6.0 |

*Sources:* P. Jay in D. Kavanagh and A. Seldon (eds), *The Major Effect* (Basingstoke: Macmillan, 1994), pp. 170–1; D. Butler and D. Kavanagh, *The British General Election of 1997* (Basingstoke: Macmillan, 1997), pp. 4–5.

dicted. Yet the US economy remained strong, and, in Britain, the Labour Chancellor of the Exchequer, Gordon Brown, claimed that prudent government measures were ensuring that recession would be kept at bay: services were doing well, manufacture, constantly subject to threats of closure and redundancies, rather badly. Over-production, the strong pound, expensive (but essential) new health and safety procedures, continental resistance to the purchase of British meat, and the collapse of the Russian market for sheepskins brought crisis to British agriculture in the late summer of 1999.

The slump in GDP is apparent from the second half of 1990 onwards (see table 6.1), with no clear recovery until 1994. Unemployment starts going up in 1991 and remains very high, even with the slight recovery in 1994 and 1995. Inflation reaches historically very low figures in the still depressed year of 1993, but then, though still relatively low, goes up again. The balance of payments figures are atrocious throughout, showing fleetingly encouraging signs in 1995 and 1996, and looking good in 1997, by which year GDP is again steadily rising. With some fluctuations, interest rates did come down from the very high ones introduced to try to contain the Lawson boom, but remained high by European standards. High unemployment meant high public expenditure on unemployment benefits, so that in 1993–4 the Public Sector Borrowing Requirement topped 7 per cent of GDP, a proportion nearly as high as that of the mid-1970s.

Margaret Thatcher had aimed to destroy socialism and to convert the British people to a belief in market economics and the minimalist state. She was aided in the first aim by the continuing association of 'socialism' with 'loony-left' policies and by the collapse of the Soviet Empire. She was rather less successful, as we have seen, in changing the social attitudes of the British people. She had given great encouragement to those who had always inclined to the politics of extreme individualism and had built up a new type of Conservative supporter among the upper-working class and lower-middle class who had prospered during the Thatcher years, sometimes defined as 'Essex man', and seemingly typified by the population of Basildon in Essex. At least as important, powerful interests welcomed the ratification of ruthless profit-seeking and massive salaries. She had very nearly destroyed the 'one-nation' tradition within the Conservative party itself. Aided by the severe recession at the beginning of the eighties she had drastically reduced the power of the leaders of the big trade unions. The decline in the size of the working class had continued, and within the workforce as a whole, trade union membership had fallen particularly sharply during the eighties. Meantime the proportion of those owning their own homes had greatly increased: in 1950 the figure for home ownership had been only 29 per cent; by 1990 it was 67 per cent. In 1950 manual workers had made up 68 per cent of the workforce; by 1990 this figure was down to 48 per cent. Between 1979 and 1990 trade union membership fell from 50 per cent to 36 per cent of the workforce.[2] No more than 42 per cent of the electorate voted Conservative, but the figures were suggesting that Labour had become practically unelectable. The gap between the two parties in the 1979 election was 7.6 per cent. This went up to 14.8 per cent in the 1983 election, and was still up at the unusually high figure, for the post-war years, of 11.5 per cent in 1987.

What had definitely gone compared with the period up until the middle seventies, was the spirit of consensus in British politics. This showed itself most strongly in the triumphalism and grasp for control over all aspects of politics and society apparent in governing circles and the disaffection from government apparent in many sectors of society. Left-wingers, such as Tony Benn, continued to argue that what Labour must do was to put forward a vigorous socialist alternative to the Conservatives – though all the evidence suggested that most electors preferred parties to remain within a certain middle ground of agreement and rejected extremist policies. The bulk of the Labour leadership could not but be aware that some adjustments to traditional policies would be essential if Labour were ever to be elected again. Kinnock as leader did succeed in detaching the party from its unpopular unilateral disarmament policy and gained credit for his denunciations of Derek Hatton and the Left. But the truly painful readjustment in Labour policies, resulting eventually in 'New Labour' and 'The Third Way', with most of the leadership trying to project a social democratic, rather than a socialist image, did not come till the mid-nineties. In important sections of the party the 'ethical socialism' of Clement Attlee remained strong, while fundamentalist socialism, if somewhat marginalized, was very far from eradicated. Globalization, further structural changes in the British economy, the unfortunate legacy of the seventies and continuing electoral failure, and the indisputable, if circumscribed, successes of Thatcherism forced Labour towards fundamental reappraisals, particularly of taxation and of the respective roles of the state and of private enterprise.

On becoming Prime Minister (28 November 1990) John Major declared that he hoped to create a society 'at ease with itself' and, indeed, 'a classless society'.[3] In many quarters hopes were high that the triumphalism and 'continuous revolution' of Thatcherism would now be brought to an end and that there would be some restoration of 'one-nation' values. But vested interests in the continuation of Thatcherite policies were strong. Recession, a high PSBR, and appalling balance of trade figures did not augur well for generous social policies. Moderate Conservatism had lost its voice and tended to be ridiculed in Conservative circles. The pressures for more of the same were rather strong. For a real break to have been made, it would have taken a strong Prime Minister of real intellectual quality. Or, of course, an Opposition capable of providing a gifted alternative leader.

## JOHN MAJOR AND A SOCIETY AT ODDS WITH ITSELF

### *THE RISE OF JOHN MAJOR*

'The middle class' is one of the most loosely used terms in British historical writing, particularly that of a Marxist tendency, where, without any clear sense being given of its size, it stands for the dominant class, the ruling class, the 'wicked bourgeoisie'. In fact, if language has any meaning, the dominant class is the upper class, which, along with the working class (despite its shrinkage), is one of the two truly homogeneous classes in British society. The aggregation in between is so miscellaneous as to merit the label 'middle classes' in the plural. No one better demonstrated the weird background which could be concealed by the label 'middle-class' than John Major. Indeed, it would take a Dickens to do justice to the strange boyhood of the young Major, even if it would have to be left to a C. P. Snow to chronicle the dull prime ministership in which the odd, and sometimes brave, apprenticeship culminated.

The paternal grandparents of the man who succeeded Margaret Thatcher as Prime Minister, by the name of Ball, were firmly working-class, the grandfather being a master bricklayer in the West Midlands.[4] Major's father, Tom Ball, took up various occupations on the fringes between working class and lower-middle class, including being a trapeze artist in a travelling variety troupe (where he took the stage name of 'Tom Major'), a builder and a salesman, before setting himself up as a manufacturer of garden ornaments. Tom Ball was 64 in 1943 when the son christened John Major was born to his second wife, 26 years younger than him, the daughter of a grocer's assistant. The family were living in a pleasant bungalow, set in a large garden, in the middle-class suburb of Worcester Park in south-west London when the young Major won a place at grammar school in Merton, three miles away. A sharp decline in the family business meant that while he was still there, the family, in 1955, had to move to a two-room rented flat, with a communal bathroom, in predominantly working-class Brixton.

Major did poorly at his grammar school. Leaving at the age of sixteen he first took a job as a clerk in an insurance brokers. Then for a while he settled into doing manual labour for the company which had taken over his father's business. After his father's death in 1962 he returned to settled work as a clerk at the London Electricity Board. He had found a purpose in life through his membership of Brixton Young Conservatives; a year later he became Chairman. He began an affair with a divorcee, 13 years older than himself, behaving as a father to her two children.[5] Bright working-class lads with political ambitions could make their way through the trade unions and the Labour party; in many ways, Major, as a member of the rootless lower-middle class, had it tougher. Some working-class young people exploited post-war educational opportunities to go on and take university degrees, something John Major never did. He moved to a local branch of the District Bank, and embarked on serious study for banking qualifications – a pattern of in-work study not altogether different from that followed by many working-class young people. Equipped with his first lot of banking qualifications he moved to an international bank in the City, the Standard Bank. He was sent out to Nigeria where he was given managerial responsibilities which would not have fallen to him at home. The shattering of his kneecap when the car being driven by a colleague crashed, meant his being invalided back to Britain. Not a piece of fortune to be equated with Margaret Thatcher's marrying a millionaire, this nonetheless meant his escape from Africa, and the opportunity to begin the building of serious political and professional careers back home. He continued with his studies so that, in the bank, he was now, as his biographer Anthony Seldon puts it, 'on a par with someone who had come in as a graduate', but never, of course, on a par with those who had debated in the unions of Cambridge or Oxford. In May 1968, profiting from a period of intense unpopularity for the then Labour Government, Major won a formerly safe Labour seat and joined the Lambeth Council. He advanced rapidly both in politics and in banking, collecting invaluable experience as he went. He rapidly became Vice-Chairman and then Chairman of the Lambeth Housing Committee. In October 1968 he joined the investment and international division of his bank, just at the time when the foreign exchange and Euro dollar markets were enjoying their modest beginnings. Then he moved to the business development division; by the time the bank had been merged into the major international player Standard Chartered, Major had moved to another growth area, marketing.

Had he been a young member of the upper class, Major would probably have been given a safe parliamentary seat by this time; as it was, he was not yet 29 when he was adopted for the safe Labour seat of St Pancras North. Defeat there led him to decide to give up politics altogether for banking, when the safe Conservative seat of Huntingdonshire fell vacant. Major was one of 250 hopefuls to put their names forward. Eliminated in the first round of selection were such future Conservative luminaries as Michael Howard, Peter Lilley, and Chris Patten. Major's qualities of courtesy combined with dedication and mastery of detail, together perhaps with a sense among the constituency party that Major might have a particular appeal to the skilled workers who were now moving into the more urbanized parts of the county (those later considered to belong to the prototype 'Essex Man') took him through (a stunning achievement in itself) to the final short-list of four, interviewed on 19 November 1976. Major's rivals were: the heir to the Duke of Wellington, and two former MPs, one definitely upper-class, the other on the fringes of the upper class. Major's victory was a true portent of the Thatcher era just beginning its pre-history.

Major lacked the traditional advantages of many in the new entry of 1979. But once he got his opportunities (some by, for him, fortunate conjunctions of circumstances) he always, discreetly and without alienating people, exploited them to the full. His 'assiduous hard work and pleasant manner', as Seldon puts it, found favour with the whips, and brought his own first job as a whip, in January 1983. His 'attention to detail, accurate reading of people and congenial personality' brought substantial advance as Minister for Social Security in 1985: here he demonstrated 'an outstanding ability to master his brief' and 'proved himself sensitive in dealing with individual cases of hardship as well as a surprisingly effective and occasionally rebarbative parliamentary performer'.[6] As a former banker, Major was certainly highly qualified for the post of Chief Secretary at the Treasury; it was his good fortune that Nigel Lawson actually fought to win him this Cabinet appointment. Then, having ousted Geoffrey Howe, Margaret Thatcher found herself in urgent need of a Foreign Secretary, and, she reflected, if Major were to have a chance of succeeding her, 'it would be better if he had held one of the three great offices of state'.[7] Major was consummate in managing his relations with her, he was self-made and of the new youthful generation uncontaminated by any association with Heath. His run of fortune continued with Lawson's resignation as Chancellor of the Exchequer. Thatcher wanted the abrasive Nicholas Ridley (shortly forced to resign because of some outrageous anti-German remarks) but was warned off him by the whips, and so Major got the post. Major, perhaps reflecting the natural prejudices of his family background, shared Thatcher's faith in market economics, low taxation, and control of both inflation and bureaucracy. But, unlike her, he had a genuine sympathy for the underdog (he was only ceasing to be one himself), and he did not have her instinctive, xenophobic anti-Europeanism. Indeed, Major was responsible for taking Britain into the European Exchange Rate Mechanism in October 1990, thus pinning the pound to the German mark and the other European currencies within a very limited band of fluctuation – 6 per cent on either side of DM 2.95. Major's speech on this matter was warmly applauded at the Conservative Party Conference; most of the Labour leadership, too, was by this time wholly in favour of this gesture towards Europeanism and attempt to bring stability to the pound. Unfortunately, though perhaps, given the prevailing ideology, inevitably, the rate chosen involved an overvalued pound.

Major, as we saw, did not win outright on the second ballot for the Conservative leadership. Had Thatcher stood again, as was her original intention, he would have been out of the race, since he had again, very reluctantly, agreed to second Hurd's nomination of her. Had Thatcher gone ahead, the likelihood is that Heseltine would have won. But most of the leading Conservative parliamentarians, including Major himself, believed it was very much in the interests of the party that Thatcher should go. This opinion did get through very strongly to Thatcher which explains why, though so close to outright victory in the first ballot, she gave up. She then let it be known that Major was her own choice as successor. Major thus got about 80 per cent of the right-wing vote in the parliamentary party. Left-wing votes went to Heseltine, but Major scored heavily among the 'floating centre'.[8] This was, first, because, over the years, he had assiduously cultivated individual MPs; secondly, because his campaign was run extremely efficiently by Norman Lamont, who had succeeded Major as Chief Secretary to the Treasury – by no means a fan, but someone who was counting on his reward if Major did indeed win; and thirdly, because, unlike Hurd, he really did desperately want to win. Beyond that, partly because of skilful lobbying, Major both won the support of the majority of the Conservative press, and emerged as the popular man in the constituencies; finally, opinion polls showed that the public would be just as willing to vote for him as for Heseltine – despite Thatcher's own support, not announced publicly, he had done enough to demonstrate that, as he himself put it in a television interview, he was not 'son of Thatcher'.

Heseltine was applauded for not going to a third ballot: realistically he had no alternative. At 47, Major was the youngest Prime Minister since Lord Rosebery in 1894. His campaign had shown his driving ambition and his consummate political skills. The latter were felt to be further demonstrated by the way in which the new Prime Minister reconstructed the Cabinet. Heseltine was offered Environment, with a special responsibility for settling on the future of the poll tax. Lamont, very much a Thatcherite, got his reward as Chancellor of the Exchequer. Chris Patten, a 'wet', who, however, as Minister for the Environment, had been responsible for introducing the poll tax, and a close friend of Major's, though he had actually supported Hurd in the recent leadership election, was made Party Chairman. This meant that the staunch Thatcherite Kenneth Baker had to be moved to the Home Office. Cecil Parkinson helped by voluntarily withdrawing. Otherwise most of Thatcher's ministers, including Hurd as Foreign Secretary and Clarke as Education Secretary, remained in post. As throughout the Thatcher years, this was an upper- and upper-middle-class Cabinet, with Major himself the only credible representative of that classlessness to which he claimed to aspire. The Cabinet contained not one single woman, though a woman – an upper-class one, Sarah Hogg, daughter of Lord Boyd-Carpenter, and wife of the son of Lord Hailsham – was chosen as head of Major's Policy Unit.

## *End of the Poll Tax: to 'the heart of Europe'*

The first problem the new Major Government had to deal with was that of the hugely unpopular poll tax, at the same time operating within the context of both deepening depression and a rapidly escalating balance of payments deficit. It would also have to clarify its position towards a Europe moving ever closer towards integration. But first there was that nasty problem of 'events', in this case a war looming in the Middle East. In western eyes the great villain in the Middle East had for long been Iran, under its fundamentalist Islamic regime. The Iraq of Saddam Hussein was seen as a force for stability, and had been supplied with arms by America, Britain and other western powers. However, on 2 August 1990, Iraq, declaring its small, oil-rich neighbour, Kuwait, part of its own historic territories, had invaded that country, six days later declaring it incorporated within these territories. Iraq's actions were condemned by the United Nations, by the United States, and also by both what was now the Confederation of Russian States and the Arab League. The United States, under President George Bush, took the initiative in preparing what would in the first instance be a massive air war against Iraq, to be followed by a counter-invasion of land forces. Margaret Thatcher announced her immediate support, and was seconded both by Labour and by the Liberal Democrats. The crucial development was the United Nations Security Council Resolution 678 of 29 November, which set a deadline of 15 January 1991 for total Iraqi withdrawal from Kuwait, and authorized the use of 'all necessary force' if the resolution was not acted upon. The military preparations and, as important, the building up of an international coalition took time. The aerial part of what was designated Operation Desert Storm began on 16 January 1991. It is a military truism that no victory can be achieved by aerial bombardment alone; and it is another one that a land invasion is nearly always very costly in lives. There was great trepidation in the west that the Gulf War would be immensely destructive, would involve high loss of life, and would do great damage to the environment and could involve Iraqi terrorist attacks throughout the world; the use by the Iraqis of chemical and biological weapons was particularly feared. Thatcher committed a British force of 30,000 to the cause. Major, on a special mission to America in December, though hopeful that military action might not in the end be necessary, confirmed the British commitment to the Americans. Land action began on Sunday, 24 February, being brought to an unexpectedly swift end on Wednesday, 28 February. On the whole, President Bush's motives were honourable in bringing to an end the slaughter of inexperienced Iraqi troops, the moment the basic United Nations objective had been attained. But, a vexing problem for the future, Saddam Hussein himself had not been removed. The general view, both at the time and since, is that Major comported himself well during this crisis. He projected great calm, and eschewed any kind of Thatcherite triumphalism. He established warm relations with Bush, and his actions in sharing information with the Opposition leaders, Neil Kinnock and Paddy Ashdown, gained him high praise.

Already intensive discussions over what to do with the poll tax were under way. The alternatives were 'big Bertha' (a massive gun of First World War vintage) or 'salami slicer' – that is to say either a one-off cut in the basic figure, or a series of smaller reductions, with special relief schemes for politically sensitive groups. In the end Major went for 'big Bertha', forcing Lamont, against his own judgement, to find £4 billion–£5 billion for a one-off reduction in the poll tax. In his budget on 19 March 1991 Lamont announced that the average poll tax bill would be reduced by £140, the cost being met by increasing VAT from 15 per cent to 17.5 per cent. The obvious danger of local authority expenditure running out of control was to be met with additional capping powers. There were some cuts in business taxation, met by increased direct taxation on alcohol and tobacco. The Conservatives were to continue to claim that they were the natural party of low taxation, but were increasingly taunted by Labour with the heavy increases in National Insurance contributions and indirect taxation throughout their period of office (the 1979 increase of VAT from 8 per cent to 15 per cent was never to be forgotten).

Brutal, stupid, and undemocratic, the poll tax was the very emblem of the far side of Thatcherite ideology. It fell equally upon rich and poor alike and was intended to keep local authority expenditure down to a level acceptable to the rich; it was extremely expensive to collect and encouraged massive evasion, the most effective form of which was to disappear from the electoral register, which entailed disenfranchisement. What, then, should happen to this accursed tax? Here was Major's big opportunity to demonstrate that he was no 'son of Thatcher', to make a significant strike in the direction of 'a society at ease with itself' and to face down the right-wing atavism of the Conservative party in the country as all Conservative leaders before Thatcher had faced it down. Instead he earned the first accusations of indecisiveness and weak leadership. Perhaps these were slightly unfair. Both the government, and the party at large, were sharply divided over the poll tax, with many determined on its retention as a symbol of keeping the faith with Thatcherism. Many ministers resented Heseltine's eagerness, as one of them put it, 'to obtain the scalp of the poll tax to place on Mrs Thatcher's grave'. But two leading Thatcherites, Lamont and Michael Portillo, did, on practical grounds, swing round against the tax, the setting up, administering and replacing of which cost at least £1.5 billion. In the end, the replacement, the Council Tax, announced in the Queen's Speech in November 1991, and rapidly enacted in 1992, to come into effect from April 1993, was sensible. Like the old rates, the tax was essentially on the value of the property, each property being allocated (in England) to one of eight bands – the eighth band, for properties over £320,000, being insisted upon by Heseltine; at the same time there was a discount for those in single occupation.

Among the most persistent criticisms of Major was the one that he had no coherent political philosophy, no 'Big Idea', though he did choose two domestic issues to identify himself with: education and improving the quality of public services. On education, he at first established a very positive image, in effect stepping in front of his Education Secretary, Clarke, to present two seminal White Papers in May 1991: *Education and Training for the 21st Century,* proposing the introduction of National Vocational Qualifications (NVQs) for those over 16, the publication of examination results by schools and colleges, and the ending of local authority control of sixth-form and further education colleges; and *Higher Education: A New Framework*, announcing the ending of the snobbish 'binary' distinction between universities and polytechnics. The latter, together with some other higher education institutions, were to be given the right to assume university status, raising the total number of British universities to over 90. Provision for regular school inspections was embodied in the 1992 Education Act. Major's struggle, particularly with the Treasury, to bring forward his own special project, the Citizen's Charter, revealed the key to what in the end was to be the rather shabby record in social policy of the Major governments: with the country's external debt constantly mounting, the watchwords became 'don't do anything which may cost money' and 'if you do do anything, make sure it saves money'. Major should be given credit for winning the struggle, so that he himself presented the White Paper to the House of Commons on Monday, 22 July 1991. But the paper revealed many of the intrinsic weaknesses of the Major political stance. At the heart of the document was the proposed Citizen's Charter, the aims of which were entirely laudable. But its mechanisms of performance targets, inspectors, league tables and financial compensation where targets were not met, were redolent of the most naive Thatcherite ideas of market incentives and disincentives. The White Paper contained other extensions of Thatcherism: privatization of British Rail, deregulation of London buses, further contracting out of civil service responsibilities. Thatcher had encouraged an intensified selfishness amongst the powerful, a fixation on profits rather than service: the further deployment of Thatcherite devices was not the way to reverse that process. The Citizen's Charter hinted at what was to prove Major's greatest weakness, one which shortly overcame education policy and social policy generally: his resort to platitudes which might sound well in a pub conversation or schoolboy debate, but which took little account of the true realities and full complexities of any situation.

Nowhere was this more true than in Major's involvement with Europe. Margaret Thatcher had not only spoken strongly against European integration (her September 1988 speech at Bruges against a 'European super-state' had led to the creation of the Conservative Europhobe Bruges Group), she kept less than complete control over her anti-German sentiments. Thus, advised by the pro-European Chris Patten and Sarah Hogg, and by the British Ambassador in Bonn, Major chose the then German capital for the speech which Seldon has called 'the most controversial of his premiership'. No doubt the words were written for him, but nonetheless an obligation lay upon the Prime Minister to think out very carefully just exactly what he was saying:

> My aims for Britain in the Community can be simply stated: I want us to be where we belong. At the very heart of Europe. Working with our partners in building the future.[9]

Major unloaded another platitude in the same speech – 'Europe is made up of nation states: their vitality and diversity are sources of strength': how exactly were these platitudes to be reconciled?

Whatever the attitudes of British politicians might be, the European Economic Community was already set firmly on a course towards becoming the European Union, which would eventually be underpinned by the introduction of a single currency (EMU, European Monetary Union). The European summit to establish the European Union and single European market was scheduled for Maastricht, in the Netherlands, for 9–10 December, where the British representatives were Major, Hurd, Lamont and Garel-Jones, the Foreign Office Minister responsible for Europe. To the consternation of the British, the French, supported by the Italians, succeeded in writing in a resolution that EMU would begin in 1999. However, the British delegation (along with the Danish) were able to secure an opt-out from joining the EMU. Although the European Economic Community had long been pilloried by the British Left as a 'rich man's club', an important element in the treaty due to be signed at Maastricht was the Social Chapter, committing all countries to moderate social welfare policies. Such a commitment was anathema to Thatcherites. To Major goes the credit (if that is the right word) for both patience and energy, against great resistance, in negotiating an opt-out on this matter as well. In the Maastricht debate on 18–19 December, only seven extreme Europhobes (always, with all the inadequacy of English gentility, called 'Eurosceptics'), led by Norman Tebbit, voted against the government, with three abstentions, including Thatcher. Labour, opposed in particular to the opt-out from the Social Chapter, also abstained. Major should probably have proceeded immediately to securing the passing of the European Community (Amendment) Bill, ratifying the Maastricht Treaty, but, hoping that Conservative hostility would melt away still further, he delayed until 1993, when, in fact, it had solidified greatly.

## *Election victory and the emergence of Tony Blair*

Lamont's budget of 11 March 1992 introduced a new twenty pence income tax band (the standard rate was 25p) for the first £2,000 of taxable income, which would benefit four million of the lowest-paid. Income support was raised for pensioners. This was a moderately, but certainly not excessively, vote-catching budget: Major shortly decided on 9 April as the date for a General Election. An election in the depths of a depression when many middle-class voters were suffering was not an ideal option for a Conservative Government; but adverse economic circumstances could also focus voters' attention on fears about Labour's economic competence. Neil Kinnock was, all informed critics agreed, doing an excellent job in 'modernizing' the Labour party and extending its appeal. As the election approached, the polls gave Labour a slight lead. Private Labour surveys suggested that the public rated Labour's front bench more highly than the Government, but Major consistently came out with higher ratings than Kinnock. Canvassers continued to find distrust of Labour and doubts about its tax plans (John Smith, Labour's Shadow Chancellor, published a 'Shadow Budget', where higher welfare benefits, it seemed clear, would be financed by higher taxation), and, most notably, hostility towards Kinnock. Because of a flaw in their methods (since corrected) the opinion polls were actually overstating the Labour vote, so that the odds, in reality, remained slightly in favour of the Conservatives. It is just possible that a truly charismatic leader, without previous associations with the Left, might, in a situation tilting away from Labour, have managed to attain the hung parliament that preoccupied so many commentators. But, in the event, the Conservative victory, 7.6 per cent over Labour in votes cast, 64 seats over Labour, and 21 overall, was not really very surprising.

**Table 6.2** General Election, 9 April 1992

| | *Electorate 43.25 million* | | *Turnout 77.7 per cent* | | |
|---|---|---|---|---|---|
| | *Conservative* | *Labour* | *Liberal Democrat* | *Nationalist* | *Other (mainly N. Ireland)* |
| Votes | 14,092,891 | 11,559,735 | 5,999,384 | 783,991 | 1,176,692 |
| Percentage of votes cast | 42.3 | 35.2 | 18.3 | 2.3 | 3.2 |
| Seats | 336 | 271 | 20 | 7 | 17 |

Labour's triumphalist eve-of-the-poll rally in Sheffield was considered a mistake by many, but beyond perhaps confirming an adverse image of Kinnock already held, it seems unlikely that it had a critical effect on the result. The press was overwhelmingly against Labour anyway, and the *Sun* had run a particularly virulent anti-Labour and anti-Kinnock campaign (Kinnock *was* vulnerable). Notoriously, the *Sun* claimed: 'It's The Sun Wot Won It': true or false, politicians were subsequently to betray an extreme anxiety over the prospect of alienating the *Sun*. The Labour-leaning *Today* did go so far as to say:

> One man and one man alone is responsible for the results for the General Election. No, it is not John Major, it is Neil Kinnock. Mr. Major did not win the election. Mr. Kinnock lost it.

Peter Jenkins in the *Independent* proposed a corrective: 'Blaming Kinnock will not do. Labour lost because it was Labour.'[10] For the time being most

Conservatives were prepared to agree that it was Mr Major who had won the election. His own majority in Huntingdonshire was over 35,000, the largest majority in the country (in, however, an over-sized constituency of 93,000 voters).

One heavy blow for Major was the defeat at Bath of Chris Patten. Patten had demeaned himself by adopting a profoundly phoney Cockney slang in referring to Labour's porkies (i.e. 'pork pies', i.e. 'lies'), but his crime was to have been the minister who introduced the poll tax. The election also brought in a new cohort of right-wing Europhobes. Patten's post as Party Chairman was filled by the colourless, but trusty, Norman Fowler. Kenneth Clarke moved up to Home Secretary, Michael Heseltine to the Department of Trade and Industry (where he insisted on the historic title of President of the Board of Trade) and Michael Howard to Environment. Tom King and Peter Brooke left more or less willingly; Kenneth Baker not so willingly. Some other posts were shuffled around. Patrick Mayhew came in as Northern Ireland Secretary, Michael Portillo as Chief Secretary to the Treasury, with the apparently leftish John Patten as Education Secretary. Two women entered the cabinet, Gillian Shephard at Employment, and Virginia Bottomley at Health. Kinnock and Hattersley resigned from the Labour leadership, being succeeded respectively by the earnest, honest, moderate, and wickedly witty Shadow Chancellor John Smith, and Margaret Beckett. Son of a Scottish Presbyterian minister, Smith was a graduate of Glasgow University and a QC. Crucially supported at the party conference by John Prescott, one of the party's dwindling number of trade union figures, Smith pushed modernization further forward by replacing the old system of trade union block voting by 'one member, one vote'.

Even social historians, I have suggested, have to take account of events, convergences, contingencies. Evaluating the significance of the death of someone in public life is not the most tasteful of their tasks. On 12 May 1994, Smith, at the age of 55, died from a heart attack. To take matters in chronological order, Labour had done well in the local elections of 5 May under his leadership; in the elections to the European Parliament of 9 June, they did at least as well without him. On a turnout fractionally up on 1989 (36.1 as against 35.9) Labour greatly increased the lead they had then had over the Conservatives (44.24 per cent against 40.1 per cent), to 47.83 per cent against 34.7 per cent, winning 62 (previously 45) of the 84 seats allocated to the United Kingdom, against only 18 for the Conservatives (previously 32). With two seats for 16.72 per cent of the vote, the Liberals gained representation for the first time. The Scottish Nationalist Party got over 32 per cent of the vote in Scotland, doubling its seats from one to two. On the same day five by-elections were held, in four of which, Labour greatly increased its majorities, while the Liberal Democrats won Eastleigh from the Conservatives. The setback for Major was palpable. Unlike Thatcher he had deliberately involved himself in the European elections, taking a distinctly Eurosceptic line. In a key pointer to the future, Labour promised that there would be a referendum before it would ever take the country into EMU. Predictions had been that the Conservatives would do much worse, so Major drew comfort from the results and from the informed view that the Conservatives would be unlikely to do any better under a different leader. What worried Major most was what he perceived as the likely consequence of John Smith's death: the advent to the Labour leadership of the formidably personable, and youthful, Tony Blair.

The expected successor to Smith had been the Shadow Chancellor, Gordon Brown, another Scottish son of the Manse; at 43 he had been something of a mentor to the 41-year-old Blair in a very close relationship. Blair had wanted Brown to stand as a modernizing candidate in 1992, against Smith, whom he saw as a traditionalist. At the time of Smith's death, Peter Mandelson, Labour's Director of Communications, and the man responsible for the generally excellent campaign fought by Labour in 1992 (when the genteel symbol of the red rose was introduced), still believed that Brown was the right man for the leadership. But in those two years Blair, performing brilliantly as Shadow Home Secretary facing the unappealing Howard, had emerged as the figure who most completely embodied the idea of Labour making a new start. He was prepared, in a way almost unheard of in a Labour leader, to accept that some Conservative policies were here to stay. Brown shared Blair's ideas, but perhaps seemed a little too like Smith; evidence was emerging that within the party Blair was likely to have the wider support. Smiling Blair, with his posh-casual English accent, was better equipped to win vital seats in the south than the dour Brown. If they stood against each other, there was a strong risk of a non-modernizer winning, so in a trendy restaurant in Islington, Brown made the self-denying agreement with Blair that he would not stand while, in return, in any future Labour government, he would, as director of Labour's economic policies, have extensive powers. The three candidates were Beckett, a graduate of Manchester College of Science and Technology; Prescott, a former merchant seaman and union official, with a degree from Hull University; and Blair. In Labour's new electoral college, Blair took 57 per cent of the votes, to 24.1 for Prescott and 18.9 for Beckett. In the election for deputy leader, Prescott took 56.5 per cent to 43.5 per cent for Beckett.

If one wanted to pursue the theme of the curious composition of the British middle classes, Blair could form another case in point. His paternal grandparents were English actors, their son Leo being fostered out to the Glasgow working-class Blair family. Leo, at the age of 17, worked as a clerk for Glasgow Corporation, before being called up in 1942. Like Edward Heath he had an upwardly mobile war: demobilized as a major in 1947 he went to Edinburgh University to study law. In 1945 Leo Blair voted Labour, but as a law lecturer at Durham and a barrister in Newcastle (and then a judge), he developed a burning ambition to become a Conservative Prime Minister (his political ambitions being tragically cut short by a stroke). His political conversion he attributed to 'the great change from living in a tenement in Govan [an area populated almost entirely by working-class Rangers supporters] to life in an officers' mess'. Tony Blair was born on 6 May 1953 in the Queen Mary Maternity Home, Edinburgh, his mother being from a Donegal Protestant farming family. In Durham the young Blair went to a private preparatory school, in 1966 winning a scholarship to a public school, Fettes, a very English place, though situated in Edinburgh. He was good at sports and very strongly religious. At Oxford, 1972–5, where he studied law, he was lead singer in the rock band Ugly Rumours.

Blair married a high-earning barrister, Cherie Booth, the daughter of a dissolute actor. Though a member of CND, Blair was strongly opposed to the Bennite wing of the party. He was adopted as the candidate for Sedgfield, in the north-east, just in time for the 1983 election.[11]

In a way in which no one else could have done, Blair set out deliberately to present Labour as having made a clean break with the past. This seemed to give Labour an appeal with the public never ever achieved before. Blair had launched the slogan 'New Labour, New Britain' at the 1994 October party conference; Labour's rating rose to an amazing 60 per cent in the opinion polls. Following an assiduous campaign, he managed to persuade a special conference, held at the Methodist Central Hall, London, on 29 April 1995, to drop the famous Clause Four of the party's constitution committing it to 'common ownership' or nationalization. The replacement clause expressed a desire to create a community 'in which power, wealth and opportunity are in the hands of the many, not the few, where the rights we enjoy reflect the duties we owe, and where we live together, freely, in a spirit of solidarity, tolerance and respect'. If that was a break with the Labour past, it was also a break from what was being practised by the Major government. But in a manner reflecting the Thatcher revolution, the revised constitution also included phrases calling for: 'A dynamic economy serving the public interest' in which 'the enterprise of the market and the vigour of competition are joined with the forces of partnership and co-operation.' Again, Thatcher would not have accepted these final phrases; Major might have preached them but he scarcely practised them. Appalling to say, it was Smith's death which had created this opportunity. At last, the Labour party had elected a potential winner as leader. The Conservatives did not know how to react to him, and in fact stumbled into the worst possible option, seeking to establish 'clear blue water' between themselves and what Blair insistently referred to as 'New Labour', that is, they moved further into extremism.

### *Trials and tribulations of the Major Government*

At the end of August 1992 massive international currency movements were putting pressure on Europe's four weakest currencies, the escudo, the peseta, the lira and the pound. The government announced its commitment to keeping the pound within the ERM band. On 13 September the lira was devalued; Chancellor Lamont rejected the very notion of any devaluation of the pound. On the morning of 16 September the Bank of England was desperately buying sterling; at 11.00 a.m. the interest rate was put up from 10 to 12 per cent; at 2.15 p.m. to 15 per cent; at 7.30 p.m. down to 12 per cent again, as Lamont at the same time announced Britain's withdrawal from the ERM; and next day back to 10 per cent. The blow to the government in what was immediately referred to as Black Wednesday (16 September 1992) was shattering (though it should be remembered that Labour had also been in favour of joining the ERM). In fact, as the pound slipped down (by about 15 per cent) to a realistic value, exports benefited. But during the first part of 1993 the government had had an appalling time trying to get the European Community (Amendment) Bill through parliament. The 'Eurosceptics' exploited every device to obstruct progress. Government ministers had to make constant appeals for loyalty, and were, in fact, dependent on Labour support. The third reading was not achieved until 20 May, when a majority was secured of 292 to 112, with 46 Conservative MPs voting against the government. A month before, Major had made a strongly pro-European speech to the Conservative Group for Europe. But his peroration not only reeked of the old dither, it was plain ridiculous, as he evoked his love of Britain:

> the country of long shadows on county grounds, warm beer, invincible green suburbs, dog lovers and pools fillers, and as George Orwell said old maids bicycling to communion through the morning mist . . . Britain will survive, unamendable in all essentials.[12]

On Thursday, 22 July 1993, the government was actually defeated by 324 to 316 votes, with 26 Conservatives voting against the motion to 'note' the opt-out on the Social Chapter. But the rebels had no wish for an early General Election, so Major comfortably won the Confidence vote the next day. That evening, Friday, 23 July 1993, Major was interviewed on television by ITN's Michael Brunson. After the camera had been switched off, Major confided his woes to the interviewer. Trouble was being caused by three right-wing members of the Cabinet threatening to resign. The problem, Major indicated, lay in finding replacements: 'We don't want another three more of the bastards out there.' The sound had not been switched off; Major's words were recorded, and leaked to the press.

Arguments may legitimately rage over economic policy; one cannot assume that a Labour government at this time would have done better. But on the matter of the collapse of standards in public life there can be no debate. On 17 January 1994 the Committee of Public Accounts of the House of Commons (an all-party committee whose membership reflected the overall Conservative majority in the House, but which was chaired by a widely respected Labour MP) published one of the key documents of the time, a report entitled *The Proper Conduct of Public Business*. It began in the thunderous yet measured tones of such documents down the years:

1 In recent years we have seen and reported on a number of serious failures in administrative and financial systems and controls within departments and other public bodies, which have led to money being wasted or otherwise improperly spent.
2 There have recently been fundamental changes in the way in which government departments and public bodies such as those in the NHS carry out their work . . .
3 But at a time of change it is important to ensure that proper standards are maintained in the conduct of public business. Annexe 1 to this report sets out a number of failings on which we have reported in key areas of financial control, compliance with rules, the stewardship of public money and assets, and generally getting value for the taxpayer's money.

The 'fundamental changes' originated in the third Thatcher Government's Next Steps Initiative of 1988, aimed at reducing the number of civil servants and contracting out government work, and the National Health Service and Community Care Act of 1990, and were enthusiastically extended by the Major governments (notably in the 'Efficiency Measures' of 1991). Basically they involved transferring power from civil service departments, from elected local authorities and from bodies of professional experts (scientists, doctors, academics, etc.) to agencies staffed by government nominees (right-wing businessmen and Thatcherite politicians) – the notorious 'quangos' (quasi-autonomous non-governmental organizations), which had existed under Labour governments but which now numbered over 1,500 and exercised power in a hitherto unheard-of fashion.

Among traditional local authorities it was generally Labour councils which stood accused of misuse of public funds. But in January 1994 it became public knowledge that throughout the eighties the Conservative council in Westminster had been following policies described by the District Auditor as 'disgraceful and improper'. In brief, the council had been using housing funds and housing stock to bring into marginal wards owner-occupiers who would be likely to vote Conservative, while deliberately denying rented accommodation to homeless families who would be likely to vote Labour. In 1995 the multiple scandal that attracted most attention was concerned with the manner in which the privatization policy initiated by Thatcher had been, and was being, carried out. Almost as a matter of routine, government ministers who had been involved in privatizing a particular industry soon appeared among the directors of the newly privatized firms; in almost every case, shares in the new companies had been sold at bargain prices; the new privatized utilities both followed pricing and service policies that were unfriendly, or even punitive, towards their poorest customers, and instituted large-scale redundancies among their work people; at the same time their directors granted themselves 'rolling' payments and share options which offered total insurance against ever being dismissed, and took grotesque pay rises – the *cause célèbre* among the 'fat cats' was that of Cedric Brown, Head of British Gas, who in late 1994 received an increase of 75 per cent which took his salary to £475,000, which was not actually an exceptional figure.

The major issues of quangos, corruption, privatization and greed apart, these years were marked by a series of remarkable and often hilarious episodes in which Conservative ministers and MPs were caught with their trousers down or their hands in the till. The sexual transgressions would scarcely have been of any account had not the Prime Minister, once again demonstrating his addiction to feeble platitudes, not declared a (quickly buried) campaign of 'back to basics', but incidents culminating in a *Sunday Times* revelation that two ministers had been prepared to accept bribes to ask parliamentary questions, and allegations against a third of improperly accepting hospitality, brought into general currency one word to describe the state of politics, 'sleaze'. On 25 October 1994 the Prime Minister announced the establishment of a Committee on Standards in Public Life, under Lord Nolan, whose *Report* led to the appointment of a Parliamentary Commissioner for Standards. In 1997 Nolan was succeeded by Lord Neill of Bladon.[13] Shortly the Scott Enquiry, into whether ministers in the last Thatcher Government had tried to mislead parliament (and the courts) over changes in the professed policy of a ban on arms sales to Iraq, reported – somewhat ambiguously, but clearly indicating that all had certainly been far from well.

## *SOCIAL POLICY (STINGY) AND PUBLIC SERVICE (LOUSY)*

Anthony Seldon stresses Major's 'relative liberalism' on race, sexual equality, and homosexuality.[14] In February 1993 he went with the middle-of-the-road majority in parliament in seeing the homosexual age of consent brought down to 18 (rather than 16, the age for heterosexual consent and that for homosexual consent in most other European countries). But, although opposed to capital punishment, Major was very much the Tory atavist on questions of law and order. He was outraged by the 'progressive' Criminal Justice Act of 1991, largely prepared under the Thatcher regime by the liberal establishment at the Home Office. He pressured first Clarke and then Howard to put policy into sharp reverse. Surveys showed that crime was a priority concern throughout the country. In England and Wales recorded crime had doubled between 1979 and 1992; with the beginning of economic recovery there was a slight easing, though the annual rate was still equivalent to one crime for every ten people.[15] Howard was happy to put himself forward as the protagonist of tough treatment for criminals, trouble-makers, and even mere suspects, and this approach was embodied in the massive Criminal Justice Act which finally reached the statute book in 1994 after an extremely troubled passage. Applause can be cheaply won at Conservative party conferences, but seldom more cheaply than when Howard declared to the 1993 conference that 'prison works'. Under his tutelage, prison most assuredly did not 'work', both in the general sense that overcrowded and under-staffed jails were quite obviously serving as forcing grounds for criminal and other antisocial activities, and in the simple sense of failing to keep prisoners safely confined: in September 1994 five IRA terrorists and a highly dangerous armed robber shot their way out of the special secure unit in the custom-built maximum security Whitemoor prison in Cambridgeshire; on the last day of the year the imprisoned serial murderer Frederick West escaped by hanging himself in his prison cell; on 3 January two very violent murderers and an arsonist got clean away from the Parkhurst maximum security jail on the Isle of Wight; while the three were still at large, three more prisoners escaped from Littlehey prison near Huntingdon. Howard encountered further humiliations when his high-handed actions were rejected in the House of Lords and in the courts. The comment of the *Observer* Home Affairs correspondent on Howard was: 'The direction is towards America – a society at war with itself, with an ever-higher proportion of the population in jail.' A number of spectacular cases (notably, the 'Guildford Four' and the 'Birmingham Six', all wrongly accused of being IRA terrorists), in which, on appeal, prisoners serving long sentences were released after it had been conclusively demonstrated that the original prosecution evidence was deeply unsound, raised grave doubts about the English judicial system.

The act making possible the privatization of British Rail was passed in November 1993, Major facing down some opposition within the Cabinet itself. Privatization was to be carried out in the manner which would appeal most to speculators and thus bring money into the Treasury as quickly as possible, without regard to the public interest. First the railway tracks themselves, together with the accompanying property, were to be sold off as Railtrack, offering enticing prospects for asset-stripping, while ignoring the prospect that the disjunction between the ownership and responsibility for tracks and signalling, and the running of the trains by the different private companies, would prove a crassly unwise one. The actual sell-off of the railways took place during 1996 and 1997, the privatized companies quickly setting new standards in abysmal service.

Delays in the under-funded, and sometimes mismanaged, ambulance services could prove lethal. Privatized gas and electricity showrooms stopped servicing gas and electrical appliances and concentrated on selling them. Privatized bus services got more expensive, more infrequent and more chaotic. Meantime there was a 'rising storm of complaints' (*The Times*, 29 November 1991) against banks, which never had been nationalized, and so were never privatized, but which were joining in the general stampede towards putting shareholders first and customers last. Small businessmen complained of exorbitant loan charges, while the Consumers' Association reported on 'huge charges, imposed without warning, by banks which bungled time and time again'; *Times* cartoonist Calman had a marvellous little drawing in which a bank manager is saying to a protesting customer: 'We're a Caring Bank – we care about making lots of money.' 'Making lots of money' was the undoing of the old-established overseas investment bank, Baring's: greed, and unbelievably lax supervision, permitted a working-class yuppie, and Far East rogue trader, Nick Leeson, to run up disastrous losses in the future's market.

Implementation of the culminating act in Thatcher's reform of the NHS, the National Health Service and Community Care Act of 1990, fell to the Major governments. Informed opinion had become very critical of the way care for elderly and physically or mentally disabled people had been available only in hospitals or special institutions. Thus there could be no disagreeing with the principle embodied in the Act of Care in the Community, which, in theory, would end the isolation and ostracizing of those with special needs. But Care in the Community was implemented in a lax and penny-pinching way, resulting in several tragic cases in which mental patients loose in the community carried out murders. In the nature of things, GP fundholding did not quite carry all before it in the manner of the NHS trusts (many practices were simply not big enough), but by April 1994, 36 per cent of the population of Britain were registered with one of the 8,800 GPs in over 2,000 fundholding practices. Quality of service was to be guaranteed – or so Major appeared to believe – by one general Patient's Charter, and several specific ones related to individual aspects of the NHS. Patients now had three new rights: to be given detailed information on local health services, including quality standards and maximum waiting times; to be guaranteed admission for treatment no later than two years from the date of being placed on a waiting list; and to have any complaint about NHS services investigated, and receive a full reply as soon as possible.

One of the long-standing charges against the NHS had been that it was entirely preoccupied with curing sickness rather than promoting health. The 1992 White Paper *The Health of the Nation* was a genuine attempt to meet that criticism and work out a strategy for the nation's health, setting targets for improvements with regard to certain specified harbingers of death and serious illness (coronary heart disease and stroke, cancers, accidents, mental illness, HIV/AIDS and sexual health) and for reducing risk behaviour, such as smoking. The other main Health Service initiative aroused much opposition, the plan launched in February 1993 to reduce the number of hospitals in London, together with a general policy of redistributing resources from inner cities to the regions. Initially, these moves did have the weight of professional opinion behind them, but when that opinion changed, the government remained inflexible. A cut in hospital spending in 1993 of £1.6 billion and a programme of closing down 40 per cent of hospital beds over eight years created crisis situations in many trust hospitals. The most telling criticism of the NHS reforms came early in 1995 from a recent chairman of the British Medical Association, who, as a Conservative, had tried to cooperate with the Major government's policies; now, as he explained in the *British Medical Association News Review*, he was taking early retirement from his post as a consultant haematologist,

> because I am fed up with what is going on. They are driven by dogma more in tune with the eastern bloc . . . for three years I negotiated with the government. It was just like slipping down a cliff.

The cry of 'children in danger' had been raised in the mid-eighties, leading indeed to the Children Act of 1989: the general thrust in implementing the act was the laudable, though in practice not necessarily successful, one that children with special needs should wherever possible remain at home with their families. No doubt it would have taken genius well beyond the talents available in the British political establishment to have found answers to all the complications of the horrifying issue of child abuse. There were guidelines and training initiatives. It was made possible for children under fourteen to testify in court through video-recorded interviews. Unfortunately this well-intentioned move did not prove particularly successful in obtaining convictions, and did not help in mitigating the trauma suffered by the children.

Children (allegedly, at least) were also at the centre of the biggest (and most controversial) initiative in the realm of Social Security. It is important to stress that, in principle, the setting up of the Child Support Agency (CSA) in April 1993 had overwhelming professional and political support. Single mothers endeavouring to bring up children were among the most deprived groups in society, with serious consequences for the health and wellbeing of both themselves and their children. Their only formal means of securing maintenance payments from absent fathers was through the courts, which was reasonably effective with respect to agreed divorce settlements between the relatively prosperous but almost totally irrelevant to women who had been deserted or who had never had stable relationships. It was intended that the CSA would assume responsibility for assessing, collecting and enforcing child maintenance payments and for tracking down absent fathers. As operated the CSA was a microcosm of everything that was wrong with the government's attitude to social policy. A prize example of a 'Next Steps' autonomous agency, it was headed by a chief executive, Ros Hepplewhite, who, in marked contrast with the formal neutrality traditionally expected of old-style civil servants, declared herself a hearty supporter of government policies; she was on a target-related bonus, the target having nothing to do with the number of children rescued from poverty, but everything to do with the amount of cash the agency succeeded in collecting from fathers. The morality of the CSA was thus that of the ordinary strong-arm debt-collector. Single mothers were harassed into naming fathers when often they had the most pressing reasons, to do with their personal safety and that of their children, for wishing to avoid all contact with their former sexual partners. Fathers who were already making provision for their children (often through court-approved settlements) were much easier and cheaper to trace than the true fly-by-night defaulters, so that such fathers, now usually with second families to support, were forced to make unreasonably high payments, driving some to suicide, and others, by mutual agreement, to part from their second wives. Against a background of protests and demonstrations, Ms. Hepplewhite resigned; in January 1995, the Parliamentary Commissioner (or 'Ombudsman') published a damning indictment of 'failures and mistakes' causing 'undue worry and distress to parents'. Amendments meeting some of the worst abuses were then proposed in the White Paper *Improving Child Support*, which set limits upon the claims that could be made against absent fathers and gave some recognition to court settlements and to the needs of second families. Even so, the Child Poverty Action Group still concluded that there was 'practically nothing to combat the poverty of lone parents and their children'.

The Ombudsman had also criticized maladministration in the other main Next Steps 'executive agency', the Benefits Agency, responsible for paying the benefits defined in the 1986 Act: its main target for 1994 to 1995 was to save £654 million through its anti-fraud work. With the specific aim of reducing the numbers claiming either sickness or invalidity benefit, the Social Security (Incapacity for Work) Act of 1994 replaced these benefits, from April 1995, with a single Incapacity Benefit, which was subject to stringent medical tests. From April 1996 unemployment benefit and income support for unemployed people were to be replaced by a Job Seekers' Allowance, which would require all unemployed people to enter into a 'job seekers' agreement', committing them to a plan of action to seek work; they would also be means-tested. Meantime, on the testimony of the City's own financial watchdog, the Securities and Investments Board, it emerged that up to one-and-a-half million people who had followed government advice in switching since 1988 to personal pensions had lost heavily thereby; compensation for the 350,000 most urgent cases could (if the financial advisers and insurers involved were ever forced to pay up) amount to over £2 billion. In 1993 wages councils, which set minimum wages for two million workers, most of them women, were abolished, giving immediate impetus to a trade union and Labour party campaign in favour of a statutory minimum hourly wage rate.

Though meant to represent the wets in the Cabinet, John Patten as Education Minister simply stirred up an atmosphere of resistance and confrontation among teachers. Gillian Shephard brought much-needed elements of negotiation and compromise. The National Curriculum was made more flexible; teachers moved towards acquiescence in modified national testing, and even in 'league tables', if these included appropriate information on a school's social circumstances and problems. In March 1996 Major announced the objectives of greater selection and choice for parents, without reflecting on whether the two were in fact compatible, and the ultimate Majorism, 'a grammar school in every town'. Peace scarcely broke out in the 'condition of war' between universities and government. Research and teaching assessments imposed further burdens on academics; management consultants were everywhere in the ascendant; glossy brochures and mission statements proliferated. Going to university was becoming less of a privilege or a right, more a commercial transaction: there were strong suspicions that standards were dropping.

No longer a major social responsibility of the Ministry of Health, housing now fell within the purview of the Ministry of the Environment. In the worst conditions of recession houses were standing empty and unsold, while, of course, many people were homeless or living in squalor. In November 1992 a 'housing market package' of £750 million was announced, to facilitate the purchase of such houses and make them available to meet social needs. In England £580 million was used to enable housing associations to buy 18,000 new, empty or refurbished properties for letting to homeless families. A further £50 million was used to provide cash incentives to housing association and local authority tenants to, in the words of the official handbook, *Britain 1994*, 'enable them to buy homes on the open market and release their existing accommodation for housing homeless families' (p. 329). The Leasehold Reform, Housing and Urban Development Act of 1993 gave residential leaseholders in blocks of flats in England and Wales the right to acquire the freehold of their block collectively at market price. The number of would-be home-owners being dispossessed because of inability to keep up mortgage payments had shot up in the 1980s and shot up again in the early nineties, peeking in 1991, but remaining excessively high in 1992, 1993 and 1994.

For both Londoners and visitors one of the most evident consequences of the Thatcher revolution was the sight of street beggars and rough sleepers, in doorways and in the 'cardboard cities' set up in squares and open spaces. In 1990 the Thatcher Government had introduced its 'Rough Sleepers Initiative', a three-year programme, costing £96 million, which provided about 950 new places in short-term hostels, and about 2,200 permanent and 700 leased places in accommodation for hostel dwellers to move into. The Major Government made £86 million available in 1994 to continue the initiative until 1996.

As I have remarked several times, much of what happened in Britain was governed by international trends, including trends in science and technology – most obviously the continuing and accelerating IT revolution. Of major scientific and technological discoveries, a smaller proportion than at any time for two centuries was emanating from Britain. The reduction in scientific investment initiated by Thatcher continued under Major. William Waldegrave's White Paper, *Realising Our Potential: A Strategy for Science, Engineering and Technology* (May 1993), announced that there was to be no advance on the £6 billion currently allocated to research; in the authentic Thatcherite style the research councils were to be reconstituted under the control of chief executives, scientists themselves being sidelined; the number of science PhDs was to be cut. Denied essential resources, leading scientists were already leaving the country, two or three a year.

### *A SEA OF TROUBLES*

At the end of May 1993 Major dismissed his Chancellor, Lamont (by the device of offering him Environment). Within the framework of his Thatcherite views, Lamont was technically a more effective and assiduous Chancellor than either Lawson had been, or Clarke, his successor, was to prove (Clarke was an excellent self-publicist). Against Lamont were his odd, satyr-like appearance, the even odder stories which circulated about him (about his credit cards, about a prostitute living in a basement he owned), his silly, self-centred pronouncements (economic hardship for the public was 'a price well worth paying', 'Je ne regrette rien'), and the fact that he and Major hated each other. Two weeks later Lamont got his revenge in the House of Commons:

> There is too much short-termism, too much reacting to events, not enough shaping of events. We give the impression of being in office but not in power.[16]

Major's biggest ever reshuffle was announced on 20 July 1994; much-needed, but also a wheeze to upstage Blair's appointment as Labour leader the following day. The class composition of the reconstructed Cabinet is interesting. The only low-born member, apart from Major himself, was Kenneth Clarke, Cambridge-educated, but the son of a Nottingham miner who had left the pits to open a jeweller's shop after the war. Of Thatcher's aristocrats only Hurd (Foreign Secretary), grandson of a knight, son of a baron, educated at Eton and Trinity College, Cambridge, remained; but he had been joined by two even grander figures, William Waldegrave (Agriculture), younger son of the Twelfth Earl of Waldegrave, and Viscount Cranborne, from the majestic Cecil, or Salisbury, family (Lord Privy Seal), and five others of lesser rank. These were: Jonathan Aitken, son of Sir William Aitken, and scion of the powerful Beaverbrook connection, educated at Eton and Christ Church, Oxford (Financial Secretary to the Treasury); Ian Lang, from a prestigious family of Scottish insurance brokers, educated at a Scottish prep school, Rugby and Sidney Sussex, Cambridge (Scottish Secretary); Sir Patrick Mayhew, son of an oil executive, himself a barrister and farmer and ex-Dragoon Guardsman, educated at Tonbridge and Balliol, Oxford (Irish Secretary); Virginia Bottomley (Health Secretary), from a family of public servants (some with left-wing leanings) – her grandfather was Secretary of the League of Nations Union, her father, Dr Maxwell Garnett CBE, who was educated at Rugby and Trinity, Cambridge, ran the Industrial Society, her uncle and aunt were the Labour patricians Douglas and Peggy Jay, and her husband, a Conservative MP, was second son of Sir James Bottomley, former Ambassador to the United States; and Stephen Dorrell, from a traditional family firm of overall manufacturers, educated at prep school, Uppingham and Brasenose, Oxford (National Heritage Secretary). Dorrell had been an old-fashioned supporter of industry against the flash, lower-class manipulators of money who were coming to dominate the Conservative party. And then there was Michael Heseltine (President of the Board of Trade) whose father had been a Swansea colonel, educated at Shrewsbury and Pembroke College, Oxford with his home outside Banbury visibly establishing him in that upper class recognized by Margaret Stacey in her pioneering survey of Banbury.[17] That gives nine indisputably upper-class figures. Newcomer Jeremy Hanley (Conservative Party Chairman), an accountant with the prestigious firm of Peat, Marwick, Mitchell, was the son of a well-known actor and a famous actress, and had married the ex-wife of Viscount Villiers. The rest of the Cabinet were much more solidly upper-middle class than Thatcher's last Cabinet had been. Michael Howard (Home Secretary), John Gummer (Environment), Peter Lilley (Social Security) and Michael Portillo (Employment) were all Cambridge graduates; Tony Newton (Leader of the House), Gillian Shephard (Education) and John Redwood (Wales) were Oxford ones. Lord Mackay (Lord Chancellor) came from a fraction lower in the solid Scottish middle class than Malcolm Rifkind (Defence Secretary). Brian Mawhinney (Transport) was from the equally solid Northern Ireland middle class. David Hunt (Chancellor of the Duchy of Lancaster, responsible for the *Citizen's Charter*, and Science) was a graduate of Montpellier University in France, and Bristol University. Britain was no classless society; and this was a classless cabinet only in the sense that all of its members came from the upper, or the upper-middle, class.

Was Major responsible for the sea of troubles which practically enveloped him, or were the 'Eurosceptics', 'the bastards', to blame? Major, with the usual necessary amount of luck, had got the job he had desperately wanted; he really wasn't in a position to complain. He was a moderately nice man with some impulses that might be called nasty if they had not been so banal, in a party and government which he led, and which had become pretty thoroughly nasty. He can be given credit for seeing that he simply could not give the guarantee that he would never take Britain into a single European currency, which was the one thing which would have won him the support of the Eurosceptics. The two things which destroyed him were the deterioration of a party too long in office – *his* party; and Europe – but then Europe *was* the big issue. By-election after by-election was lost: that is what happens to rotten, unpopular governments. The Conservative majority of twenty-one in 1992 had become a mere eleven by the end of 1994. Technically it disappeared when nine extreme Eurosceptics had the whip withdrawn – however, in one of Major's feeblest acts, they got it back again after six months without giving any guarantees of good behaviour. More serious were the defections of Alan Howarth to Labour, and of Emma Nicholson and Peter Thurnham to the Liberal Democrats. When the Conservative MP for Wirral South died on 3 November 1996,

Major's majority totally evaporated. Already by December 1993 the government was 20 per cent behind Labour in the opinion polls, and there it broadly remained for the remainder of the parliament. Major's own ratings were the lowest ever in fifty years of opinion polling. His most important action against his sea of troubles revealed the mind of a sergeant major rather than that of a field marshal. On 22 June 1995 he resigned as leader with the specific purpose of seeking re-election. In the contest with John Redwood he won 218 to 89, with 22 abstaining. On 5 July, Heseltine, the most prominent and vocal pro-European, was given the title of Deputy Prime Minister. Hurd, still perhaps something of an upholder of older Tory values, slipped out of office to be replaced by Rifkind.

One success claimed for the Majorite continuation of Thatcherite policies was that in 1994 the statistics for strikes were the lowest ever since records began in 1891; it really did appear that the days of great industrial struggles were over. And there was one achievement which will stand as the one true memorial to the Major years: the launch of the National Lottery – a 'pet project', as Seldon assures us several times – was celebrated on 21 November 1994. This was really an immensely popular, and entirely voluntary, form of national taxation, with fun attached, providing funds for charities, the arts and sport.

Meantime the world economy, and therefore the British economy (with the continental Europeans lagging somewhat behind), was moving out of recession. By the beginning of 1995 some of the figures were looking quite impressive: 3.5 per cent growth in 1994; unemployment (on the government's own widely distrusted figures) down well below three million; inflation at a 27-year low of 2 per cent. Yet, as opinion polls amply demonstrated, there was no sense of wellbeing throughout the country; government plans to increase VAT on domestic heating drew attention to the fact that overall people were being more highly taxed under the Conservatives than they had been at the end of the last Labour government. That a back-bench revolt inflicted a humiliating defeat on this issue scarcely served to raise the credibility of the government.

The last, massive blow to strike John Major's government was an almost pure product of the Thatcherism which he had never repudiated and, indeed, had done so much to extend and accelerate – the authoritarian Thatcherism which privileged deregulation and untrammelled profit-making and suppressed all questioning, all dissent. It is true that two elements in the great BSE crisis pre-dated Thatcherism: the encouragement of intensive farming, including the feeding of meat-and-bone meal ('supplementary feedstuffs') to cows, and the flaw in government structure whereby in the combined Ministry of Agriculture, Food, and Fisheries consumer interests were completely swamped by those of producers. But it was deregulation under Thatcher which permitted the switch in 1981–2 to cost-cutting processing of 'supplementary feedstuffs' at lower temperatures with reduced use of solvents;[18] this permitted contaminated protein, almost certainly the source of BSE (Bovine Spongiform Encephalopathy), or 'mad cow disease', to be fed to cows.[19] The first 'mad cow' was noted in Kent in April 1985, the first official confirmation issued in November 1986; already there were over 200,000 infected cattle, but BSE was not made a notifiable disease till 21 June 1988. It was at the same time decided that the feeding to ruminants of feedstuffs derived from animal remnants should be banned, but the ban was delayed for one month, so that existing (contaminated) stocks could be used up, thus infecting thousands more animals. In June the government was also advised that all BSE-infected animals should be destroyed, but took no action till August. Meantime, since there was a possibility of BSE being communicated to humans, the government set up the Southwood Committee, which eventually became the permanent Spongiform Encephalopathy Advisory Committee (SEAC).[20] The government kept up an unjustifiably confident façade, with, in 1990, John Gummer, Agriculture Secretary, blustering in public, and attempting to force-feed a hamburger to his daughter. On the recommendation of Southwood, in November 1989 the sale of specified bovine offal for human consumption was banned, but, again in the spirit of deregulation and cost-cutting, inspection procedures were sloppy and inadequate. Research was discouraged and evidence suppressed. The Americans wisely banned imports of British beef, but even that was not sufficient to upset government complacency. The maximum extraction – and maximum profit – policies of the food industry meant that cheap pies and hamburgers were particularly suspect.[21] Deaths began to occur among young people, and could often be linked to the consumption of cheap beef products.

If the issue was dormant, it certainly should not have been, and it blew up in March 1996. The fact that SEAC was about to make a statement of new evidence on the putative link between the spread of BSE in cattle and ten new cases of New Variant Creutzfeldt-Jakob brain disease (CJD) in young people in the previous two years was recorded in a memo written by the Ministers of Agriculture and of Health, Douglas Hogg and Stephen Dorrell, on 18 March 1996. (There were two further cases the following year, and by the end of 1998 there had been 27 cases in all.) The government decided on a parliamentary statement to be made on the afternoon of 20 March; but the news was leaked in that morning's *Daily Mirror*. Dorrell's statement intimated that CJD cases might be linked to the eating of beef before the introduction of the specified bovine offal ban in 1989. It was not so clear that the precautions taken in 1989 were sufficient, nor indeed that they were being rigorously enforced. On 25 March the veterinary committee of the European Commission imposed a worldwide ban on the import of British beef and beef by-products.

The European Commission acted very rationally, promising Britain financial help for the destruction of older cattle, and expressing the hope that the ban could be lifted once measures acceptable to the European Union had been agreed. But Major chose to behave in a petulant and obstructive manner, announcing on 21 May that Britain would pursue a policy of 'non-cooperation' with Europe. The agreement reached with the European Union in mid-June that subject to European scrutiny of the cattle-slaughtering programme there would be a progressive lifting of the ban, was readily represented as a climbdown on the part of Major. Officially, the government embarked on a programme of slaughtering 60,000 head of cattle over three years old, every week. But facilities for burning carcasses were inadequate; stories continued to surface of dangerous conditions in slaughter houses where younger cattle were being slaughtered for the market, and of infected carcasses simply being buried in shallow graves. If ever regulation was needed, it was now; but resources were thin, the ethos of responsibility threadbare.

In his November budget Clarke took 1p off income tax, resisting advice from the Bank of England to raise interest rates. In January 1997 Gordon Brown announced that if Labour did come into power it would, for its first two years, keep to Conservative spending limits. On 18 March the election was announced for 1 May.

## *IRELAND*

The Irish problem was brought home to Major when an IRA mortar attack on 10 Downing Street on 7 February 1991 might well have killed the Prime Minister and several of his colleagues, though it failed to do so. There were a number of other mainland bomb attacks, including one in March 1993 when two small boys were killed in a busy shopping centre in Warrington.

In appointing Mayhew as Northern Ireland Secretary, Major indicated that Ireland would have high priority. For this he deserves applause, as for his devotion, patience and hard work, though there were traditional weaknesses in his approach. These weaknesses were all the more difficult to overcome because of Major's incredible shrinking parliamentary majority, which made him openly dependent on the Ulster Unionists. Furthermore, Patrick Mayhew, decent and dedicated, was, unfortunately, upper-class in speech, manner and body language, to such a degree as to seem almost a parody. Given that those he had to negotiate with were, on all sides, at just about the furthest remove possible from English upper-class lifestyles and attitudes, this did add to the basic problem, which had always been one of a failure to understand fully the several separate dimensions which simultaneously constituted the Northern Ireland question. Openly, Mayhew was involved in discussions with both the Unionist and Nationalist parties in Northern Ireland – which got nowhere. Secretly, he was in contact with Sinn Féin and the Provisional IRA, conveying the message that the British Government would certainly be interested in publicly entering into negotiations if there were a ceasefire. More important, discussions reopened between Hume and Adams. In a joint statement of late April 1993 they declared that there could be no internal Northern Ireland political settlement without recognition of the Irish dimension. As so often in Northern Ireland, an apparent advance simply produced intensified violence, first on the Loyalist side, and then on 23 October 1993 in the form of a Provisional IRA bomb exploding in a fish shop on the Shankill Road, Belfast. Nine Protestant shoppers were killed (together with one of the bombers) and 57 injured. Loyalist paramilitary attacks resulted in four Catholic deaths and then on 30 October UFF gunmen opened fire on the Rising Sun bar in Greysteel, County Londonderry, killing seven Catholics and one Protestant. That October, 27 people were killed, the highest death toll for a single month since October 1976.

Urgent talks were arranged between the British and Irish governments. These resulted in the Downing Street Declaration of December 1993, which must, most certainly, be acknowledged as a vital stage in advancing the peace process. The British Government could not agree to the Sinn Féin demand that it become a 'persuader' on behalf of Irish union, nor to their demand that any referendum should be taken in Ireland as a whole, rather than in the two separate parts. It did

> agree that it is for the people of the island of Ireland alone, by agreement between the two parts respectively, to exercise the right of self-determination on the basis of consent, freely and concurrently given, North and South, to bring about a united Ireland, if that is their wish.[22]

It also declared that Britain had 'no selfish strategic or economic interest in Northern Ireland'. The Irish Taoiseach, Albert Reynolds, accepted the rights of the majority in Northern Ireland, and confirmed that, in the event of an overall political settlement, the Irish Government would remove from its constitution the claim to Northern Ireland. On Wednesday, 31 August 1994 the Provisional IRA announced an immediate ceasefire. Unfortunately, if in many ways understandably, the British Government did not feel able to respond in a manner which might have got the peace process really moving forward. Of course, without the participation of the Unionists, there really couldn't be a serious peace process, and the Unionists totally distrusted the IRA. Right from the start the Unionists were calling for the IRA to destroy their weapons, while the British Government were insisting that there must be evidence that the ceasefire was a permanent one. Thus, there was no bringing of Sinn Féin into political discussions. Among Unionists, and in the British Government as well, there was a perception of the IRA as murderous criminals (which some, undoubtedly, were). Wittingly or not, the British projected a sense of wanting the IRA to admit the error of their ways; indeed, to, as the IRA perceived it, surrender. The British Government could not quite see that the urgent prior problem was that of conflict resolution, not of rights and wrongs, while Sinn Féin could not avoid seeing how dependent Major was on the Irish Unionists for his parliamentary majority. One very immediate danger was of the Protestant paramilitaries reacting to the possibility of any kind of agreement with increased violence. Sensibly, the British Government issued reassurances that it was certainly not committed to a United Ireland, and that there could be no question of the people of Northern Ireland being forced into such a union. The Protestant paramilitaries, assured that there had been no secret deal with the Provisionals, declared a ceasefire of their own on 13 October 1996.

Meantime, quite independently of anything the British could do, a change took place which Sinn Féin regarded as unfavourable to their cause. Reynolds's pro-Nationalist Coalition was replaced by a government led by the Fine Gael John Bruton, with Labour's Dick Spring as Foreign Secretary. In February 1995 the new Irish Government, along with the British Government, published discussion documents, *Frameworks for the Future*. A new one-chamber Northern Ireland Assembly of 90 members elected by PR was proposed, to be chaired by a directly elected panel of three people, with all-party committees to oversee the work of the Northern Ireland departments. The aim, once more, was to involve the Catholic minority in the government of Northern Ireland. The other half of the proposals concerned, once more also, the creation of a main north–south body, and various north–south institutions. The immediate rejection of these proposals by the Unionists can be taken as demonstrating just how terribly difficult the British Government's task was, or perhaps as suggesting that it could just as well have been far more bold in its response to the IRA ceasefire.

The British Government failed to understand that to the IRA and Sinn Féin the very ceasefire itself was an enormous concession, from which reciprocal concessions were to be expected. It was true that the IRA continued many of its other unpleasant activities, particularly the imposition of discipline within its own communities in the form of kneecappings and punishment beatings. Unionists, perhaps, could be forgiven for seeing the ceasefire as simply a tactical device, with the IRA, if they did not get their own way in negotiations, ready to resume operations. But the British Government showed less eagerness to follow this line, recognizing that the ceasefire in itself was a positive good. Obviously there was the problem of possible divisions within Republican ranks, and in particular between Sinn Féin and the Provisionals. Perhaps, then, it would have been best to give as much support as possible to the Sinn Féin leaders Gerry Adams and Martin MacGuiness.

Still, the Protestants certainly didn't help. Very soon it was to seem that one disruptive annual fixture that would not go away was that at Drumcree. Trying to show sensitivity to Nationalist sentiment, the RUC prohibited Orangemen from marching from the church at Drumcree back along the nationalist Garvaghy Road in Portadown, the route they considered to be hallowed by tradition. David Trimble, law lecturer at Belfast University and MP for Upper Bann, emerged as a leading and uncompromising spokesman for the Orangemen. As Orange support grew, the RUC felt the protest could not be contained, certainly without a very high level of violence, and gave way, thus losing whatever credit it might have gained with the Nationalist community. Really, the prospects for the peace process seemed bleak if there was no will to peace among the communities themselves. A further Drumcree confrontation the next year suggested that perhaps there wasn't any.

The Unionist rejection of the Frameworks documents led to the resignation of the Ulster Unionist party leader, James Molyneaux. Trimble was elected in his place. For the moment this suggested still greater intransigence amongst the Unionists. Clearly what was needed was some *deus ex machina.* And so indeed President Bill Clinton of the United States arrived in November 1995 for visits both to Northern Ireland and to the Republic, anxious to contribute positively to the peace process. His rapturous welcome in Belfast did suggest that he was someone who could bring out the longing for peace in both communities in a way that neither Major nor Mayhew could. A major initiative was the establishing of an international body chaired by the former US Senator George Mitchell, to deal with the decommissioning of weapons and the initiation of all-party talks. To its credit the Major Government made no fuss about its own prerogatives in the matter.

The Mitchell Report, accepted by the British Government, was delivered on 24 January 1996. It recognized that the paramilitary organizations would not undertake decommissioning in advance of all-party talks. It therefore suggested that decommissioning should take place *during* all-party negotiations, not *before* as the British had been insisting, or *after*, which was the Sinn Féin position. A central point was that everyone involved in all-party negotiations should commit themselves to a number of fundamental principles of democracy and non-violence. These were: democratic and exclusively peaceful means of resolving political issues; total disarmament of all paramilitary organizations, such disarmament being verifiable by an independent commission; renunciation, and opposition to, any efforts to use force or threats of force to influence the course of all-party negotiations; agreement to abide by the terms of any agreement reached in all-party negotiations with any subsequent attempts to alter that agreement confined to democratic and peaceful means; and the taking of effective steps to prevent punishment killings and beatings.

The British Government appeared confident that progress was being made, but if it was now prepared to believe in the permanence of the ceasefire, it was too late. On 4 February 1996 a massive bomb at Canary Wharf in London, which killed two, and injured over a hundred, with more than £85 million worth of damage, announced the end of the IRA ceasefire. Enormous damage, many casualties, though no deaths, were caused by another huge bomb in the centre of Manchester on Saturday, 15 June 1996. The Government could tell itself that all its worst suspicions of the IRA had been fully justified. But really it had failed to grasp that if this complex, multi-dimensional conflict were ever to be resolved, other policies would have to be pursued, old banalities would have to be abandoned.

## CONSENSUS REGAINED?

Since, rather in the style of 1945, the 1997 election gave rise to a certain mythology, it is important to scrutinize the actual results very closely.

Had the country unified behind 'New Labour'? Had Tony Blair been given an overwhelming popular mandate? It is worth flicking to page 343 to have a look at the 1992 figures, and the numbers voting for John Major and the Conservatives. Well, for a start, we can see that Blair actually got nearly half a

**Table 6.3** General Election, 1 May 1997

| | *Electorate 43.85 million* | | *Turnout 71.2 per cent* | | |
|---|---|---|---|---|---|
| | *Labour* | *Conservative* | *Liberal Democrat* | *Nationalist* | *Others (mainly Northern Ireland)* |
| Total votes | 13,518,167 | 9,600,943 | 5,242,947 | 782,580 | 2,141,647 |
| Percentage | 43.2 | 30.7 | 16.8 | 2.5 | 6.8 |
| Seats | 418 | 165 | 46 | 4 PC 6 SNP | 20 |

million fewer votes than Major, and just 1.3 per cent more of the total vote – 43.2 per cent scarcely being an overwhelming endorsement. The turnout was nearly 6.5 per cent down, indicating that the electorate did not turn out in their enthusiastic droves to sweep Blair into power. Subsequent to the election, Labour's score in public opinion polls did reach some astonishing heights, and some polls indicated that people were claiming to have voted for Labour and Blair when manifestly they could not have done so. But the point I want to make is that, *at the time of the election*, the landslide apparently indicated by Labour's massive majority in parliamentary seats was not an accurate reflection of voters' reactions in the country at large, though the low poll for the Conservatives, 4 per cent below that of Kinnock in 1992, certainly is noteworthy.

And if we wanted further evidence of the oddities of the first-past-the-post system we could note that the Liberal Democrats – still, of course, unfairly treated overall – had doubled their number of seats on a poll one per cent lower than in 1992. What this suggested, above all, was tactical voting, with Labour voters supporting the Liberal Democrat where their own candidate had no real chance against the Conservative. Labour almost certainly similarly benefited from Liberal Democrat votes. The voting behaviour of ordinary people, therefore, provided some ratification for the notion of Labour and Liberal Democrats working together in some areas, without in any sense merging. A new right-wing Europhobe party, bankrolled by millionaire Sir James Goldsmith, and largely made up of disgruntled Conservatives, had entered the election, seeming at the time like yet another horrible twist of the knife for Major. The abysmal performance of 'The Referendum Party' might have brought him some joy, save that, having been buoyed up by his usual facile optimism, he was absolutely devastated by Labour's victory.[23] His public comment could not have been more Majorish: 'politics is a rough old game'. Another new party on the British electoral scene deserves as much attention, and as quick a dismissal. The appearance of anti-abortion, 'Pro-Life' candidates conjured up fears of the arrival in Britain of the unscrupulous and ultra-violent American movement. Standing in 51 seats, these candidates in fact polled the derisory average of 345 votes each, less than the perennial joke candidate, Screaming Lord Sutch. My point about the steady growth of libertarian sentiment in Britain since the 1960s is strikingly upheld.

What I am now going to do is to nominate the 'Top Ten' contentious issues of the nineties, issues central to the fracturing and polarization of Britain. How did they stand after two years of Blair government? I shall conclude with discussions of national identity, the Americanization of Britain, and Britain's relationship with Europe.

## *TEN CONTENTIOUS ISSUES*

### *1 The economy*

When Labour took office in May 1997 the economy was quite definitely moving into recovery. How far recovery was due to the skill of Conservative economic management, and how far to global changes, is the obvious question; my money would go on the latter explanation. America had moved into an unusually sustained period of prosperity; on the other hand, it was true that the European countries were scarcely out of recession yet and generally suffering higher levels of unemployment. Largely because of continuing unemployment in Britain, the public sector borrowing requirement remained dangerously high; still worse was the overseas trade deficit. Perhaps the fairest comment in conventional economic terms would be that the situation Labour inherited from Major in 1997 was a good deal better than the situation Major inherited from Thatcher and Lawson in 1990. There were important productivity and efficiency gains from the Thatcher years, but as Lawson himself had suggested, there had been no escape from boom and bust, no discovery of the secret of steady, inflation-free, growth. Thanks to the first Thatcher years, the manufacturing base looked to be too small to take full advantage of improving world conditions.

Labour's Chancellor of the Exchequer, Gordon Brown, quickly earned the epithet 'The Iron Chancellor'. He was governed both by the Conservative economic legacy, and by the New Labour ideology which sought above all to escape from Labour's past reputation for high inflation, high taxation, 'bust' if not too much 'boom', and the fostering of a 'dependency culture' with too many people on public handouts, and thus excluded from mainstream society, rather than participating in the common task of wealth creation. Labour's public commitment to 'education – education – education' had more to do with economic efficiency than social equality, yet enough of ethical socialism remained for there to be a wish to directly help the poor and to protect the NHS. The biggest gesture towards demonstrating that this was to be a government of economic virtue, a government which would forswear both an important feature of Keynesian demand management, and fiddling with interest rates for purely political reasons (like winning elections), was the commitment that the Bank of England would have complete independence in making its decisions on interest rates (a complete reversal, this, of the Attlee Government's nationalization of the Bank of England, and a strong echo of the way in which the European Central Bank was intended to operate once the single currency was in operation). If the aim of getting rid of the trade deficit could be made to sound like Roy Jenkins at the end of the sixties, the aim of keeping inflation down at 2.5 per cent (the Major Government had achieved this before things had begun to loosen again under Clarke) sounded very traditionally Tory. With Labour in power, the newly independent Bank duly did put up the minimum lending rate. Only slowly, and in painfully small slices, were rates reduced over the first two years of Labour government. The consequence was a high pound and a heavy burden on British exporters. However, one little sign that there was possibly now a more consensual, more caring, spirit in high places was the statement by the Governor, Eddie George, himself that he did recognize that Bank policy must not be confined to economic orthodoxy, but must take account of the interests of everyone in the community, including the unemployed.

In July 1997 Brown put into place a five-year deficit reduction plan, involving, in particular, additional indirect taxation and high interest rates. To show himself a friend of business he brought corporation tax down 2 per cent to 31 per cent. The Windfall Tax on the excessive profits made by the privatized utilities, promised before the election, was put into operation to fund a programme for creating job opportunities for the young unemployed; £400,000 million was immediately set aside for education. In the budget of 17 March 1998, Corporation Tax was cut by a further one per cent, to a main rate of 30 per cent, and to 20 per cent for small businesses. Petrol and diesel duties were put up within the range 4.4p to 5.5p. There was 21p on a packet of twenty cigarettes, 1p on a pint of beer, and 4p on a bottle of wine. Yet, in a broadly neutral budget, a number of small things were done which did suggest a sharp break with the budgets of the past 19 years. Through combined reforms in the tax and benefits system Brown aimed to provide a guaranteed family income of at least £180 a week, while at the same time increasing child benefit by £2.50 a week. The calculation was that 5.5 million households with children would get an increase in disposable income, amounting on average to £250 a year. The poorest fifth of households with children, embracing 3.8 million children, would benefit by an average of £500. A £1.5 billion surplus in the year's finances was used to provide a further £500 million for the NHS, £250 million for schools and £175 million for transport, including a £50 million annual fund for rural transport. Also of great potential significance was Brown's initiation of strong measures to combat tax evasion by the wealthy.[24]

During 1997 and into 1998 there was a series of banking collapses in the Far East. Britain's chronic lack of domestic investment was immediately exposed, as a number of Japanese, and other Far Eastern companies, withdrew from involvement in Britain, resulting in redundancies being declared in a number of particularly sensitive areas, including the Prime Minister's own constituency. The onset of recession in Britain was widely predicted, and prospects were not improved by the massive collapse in Brazil at the end of the year. The government claimed that the prudent measures it had been taking were serving to insulate the British economy, and at the beginning of 1999 announced that unemployment had now fallen to its lowest figure since 1980; it rose again slightly in March to 1.8 million, then began falling again. Meantime the German company BMW threatened to cancel its £1.7 billion project to build a new medium-sized Rover car at the Longbridge plant in Birmingham, followed shortly by the announcement that the last Clyde shipyard was to be sold by its Norwegian owners. At the beginning of April 1999 Longbridge was saved by the distinctly 'old Labour' device of a £150 million aid package.[25] The Clyde workers faced the prospect of unemployment.

With regard to issues of poverty and social exclusion the trends of 19 years were not going to be easily reversed, and, manifestly, their reversal was not, compared with establishing long-term economic stability, the government's highest priority. The Secretary of State for Health, Frank Dobson, did appoint a former government chief medical officer, Sir Donald Acheson, to examine what could be done to reduce health inequalities between rich and poor. Sir Donald reported that the gap in health statistics and mortality rates between rich and poor was continuing to widen and that, partly because of the growth in out-of-town supermarkets, and the decline of city-centre shops, many of the poor in Britain were going hungry.

*2 Education*

Britain's inadequate and class-divided education system could very plausibly be blamed for persistent economic failings, as well as the many lapses into antisocial and insensitive behaviour: one victim was the coach of the English National Football Team, Glenn Hoddle, whose uneducated, incoherent burblings about the links between being disabled and sins committed in a previous incarnation cost him his job in February 1999. Employers claimed that even graduates turned up without appropriate skills, while international tables consistently showed British children far down in basic literacy and numeracy. To those on the Right, which included practically the whole of the Conservative party, it was a matter of opportunity and choice, of giving special encouragement to the able, and of, above all, freeing education from the ideological hand of local authority control. To the Left (that is to say a majority of the Labour party, but not its New Labour leaders), it was a matter of abolishing all grammar schools, independent schools, whether fee-paying or not, and all private schools, so that every child would go to the local comprehensive. Both left and right were barking up the wrong trees. Selection inevitably entailed the very heavy risk of rejection and therefore the exact opposite of choice or opportunity for the majority: Conservative policy really meant backing a favoured few and condemning the rest to lower-grade, dead-end non-education. The ideological Left ignored the fact that standards in some local schools were abysmally low, and that it was perfectly natural that caring parents would seek all possible methods to get their children to schools with a decent reputation. One method was to be sure to live in a (sufficiently expensive) area where the local comprehensives were high-quality (as many were). Labour front-bencher Harriet Harman incurred the hatred of the Left for sending her son to a fee-paying grammar school; Tony Blair was similarly excoriated for sending his children out of Islington and across London to non-fee-paying, but high-quality, Catholic schools. The Conservatives joined in the criticism, alleging hypocrisy, though it was difficult to discern any logic in their position. Black television producer Trevor Phillips, a putative Labour candidate for the Mayorship of London, saw his chances of winning the Labour nomination as being weakened by the fact that he had sent both of his daughters to a private school. In an interview,[26] which gets far nearer to the realities of British educational problems than the ideological posturing of both right and left, Phillips robustly explained the decisions which had horrified his Indian wife, brought up in France 'where everyone attends the neighbourhood school'. However, the designated secondary school in Haringey was White Hart Lane Comprehensive, where he and his sister had been pupils and where the number of children with five GCSE passes in the most recent league tables was just 14 per cent. 'And in the year my older daughter would have gone there, 1995,' Phillips commented, 'the proportion of children getting five GCSE passes was 4 per cent.'

> This wasn't somewhere working-class children might suffer but middle-class ones would do okay. Something was so drastically wrong you are effectively saying to your children I don't care if you fail to fulfil your potential.

Phillips felt he had to cast around for the best available option in London, which meant, since he was able to afford it, a fee-paying school.

> People will say why didn't you find a nice grant-maintained school, move across the borough borders or whatever: I have no particular quarrel with people who do that. But once you say that you can't put your children in your local neighbourhood school, then whatever else you do is irrelevant.
>
> The thing that upsets me about this is that people raise it about me as if I have committed a crime . . . The issue is not whether it makes me into some kind of bloated plutocrat but why most London parents are confronted with the situation where they are asked to see their children fail and smile about it.

Other black families sympathized with the Phillips position, and black MP Bernie Grant had supported Harriet Harman in her crisis:

> This goes beyond the old left–right divide. It's really an argument between people who want to confront a real problem and people who want to pretend it doesn't exist and stick to the old slogans.

The absolutely fundamental task was to get standards up. Once all comprehensive schools were achieving the highest standards and offering the necessary range of specialist options, that would be the time to phase out the schools which, it could reasonably be argued, tended, even if unwittingly, to inculcate snobbery and class-awareness. In fact Labour's Education Secretary, David Blunkett, very much followed lines set down by the previous Conservative governments – tests, inspections, tables, take-overs of failing schools – but with greater energy. There was some opposition from the teachers' unions, of whom it could fairly be said that like almost all of Britain's overly traditional and hidebound unions, they had failed over the years to secure their members decent remuneration. One incontrovertible fact was the sheer shortage of well-qualified teachers and head teachers. It was not at all clear that the government, with its attempted reintroduction of nineteenth-century 'payment by results' policies, had grasped the point that without a significant rise in the status and remuneration of the teaching profession, the recruitment necessary was unlikely to be forthcoming. Before the election, Labour had set up reduction in class sizes in primary schools as a gauge of the success of its educational policies: two-and-a-half years on it had not achieved its target.

Since the post-war reforms, university education had been free to the privileged minority, including a bigger proportion of working-class students than was to be found anywhere on the continent. The great need was to produce more graduates, that is to say to widen access to the universities. At the same time standards, which in some places seemed to be slipping under the Conservatives, had to be maintained. Maintaining university standards costs lots of money. The National Committee of Inquiry into Higher Education under Lord Dearing having identified fee-paying as 'the least worst option', the Teaching and Higher Education Act of July 1998 laid down that higher education students must pay up to £1,025 per year of their tuition costs, while at the same time it reconstructed the loan system for both fees and maintenance.[27] Despite the hostility from left as well as right, the policy was actually a socialistic, anti-middle-class one. Only a third of students were liable for the full amount (those whose family income was above £26,000 – not a princely sum when compared with fat-cat salaries!); another third (with family incomes below £16,000) paid nothing. Loans were available and only repayable when the successful graduate's income reached a certain level.

*3 'Sleaze' and contempt for authority*

The Conservative Government had been suffocating in sleaze. It was perhaps unrealistic to expect the new regime to remain whiter than white for long, though that was what 'New Labour' promised. Just as the Conservatives had plaintively complained that they were at heart the party of low taxes, even as taxation rose, Blair tended to claim that he was a man of upright Christian virtue, as if that automatically purified all dubious associations. Most dubious was the association with the media monopolist Rupert Murdoch. Though continuing to be hysterically anti-European, the *Sun* had supported Blair in the General Election. Obviously Blair was not going to go out of his way to lose the support of the Murdoch press, especially since a central calculation behind many of his actions was that if Labour was to carry through its modernization of Britain, it must do what no previous Labour government had ever achieved, win a second full term in office.

Still, on 9 April 1999, the Trade and Industry Secretary, Stephen Byers, ruled that Murdoch's British Sky Broadcasting (B Sky B) could not take over England's most successful football club, Manchester United (managed by Scotsman, Alex Ferguson). 'The most remarkable thing,' said Michael Crick, broadcaster and United fan, 'is that a politician has at last stood up to Rupert Murdoch.'[28] Given the abysmal Conservative performance and Blair's appeal as a moderate, it was not surprising that Labour's election campaign had been backed by a number of very wealthy people. When the government came to implement its promise to abolish tobacco sponsorship of sporting events, it put itself in a very bad light when it exempted motor racing, whose leading figure Bernie Ecclestone had donated one million pounds to Labour Party funds. The real corruption was out in the cities where Labour had dominated for so long that, not merely old Labour, it was putrefying Labour. Throughout the first years of Labour government there were scandals in Lambeth, Doncaster, Hull, Tyneside, Lanarkshire, Paisley and Glasgow, 'one-party fiefdoms' said journalist Andrew Rawnsley, 'enveloped in clouds of sleaze'.[29]

At the end of 1998 the government was said to have suffered a 'Black Christmas'. Two Cabinet ministers, Peter Mandelson and Geoffrey Robinson, both very close friends of the Prime Minister, had to resign, followed by Gordon Brown's political secretary. Robinson, who was very rich, and revealed no more about his complex interests and paid no more tax than he was legally obliged to, had loaned money to Mandelson to enable him to buy a house in an upper-class enclave in Notting Hill Gate. Mandelson, at the Department of Trade and Industry, had not declared the loan, though his department (not Mandelson himself) was involved in investigating Robinson's financial interests. There was talk of an axis between Brown and Prescott to propagate 'traditional Labour values' as against those of New Labour. Black Christmas was taken as having weakened Blair's position, confirmed that there were damaging divisions between him and Brown, and shown that Labour ministers could be just as venal as Conservative ones. The most significant fact, actually, was that Labour still stood at 50 per cent or more in the opinion polls, with the Conservatives down in the twenties. However, polls also suggested that people were beginning to feel that Labour was not that different from the Conservatives, and was failing to deliver on its promises.[30]

In January 1998, it was revealed that a secret 'ghost' squad of anti-corruption officers, set up in 1993, had discovered that:

> up to 250 officers, mostly senior detectives working in some of the force's most prestigious squads, were involved in major criminal activities. Serving and retired officers, up to the rank of Commander, are suspected of earning tens of thousands of pounds from bribes and corruption, some by working with London's top crime gangs.

The announcement followed

> the biggest anti-corruption operation ever mounted earlier this week, when raids were carried out on the homes and offices of nineteen serving and former officers from the Flying Squad. Thirteen officers have so far been suspended and enquiries are continuing.[31]

This came at a time when the inquiry into the handling of the murder in 1993 of a black teenager, Stephen Lawrence, was revealing unparalleled police incompetence, and worse (see issue 6 below). Possibly the Blair Government, which at about the same time announced a new judicial inquiry into the killings by British soldiers in Londonderry on Bloody Sunday, 30 January 1972, could be credited with marking the beginning of the end of cover-up. But restoration of confidence in the police, the civil service, and politicians national as well as local – opinion polls gave politicians, as a class, respect rating of 4 per cent[32] – seemed a long way off.

*4 Service, safety and quality of life*

According to opinion surveys, the public did not feel that services generally had improved under Labour, and some people were prepared to date such improvements as could be detected to the period of Major's government. The domain which embraces most of the sub-issues involved here is that of transport, the special responsibility of the Deputy Prime Minister, John Prescott. As details came out of the gross squandering of public money involved in the Major Government's privatization of the railways,[33] complaints mounted about late-running and cancelled trains, the difficulties of obtaining advance information about train services, dirty and overcrowded trains, unjustified fare rises and withdrawal of economy fares. Figures released in February 1999 revealed a further deterioration over the previous year, with only one company (on the Isle of Wight!) out of 25 scoring top marks for punctuality and reliability. There were frequent reports of inadequacies in track maintenance and failure to maintain safety systems on trains. Then came successive crashes outside Paddington Station, at Southall (19 September, 1997) when seven people were killed and thirteen seriously injured[34], and Ladbroke Grove (5 October 1999) when 31 died. Although the July 1998 White Paper, *A New Deal for Transport*, promised an integrated transport system,[35] proposals designed to deter the use of private cars were not matched by improvements in public transport. The London tube system was literally crumbling (with closures being imposed during the summer of 1999).

Rather suddenly, a *soi-disant* Countryside Movement came to prominence, with a somewhat mixed, and even contradictory agenda. Some complained about the devastating effect on rural life of the decline in rural transport. Others, however, owning cars as big as small houses, were more concerned about the possibility of legislation banning hunting. Such legislation had been a Labour-supported objective, but had apparently succumbed to Blair's determination never to stir up powerful enmities.

5 *Social policy, the poor*

The government did introduce a statutory minimum wage, though at the low rate of £3.60 per hour, and Brown's third budget, in March 1998, made some small, but concrete, steps towards improving the lot of the very poorest families. The most positive, if in some ways most nebulous, drive behind Labour's social welfare policy was the notion of 'social inclusion' (which replaced the earlier notion of a 'stakeholder society' since few people knew what a 'stakeholder' was). A very strong contrary force was the insistence on preserving low levels of taxation and keeping down expenditure. Much was made of the high costs of having people out of work and paying them benefits; attention, too, was focused on benefit fraud, estimated at £2.8 billion per annum. So emerged the central concept of 'welfare to work', which sounded very conservative (even Republican, in the American party-political sense). However, having everyone who was able to contribute to the community do so, rather than being (allegedly) cut off in a dependency culture, was an important part of social inclusion. It was seen as a daring move when Frank Field, protagonist of radical reform of the welfare system, was appointed to support Harriet Harman at Social Security. The government's first real crisis came when Harman and Field, who had been unable to work with each other, were both removed from their posts. After a number of pilot schemes which, the government claimed, had found work for seven out of ten jobless young people, the nationwide 'New Deal' was launched on 6 April 1998. However, it was also revealed that there were fewer placings into unsubsidized jobs than originally estimated. The subsidized jobs were funded by the £4 billion raised by the windfall levy on the privatized utilities. More than 118,000 young people were eligible for the scheme, with some 4,000 employers agreeing to offer more than 14,000 jobs, each carrying a £60 subsidy. As the number of young unemployed turned out to be smaller than expected, the scheme was subsequently opened to the older unemployed. The Welfare Bill published in February 1999 made it clear that the government was determined upon a 'welfare to work', root-and-branch reform of the welfare state by 2000. There would be a 'single gateway' for all benefit claimants of working age, including lone parents and the disabled, who would have to attend personal interviews about employment possibilities. Incapacity benefit would be means-tested. Given the manifest weakness of the social security system, there was much to commend this approach. But the Prime Minister's declaration of 'the end of something for nothing' was offensive and threatening to those who had, after all, not created the system in which they were entrapped.[36] On the positive side, child benefit was to be increased by £2.95 to £14.40 a week, there was to be a new minimum income guarantee to give the poorest pensioners at least £75 a week, and pensioner couples £116.60 a week, and there was to be a £30 million fund to help the disabled into work, including the provision of 1,500 new jobs for the severely disabled. The Child Support Agency moved definitively from grabbing what it could, to a fixed-levy basis.

With regard to the NHS the objective was to keep the crisis-prone system going – there had been no doubt about Major's own personal commitment to the NHS, but it had been apparent that many in the Conservative party wished to move to a largely privatized service, with the NHS serving only the very poor. Labour ended the internal market, claiming thereby to have released funds previously spent on bureaucracy. From 1 April 1999, GP Fundholders were replaced by Primary Care Groups, clusters of GP practices serving populations of 100,000. The usual swell of Christmas flu cases at the end of 1998 produced a recurrence of not unfamiliar tales of the NHS in crisis: 'on its knees', the *Observer* reported, 'as bodies are stored in meat lorries, blood supplies run low and patients wait in corridors'.[37] Surprisingly, the distinctively 'old Labour' Health Secretary, Frank Dobson, seemed relatively unscathed, gaining some credit for being open and honest about the nature of the crisis, and his own failure to get waiting lists down. The essence of the problem was a shortage of nurses, in turn related to low pay and unsatisfactory conditions. Improvements were on the way from April 1999. A less-publicized problem was that with more and more dentists taking only private patients, an NHS in dental care was ceasing to exist in many areas.

### 6 *Class, race, gender*

According to Blair, speaking in December 1998: 'slowly but surely, the old establishment is being replaced by a new, larger, more meritocratic middle class'. In that same month the old official classification of people into classes AB, C1, C2, DE, which dated from 1911, was replaced by a more complex system, broadly suggesting that almost everyone was now middle class. Had the working class disappeared, the fortunates moving into the middle class, the unfortunates into an underclass? With manufacturing now contributing only 20 per cent of GDP the traditional working class certainly had shrunk, but it had not disappeared, nor had age-old working-class attitudes. Although trade union membership had dropped greatly, the view that it was no part of a worker's responsibility to participate in any way in management – a sentiment echoed by many managers, and one still at the heart of many of the country's economic difficulties – persisted.

Issues of gender, social mobility, and class were combined in the person of Dr

Marjorie ('Mo') Mowlam, Secretary for Northern Ireland, and consistently voted the most popular member of the government after Blair. Mowlam, daughter of an alcoholic postal worker, had gone to a comprehensive in Coventry, then on to élitist Durham University, to study social anthropology. After that she took a PhD in Iowa, lectured first in Florida, and then back in Britain at Newcastle. If anything could be called 'classless', perhaps it was her down-to-earth, utterly unpretentious manner, which obviously belonged to the genuinely middle reaches of society, not, as with her predecessor, to the upper ones.

Through deliberate positive discrimination (subsequently ruled illegal) Labour had ensured that there were 101 women among its ranks in parliament. Palpable evidence of discrimination remained, though also some of able women achieving high positions in business and government. Women constituted 45 per cent of the workforce, but only 5 per cent of company directors, 7 per cent of university professors, and 10 per cent of judges; for the situation in the police see table 6.4.

**Table 6.4** Numbers of police officers in England and Wales, by rank and gender, 1998

| | *Males* | *Females* |
|---|---|---|
| Chief Constable | 47 | 2 |
| Assistant Chief Constable | 135 | 8 |
| Superintendent | 1,188 | 46 |
| Chief Inspector | 5,732 | 90 |
| Inspector | 1,520 | 320 |
| Sergeant | 17,221 | 1,395 |
| Constable | 79,349 | 17,745 |
| All ranks | 105,192 | 19,606 |

*Source: Social Trends 29* (1999), p. 165.

Some role reversals were not entirely happy ones. Because of the shrinkage in traditional male manufacturing jobs, in many households the principal earner was a woman, often herself on low wages. But at school, and increasingly at university, girls, showing great powers of application, as well as confidence that there were jobs to be obtained in telecommunications, design, teaching, information technology, office administration and the liberal professions, were outperforming boys. This created the problem of a rising number of young men adrift from the world of work and marriage, whose teenage misdemeanours were leading inexorably to an adult life of dereliction and crime; a problem so serious that Blair set up a special ministerial team to address it. In the sixties the all-conquering British rock/pop groups had all been male. Perhaps the greatest portent of what, rather politically incorrectly, it had become fashionable to call 'girl power' was the immense success of the Spice Girls, the all-female, multi-ethnic, Beatles of the nineties.

The most significant events in highlighting continuing racism in Britain were

**Table 6.5** Population by ethnic group and age (percentages), 1996

| | *Under 16* | *16–34* | *35–54* | *55 and over* | *all ages (= 100%) (thousands)* |
|---|---|---|---|---|---|
| White | 20 | 27 | 27 | 26 | 52,942 |
| Black Caribbean | 23 | 36 | 24 | 17 | 477 |
| Black African | 28 | 43 | 23 | 6 | 281 |
| Other Black | 49 | 38 | 12 | * | 117 |
| Indian | 27 | 32 | 29 | 12 | 877 |
| Pakistani | 40 | 33 | 19 | 8 | 579 |
| Bangladeshi | 40 | 35 | 17 | 8 | 183 |
| Chinese | 16 | 40 | 30 | 15 | 126 |
| Other Asian | 27 | 31 | 36 | 6 | 161 |
| Other ethnic minorities | 51 | 30 | 15 | 5 | 506 |
| All ethnic groups | 21 | 27 | 27 | 25 | 56,241 |

*Source: Social Trends 27* (1997), p. 31. * This figure (almost negligible) is unavailable.

the triple enquiries into how the Metropolitan police had conducted their investigations of the murder in south-east London, back in April 1993, of a gifted, 18-year-old student, Stephen Lawrence, by a white gang. The police made such a mess of the investigation that even when they eventually did bring three young men, believed to be members of the gang, to the Old Bailey, the prosecution failed. Investigations by the Kent police and the Police Complaints Authority (PCA) began before the general election. The PCA inquiry felt that five detectives on the case ought to face charges of neglect of duty. Four of the officers had already retired, and the fifth shortly seized the opportunity to do so too. More important, the exhaustive public inquiry, chaired by Sir William Macpherson, found the Metropolitan police guilty of institutional racism. Officers had failed to give Stephen first aid, to record evidence against the white gang, to arrest them speedily, had suspected Stephen's black companion of the murder, and had been grossly insensitive in their handling of Stephen's parents. It should not, of course, have needed the destruction of a promising life, and the dedicated efforts of the Lawrence parents, to bring this all out and expose the original attempted whitewash on the part of the Metropolitan police. The escape from justice by the defaulting officers was a regrettable quirk in the system which Home Secretary Jack Straw declared he would rectify. New race awareness training was introduced in an effort to extirpate racism from the force. The earlier introduction of community-policing officers, liasing with minority communities, had had a definite effect in improving relationships in areas which had formerly been prone to rioting, but a further report found a substantial minority of policing areas totally negligent in this respect, while unemployment remained high among ethnic minorities (see table 6.6). Racism was not an easy problem to address, and indeed one study by the Institute for Public Policy Research showed that there was considerable racial prejudice between ethnic communities, particularly between black and

Asian people. The growing proportion of minorities born in the UK, usually speaking with regional British accents, and falling into the younger age groups (see table 6.5), together with such phenomena as the high proportion of star black players in English football teams, helped to create a situation which, while giving no cause for complacency, was probably more satisfactory than that obtaining in either Germany or France. The strongest indicator of a decline in racism is the rise in the number of sexual relationships taking place across racial boundaries: such relationships between whites and members of ethnic minorities were far more prevalent than any between members of different ethnic minorities.

The intensification of Scottish and Welsh nationalism, under the stimulus of devolution, created fascinating new cross-currents with regard to questions of both race and identity. Expatriate Scottish journalist Gavin Essler reported (*Independent*, 15 May 1999) on his brief return to Scotland:

> You can have many layers of identity even if you call yourself a nationalist. Bashir Ahmed, of Scots Asians for Independence, is simultaneously a Scot, an Asian, a Glaswegian, a Muslim, a Scottish National party candidate for the Scottish Parliament and a British citizen. 'Scotland to me is everything', he says rapturously, recounting how he was welcomed after he left Pakistan in the Sixties. Un-self-consciously, Bashir Ahmed uses the word 'we' to describe the new Scottish national mosaic of which he is a part. 'After 300 years, we are getting our Scottish parliament back. A short time ago we got our Stone of Destiny back. So we are getting everything back'.

**Table 6.6** Unemployed rates (in percentages) in Great Britain by ethnic group and age, 1997–1998 (men up to age 64, women up to age 59)

| | *16–24* | *25–34* | *35–44* | *45–59/64* | *All aged 15–59/64* |
|---|---|---|---|---|---|
| White | 13 | 6 | 5 | 5 | 6 |
| Black | 39 | 18 | 12 | 16 | 19 |
| Indian | 18 | 7 | 6 | 7 | 8 |
| Pakistani/Bangladeshi | 29 | 16 | 13 | 26 | 21 |
| Other groups | 22 | 13 | 10 | 8 | 13 |
| All ethnic groups | 14 | 7 | 5 | 5 | 7 |

*Source: Social Trends 29* (1999), p. 82.

### 7 *Crime*

Two of the main issues at the beginning of 1999 were levels of policing, and levels of punishment. For all the exposures of police frailty, the public continued to tell pollsters that what they most wanted was more policemen on the beat. Tight spending controls meant that, in the eyes of many, policing levels were too low. Though by no means in the same mould as his predecessor, Straw definitely projected a tough image, at the end of 1998 implementing his predecessor's policy (and one imitative of American policies) of setting a minimum prison sentence for those committing a third burglary, though with the introduction of some discretion for the courts. Britain had the largest prison population in Europe: the government's response that this showed that Britain was catching more criminals suggested a lamentable failure to give the crime problem the serious, professional attention it needed.

Two areas of criminal activity attracted special attention. The European Commission's *1998 Annual Report* on the state of the drugs problem in the European Union reported that in Britain, among both teenagers and adults, consumption of drugs was higher than anywhere else in Europe. Huge drug seizures were announced from time to time, but the problem seemed to get only worse, increased drug-taking being reported first among pre-teen boys, and then among teenage girls. Again in imitation of America, a 'drugs czar' was appointed, an ex-miner who had risen to the status of Chief Constable, Keith Hellawell. The government were resolutely opposed to the decriminalization of even the 'soft' drug, cannabis. However, at the end of May 1999, an imaginative new strategy was announced, aimed at rehabilitation, rather than punishment, for drug offences.

Britain was 'the drugs capital of Europe'. It was probably not the 'paedophilia capital of Europe', that dishonour perhaps belonging to Belgium. But from the mid-nineties onwards there was a spate of well-documented cases of child abuse: the stories children, and adults, told were now (rightly) being listened to, when previously they were being dismissed. At Ashworth secure mental hospital, it was actually a patient, in October 1996, whose complaints of paedophilia, and other goings on, prompted the setting up of an inquiry in February 1997 which produced a disturbing report at the end of 1998.[38] The presence, in any area, of a known paedophile was a nightmare for parents. Legislation was introduced in a not wholly successful attempt to keep track of convicted paedophiles released from prison; but the menace of paedophiles not covered by the new legislation continued.

### 8 *Constitutional reforms*

Devolution for Scotland and Wales, and abolition of the House of Lords, had been under discussion since the later nineteenth century. Always the devil had been in the detail, and the devil had always been strong enough to prevent any proposals going ahead. The problem with devolution was that the United Kingdom did not readily lend itself to a federal solution, as did the United States with its 50 separate states, or Germany with its roughly equal *Länder*, specially created at the end of the war. England was very large and heavily populated, Scotland, and still more so Wales, small. But they were not regions, or artificially created states, they were nations. If Scotland had a separate parliament, shouldn't England have a separate one too? Or, despite the fact that a region could not be fully equated with a nation, should England be divided up into regions each with at least a local assembly? If Scotland had a separate parliament, but nothing was done about England, how could it be right for Scottish MPs still to come to Westminster and discuss matters purely relating to England? This last point became known as the 'West Lothian question' since it was posed by the upper-class, Catholic, MP for West Lothian in Scotland, Tam Dalyell, who was as opposed to Scottish self-government as he was to foreign ventures by the British Government.

The question which always bedevilled Lords reform was that of what was to be put in the place of the hereditary house. Creating another elected house would derogate from the prestige and powers of the House of Commons. Because Britain was not naturally a federal country, the kind of senate which existed in the United States could not readily be created, though was surely not impossible to devise. The Blair Government appreciated that if questions of detail were to be settled first neither devolution nor Lords reform would ever be carried through. On devolution, referendums were held in Scotland and Wales in September 1997. This time the Scottish vote could scarcely have been more decisive, the Welsh scarcely less. The Scots voted by 1,775,045 votes (74.3 per cent) to 614,400 (25.7 per cent) for a Scottish Parliament, and by 63.5 per cent to 36.5 per cent in favour of that parliament having the power to vary income tax by up to three pence in the pound. In Wales the vote for a National Assembly was 559,419 (50.3 per cent), against 552,698 (49.7 per cent). The government fired ahead on both barrels, with elections being held on 9 May 1999. The Scottish Parliament had 129 MSPs (in the 'additional member' proportional representation system, 73 represented existing single-member constituencies, 56, chosen from party lists, represented the eight European Parliament constituencies). The Welsh Assembly (see plate 12) had 60 members, similarly divided 40/20.[39] On the question of the second chamber, with the Conservatives claiming that Blair intended a house of 'Tony's

**Plate 12** Computer-generated view of the proposed National Assembly for Wales building, designed by Richard Rogers Partnership. On the left is the Pierhead Building, symbol of Victorian prosperity. The notorious Tiger Bay area, birthplace of singer Shirley Bassey, has been completely cleared. Courtesy of Hayes Davidson/John Maclean.

cronies', an interim compromise was reached, whereby 91 hereditary peers would retain their seats until a Royal Commission had had time to make proposals. William Hague went along with the scheme, but sacked its begetter, the Conservative leader in the House of Lords, Lord Cranborne.

On the question of changing the UK electoral system, the government acted with rather less celerity. In 1998 a commission under Lord Jenkins (founding member of the SDP, now a Liberal Democrat peer) proposed a system basically employing the alternative vote, but topped up with national lists of candidates to be selected by proportional representation. Such a system would not be introduced until there had been a nationwide referendum; increasingly it seemed likely that that would not come until after another general election. Meantime plans were being laid to restore government to the conurbations, above all, London, with the added ingredient of directly elected mayors. For the European elections on 10 June 1999 proportional representation with party lists was used for the first time; a disconcertingly low poll (23 per cent), from which the Conservatives emerged triumphant (36 seats to Labour's 29), indicated not just apathy, but accelerating hostility to EMU; Britain, it could be noted, was the only country with non-white candidates.

The monarchy, of which Blair was a strong supporter, made some moves towards rendering itself more human, and less of a burden on the taxpayer. Some associated these changes with the great outburst of feeling among many sections of the public over the tragic death in a car accident in Paris of Diana, Princess of Wales, in September 1997, but this was officially denied. Historian Ben Pimlott, biographer of the Queen, adjudged:

> A lot of changes to the royal family were already taking place, but it is clear that the mood created by Diana's death has increased the sense of urgency both inside and outside the Palace.[40]

A constitutional innovation of a different sort was Blair's attempt 'to end tribalism' in politics through seeking to work with Liberal Democrat leaders in areas where there was agreement, including, in particular, constitutional and voting reform. Early on, a new Cabinet Council was created, which Paddy Ashdown was invited to attend. With Ashdown's announcement that he would step down from the Liberal Democrat leadership during 1999, and the open rejoicing in 'tribalism' of John Prescott and other leading Labour figures, the permanence of the innovation could not be guaranteed. Much might depend on the success of the Labour–Liberal Democrat Coalition formed in Scotland under First Minister Donald Dewar.

### 9 *Values: permissiveness, piety, selfishness, consensus*

One of my central themes in the second half of this book has been that the permissive values of the sixties continued to develop and accelerate, even when radical Conservative governments were trying to propagate very different attitudes. This seems to be confirmed by the results of an *Observer/ICM* poll in October 1998, published in the *Observer*, 25 October 1998 (see table 6.7).

Within the clear and impressive broad picture, the following may be noted:

**Table 6.7** Permissiveness, October 1998

(a) Percentage 'agree', 'disagree', and 'don't know'

| | *Agree* | *Disagree* | *Don't Know* |
|---|---|---|---|
| 'Divorce in Britain should be more difficult to obtain' | 47 | 44 | 9 |
| 'Married parents should always stay together while their children are young, no matter how badly mother and father get on together' | 28 | 67 | 6 |
| 'It is always wrong for couples to sleep together before they are married' | 21 | 75 | 4 |
| 'Parents who live together without getting married cannot care for their children as well as parents who are married' | 17 | 80 | 3 |
| 'As long as they have enough money, single parents can bring up children just as well as parents who are married' | 68 | 29 | 3 |
| 'Gay couples should be allowed to get married' | 36 | 55 | 9 |
| 'It is possible for married people to have an affair without harming their marriage' | 12 | 85 | 3 |

(b) Which of the following statements comes closest to your view:

| | |
|---|---|
| 'The government should actively support family values and encourage couples to get married and then stay together' | 40% |
| OR | |
| 'It is none of the government's business how people conduct their lives, as long as they stay with the law' | 58% |
| 'Don't know' | 2% |

(c) Percentage of respondents saying they are:

| | *Very permissive* | *Fairly permissive* | *Neither* | *Fairly traditional* | *Very traditional* |
|---|---|---|---|---|---|
| All | 14 | 39 | 30 | 14 | 2 |
| Men | 10 | 37 | 34 | 16 | 3 |
| Women | 18 | 41 | 28 | 11 | 2 |
| Age: | | | | | |
| 18–24 | 16 | 50 | 23 | 9 | 1 |
| 25–34 | 21 | 50 | 25 | 4 | 0 |
| 35–44 | 18 | 46 | 23 | 10 | 1 |
| 45–54 | 15 | 40 | 32 | 13 | 1 |
| 55–64 | 10 | 28 | 37 | 19 | 5 |
| 65+ | 4 | 22 | 40 | 26 | 8 |

(c) Percentage of respondents saying they are: *cont'd*

| | *Very permissive* | *Fairly permissive* | *Neither* | *Fairly traditional* | *Very traditional* |
|---|---|---|---|---|---|
| Social class: | | | | | |
| AB | 16 | 38 | 32 | 13 | 2 |
| C1 | 18 | 42 | 26 | 13 | 1 |
| C2 | 16 | 44 | 26 | 10 | 3 |
| DE | 8 | 33 | 36 | 18 | 5 |

opposition to gay marriages; the realistic recognition that affairs are likely to harm a marriage; the fact that women see themselves as much more permissive than men see themselves (certainly a very sharp reversal from what opinion polls were reporting in the 1950s); that only the over-65s come out as more traditional than permissive, with the most permissive being in the 25–34 age group, while all 'class' groups are more permissive than not, the most working-class group (DE) is least permissive.

The fundamental facts of family life in Britain are such: it has the highest proportion of divorces, and the highest proportion of single-parent families in Europe. Average household size was now 2.4. The proportion of households consisting of a single person was 27 per cent, with the fastest growth being in single male adult households.[41] Some commentators deduced from these figures, from the greater stress and competitiveness in the work place, and from the attitudes which the Thatcher and Major governments had tried to inculcate, that the British people had become 'more selfish', with, as the Director of Consumer Consultancy at the Henley Business Centre put it, 'less of our life taken up by other people'. Social attitude surveys and opinion polls did not bear out that conclusion;[42] but perhaps that is soft evidence, trumped by the hard statistics presented in the Institute of Directors report of May 1999, *The End of Altruism?*, which showed that in real terms charitable donations had dropped by a third since 1993. Also in May 1999, the *British Medical Journal* came out with another dismal British 'best'. Though uninhibited sexual activity among young people was no greater than that in other northern European countries, the prevalence of sexually-transmitted diseases was. The blame was put on Britain's exceptionally large number of poor, the 'socially excluded', among whom ignorance prevailed, and state and parental care was lacking.

*10 The arts and media*

The arts did not die in Britain in the nineties. Nor did they suddenly leap into glorious summer with the return of the Blair Government and the flashing around for a time of the empty slogan 'Cool Britannia'. The art which can shock without actually having to be viewed – featured in the Royal Academy 1997 Exhibition, *Sensation*, and the 1999 Saatchi Gallery Exhibition, *Neurotic Realism* – remained the height of fashion, while the deep human craving for art as rich visual experience was demonstrated by the unprecedented financial success of the 1999 Royal Academy Monet Exhibition. The label 'National Heritage' was abolished, and Chris Smith was appointed Minister for Culture, Media and Sport. At least, like any decent European minister of culture, he did, at last, introduce tax concessions for films made in the UK. (There was a great outcry *Braveheart* (1997), an inspiration to the SNP (the Scottish National Party), had been filmed in the Irish Republic.) Whether the Royal Opera House, notorious for wastefulness and lax management, while chronically underfunded by continental standards, would cease to be the focus for corporate entertainment, and generally become an accessible natural asset, remained to be seen. The difficulty of making instant judgements is well illustrated by the American successes of British theatre. During 1998 British productions overwhelmingly dominated Broadway. But this was not entirely due to their inherent quality: Broadway owners reckoned proven and well-advertised British successes much safer investments than untested American plays.[43] This was rather like what was happening in British football, where more and more premier division stars were foreign imports: it was easier and more profitable to buy in your stars ready-made, than to try to rear them at home. The 5,000 school sports grounds sold off during the Conservative years would not readily be replaced – and the Labour Government, to its shame, showed no signs of reversing that disgraceful policy. To stick with drama: when *Amy's View*, total sell-out at the National Theatre from June 1997 until its successful transfer to the West End in January 1998, was followed by a sell-out revival of *Plenty* (1977), it was clear that playwright David Hare, product of the cultural revolution, had joined the ranks of the canonized dramatists of earlier in the century.[44] Even without tax concessions, the British cinema industry, the biggest in Europe, still produced a respectable number of critical and commercial successes, including the four comedies: *Four Weddings and a Funeral* (1994), about leisure and love among the still very-much-alive upper class, which made £60 million; *The Full Monty* (1997), about former steel-workers in deindustrialized Sheffield who become male strippers (£73 m); and *Shakespeare in Love*, postmodernist in its deliberate anachronisms (£74m); and *Notting Hill*, biggest seller of the four. Television had played an as yet scarcely acknowledged part in the undoing of John Major: soap opera after soap opera, about the emergency services, about medical practice, about the police and the law, paraded the effects of Conservative cuts. But by the end of the decade all the companies – once great sponsors of British creativity – were economizing on actors and creative writers and putting on more and more low-cost fly-on-the-wall or docu-drama series.

Lola Young, black, professor of Cultural Studies at Middlesex University, author of a brilliant critical study, *Fear of the Dark: 'Race', Gender and Sexuality in the Cinema* (1996), spoke of novels which 'tended towards the domestic in a piddling sort of way'. True, perhaps, of the hilarious novels about single thirty-somethings of which *Bridget Jones's Diary* (1998) by Helen Fielding was the prototype. But, to choose two of the decade's outstanding works, Rose Tremain's *The Way I Found Her* (1997), set in Paris, told by a 13-year-old boy about the disappearance of a Russian beauty, is an incredible work of creative imagination; while *Birdsong* (1994) by Sebastian Faulks ranks with the greatest twentieth-century war novels.

## IDENTITIES: IRELAND, AMERICA, EUROPE

In the 1997 election Sinn Féin took 17 per cent of the Northern Ireland vote, winning two seats (though it still refused to send its two members to Westminster). It could now claim that it did have a legitimate electoral base. The SDLP had remained stuck on three seats for 24 per cent of the vote. With a second IRA ceasefire being declared in July 1997, a new phase of intensive all-party discussions began. In September an Independent International Commission on Decommissioning (of weapons), consisting of Commissioners and staff from the US, Canada and Finland, and chaired by the Canadian General John de Chastelain, was set up by the British and Irish Governments. Up to the last, the multi-party talks in Belfast always seemed at risk of breaking down, but, helped perhaps by the direct intervention of Tony Blair, the 'Good Friday Agreement' was concluded on 10 April 1998. The Agreement was first to be submitted to referendums in Northern Ireland and the Republic. A new Northern Ireland Assembly of 108 members was to be elected on 25 June. By 10 March 1999 that Assembly was to have appointed a multi-party Executive (proportional to party strengths in the Assembly) to which responsibility for governing the province would be transferred. There was to be both a north/south Ministerial Council, together with 'implementation bodies', and a British–Irish Council, which would bring in representatives of the devolved governments of Scotland and Wales. Both governments recognized that Northern Ireland would remain a part of the United Kingdom as long as a majority of its people so wished, the Irish Government undertaking to remove the claim to Northern Ireland from the Irish Constitution; and should the Northern Ireland people ever decide for a United Ireland, the British Government would immediately facilitate this.

All parties to the Agreement committed themselves to use their best efforts to achieve decommissioning of all paramilitary weapons within two years of the referendum (i.e. by 22 May 2000) and to work with the Independent International Commission. An independent commission (former Conservative Party Chairman, and then Governor of Hong Kong, Chris Patten, was appointed to head this) would report on the future of the RUC – still greatly mistrusted by Catholics. (This mistrust was suddenly recharged with the ghastly assassination by car bomb on 16 March 1999 of solicitor Mrs Rosemary Nelson, notorious in RUC circles for her successful defence of the IRA suspects they arrested (see plate 13).) Arrangements would be made for an accelerated programme for release under licence of paramilitary prisoners (ratified at Westminster by legislation of July 1998). On 22 May, 80.9 per cent of the Northern Ireland electorate took part in the referendum; there was a 55.5 per cent turnout in the Irish Republic. The votes in favour of the Good Friday Agreement were, respectively, 71.1 per cent for to 28.8 per cent against, and 94.3 per cent for to 5.6 per cent against. In the elections for the new Assembly the results (six members coming from each of the 18 existing constituencies) were as in table 6.8.[45]

Trimble became First Minister, with Seamus Mallon of the SDLP as his Deputy.

**Table 6.8** Results of Northern Ireland Assembly election, 25 June 1998

| *Party* | *Seats* |
|---|---|
| Ulster Unionist | 28 |
| SDLP | 24 |
| Democratic Unionist | 20 |
| Sinn Féin | 18 |
| Alliance | 6 |
| UK Unionist | 5 |
| Progressive Unionist | 2 |
| Northern Ireland Women's Coalition | 2 |
| Others | 3 |

Extremists were not reconciled to the Agreement, the splinter group Continuity IRA carrying out an atrocious attack, in which 29 people were killed, at Omagh in August 1998. From being an annual event fraught with danger, Drumcree had become a permanent one. Under heavy siege from Orangemen, the RUC strove to hold out against any attempted march down the Garvaghy Road. As the deadline for handover of power approached, many obstacles lay in the way of completing the setting up of the Executive. Trimble maintained that the Unionists could not permit representatives of Sinn Féin to take up

**Plate 13** Belfast wall mural – Republican reactions to the murder of Rosemary Nelson. Courtesy of Pachemaker Press International.

places on the Executive until decommissioning of IRA weapons had begun. Sinn Féin maintained that there was no possibility of their influencing the IRA on this (Adams said he 'would be laughed out of the room') and that, in any case, decommissioning at this stage was not laid down in the Agreement. Also of concern was the continuance of punishment shootings and beatings by the paramilitaries. At Easter 1999 the new cross-party Executive was still not in place; the British and Irish Prime Ministers issued the Hillsborough Declaration calling on the IRA to put a token quantity of weapons 'beyond use'. Sinn Féin rejected this. With magnificent energy and devotion Blair and Aherne continued with their efforts, in mid-May 1999 producing proposals that the Executive should be formed, with the IRA committed to beginning decommissioning shortly thereafter. The Unionists rejected this. There matters stood, when, on 11 October 1999, Peter Mandelson returned to office as Northern Ireland Secretary.

Meantime ex-Senator George Mitchell had been persuaded to chair further talks between the parties. After ten weeks, peace seemed to break out, with remarkably conciliatory statements by the Ulster Unionists and by Sinn Féin on 16 November, and by the IRA on 17 November. The power-sharing Executive was (at last) to take office, with the IRA on the same day appointing a representative to discuss decommissioning with General de Chastelain. Meeting on Saturday 27 November the Ulster Unionist Council voted by 480 to 349 to accept the latest agreement, but with the warning that if decommissioning had not begun by February 2000, the process would stall once again.

That the peace process had progressed so far owed much to President Clinton and ex-Senator Mitchell. Relationships between the American President and the British Prime Minister were warm: they both, allowing for the different circumstances of the two countries, favoured the 'Third Way' in politics. Probably only a temporary convergence, but there did again seem to be some substance in the notion of a 'special relationship', especially when, in December 1998, Britain was the only country to join with the Americans in air attacks on Iraq, provoked by Saddam Hussein's interference with UN weapons inspections.

But much more powerful forces were drawing Britain into Europe. For many years the annual *Britain* publications had been printing tables showing how Britain's overseas trade was steadily swinging away from the rest of the world towards Europe. Table 6.9 reprints the latest one.

**Table 6.9** Percentage distribution of UK overseas trade

| | *Exports* | *Imports* |
|---|---|---|
| European Union | 55.8 | 54.5 |
| Other Western Europe | 4.6 | 5.9 |
| North America | 13.9 | 14.8 |
| Other OECD countries | 6.3 | 7.9 |
| Oil-exporting countries | 5.5 | 1.8 |
| Rest of the world | 14.0 | 15.2 |

*Source: Britain*, 1999, p. 404.

**Table 6.10** Contributions to and receipts from the European budget, 1997 in £ billion

| | *Contributions* | *Receipts* | *Balance* |
|---|---|---|---|
| Germany | 14.6 | 6.9 | –7.7 |
| Netherlands | 3.3 | 1.7 | –1.6 |
| UK | 6.2 | 4.9 | –1.3 |
| Sweden | 1.6 | 0.8 | –0.8 |
| Belgium | 2.0 | 1.4 | –0.7 |
| France | 9.1 | 8.4 | –0.7 |
| Austria | 1.5 | 0.9 | –0.5 |
| Italy | 6.0 | 5.8 | –0.2 |
| Luxembourg | 0.1 | 0.1 | 0.0 |
| Finland | 0.7 | 0.7 | 0.0 |
| Denmark | 1.0 | 1.1 | 0.1 |
| Portugal | 0.7 | 2.5 | 1.8 |
| Irish Republic | 0.5 | 2.3 | 1.8 |
| Greece | 0.8 | 3.7 | 2.9 |
| Spain | 3.7 | 7.7 | 4.0 |
| All EU countries | 51.8 | 48.9 | -3.1 |

*Source: Social Trends 29* (1999), p. 117.

**Table 6.11** British people's views on the single currency

If there were to be a referendum, would you vote to join a European single currency or not?

| | *All* | *Labour* | *Conservative* |
|---|---|---|---|
| Vote to join | 30% | 38% | 20% |
| Vote not to join | 54% | 48% | 70% |
| Don't know/would not vote | 16% | 14% | 10% |

Do you agree or disagree with the statement: 'if the European single currency turns out to be a success, Britain can't afford to stay out of it'?

| | *All* | *Labour* | *Conservative* |
|---|---|---|---|
| Agree | 58% | 64% | 42% |
| Disagree | 30% | 23% | 50% |
| Neither/don't know | 12% | 13% | 8% |

The 'Rest of the world' is there; 'North America' is there; 'The Commonwealth', it may be noted, is not (and had not been for many years). The reality of Britain's economic interests was over-powering.

But Britain was still opted out from joining the common currency. More immediately, following the election victory of the Social Democrats in Germany, moves were being concerted to end the rebate Thatcher had negotiated on Britain's contributions to the EU. Table 6.10 helps to explain Germany's concern in this matter.

On 24 June 1998, the *Sun* printed a picture of Tony Blair on its front page, with the massive headline: 'Is this the most dangerous man in Britain?', the reference being to the possibility that Blair would decide positively for the single currency. An *Observer/ICM* poll (table 6.11) in December 1998 (*Observer*, 6 December 1998) confirmed that the British people were still not enthusiastic, but at the same time felt that if the currency were a success, Britain could scarcely afford to stay out.[46]

The European single currency did come into being on 1 January 1999. For Britain, the likely scenario was a referendum following the next General Election (provided Labour won it) with the government then positively recommending that Britain should join (a referendum would be less likely if it became clear that opion was continuing to harden against Britain joining EMU). Whatever the big reforms, whatever the moves towards restoring consensus, retaining middle-class support, and winning that election would remain primary concerns of the Blair Government.

## LABOUR'S MID-TERM: GENERAL CONCLUSIONS

If we attempt a mid-term balance-sheet of Blair's successes and failures, we find ourselves re-encountering themes and dilemmas discussed throughout this book: the (changing) structural, ideological, and institutional limits within which politicians operate; the sad facts that no solutions are ever perfect, and that as one problem is solved others are created; the way events take unforeseen turns. As governments contemplate welfare expenditure, good intentions are not enough: ministers have to recognize that population size is levelling off (and actually declining in Scotland), while the proportion of the population not working, but requiring pensions, is steadily increasing. In 1961, around 12 per cent of the population were aged 65 and over and 4 per cent were aged 75 and over. In 1997 these figures had increased respectively to 16 per cent and 7 per cent. The other limiting structural factor that I keep stressing is the extent to which a small and vulnerable manufacturing sector is foreign-owned and foreign-managed.

Over the century, particularly during and after the two total wars, during the sixties, and during the Thatcher revolution, changes took place in what was thinkable and therefore in what was do-able. The public discourse of today, all Viagra, AIDS and bonking, would have appalled Britons in the twenties. As, too, would the literary work of Edinburgh working-class dropout and drug addict Irvine Welsh, who subsequently (again driving home the complexities of class) took business management qualifications: scatological, drug-ridden *Trainspotting* (1993, turned and slightly sentimentalized into a successful film – £23m, 1996), *Acid House* (1994), *Ecstasy* (1996), and *Filth* (1998); best-selling novels of the nineties which were certainly neither 'domestic' nor 'piddling'. A most notable change in ideological perspective was in that relating to children: the banning of corporal punishment in state schools since 15 August 1987,[47] and the concern over child abuse constrasted sharply with the harsh attitudes earlier in the century. Yet politicians at the end of the second millennium dare not contemplate even *investigating* the pros and cons of decriminalizing the consumption of drugs. After the tragic fiasco of Bosnia, the West should have known that it could not trust Slobodan Milosevic of Serbia to refrain from carrying his brutal 'ethnic cleansing' policies to Kosovo. When the NATO bombing of Yugoslavia began on 24 March 1999, the eviction and killings of Kosovar Albanians intensified, and obviously, when the operation was formally ended on 20 June, there was an immense task of reconstruction. But criticisms from left and right simply revealed the continuance of, respectively, an entrenched, robotic anti-Americanism, and an entrenched, none-of-our-business certainty that foreigners should be left to get on with slaughtering each other.

Ironically, while acting genuinely in the cause of Kosovars ejected from their land, the government was also attempting to enact an Immigration and Asylum Bill of distinctly illiberal character. There was something rather unpalatable too about the cuts in disablement benefit proposed in the Welfare Reform and Pension Bill, against which 80 Labour MPs voted at Committee stage. From the much delayed, and (compared with Labour promises) much-weakened Freedom of Information Bill, it appeared that a good measure of the old authoritarian secretiveness, which, at times, Blair appeared to favour, would continue. Still awaited was the Food Standards Agency: would this be powerful enough to avert another BSE-style disaster, or to resolve current concerns about genetically modified (GM) crops? While Blair was at his best in the Kosovo crisis, principled and unflinching (on the evening of 9 June 1999, Serbia's top generals signed a military agreement with the NATO commander, British General Sir Michael Jackson, on their immediate withdrawal from Kosovo), he was at his worst on GM crops: 'trust me, I'm a Christian', was compounded with 'trust me, I'm a man of science and enterprise'. On the other hand, the Social Exclusion Unit, bringing several departments to bear ('joined-up government', Blair called it) on the many interlinked problems of the dispossessed, and the making of Citizenship a compulsory subject in the National Curriculum were both, in their different ways, direct, pragmatic responses to deep failings in British society.

'Revolution' has become a rather over-used word; like 'consensus' it must be seen as a relative term, and it is in that sense that I have written of a 'Thatcherite Revolution'. The Blair regime was characterized by energy, freedom from dogma, pragmatic and untiring problem-solving, together with that inclusiveness and sensitivity to the lot of the misfortunate which had always appertained to the best of British politics. The advent of New Labour was a Restoration, not a Revolution. But a Restoration with an unprecedented youthful bounce, and an up-to-the-minute smoothness in keeping with a world which had undergone a communications revolution (that word again!).

A real sensitivity to what motivated both Republicans and Loyalists had made possible the drama-filled days of November, culminating in the legally-approved establishment of the devolved power-sharing Executive, the appointment of an IRA decommissioning go-between, and the abandonment of the Republic's claim to Northern Ireland, all on 2 December. On Europe the government was slowly opening the minds of the public to the possible benefits of joining EMU. There would never be a perfect moment. As with air strikes on Yugoslavia, the decision would involve a balancing of advantages against disadvantages. It was ever thus.

Is that a decent ending? 'History' is not 'the Past', but 'knowledge about the past produced by historians'. Individual contributions to that knowledge, and (as is the case for most of this book) to communicating that knowledge, should involve a dialogue between historian and reader. As a final exercise, I suggest that you, the reader, look at the endings to the various twentieth-century, or contemporary, histories to be found in my Further Reading. Do you see the difficulties? Which one most takes your fancy? Amusingly, if a trifle incestuously, Kenneth Morgan, in bringing his up-dated *The People's Peace* (1999) to a rousing finish, seizes upon the title given by Peter Clarke to his history of Britain 1900–1990, *Hope and Glory*: 'The glory had mostly departed but the hope lived on.' How important – do you remember the discussion in the Preface? – is a title?

## NOTES

1 Nigel Lawson, *Britain's Economy: A Mid-Term Report* (1985), p. 6.
2 G. C. Peden, *British Economic and Social Policy: Lloyd George to Margaret Thatcher* (1991), p. 215.
3 Anthony Seldon, *John Major: A Political Life* (1997, paperback 1998), pp. 131–4.
4 Ibid., p. 7.
5 The credit for making the discovery belongs to Michael Crick – see Michael Crick, 'John Major and the Older Woman', *Esquire*, March 1995; also Seldon, *Major*, pp. 20–5.
6 Quotations from Seldon, *Major*, pp. 25, 42, 62ff.
7 Margaret Thatcher, *The Downing Street Years* (1993, paperback 1995), p. 757.
8 Seldon, *Major*, pp. 122–8.
9 Quotations from ibid., pp. 155, 167; Hugo Young, *This Blessed Plot: Britain and Europe from Churchill to Blair* (1998), pp. 424–5.
10 David Butler and Dennis Kavanagh, *The British General Election of 1992* (1993), pp. 269, 278.
11 John Rentoul, *Tony Blair* (1995, paperback 1996), pp. 14–15, 17–18, 23, 33, 95.
12 Seldon, *Major*, p. 370.
13 Office for National Statistics, *Britain 1999: The Official Yearbook of the United Kingdom* (1998), pp. 56, 45.
14 Seldon, *Major*, p. 215.
15 For crime statistics see Office for National Statistics, *Social Trends 29* (1999), pp. 151–7.
16 Seldon, *Major*, p. 378.
17 Margaret Stacey, *Tradition and Change: A Study of Banbury* (1960), ch. 8.
18 Brian J. Ford, *BSE: The Facts. Mad Cow Disease and the Risk to Mankind* (1996), pp. 23–6, 156. It should be recorded that this view is contested by Rosalind M.

Ridley, *Fatal Protein: The Story of CJD, BSE, and Other Prion Diseases* (1998), p. 198.

19 Ridley, *Fatal Protein*, pp. 150–69, 190–201.

20 The case that preventive action should have been taken in 1988–9 and that the government was dishonest throughout is most strongly presented in Richard W. Lacey, *Mad Cow Disease: The History of BSE in Britain* (1994).

21 Ridley, *Fatal Protein*, pp. 190–201.

22 Seldon, *Major*, p. 287.

23 Ibid., pp. 732–4.

24 *Britain 1999*, pp. 387–97.

25 *Sunday Times*, 4 April 1999.

26 *Independent*, 3 December 1998.

27 *Britain 1999*, p. 141.

28 *Independent*, 10 April 1999. For Michael Crick, see note 6.

29 *Observer*, 15 March 1998.

30 *Observer*, 17 January 1998.

31 *Independent*, 30 January 1998.

32 MORI Poll in *The Evening Standard*, 3 February 1999. In 1993 an NOP poll had given politicians 5 per cent, civil servants 20 per cent, and judges 27 per cent – *Independent*, 13 December 1993.

33 Amounting to £1.2 billion. *Independent*, 4 June 1998.

34 Stanley Hall, *Railway Accidents* (1997), p. 103.

35 *Britain 1999*, p. 361.

36 *Observer*, 21 March 1999.

37 *Observer*, 10 January 1999. See *Social Trends 29*, p. 140, table 8.9.

38 *Report of the Committee of Inquiry into the Personality Disorder Unit, Ashworth Special Hospital*, 2 vols (1999). On paedophilia generally see Department of Health, *The Government's Response to the Children's Safeguards Review* (November 1998).

39 *Britain 1999*, pp. 20–1, 26.

40 *Observer*, 8 March 1998.

41 *Social Trends 29*, p. 42.

42 *Observer*, 10 January 1999. For a rebuttal see, in particular, NOP poll in *Sunday Mirror*, 31 January 1999.

43 *Observer*, 15 November 1998.

44 An excellent up-to-date history of recent British theatre is Dominic Shellard, *British Theatre Since the War* (1999).

45 The entire process is summarized in *Britain 1999*, pp. 14–18.

46 For the Labour party and Europe see Young, *Blessed Plot*, pp. 472ff.

47 By sections 47 and 48 of the Education (No. 2) Act, 1986. See *House of Commons Debates*, vol. 107, Written Answers, Col. 457, 16 December, 1986.

# Further Reading

Bibliographies are dangerous: reviewers always look to see if their own books are listed. Let me therefore stress, first, that guidance regarding further reading on individual sub-periods and sub-topics should be sought in the chapter notes; with very few exceptions, books appearing there are not re-listed here. Second, this section on 'Further Reading' simply sets out the different types of book available, and gives a few examples. All the major works have extensive bibliographies; the skill of building up reading lists of one's own, once one has identified a couple of key works, is an important one.

The chapter notes do contain a few primary sources, just to give some flavour of the sorts of primary sources historians of twentieth-century Britain make use of. You could, as a simple exercise in methodology, go through the notes picking out the primary sources – not always as obvious as might be thought.

## 1 Redoubtable pioneers

While almost all aspects of nineteenth-century history have been worked over several times (a tad tediously, one sometimes thinks), the twentieth century only became open to full scholarly research with the release, beginning in the late sixties, of the public records under the new thirty-year rule, and the opening of many important collections of private papers. A band of redoubtable pioneers, from the seventies and eighties onwards, have produced the fundamental knowledge to which all further studies must refer or react. Here are some of them:


Addison, Paul, *The Road to 1945: British Politics in the Second World War* (1975).
Bentley, Michael, *The Liberal Mind, 1914–29* (Cambridge, 1977).
Briggs, Asa, *History of Broadcasting in the United Kingdom*, 5 vols (1961–87).
Brooke, Stephen, *Labour's War: The Labour Party During the Second World War* (Oxford, 1992).
Burk, Kathleen, and Cairncross, Alec, *Goodbye, Great Britain: The 1976 IMF Crisis* (1991).
Clarke, Peter, *The Keynesian Revolution in the Making* (1988).
French, David, *British Strategy and War Aims, 1914–1916* (Oxford, 1986).
French, David, *The Strategy of the Lloyd George Coalition, 1916–1918* (Oxford, 1995).

Hennessy, Peter, *Never Again: Britain 1945–51* (1992).
Howson, Susan, *British Monetary Policy 1945–51* (Oxford, 1993).
McLaine, Iain, *Ministry of Morale: Home Front Morale and the Ministry of Information in World War Two* (1979).
Morgan, Kenneth O., *Consensus and Disunity: The Lloyd George Coalition Government 1918–1932* (1979).
Morgan, Kenneth O., *Labour in Power 1945–1951* (1984).
Morgan, Kenneth O., *The People's Peace: British History since 1945* (new edition, 1999). Informed by, rather than based on, Morgan's extensive knowledge of the available archive materials, this also has the qualities of a highly superior textbook, now going up (in a rather brief chapter) to 1998.
Peden, G. C., *British Rearmament and the Treasury* (1980).
Pelling, Henry, *The Labour Governments 1945–51* (1984).
Ramsden, John, *The Age of Churchill and Eden, 1940–1957* (1995).
Ramsden, John, *The Winds of Change: Macmillan to Heath 1957–1975* (1996).
Seldon, Anthony, *Churchill's Indian Summer: The Conservative Government 1951–1955* (1981).
Tanner, Duncan, *Political Change and the Labour Party, 1900–18* (Cambridge, 1990).
Turner, John, *British Politics and the Great War: Coalition and Conflict 1915–1918* (1992).
Webster, Charles, *The Health Services Since the War, vol.1* (1988); *vol. 2* (1997).
Williamson, Philip, *National Crisis and National Government: British Politics, the Economy and Empire 1926–32* (Cambridge, 1992).

## 2 *Biographies*

Biographers can no longer get away with simply exploiting privileged access to their biographees' private papers; they now pursue their subject's activities through *all* the relevant sources, thus producing contributions to history whose value goes far beyond the merely biographical. The work of journalists and specialist biographers has sometimes rivalled that of professional historians.

The mother and father of all biographies is *Winston S. Churchill*, vols III to VIII (1971–88) by Martin Gilbert. A few others, roughly cut to appropriate size, are (biographies are easily located by keying-in, or looking up, the *biographee*):

Addison, Paul, *Churchill on the Home Front, 1900–1955* (1992).
Burridge, Trevor, *Clement Attlee: A Political Biography* (1985).
Campbell, John, *Nye Bevan and the Mirage of British Socialism* (1987).
Dilks, David, *Neville Chamberlain, vol.1, Pioneering and Reform, 1869–1929* (Cambridge, 1984).
Grigg, John, *Lloyd George: From Peace to War 1912–1916* (1985).
Horne, Alastair, *Harold Macmillan* (2 vols, 1988, 1989).
Howard, Anthony, *RAB: The Life of R. A. Butler* (1987).
Pimlott, Ben, *Harold Wilson* (1992).
Pimlott, Ben, *Hugh Dalton* (1985).
Routledge, Paul, *Gordon Brown: The Biography* (1998).

## 3 *COLLECTIVE ENTERPRISE*

It is easier to write a learned article than it is to write a learned book. Stick a number of articles together, and, lo!, you have a book – of sorts. Some collections, and certain articles within collections, in particular, are invaluable, presenting important ideas and information in a brief and accessible way. On the down side, the same historians, on the same topics, do turn up rather too frequently in the different collections.

Here is a select list:

Brivati, Brian, and Bale, Tim (eds), *New Labour in Power: Precedents and Perspectives* (1997). Since the conference out of which this book was manufactured took place within weeks of the election of the Blair Government, the main title perpetrates a silly confidence trick. This is not instant history, but instant obsolescence.

Burk, Kathleen (ed.), *War and the State* (1982). Essential reading for effects of World War I.

Coopey, Richard, and Woodward, Nicholas (eds), *Britain in the 1970s: The Troubled Economy* (1996). Splendid collection, headed by the editors' brilliant overview.

Floud, Roderick, and McCloskey, Donald (eds), *The Economic History of Britain since 1700*, vols 2 and 3 (Cambridge, 1994). Top-class stuff.

Halsey, A. H. (ed.), *British Social Trends since 1900* (1988). Packed with useful information.

Hennessy, Peter, and Seldon, Anthony (eds), *Ruling Performance: British Governments from Attlee to Thatcher* (1987). Mustering the stage army; but they do well.

Johnson, Paul (ed.), *20th Britain: Economic, Social and Cultural Change* (1994). Highly professional, particularly on economics. But there are too many gaps in the coverage for this to serve as a textbook.

Smith, Harold (ed.), *War and Social Change: British Society in the Second World War* (Manchester, 1986). Meant to combat the alleged Marwick 'War and Social Change' thesis, many of the specialist contributions attest to the changes wrought by the war experience.

Thompson, F. M. L. (ed.), *The Cambridge Social History of Britain 1750–1950, vol. 3* (1990). A roll-call of distinguished historians.

Tiratsoo, Nick (ed.), *From Blitz to Blair: A New History of Britain since 1939* (1997). Sets up Thatcherite propaganda about Britain's recent past as if it were serious historical analysis, thus creating soft target.

## 4 *SPECIALIST WORKS OF SPECIAL INTEREST (NOT MENTIONED ELSEWHERE)*

Beddoe, Deirdre, *Back to Home and Duty: Women Between the Wars* (1991). Back to a basic topic.

Benson, John, *The Rise of Consumer Society in Britain, 1880–1980* (1994). Useful pioneering work.

Butler, David, Adonis, Andrew, and Travers, Tony, *Failure in British Government: The Politics of the Poll Tax* (1994). And what a failure!

Cairncross, Alec, *Managing the British Economy in the 1960s: A Treasury Perspective* (1996). Sober stuff.

Calder, Angus, *The People's War: Britain 1939–45* (1969). Few commentators appreciated that the title was intended ironically, probably because the rich content did not altogether support the author's conclusion that the war had merely hastened Britain on its wicked capitalist way.

Cannadine, David, *Class in Britain* (1998). Stresses continuing importance of historical perceptions of class.

Chapman, James, *The British at War: Cinema, State and Propaganda* (1998). Fresh approach to multi-faceted topic.

Cockett, Richard, *Thinking the Unthinkable: Think Tanks and the Economic Counter-Revolution 1931–1983* (1994). Makes you think.

Crowther, Ann, *British Social Policy, 1914–1939* (1988). Clear and informative.

Dockrill, Michael, *British Defence since 1945* (1988). Clear guide to crucial topic.

Freedman, Lawrence, *Britain and Nuclear Weapons* (1980). Leading authority on defence matters.

Fussell, Paul, *The Great War and Modern Memory* (1975). The classic on World War I and literature.

Harvie, Christopher, *Scotland and Nationalism* (second edition, 1994). Expert stuff by the expert.

Hennessy, Peter, *Whitehall* (1989). A master on his home ground.

Hiro, Dilip, *Black British White British: A History of Race Relations in Britain* (1991). Vital book on vital topic.

Holmes, Colin, *John Bull's Island: Immigration and British Society, 1871–1971* (1988). Comprehensive.

Jefferys, Kevin, *Retreat from New Jerusalem: British Politics, 1951–64*. Brief, but archive-based.

Lewis, Jane, *Women in Britain since 1945* (1992).

Lewis, Jane, *Women in England, 1870–1950* (1984). Two basic but essential books.

Mallie, Eamonn and McKittrick, David, *The Fight for Peace: The Secret Story behind the Irish Peace Process* (1997). Rich account by two distinguished journalists.

McKibbin, Ross, *Class and Cultures: England 1918–1951* (1998). Excellent on class. Locked away in his Oxford ivory tower, McKibbin is unaware that I pioneered the cultural, non-sociological, approach to class twenty years ago.

Middlemas, Keith, *Power, Competition and the State*, Vols 1–3 (1986–1991). Central work with respect to the 'corporatist' thesis.

Morris, Terence, *Crime and Criminal Justice in Britain since 1945* (1989). Excellent textbook.

Parsons, Gerald, *The Growth of Religious Diversity: Britain since 1945*, 2 vols (1993, 1994). Splendid introduction.

Pedersen, Susan, *Family Dependence, and the Origins of the Welfare State: Britain and France, 1914–1945* (1993). Interesting angle in valuable comparative perspective.

Perkin, Harold, *The Rise of Professional Society: England since 1880* (1989). All students need to be familiar with the challenging thesis of Britain's leading Weberian scholar and pioneer social historian.

Pugh, Martin, *Women and the Women's Movement in Britain, 1914–1959* (1992). Careful study, holding that war had little, if any, influence.

Rubinstein, W. D., *Men of Property: The Very Wealthy in Britain since the Industrial Revolution* (1981). Essential for any serious study of class.

Summerfield, Penny, *Reconstructing Women's Wartime Lives: Discourse and Subjectivity in Oral Histories of the Second World War* (Manchester, 1998). Distinguished pioneer, fallen among postmodernists (see Note at end of Further Reading).

Vincent, David, *Poor Citizens: The State and the Poor in Twentieth Century Britain* (1991). Superior textbook.

Wilson, Trevor, *The Myriad Faces of War* (1986). Fantastic resource. Contains everything about World War I, including the kitchen sink, but very little analysis.

Winter, J. M., *The Great War and the British People* (1985). Essential for any study of the 'war and social change' theme.

## 5 GENERAL TEXTBOOKS

Childs, David, *Britain since 1945: A Political History* (1997). Stuffed with essential information.

Clarke, Peter, *Hope and Glory: Britain 1900–1990* (1996). Miracle of compression, brilliantly presented.

Lee, Stephen J., *Aspects of British Political History 1914–1995* (1996). Aimed at sixth-formers. Reads at times as if written by one. Certainly the summaries of 'historical debates' are naive and misleading.

Lloyd, T. O., *Empire, Welfare State, Europe: England 1880–1990* (Oxford, 1994). Full of information, though only an Old Etonian, teaching in Canada, would feature 'England' in the title of a book really intended to cover Scotland, Wales and Northern Ireland.

Pearce, Malcolm, and Geoffrey, Stewart, *British Political History 1867–1995: Democracy and Decline* (1996). Quite specifically, and efficiently, aimed at A-level students, and the 'themes' they study; but history, cut-up and dried-out, can lack real explanatory force.

Pugh, Martin, *State and Society: British Political and Social History 1870–1997* (1999). Sophisticated, yet very lucid. New edition ends in deep gloom.

Robbins, Keith, *The Eclipse of a Great Power: Modern Britain 1870–1992* (1994). An amazing number of one-clause sentences, and equally amazing absence of colons or semi-colons, presenting much information on all parts of the British Isles, while ending in rejection of 'easy generalizations'; Robbins, in particular, denies any special significance to the two total wars.

Seaman, L. C. B., *Post-Victorian Britain 1902–1951* (1966). With a splendidly archaic title like that, who needs critics? It must be some kind of tribute to the author that this work, unrevised, continues to be reprinted.

Sked, Alan, and Cook, Chris, *Post-War Britain: A Political History* (1993). Expert text-book compilers on form: 'not to be read with joy but to be consulted with confidence', Roy Hattersley wrote in the *Guardian*.

## 6 AUTOBIOGRAPHIES, MEMOIRS AND PUBLISHED DIARIES

All books, even secondary works by the most distinguished professional historians, have to be approached with critical awareness kept switched on. These books, being of a primary character, have an invaluable immediacy, but, given the vast extent of human frailty, must, of course, be treated with a special scepticism.

Ali, Tariq, *Streetfighting Years* (1987).

Benn, Tony, *Diaries* (5 vols, 1987–91).

Castle, Barbara, *The Castle Diaries, 1964–70* (1984).

Clarke, Alan, *Diaries* (1993).

Colville, John, *The Fringes of Power: Downing Street Diaries 1939–1955* (1985).
Crossman, Richard, *The Diaries of a Cabinet Minister, 1961–70* (3 vols, 1975–7).
Donoughue, Bernard, *Prime Minister: The Conduct of Policy under Wilson and Callaghan* (1987). Insider writing.
Jenkins, Roy, *A Life at the Centre* (1991).
Lloyd George, David, *War Diaries* (2 vols, 1938). All the revelation, and all the concealment, of a stunning primary source.
Macmillan, Harold, *Tides of Fortune, 1945–1955* (1969).
Pimlott, Ben (ed.), *The Political Diary of Hugh Dalton, 1918–40, 1945–60* (1987).
Pimlott, Ben (ed.), *The Second World War Diary of Hugh Dalton 1940–1945* (1986).
Taylor, A. J. P. (ed.), *Lloyd George: A Diary by Frances Stevenson* (1971).
Williams, Philip (ed.), *The Diary of Hugh Gaitskell 1945–1955* (1983).
Wilson, Harold, *Final Term: The Labour Government, 1974–1976* (1979).

## 7 *Collections of primary documents*

Remember you will only be getting someone else's selection, and their pre-selected extracts at that. Still, even working from pre-selected, printed primary sources gives you some sense of what it is like to be a historian working from sources in the archives.

Six of the volumes of Martin Gilbert's massive biography of Churchill have companion volumes of relevant documents. The most wide-ranging collection of pre-selected documents is contained in the two volumes edited by Lawrence Butler and Harriet Jones, *Britain in the Twentieth Century: A Documentary Reader, vol. 1: 1900–1939, vol. 2: 1939–1970* (1994). The individual volumes in such series as 'Seminar Studies in History' and 'Documents and Debates' contain extracts from key documents. Examples are:

Ball, Stuart, *The Conservative Party and British Politics, 1902–1951.*
Boxer, Andrew, *The Conservative Governments 1899–1951.*
Brown, Richard, *Twentieth-Century Britain* (1982).
May, Alex Charles, *Britain and Europe since 1945* (1999).
Reekes, Andrew, *The Rise of Labour 1899–1951.*

Extracts from the most important pieces of social investigation in the inter-war years are contained in Stevenson, John, *Social Conditions in Britain Between the Wars* (1977).

## 8 *Oral History*

A misnomer for collections of Oral Testimony useful for *our* age, though inapplicable to earlier ones, apart from Summerfield, examples are:

Blackwell, Trevor, and Seabrook, Jeremy, *Talking Work: An oral history* (1996).
Courtney, Cathy, and Thompson, Paul, *City Lives: the changing voice of British Finance* (1996).

Roberts, Elizabeth, *A Woman's Place: an oral history of working-class women, 1890–1940* (1985).

## 9 Reference works

A few facts never did any harm. Instead of inventing 'the bourgeoisie' one can track actual origins and destinations in the volumes of *The Dictionary of National Biography*, *Who's Who?* and *Who Was Who?*, and also in *The Dictionary of Labour Biography* (Joyce M. Bellamy and John Saville, eds). For definitive election results, and much, much more, David Butler and Gareth Butler, *British Political Facts 1900–1994* (1994) is unsurpassable.

## Note on History, Cultural Studies, Gender and Postmodernism

It is impossible to study history today without being aware of the attacks on it by the apostles of postmodernism, led by the former Professor of Comparative Literature at Stanford University, Hayden White, and supported in this country by Patrick Joyce, Alun Munslow and Keith Jenkins. Most (not all) postmodernist discourse inclines to the support of leftist causes (Hayden White is quite open in his total commitment to Marxism). Many historians, being left-leaning themselves, are reluctant to adopt any posture other than gentlemanly tolerance; others feel ill-equipped to enter upon the philosophical ground which postmodernists claim to be occupying – their claims, actually, are pretty thoroughly undermined in recent books by John Searle and Sokal and Bricmont. (John Searle, *Mind, Language and Society: Doing Philosophy in the Real World* (1999); Alan Sokal and Jean Bricmont, *Intellectual Impostures: Postmodern Philosophers' Abuse of Science* (1998).) Some historians feel that they must show themselves to be in the height of fashion by adopting postmodernist phrases and concepts without always realizing the full implications of what they are saying; they, if I may deliberately rewrite a weary cliché, hunt with the hare and run with the hounds. In some circles, instead of making precise distinctions between structural, ideological and institutional circumstances, it has become a ritual to insist that all historical phenomena are 'culturally constructed'. Thus, Sean O'Connell, in his excellent *The Car in British Society* (1998), in a series avowedly aimed at merging cultural studies and social history, declares the technology of the internal combustion engine to be culturally constructed in that it led to the private ownership of the motor car rather than universal public transport; presumably, then, the technology of the steam locomotive, also being culturally constructed, *could*, in a different cultural context, have resulted in little privately-owned locomotives racing up and down country roads. In fact, of course, the determining factor is the structural one, the nature of the technology itself. In his informative *British Youth since 1945* (1997) Bill Osgerby insists that 'youth' is culturally constructed. Presumably, therefore, to be consistent, Osgerby must believe that old age and death are also culturally constructed; if so, he's in for a shock.

Along with 'Cultural Studies', 'Gender Studies' has become very fashionable. As always, it is important to scrutinize the language being used. In an excellent article on the rise of Gender Studies, Jane Rendall recognizes that the term 'gender' was originally purely grammatical (Jane Rendall, '"Uneven Developments": Women's History and Gender History in Great Britain', in Karen Offan, Ruth Roach Pierson and Jane Rendall, *Writing Women's History: International Perspectives* (1991)). Since the word 'sex' simply signified the physiological differences between males and females, feminists and poststructuralists brought the word 'gender' into use to represent the notion that the differences between males and females were largely (wait for it) 'culturally constructed'. As the word 'sex' more and more came to denote 'sexual activity', the word 'gender' slipped into use as a harmless replacement, without necessarily implying any elements of cultural construction: in 1995, even British government surveys started speaking of 'gender' rather than 'sex'. 'Gender' is now a deeply ambiguous word, and it is all too easy for polemicists to slide from one meaning to the other. Gender Studies, in fact, as Rendall shows, is very fully imbricated with postmodernist assumptions about cultural construction, even though these assumptions have never been properly tested against scientific work in the fields of social biology and evolutionary psychology (this contains its own measure of dubious theory, but it is a fundamental of academic endeavour that we do not rush to conclusions without considering all the options). Social phenomena are not culturally *constructed* (who does the 'constructing'? – presumably the usual suspect, 'the dominant class' – the 'bourgeoisie'!), though they are culturally *influenced*: prevailing ideological circumstances, I suggested in chapter 1 (remember the *Punch* cartoon), establish the boundaries within which relationships between men and women operate.

An obvious piece of further reading for students of twentieth-century Britain might well seem to be *Making Peace: The Reconstruction of Gender in Interwar Britain* (1993) by Susan Kingsley Kent. But maybe not. Consider this paragraph from the end of the opening chapter:

> It will be evident that I am drawing on poststructuralist theories of language in my analysis of war, gender, sexuality, and feminism. Such an approach starts with the assumption that every language act produces meanings that exceed the author's intention; that all texts create multiple meanings; that these meanings may contradict one another; and that interpretation of the text does not recover a 'true' or original meaning but is itself a part of the play of signification that produces textuality. I do not wish to imply that the meanings I have attributed to the texts, particularly the literary ones, quoted throughout this book, are the only ones, but rather to argue that the texts produce at least the meanings I identify. (p. 11)

The first thing to say is that this is not a model anyone attempting to write history – whether a student essay, or perhaps a piece of personal or local history – should imitate. Historical writing should always be precise and explicit. Specially invented terms like 'textuality' are to be avoided. I am far from sure myself that any such thing exists; certainly the very use of the word implies a freight of insecure assumptions. If we do take care to be precise and explicit in our writing then it is possible to say exactly what we mean: we will not 'exceed' our 'intention'. Undoubtedly, given the temptations of slipping into cliché or other forms of sloppy writing, or of striving for some high-falutin' rhetoric, expressing exactly what we mean is far from easy, particularly in a complex subject like history. But, contrary to Kent's 'assumption', language can be made to operate as a very exact tool, though usually only after much effort and much rewriting.

'Texts', or, as we should prefer to say, 'primary sources', are certainly not transparent: but provided we have a precise topic in mind, have sufficient contextual knowledge, and can practise the quite complicated technical skills of source analysis, we will be able to extract firm information relevant to our topic. We are not looking for a 'true' meaning, but for pieces of evidence which will have to be put together and collated with masses of other evidence (which may well be contradictory), winnowed out of other pertinent primary sources. Often the 'unwitting testimony' of a particular source is of greater importance to the historian than the 'witting testimony'. George V's speech on Ireland, briefly quoted in chapter 2, may not have greatly affected the course of events, but, as I suggested there, his unwitting use of the word 'race' is very revealing of basic assumptions and attitudes. Historians have been wrestling with sources, and with language, for generations. They have nothing to fear from the misunderstandings and convoluted utterances of the postmodernists.

# Index

Lightning Source UK Ltd.
Milton Keynes UK
UKOW010251280312

189658UK00003B/4/P